# GOD PASSES BY

By Shoghi Effendi

*THE ADVENT OF DIVINE JUSTICE*
*THE PROMISED DAY IS COME*

Collections of Letters and Messages

*THE WORLD ORDER OF BAHÁ'U'LLÁH*
*MESSAGES TO THE BAHÁ'Í WORLD*
*CITADEL OF FAITH*
*BAHÁ'Í ADMINISTRATION*

Translations

*THE DAWN-BREAKERS*
*THE KITÁB-I-ÍQÁN*
*EPISTLE TO THE SON OF THE WOLF*
*GLEANINGS FROM THE WRITINGS OF BAHÁ'U'LLÁH*
*PRAYERS AND MEDITATIONS*
*THE HIDDEN WORDS*

# GOD PASSES BY

SHOGHI EFFENDI

Introduction by
GEORGE TOWNSHEND, M.A.
Canon of St. Partick's Cathedral Dublin
Archdeacon of Clonfert

*Bahá'í Publishing Trust*
WILMETTE, ILLINOIS

New Edition 1974

Sixth Printing 2004

ISBN 0-87743-020-9 (cloth)
0-87743-034-9 (paper)
Library of Congress Catalog Card No. 44-51036

Printed in the United States of America

# INTRODUCTION

Here is a history of our times written on an unfamiliar theme—a history filled with love and happiness and vision and strength, telling of triumphs gained and wider triumphs yet to come: and whatever it holds of darkest tragedy it leaves mankind at its close not facing a grim inhospitable future but marching out from the shadows on the high road of an inevitable destiny towards the opened gates of the Promised City of Eternal Peace.

These hundred years as we have known them have been distinguished by human achievements and marvels unparalleled in any annals, and also by unparalleled disillusion and loss. But this history tells of wonders greater, mightier, more beneficent, wrought in the same period: and its tidings instead of tears and sorrow are of long forgotten Joy and vanished Power descended from heaven once more into the world of action and the lives of mortal men. It tells of things divine: of the birth of a new World Faith in our midst—a Faith which comes in succession to all the World Faiths of the past, acknowledging all, fulfilling all, carrying the common purpose of all to its consummation: and bearing to the Christians, "the People of the Gospel," a special summons to rise and help speed its propagation through the whole earth.

The narrative centers round one majestic lonely Figure, and its animating motive is the infinite transcendent love He bears for all mankind and the answering love which He draws forth from the hearts of the faithful.

The theme on its human side is that of Love and Struggle and Death. It tells of men and women like ourselves, adventuring all they had and all they were for sheer love's sake, of desolated homes, of breaking hearts, of bereavement and exile and suffering and indomitable purpose.

For long it seemed as if the world were too unhappy, too content with trivial pursuits to be able to accept in practice a Revelation so spiritual, so universal. Time and again the violent extirpation of the Faith at the hands of tyranny seemed assured. Many there were in high places in diverse lands who knew of the Faith, who were informed of the cruel wrongs inflicted on its votaries and heard their protests and appeals for justice. But there was none who heeded or who helped.

Strange and pitiful that an eager, inquiring Age which discovered so much of truth should have left the spiritual realm unexplored and should have missed the most important truth of all.

No Prophet has ever come into the world with greater proofs of His identity than Bahá'u'lláh: nor in the first century of its activity has any older Faith achieved so much or spread so far across the globe as this.

The mightiest proof of a Prophet has ever been found in Himself and in the efficacy of His word. Bahá'u'lláh rekindled the fires of faith and of happiness in the hearts of men. His knowledge was innate and spontaneous, not acquired in any school. None could gainsay or resist His wisdom and even His worst enemies admitted His greatness. All human perfections were embodied in Him. His strength was infinite. Trials and sufferings increased His firmness and power. As a divine physician He diagnosed the malady of the Age and prescribed the remedy. His teachings were universal and conferred illumination on all mankind. His power has been poured forth more abundantly since His death. In His prescience He stood alone and events have proved and are still proving its accuracy.

A second proof which every Prophet has brought with Him has been the witness of the past: the evidence of Ancient Prophecy.

The fulfillment in this Day of the prophecies contained in the Qur'án and in Muslim tradition has not prevented Islám from persecuting the Bahá'í Faith but it has been startling and notorious.

The fulfillment of the prophecies of Christ and of the Bible has been over a period of a hundred years or more matter of common knowledge and remark in the West. But the full extent of that fulfillment is only seen in Bahá'u'lláh. The proclamation of His Faith was made in 1844, the year when the strict exclusion of the Jews from their own land enforced by the Muslims for some twelve centuries was at last relaxed by the Edict of Toleration and "the times of the Gentiles" were "fulfilled."[1] The Advent has been long delayed and has fallen in a time of oppression and iniquity of religious unreality and disbelief, when love for God and man had grown cold,[2] when men were immersed in material business[3] and pleasure. The Prophet came like a thief[4] in the night and was here in our midst while people were wrapped in deep spiritual slumber. He tried and tested souls, separated the spiritual from the unspiritual, true from false believers, the sheep from the goats;[5] and the people taken un-

[1] Luke c. 21, v. 24; [2] Matt. c. 24, vv. 12, 48; [3] Matt. c. 24, v. 38; [4] Matt. c. 24, v. 43; [5] Matt. c. 25, v. 33.

awares were caught as in a snare[1] and knew not their danger till the retributive justice of God closed in upon them. Yet the appearance of the Faith and the rapidity and direction of its extension was as the lightning which flashes from the East to the West.[2] Christianity in contrast to the Revelation of Muḥammad had spread from the East to the West and has been predominantly a Western Faith. The Bahá'í Faith likewise has moved westward but with even greater speed and momentum than Christianity.

From the beginning of the Era, from the days of the Herald of the Faith, the Báb, the chronicles show a conscious sympathy of Christians with the New Teaching, which was in marked contrast with the attitude of their Muslim neighbors. The earliest instance of this perhaps is the kindly tribute of Dr. Cormick, an English Physician resident in Ṭihrán to the Báb whom he attended in prison when suffering from the effects of torture, and his record of the prevalent opinion that the Teaching of the Báb resembled Christianity. The first Western historian of the Movement, Count Gobineau, a French diplomat, wrote (1865) with enthusiasm of the Báb's saintliness, of the loftiness of His ideals, of His charm, His eloquence, and of the astonishing power of His words over both friend and foe: Ernest Renan in "Les Apôtres" (1866), Lord Curzon in "Persia," Professor Browne of Cambridge in several works, and many Christian men of letters of later date have written in a similar strain.

But among the many instances of this instinctive sympathy, the most spectacular is that which marked the execution of the Báb in the market square of Tabríz on July 9th, 1850. The officer in charge of the firing party was a Christian. He approached the Báb and prayed Him that on this account and because he had no enmity towards Him in his heart he might be spared the guilt of perpetrating so heinous a crime. The Báb replied that if his prayer were sincere God was able to fulfill his desire. The remarkable miracle by which this prayer was granted, and the martyrdom of the Báb carried out by another regiment under a Muslim officer, is a part of history.

The Christian West, though far from the scene of the Prophet's ministry, felt and responded practically to the divine World Impulse decades before the East. Poets, major and minor, Shelley and Wordsworth and many another, sang of a new Dawn. A new missionary effort spread the Christian Gospel through the earth: spiritual men and women sought to revive reality in religion: reformers arose to redress long standing evils; novelists used their art for a social pur-

[1] Luke c. 21, v. 35; [2] Matt. c. 24, v. 27.

pose. How different all this from the action of the corrupt, fanatical, persecuting East!

The Báb Himself identified His Teaching in spirit and purpose with that of Christ which was a preparation for His own: and He quoted some of Christ's Instructions to His disciples as part of His own Ordination Address to the "Letters of the Living."

Bahá'u'lláh from the beginning seems to have realized the special capacity of the progressive and enterprising West. He took the most vigorous steps possible to bring the Truth of the Age to the knowledge of the West and its leaders. Debarred from delivering His message to Europe in person, He wrote from a Turkish prison a general Tablet to the Christians, and another Tablet to the Sovereigns and leading men of the world but especially to the rulers of Christendom: and He also addressed five personal Tablets, one to the Czar, another to the Pope, another to Queen Victoria and two to Napoleon III. In these, in ringing tones of power and majesty such as would become the King of Kings imposing commands upon His vassals, He declared this Age the Supreme Day of God and Himself the Lord of Lords, the Father Who had come in His most great glory. All that had been mentioned in the Gospel had been fulfilled. Jesus had announced this Light and His signs had been spread in the West, that His followers might in this Day set their faces towards Bahá'u'lláh.

These letters are indeed pronouncements of a far-sighted Providence: and the catastrophe of the West which has occurred since they were written gives to them now a tragic and a terrible interest. They are of some length but their drift may be generally indicated in a few paragraphs.

In His Tablet to Queen Victoria He commends Her Majesty for ending the slave trade and for "entrusting the reins of counsel into the hands of the representatives of the people." But they who entered the Assembly should do so in a spirit of prayer to God and of trusteeship for the best interests of all mankind. The human race was one whole and should be regarded as the human body which though created perfect had become afflicted with grave disorders. It lay at the mercy of rulers so drunk with pride that they could not see their own best advantage, much less recognize this mighty Revelation. The one real remedy for the world's ills was the union of all its peoples in one universal Cause, one common Faith. This could be brought to pass only through the Divine Physician. He called on the Queen to ensure peace, to be just and considerate to her subjects, to avoid excessive taxation, to effect an international union for the reduction of armaments and the joint resistance of all nations to any aggressor Power.

His Tablet to the Pope contains an impassioned, loving appeal to Christians that they will recognize this, the Promised Day of God, that they will come forth into its light and acclaim their Lord, and enter the Kingdom in His name. They were created for the light and He likes not to see them in the darkness. Christ purified the world with Love and with the Spirit that in this Day it might be able to receive Life at the hands of the Merciful. This is the coming of the Father of whom Isaiah spoke: the teaching which He now reveals is that which Christ withheld when He said, "other things I have to say unto you but ye cannot bear them now." He bids the Pontiff take the Cup of Life and drink therefrom and "offer it then to such as turn towards it amongst the peoples of all Faiths."

The Tablet to Alexander II is in answer to a prayer addressed by the Czar to His Lord and in recognition of a kindness shown to Bahá'u'lláh when in prison and in chains by an ambassador of the Czar. He impresses on the Czar the supreme greatness of this Manifestation, tells him how the Prophet has subjected Himself to a thousand calamities for the salvation of the world and, having brought life to men, is threatened by them with death. He bids him expose this injustice, and in love for God and God's Kingdom offer himself as a ransom in God's path: no harm will come to him but a reward in this world and the next. Great, great the blessing in store for the king who gives his heart to his Lord.

In His two Tablets to Napoleon III, Bahá'u'lláh impresses on the Emperor the oneness of mankind whose many maladies will not be cured unless the nations, abandoning the pursuit of their several interests, agree together and unite in common obedience to the plan of God. The human race should be as one body and one soul. A far higher degree of faith than the world has ever reached before is demanded by God of every man in this Era. All are commanded to teach the truth and to work for God's cause: but no one will produce good results in this service unless he first purify and ennoble his own character.

Bahá'u'lláh bids the clergy give up their seclusion, mingle in the life of the people and marry. God is calling men to Him in this Age and any theology which takes its own theses as a standard of truth and turns away from Him is deprived of value and efficacy.

He has come to regenerate and unite all mankind in very deed and truth and He will gather them at the one table of His bounty.

Let the Emperor call on His name and declare His truth to the people.

Grave warnings and open or implicit threats if the kings do not acknowledge the Manifestation and obey His commands are contained in all these Tablets, especially in this to Napoleon III. The collective Tablet addressed to all the kings is however stern and minatory beyond the rest. Bahá'u'lláh warns the rulers that if they do not treat the poor amongst them as a trust from God; if they do not observe the strictest justice; if they do not compose their differences, heal the dissensions that estrange them and reduce their armaments, and follow the other counsels now given them by the Prophet, "Divine chastisement shall assail you from every direction and the sentence of His justice shall be pronounced against you. On that day ye shall have no power to resist Him and shall recognize your own impotence. Have mercy on yourselves and on those beneath you."

Christ long centuries before had wept over the city whose children had ignored His visitation and refused His protection. Now at His second coming the same event recurred. But they who brought down the wrath of God on themselves were not the members of a nation but of an entire world.

Before He passed away Bahá'u'lláh proclaimed: "The hour is approaching when the most great convulsion will have appeared." And again, "The time for the destruction of the world and its people hath arrived."

More than forty years after the dispatch of these Tablets 'Abdu'l-Bahá, the son of the Prophet and the appointed Exemplar of His Faith, being freed at last from prison by the Young Turks, made a three years' tour of Europe and America. Saddened by many things He saw, and knowing the doom to which the heedlessness of the nations was hurrying them, He was sparing of denunciation, reproach or criticism; instead, with words of cheer and undiscriminating love He summoned His hearers to high, heroic action. He spoke much of the spiritual and social goal set by God for this enlightened Age: "The Most Great Peace." He Himself in His joy, in His serenity, in His love for all, in His wisdom, His strength and resolution and utter submissiveness to God, seemed the incarnation of the Spirit of that Peace. His very presence brought receptive souls into touch with a state of being of which they might have heard but which none of them had ever known. Through many months of missionary work He explained the moral and spiritual conditions which would make possible the Most Great Peace, and developed in many addresses the practical means by which it could be approached. In the United

States, at Wilmette on the shores of Lake Michigan, He laid the foundation stone of the first Bahá'í Temple of the West, round which are to be grouped buildings devoted to social, humanitarian, educational and scientific purposes, the whole to be dedicated as one scheme to the glory of God and the service of man. He also saw in America the first beginnings of the building of the Administrative Order of Bahá'u'lláh.

But the general response of the public was not sufficient to stem the tides flowing towards war. Before He left the United States, 'Abdu'l-Bahá foretold the outbreak of hostilities in two years' time.

When at last peace was made, He declared that the League of Nations as constituted could not prevent war; and before He passed away in 1921 He announced to His followers the outbreak of another war fiercer than the last.

To many, at the opening of the second Bahá'í century, mankind seems to be drifting in a helmless barque upon a stormy and uncharted sea. But to the Bahá'ís another vision is revealed. The barriers by which men blocked their path to progress are torn down. Human pride is abased, human wisdom stultified. The anarchy of nationalism and the insufficiency of secularism are thoroughly exposed.

Slowly the veil lifts from the future. Along whatever road thoughtful men look out they see before them some guiding truth, some leading principle, which Bahá'u'lláh gave long ago and which men rejected. The sum and essence of the best hopes of the best minds today is garnered in such a simple statement as that of 'Abdu'l-Bahá's "Twelve Points." 1. Unfettered search after truth. 2. The oneness of mankind. 3. Religion a cause of love and harmony. 4. Religion hand in hand with science. 5. Universal peace. 6. An international language. 7. Education for all. 8. Equal opportunities for both sexes. 9. Justice for all. 10. Work for all. 11. Abolition of extremes of poverty and wealth. 12. The Holy Spirit to be the prime motive power in life.

The immense, complex, baffling task of unifying all peoples is set forth in its complete and inmost simplicity by 'Abdu'l-Bahá in seven pregnant phrases. 1. Unity in the political realm. 2. Unity of thought in world undertakings. 3. Unity of freedom. 4. Unity in religion. 5. Unity of nations. 6. Unity of races. 7. Unity of language.

Already the Bahá'ís have begun in deed and in fact to build the instrument destined to be the model and the nucleus of the Most Great Peace. The Administrative Order is as simple as it is profoundly conceived, and it can only be conducted by those whose lives are animated by love and fear of God. It is a system in which such opposites as unity and universality, the practical and the spiritual, the rights of the individual and the rights of society, are perfectly balanced not through arranging a compromise but through the revelation of an inner harmony. Those who have the experience of operating the Order testify that it seems to them like a human body which is made to express the soul within.

On the lake shore at Wilmette stands the completed Temple of Praise, a sign of the Spirit of the Most Great Peace and of the Splendor of God that has come down to dwell among men. The walls of the Temple are transparent, made of an open tracery cut as in sculptured stone, and lined with glass. All imaginable symbols of light are woven together into the pattern, the lights of the sun and the moon and the constellations, the lights of the spiritual heavens unfolded by the great Revealers of today and yesterday, the Cross in various forms, the Crescent and the nine pointed Star (emblem of the Bahá'í Faith). No darkness invades the Temple at any time; by day it is lighted by the sun whose rays flood in from every side through the exquisitely perforated walls, and by night it is artificially illuminated and its ornamented shape is etched with light against the dark. From whatever side the visitor approaches, the aspiring form of the Temple appears as the spirit of adoration; and seen from the air above it has the likeness of a Nine-Pointed Star come down from heaven to find its resting place on the earth.

But for the leading of the peoples into the Promised Land, for the spiritualizing of mankind, for the attainment of the Most Great Peace the world awaits the arising of those whom the King of Kings has summoned to the task—the Christians and the Churches of the West.

"Verily Christ said 'Come that I may make you fishers of men' and today We say 'Come, that We may make you quickeners of the world' . . . Lo! This is the Day of Grace! Come ye that I may make you kings of the realm of My Kingdom. If ye obey Me you will see that which We have promised you, and I will make you the friends of My Soul in the realm of My Greatness and the Companions of My Beauty in the heaven of My Might for ever."

*G. Townshend*

# FOREWORD

On the 23rd of May of this auspicious year the Bahá'í world will celebrate the centennial anniversary of the founding of the Faith of Bahá'u'lláh. It will commemorate at once the hundreth anniversary of the inception of the Bábí Dispensation, of the inauguration of the Bahá'í Era, of the commencement of the Bahá'í Cycle, and of the birth of 'Abdu'l-Bahá. The weight of the potentialities with which this Faith, possessing no peer or equal in the world's spiritual history, and marking the culmination of a universal prophetic cycle, has been endowed, staggers our imagination. The brightness of the millennial glory which it must shed in the fullness of time dazzles our eyes. The magnitude of the shadow which its Author will continue to cast on successive Prophets destined to be raised up after Him eludes our calculation.

Already in the space of less than a century the operation of the mysterious processes generated by its creative spirit has provoked a tumult in human society such as no mind can fathom. Itself undergoing a period of incubation during its primitive age, it has, through the emergence of its slowly-crystallizing system, induced a fermentation in the general life of mankind designed to shake the very foundations of a disordered society, to purify its life-blood, to reorientate and reconstruct its institutions, and shape its final destiny.

To what else can the observant eye or the unprejudiced mind, acquainted with the signs and portents heralding the birth, and accompanying the rise, of the Faith of Bahá'ulláh ascribe this dire, this planetary upheaval, with its attendant destruction, misery and fear, if not to the emergence of His embryonic World Order, which, as He Himself has unequivocally proclaimed, has *"deranged the equilibrium of the world and revolutionized mankind's ordered life"*? To what agency, if not to the irresistible diffusion of that world-shaking, world-energizing, world-redeeming spirit, which the Báb has affirmed is *"vibrating in the innermost realities of all created things"* can the origins of this portentous crisis, incomprehensible to man, and admittedly unprecedented in the annals of the human race, be attributed? In the convulsions of contemporary society, in the frenzied, world-wide ebullitions of men's thoughts, in the fierce antagonisms inflaming races, creeds and classes, in the shipwreck of nations, in the downfall of kings, in the dismemberment of empires, in the extinction of dynasties, in the collapse of ecclesiastical hierarchies, in the deterioration of time-honored institutions, in the dissolution of ties, secular as well as religious, that had for so long held together the members of the human race—all manifesting themselves with ever-increasing gravity since the outbreak of the first World War that immediately preceded the opening years of the Formative Age of the Faith of Bahá'u'lláh—in these we can readily recognize the evidences of the travail of an age that has sustained the impact of His Revelation, that has ignored His summons, and is now laboring to be delivered of its burden, as a direct consequence of the impulse communicated to it by the generative, the purifying, the transmuting influence of His Spirit.

It is my purpose, on the occasion of an anniversary of such profound significance, to attempt in the succeeding pages a survey of the outstanding events of the century that has seen this Spirit burst forth upon the world, as well as the initial stages of its subsequent incarnation in a System that must evolve into an Order designed to embrace the whole of mankind, and capable of fulfilling the high destiny that awaits man on this planet. I shall endeavor to review, in their proper perspective and despite the comparatively brief space of time which separates us from them, the events which the revolution of a hundred years, unique alike in glory and tribulation, has unrolled before our eyes. I shall seek to represent and correlate, in however cursory a manner, those momentous happenings which have insensibly, relentlessly, and under the very eyes of successive generations, perverse, indifferent or hostile, transformed a heterodox and seemingly negligible offshoot of the Shaykhí school of the Ithná-'Asharíyyih sect of Shí'ah Islám into a world religion whose unnumbered followers are organically and indissolubly united; whose light has overspread the earth as far as Iceland in the North and Magellanes in the South; whose ramifications have spread to no less than sixty countries of the world; whose literature has been translated and disseminated in no less than forty languages; whose endowments in the five continents of the globe, whether local, national or international, already run into several million dollars; whose incorporated elective bodies have secured the official recognition of a number of governments in East and West; whose adherents are recruited from the diversified races and chief religions of mankind; whose representatives are to be found in hundreds of cities in both Persia and the United States of America; to whose verities royalty has publicly and repeatedly testified; whose independent status its enemies, from the ranks of its parent religion and in the leading center of both the Arab and Muslim worlds, have proclaimed and demonstrated; and whose claims have been virtually recognized, entitling it to rank as the fourth religion of a Land in which its world spiritual center has been established, and which is at once the heart of Christendom, the holiest shrine of the Jewish people, and, save Mecca alone, the most sacred spot in Islám.

It is not my purpose—nor does the occasion demand it,—to write a detailed history of the last hundred years of the Bahá'í Faith, nor do I intend to trace the origins of so tremendous a Movement, or to portray the conditions under which it was born, or to examine the character of the religion from which it has sprung, or to arrive at an estimate of the effects which its impact upon the fortunes of mankind has produced. I shall rather content myself with a review of the salient features of its birth and rise, as well as of the initial stages in the establishment of its administrative institutions—institutions which must be regarded as the nucleus and herald of that World Order that must incarnate the soul, execute the laws, and fulfill the purpose of the Faith of God in this day.

Nor will it be my intention to ignore, whilst surveying the panorama which the revolution of a hundred years spreads before our gaze, the swift interweaving of seeming reverses with evident victories, out of which the hand of an inscrutable Providence has chosen to form the pattern of the Faith from its earliest days, or to minimize those disasters that have so often proved themselves to be the prelude to fresh triumphs which have, in turn, stimulated its growth and consolidated its past achievements. Indeed, the history of the first hundred years of its evolution resolves itself into a series of internal and external crises, of varying severity, devastating in their immediate effects, but each mysteriously releasing a corresponding measure of divine power, lending thereby a fresh impulse to its unfoldment, this further unfoldment engendering in its turn a still graver calamity, followed by a still more liberal effusion of celestial grace enabling its upholders to accelerate still further its march and win in its service still more compelling victories.

In its broadest outline the first century of the Bahá'í Era may be said to comprise the Heroic, the Primitive, the Apostolic Age of the Faith of Bahá'u'lláh, and also the initial stages of the Formative, the Transitional, the Iron Age which is to witness the crystallization and shaping of the creative energies released by His Revelation. The first eighty years of this century may roughly be said to have covered the entire period of the first age, while the last two decades may be regarded as having witnessed the beginnings of the second. The former commences with the Declaration of the Báb, includes the mission of Bahá'u'lláh, and terminates with the passing of 'Abdu'l-Bahá. The latter is ushered in by His Will and Testament, which defines its character and establishes its foundation.

The century under our review may therefore be considered as falling into four distinct periods, of unequal duration, each of specific import and of tremendous and indeed unappraisable significance. These four periods are closely interrelated, and constitute successive acts of one, indivisible, stupendous and sublime drama, whose mystery no intellect can fathom, whose climax no eye can even dimly perceive, whose conclusion no mind can adequately foreshadow. Each of these acts revolves around its own theme, boasts of its own heroes, registers its own tragedies, records its own triumphs, and contributes its own share to the execution of one common, immutable Purpose. To isolate any one of them from the others, to dissociate the later manifestations of one universal, all-embracing Revelation from the pristine purpose that animated it in its earliest days, would be tantamount to a mutilation of the structure on which it rests, and to a lamentable perversion of its truth and of its history.

The first period (1844-1853), centers around the gentle, the youthful and irresistible person of the Báb, matchless in His meekness, imperturbable in His serenity, magnetic in His utterance, unrivaled in the dramatic episodes of His swift and tragic ministry. It begins with the Declaration of His Mission, culminates in His martyrdom, and ends in a veritable orgy of religious massacre revolting in its hideousness. It is characterized by nine years of fierce and relentless contest, whose theatre was the whole of Persia, in which above ten thousand heroes laid down their lives, in which two sovereigns of the Qájár dynasty and their wicked ministers participated, and which was supported by the entire Shí'ah ecclesiastical hierarchy, by the military resources of the state, and by the implacable hostility of the masses. The second period (1853-1892) derives its inspiration from the august figure of Bahá'u'lláh, preeminent in holiness, awesome in the majesty of His strength and power, unapproachable in the transcendent brightness of His glory. It opens with the first stirrings, in the soul of Bahá'u'lláh while in the Síyáh-Chál of Ṭihrán, of the Revelation anticipated by the Báb, attains its plenitude in the proclamation of that Revelation to the kings and ecclesiastical leaders of the earth, and terminates in the ascension of its Author in the vicinity of the prison-town of 'Akká. It extends over thirty-nine years of continuous, of unprecedented and overpowering Revelation, is marked by the propagation of the Faith to the neighboring territories of Turkey, of Russia, of 'Iráq, of Syria, of Egypt and of India, and is distinguished by a corresponding aggravation of hostility, represented by the united attacks launched by the S͟háh of Persia and the Sulṭán of Turkey, the two admittedly most powerful potentates of the East, as well as by the opposition of the twin sacerdotal orders of S͟hí'ah and Sunní Islám. The third period (1892-1921) revolves around the vibrant personality of 'Abdu'l-Bahá, mysterious in His essence, unique in His station, astoundingly potent in both the charm and strength of His character. It commences with the announcement of the Covenant of Bahá'u'lláh, a document without parallel in the history of any earlier Dispensation, attains its climax in the emphatic assertion by the Center of that Covenant, in the City of the Covenant, of the unique character and far-reaching implications of that Document, and closes with His passing and the interment of His remains on Mt. Carmel. It will go down in history as a period of almost thirty years' duration, in which tragedies and triumphs have been so intertwined as to eclipse at one time the Orb of the Covenant, and at another time to pour forth its light over the continent of Europe, and as far as Australasia, the Far East and the North American continent. The fourth period (1921-1944) is motivated by the forces radiating from the Will and Testament of 'Abdu'l-Bahá, that Charter of Bahá'u'lláh's New World Order, the offspring resulting from the mystic intercourse between Him Who is the Source of the Law of God and the mind of the One Who is the vehicle and interpreter of that Law. The inception of this fourth, this last period of the first Bahá'í century synchronizes with the birth of the Formative Age of the Bahá'í Era, with the founding of the Administrative Order of the Faith of Bahá'u'lláh—a system which is at once the harbinger, the nucleus and pattern of His World Order. This period, covering the first twenty-three years of this Formative Age, has already been distinguished by an outburst of further hostility, of a different character, accelerating on the one hand the diffusion of the Faith over a still wider area in each of the five continents of the globe, and resulting on the other in the emancipation and the recognition of the independent status of several communities within its pale.

These four periods are to be regarded not only as the component, the inseparable parts of one stupendous whole, but as progressive stages in a single evolutionary process, vast, steady and irresistible. For as we survey the entire range which the operation of a century-old Faith has unfolded before us, we cannot escape the conclusion that from whatever angle we view this colossal scene, the events associated with these periods present to us unmistakable evidences of a slowly maturing process, of an orderly development, of internal consolidation, of external expansion, of a gradual emancipation from the fetters of religious orthodoxy, and of a corresponding diminution of civil disabilities and restrictions.

Viewing these periods of Bahá'í history as the constituents of a single entity, we note the chain of events proclaiming successively the rise of a Forerunner, the Mission of One Whose advent that Forerunner had promised, the establishment of a Covenant generated through the direct authority of the Promised One Himself, and lastly the birth of a System which is the child sprung from both the Author of the Covenant and its appointed Center. We observe how the Báb, the Forerunner, announced the impending inception of a divinely-conceived Order, how Bahá'u'lláh, the Promised One, formulated its laws and ordinances, how 'Abdu'l-Bahá, the appointed Center, delineated its features, and how the present generation of their followers have commenced to erect the framework of its institutions. We watch, through these periods, the infant light of the Faith diffuse itself from its cradle, eastward to India and the Far East, westward to the neighboring territories of 'Iráq, of Turkey, of Russia, and of Egypt, travel as far as the North American continent, illuminate subsequently the major countries of Europe, envelop with its radiance, at a later stage, the Antipodes, brighten the fringes of the Arctic, and finally set aglow the Central and South American horizons. We witness a corresponding increase in the diversity of the elements within its fellowship, which from being confined, in the first period of its history, to an obscure body of followers chiefly recruited from the ranks of the masses in Shí'ah Persia, has expanded into a fraternity representative of the leading religious systems of the world, of almost every caste and color, from the humblest worker and peasant to royalty itself. We notice a similar development in the extent of its literature—a literature which, restricted at first to the narrow range of hurriedly transcribed, often corrupted, secretly circulated, manuscripts, so furtively perused, so frequently effaced, and at times even eaten by the terrorized members of a proscribed sect, has, within the space of a century, swelled into innumerable editions, comprising tens of thousands of printed volumes, in diverse scripts, and in no less than forty languages, some elaborately reproduced, others profusely illustrated, all methodically and vigorously disseminated through the agency of world-wide, properly constituted and specially organized committees and Assemblies. We perceive a no less apparent evolution in the scope of its teachings, at first designedly rigid, complex and severe, subsequently recast, expanded, and liberalized under the succeeding Dispensation, later expounded, reaffirmed and amplified by an appointed Interpreter, and lastly systematized and universally applied to both individuals and institutions. We can discover a no less distinct gradation in the character of the opposition it has had to encounter—an opposition, at first kindled in the bosom of S͟hí'ah Islám, which, at a later stage, gathered momentum with the banishment of Bahá'u'lláh to the domains of the Turkish Sulṭán and the consequent hostility of the more powerful Sunní hierarchy and its Caliph, the head of the vast majority of the followers of Muḥammad—an opposition which, now, through the rise of a divinely appointed Order in the Christian West, and its initial impact on civil and ecclesiastical institutions, bids fair to include among its supporters established governments and systems associated with the most ancient, the most deeply entrenched sacerdotal hierarchies in Christendom. We can, at the same time, recognize, through the haze of an ever-widening hostility, the progress, painful yet persistent, of certain communities within its pale through the stages of obscurity, of proscription, of emancipation, and of recognition—stages that must needs culminate in the course of succeeding centuries, in the establishment of the Faith, and the founding, in the plenitude of its power and authority, of the world-embracing Bahá'í Commonwealth. We can likewise discern a no less appreciable advance in the rise of its institutions, whether as administrative centers or places of worship—institutions, clandestine and subterrene in their earliest beginnings, emerging imperceptibly into the broad daylight of public recognition, legally protected, enriched by pious endowments, ennobled at first by the erection of the Mas͟hriqu'l-Ad͟hkár of 'Is͟hqábád, the first Bahá'í House of Worship, and more recently immortalized, through the rise in the heart of the North American continent of the Mother Temple of the West, the forerunner of a divine, a slowly maturing civilization. And finally, we can even bear witness to the marked improvement in the conditions surrounding the pilgrimages performed by its devoted adherents to its consecrated shrines at its world center—pilgrimages originally arduous, perilous, tediously long, often made on foot, at times ending in disappointment, and confined to a handful of harassed Oriental followers, gradually attracting, under steadily improving circumstances of security and comfort, an ever swelling number of new converts converging from the four corners of the globe, and culminating in the widely publicized yet sadly frustrated visit of a noble Queen, who, at the very threshold of the city of her heart's desire, was compelled, according to her own written testimony, to divert her steps, and forego the privilege of so priceless a benefit.

## CONTENTS

## SECOND PERIOD: THE MINISTRY OF BAHÁ'U'LLÁH 1853-1892

## FOURTH PERIOD: THE INCEPTION OF THE FORMATIVE AGE OF THE BAHÁ'Í FAITH 1921-1944

FIRST PERIOD

# THE MINISTRY OF THE BÁB
## 1844-1853

## CHAPTER I

# The Birth of the Bábí Revelation

May 23, 1844, signalizes the commencement of the most turbulent period of the Heroic Age of the Bahá'í Era, an age which marks the opening of the most glorious epoch in the greatest cycle which the spiritual history of mankind has yet witnessed. No more than a span of nine short years marks the duration of this most spectacular, this most tragic, this most eventful period of the first Bahá'í century. It was ushered in by the birth of a Revelation whose Bearer posterity will acclaim as the *"Point round Whom the realities of the Prophets and Messengers revolve,"* and terminated with the first stirrings of a still more potent Revelation, *"whose day,"* Bahá'u'lláh Himself affirms, *"every Prophet hath announced,"* for which *"the soul of every Divine Messenger hath thirsted,"* and through which *"God hath proved the hearts of the entire company of His Messengers and Prophets."* Little wonder that the immortal chronicler of the events associated with the birth and rise of the Bahá'í Revelation has seen fit to devote no less than half of his moving narrative to the description of those happenings that have during such a brief space of time so greatly enriched, through their tragedy and heroism, the religious annals of mankind. In sheer dramatic power, in the rapidity with which events of momentous importance succeeded each other, in the holocaust which baptized its birth, in the miraculous circumstances attending the martyrdom of the One Who had ushered it in, in the potentialities with which it had been from the outset so thoroughly impregnated, in the forces to which it eventually gave birth, this nine-year period may well rank as unique in the whole range of man's religious experience. We behold, as we survey the episodes of this first act of a sublime drama, the figure of its Master Hero, the Báb, arise meteor-like above the horizon of Shíráz, traverse the sombre sky of Persia from south to north, decline with tragic swiftness, and perish in a blaze of glory. We see His satellites, a galaxy of God-intoxicated heroes, mount above that same horizon, irradiate that same incandescent light, burn themselves out with that self-same swiftness, and impart in their turn an added impetus to the steadily gathering momentum of God's nascent Faith.

He Who communicated the original impulse to so incalculable a Movement was none other than the promised Qá'im (He who ariseth), the Ṣáḥibu'z-Zamán (the Lord of the Age), Who assumed the exclusive right of annulling the whole Qur'ánic Dispensation, Who styled Himself *"the Primal Point from which have been generated all created things . . . the Countenance of God Whose splendor can never be obscured, the Light of God Whose radiance can never fade."* The people among whom He appeared were the most decadent race in the civilized world, grossly ignorant, savage, cruel, steeped in prejudice, servile in their submission to an almost deified hierarchy, recalling in their abjectness the Israelites of Egypt in the days of Moses, in their fanaticism the Jews in the days of Jesus, and in their perversity the idolators of Arabia in the days of Muḥammad. The arch-enemy who repudiated His claim, challenged His authority, persecuted His Cause, succeeded in almost quenching His light, and who eventually became disintegrated under the impact of His Revelation was the S͟hí'ah priesthood. Fiercely fanatic, unspeakably corrupt, enjoying unlimited ascendancy over the masses, jealous of their position, and irreconcilably opposed to all liberal ideas, the members of this caste had for one thousand years invoked the name of the Hidden Imám, their breasts had glowed with the expectation of His advent, their pulpits had rung with the praises of His world-embracing dominion, their lips were still devoutly and perpetually murmuring prayers for the hastening of His coming. The willing tools who prostituted their high office for the accomplishment of the enemy's designs were no less than the sovereigns of the Qájár dynasty, first, the bigoted, the sickly, the vacillating Muḥammad S͟háh, who at the last moment cancelled the Báb's imminent visit to the capital, and, second, the youthful and inexperienced Náṣiri'd-Dín S͟háh, who gave his ready assent to the sentence of his Captive's death. The arch villains who joined hands with the prime movers of so wicked a conspiracy were the two grand vizirs, Ḥájí Mírzá Áqásí, the idolized tutor of Muḥammad S͟háh, a vulgar, false-hearted and fickle-minded schemer, and the arbitrary, bloodthirsty, reckless Amír-Niẓám, Mírzá Taqí K͟hán, the first of whom exiled the Báb to the mountain fastnesses of Ád͟hirbáyján, and the latter decreed His death in Tabríz. Their accomplice in these and other heinous crimes was a government bolstered up by a flock of idle, parasitical princelings and governors, corrupt, incompetent, tenaciously holding to their ill-gotten privileges, and utterly subservient to a notoriously degraded clerical order. The heroes whose deeds shine upon the record of this fierce spiritual contest, involving at once people, clergy, monarch and government, were the Báb's chosen disciples, the Letters of the Living, and their companions, the trail-breakers of the New Day, who to so much intrigue, ignorance, depravity, cruelty, superstition and cowardice opposed a spirit exalted, unquenchable and awe-inspiring, a knowledge surprisingly profound, an eloquence sweeping in its force, a piety unexcelled in fervor, a courage leonine in its fierceness, a self-abnegation saintly in its purity, a resolve granite-like in its firmness, a vision stupendous in its range, a veneration for the Prophet and His Imáms disconcerting to their adversaries, a power of persuasion alarming to their antagonists, a standard of faith and a code of conduct that challenged and revolutionized the lives of their countrymen.

The opening scene of the initial act of this great drama was laid in the upper chamber of the modest residence of the son of a mercer of Shíráz, in an obscure corner of that city. The time was the hour before sunset, on the 22nd day of May, 1844. The participants were the Báb, a twenty-five year old siyyid, of pure and holy lineage, and the young Mullá Ḥusayn, the first to believe in Him. Their meeting immediately before that interview seemed to be purely fortuitous. The interview itself was protracted till the hour of dawn. The Host remained closeted alone with His guest, nor was the sleeping city remotely aware of the import of the conversation they held with each other. No record has passed to posterity of that unique night save the fragmentary but highly illuminating account that fell from the lips of Mullá Ḥusayn.

"I sat spellbound by His utterance, oblivious of time and of those who awaited me," he himself has testified, after describing the nature of the questions he had put to his Host and the conclusive replies he had received from Him, replies which had established beyond the shadow of a doubt the validity of His claim to be the promised Qá'im. "Suddenly the call of the Mu'adhdhin, summoning the faithful to their morning prayer, awakened me from the state of ecstasy into which I seemed to have fallen. All the delights, all the ineffable glories, which the Almighty has recounted in His Book as the priceless possessions of the people of Paradise—these I seemed to be experiencing that night. Methinks I was in a place of which it could be truly said: *'Therein no toil shall reach us, and therein no weariness shall touch us;' 'no vain discourse shall they hear therein, nor any falsehood, but only the cry, "Peace! Peace!"'; 'their cry therein shall be, "Glory be to Thee, O God!" and their salutation therein, "Peace!",* and the close of their cry, *"Praise be to God, Lord of all creatures!"'*

Sleep had departed from me that night. I was enthralled by the music of that voice which rose and fell as He chanted; now swelling forth as He revealed verses of the Qayyúmu'l-Asmá', again acquiring ethereal, subtle harmonies as He uttered the prayers He was revealing. At the end of each invocation, He would repeat this verse: *'Far from the glory of thy Lord, the All-Glorious, be that which His creatures affirm of Him! And peace be upon His Messengers! And praise be to God, the Lord of all beings!'* "

"This Revelation," Mullá Ḥusayn has further testified, "so suddenly and impetuously thrust upon me, came as a thunderbolt which, for a time, seemed to have benumbed my faculties. I was blinded by its dazzling splendor and overwhelmed by its crushing force. Excitement, joy, awe, and wonder stirred the depths of my soul. Predominant among these emotions was a sense of gladness and strength which seemed to have transfigured me. How feeble and impotent, how dejected and timid, I had felt previously! Then I could neither write nor walk, so tremulous were my hands and feet. Now, however, the knowledge of His Revelation had galvanized my being. I felt possessed of such courage and power that were the world, all its peoples and its potentates, to rise against me, I would, alone and undaunted, withstand their onslaught. The universe seemed but a handful of dust in my grasp. I seemed to be the voice of Gabriel personified, calling unto all mankind: 'Awake, for, lo! the morning Light has broken. Arise, for His Cause is made manifest. The portal of His grace is open wide; enter therein, O peoples of the world! For He Who is your promised One is come!' "

A more significant light, however, is shed on this episode, marking the Declaration of the Mission of the Báb, by the perusal of that *"first, greatest and mightiest"* of all books in the Bábí Dispensation, the celebrated commentary on the Súrih of Joseph, the first chapter of which, we are assured, proceeded, in its entirety, in the course of that night of nights from the pen of its divine Revealer. The description of this episode by Mullá Ḥusayn, as well as the opening pages of that Book attest the magnitude and force of that weighty Declaration. A claim to be no less than the mouthpiece of God Himself, promised by the Prophets of bygone ages; the assertion that He was, at the same time, the Herald of One immeasurably greater than Himself; the summons which He trumpeted forth to the kings and princes of the earth; the dire warnings directed to the Chief Magistrate of the realm, Muḥammad S͟háh; the counsel imparted to Ḥájí Mírzá Áqásí to fear God, and the peremptory command to abdicate his authority as grand vizir of the S͟háh and submit to the One Who is the *"Inheritor of the earth and all that is therein"*; the challenge issued to the rulers of the world proclaiming the self-sufficiency of His Cause, denouncing the vanity of their ephemeral power, and calling upon them to *"lay aside, one and all, their dominion,"* and deliver His Message to *"lands in both the East and the West"*—these constitute the dominant features of that initial contact that marked the birth, and fixed the date, of the inception of the most glorious era in the spiritual life of mankind.

With this historic Declaration the dawn of an Age that signalizes the consummation of all ages had broken. The first impulse of a momentous Revelation had been communicated to the one *"but for whom,"* according to the testimony of the Kitáb-i-Íqán, *"God would not have been established upon the seat of His mercy, nor ascended the throne of eternal glory."* Not until forty days had elapsed, however, did the enrollment of the seventeen remaining Letters of the Living commence. Gradually, spontaneously, some in sleep, others while awake, some through fasting and prayer, others through dreams and visions, they discovered the Object of their quest, and were enlisted under the banner of the new-born Faith. The last, but in rank the first, of these Letters to be inscribed on the Preserved Tablet was the erudite, the twenty-two year old Quddús, a direct descendant of the Imám Ḥasan and the most esteemed disciple of Siyyid Káẓim. Immediately preceding him, a woman, the only one of her sex, who, unlike her fellow-disciples, never attained the presence of the Báb, was invested with the rank of apostleship in the new Dispensation. A poetess, less than thirty years of age, of distinguished birth, of bewitching charm, of captivating eloquence, indomitable in spirit, unorthodox in her views, audacious in her acts, immortalized as Ṭáhirih (the Pure One) by the "Tongue of Glory," and surnamed Qurratu'l-'Ayn (Solace of the Eyes) by Siyyid Káẓim, her teacher, she had, in consequence of the appearance of the Báb to her in a dream, received the first intimation of a Cause which was destined to exalt her to the fairest heights of fame, and on which she, through her bold heroism, was to shed such imperishable luster.

These *"first Letters generated from the Primal Point,"* this *"company of angels arrayed before God on the Day of His coming,"* these *"Repositories of His Mystery,"* these *"Springs that have welled out from the Source of His Revelation,"* these first companions who, in the words of the Persian Bayán, *"enjoy nearest access to God,"* these *"Luminaries that have, from everlasting, bowed down, and will ever-*

*lastingly continue to bow down, before the Celestial Throne,"* and lastly these *"elders"* mentioned in the Book of Revelation as *"sitting before God on their seats," "clothed in white raiment"* and wearing on their heads *"crowns of gold"*—these were, ere their dispersal, summoned to the Báb's presence, Who addressed to them His parting words, entrusted to each a specific task, and assigned to some of them as the proper field of their activities their native provinces. He enjoined them to observe the utmost caution and moderation in their behavior, unveiled the loftiness of their rank, and stressed the magnitude of their responsibilities. He recalled the words addressed by Jesus to His disciples, and emphasized the superlative greatness of the New Day. He warned them lest by turning back they forfeit the Kingdom of God, and assured them that if they did God's bidding, God would make them His heirs and spiritual leaders among men. He hinted at the secret, and announced the approach, of a still mightier Day, and bade them prepare themselves for its advent. He called to remembrance the triumph of Abraham over Nimrod, of Moses over Pharaoh, of Jesus over the Jewish people, and of Muḥammad over the tribes of Arabia, and asserted the inevitability and ultimate ascendancy of His own Revelation. To the care of Mullá Ḥusayn He committed a mission, more specific in character and mightier in import. He affirmed that His covenant with him had been established, cautioned him to be forbearing with the divines he would encounter, directed him to proceed to Ṭihrán, and alluded, in the most glowing terms, to the as yet unrevealed Mystery enshrined in that city—a Mystery that would, He affirmed, transcend the light shed by both Ḥijáz and S͟híráz.

Galvanized into action by the mandate conferred upon them, launched on their perilous and revolutionizing mission, these lesser luminaries who, together with the Báb, constitute the First Váḥid (Unity) of the Dispensation of the Bayán, scattered far and wide through the provinces of their native land, where, with matchless heroism, they resisted the savage and concerted onslaught of the forces arrayed against them, and immortalized their Faith by their own exploits and those of their co-religionists, raising thereby a tumult that convulsed their country and sent its echoes reverberating as far as the capitals of Western Europe.

It was not until, however, the Báb had received the eagerly anticipated letter of Mullá Ḥusayn, His trusted and beloved lieutenant, communicating the joyful tidings of his interview with Bahá'u'lláh, that He decided to undertake His long and arduous pilgrimage to the

Tombs of His ancestors. In the month of S͟ha'bán, of the year 1260 A.H. (September, 1844) He Who, both on His father's and mother's side, was of the seed of the illustrious Fáṭimih, and Who was a descendant of the Imám Ḥusayn, the most eminent among the lawful successors of the Prophet of Islám, proceeded, in fulfillment of Islamic traditions, to visit the Kaaba. He embarked from Bus͟hihr on the 19th of Ramaḍán (October, 1844) on a sailing vessel, accompanied by Quddús whom He was assiduously preparing for the assumption of his future office. Landing at Jaddih after a stormy voyage of over a month's duration, He donned the pilgrim's garb, mounted a camel, and set out for Mecca, arriving on the first of D͟hi'l-Ḥajjih (December 12). Quddús, holding the bridle in his hands, accompanied his Master on foot to that holy Shrine. On the day of 'Arafih, the Prophet-pilgrim of S͟híráz, His chronicler relates, devoted His whole time to prayer. On the day of Nahr He proceeded to Muná, where He sacrificed according to custom nineteen lambs, nine in His own name, seven in the name of Quddús, and three in the name of the Ethiopian servant who attended Him. He afterwards, in company with the other pilgrims, encompassed the Kaaba and performed the rites prescribed for the pilgrimage.

His visit to Ḥijáz was marked by two episodes of particular importance. The first was the declaration of His mission and His open challenge to the haughty Mírzá Muhít-i-Kirmání, one of the most outstanding exponents of the S͟hayk͟hí school, who at times went so far as to assert his independence of the leadership of that school assumed after the death of Siyyid Káẓim by Ḥájí Muḥammad Karím K͟hán, a redoubtable enemy of the Bábí Faith. The second was the invitation, in the form of an Epistle, conveyed by Quddús, to the Sherif of Mecca, in which the custodian of the House of God was called upon to embrace the truth of the new Revelation. Absorbed in his own pursuits the Sherif however failed to respond. Seven years later, when in the course of a conversation with a certain Ḥájí Níyáz-i-Bag͟hdádí, this same Sherif was informed of the circumstances attending the mission and martyrdom of the Prophet of S͟híráz, he listened attentively to the description of those events and expressed his indignation at the tragic fate that had overtaken Him.

The Báb's visit to Medina marked the conclusion of His pilgrimage. Regaining Jaddih, He returned to Bús͟hihr, where one of His first acts was to bid His last farewell to His fellow-traveler and disciple, and to assure him that he would meet the Beloved of their hearts. He, moreover, announced to him that he would be crowned with a martyr's death, and that He Himself would subsequently suffer a similar fate at the hands of their common foe.

The Báb's return to His native land (Ṣafar 1261) (February-March, 1845) was the signal for a commotion that rocked the entire country. The fire which the declaration of His mission had lit was being fanned into flame through the dispersal and activities of His appointed disciples. Already within the space of less than two years it had kindled the passions of friend and foe alike. The outbreak of the conflagration did not even await the return to His native city of the One Who had generated it. The implications of a Revelation, thrust so dramatically upon a race so degenerate, so inflammable in temper, could indeed have had no other consequence than to excite within men's bosoms the fiercest passions of fear, of hate, of rage and envy. A Faith Whose Founder did not content Himself with the claim to be the Gate of the Hidden Imám, Who assumed a rank that excelled even that of the Ṣáḥibu'z-Zamán, Who regarded Himself as the precursor of one incomparably greater than Himself, Who peremptorily commanded not only the subjects of the S͟háh, but the monarch himself, and even the kings and princes of the earth, to forsake their all and follow Him, Who claimed to be the inheritor of the earth and all that is therein—a Faith Whose religious doctrines, Whose ethical standards, social principles and religious laws challenged the whole structure of the society in which it was born, soon ranged, with startling unanimity, the mass of the people behind their priests, and behind their chief magistrate, with his ministers and his government, and welded them into an opposition sworn to destroy, root and branch, the movement initiated by One Whom they regarded as an impious and presumptuous pretender.

With the Báb's return to S͟híráz the initial collision of irreconcilable forces may be said to have commenced. Already the energetic and audacious Mullá 'Alíy-i-Basṭámí, one of the Letters of the Living, "the first to leave the House of God (S͟híráz) and the first to suffer for His sake," who, in the presence of one of the leading exponents of S͟hí'ah Islám, the far-famed S͟hayk͟h Muḥammad Ḥasan, had audaciously asserted that from the pen of his new-found Master within the space of forty-eight hours, verses had streamed that equalled in number those of the Qur'án, which it took its Author twenty-three years to reveal, had been excommunicated, chained, disgraced, imprisoned, and, in all probability, done to death. Mullá Ṣádiq-i-K͟hurásání, impelled by the injunction of the Báb in the K͟hasá'il-i-Sab'ih to alter the sacrosanct formula of the ad͟hán, sounded it in its amended form before a scandalized congregation in S͟híráz, and was instantly arrested, reviled, stripped of his garments, and scourged with a thousand lashes. The villainous Ḥusayn K͟hán, the Niẓámu'd-Dawlih, the governor of Fárs, who had read the challenge thrown out in the Qayyúmu'l-Asmá', having ordered that Mullá Ṣádiq together with Quddús and another believer be summarily and publicly punished, caused their beards to be burned, their noses pierced, and threaded with halters; then, having been led through the streets in this disgraceful condition, they were expelled from the city.

The people of S͟híráz were by that time wild with excitement. A violent controversy was raging in the masjids, the madrisihs, the bazaars, and other public places. Peace and security were gravely imperiled. Fearful, envious, thoroughly angered, the mullás were beginning to perceive the seriousness of their position. The governor, greatly alarmed, ordered the Báb to be arrested. He was brought to S͟híráz under escort, and, in the presence of Ḥusayn K͟hán, was severely rebuked, and so violently struck in the face that His turban fell to the ground. Upon the intervention of the Imám-Jum'ih He was released on parole, and entrusted to the custody of His maternal uncle Ḥájí Mírzá Siyyid'Alí. A brief lull ensued, enabling the captive Youth to celebrate the Naw-Rúz of that and the succeeding year in an atmosphere of relative tranquillity in the company of His mother, His wife, and His uncle. Meanwhile the fever that had seized His followers was communicating itself to the members of the clergy and to the merchant classes, and was invading the higher circles of society. Indeed, a wave of passionate inquiry had swept the whole country, and unnumbered congregations were listening with wonder to the testimonies eloquently and fearlessly related by the Báb's itinerant messengers.

The commotion had assumed such proportions that the S͟háh, unable any longer to ignore the situation, delegated the trusted Siyyid Yaḥyáy-i-Dárábí, surnamed Vaḥíd, one of the most erudite, eloquent and influential of his subjects—a man who had committed to memory no less than thirty thousand traditions—to investigate and report to him the true situation. Broad-minded, highly imaginative, zealous by nature, intimately associated with the court, he, in the course of three interviews, was completely won over by the arguments and personality of the Báb. Their first interview centered around the metaphysical teachings of Islám, the most obscure passages of the Qur'án, and the traditions and prophecies of the Imáms. In the course of the second interview Vaḥíd was astounded to find that the questions which he had intended to submit for elucidation had been effaced from his retentive memory, and yet, to his utter amazement, he discovered that the Báb was answering the very questions he had forgotten. During the third interview the circumstances attending the revelation of the Báb's commentary on the súrih of Kawt͟har, comprising no less than two thousand verses, so overpowered the delegate of the S͟háh that he, contenting himself with a mere written report to the Court Chamberlain, arose forthwith to dedicate his entire life and resources to the service of a Faith that was to requite him with the crown of martyrdom during the Nayríz upheaval. He who had firmly resolved to confute the arguments of an obscure siyyid of S͟híráz, to induce Him to abandon His ideas, and to conduct Him to Ṭihrán as an evidence of the ascendancy he had achieved over Him, was made to feel, as he himself later acknowledged, as "lowly as the dust beneath His feet." Even Ḥusayn K͟hán, who had been Vaḥíd's host during his stay in S͟híráz, was compelled to write to the S͟háh and express the conviction that his Majesty's illustrious delegate had become a Bábí.

Another famous advocate of the Cause of the Báb, even fiercer in zeal than Vaḥíd, and almost as eminent in rank, was Mullá Muḥammad-'Alíy-i-Zánjání, surnamed Ḥujjat. An Ak͟hbárí, a vehement controversialist, of a bold and independent temper of mind, impatient of restraint, a man who had dared condemn the whole ecclesiastical hierarchy from the Abváb-i-Arba'ih down to the humblest mullá, he had more than once, through his superior talents and fervid eloquence, publicly confounded his orthodox S͟hí'ah adversaries. Such a person could not remain indifferent to a Cause that was producing so grave a cleavage among his countrymen. The disciple he sent to S͟híráz to investigate the matter fell immediately under the spell of the Báb. The perusal of but a page of the Qayyúmu'l-Asmá', brought by that messenger to Ḥujjat, sufficed to effect such a transformation within him that he declared, before the assembled 'ulamás of his native city, that should the Author of that work pronounce day to be night and the sun to be a shadow he would unhesitatingly uphold his verdict.

Yet another recruit to the ever-swelling army of the new Faith was the eminent scholar, Mírzá Aḥmad-i-Azghandí, the most learned, the wisest and the most outstanding among the 'ulamás of K͟hurásán, who, in anticipation of the advent of the promised Qá'im, had compiled above twelve thousand traditions and prophecies concerning the time and character of the expected Revelation, had circulated them among His fellow-disciples, and had encouraged them to quote them extensively to all congregations and in all meetings.

While the situation was steadily deteriorating in the provinces, the bitter hostility of the people of Shíráz was rapidly moving towards a climax. Ḥusayn Khán, vindictive, relentless, exasperated by the reports of his sleepless agents that his Captive's power and fame were hourly growing, decided to take immediate action. It is even reported that his accomplice, Ḥájí Mírzá Áqásí, had ordered him to kill secretly the would-be disrupter of the state and the wrecker of its established religion. By order of the governor the chief constable, 'Abdu'l-Ḥamíd Khán, scaled, in the dead of night, the wall and entered the house of Ḥájí Mírzá Siyyid'Alí, where the Báb was confined, arrested Him, and confiscated all His books and documents. That very night, however, took place an event which, in its dramatic suddenness, was no doubt providentially designed to confound the schemes of the plotters, and enable the Object of their hatred to prolong His ministry and consummate His Revelation. An outbreak of cholera, devastating in its virulence, had, since midnight, already smitten above a hundred people. The dread of the plague had entered every heart, and the inhabitants of the stricken city were, amid shrieks of pain and grief, fleeing in confusion. Three of the governor's domestics had already died. Members of his family were lying dangerously ill. In his despair he, leaving the dead unburied, had fled to a garden in the outskirts of the city. 'Abdu'l-Ḥamíd Khán, confronted by this unexpected development, decided to conduct the Báb to His own home. He was appalled, upon his arrival, to learn that his son lay in the death-throes of the plague. In his despair he threw himself at the feet of the Báb, begged to be forgiven, adjured Him not to visit upon the son the sins of the father, and pledged his word to resign his post, and never again to accept such a position. Finding that his prayer had been answered, he addressed a plea to the governor begging him to release his Captive, and thereby deflect the fatal course of this dire visitation. Ḥusayn Khán acceded to his request, and released his Prisoner on condition of His quitting the city.

Miraculously preserved by an almighty and watchful Providence, the Báb proceeded to Iṣfahán (September, 1846), accompanied by Siyyid Kaẓim-i-Zanjání. Another lull ensued, a brief period of comparative tranquillity during which the Divine processes which had been set in motion gathered further momentum, precipitating a series of events leading to the imprisonment of the Báb in the fortresses of Máh-Kú and C̱h̲ihríq, and culminating in His martyrdom in the barrack-square of Tabríz. Well aware of the impending trials that were to afflict Him, the Báb had, ere His final separation from His family, bequeathed to His mother and His wife all His possessions, had confided to the latter the secret of what was to befall Him, and revealed for her a special prayer the reading of which, He assured her, would resolve her perplexities and allay her sorrows. The first forty days of His sojourn in Iṣfahán were spent as the guest of Mírzá Siyyid Muḥammad, the Sulṭanu'l-'Ulamá, the Imám-Jum'ih, one of the principal ecclesiastical dignitaries of the realm, in accordance with the instructions of the governor of the city, Manuc̱h̲ihr K̲h̲án, the Mu 'Tamidu'd-Dawlih, who had received from the Báb a letter requesting him to appoint the place where He should dwell. He was ceremoniously received, and such was the spell He cast over the people of that city that, on one occasion, after His return from the public bath, an eager multitude clamored for the water that had been used for His ablutions. So magic was His charm that His host, forgetful of the dignity of his high rank, was wont to wait personally upon Him. It was at the request of this same prelate that the Báb, one night, after supper, revealed His well-known commentary on the súrih of Va'l-'Aṣr. Writing with astonishing rapidity, He, in a few hours, had devoted to the exposition of the significance of only the first letter of that súrih—a letter which S̲h̲ayk̲h̲ Aḥmad-i-Aḥsá'í had stressed, and which Bahá'u'lláh refers to in the Kitáb-i-Aqdas—verses that equalled in number a third of the Qur'án, a feat that called forth such an outburst of reverent astonishment from those who witnessed it that they arose and kissed the hem of His robe.

The tumultuous enthusiasm of the people of Iṣfahán was meanwhile visibly increasing. Crowds of people, some impelled by curiosity, others eager to discover the truth, still others anxious to be healed of their infirmities, flocked from every quarter of the city to the house of the Imám-Jum'ih. The wise and judicious Manúc̱h̲ihr K̲h̲án could not resist the temptation of visiting so strange, so intriguing a Personage. Before a brilliant assemblage of the most accomplished divines he, a Georgian by origin and a Christian by birth, requested the Báb to expound and demonstrate the truth of Muḥammad's specific mission. To this request, which those present had felt compelled to decline, the Báb readily responded. In less than two hours, and in the space of fifty pages, He had not only revealed a minute, a vigorous and original dissertation on this noble theme, but had also linked it with both the coming of the Qá'im and the return of the Imám Ḥusayn—an exposition that prompted Manúchihr Khán to declare before that gathering his faith in the Prophet of Islám, as well as his recognition of the supernatural gifts with which the Author of so convincing a treatise was endowed.

These evidences of the growing ascendancy exercised by an unlearned Youth on the governor and the people of a city rightly regarded as one of the strongholds of Shí'ah Islám, alarmed the ecclesiastical authorities. Refraining from any act of open hostility which they knew full well would defeat their purpose, they sought, by encouraging the circulation of the wildest rumors, to induce the Grand Vizir of the Sháh to save a situation that was growing hourly more acute and menacing. The popularity enjoyed by the Báb, His personal prestige, and the honors accorded Him by His countrymen, had now reached their high watermark. The shadows of an impending doom began to fast gather about Him. A series of tragedies from then on followed in rapid sequence destined to culminate in His own death and the apparent extinction of the influence of His Faith.

The overbearing and crafty Ḥájí Mírzá Áqásí, fearful lest the sway of the Báb encompass his sovereign and thus seal his own doom, was aroused as never before. Prompted by a suspicion that the Báb possessed the secret sympathies of the Mu'tamid, and well aware of the confidence reposed in him by the Sháh, he severely upbraided the Imám-Jum'ih for the neglect of his sacred duty. He, at the same time, lavished, in several letters, his favors upon the 'ulamás of Iṣfahán, whom he had hitherto ignored. From the pulpits of that city an incited clergy began to hurl vituperation and calumny upon the Author of what was to them a hateful and much to be feared heresy. The Sháh himself was induced to summon the Báb to his capital. Manúchihr Khán, bidden to arrange for His departure, decided to transfer His residence temporarily to his own home. Meanwhile the mujtahids and 'ulamás, dismayed at the signs of so pervasive an influence, summoned a gathering which issued an abusive document signed and sealed by the ecclesiastical leaders of the city, denouncing the Báb as a heretic and condemning Him to death. Even the Imám-Jum'ih was constrained to add his written testimony that the Accused was devoid of reason and judgment. The Mu'tamid, in his great embarrassment, and in order to appease the rising tumult, conceived a plan whereby an increasingly restive populace were made to believe that the Báb had left for Ṭihrán, while he succeeded in insuring for Him a brief respite of four months in the privacy of the 'Imárat-i-Khurshíd, the governor's private residence in Iṣfahán. It was in those days that the host expressed the desire to consecrate all his possessions, evaluated by his contemporaries at no less than forty million francs, to the furtherance of the interests of the new Faith, declared his intention of converting Muḥammad S̲h̲áh, of inducing him to rid himself of a shameful and profligate minister, and of obtaining his royal assent to the marriage of one of his sisters with the Báb. The sudden death of the Mu'tamid, however, foretold by the Báb Himself, accelerated the course of the approaching crisis. The ruthless and rapacious Gurgín K̲h̲án, the deputy governor, induced the S̲h̲áh to issue a second summons ordering that the captive Youth be sent in disguise to Ṭihrán, accompanied by a mounted escort. To this written mandate of the sovereign the vile Gurgín K̲h̲án, who had previously discovered and destroyed the will of his uncle, the Mu'tamid, and seized his property, unhesitatingly responded. At the distance of less than thirty miles from the capital, however, in the fortress of Kinár-Gird, a messenger delivered to Muḥammad Big, who headed the escort, a written order from Ḥájí Mírzá Áqásí instructing him to proceed to Kulayn, and there await further instructions. This was, shortly after, followed by a letter which the S̲h̲áh had himself addressed to the Báb, dated Rabí'u'th̲-thání 1263 (March 19-April 17, 1847), and which, though couched in courteous terms, clearly indicated the extent of the baneful influence exercised by the Grand Vizir on his sovereign. The plans so fondly cherished by Manúchihr K̲h̲án were now utterly undone. The fortress of Máh-Kú, not far from the village of that same name, whose inhabitants had long enjoyed the patronage of the Grand Vizir, situated in the remotest northwestern corner of Ád̲h̲irbáyján, was the place of incarceration assigned by Muḥammad S̲h̲áh, on the advice of his perfidious minister, for the Báb. No more than one companion and one attendant from among His followers were allowed to keep Him company in those bleak and inhospitable surroundings. All-powerful and crafty, that minister had, on the pretext of the necessity of his master's concentrating his immediate attention on a recent rebellion in K̲h̲urásán and a revolt in Kirmán, succeeded in foiling a plan, which, had it materialized, would have had the most serious repercussions on his own fortunes, as well as on the immediate destinies of his government, its ruler and its people.

## CHAPTER II

# The Báb's Captivity in Ádhirbáyján

The period of the Báb's banishment to the mountains of Ádhirbáyján, lasting no less than three years, constitutes the saddest, the most dramatic, and in a sense the most pregnant phase of His six year ministry. It comprises His nine months' unbroken confinement in the fortress of Máh-Kú, and His subsequent incarceration in the fortress of Chihríq, which was interrupted only by a brief yet memorable visit to Tabríz. It was overshadowed throughout by the implacable and mounting hostility of the two most powerful adversaries of the Faith, the Grand Vizir of Muḥammad Sháh, Ḥájí Mírzá Áqásí, and the Amír-Niẓám, the Grand Vizir of Náṣiri'd-Dín Sháh. It corresponds to the most critical stage of the mission of Bahá'u'lláh, during His exile to Adrianople, when confronted with the despotic Sulṭán 'Abdu'l-'Azíz and his ministers, 'Álí Páshá and Fu'ád Páshá, and is paralleled by the darkest days of 'Abdu'l-Bahá's ministry in the Holy Land, under the oppressive rule of the tyrannical 'Abdu'l-Ḥamíd and the equally tyrannical Jamál Páshá. Shíráz had been the memorable scene of the Báb's historic Declaration; Iṣfahán had provided Him, however briefly, with a haven of relative peace and security; whilst Ádhirbáyján was destined to become the theatre of His agony and martyrdom. These concluding years of His earthly life will go down in history as the time when the new Dispensation attained its full stature, when the claim of its Founder was fully and publicly asserted, when its laws were formulated, when the Covenant of its Author was firmly established, when its independence was proclaimed, and when the heroism of its champions blazed forth in immortal glory. For it was during these intensely dramatic, fate-laden years that the full implications of the station of the Báb were disclosed to His disciples, and formally announced by Him in the capital of Ádhirbáyján, in the presence of the Heir to the Throne; that the Persian Bayán, the repository of the laws ordained by the Báb, was revealed; that the time and character of the Dispensation of *"the One Whom God will make manifest"* were unmistakably determined; that the Conference of Badasht proclaimed the annulment of the old order; and that the great conflagrations of Mázindarán, of Nayríz and of Zanján were kindled.

And yet, the foolish and short-sighted Ḥájí Mírzá Áqásí fondly imagined that by confounding the plan of the Báb to meet the S͟háh face to face in the capital, and by relegating Him to the farthest corner of the realm, he had stifled the Movement at its birth, and would soon conclusively triumph over its Founder. Little did he imagine that the very isolation he was forcing upon his Prisoner would enable Him to evolve the System designed to incarnate the soul of His Faith, and would afford Him the opportunity of safeguarding it from disintegration and schism, and of proclaiming formally and unreservedly His mission. Little did he imagine that this very confinement would induce that Prisoner's exasperated disciples and companions to cast off the shackles of an antiquated theology, and precipitate happenings that would call forth from them a prowess, a courage, a self-renunciation unexampled in their country's history. Little did he imagine that by this very act he would be instrumental in fulfilling the authentic tradition ascribed to the Prophet of Islám regarding the inevitability of that which should come to pass in Ád͟hirbáyján. Untaught by the example of the governor of S͟híráz, who, with fear and trembling, had, at the first taste of God's avenging wrath, fled ignominiously and relaxed his hold on his Captive, the Grand Vizir of Muḥammad S͟háh was, in his turn, through the orders he had issued, storing up for himself severe and inevitable disappointment, and paving the way for his own ultimate downfall.

His orders to 'Alí K͟hán, the warden of the fortress of Máh-Kú, were stringent and explicit. On His way to that fortress the Báb passed a number of days in Tabríz, days that were marked by such an intense excitement on the part of the populace that, except for a few persons, neither the public nor His followers were allowed to meet Him. As He was escorted through the streets of the city the shout of "Alláh-u-Akbar" resounded on every side. So great, indeed, became the clamor that the town crier was ordered to warn the inhabitants that any one who ventured to seek the Báb's presence would forfeit all his possessions and be imprisoned. Upon His arrival in Máh-Kú, surnamed by Him Jabal-i-Básiṭ (the Open Mountain) no one was allowed to see Him for the first two weeks except His amanuensis, Siyyid Ḥusayn, and his brother. So grievous was His plight while in that fortress that, in the Persian Bayán, He Himself has stated that at night-time He did not even have a lighted lamp, and that His solitary chamber, constructed of sun-baked bricks, lacked even a door, while, in His Tablet to Muḥammad S͟háh, He has complained that the inmates of the fortress were confined to two guards and four dogs.

Secluded on the heights of a remote and dangerously situated mountain on the frontiers of the Ottoman and Russian empires; imprisoned within the solid walls of a four-towered fortress; cut off from His family, His kindred and His disciples; living in the vicinity of a bigoted and turbulent community who, by race, tradition, language and creed, differed from the vast majority of the inhabitants of Persia; guarded by the people of a district which, as the birthplace of the Grand Vizir, had been made the recipient of the special favors of his administration, the Prisoner of Máh-Kú seemed in the eyes of His adversary to be doomed to languish away the flower of His youth, and witness, at no distant date, the complete annihilation of His hopes. That adversary was soon to realize, however, how gravely he had misjudged both his Prisoner and those on whom he had lavished his favors. An unruly, a proud and unreasoning people were gradually subdued by the gentleness of the Báb, were chastened by His modesty, were edified by His counsels, and instructed by His wisdom. They were so carried away by their love for Him that their first act every morning, notwithstanding the remonstrations of the domineering 'Alí Khán, and the repeated threats of disciplinary measures received from Ṭihrán, was to seek a place where they could catch a glimpse of His face, and beseech from afar His benediction upon their daily work. In cases of dispute it was their wont to hasten to the foot of the fortress, and, with their eyes fixed upon His abode, invoke His name, and adjure one another to speak the truth. 'Alí Khán himself, under the influence of a strange vision, felt such mortification that he was impelled to relax the severity of his discipline, as an atonement for his past behavior. Such became his leniency that an increasing stream of eager and devout pilgrims began to be admitted at the gates of the fortress. Among them was the dauntless and indefatigable Mullá Ḥusayn, who had walked on foot the entire way from Mashad in the east of Persia to Máh-Kú, the westernmost outpost of the realm, and was able, after so arduous a journey, to celebrate the festival of Naw-Rúz (1848) in the company of his Beloved.

Secret agents, however, charged to watch 'Alí Khán, informed Ḥájí Mírzá Áqásí of the turn events were taking, whereupon he immediately decided to transfer the Báb to the fortress of Chihríq (about April 10, 1848), surnamed by Him the Jabal-i-Shadíd (the Grievous Mountain). There He was consigned to the keeping of Yaḥya Khán, a brother-in-law of Muḥammad S͟háh. Though at the outset he acted with the utmost severity, he was eventually compelled to yield to the fascination of his Prisoner. Nor were the kurds, who lived in the village of C͟hihríq, and whose hatred of the S͟hí'ahs exceeded even that of the inhabitants of Máh-Kú, able to resist the pervasive power of the Prisoner's influence. They too were to be seen every morning, ere they started for their daily work, to approach the fortress and prostrate themselves in adoration before its holy Inmate. "So great was the confluence of the people," is the testimony of a European eye-witness, writing in his memoirs of the Báb, "that the courtyard, not being large enough to contain His hearers, the majority remained in the street and listened with rapt attention to the verses of the new Qur'án."

Indeed the turmoil raised in C͟hihríq eclipsed the scenes which Máh-Kú had witnessed. Siyyids of distinguished merit, eminent 'ulamás, and even government officials were boldly and rapidly espousing the Cause of the Prisoner. The conversion of the zealous, the famous Mírzá Asadu'lláh, surnamed Dayyán, a prominent official of high literary repute, who was endowed by the Báb with the "hidden and preserved knowledge," and extolled as the "repository of the trust of the one true God," and the arrival of a dervish, a former navváb, from India, whom the Báb in a vision had bidden renounce wealth and position, and hasten on foot to meet Him in Ád͟hirbáyján, brought the situation to a head. Accounts of these startling events reached Tabríz, were thence communicated to Ṭihrán, and forced Ḥájí Mírzá Áqásí again to intervene. Dayyán's father, an intimate friend of that minister, had already expressed to him his grave apprehension at the manner in which the able functionaries of the state were being won over to the new Faith. To allay the rising excitement the Báb was summoned to Tabríz. Fearful of the enthusiasm of the people of Ád͟hirbáyján, those into whose custody He had been delivered decided to deflect their route, and avoid the town of K͟huy, passing instead through Urúmíyyih. On His arrival in that town Prince Malik Qásim Mírzá ceremoniously received Him, and was even seen, on a certain Friday, when his Guest was riding on His way to the public bath, to accompany Him on foot, while the Prince's footmen endeavored to restrain the people who, in their overflowing enthusiasm, were pressing to catch a glimpse of so marvelous a Prisoner. Tabríz, in its turn in the throes of wild excitement, joyously hailed His arrival. Such was the fervor of popular feeling that the Báb was assigned a place outside the gates of the city.

This, however, failed to allay the prevailing emotion. Precautions, warnings and restrictions served only to aggravate a situation that had already become critical. It was at this juncture that the Grand Vizir issued his historic order for the immediate convocation of the ecclesiastical dignitaries of Tabríz to consider the most effectual measures which would, once and for all, extinguish the flames of so devouring a conflagration.

The circumstances attending the examination of the Báb, as a result of so precipitate an act, may well rank as one of the chief landmarks of His dramatic career. The avowed purpose of that convocation was to arraign the Prisoner, and deliberate on the steps to be taken for the extirpation of His so-called heresy. It instead afforded Him the supreme opportunity of His mission to assert in public, formally and without any reservation, the claims inherent in His Revelation. In the official residence, and in the presence, of the governor of Ádhirbáyján, Náṣiri'd-Dín Mírzá, the heir to the throne; under the presidency of Ḥájí Mullá Maḥmúd, the Niẓámu'l-'Ulamá, the Prince's tutor; before the assembled ecclesiastical dignitaries of Tabríz, the leaders of the Shaykhi community, the Shaykhu'l-Islám, and the Imám-Jum'ih, the Báb, having seated Himself in the chief place which had been reserved for the Valí-'Ahd (the heir to the throne), gave, in ringing tones, His celebrated answer to the question put to Him by the President of that assembly. *"I am,"* He exclaimed, *"I am, I am the Promised One! I am the One Whose name you have for a thousand years invoked, at Whose mention you have risen, Whose advent you have longed to witness, and the hour of Whose Revelation you have prayed God to hasten. Verily, I say, it is incumbent upon the peoples of both the East and the West to obey My word, and to pledge allegiance to My person."*

Awe-struck, those present momentarily dropped their heads in silent confusion. Then Mullá Muḥammad-i-Mamáqání, that one-eyed white-bearded renegade, summoning sufficient courage, with characteristic insolence, reprimanded Him as a perverse and contemptible follower of Satan; to which the undaunted Youth retorted that He maintained what He had already asserted. To the query subsequently addressed to Him by the Niẓámu'l-'Ulamá the Báb affirmed that His words constituted the most incontrovertible evidence of His mission, adduced verses from the Qur'án to establish the truth of His assertion, and claimed to be able to reveal, within the space of two days and two nights, verses equal to the whole of that Book. In answer to a criticism calling His attention to an infraction by Him of the rules of grammar, He cited certain passages from the Qur'án as corroborative evidence, and, turning aside, with firmness and dignity, a frivolous and irrelevant remark thrown at Him by one of those who were present, summarily disbanded that gathering by Himself rising and quitting the room. The convocation thereupon dispersed, its members confused, divided among themselves, bitterly resentful and humiliated through their failure to achieve their purpose. Far from daunting the spirit of their Captive, far from inducing Him to recant or abandon His mission, that gathering was productive of no other result than the decision, arrived at after considerable argument and discussion, to inflict the bastinado on Him, at the hands, and in the prayer-house of the heartless and avaricious Mírzá 'Alí-Aṣghar, the Shaykhu'l-Islám of that city. Confounded in his schemes Ḥájí Mírzá Áqásí was forced to order the Báb to be taken back to Chihríq.

This dramatic, this unqualified and formal declaration of the Báb's prophetic mission was not the sole consequence of the foolish act which condemned the Author of so weighty a Revelation to a three years' confinement in the mountains of Ádhirbáyján. This period of captivity, in a remote corner of the realm, far removed from the storm centers of Shíráz, Iṣfahán, and Ṭihrán, afforded Him the necessary leisure to launch upon His most monumental work, as well as to engage on other subsidiary compositions designed to unfold the whole range, and impart the full force, of His short-lived yet momentous Dispensation. Alike in the magnitude of the writings emanating from His pen, and in the diversity of the subjects treated in those writings, His Revelation stands wholly unparalleled in the annals of any previous religion. He Himself affirms, while confined in Máh-Kú, that up to that time His writings, embracing highly diversified subjects, had amounted to more than five hundred thousand verses. *"The verses which have rained from this Cloud of Divine mercy,"* is Bahá'u'lláh's testimony in the Kitáb-i-Íqán, *"have been so abundant that none hath yet been able to estimate their number. A score of volumes are now available. How many still remain beyond our reach! How many have been plundered and have fallen into the hands of the enemy, the fate of which none knoweth!"* No less arresting is the variety of themes presented by these voluminous writings, such as prayers, homilies, orations, Tablets of visitation, scientific treatises, doctrinal dissertations, exhortations, commentaries on the Qur'án and on various traditions, epistles to the highest religious and ecclesiastical dignitaries of the realm, and laws and ordinances for the consolidation of His Faith and the direction of its activities.

Already in <u>Sh</u>íráz, at the earliest stage of His ministry, He had revealed what Bahá'u'lláh has characterized as *"the first, the greatest, and mightiest of all books"* in the Bábí Dispensation, the celebrated commentary on the súrih of Joseph, entitled the Qayyúmu'l-Asmá', whose fundamental purpose was to forecast what the true Joseph (Bahá'u'lláh) would, in a succeeding Dispensation, endure at the hands of one who was at once His arch-enemy and blood brother. This work, comprising above nine thousand three hundred verses, and divided into one hundred and eleven chapters, each chapter a commentary on one verse of the above-mentioned súrih, opens with the Báb's clarion-call and dire warnings addressed to the *"concourse of kings and of the sons of kings;"* forecasts the doom of Muḥammad <u>Sh</u>áh; commands his Grand Vizir, Ḥájí Mírzá Áqásí, to abdicate his authority; admonishes the entire Muslim ecclesiastical order; cautions more specifically the members of the <u>Sh</u>í'ah community; extols the virtues, and anticipates the coming, of Bahá'u'lláh, the "Remnant of God," the "Most Great Master;" and proclaims, in unequivocal language, the independence and universality of the Bábí Revelation, unveils its import, and affirms the inevitable triumph of its Author. It, moreover, directs the *"people of the West"* to *"issue forth from your cities and aid the Cause of God;"* warns the peoples of the earth of the *"terrible, the most grievous vengeance of God;"* threatens the whole Islamic world with *"the Most Great Fire"* were they to turn aside from the newly-revealed Law; foreshadows the Author's martyrdom; eulogizes the high station ordained for the people of Bahá, the *"Companions of the crimson-colored ruby Ark;"* prophesies the fading out and utter obliteration of some of the greatest luminaries in the firmament of the Bábí Dispensation; and even predicts *"afflictive torment,"* in both the *"Day of Our Return"* and in *"the world which is to come,"* for the usurpers of the Imamate, who *"waged war against Ḥusayn* (Imám Ḥusayn) *in the Land of the Euphrates."*

It was this Book which the Bábís universally regarded, during almost the entire ministry of the Báb, as the Qur'án of the people of the Bayán; whose first and most challenging chapter was revealed in the presence of Mullá Ḥusayn, on the night of its Author's Declaration; some of whose pages were borne, by that same disciple, to Bahá'u'lláh, as the first fruits of a Revelation which instantly won His enthusiastic allegiance; whose entire text was translated into Persian by the brilliant and gifted Táhirih; whose passages inflamed the hostility of Ḥusayn Khán and precipitated the initial outbreak of persecution in Shíráz; a single page of which had captured the imagination and entranced the soul of Ḥujjat; and whose contents had set afire the intrepid defenders of the Fort of Shaykh Ṭabarsí and the heroes of Nayríz and Zanján.

This work, of such exalted merit, of such far-reaching influence, was followed by the revelation of the Báb's first Tablet to Muḥammad Sháh; of His Tablets to Sulṭán 'Abdu'l-Majíd and to Najíb Páshá, the Válí of Baghdád; of the Ṣaḥífiy-i-baynu'l-Ḥaramayn, revealed between Mecca and Medina, in answer to questions posed by Mírzá Muḥít-i-Kirmání; of the Epistle to the Sherif of Mecca; of the Kitábu'r-Ruḥ, comprising seven hundred súrihs; of the Khasá'il-i-Sab'ih, which enjoined the alteration of the formula of the adhán; of the Risaliy-i-Furu'-i-'Adliyyih, rendered into Persian by Mullá Muḥammad-Taqíy-i-Harátí; of the commentary on the súrih of Kawthar, which effected such a transformation in the soul of Vaḥíd; of the commentary on the súrih of Va'l-'Asr, in the house of the Imám-Jum'ih of Iṣfahán; of the dissertation on the Specific Mission of Muḥammad, written at the request of Manúchihr Khán; of the second Tablet to Muḥammad Sháh, craving an audience in which to set forth the truths of the new Revelation, and dissipate his doubts; and of the Tablets sent from the village of Síyah-Dihán to the 'ulamás of Qasvín and to Ḥájí Mírzá Áqásí, inquiring from him as to the cause of the sudden change in his decision.

The great bulk of the writings emanating from the Báb's prolific mind was, however, reserved for the period of His confinement in Máh-Kú and Chihríq. To this period must probably belong the unnumbered Epistles which, as attested by no less an authority than Bahá'u'lláh, the Báb specifically addressed to the divines of every city in Persia, as well as to those residing in Najaf and Karbilá, wherein He set forth in detail the errors committed by each one of them. It was during His incarceration in the fortress of Máh-Kú that He, according to the testimony of Shaykh Ḥasan-i-Zunúzí, who transcribed during those nine months the verses dictated by the Báb to His amanuensis, revealed no less than nine commentaries on the whole of the Qur'án—commentaries whose fate, alas, is unknown, and one of which, at least the Author Himself affirmed, surpassed in some respects a book as deservedly famous as the Qayyúmu'l-Asmá.

Within the walls of that same fortress the Bayán (Exposition)—that monumental repository of the laws and precepts of the new Dispensation and the treasury enshrining most of the Báb's references and tributes to, as well as His warning regarding, *"Him Whom God will make manifest"*—was revealed. Peerless among the doctrinal works of the Founder of the Bábí Dispensation; consisting of nine Váḥids (Unities) of nineteen chapters each, except the last Váḥid comprising only ten chapters; not to be confounded with the smaller and less weighty Arabic Bayán, revealed during the same period; fulfilling the Muḥammadan prophecy that "a Youth from Bani-Háshim . . . will reveal a new Book and promulgate a new Law;" wholly safeguarded from the interpolation and corruption which has been the fate of so many of the Báb's lesser works, this Book, of about eight thousand verses, occupying a pivotal position in Bábí literature, should be regarded primarily as a eulogy of the Promised One rather than a code of laws and ordinances designed to be a permanent guide to future generations. This Book at once abrogated the laws and ceremonials enjoined by the Qur'án regarding prayer, fasting, marriage, divorce and inheritance, and upheld, in its integrity, the belief in the prophetic mission of Muḥammad, even as the Prophet of Islám before Him had annulled the ordinances of the Gospel and yet recognized the Divine origin of the Faith of Jesus Christ. It moreover interpreted in a masterly fashion the meaning of certain terms frequently occurring in the sacred Books of previous Dispensations such as Paradise, Hell, Death, Resurrection, the Return, the Balance, the Hour, the Last Judgment, and the like. Designedly severe in the rules and regulations it imposed, revolutionizing in the principles it instilled, calculated to awaken from their age-long torpor the clergy and the people, and to administer a sudden and fatal blow to obsolete and corrupt institutions, it proclaimed, through its drastic provisions, the advent of the anticipated Day, the Day when "the Summoner shall summon to a stern business," when He will "demolish whatever hath been before Him, even as the Apostle of God demolished the ways of those that preceded Him."

It should be noted, in this connection, that in the third Váḥid of this Book there occurs a passage which, alike in its explicit reference to the name of the Promised One, and in its anticipation of the Order which, in a later age, was to be identified with His Revelation, deserves to rank as one of the most significant statements recorded in any of the Báb's writings. *"Well is it with him,"* is His prophetic announcement, *"who fixeth his gaze upon the Order of Bahá'u'lláh, and rendereth thanks unto his Lord. For He will assuredly be made manifest. God hath indeed irrevocably ordained it in the Bayán."* It is with that self-same Order that the Founder of the promised

Revelation, twenty years later—incorporating that same term in His Kitáb-i-Aqdas—identified the System envisaged in that Book, affirming that *"this most great Order"* had deranged the world's equilibrium, and revolutionized mankind's ordered life. It is the features of that self-same Order which, at a later stage in the evolution of the Faith, the Center of Bahá'u'lláh's Covenant and the appointed Interpreter of His teachings, delineated through the provisions of His Will and Testament. It is the structural basis of that self-same Order which, in the Formative Age of that same Faith, the stewards of that same Covenant, the elected representatives of the world-wide Bahá'í community, are now laboriously and unitedly establishing. It is the superstructure of that self-same Order, attaining its full stature through the emergence of the Bahá'í World Commonwealth—the Kingdom of God on earth—which the Golden Age of that same Dispensation must, in the fullness of time, ultimately witness.

The Báb was still in Máh-Kú when He wrote the most detailed and illuminating of His Tablets to Muḥammad S̲h̲áh. Prefaced by a laudatory reference to the unity of God, to His Apostles and to the twelve Imáms; unequivocal in its assertion of the divinity of its Author and of the supernatural powers with which His Revelation had been invested; precise in the verses and traditions it cites in confirmation of so audacious a claim; severe in its condemnation of some of the officials and representatives of the S̲h̲áh's administration, particularly of the *"wicked and accursed"* Ḥusayn K̲h̲án; moving in its description of the humiliation and hardships to which its writer had been subjected, this historic document resembles, in many of its features, the Lawḥ-i-Sulṭán, the Tablet addressed, under similar circumstances, from the prison-fortress of 'Akká by Bahá'u'lláh to Náṣiri'd-Dín S̲h̲áh, and constituting His lengthiest epistle to any single sovereign.

The Dalá'il-i-Sab'ih (Seven Proofs), the most important of the polemical works of the Báb, was revealed during that same period. Remarkably lucid, admirable in its precision, original in conception, unanswerable in its argument, this work, apart from the many and divers proofs of His mission which it adduces, is noteworthy for the blame it assigns to the *"seven powerful sovereigns ruling the world"* in His day, as well as for the manner in which it stresses the responsibilities, and censures the conduct, of the Christian divines of a former age who, had they recognized the truth of Muḥammad's mission, He contends, would have been followed by the mass of their co-religionists.

During the Báb's confinement in the fortress of Chihríq, where He spent almost the whole of the two remaining years of His life, the Lawḥ-i-Ḥuru'fát (Tablet of the Letters) was revealed, in honor of Dayyán—a Tablet which, however misconstrued at first as an exposition of the science of divination, was later recognized to have unravelled, on the one hand, the mystery of the Mustagháth, and to have abstrusely alluded, on the other, to the nineteen years which must needs elapse between the Declaration of the Báb and that of Bahá'u'lláh. It was during these years—years darkened throughout by the rigors of the Báb's captivity, by the severe indignities inflicted upon Him, and by the news of the disasters that overtook the heroes of Mázindarán and Nayríz—that He revealed, soon after His return from Tabríz, His denunciatory Tablet to Ḥájí Mírzá Áqásí. Couched in bold and moving language, unsparing in its condemnation, this epistle was forwarded to the intrepid Ḥujjat who, as corroborated by Bahá'u'lláh, delivered it to that wicked minister.

To this period of incarceration in the fortresses of Máh-Kú and Chihríq—a period of unsurpassed fecundity, yet bitter in its humiliations and ever-deepening sorrows—belong almost all the written references, whether in the form of warnings, appeals or exhortations, which the Báb, in anticipation of the approaching hour of His supreme affliction, felt it necessary to make to the Author of a Revelation that was soon to supersede His own. Conscious from the very beginning of His twofold mission, as the Bearer of a wholly independent Revelation and the Herald of One still greater than His own, He could not content Himself with the vast number of commentaries, of prayers, of laws and ordinances, of dissertations and epistles, of homilies and orations that had incessantly streamed from His pen. The Greater Covenant into which, as affirmed in His writings, God had, from time immemorial, entered, through the Prophets of all ages, with the whole of mankind, regarding the newborn Revelation, had already been fulfilled. It had now to be supplemented by a Lesser Covenant which He felt bound to make with the entire body of His followers concerning the One Whose advent He characterized as the fruit and ultimate purpose of His Dispensation. Such a Covenant had invariably been the feature of every previous religion. It had existed, under various forms, with varying degrees of emphasis, had always been couched in veiled language, and had been alluded to in cryptic prophecies, in abstruse allegories, in unauthenticated traditions, and in the fragmentary and obscure passages of the sacred Scriptures. In the Bábí Dispensation, however, it was destined to be established in clear and unequivocal language, though not embodied in a separate document. Unlike the Prophets gone before Him, Whose Covenants were shrouded in mystery, unlike Bahá'u'lláh, Whose clearly defined Covenant was incorporated in a specially written Testament, and designated by Him as *"the Book of My Covenant,"* the Báb chose to intersperse His Book of Laws, the Persian Bayán, with unnumbered passages, some designedly obscure, mostly indubitably clear and conclusive, in which He fixes the date of the promised Revelation, extols its virtues, asserts its pre-eminent character, assigns to it unlimited powers and prerogatives, and tears down every barrier that might be an obstacle to its recognition. *"He, verily,"* Bahá'u'lláh, referring to the Báb in His Kitáb-i-Badí', has stated, *"hath not fallen short of His duty to exhort the people of the Bayán and to deliver unto them His Message. In no age or dispensation hath any Manifestation made mention, in such detail and in such explicit language, of the Manifestation destined to succeed Him."*

Some of His disciples the Báb assiduously prepared to expect the imminent Revelation. Others He orally assured would live to see its day. To Mullá Báqir, one of the Letters of the Living, He actually prophesied, in a Tablet addressed to him, that he would meet the Promised One face to face. To Sayyáḥ, another disciple, He gave verbally a similar assurance. Mullá Ḥusayn He directed to Ṭihrán, assuring him that in that city was enshrined a Mystery Whose light neither Ḥijáz nor S͟hīráz could rival. Quddús, on the eve of his final separation from Him, was promised that he would attain the presence of the One Who was the sole Object of their adoration and love. To S͟hayk͟h Ḥasan-i-Zunúzí He declared while in Máh-Kú that he would behold in Karbilá the countenance of the promised Ḥusayn. On Dayyán He conferred the title of *"the third Letter to believe in Him Whom God shall make manifest,"* while to 'Azím He divulged, in the Kitáb-i-Panj-S͟ha'n, the name, and announced the approaching advent, of Him Who was to consummate His own Revelation.

A successor or vicegerent the Báb never named, an interpreter of His teachings He refrained from appointing. So transparently clear were His references to the Promised One, so brief was to be the duration of His own Dispensation, that neither the one nor the other was deemed necessary. All He did was, according to the testimony of 'Abdu'l-Bahá in "A Traveller's Narrative," to nominate, on the advice of Bahá'u'lláh and of another disciple, Mírzá Yaḥyá, who would act solely as a figure-head pending the manifestation of the

Promised One, thus enabling Bahá'u'lláh to promote, in relative security, the Cause so dear to His heart.

"*The Bayán*," the Báb in that Book, referring to the Promised One, affirms, "*is, from beginning to end, the repository of all of His attributes, and the treasury of both His fire and His light.*" "*If thou attainest unto His Revelation*," He, in another connection declares, "*and obeyest Him, thou wilt have revealed the fruit of the Bayán; if not, thou art unworthy of mention before God.*" "*O people of the Bayán!*" He, in that same Book, thus warns the entire company of His followers, "*act not as the people of the Qur'án have acted, for if ye do so, the fruits of your night will come to naught.*" "*Suffer not the Bayán*," is His emphatic injunction, "*and all that hath been revealed therein to withhold you from that Essence of Being and Lord of the visible and invisible.*" "*Beware, beware*," is His significant warning addressed to Vaḥíd, "*lest in the days of His Revelation the Váḥid of the Bayán* (eighteen Letters of the Living and the Báb) *shut thee out as by a veil from Him, inasmuch as this Váḥid is but a creature in His sight.*" And again: "*O congregation of the Bayán, and all who are therein! Recognize ye the limits imposed upon you, for such a One as the Point of the Bayán Himself hath believed in Him Whom God shall make manifest before all things were created. Therein, verily, do I glory before all who are in the kingdom of heaven and earth.*"

"*In the year nine*," He, referring to the date of the advent of the promised Revelation, has explicitly written, "*ye shall attain unto all good.*" "*In the year nine, ye will attain unto the presence of God.*" And again: "*After Ḥín* (68) *a Cause shall be given unto you which ye shall come to know.*" "*Ere nine will have elapsed from the inception of this Cause*," He more particularly has stated, "*the realities of the created things will not be made manifest. All that thou hast as yet seen is but the stage from the moist germ until We clothed it with flesh. Be patient, until thou beholdest a new creation. Say: 'Blessed, therefore, be God, the most excellent of Makers!'*" "*Wait thou*," is His statement to 'Azím, "*until nine will have elapsed from the time of the Bayán. Then exclaim: 'Blessed, therefore, be God, the most excellent of Makers!'*" "*Be attentive*," He, referring in a remarkable passage to the year nineteen, has admonished, "*from the inception of the Revelation till the number of Váḥid* (19)." "*The Lord of the Day of Reckoning*," He, even more explicitly, has stated, "*will be manifested at the end of Váḥid* (19) *and the beginning of eighty* (1280 A.H.)." "*Were He to appear this very moment*," He, in His eagerness to insure that the proximity of the promised Revelation should not withhold men from the Promised One, has revealed, *"I would be the first to adore Him, and the first to bow down before Him."*

*"I have written down in My mention of Him,"* He thus extols the Author of the anticipated Revelation, *"these gem-like words: 'No allusion of Mine can allude unto Him, neither anything mentioned in the Bayán.'"* *"I, Myself, am but the first servant to believe in Him and in His signs. . . ."* *"The year-old germ,"* He significantly affirms, *"that holdeth within itself the potentialities of the Revelation that is to come is endowed with a potency superior to the combined forces of the whole of the Bayán."* And again: *"The whole of the Bayán is only a leaf amongst the leaves of His Paradise."* *"Better is it for thee,"* He similarly asserts, *"to recite but one of the verses of Him Whom God shall make manifest than to set down the whole of the Bayán, for on that Day that one verse can save thee, whereas the entire Bayán cannot save thee."* *"Today the Bayán is in the stage of seed; at the beginning of the manifestation of Him Whom God shall make manifest its ultimate perfection will become apparent."* *"The Bayán deriveth all its glory from Him Whom God shall make manifest."* *"All that hath been revealed in the Bayán is but a ring upon My hand, and I Myself am, verily, but a ring upon the hand of Him Whom God shall make manifest . . . He turneth it as He pleaseth, for whatsoever He pleaseth, and through whatsoever He pleaseth. He, verily, is the Help in Peril, the Most High."* *"Certitude itself,"* He, in reply to Vaḥíd and to one of the Letters of the Living who had inquired regarding the promised One, had declared, *"is ashamed to be called upon to certify His truth . . . and Testimony itself is ashamed to testify unto Him."* Addressing this same Vaḥíd, He moreover had stated: *"Were I to be assured that in the day of His manifestation thou wilt deny Him, I would unhesitatingly disown thee . . . If, on the other hand, I be told that a Christian, who beareth no allegiance to My Faith, will believe in Him, the same will I regard as the apple of My eye."*

And finally is this, His moving invocation to God: *"Bear Thou witness that, through this Book, I have covenanted with all created things concerning the mission of Him Whom Thou shalt make manifest, ere the covenant concerning My own mission had been established. Sufficient witness art Thou and they that have believed in Thy signs."* *"I, verily, have not fallen short of My duty to admonish that people,"* is yet another testimony from His pen, *". . . If on the day of*

*His Revelation all that are on earth bear Him allegiance, Mine inmost being will rejoice, inasmuch as all will have attained the summit of their existence. . . . If not, My soul will be saddened. I truly have nurtured all things for this purpose. How, then, can any one be veiled from Him?"*

The last three and most eventful years of the Báb's ministry had, as we have observed in the preceding pages, witnessed not only the formal and public declaration of His mission, but also an unprecedented effusion of His inspired writings, including both the revelation of the fundamental laws of His Dispensation and also the establishment of that Lesser Covenant which was to safeguard the unity of His followers and pave the way for the advent of an incomparably mightier Revelation. It was during this same period, in the early days of His incarceration in the fortress of Chihríq, that the independence of the new-born Faith was openly recognized and asserted by His disciples. The laws underlying the new Dispensation had been revealed by its Author in a prison-fortress in the mountains of Ádhirbáyján, while the Dispensation itself was now to be inaugurated in a plain on the border of Mázindarán, at a conference of His assembled followers.

Bahá'u'lláh, maintaining through continual correspondence close contact with the Báb, and Himself the directing force behind the manifold activities of His struggling fellow-disciples, unobtrusively yet effectually presided over that conference, and guided and controlled its proceedings. Quddús, regarded as the exponent of the conservative element within it, affected, in pursuance of a pre-conceived plan designed to mitigate the alarm and consternation which such a conference was sure to arouse, to oppose the seemingly extremist views advocated by the impetuous Ṭáhirih. The primary purpose of that gathering was to implement the revelation of the Bayán by a sudden, a complete and dramatic break with the past—with its order, its ecclesiasticism, its traditions, and ceremonials. The subsidiary purpose of the conference was to consider the means of emancipating the Báb from His cruel confinement in Chihríq. The first was eminently successful; the second was destined from the outset to fail.

The scene of such a challenging and far-reaching proclamation was the hamlet of Badasht, where Bahá'u'lláh had rented, amidst pleasant surroundings, three gardens, one of which He assigned to Quddús, another to Ṭáhirih, whilst the third He reserved for Himself. The eighty-one disciples who had gathered from various provinces were His guests from the day of their arrival to the day they dispersed. On each of the twenty-two days of His sojourn in that hamlet He revealed a Tablet, which was chanted in the presence of the assembled believers. On every believer He conferred a new name, without, however, disclosing the identity of the one who had bestowed it. He Himself was henceforth designated by the name Bahá. Upon the Last Letter of the Living was conferred the appellation of Quddús, while Qurratu'l-'Ayn was given the title of Ṭáhirih. By these names they were all subsequently addressed by the Báb in the Tablets He revealed for each one of them.

It was Bahá'u'lláh Who steadily, unerringly, yet unsuspectedly, steered the course of that memorable episode, and it was Bahá'u'lláh Who brought the meeting to its final and dramatic climax. One day in His presence, when illness had confined Him to bed, Ṭáhirih, regarded as the fair and spotless emblem of chastity and the incarnation of the holy Fáṭimih, appeared suddenly, adorned yet unveiled, before the assembled companions, seated herself on the right-hand of the affrighted and infuriated Quddús, and, tearing through her fiery words the veils guarding the sanctity of the ordinances of Islám, sounded the clarion-call, and proclaimed the inauguration, of a new Dispensation. The effect was electric and instantaneous. She, of such stainless purity, so reverenced that even to gaze at her shadow was deemed an improper act, appeared for a moment, in the eyes of her scandalized beholders, to have defamed herself, shamed the Faith she had espoused, and sullied the immortal Countenance she symbolized. Fear, anger, bewilderment, swept their inmost souls, and stunned their faculties. 'Abdu'l-Kháliq-i-Iṣfahání, aghast and deranged at such a sight, cut his throat with his own hands. Spattered with blood, and frantic with excitement, he fled away from her face. A few, abandoning their companions, renounced their Faith. Others stood mute and transfixed before her. Still others must have recalled with throbbing hearts the Islamic tradition foreshadowing the appearance of Fáṭimih herself unveiled while crossing the Bridge (Ṣirát) on the promised Day of Judgment. Quddús, mute with rage, seemed to be only waiting for the moment when he could strike her down with the sword he happened to be then holding in his hand.

Undeterred, unruffled, exultant with joy, Ṭáhirih arose, and, without the least premeditation and in a language strikingly resembling that of the Qur'án, delivered a fervid and eloquent appeal to the remnant of the assembly, ending it with this bold assertion: "I am the Word which the Qá'im is to utter, the Word which shall put to flight the chiefs and nobles of the earth!" Thereupon, she invited them to embrace each other and celebrate so great an occasion.

On that memorable day the *"Bugle"* mentioned in the Qur'án was sounded, the *"stunning trumpet-blast"* was loudly raised, and the *"Catastrophe"* came to pass. The days immediately following so startling a departure from the time-honored traditions of Islám witnessed a veritable revolution in the outlook, habits, ceremonials and manner of worship of these hitherto zealous and devout upholders of the Muḥammadan Law. Agitated as had been the Conference from first to last, deplorable as was the secession of the few who refused to countenance the annulment of the fundamental statutes of the Islamic Faith, its purpose had been fully and gloriously accomplished. Only four years earlier the Author of the Bábí Revelation had declared His mission to Mullá Ḥusayn in the privacy of His home in Shíráz. Three years after that Declaration, within the walls of the prison-fortress of Máh-Kú, He was dictating to His amanuensis the fundamental and distinguishing precepts of His Dispensation. A year later, His followers, under the actual leadership of Bahá'u'lláh, their fellow-disciple, were themselves, in the hamlet of Badasht, abrogating the Qur'ánic Law, repudiating both the divinely-ordained and man-made precepts of the Faith of Muḥammad, and shaking off the shackles of its antiquated system. Almost immediately after, the Báb Himself, still a prisoner, was vindicating the acts of His disciples by asserting, formally and unreservedly, His claim to be the promised Qá'im, in the presence of the Heir to the Throne, the leading exponents of the Shaykhí community, and the most illustrious ecclesiastical dignitaries assembled in the capital of Ádhirbáyján.

A little over four years had elapsed since the birth of the Báb's Revelation when the trumpet-blast announcing the formal extinction of the old, and the inauguration of the new Dispensation was sounded. No pomp, no pageantry marked so great a turning-point in the world's religious history. Nor was its modest setting commensurate with such a sudden, startling, complete emancipation from the dark and embattled forces of fanaticism, of priestcraft, of religious orthodoxy and superstition. The assembled host consisted of no more than a single woman and a handful of men, mostly recruited from the very ranks they were attacking, and devoid, with few exceptions, of wealth, prestige and power. The Captain of the host was Himself an absentee, a captive in the grip of His foes. The arena was a tiny hamlet in the plain of Badasht on the border of Mázindarán. The trumpeter was a lone woman, the noblest of her sex in that Dispensation, whom even some of her co-religionists pronounced a heretic. The call she sounded was the death-knell of the twelve hundred year old law of Islám.

Accelerated, twenty years later, by another trumpet-blast, announcing the formulation of the laws of yet another Dispensation, this process of disintegration, associated with the declining fortunes of a superannuated, though divinely revealed Law, gathered further momentum, precipitated, in a later age, the annulment of the S̲harí'aḥ canonical Law in Turkey, led to the virtual abandonment of that Law in S̲hí'ah Persia, has, more recently, been responsible for the dissociation of the System envisaged in the Kitáb-i-Aqdas from the Sunní ecclesiastical Law in Egypt, has paved the way for the recognition of that System in the Holy Land itself, and is destined to culminate in the secularization of the Muslim states, and in the universal recognition of the Law of Bahá'u'lláh by all the nations, and its enthronement in the hearts of all the peoples, of the Muslim world.

# CHAPTER III

## Upheavals in Mázindarán, Nayríz and Zanján

The Báb's captivity in a remote corner of Á<u>dh</u>irbáyján, immortalized by the proceedings of the Conference of Bada<u>sh</u>t, and distinguished by such notable developments as the public declaration of His mission, the formulation of the laws of His Dispensation and the establishment of His Covenant, was to acquire added significance through the dire convulsions that sprang from the acts of both His adversaries and His disciples. The commotions that ensued, as the years of that captivity drew to a close, and that culminated in His own martyrdom, called forth a degree of heroism on the part of His followers and a fierceness of hostility on the part of His enemies which had never been witnessed during the first three years of His ministry. Indeed, this brief but most turbulent period may be rightly regarded as the bloodiest and most dramatic of the Heroic Age of the Bahá'í Era.

The momentous happenings associated with the Báb's incarceration in Máh-Kú and <u>Ch</u>ihríq, constituting as they did the high watermark of His Revelation, could have no other consequence than to fan to fiercer flame both the fervor of His lovers and the fury of His enemies. A persecution, grimmer, more odious, and more shrewdly calculated than any which Ḥusayn <u>Kh</u>án, or even Ḥájí Mírzá Áqásí, had kindled was soon to be unchained, to be accompanied by a corresponding manifestation of heroism unmatched by any of the earliest outbursts of enthusiasm that had greeted the birth of the Faith in either <u>Sh</u>íráz or Iṣfahán. This period of ceaseless and unprecedented commotion was to rob that Faith, in quick succession, of its chief protagonists, was to attain its climax in the extinction of the life of its Author, and was to be followed by a further and this time an almost complete elimination of its eminent supporters, with the sole exception of One Who, at its darkest hour, was entrusted, through the dispensations of Providence, with the dual function of saving a sorely-stricken Faith from annihilation, and of ushering in the Dispensation destined to supersede it.

The formal assumption by the Báb of the authority of the promised Qá'im, in such dramatic circumstances and in so challenging a tone, before a distinguished gathering of eminent <u>Sh</u>í'ah ecclesiastics, powerful, jealous, alarmed and hostile, was the explosive force that loosed a veritable avalanche of calamities which swept down upon the Faith and the people among whom it was born. It raised to fervid heat the zeal that glowed in the souls of the Báb's scattered disciples, who were already incensed by the cruel captivity of their Leader, and whose ardor was now further inflamed by the outpourings of His pen which reached them unceasingly from the place of His confinement. It provoked a heated and prolonged controversy throughout the length and breadth of the land, in bazaars, masjids, madrisihs and other public places, deepening thereby the cleavage that had already sundered its people. Muḥammad S̲h̲áh, at so perilous an hour, was meanwhile rapidly sinking under the weight of his physical infirmities. The shallow-minded Ḥájí Mírzá Áqásí, now the pivot of state affairs, exhibited a vacillation and incompetence that seemed to increase with every extension in the range of his grave responsibilities. At one time he would feel inclined to support the verdict of the 'ulamás; at another he would censure their aggressiveness and distrust their assertions; at yet another, he would relapse into mysticism, and, wrapt in his reveries, lose sight of the gravity of the emergency that confronted him.

So glaring a mismanagement of national affairs emboldened the clerical order, whose members were now hurling with malignant zeal anathemas from their pulpits, and were vociferously inciting superstitious congregations to take up arms against the upholders of a much hated creed, to insult the honor of their women folk, to plunder their property and harass and injure their children. "What of the signs and prodigies," they thundered before countless assemblies, "that must needs usher in the advent of the Qá'im? What of the Major and Minor Occultations? What of the cities of Jábulqá and Jábulsá? How are we to explain the sayings of Ḥusayn-ibn-Rúḥ, and what interpretation should be given to the authenticated traditions ascribed to Ibn-i-Mihríyár? Where are the Men of the Unseen, who are to traverse, in a week, the whole surface of the earth? What of the conquest of the East and West which the Qá'im is to effect on His appearance? Where is the one-eyed Anti-Christ and the ass on which he is to mount? What of Sufyán and his dominion?" "Are we," they noisily remonstrated, "are we to account as a dead letter the indubitable, the unnumbered traditions of our holy Imáms, or are we to extinguish with fire and sword this brazen heresy that has dared to lift its head in our land?"

To these defamations, threats and protestations the learned and resolute champions of a misrepresented Faith, following the example of their Leader, opposed unhesitatingly treatises, commentaries and refutations, assiduously written, cogent in their argument, replete with testimonies, lucid, eloquent and convincing, affirming their belief in the Prophethood of Muḥammad, in the legitimacy of the Imáms, in the spiritual sovereignty of the Ṣáḥibu'z-Zamán (the Lord of the Age), interpreting in a masterly fashion the obscure, the designedly allegorical and abstruse traditions, verses and prophecies in the Islamic holy Writ, and adducing, in support of their contention, the meekness and apparent helplessness of the Imám Ḥusayn who, despite his defeat, his discomfiture and ignominious martyrdom, had been hailed by their antagonists as the very embodiment and the matchless symbol of God's all-conquering sovereignty and power.

This fierce, nation-wide controversy had assumed alarming proportions when Muḥammad Sháh finally succumbed to his illness, precipitating by his death the downfall of his favorite and all-powerful minister, Ḥájí Mírzá Áqásí, who, soon stripped of the treasures he had amassed, fell into disgrace, was expelled from the capital, and sought refuge in Karbilá. The seventeen year old Náṣiri'd-Dín Mírzá ascended the throne, leaving the direction of affairs to the obdurate, the iron-hearted Amír-Niẓám, Mírzá Taqí Khán, who, without consulting his fellow-ministers, decreed that immediate and condign punishment be inflicted on the hapless Bábís. Governors, magistrates and civil servants, throughout the provinces, instigated by the monstrous campaign of vilification conducted by the clergy, and prompted by their lust for pecuniary rewards, vied in their respective spheres with each other in hounding and heaping indignities on the adherents of an outlawed Faith. For the first time in the Faith's history a systematic campaign in which the civil and ecclesiastical powers were banded together was being launched against it, a campaign that was to culminate in the horrors experienced by Bahá'u'lláh in the Síyáh-Chál of Ṭihrán and His subsequent banishment to 'Iráq. Government, clergy and people arose, as one man, to assault and exterminate their common enemy. In remote and isolated centers the scattered disciples of a persecuted community were pitilessly struck down by the sword of their foes, while in centers where large numbers had congregated measures were taken in self-defense, which, misconstrued by a cunning and deceitful adversary, served in their turn to inflame still further the hostility of the authorities, and multiply the outrages perpetrated by the oppressor. In the East at Shaykh Ṭabarsí, in the south in Nayríz, in the west in Zanján, and in the capital itself, massacres, upheavals, demonstrations, engagements, sieges, acts of treachery proclaimed, in rapid succession, the violence of the storm which had broken out, and exposed the bankruptcy, and blackened the annals, of a proud yet degenerate people.

The audacity of Mullá Ḥusayn who, at the command of the Báb, had attired his head with the green turban worn and sent to him by his Master, who had hoisted the Black Standard, the unfurling of which would, according to the Prophet Muḥammad, herald the advent of the vicegerent of God on earth, and who, mounted on his steed, was marching at the head of two hundred and two of his fellow-disciples to meet and lend his assistance to Quddús in the Jazíriy-i-Khaḍrá (Verdant Isle)—his audacity was the signal for a clash the reverberations of which were to resound throughout the entire country. The contest lasted no less than eleven months. Its theatre was for the most part the forest of Mázindarán. Its heroes were the flower of the Báb's disciples. Its martyrs comprised no less than half of the Letters of the Living, not excluding Quddús and Mullá Ḥusayn, respectively the last and the first of these Letters. The directive force which however unobtrusively sustained it was none other than that which flowed from the mind of Bahá'u'lláh. It was caused by the unconcealed determination of the dawn-breakers of a new Age to proclaim, fearlessly and befittingly, its advent, and by a no less unyielding resolve, should persuasion prove a failure, to resist and defend themselves against the onslaughts of malicious and unreasoning assailants. It demonstrated beyond the shadow of a doubt what the indomitable spirit of a band of three hundred and thirteen untrained, unequipped yet God-intoxicated students, mostly sedentary recluses of the college and cloister, could achieve when pitted in self-defense against a trained army, well equipped, supported by the masses of the people, blessed by the clergy, headed by a prince of the royal blood, backed by the resources of the state, acting with the enthusiastic approval of its sovereign, and animated by the unfailing counsels of a resolute and all-powerful minister. Its outcome was a heinous betrayal ending in an orgy of slaughter, staining with everlasting infamy its perpetrators, investing its victims with a halo of imperishable glory, and generating the very seeds which, in a later age, were to blossom into world-wide administrative institutions, and which must, in the fullness of time, yield their golden fruit in the shape of a world-redeeming, earth-encircling Order.

It will be unnecessary to attempt even an abbreviated narrative of this tragic episode, however grave its import, however much misconstrued by adverse chroniclers and historians. A glance over its salient features will suffice for the purpose of these pages. We note, as we conjure up the events of this great tragedy, the fortitude, the intrepidity, the discipline and the resourcefulness of its heroes, contrasting sharply with the turpitude, the cowardice, the disorderliness and the inconstancy of their opponents. We observe the sublime patience, the noble restraint exercised by one of its principal actors, the lion-hearted Mullá Ḥusayn, who persistently refused to unsheathe his sword until an armed and angry multitude, uttering the foulest invectives, had gathered at a farsang's distance from Bárfurúsh to block his way, and had mortally struck down seven of his innocent and staunch companions. We are filled with admiration for the tenacity of faith of that same Mullá Ḥusayn, demonstrated by his resolve to persevere in sounding the adhán, while besieged in the caravanserai of Sabsih-Maydán, though three of his companions, who had successively ascended to the roof of the inn, with the express purpose of performing that sacred rite, had been instantly killed by the bullets of the enemy. We marvel at the spirit of renunciation that prompted those sore pressed sufferers to contemptuously ignore the possessions left behind by their fleeing enemy; that led them to discard their own belongings, and content themselves with their steeds and swords; that induced the father of Badí‘, one of that gallant company, to fling unhesitatingly by the roadside the satchel, full of turquoises which he had brought from his father's mine in Níshápúr; that led Mírzá Muḥammad-Taqíy-i-Juvayní to cast away a sum equivalent in value in silver and gold; and impelled those same companions to disdain, and refuse even to touch, the costly furnishings and the coffers of gold and silver which the demoralized and shame-laden Prince Mihdí-Qulí Mírzá, the commander of the army of Mázindarán and a brother of Muḥammad Sháh, had left behind in his headlong flight from his camp. We cannot but esteem the passionate sincerity with which Mullá Ḥusayn pleaded with the Prince, and the formal assurance he gave him, disclaiming, in no uncertain terms, any intention on his part or that of his fellow-disciples of usurping the authority of the Sháh or of subverting the foundations of his state. We cannot but view with contempt the conduct of that arch-villain, the hysterical, the cruel and overbearing Sa‘ídu'l-‘Ulamá, who, alarmed at the approach of those same companions, flung, in a frenzy of excitement, and before an immense crowd of men and women, his turban to the ground, tore open the neck of his shirt, and, bewailing the plight into which Islám had fallen, implored his congregation to fly to arms and cut down the approaching band. We are struck with wonder as we contemplate the super-human prowess of Mullá Ḥusayn which enabled him, notwithstanding his fragile frame and trembling hand, to slay a treacherous foe who had taken shelter behind a tree, by cleaving with a single stroke of his sword the tree, the man and his musket in twain. We are stirred, moreover, by the scene of the arrival of Bahá'u'lláh at the Fort, and the indefinable joy it imparted to Mullá Ḥusayn, the reverent reception accorded Him by His fellow-disciples, His inspection of the fortifications which they had hurriedly erected for their protection, and the advice He gave them, which resulted in the miraculous deliverance of Quddús, in his subsequent and close association with the defenders of that Fort, and in his effective participation in the exploits connected with its siege and eventual destruction. We are amazed at the serenity and sagacity of that same Quddús, the confidence he instilled on his arrival, the resourcefulness he displayed, the fervor and gladness with which the besieged listened, at morn and at even-tide, to the voice intoning the verses of his celebrated commentary on the Ṣád of Ṣamad, to which he had already, while in Sárí, devoted a treatise thrice as voluminous as the Qur'án itself, and which he was now, despite the tumultuary attacks of the enemy and the privations he and his companions were enduring, further elucidating by adding to that interpretation as many verses as he had previously written. We remember with thrilling hearts that memorable encounter when, at the cry "Mount your steeds, O heroes of God!" Mullá Ḥusayn, accompanied by two hundred and two of the beleaguered and sorely-distressed companions, and preceded by Quddús, emerged before daybreak from the Fort, and, raising the shout of "Yá Ṣáḥibu'z-Zamán!", rushed at full charge towards the stronghold of the Prince, and penetrated to his private apartments, only to find that, in his consternation, he had thrown himself from a back window into the moat, and escaped bare-footed, leaving his host confounded and routed. We see relived in poignant memory that last day of Mullá Ḥusayn's earthly life, when, soon after midnight, having performed his ablutions, clothed himself in new garments, and attired his head with the Báb's turban, he mounted his charger, ordered the gate of the Fort to be opened, rode out at the head of three hundred and thirteen of his companions, shouting aloud "Yá Ṣáḥibu'z-Zamán!", charged successively the seven barricades erected by the enemy, captured every one of them, notwithstanding the bullets that were raining upon him, swiftly dispatched their defenders, and had scattered their forces when, in the ensuing tumult, his steed became suddenly entangled in the rope of a tent, and before he could extricate himself he was struck in the breast by a bullet which the cowardly 'Abbás-Qulí Khán-i-Láríjání had discharged, while lying in ambush in the branches of a neighboring tree. We acclaim the magnificent courage that, in a subsequent encounter, inspired nineteen of those stout-hearted companions to plunge headlong into the camp of an enemy that consisted of no less than two regiments of infantry and cavalry, and to cause such consternation that one of their leaders, the same 'Abbás-Qulí Khán, falling from his horse, and leaving in his distress one of his boots hanging from the stirrup, ran away, half-shod and bewildered, to the Prince, and confessed the ignominious reverse he had suffered. Nor can we fail to note the superb fortitude with which these heroic souls bore the load of their severe trials; when their food was at first reduced to the flesh of horses brought away from the deserted camp of the enemy; when later they had to content themselves with such grass as they could snatch from the fields whenever they obtained a respite from their besiegers; when they were forced, at a later stage, to consume the bark of the trees and the leather of their saddles, of their belts, of their scabbards and of their shoes; when during eighteen days they had nothing but water of which they drank a mouthful every morning; when the cannon fire of the enemy compelled them to dig subterranean passages within the Fort, where, dwelling amid mud and water, with garments rotting away with damp, they had to subsist on ground up bones; and when, at last, oppressed by gnawing hunger, they, as attested by a contemporary chronicler, were driven to disinter the steed of their venerated leader, Mullá Ḥusayn, cut it into pieces, grind into dust its bones, mix it with the putrified meat, and, making it into a stew, avidly devour it.

Nor can reference be omitted to the abject treachery to which the impotent and discredited Prince eventually resorted, and his violation of his so-called irrevocable oath, inscribed and sealed by him on the margin of the opening súrih of the Qur'án, whereby he, swearing by that holy Book, undertook to set free all the defenders of the Fort, pledged his honor that no man in his army or in the neighborhood would molest them, and that he would himself, at his own expense, arrange for their safe departure to their homes. And lastly, we call to remembrance, the final scene of that sombre tragedy, when, as a result of the Prince's violation of his sacred engagement, a number of the betrayed companions of Quddús were assembled in the camp of the enemy, were stripped of their possessions, and sold as slaves, the rest being either killed by the spears and swords of the officers, or torn asunder, or bound to trees and riddled with bullets, or blown from the mouths of cannon and consigned to the flames, or else being disemboweled and having their heads impaled on spears and lances. Quddús, their beloved leader, was by yet another shameful act of the intimidated Prince surrendered into the hands of the diabolical Sa'ídu'l-'Ulamá who, in his unquenchable hostility and aided by the mob whose passions he had sedulously inflamed, stripped his victim of his garments, loaded him with chains, paraded him through the streets of Bárfurúsh, and incited the scum of its female inhabitants to execrate and spit upon him, assail him with knives and axes, mutilate his body, and throw the tattered fragments into a fire.

This stirring episode, so glorious for the Faith, so blackening to the reputation of its enemies—an episode which must be regarded as a rare phenomenon in the history of modern times—was soon succeeded by a parallel upheaval, strikingly similar in its essential features. The scene of woeful tribulations was now shifted to the south, to the province of Fárs, not far from the city where the dawning light of the Faith had broken. Nayríz and its environs were made to sustain the impact of this fresh ordeal in all its fury. The Fort of Khájih, in the vicinity of the Chinár-Súkhtih quarter of that hotly agitated village became the storm-center of the new conflagration. The hero who towered above his fellows, valiantly struggled, and fell a victim to its devouring flames was that "unique and peerless figure of his age," the far-famed Siyyid Yaḥyáy-i-Dárábí, better known as Vaḥíd. Foremost among his perfidious adversaries, who kindled and fed the fire of this conflagration was the base and fanatical governor of Nayríz, Zaynu'l-'Ábidín Khán, seconded by 'Abdu'lláh Khán, the Shujá'u'l-Mulk, and reinforced by Prince Fírúz Mírzá, the governor of Shíráz. Of a much briefer duration than the Mázindarán upheaval, which lasted no less than eleven months, the atrocities that marked its closing stage were no less devastating in their consequences. Once again a handful of men, innocent, law-abiding, peace-loving, yet high-spirited and indomitable, consisting partly, in this case, of untrained lads and men of advanced age, were surprised, challenged, encompassed and assaulted by the superior force of a cruel and crafty enemy, an innumerable host of able-bodied men who, though well-trained, adequately equipped and continually reinforced, were impotent to coerce into submission, or subdue, the spirit of their adversaries.

This fresh commotion originated in declarations of faith as fearless and impassioned, and in demonstrations of religious enthusiasm almost as vehement and dramatic, as those which had ushered in the Mázindarán upheaval. It was instigated by a no less sustained and violent outburst of uncompromising ecclesiastical hostility. It was accompanied by corresponding manifestations of blind religious fanaticism. It was provoked by similar acts of naked aggression on the part of both clergy and people. It demonstrated afresh the same purpose, was animated throughout by the same spirit, and rose to almost the same height of superhuman heroism, of fortitude, courage, and renunciation. It revealed a no less shrewdly calculated coordination of plans and efforts between the civil and ecclesiastical authorities designed to challenge and overthrow a common enemy. It was preceded by a similar categorical repudiation, on the part of the Bábís, of any intention of interfering with the civil jurisdiction of the realm, or of undermining the legitimate authority of its sovereign. It provided a no less convincing testimony to the restraint and forbearance of the victims, in the face of the ruthless and unprovoked aggression of the oppressor. It exposed, as it moved toward its climax, and in hardly less striking a manner, the cowardice, the want of discipline and the degradation of a spiritually bankrupt foe. It was marked, as it approached its conclusion, by a treachery as vile and shameful. It ended in a massacre even more revolting in the horrors it evoked and the miseries it engendered. It sealed the fate of Vaḥíd who, by his green turban, the emblem of his proud lineage, was bound to a horse and dragged ignominiously through the streets, after which his head was cut off, was stuffed with straw, and sent as a trophy to the feasting Prince in S͟híráz, while his body was abandoned to the mercy of the infuriated women of Nayríz, who, intoxicated with barbarous joy by the shouts of exultation raised by a triumphant enemy, danced, to the accompaniment of drums and cymbals, around it. And finally, it brought in its wake, with the aid of no less than five thousand men, specially commissioned for this purpose, a general and fierce onslaught on the defenseless Bábís, whose possessions were confiscated, whose houses were destroyed, whose stronghold was burned to the ground, whose women and children were captured, and some of whom, stripped almost naked, were mounted on donkeys, mules and camels, and led through rows of heads hewn from the lifeless bodies of their fathers, brothers, sons and husbands, who previously had been either branded, or had their nails torn out, or had been lashed to death, or had spikes hammered into their hands and feet, or had incisions made in their noses through which strings were passed, and by which they were led through the streets before the gaze of an irate and derisive multitude.

This turmoil, so ravaging, so distressing, had hardly subsided when another conflagration, even more devastating than the two previous upheavals, was kindled in Zanján and its immediate surroundings. Unprecedented in both its duration and in the number of those who were swept away by its fury, this violent tempest that broke out in the west of Persia, and in which Mullá Muḥammad-'Alíy-i-Zanjání, surnamed Ḥujjat, one of the ablest and most formidable champions of the Faith, together with no less than eighteen hundred of his fellow-disciples, drained the cup of martyrdom, defined more sharply than ever the unbridgeable gulf that separated the torchbearers of the newborn Faith from the civil and ecclesiastical exponents of a gravely shaken Order. The chief figures mainly responsible for, and immediately concerned with, this ghastly tragedy were the envious and hypocritical Amír Arslán Khán, the Majdu'd-Dawlih, a maternal uncle of Náṣiri'd-Dín Sháh, and his associates, the Ṣadru'd-Dawliy-i-Iṣfáhání and Muḥammad Khán, the Amír-Túmán, who were assisted, on the one hand, by substantial military reinforcements dispatched by order of the Amír-Niẓám, and aided, on the other, by the enthusiastic moral support of the entire ecclesiastical body in Zanján. The spot that became the theatre of heroic exertions, the scene of intense sufferings, and the target for furious and repeated assaults, was the Fort of 'Alí-Mardán Khán, which at one time sheltered no less than three thousand Bábís, including men, women and children, the tale of whose agonies is unsurpassed in the annals of a whole century.

A brief reference to certain outstanding features of this mournful episode, endowing the Faith, in its infancy, with measureless potentialities, will suffice to reveal its distinctive character. The pathetic scenes following upon the division of the inhabitants of Zanján into two distinct camps, by the order of its governor—a decision dramatically proclaimed by a crier, and which dissolved ties of worldly interest and affection in favor of a mightier loyalty; the reiterated exhortations addressed by Ḥujjat to the besieged to refrain from aggression and acts of violence; his affirmation, as he recalled the tragedy of Mázindarán, that their victory consisted solely in sacrificing their all on the altar of the Cause of the Ṣáḥibu'z-Zamán, and his declaration of the unalterable intention of his companions to serve their sovereign loyally and to be the well-wishers of his people; the astounding intrepidity with which these same companions repelled the ferocious onslaught launched by the Ṣadru'd-Dawlih, who eventually was obliged to confess his abject failure, was reprimanded by the S͟háh and was degraded from his rank; the contempt with which the occupants of the Fort met the appeals of the crier seeking on behalf of an exasperated enemy to inveigle them into renouncing their Cause and to beguile them by the generous offers and promises of the sovereign; the resourcefulness and incredible audacity of Zaynab, a village maiden, who, fired with an irrepressible yearning to throw in her lot with the defenders of the Fort, disguised herself in male attire, cut off her locks, girt a sword about her waist, and, raising the cry of "Yá Ṣáḥibu'z-Zamán!" rushed headlong in pursuit of the assailants, and who, disdainful of food and sleep, continued, during a period of five months, in the thick of the turmoil, to animate the zeal and to rush to the rescue of her men companions; the stupendous uproar raised by the guards who manned the barricades as they shouted the five invocations prescribed by the Báb, on the very night on which His instructions had been received—an uproar which precipitated the death of a few persons in the camp of the enemy, caused the dissolute officers to drop instantly their wine-glasses to the ground and to overthrow the gambling-tables, and hurry forth bare-footed, and induced others to run half-dressed into the wilderness, or flee panic-stricken to the homes of the 'ulamás—these stand out as the high lights of this bloody contest. We recall, likewise, the contrast between the disorder, the cursing, the ribald laughter, the debauchery and shame that characterized the camp of the enemy, and the atmosphere of reverent devotion that filled the Fort, from which anthems of praise and hymns of joy were continually ascending. Nor can we fail to note the appeal addressed by Ḥujjat and his chief supporters to the S͟háh, repudiating the malicious assertions of their foes, assuring him of their loyalty to him and his government, and of their readiness to establish in his presence the soundness of their Cause; the interception of these messages by the governor and the substitution by him of forged letters loaded with abuse which he dispatched in their stead to Ṭihrán; the enthusiastic support extended by the female occupants of the Fort, the shouts of exultation which they raised, the eagerness with which some of them, disguised in the garb of men, rushed to reinforce its defences and to supplant their fallen brethren, while others ministered to the sick, and carried on their shoulders skins of water for the wounded, and still others, like the Carthaginian women of old, cut off their long hair and bound the thick coils around the guns to reinforce them; the foul treachery of the besiegers, who, on the very day they had drawn up and written out an appeal for peace and, enclosing with it a sealed copy of the Qur'án as a testimony of their pledge, had sent it to Ḥujjat, did not shrink from throwing into a dungeon the members of the delegation, including the children, which had been sent by him to treat with them, from tearing out the beard of the venerated leader of that delegation, and from savagely mutilating one of his fellow-disciples. We call to mind, moreover, the magnanimity of Ḥujjat who, though afflicted with the sudden loss of both his wife and child, continued with unruffled calm in exhorting his companions to exercise forbearance and to resign themselves to the will of God, until he himself succumbed to a wound he had received from the enemy; the barbarous revenge which an adversary incomparably superior in numbers and equipment wreaked upon its victims, giving them over to a massacre and pillage, unexampled in scope and ferocity, in which a rapacious army, a greedy populace and an unappeasable clergy freely indulged; the exposure of the captives, of either sex, hungry and ill-clad, during no less than fifteen days and nights, to the biting cold of an exceptionally severe winter, while crowds of women danced merrily around them, spat in their faces and insulted them with the foulest invectives; the savage cruelty that condemned others to be blown from guns, to be plunged into ice-cold water and lashed severely, to have their skulls soaked in boiling oil, to be smeared with treacle and left to perish in the snow; and finally, the insatiable hatred that impelled the crafty governor to induce through his insinuations the seven year old son of Ḥujjat to disclose the burial-place of his father, that drove him to violate the grave, disinter the corpse, order it to be dragged to the sound of drums and trumpets through the streets of Zanján, and be exposed, for three days and three nights, to unspeakable injuries. These, and other similar incidents connected with the epic story of the Zanján upheaval, characterized by Lord Curzon as a "terrific siege and slaughter," combine to invest it with a sombre glory unsurpassed by any episode of a like nature in the records of the Heroic Age of the Faith of Bahá'u'lláh.

To the tide of calamity which, during the concluding years of the Báb's ministry, was sweeping with such ominous fury the provinces of Persia, whether in the East, in the South, or in the West, the heart and center of the realm itself could not remain impervious. Four months before the Báb's martyrdom Ṭihrán in its turn was to participate, to a lesser degree and under less dramatic circumstances, in the carnage that was besmirching the face of the country. A tragedy was being enacted in that city which was to prove but a prelude to the orgy of massacre which, after the Báb's execution, convulsed its inhabitants and sowed consternation as far as the outlying provinces. It originated in the orders and was perpetrated under the very eyes of the irate and murderous Amír-Niẓám, supported by Maḥmúd Khán-i-Kalantar, and aided by a certain Ḥusayn, one of the 'ulamás of Kashán. The heroes of that tragedy were the Seven Martyrs of Ṭihrán, who represented the more important classes among their countrymen, and who deliberately refused to purchase life by that mere lip-denial which, under the name of taqíyyih, Shí'ah Islám had for centuries recognized as a wholly justifiable and indeed commendable subterfuge in the hour of peril. Neither the repeated and vigorous intercessions of highly placed members of the professions to which these martyrs belonged, nor the considerable sums which, in the case of one of them—the noble and serene Ḥájí Mírzá Siyyid 'Alí, the Báb's maternal uncle—affluent merchants of Shíráz and Ṭihrán were eager to offer as ransom, nor the impassioned pleas of state officials on behalf of another—the pious and highly esteemed dervish, Mírzá Qurbán-'Alí—nor even the personal intervention of the Amír-Niẓám, who endeavored to induce both of these brave men to recant, could succeed in persuading any of the seven to forego the coveted laurels of martyrdom. The defiant answers which they flung at their persecutors; the ecstatic joy which seized them as they drew near the scene of their death; the jubilant shouts they raised as they faced their executioner; the poignancy of the verses which, in their last moments, some of them recited; the appeals and challenges they addressed to the multitude of onlookers who gazed with stupefaction upon them; the eagerness with which the last three victims strove to precede one another in sealing their faith with their blood; and lastly, the atrocities which a bloodthirsty foe degraded itself by inflicting upon their dead bodies which lay unburied for three days and three nights in the Sabzih-Maydán, during which time thousands of so-called devout Shí'ahs kicked their corpses, spat upon their faces, pelted, cursed, derided, and heaped refuse upon them—these were the chief features of the tragedy of the Seven Martyrs of Ṭihrán, a tragedy which stands out as one of the grimmest scenes witnessed in the course of the early unfoldment of the Faith of Bahá'u'lláh. Little wonder that the Báb, bowed down by the weight of His accumulated sorrows in the Fortress of Chihríq, should have acclaimed and glorified them, in the pages of a lengthy eulogy which immortalized their fidelity to His Cause, as those same "Seven Goats" who, according to Islamic tradition, should, on the Day of Judgment, "walk in front" of the promised Qá'im, and whose death was to precede the impending martyrdom of their true Shepherd.

## CHAPTER IV

# The Execution of the Báb

The waves of dire tribulation that violently battered at the Faith, and eventually engulfed, in rapid succession, the ablest, the dearest and most trusted disciples of the Báb, plunged Him, as already observed, into unutterable sorrow. For no less than six months the Prisoner of Chihríq, His chronicler has recorded, was unable to either write or dictate. Crushed with grief by the evil tidings that came so fast upon Him, of the endless trials that beset His ablest lieutenants, by the agonies suffered by the besieged and the shameless betrayal of the survivors, by the woeful afflictions endured by the captives and the abominable butchery of men, women and children, as well as the foul indignities heaped on their corpses, He, for nine days, His amanuensis has affirmed, refused to meet any of His friends, and was reluctant to touch the meat and drink that was offered Him. Tears rained continually from His eyes, and profuse expressions of anguish poured forth from His wounded heart, as He languished, for no less than five months, solitary and disconsolate, in His prison.

The pillars of His infant Faith had, for the most part, been hurled down at the first onset of the hurricane that had been loosed upon it. Quddús, immortalized by Him as Ismu'lláhi'l-Ákhir (the Last Name of God); on whom Bahá'u'lláh's Tablet of Kullu'ṭ-Ṭa'ám later conferred the sublime appellation of Nuqṭiy-i-Ukhrá (the Last Point); whom He elevated, in another Tablet, to a rank second to none except that of the Herald of His Revelation; whom He identifies, in still another Tablet, with one of the *"Messengers charged with imposture"* mentioned in the Qur'án; whom the Persian Bayán extolled as that fellow-pilgrim round whom mirrors to the number of eight Váḥids revolve; on whose *"detachment and the sincerity of whose devotion to God's will God prideth Himself amidst the Concourse on high;"* whom 'Abdu'l-Bahá designated as the *"Moon of Guidance;"* and whose appearance the Revelation of St. John the Divine anticipated as one of the two "Witnesses" into whom, ere the *"second woe is past,"* the *"spirit of life from God"* must enter—such a man had, in the full bloom of his youth, suffered, in the Sabzih-Maydán of Bárfurúsh, a death which even Jesus Christ, as attested by Bahá'u'lláh, had not faced in the hour of His greatest agony. Mullá Ḥusayn, the first Letter of the Living, surnamed the Bábu'l-Báb (the Gate of the Gate); designated as the *"Primal Mirror;"* on whom eulogies, prayers and visiting Tablets of a number equivalent to thrice the volume of the Qur'án had been lavished by the pen of the Báb; referred to in these eulogies as *"beloved of My Heart;"* the dust of whose grave, that same Pen had declared, was so potent as to cheer the sorrowful and heal the sick; whom *"the creatures, raised in the beginning and in the end"* of the Bábí Dispensation, envy, and will continue to envy till the *"Day of Judgment;"* whom the Kitáb-i-Íqán acclaimed as the one but for whom *"God would not have been established upon the seat of His mercy, nor ascended the throne of eternal glory;"* to whom Siyyid Káẓim had paid such tribute that his disciples suspected that the recipient of such praise might well be the promised One Himself—such a one had likewise, in the prime of his manhood, died a martyr's death at Ṭabarsí. Vaḥíd, pronounced in the Kitáb-i-Íqán to be the *"unique and peerless figure of his age,"* a man of immense erudition and the most preeminent figure to enlist under the banner of the new Faith, to whose *"talents and saintliness,"* to whose *"high attainments in the realm of science and philosophy"* the Báb had testified in His Dalá'il-i-Sab'ih (Seven Proofs), had already, under similar circumstances, been swept into the maelstrom of another upheaval, and was soon to quaff in his turn the cup drained by the heroic martyrs of Mázindarán. Ḥujjat, another champion of conspicuous audacity, of unsubduable will, of remarkable originality and vehement zeal, was being, swiftly and inevitably, drawn into the fiery furnace whose flames had already enveloped Zanján and its environs. The Báb's maternal uncle, the only father He had known since His childhood, His shield and support and the trusted guardian of both His mother and His wife, had, moreover, been sundered from Him by the axe of the executioner in Ṭihrán. No less than half of His chosen disciples, the Letters of the Living, had already preceded Him in the field of martyrdom. Ṭáhirih, though still alive, was courageously pursuing a course that was to lead her inevitably to her doom.

A fast ebbing life, so crowded with the accumulated anxieties, disappointments, treacheries and sorrows of a tragic ministry, now moved swiftly towards its climax. The most turbulent period of the Heroic Age of the new Dispensation was rapidly attaining its culmination. The cup of bitter woes which the Herald of that Dispensation had tasted was now full to overflowing. Indeed, He Himself had already foreshadowed His own approaching death. In the Kitáb-i-Panj-Sha'n, one of His last works, He had alluded to the fact that the sixth Naw-Rúz after the declaration of His mission would be the last He was destined to celebrate on earth. In His interpretation of the letter Há, He had voiced His craving for martyrdom, while in the Qayyúmu'l-Asmá' He had actually prophesied the inevitability of such a consummation of His glorious career. Forty days before His final departure from Chihríq He had even collected all the documents in His possession, and placed them, together with His pen-case, His seals and His rings, in the hands of Mullá Báqir, a Letter of the Living, whom He instructed to entrust them to Mullá 'Abdu'l-Karím-i-Qazvíní, surnamed Mírzá Aḥmad, who was to deliver them to Bahá'u'lláh in Ṭihrán.

While the convulsions of Mázindarán and Nayríz were pursuing their bloody course the Grand Vizir of Náṣiri'd-Dín Sháh, anxiously pondering the significance of these dire happenings, and apprehensive of their repercussions on his countrymen, his government and his sovereign, was feverishly revolving in his mind that fateful decision which was not only destined to leave its indelible imprint on the fortunes of his country, but was to be fraught with such incalculable consequences for the destinies of the whole of mankind. The repressive measures taken against the followers of the Báb, he was by now fully convinced, had but served to inflame their zeal, steel their resolution and confirm their loyalty to their persecuted Faith. The Báb's isolation and captivity had produced the opposite effect to that which the Amír-Niẓám had confidently anticipated. Gravely perturbed, he bitterly condemned the disastrous leniency of his predecessor, Ḥájí Mírzá Áqásí, which had brought matters to such a pass. A more drastic and still more exemplary punishment, he felt, must now be administered to what he regarded as an abomination of heresy which was polluting the civil and ecclesiastical institutions of the realm. Nothing short, he believed, of the extinction of the life of Him Who was the fountain-head of so odious a doctrine and the driving force behind so dynamic a movement could stem the tide that had wrought such havoc throughout the land.

The siege of Zanján was still in progress when he, dispensing with an explicit order from his sovereign, and acting independently of his counsellors and fellow-ministers, dispatched his order to Prince Ḥamzih Mírzá, the Ḥishmatu'd-Dawlih, the governor of Ádhirbáyján, instructing him to execute the Báb. Fearing lest the infliction of such condign punishment in the capital of the realm would set in motion forces he might be powerless to control, he ordered that his Captive be taken to Tabríz, and there be done to death. Confronted with a flat refusal by the indignant Prince to perform what he regarded as a flagitious crime, the Amír-Niẓám commissioned his own brother, Mírzá Ḥasan K͟hán, to execute his orders. The usual formalities designed to secure the necessary authorization from the leading mujtahids of Tabríz were hastily and easily completed. Neither Mullá Muḥammad-i-Mamáqání, however, who had penned the Báb's death-warrant on the very day of His examination in Tabríz, nor Ḥájí Mírzá Báqir, nor Mullá Murtaḍá-Qulí, to whose houses their Victim was ignominiously led by the farrás͟h-bás͟hí, by order of the Grand Vizir, condescended to meet face to face their dreaded Opponent.

Immediately before and soon after this humiliating treatment meted out to the Báb two highly significant incidents occurred, incidents that cast an illuminating light on the mysterious circumstances surrounding the opening phase of His martyrdom. The farrás͟h-bás͟hí had abruptly interrupted the last conversation which the Báb was confidentially having in one of the rooms of the barracks with His amanuensis Siyyid Ḥusayn, and was drawing the latter aside, and severely rebuking him, when he was thus addressed by his Prisoner: *"Not until I have said to him all those things that I wish to say can any earthly power silence Me. Though all the world be armed against Me, yet shall it be powerless to deter Me from fulfilling, to the last word, My intention."* To the Christian Sám K͟hán—the colonel of the Armenian regiment ordered to carry out the execution—who, seized with fear lest his act should provoke the wrath of God, had begged to be released from the duty imposed upon him, the Báb gave the following assurance: *"Follow your instructions, and if your intention be sincere, the Almighty is surely able to relieve you of your perplexity."*

Sám K͟hán accordingly set out to discharge his duty. A spike was driven into a pillar which separated two rooms of the barracks facing the square. Two ropes were fastened to it from which the Báb and one of his disciples, the youthful and devout Mírzá Muḥammad-'Alí-i-Zunúzí, surnamed Anís, who had previously flung himself at the feet of his Master and implored that under no circumstances he be sent away from Him, were separately suspended. The firing squad ranged itself in three files, each of two hundred and fifty men. Each file in turn opened fire until the whole detachment had discharged its bullets. So dense was the smoke from the seven hundred and fifty rifles that the sky was darkened. As soon as the smoke had cleared away the astounded multitude of about ten thousand souls, who had crowded onto the roof of the barracks, as well as the tops of the adjoining houses, beheld a scene which their eyes could scarcely believe.

The Báb had vanished from their sight! Only his companion remained, alive and unscathed, standing beside the wall on which they had been suspended. The ropes by which they had been hung alone were severed. "The Siyyid-i-Báb has gone from our sight!" cried out the bewildered spectators. A frenzied search immediately ensued. He was found, unhurt and unruffled, in the very room He had occupied the night before, engaged in completing His interrupted conversation with His amanuensis. *"I have finished My conversation with Siyyid Ḥusayn"* were the words with which the Prisoner, so providentially preserved, greeted the appearance of the farrá<u>sh</u>-bá<u>sh</u>í, *"Now you may proceed to fulfill your intention."* Recalling the bold assertion his Prisoner had previously made, and shaken by so stunning a revelation, the farrá<u>sh</u>-bá<u>sh</u>í quitted instantly the scene, and resigned his post.

Sám <u>Kh</u>án, likewise, remembering, with feelings of awe and wonder, the reassuring words addressed to him by the Báb, ordered his men to leave the barracks immediately, and swore, as he left the courtyard, never again, even at the cost of his life, to repeat that act. Áqá Ján-i-<u>Kh</u>amsih, colonel of the body-guard, volunteered to replace him. On the same wall and in the same manner the Báb and His companion were again suspended, while the new regiment formed in line and opened fire upon them. This time, however, their breasts were riddled with bullets, and their bodies completely dissected, with the exception of their faces which were but little marred. *"O wayward generation!"* were the last words of the Báb to the gazing multitude, as the regiment prepared to fire its volley, *"Had you believed in Me every one of you would have followed the example of this youth, who stood in rank above most of you, and would have willingly sacrificed himself in My path. The day will come when you will have recognized Me; that day I shall have ceased to be with you."*

Nor was this all. The very moment the shots were fired a gale of exceptional violence arose and swept over the city. From noon till night a whirlwind of dust obscured the light of the sun, and blinded the eyes of the people. In <u>Sh</u>íráz an "earthquake," foreshadowed in no less weighty a Book than the Revelation of St. John, occurred in 1268 A.H. which threw the whole city into turmoil and wrought havoc amongst its people, a havoc that was greatly aggravated by the outbreak of cholera, by famine and other afflictions. In that same year no less than two hundred and fifty of the firing squad, that had replaced Sám Khán's regiment, met their death, together with their officers, in a terrible earthquake, while the remaining five hundred suffered, three years later, as a punishment for their mutiny, the same fate as that which their hands had inflicted upon the Báb. To insure that none of them had survived, they were riddled with a second volley, after which their bodies, pierced with spears and lances, were exposed to the gaze of the people of Tabríz. The prime instigator of the Báb's death, the implacable Amír-Niẓám, together with his brother, his chief accomplice, met their death within two years of that savage act.

On the evening of the very day of the Báb's execution, which fell on the ninth of July 1850 (28th of Sha'bán 1266 A.H.), during the thirty-first year of His age and the seventh of His ministry, the mangled bodies were transferred from the courtyard of the barracks to the edge of the moat outside the gate of the city. Four companies, each consisting of ten sentinels, were ordered to keep watch in turn over them. On the following morning the Russian Consul in Tabríz visited the spot, and ordered the artist who had accompanied him to make a drawing of the remains as they lay beside the moat. In the middle of the following night a follower of the Báb, Ḥájí Sulaymán Khán, succeeded, through the instrumentality of a certain Ḥájí Alláh-Yár, in removing the bodies to the silk factory owned by one of the believers of Mílán, and laid them, the next day, in a specially made wooden casket, which he later transferred to a place of safety. Meanwhile the mullás were boastfully proclaiming from the pulpits that, whereas the holy body of the Immaculate Imám would be preserved from beasts of prey and from all creeping things, this man's body had been devoured by wild animals. No sooner had the news of the transfer of the remains of the Báb and of His fellow-sufferer been communicated to Bahá'u'lláh than He ordered that same Sulaymán Khán to bring them to Ṭihrán, where they were taken to the Imám-Zádih-Ḥasan, from whence they were removed to different places, until the time when, in pursuance of 'Abdu'l-Bahá's instructions, they were transferred to the Holy Land, and were permanently and ceremoniously laid to rest by Him in a specially erected mausoleum on the slopes of Mt. Carmel.

Thus ended a life which posterity will recognize as standing at the confluence of two universal prophetic cycles, the Adamic Cycle stretching back as far as the first dawnings of the world's recorded religious history and the Bahá'í Cycle destined to propel itself across the unborn reaches of time for a period of no less than five thousand centuries. The apotheosis in which such a life attained its consummation marks, as already observed, the culmination of the most heroic phase of the Heroic Age of the Bahá'í Dispensation. It can, moreover, be regarded in no other light except as the most dramatic, the most tragic event transpiring within the entire range of the first Bahá'í century. Indeed it can be rightly acclaimed as unparalleled in the annals of the lives of all the Founders of the world's existing religious systems.

So momentous an event could hardly fail to arouse widespread and keen interest even beyond the confines of the land in which it had occurred. "C'est un des plus magnifiques exemples de courage qu'il ait été donné à l'humanité de contempler," is the testimony recorded by a Christian scholar and government official, who had lived in Persia and had familiarized himself with the life and teachings of the Báb, "et c'est aussi une admirable preuve de l'amour que notre héros portait à ses concitoyens. Il s'est sacrifié pour l'humanité: pour elle il a donné son corps et son âme, pour elle il a subi les privations, les affronts, les injures, la torture et le martyre. Il a scellé de son sang le pacte de la fraternité universelle, et comme Jésus il a payé de sa vie l'annonce du règne de la concorde, de l'équité et de l'amour du prochain." "Un fait étrange, unique dans les annales de l'humanité," is a further testimony from the pen of that same scholar commenting on the circumstances attending the Báb's martyrdom. "A veritable miracle," is the pronouncement made by a noted French Orientalist. "A true God-man," is the verdict of a famous British traveler and writer. "The finest product of his country," is the tribute paid Him by a noted French publicist. "That Jesus of the age . . . a prophet, and more than a prophet," is the judgment passed by a distinguished English divine. "The most important religious movement since the foundation of Christianity," is the possibility that was envisaged for the Faith the Báb had established by that far-famed Oxford scholar, the late Master of Balliol.

*"Many persons from all parts of the world,"* is 'Abdu'l-Bahá's written assertion, *"set out for Persia and began to investigate wholeheartedly the matter."* The Czar of Russia, a contemporary chronicler has written, had even, shortly before the Báb's martyrdom, instructed the Russian Consul in Tabríz to fully inquire into, and report the circumstances of so startling a Movement, a commission that could not be carried out in view of the Báb's execution. In countries as

remote as those of Western Europe an interest no less profound was kindled, and spread with great rapidity to literary, artistic, diplomatic and intellectual circles. "All Europe," attests the above-mentioned French publicist, "was stirred to pity and indignation . . . Among the littérateurs of my generation, in the Paris of 1890, the martyrdom of the Báb was still as fresh a topic as had been the first news of His death. We wrote poems about Him. Sarah Bernhardt entreated Catulle Mendès for a play on the theme of this historic tragedy." A Russian poetess, member of the Philosophic, Oriental and Bibliological Societies of St. Petersburg, published in 1903 a drama entitled "The Báb," which a year later was played in one of the principal theatres of that city, was subsequently given publicity in London, was translated into French in Paris, and into German by the poet Fiedler, was presented again, soon after the Russian Revolution, in the Folk Theatre in Leningrad, and succeeded in arousing the genuine sympathy and interest of the renowned Tolstoy, whose eulogy of the poem was later published in the Russian press.

It would indeed be no exaggeration to say that nowhere in the whole compass of the world's religious literature, except in the Gospels, do we find any record relating to the death of any of the religion-founders of the past comparable to the martyrdom suffered by the Prophet of S͟híráz. So strange, so inexplicable a phenomenon, attested by eye-witnesses, corroborated by men of recognized standing, and acknowledged by government as well as unofficial historians among the people who had sworn undying hostility to the Bábí Faith, may be truly regarded as the most marvelous manifestation of the unique potentialities with which a Dispensation promised by all the Dispensations of the past had been endowed. The passion of Jesus Christ, and indeed His whole public ministry, alone offer a parallel to the Mission and death of the Báb, a parallel which no student of comparative religion can fail to perceive or ignore. In the youthfulness and meekness of the Inaugurator of the Bábí Dispensation; in the extreme brevity and turbulence of His public ministry; in the dramatic swiftness with which that ministry moved towards its climax; in the apostolic order which He instituted, and the primacy which He conferred on one of its members; in the boldness of His challenge to the time-honored conventions, rites and laws which had been woven into the fabric of the religion He Himself had been born into; in the rôle which an officially recognized and firmly entrenched religious hierarchy played as chief instigator of the outrages which He was made to suffer; in the indignities heaped upon Him; in the suddenness of His arrest; in the interrogation to which He was subjected; in the derision poured, and the scourging inflicted, upon Him; in the public affront He sustained; and, finally, in His ignominious suspension before the gaze of a hostile multitude—in all these we cannot fail to discern a remarkable similarity to the distinguishing features of the career of Jesus Christ.

It should be remembered, however, that apart from the miracle associated with the Báb's execution, He, unlike the Founder of the Christian religion, is not only to be regarded as the independent Author of a divinely revealed Dispensation, but must also be recognized as the Herald of a new Era and the Inaugurator of a great universal prophetic cycle. Nor should the important fact be overlooked that, whereas the chief adversaries of Jesus Christ, in His lifetime, were the Jewish rabbis and their associates, the forces arrayed against the Báb represented the combined civil and ecclesiastical powers of Persia, which, from the moment of His declaration to the hour of His death, persisted, unitedly and by every means at their disposal, in conspiring against the upholders and in vilifying the tenets of His Revelation.

The Báb, acclaimed by Bahá'u'lláh as the *"Essence of Essences,"* the *"Sea of Seas,"* the *"Point round Whom the realities of the Prophets and Messengers revolve," "from Whom God hath caused to proceed the knowledge of all that was and shall be,"* Whose *"rank excelleth that of all the Prophets,"* and Whose *"Revelation transcendeth the comprehension and understanding of all their chosen ones,"* had delivered His Message and discharged His mission. He Who was, in the words of 'Abdu'l-Bahá, the *"Morn of Truth"* and *"Harbinger of the Most Great Light,"* Whose advent at once signalized the termination of the *"Prophetic Cycle"* and the inception of the *"Cycle of Fulfillment,"* had simultaneously through His Revelation banished the shades of night that had descended upon His country, and proclaimed the impending rise of that Incomparable Orb Whose radiance was to envelop the whole of mankind. He, as affirmed by Himself, *"the Primal Point from which have been generated all created things," "one of the sustaining pillars of the Primal Word of God,"* the *"Mystic Fane,"* the *"Great Announcement,"* the *"Flame of that supernal Light that glowed upon Sinai,"* the *"Remembrance of God"* concerning Whom *"a separate Covenant hath been established with each and every Prophet"* had, through His advent, at once fulfilled the promise of all ages and ushered in the consummation of all Revelations. He the "Qá'im" (He Who ariseth) promised to the Shí'ahs, the "Mihdí" (One Who is guided) awaited by the Sunnís, the "Return of John the Baptist" expected by the Christians, the "Ús͟hídar-Máh" referred to in the Zoroastrian scriptures, the "Return of Elijah" anticipated by the Jews, Whose Revelation was to show forth *"the signs and tokens of all the Prophets"*, Who was to *"manifest the perfection of Moses, the radiance of Jesus and the patience of Job"* had appeared, proclaimed His Cause, been mercilessly persecuted and died gloriously. The *"Second Woe,"* spoken of in the Apocalypse of St. John the Divine, had, at long last, appeared, and the first of the two *"Messengers,"* Whose appearance had been prophesied in the Qur'án, had been sent down. The first *"Trumpet-Blast"*, destined to smite the earth with extermination, announced in the latter Book, had finally been sounded. *"The Inevitable," "The Catastrophe," "The Resurrection," "The Earthquake of the Last Hour,"* foretold by that same Book, had all come to pass. The *"clear tokens"* had been *"sent down,"* and the *"Spirit"* had *"breathed,"* and the *"souls"* had *"waked up,"* and the *"heaven"* had been *"cleft,"* and the *"angels"* had *"ranged in order,"* and the *"stars"* had been *"blotted out,"* and the *"earth"* had *"cast forth her burden,"* and *"Paradise"* had been *"brought near,"* and *"hell"* had been *"made to blaze,"* and the *"Book"* had been *"set,"* and the *"Bridge"* had been *"laid out,"* and the *"Balance"* had been *"set up,"* and the *"mountains scattered in dust."* The *"cleansing of the Sanctuary,"* prophesied by Daniel and confirmed by Jesus Christ in His reference to *"the abomination of desolation,"* had been accomplished. The *"day whose length shall be a thousand years,"* foretold by the Apostle of God in His Book, had terminated. The *"forty and two months,"* during which the *"Holy City,"* as predicted by St. John the Divine, would be trodden under foot, had elapsed. The *"time of the end"* had been ushered in, and the first of the *"two Witnesses"* into Whom, *"after three days and a half the Spirit of Life from God"* would enter, had arisen and had *"ascended up to heaven in a cloud."* The *"remaining twenty and five letters to be made manifest,"* according to Islamic tradition, out of the *"twenty and seven letters"* of which Knowledge has been declared to consist, had been revealed. The *"Man Child,"* mentioned in the Book of Revelation, destined to *"rule all nations with a rod of iron,"* had released, through His coming, the creative energies which, reinforced by the effusions of a swiftly succeeding and infinitely mightier Revelation, were to instill into the entire human race the capacity to achieve its organic unification, attain maturity and thereby reach the final stage in its age-long evolution. The clarion-call addressed to the *"concourse of kings and of the sons of kings,"* marking the inception of a process which, accelerated by Bahá'u'lláh's subsequent warnings to the entire company of the monarchs of East and West, was to produce so widespread a revolution in the fortunes of royalty, had been raised in the Qayyumú'l-Asmá'. The *"Order,"* whose foundation the Promised One was to establish in the Kitáb-i-Aqdas, and the features of which the Center of the Covenant was to delineate in His Testament, and whose administrative framework the entire body of His followers are now erecting, had been categorically announced in the Persian Bayán. The laws which were designed, on the one hand, to abolish at a stroke the privileges and ceremonials, the ordinances and institutions of a superannuated Dispensation, and to bridge, on the other, the gap between an obsolete system and the institutions of a world-encompassing Order destined to supersede it, had been clearly formulated and proclaimed. The Covenant which, despite the determined assaults launched against it, succeeded, unlike all previous Dispensations, in preserving the integrity of the Faith of its Author, and in paving the way for the advent of the One Who was to be its Center and Object, had been firmly and irrevocably established. The light which, throughout successive periods, was to propagate itself gradually from its cradle as far as Vancouver in the West and the China Sea in the East, and to diffuse its radiance as far as Iceland in the North and the Tasman Sea in the South, had broken. The forces of darkness, at first confined to the concerted hostility of the civil and ecclesiastical powers of S͟hí'ah Persia, gathering momentum, at a later stage, through the avowed and persistent opposition of the Caliph of Islám and the Sunní hierarchy in Turkey, and destined to culminate in the fierce antagonism of the sacerdotal orders associated with other and still more powerful religious systems, had launched their initial assault. The nucleus of the divinely ordained, world-embracing Community—a Community whose infant strength had already plucked asunder the fetters of S͟hí'ah orthodoxy, and which was, with every expansion in the range of its fellowship, to seek and obtain a wider and still more significant recognition of its claims to be the world religion of the future, had been formed and was slowly crystallizing. And, lastly, the seed, endowed by the Hand of Omnipotence with such vast potentialities, though rudely trampled under foot and seemingly perished from the face of the earth, had, through this very process, been vouchsafed the opportunity to germinate and remanifest itself, in the shape of a still more compelling Revelation—a Revelation destined to blossom forth, in a later period into the flourishing institutions of a world-wide administrative System, and to ripen, in the Golden Age as yet unborn, into mighty agencies functioning in consonance with the principles of a world-unifying, world-redeeming Order.

## CHAPTER V

# The Attempt on the Life of the Sháh and Its Consequences

The Faith that had stirred a whole nation to its depth, for whose sake thousands of precious and heroic souls had been immolated and on whose altar He Who had been its Author had sacrificed His life, was now being subjected to the strain and stress of yet another crisis of extreme violence and far-reaching consequences. It was one of those periodic crises which, occurring throughout a whole century, succeeded in momentarily eclipsing the splendor of the Faith and in almost disrupting the structure of its organic institutions. Invariably sudden, often unexpected, seemingly fatal to both its spirit and its life, these inevitable manifestations of the mysterious evolution of a world Religion, intensely alive, challenging in its claims, revolutionizing in its tenets, struggling against overwhelming odds, have either been externally precipitated by the malice of its avowed antagonists or internally provoked by the unwisdom of its friends, the apostasy of its supporters, or the defection of some of the most highly placed amongst the kith and kin of its founders. No matter how disconcerting to the great mass of its loyal adherents, however much trumpeted by its adversaries as symptoms of its decline and impending dissolution, these admitted setbacks and reverses, from which it has time and again so tragically suffered, have, as we look back upon them, failed to arrest its march or impair its unity. Heavy indeed has been the toll which they exacted, unspeakable the agonies they engendered, widespread and paralyzing for a time the consternation they provoked. Yet, viewed in their proper perspective, each of them can be confidently pronounced a blessing in disguise, affording a providential means for the release of a fresh outpouring of celestial strength, a miraculous escape from imminent and still more dreadful calamities, an instrument for the fulfillment of age-old prophecies, an agency for the purification and revitalization of the life of the community, an impetus for the enlargement of its limits and the propagation of its influence, and a compelling evidence of the indestructibility of its cohesive strength. Sometimes at the height of the crisis itself, more often when the crisis was past, the significance of these trials has manifested itself to men's eyes, and the necessity of such experiences has been demonstrated, far and wide and beyond the shadow of a doubt, to both friend and foe. Seldom, if indeed at any time, has the mystery underlying these portentous, God-sent upheavals remained undisclosed, or the profound purpose and meaning of their occurrence been left hidden from the minds of men.

Such a severe ordeal the Faith of the Báb, still in the earliest stages of its infancy, was now beginning to experience. Maligned and hounded from the moment it was born, deprived in its earliest days of the sustaining strength of the majority of its leading supporters, stunned by the tragic and sudden removal of its Founder, reeling under the cruel blows it had successively sustained in Mázindarán, Ṭihrán, Nayríz and Zanján, a sorely persecuted Faith was about to be subjected through the shameful act of a fanatical and irresponsible Bábí, to a humiliation such as it had never before known. To the trials it had undergone was now added the oppressive load of a fresh calamity, unprecedented in its gravity, disgraceful in its character, and devastating in its immediate consequences.

Obsessed by the bitter tragedy of the martyrdom of his beloved Master, driven by a frenzy of despair to avenge that odious deed, and believing the author and instigator of that crime to be none other than the S͟háh himself, a certain Ṣádiq-i-Tabrízí, an assistant in a confectioner's shop in Ṭihrán, proceeded on an August day (August 15, 1852), together with his accomplice, an equally obscure youth named Fatḥu'lláh-i-Qumí, to Níyávarán where the imperial army had encamped and the sovereign was in residence, and there, waiting by the roadside, in the guise of an innocent bystander, fired a round of shot from his pistol at the S͟háh, shortly after the latter had emerged on horseback from the palace grounds for his morning promenade. The weapon the assailant employed demonstrated beyond the shadow of a doubt the folly of that half-demented youth, and clearly indicated that no man of sound judgment could have possibly instigated so senseless an act.

The whole of Níyávarán where the imperial court and troops had congregated was, as a result of this assault, plunged into an unimaginable tumult. The ministers of the state, headed by Mírzá Áqá K͟hán-i-Núrí, the I'timádu'd-Dawlih, the successor of the Amír-Niẓám, rushed horror-stricken to the side of their wounded sovereign. The fanfare of the trumpets, the rolling of the drums and the shrill piping of the fifes summoned the hosts of His Imperial Majesty on all sides. The S͟háh's attendants, some on horseback, others on foot, poured into the palace grounds. Pandemonium reigned in which every one issued orders, none listened, none obeyed, nor understood anything. Ardis͟hír Mírzá, the governor of Ṭihrán, having in the meantime already ordered his troops to patrol the deserted streets of the capital, barred the gates of the citadel as well as of the city, charged his batteries and feverishly dispatched a messenger to ascertain the veracity of the wild rumors that were circulating amongst the populace, and to ask for special instructions.

No sooner had this act been perpetrated than its shadow fell across the entire body of the Bábí community. A storm of public horror, disgust and resentment, heightened by the implacable hostility of the mother of the youthful sovereign, swept the nation, casting aside all possibility of even the most elementary inquiry into the origins and the instigators of the attempt. A sign, a whisper, was sufficient to implicate the innocent and loose upon him the most abominable afflictions. An army of foes—ecclesiastics, state officials and people, united in relentless hate, and watching for an opportunity to discredit and annihilate a dreaded adversary—had, at long last, been afforded the pretext for which it was longing. Now it could achieve its malevolent purpose. Though the Faith had, from its inception, disclaimed any intention of usurping the rights and prerogatives of the state; though its exponents and disciples had sedulously avoided any act that might arouse the slightest suspicion of a desire to wage a holy war, or to evince an aggressive attitude, yet its enemies, deliberately ignoring the numerous evidences of the marked restraint exercised by the followers of a persecuted religion, proved themselves capable of inflicting atrocities as barbarous as those which will ever remain associated with the bloody episodes of Mázindarán, Nayríz and Zanján. To what depths of infamy and cruelty would not this same enemy be willing to descend now that an act so treasonable, so audacious had been committed? What accusations would it not be prompted to level at, and what treatment would it not mete out to, those who, however unjustifiably, could be associated with so heinous a crime against one who, in his person, combined the chief magistracy of the realm and the trusteeship of the Hidden Imám?

The reign of terror which ensued was revolting beyond description. The spirit of revenge that animated those who had unleashed its horrors seemed insatiable. Its repercussions echoed as far as the press of Europe, branding with infamy its bloodthirsty participants. The Grand Vizir, wishing to reduce the chances of blood revenge, divided the work of executing those condemned to death among the princes and nobles, his principal fellow-ministers, the generals and officers of the Court, the representatives of the sacerdotal and merchant classes, the artillery and the infantry. Even the Sháh himself had his allotted victim, though, to save the dignity of the crown, he delegated the steward of his household to fire the fatal shot on his behalf. Ardishír Mírzá, on his part, picketed the gates of the capital, and ordered the guards to scrutinize the faces of all those who sought to leave it. Summoning to his presence the kalantar, the dárúghih and the kad-khudás he bade them search out and arrest every one suspected of being a Bábí. A youth named 'Abbás, a former servant of a well-known adherent of the Faith, was, on threat of inhuman torture, induced to walk the streets of Ṭihrán, and point out every one he recognized as being a Bábí. He was even coerced into denouncing any individual whom he thought would be willing and able to pay a heavy bribe to secure his freedom.

The first to suffer on that calamitous day was the ill-fated Ṣádiq, who was instantly slain on the scene of his attempted crime. His body was tied to the tail of a mule and dragged all the way to Ṭihrán, where it was hewn into two halves, each of which was suspended and exposed to the public view, while the Ṭihránís were invited by the city authorities to mount the ramparts and gaze upon the mutilated corpse. Molten lead was poured down the throat of his accomplice, after having subjected him to the torture of red-hot pincers and limb-rending screws. A comrade of his, Ḥájí Qásim, was stripped of his clothes, lighted candles were thrust into holes made in his flesh, and was paraded before the multitude who shouted and cursed him. Others had their eyes gouged out, were sawn asunder, strangled, blown from the mouths of cannons, chopped in pieces, hewn apart with hatchets and maces, shod with horse shoes, bayoneted and stoned. Torture-mongers vied with each other in running the gamut of brutality, while the populace, into whose hands the bodies of the hapless victims were delivered, would close in upon their prey, and would so mutilate them as to leave no trace of their original form. The executioners, though accustomed to their own gruesome task, would themselves be amazed at the fiendish cruelty of the populace. Women and children could be seen led down the streets by their executioners, their flesh in ribbons, with candles burning in their wounds, singing with ringing voices before the silent spectators: "Verily from God we come, and unto Him we return!" As some of the children expired on the way their tormentors would fling their bodies under the feet of their fathers and sisters who, proudly treading upon them, would not deign to give them a second glance. A father, according to the testimony of a distinguished French writer, rather than abjure his faith, preferred to have the throats of his two young sons, both already covered with blood, slit upon his breast, as he lay on the ground, whilst the elder of the two, a lad of fourteen, vigorously pressing his right of seniority, demanded to be the first to lay down his life.

An Austrian officer, Captain Von Goumoens, in the employ of the Sháh at that time, was, it is reliably stated, so horrified at the cruelties he was compelled to witness that he tendered his resignation. "Follow me, my friend," is the Captain's own testimony in a letter he wrote two weeks after the attempt in question, which was published in the "Soldatenfreund," "you who lay claim to a heart and European ethics, follow me to the unhappy ones who, with gouged-out eyes, must eat, on the scene of the deed, without any sauce, their own amputated ears; or whose teeth are torn out with inhuman violence by the hand of the executioner; or whose bare skulls are simply crushed by blows from a hammer; or where the bazaar is illuminated with unhappy victims, because on right and left the people dig deep holes in their breasts and shoulders, and insert burning wicks in the wounds. I saw some dragged in chains through the bazaar, preceded by a military band, in whom these wicks had burned so deep that now the fat flickered convulsively in the wound like a newly extinguished lamp. Not seldom it happens that the unwearying ingenuity of the Oriental leads to fresh tortures. They will skin the soles of the Bábí's feet, soak the wounds in boiling oil, shoe the foot like the hoof of a horse, and compel the victim to run. No cry escaped from the victim's breast; the torment is endured in dark silence by the numbed sensation of the fanatic; now he must run; the body cannot endure what the soul has endured; he falls. Give him the coup de grâce! Put him out of his pain! No! The executioner swings the whip, and—I myself have had to witness it—the unhappy victim of hundredfold tortures runs! This is the beginning of the end. As for the end itself, they hang the scorched and perforated bodies by their hands and feet to a tree head downwards, and now every Persian may try his marksmanship to his heart's content from a fixed but not too proximate distance on the noble quarry placed at his disposal. I saw corpses torn by nearly one hundred and fifty bullets." "When I read over again," he continues, "what I have written, I am overcome by the thought that those who are with you in our dearly beloved Austria may doubt the full truth of the picture, and accuse me of exaggeration. Would to God that I had not lived to see it! But by the duties of my profession I was unhappily often, only too often, a witness of these abominations. At present I never leave my house, in order not to meet with fresh scenes of horror . . . Since my whole soul revolts against such infamy . . . I will no longer maintain my connection with the scene of such crimes." Little wonder that a man as far-famed as Renan should, in his "Les Apôtres" have characterized the hideous butchery perpetrated in a single day, during the great massacre of Ṭihrán, as "a day perhaps unparalleled in the history of the world!"

The hand that was stretched to deal so grievous a blow to the adherents of a sorely-tried Faith did not confine itself to the rank and file of the Báb's persecuted followers. It was raised with equal fury and determination against, and struck down with equal force, the few remaining leaders who had survived the winnowing winds of adversity that had already laid low so vast a number of the supporters of the Faith. Ṭáhirih, that immortal heroine who had already shed imperishable luster alike on her sex and on the Cause she had espoused, was swept into, and ultimately engulfed by, the raging storm. Siyyid Ḥusayn, the amanuensis of the Báb, the companion of His exile, the trusted repository of His last wishes, and the witness of the prodigies attendant upon His martyrdom, fell likewise a victim of its fury. That hand had even the temerity to lift itself against the towering figure of Bahá'u'lláh. But though it laid hold of Him it failed to strike Him down. It imperilled His life, it imprinted on His body indelible marks of a pitiless cruelty, but was impotent to cut short a career that was destined not only to keep alive the fire which the Spirit of the Báb had kindled, but to produce a conflagration that would at once consummate and outshine the glories of His Revelation.

During those somber and agonizing days when the Báb was no more, when the luminaries that had shone in the firmament of His Faith had been successively extinguished, when His nominee, a "bewildered fugitive, in the guise of a dervish, with kas͟hkúl (alms-basket) in hand" roamed the mountains and plains in the neighborhood of Ras͟ht, Bahá'u'lláh, by reason of the acts He had performed, appeared in the eyes of a vigilant enemy as its most redoubtable adversary and as the sole hope of an as yet unextirpated heresy. His seizure and death had now become imperative. He it was Who, scarce three months after the Faith was born, received, through the envoy of the Báb, Mullá Ḥusayn, the scroll which bore to Him the first tidings of a newly announced Revelation, Who instantly acclaimed its truth, and arose to champion its cause. It was to His native city and dwelling place that the steps of that envoy were first directed, as the place which enshrined "a Mystery of such transcendent holiness as neither Ḥijáz nor Shíráz can hope to rival." It was Mullá Ḥusayn's report of the contact thus established which had been received with such exultant joy by the Báb, and had brought such reassurance to His heart as to finally decide Him to undertake His contemplated pilgrimage to Mecca and Medina. Bahá'u'lláh alone was the object and the center of the cryptic allusions, the glowing eulogies, the fervid prayers, the joyful announcements and the dire warnings recorded in both the Qayyúmu'l-Asmá' and the Bayán, designed to be respectively the first and last written testimonials to the glory with which God was soon to invest Him. It was He Who, through His correspondence with the Author of the newly founded Faith, and His intimate association with the most distinguished amongst its disciples, such as Vaḥíd, Ḥujjat, Quddús, Mullá Ḥusayn and Ṭáhirih, was able to foster its growth, elucidate its principles, reinforce its ethical foundations, fulfill its urgent requirements, avert some of the immediate dangers threatening it and participate effectually in its rise and consolidation. It was to Him, "the one Object of our adoration and love" that the Prophet-pilgrim, on His return to Búshihr, alluded when, dismissing Quddús from His presence, He announced to him the double joy of attaining the presence of their Beloved and of quaffing the cup of martyrdom. He it was Who, in the hey-day of His life, flinging aside every consideration of earthly fame, wealth and position, careless of danger, and risking the obloquy of His caste, arose to identify Himself, first in Ṭihrán and later in His native province of Mázindarán, with the cause of an obscure and proscribed sect; won to its support a large number of the officials and notables of Núr, not excluding His own associates and relatives; fearlessly and persuasively expounded its truths to the disciples of the illustrious mujtahid, Mullá Muḥammad; enlisted under its banner the mujtahid's appointed representatives; secured, in consequence of this act, the unreserved loyalty of a considerable number of ecclesiastical dignitaries, government officers, peasants and traders; and succeeded in challenging, in the course of a memorable interview, the mujtahid himself. It was solely due to the potency of the written message entrusted by Him to Mullá Muḥammad Mihdíy-i-Kandí and delivered to the Báb while in the neighborhood of the village of Kulayn, that the soul of the disappointed Captive was able to rid itself, at an hour of uncertainty and suspense, of the anguish that had settled upon it ever since His arrest in Shíráz. He it was Who, for the sake of Ṭáhirih and her imprisoned companions, willingly submitted Himself to a humiliating confinement, lasting several days—the first He was made to suffer—in the house of one of the kad-khudás of Ṭihrán. It was to His caution, foresight and ability that must be ascribed her successful escape from Qasvín, her deliverance from her opponents, her safe arrival in His home, and her subsequent removal to a place of safety in the vicinity of the capital from whence she proceeded to Khurásán. It was into His presence that Mullá Ḥusayn was secretly ushered upon his arrival in Ṭihrán, after which interview he traveled to Ádhirbáyján on his visit to the Báb then confined in the fortress of Máh-Kú. He it was Who unobtrusively and unerringly directed the proceedings of the Conference of Badasht; Who entertained as His guests Quddús, Ṭáhirih and the eighty-one disciples who had gathered on that occasion; Who revealed every day a Tablet and bestowed on each of the participants a new name; Who faced unaided the assault of a mob of more than five hundred villagers in Níyálá; Who shielded Quddús from the fury of his assailants; Who succeeded in restoring a part of the property which the enemy had plundered and Who insured the protection and safety of the continually harassed and much abused Ṭáhirih. Against Him was kindled the anger of Muḥammad Sháh who, as a result of the persistent representations of mischief-makers, was at last induced to order His arrest and summon Him to the capital—a summons that was destined to remain unfulfilled as a result of the sudden death of the sovereign. It was to His counsels and exhortations, addressed to the occupants of Shaykh Ṭabarsí, who had welcomed Him with such reverence and love during His visit to that Fort, that must be attributed, in no small measure, the spirit evinced by its heroic defenders, while it was to His explicit instructions that they owed the miraculous release of Quddús and his consequent association with them in the stirring exploits that have immortalized the Mázindarán upheaval. It was for the sake of those same defenders, whom He had intended to join, that He suffered His second imprisonment, this time in the masjid of Ámul to which He was led, amidst the tumult raised by no less than four thousand spectators,—for their sake that He was bastinadoed in the namáz-khánih of the mujtahid of that town until His feet bled, and later confined in the private residence of its governor; for their sake that He was bitterly denounced by the leading mullá, and insulted by the mob who, besieging the governor's residence, pelted Him with stones, and hurled in His face the foulest invectives. He alone was the One alluded to by Quddús who, upon his arrival at the Fort of Shaykh Ṭabarsí, uttered, as soon as he had dismounted and leaned against the shrine, the prophetic verse "The Baqíyyatu'lláh (the Remnant of God) will be best for you if ye are of those who believe." He alone was the Object of that prodigious eulogy, that masterly interpretation of the Ṣád of Ṣamad, penned in part, in that same Fort by that same youthful hero, under the most distressing circumstances, and equivalent in dimensions to six times the volume of the Qur'án. It was to the date of His impending Revelation that the Lawḥ-i-Ḥurúfat, revealed in Chihríq by the Báb, in honor of Dayyán, abstrusely alluded, and in which the mystery of the "Mustagháth" was unraveled. It was to the attainment of His presence that the attention of another disciple, Mullá Báqir, one of the Letters of the Living, was expressly directed by none other than the Báb Himself. It was exclusively to His care that the documents of the Báb, His pen-case, His seals, and agate rings, together with a scroll on which He had penned, in the form of a pentacle, no less than three hundred and sixty derivatives of the word Bahá, were delivered, in conformity with instructions He Himself had issued prior to His departure from Chihríq. It was solely due to His initiative, and in strict accordance with His instructions, that the precious remains of the Báb were safely transferred from Tabríz to the capital, and were concealed and safeguarded with the utmost secrecy and care throughout the turbulent years following His martyrdom. And finally, it was He Who, in the days preceding the attempt on the life of the Sháh, had been instrumental, while sojourning in Karbilá, in spreading, with that same enthusiasm and ability that had distinguished His earlier exertions in Mázindarán, the teachings of His departed Leader, in safeguarding the interests of His Faith, in reviving the zeal of its grief-stricken followers, and in organizing the forces of its scattered and bewildered adherents.

Such a man, with such a record of achievements to His credit, could not, indeed did not, escape either the detection or the fury of a vigilant and fully aroused enemy. Afire from the very beginning with an uncontrollable enthusiasm for the Cause He had espoused; conspicuously fearless in His advocacy of the rights of the downtrodden; in the full bloom of youth; immensely resourceful; matchless in His eloquence; endowed with inexhaustible energy and penetrating judgment; possessed of the riches, and enjoying, in full measure, the esteem, power and prestige associated with an enviably high and noble position, and yet contemptuous of all earthly pomp, rewards, vanities and possessions; closely associated, on the one hand, through His regular correspondence with the Author of the Faith He had risen to champion, and intimately acquainted, on the other, with the hopes and fears, the plans and activities of its leading exponents; at one time advancing openly and assuming a position of acknowledged leadership in the forefront of the forces struggling for that Faith's emancipation, at another deliberately drawing back with consummate discretion in order to remedy, with greater efficacy, an awkward or dangerous situation; at all times vigilant, ready and indefatigable in His exertions to preserve the integrity of that Faith, to resolve its problems, to plead its cause, to galvanize its followers, and to confound its antagonists, Bahá'u'lláh, at this supremely critical hour in its fortunes, was at last stepping into the very center of the stage so tragically vacated by the Báb—a stage on which He was destined, for no less a period than forty years, to play a part unapproached in its majesty, pathos and splendor by any of the great Founders of the world's historic religions.

Already so conspicuous and towering a figure had, through the accusations levelled against Him, kindled the wrath of Muḥammad S͟háh, who, after having heard what had transpired in Badas͟ht, had ordered His arrest, in a number of farmáns addressed to the k͟háns of Mázindarán, and expressed his determination to put Him to death. Ḥájí Mírzá Áqásí, previously alienated from the Vazír (Bahá'u'llah's father), and infuriated by his own failure to appropriate by fraud an estate that belonged to Bahá'u'lláh, had sworn eternal enmity to the One Who had so brilliantly succeeded in frustrating his evil designs. The Amír-Niẓám, moreover, fully aware of the pervasive influence of so energetic an opponent, had, in the presence of a distinguished gathering, accused Him of having inflicted, as a result of His activities, a loss of no less than five kurúrs upon the government, and had expressly requested Him, at a critical moment in the fortunes of the Faith, to temporarily transfer His residence to Karbilá. Mírzá Áqá K͟hán-i-Núrí, who succeeded the Amír-Niẓám, had endeavored, at the very outset of his ministry, to effect a reconciliation between his government and the One Whom he regarded as the most resourceful of the Báb's disciples. Little wonder that when, later, an act of such gravity and temerity was committed, a suspicion as dire as it was unfounded, should at once have crept into the minds of the S͟háh, his government, his court, and his people against Bahá'u'lláh. Foremost among them was the mother of the youthful sovereign, who, inflamed with anger, was openly denouncing Him as the would-be murderer of her son.

Bahá'u'lláh, when that attempt had been made on the life of the sovereign, was in Lavásán, the guest of the Grand Vizir, and was staying in the village of Afchih when the momentous news reached Him. Refusing to heed the advice of the Grand Vizir's brother, Ja'far-Qulí Khán, who was acting as His host, to remain for a time concealed in that neighborhood, and dispensing with the good offices of the messenger specially dispatched to insure His safety, He rode forth, the following morning, with cool intrepidity, to the headquarters of the Imperial army which was then stationed in Níyávarán, in the Shimírán district. In the village of Zarkandih He was met by, and conducted to the home of, His brother-in-law, Mírzá Majíd, who, at that time, was acting as secretary to the Russian Minister, Prince Dolgorouki, and whose house adjoined that of his superior. Apprised of Bahá'u'lláh's arrival the attendants of the Ḥájibu'd-Dawlih, Ḥájí 'Alí Khán, straightway informed their master, who in turn brought the matter to the attention of his sovereign. The Sháh, greatly amazed, dispatched his trusted officers to the Legation, demanding that the Accused be forthwith delivered into his hands. Refusing to comply with the wishes of the royal envoys, the Russian Minister requested Bahá'u'lláh to proceed to the home of the Grand Vizir, to whom he formally communicated his wish that the safety of the Trust the Russian government was delivering into his keeping should be insured. This purpose, however, was not achieved because of the Grand Vizir's apprehension that he might forfeit his position if he extended to the Accused the protection demanded for Him.

Delivered into the hands of His enemies, this much-feared, bitterly arraigned and illustrious Exponent of a perpetually hounded Faith was now made to taste of the cup which He Who had been its recognized Leader had drained to the dregs. From Níyávarán He was conducted "on foot and in chains, with bared head and bare feet," exposed to the fierce rays of the midsummer sun, to the Síyáh-Chál of Ṭihrán. On the way He several times was stripped of His outer garments, was overwhelmed with ridicule, and pelted with stones. As to the subterranean dungeon into which He was thrown, and which originally had served as a reservoir of water for one of the public baths of the capital, let His own words, recorded in His "Epistle to the Son of the Wolf," bear testimony to the ordeal which He endured in that pestilential hole. *"We were consigned for four months to a place foul beyond comparison. . . . Upon Our arrival*

*We were first conducted along a pitch-black corridor, from whence We descended three steep flights of stairs to the place of confinement assigned to Us. The dungeon was wrapped in thick darkness, and Our fellow-prisoners numbered nearly one hundred and fifty souls: thieves, assassins and highwaymen. Though crowded, it had no other outlet than the passage by which We entered. No pen can depict that place, nor any tongue describe its loathsome smell. Most of those men had neither clothes nor bedding to lie on. God alone knoweth what befell Us in that most foul-smelling and gloomy place!"* Bahá'u'lláh's feet were placed in stocks, and around His neck were fastened the Qará-Guhar chains of such galling weight that their mark remained imprinted upon His body all the days of His life. *"A heavy chain,"* 'Abdu'l-Bahá Himself has testified, *"was placed about His neck by which He was chained to five other Bábís; these fetters were locked together by strong, very heavy, bolts and screws. His clothes were torn to pieces, also His headdress. In this terrible condition He was kept for four months."* For three days and three nights, He was denied all manner of food and drink. Sleep was impossible to Him. The place was chill and damp, filthy, fever-stricken, infested with vermin, and filled with a noisome stench. Animated by a relentless hatred His enemies went even so far as to intercept and poison His food, in the hope of obtaining the favor of the mother of their sovereign, His most implacable foe—an attempt which, though it impaired His health for years to come, failed to achieve its purpose. " 'Abdu'l-Bahá," Dr. J. E. Esslemont records in his book, "tells how, one day, He was allowed to enter the prison yard to see His beloved Father, where He came out for His daily exercise. Bahá'u'lláh was terribly altered, so ill He could hardly walk, His hair and beard unkempt, His neck galled and swollen from the pressure of a heavy steel collar, His body bent by the weight of His chains."

While Bahá'u'lláh was being so odiously and cruelly subjected to the trials and tribulations inseparable from those tumultuous days, another luminary of the Faith, the valiant Ṭáhirih, was swiftly succumbing to their devastating power. Her meteoric career, inaugurated in Karbilá, culminating in Badasht, was now about to attain its final consummation in a martyrdom that may well rank as one of the most affecting episodes in the most turbulent period of Bahá'í history.

A scion of the highly reputed family of Hájí Mullá Ṣáliḥ-i-Baraqání, whose members occupied an enviable position in the Persian ecclesiastical hierarchy; the namesake of the illustrious

Fáṭimih; designated as Zarrín-Táj (Crown of Gold) and Zakíyyih (Virtuous) by her family and kindred; born in the same year as Bahá'u'lláh; regarded from childhood, by her fellow-townsmen, as a prodigy, alike in her intelligence and beauty; highly esteemed even by some of the most haughty and learned 'ulamás of her country, prior to her conversion, for the brilliancy and novelty of the views she propounded; acclaimed as 'Qurrat-i-'Ayní (solace of my eyes) by her admiring teacher, Siyyid Káẓim; entitled Ṭáhirih (the Pure One) by the "Tongue of Power and Glory;" and the only woman enrolled by the Báb as one of the Letters of the Living; she had, through a dream, referred to earlier in these pages, established her first contact with a Faith which she continued to propagate to her last breath, and in its hour of greatest peril, with all the ardor of her unsubduable spirit. Undeterred by the vehement protests of her father; contemptuous of the anathemas of her uncle; unmoved by the earnest solicitations of her husband and her brothers; undaunted by the measures which, first in Karbilá and subsequently in Baghdád, and later in Qasvín, the civil and ecclesiastical authorities had taken to curtail her activities, with eager energy she urged the Bábí Cause. Through her eloquent pleadings, her fearless denunciations, her dissertations, poems and translations, her commentaries and correspondence, she persisted in firing the imagination and in enlisting the allegiance of Arabs and Persians alike to the new Revelation, in condemning the perversity of her generation, and in advocating a revolutionary transformation in the habits and manners of her people.

She it was who while in Karbilá—the foremost stronghold of Shí'ah Islám—had been moved to address lengthy epistles to each of the 'ulamás residing in that city, who relegated women to a rank little higher than animals and denied them even the possession of a soul—epistles in which she ably vindicated her high purpose and exposed their malignant designs. She it was who, in open defiance of the customs of the fanatical inhabitants of that same city, boldly disregarded the anniversary of the martyrdom of the Imám Ḥusayn, commemorated with elaborate ceremony in the early days of Muḥarram, and celebrated instead the anniversary of the birthday of the Báb, which fell on the first day of that month. It was through her prodigious eloquence and the astounding force of her argument that she confounded the representative delegation of Shí'ah, of Sunní, of Christian and Jewish notables of Baghdád, who had endeavored to dissuade her from her avowed purpose of spreading the tidings of the new Message. She it was who, with consummate skill, defended her faith and vindicated her conduct in the home and in the presence of that eminent jurist, Shaykh Maḥmúd-i-Álúsí, the Muftí of Baghdád, and who later held her historic interviews with the princes, the 'ulamás and the government officials residing in Kirmánsháh, in the course of which the Báb's commentary on the Súrih of Kawthar was publicly read and translated, and which culminated in the conversion of the Amír (the governor) and his family. It was this remarkably gifted woman who undertook the translation of the Báb's lengthy commentary on the Súrih of Joseph (the Qayyúmu'l-Asmá') for the benefit of her Persian co-religionists, and exerted her utmost to spread the knowledge and elucidate the contents of that mighty Book. It was her fearlessness, her skill, her organizing ability and her unquenchable enthusiasm which consolidated her newly won victories in no less inimical a center than Qasvín, which prided itself on the fact that no fewer than a hundred of the highest ecclesiastical leaders of Islám dwelt within its gates. It was she who, in the house of Bahá'u'lláh in Ṭihrán, in the course of her memorable interview with the celebrated Vaḥíd, suddenly interrupted his learned discourse on the signs of the new Manifestation, and vehemently urged him, as she held 'Abdu'l-Bahá, then a child, on her lap, to arise and demonstrate through deeds of heroism and self-sacrifice the depth and sincerity of his faith. It was to her doors, during the height of her fame and popularity in Ṭihrán, that the flower of feminine society in the capital flocked to hear her brilliant discourses on the matchless tenets of her Faith. It was the magic of her words which won the wedding guests away from the festivities, on the occasion of the marriage of the son of Maḥmúd Khán-i-Kalantar—in whose house she was confined—and gathered them about her, eager to drink in her every word. It was her passionate and unqualified affirmation of the claims and distinguishing features of the new Revelation, in a series of seven conferences with the deputies of the Grand Vizir commissioned to interrogate her, which she held while confined in that same house, which finally precipitated the sentence of her death. It was from her pen that odes had flowed attesting, in unmistakable language, not only her faith in the Revelation of the Báb, but also her recognition of the exalted and as yet undisclosed mission of Bahá'u'lláh. And last but not least it was owing to her initiative, while participating in the Conference of Badasht, that the most challenging implications of a revolutionary and as yet but dimly grasped Dispensation were laid bare before her fellow-disciples and the new Order permanently divorced from the laws and institutions of Islám. Such marvelous achievements were now to be crowned by, and attain their final consummation in, her martyrdom in the midst of the storm that was raging throughout the capital.

One night, aware that the hour of her death was at hand, she put on the attire of a bride, and annointed herself with perfume, and, sending for the wife of the Kalantar, she communicated to her the secret of her impending martyrdom, and confided to her her last wishes. Then, closeting herself in her chambers, she awaited, in prayer and meditation, the hour which was to witness her reunion with her Beloved. She was pacing the floor of her room, chanting a litany expressive of both grief and triumph, when the farráshes of 'Azíz Khán-i-Sardár arrived, in the dead of night, to conduct her to the Ílkhání garden, which lay beyond the city gates, and which was to be the site of her martyrdom. When she arrived the Sardár was in the midst of a drunken debauch with his lieutenants, and was roaring with laughter; he ordered offhand that she be strangled at once and thrown into a pit. With that same silken kerchief which she had intuitively reserved for that purpose, and delivered in her last moments to the son of Kalantar who accompanied her, the death of this immortal heroine was accomplished. Her body was lowered into a well, which was then filled with earth and stones, in the manner she herself had desired.

Thus ended the life of this great Bábí heroine, the first woman suffrage martyr, who, at her death, turning to the one in whose custody she had been placed, had boldly declared: "You can kill me as soon as you like, but you cannot stop the emancipation of women." Her career was as dazzling as it was brief, as tragic as it was eventful. Unlike her fellow-disciples, whose exploits remained, for the most part unknown, and unsung by their contemporaries in foreign lands, the fame of this immortal woman was noised abroad, and traveling with remarkable swiftness as far as the capitals of Western Europe, aroused the enthusiastic admiration and evoked the ardent praise of men and women of divers nationalities, callings and cultures. Little wonder that 'Abdu'l-Bahá should have joined her name to those of Sarah, of Ásíyih, of the Virgin Mary and of Fáṭimih, who, in the course of successive Dispensations, have towered, by reason of their intrinsic merits and unique position, above the rank and file of their sex. *"In eloquence,"* 'Abdu'l-Bahá Himself has written, *"she was the calamity of the age, and in ratiocination the trouble of the world."* He, moreover, has described her as *"a brand afire with the love of God"* and *"a lamp aglow with the bounty of God."*

Indeed the wondrous story of her life propagated itself as far and as fast as that of the Báb Himself, the direct Source of her inspiration. "Prodige de science, mais aussi prodige de beauté" is the tribute paid her by a noted commentator on the life of the Báb and His disciples. "The Persian Joan of Arc, the leader of emancipation for women of the Orient . . . who bore resemblance both to the mediaeval Heloise and the neo-platonic Hypatia," thus was she acclaimed by a noted playwright whom Sarah Bernhardt had specifically requested to write a dramatized version of her life. "The heroism of the lovely but ill-fated poetess of Qasvín, Zarrín-Táj (Crown of Gold) . . . " testifies Lord Curzon of Kedleston, "is one of the most affecting episodes in modern history." "The appearance of such a woman as Qurratu'l-'Ayn," wrote the well-known British Orientalist, Prof. E. G. Browne, "is, in any country and any age, a rare phenomenon, but in such a country as Persia it is a prodigy—nay, almost a miracle. . . . Had the Bábí religion no other claim to greatness, this were sufficient . . . that it produced a heroine like Qurratu'l-'Ayn." "The harvest sown in Islamic lands by Qurratu'l-'Ayn," significantly affirms the renowned English divine, Dr. T. K. Cheyne, in one of his books, "is now beginning to appear . . . this noble woman . . . has the credit of opening the catalogue of social reforms in Persia . . . " "Assuredly one of the most striking and interesting manifestations of this religion" is the reference to her by the noted French diplomat and brilliant writer, Comte de Gobineau. "In Qasvín," he adds, "she was held, with every justification, to be a prodigy." "Many people," he, moreover has written, "who knew her and heard her at different periods of her life have invariably told me . . . that when she spoke one felt stirred to the depths of one's soul, was filled with admiration, and was moved to tears." "No memory," writes Sir Valentine Chirol, "is more deeply venerated or kindles greater enthusiasm than hers, and the influence which she wielded in her lifetime still inures to her sex." "O Ṭáhirih!" exclaims in his book on the Bábís the great author and poet of Turkey, Sulaymán Náẓim Bey, "you are worth a thousand Náṣiri'd-Dín Shãhs!" "The greatest ideal of womanhood has been Ṭáhirih" is the tribute paid her by the mother of one of the Presidents of Austria, Mrs. Marianna Hainisch, ". . . I shall try to do for the women of Austria what Ṭáhirih gave her life to do for the women of Persia."

Many and divers are her ardent admirers who, throughout the five continents, are eager to know more about her. Many are those whose conduct has been ennobled by her inspiring example, who have committed to memory her matchless odes, or set to music her poems, before whose eyes glows the vision of her indomitable spirit, in whose hearts is enshrined a love and admiration that time can never dim, and in whose souls burns the determination to tread as dauntlessly, and with that same fidelity, the path she chose for herself, and from which she never swerved from the moment of her conversion to the hour of her death.

The fierce gale of persecution that had swept Bahá'u'lláh into a subterranean dungeon and snuffed out the light of Ṭáhirih also sealed the fate of the Báb's distinguished amanuensis, Siyyid Ḥusayn-i-Yazdí, surnamed 'Azíz, who had shared His confinement in both Máh-Kú and Chihríq. A man of rich experience and high merit, deeply versed in the teachings of his Master, and enjoying His unqualified confidence, he, refusing every offer of deliverance from the leading officials of Ṭihrán, yearned unceasingly for the martyrdom which had been denied him on the day the Báb had laid down His life in the barrack-square of Tabríz. A fellow-prisoner of Bahá'u'lláh in the Síyáh-Chál of Ṭihrán, from Whom he derived inspiration and solace as he recalled those precious days spent in the company of his Master in Ádhirbáyján, he was finally struck down, in circumstances of shameful cruelty, by that same 'Azíz Khán-i-Sardár who had dealt the fatal blow to Ṭáhirih.

Another victim of the frightful tortures inflicted by an unyielding enemy was the high-minded, the influential and courageous Ḥájí Sulaymán Khán. So greatly was he esteemed that the Amír-Niẓám had felt, on a previous occasion, constrained to ignore his connection with the Faith he had embraced and to spare his life. The turmoil that convulsed Ṭihrán as a result of the attempt on the life of the sovereign, however, precipitated his arrest and brought about his martyrdom. The Sháh, having failed to induce him through the Ḥájibu'd-Dawlih to recant, commanded that he be put to death in any way he himself might choose. Nine holes, at his express wish, were made in his flesh, in each of which a lighted candle was placed. As the executioner shrank from performing this gruesome task, he attempted to snatch the knife from his hand that he might himself plunge it into his own body. Fearing lest he should attack him the executioner refused, and bade his men tie the victim's hands behind his back, whereupon the intrepid sufferer pleaded with them to pierce two holes in his breast, two in his shoulders, one in the nape of his neck, and four others in his back—a wish they complied with. Standing erect as an arrow, his eyes glowing with stoic fortitude, unperturbed by the howling multitude or the sight of his own blood streaming from his wounds, and preceded by minstrels and drummers, he led the concourse that pressed round him to the final place of his martyrdom. Every few steps he would interrupt his march to address the bewildered bystanders in words in which he glorified the Báb and magnified the significance of his own death. As his eyes beheld the candles flickering in their bloody sockets, he would burst forth in exclamations of unrestrained delight. Whenever one of them fell from his body he would with his own hand pick it up, light it from the others, and replace it. "Why dost thou not dance?" asked the executioner mockingly, "since thou findest death so pleasant?" "Dance?" cried the sufferer, "In one hand the wine-cup, in one hand the tresses of the Friend. Such a dance in the midst of the market-place is my desire!" He was still in the bazaar when the flowing of a breeze, fanning the flames of the candles now burning deep in his flesh, caused it to sizzle, whereupon he burst forth addressing the flames that ate into his wounds: "You have long lost your sting, O flames, and have been robbed of your power to pain me. Make haste, for from your very tongues of fire I can hear the voice that calls me to my Beloved." In a blaze of light he walked as a conqueror might have marched to the scene of his victory. At the foot of the gallows he once again raised his voice in a final appeal to the multitude of onlookers. He then prostrated himself in the direction of the shrine of the Imám-Zádih Ḥasan, murmuring some words in Arabic. "My work is now finished," he cried to the executioner, "come and do yours." Life still lingered in him as his body was sawn into two halves, with the praise of his Beloved still fluttering from his dying lips. The scorched and bloody remnants of his corpse were, as he himself had requested, suspended on either side of the Gate of Naw, mute witnesses to the unquenchable love which the Báb had kindled in the breasts of His disciples.

The violent conflagration kindled as a result of the attempted assassination of the sovereign could not be confined to the capital. It overran the adjoining provinces, ravaged Mázindarán, the native province of Bahá'u'lláh, and brought about in its wake, the confiscation, the plunder and the destruction of all His possessions. In the village of Tákur, in the district of Núr, His sumptuously furnished home, inherited from His father, was, by order of Mírzá Abú-Ṭálib K͟hán, nephew of the Grand Vizir, completely despoiled, and whatever could not be carried away was ordered to be destroyed, while its rooms, more stately than those of the palaces of Ṭihrán, were disfigured beyond repair. Even the houses of the people were leveled with the ground, after which the entire village was set on fire.

The commotion that had seized Ṭihrán and had given rise to the campaign of outrage and spoliation in Mázindarán spread even as far as Yazd, Nayríz and Shíráz, rocking the remotest hamlets, and rekindling the flames of persecution. Once again greedy governors and perfidious subordinates vied with each other in despoiling the innocent, in massacring the guiltless, and in dishonoring the noblest of their race. A carnage ensued which repeated the atrocities already perpetrated in Nayríz and Zanján. "My pen," writes the chronicler of the bloody episodes associated with the birth and rise of our Faith, "shrinks in horror in attempting to describe what befell those valiant men and women. . . . What I have attempted to recount of the horrors of the siege of Zanján . . . pales before the glaring ferocity of the atrocities perpetrated a few years later in Nayríz and Shíráz." The heads of no less than two hundred victims of these outbursts of ferocious fanaticism were impaled on bayonets, and carried triumphantly from Shíráz to Ábádih. Forty women and children were charred to a cinder by being placed in a cave, in which a vast quantity of firewood had been heaped up, soaked with naphtha and set alight. Three hundred women were forced to ride two by two on bare-backed horses all the way to Shíráz. Stripped almost naked they were led between rows of heads hewn from the lifeless bodies of their husbands, sons, fathers and brothers. Untold insults were heaped upon them, and the hardships they suffered were such that many among them perished.

Thus drew to a close a chapter which records for all time the bloodiest, the most tragic, the most heroic period of the first Bahá'í century. The torrents of blood that poured out during those crowded and calamitous years may be regarded as constituting the fertile seeds of that World Order which a swiftly succeeding and still greater Revelation was to proclaim and establish. The tributes paid the noble army of the heroes, saints and martyrs of that Primitive Age, by friend and foe alike, from Bahá'u'lláh Himself down to the most disinterested observers in distant lands, and from the moment of its birth until the present day, bear imperishable witness to the glory of the deeds that immortalize that Age.

*"The whole world,"* is Bahá'u'lláh's matchless testimony in the Kitáb-i-Íqán, *"marveled at the manner of their sacrifice. . . . The mind is bewildered at their deeds, and the soul marveleth at their fortitude and bodily endurance. . . . Hath any age witnessed such momentous happenings?"* And again: *"Hath the world, since the*

*days of Adam, witnessed such tumult, such violent commotion? . . . Methinks, patience was revealed only by virtue of their fortitude, and faithfulness itself was begotten only by their deeds." "Through the blood which they shed,"* He, in a prayer, referring more specifically to the martyrs of the Faith, has significantly affirmed, *"the earth hath been impregnated with the wondrous revelations of Thy might and the gem-like signs of Thy glorious sovereignty. Ere-long shall she tell out her tidings, when the set time is come."*

To whom else could these significant words of Muḥammad, the Apostle of God, quoted by Quddús while addressing his companions in the Fort of Shaykh Ṭabarsí, apply if not to those heroes of God who, with their life-blood, ushered in the Promised Day? *"O how I long to behold the countenance of My brethren, my brethren who will appear at the end of the world! Blessed are We, blessed are they; greater is their blessedness than ours."* Who else could be meant by this tradition, called Ḥadíth-i-Jábir, recorded in the Káfí, and authenticated by Bahá'u'lláh in the Kitáb-i-Íqán, which, in indubitable language, sets forth the signs of the appearance of the promised Qá'im? *"His saints shall be abased in His time, and their heads shall be exchanged as presents, even as the heads of the Turk and the Daylamite are exchanged as presents; they shall be slain and burned, and shall be afraid, fearful and dismayed; the earth shall be dyed with their blood, and lamentation and wailing shall prevail amongst their women; these are My saints indeed."*

"Tales of magnificent heroism," is the written testimony of Lord Curzon of Kedleston, "illumine the blood-stained pages of Bábí history. . . . The fires of Smithfield did not kindle a nobler courage than has met and defied the more refined torture-mongers of Ṭihrán. Of no small account, then, must be the tenets of a creed that can awaken in its followers so rare and beautiful a spirit of self-sacrifice. The heroism and martyrdom of His (the Báb) followers will appeal to many others who can find no similar phenomena in the contemporaneous records of Islám." "Bábism," wrote Prof. J. Darmesteter, "which diffused itself in less than five years from one end of Persia to another, which was bathed in 1852 in the blood of its martyrs, has been silently progressing and propagating itself. If Persia is to be at all regenerate it will be through this new Faith." "Des milliers de martyrs," attests Renan in his "Les Apôtres," "sont accourus pour lui (the Báb) avec allégresse au devant de la mort. Un jour sans pareil peut-être dans l'histoire du monde fut celui de la grande boucherie qui se fit des Bábís à Teheran." "One of those strange outbursts," declares the well-known Orientalist Prof. E. G. Browne, "of enthusiasm, faith, fervent devotion and indomitable heroism . . . the birth of a Faith which may not impossibly win a place amidst the great religions of the world." And again: "The spirit which pervades the Bábís is such that it can hardly fail to affect most powerfully all subjected to its influence. . . . Let those who have not seen disbelieve me if they will, but, should that spirit once reveal itself to them, they will experience an emotion which they are not likely to forget." "J'avoue même," is the assertion made by Comte de Gobineau in his book, "que, si je voyais en Europe une secte d'une nature analogue au Babysme se présenter avec des avantages tels que les siens, foi aveugle, enthousiasme extrême, courage et dévouement éprouvés, respect inspiré aux indifférents, terreur profonde inspirée aux adversaires, et de plus, comme je l'ai dit, un prosélytisme qui ne s'arrête pas, et donc les succès sont constants dans toutes les classes de la société; si je voyais, dis-je, tout cela exister en Europe, je n'hésiterais pas à prédire que, dans un temps donné, la puissance et le sceptre appartiendront de toute nécessité aux possesseurs de ces grands avantages."

"The truth of the matter," is the answer which 'Abbás-Qulí Khán-i-Lárījání, whose bullet was responsible for the death of Mullá Ḥusayn, is reported to have given to a query addressed to him by Prince Ahmad Mírzá in the presence of several witnesses, "is that any one who had not seen Karbilá would, if he had seen Tabarsí, not only have comprehended what there took place, but would have ceased to consider it; and had he seen Mullá Ḥusayn of Bushrúyih, he would have been convinced that the Chief of Martyrs (Imám Ḥusayn) had returned to earth; and had he witnessed my deeds, he would assuredly have said: 'This is Shimr come back with sword and lance . . .' In truth, I know not what had been shown to these people, or what they had seen, that they came forth to battle with such alacrity and joy. . . . The imagination of man cannot conceive the vehemence of their courage and valor."

What, in conclusion, we may well ask ourselves, has been the fate of that flagitious crew who, actuated by malice, by greed or fanaticism, sought to quench the light which the Báb and His followers had diffused over their country and its people? The rod of Divine chastisement, swiftly and with unyielding severity, spared neither the Chief Magistrate of the realm, nor his ministers and counselors, nor the ecclesiastical dignitaries of the religion with which his government was indissolubly connected, nor the governors who acted as his representatives, nor the chiefs of his armed forces who, in varying degrees, deliberately or through fear or neglect, contributed to the appalling trials to which an infant Faith was so undeservedly subjected. Muḥammad S͟háh himself, a sovereign at once bigoted and irresolute who, refusing to heed the appeal of the Báb to receive Him in the capital and enable Him to demonstrate the truth of His Cause, yielded to the importunities of a malevolent minister, succumbed, at the early age of forty, after sustaining a sudden reverse of fortune, to a complication of maladies, and was condemned to that *"hell-fire"* which, *"on the Day of Resurrection,"* the Author of the Qayyúmu'l-Asmá' had sworn would inevitably devour him. His evil genius, the omnipotent Ḥájí Mírzá Áqásí, the power behind the throne and the chief instigator of the outrages perpetrated against the Báb, including His imprisonment in the mountains of Ád͟hirbáyján, was, after the lapse of scarcely a year and six months from the time he interposed himself between the S͟háh and his Captive, hurled from power, deprived of his ill-gotten riches, was disgraced by his sovereign, was driven to seek shelter from the rising wrath of his countrymen in the shrine of S͟háh 'Abdu'l-'Azím, and was later ignominiously expelled to Karbilá, falling a prey to disease, poverty and gnawing sorrow—a piteous vindication of that denunciatory Tablet in which his Prisoner had foreshadowed his doom and denounced his infamy. As to the low-born and infamous Amír-Niẓám, Mírzá Taqí K͟hán, the first year of whose short-lived ministry was stained with the ferocious onslaught against the defenders of the Fort of Ṭabarsí, who authorized and encouraged the execution of the Seven Martyrs of Ṭihrán, who unleashed the assault against Vaḥíd and his companions, who was directly responsible for the death-sentence of the Báb, and who precipitated the great upheaval of Zanján, he forfeited, through the unrelenting jealousy of his sovereign and the vindictiveness of court intrigue, all the honors he had enjoyed, and was treacherously put to death by the royal order, his veins being opened in the bath of the Palace of Fín, near Kás͟hán. *"Had the Amír-Niẓám,"* Bahá'u'lláh is reported by Nabíl to have stated, *"been aware of My true position, he would certainly have laid hold on Me. He exerted the utmost effort to discover the real situation, but was unsuccessful. God wished him to be ignorant of it."* Mírzá Áqá K͟hán, who had taken such an active part in the unbridled cruelties perpetrated as a result of the attempt on the life of the sovereign, was driven from office, and placed under strict surveillance in Yazd, where he ended his days in shame and despair.

Ḥusayn Khán, the governor of Shíráz, stigmatized as a "winebibber" and a "tyrant," the first who arose to ill-treat the Báb, who publicly rebuked Him and bade his attendant strike Him violently in the face, was compelled not only to endure the dreadful calamity that so suddenly befell him, his family, his city and his province, but afterwards to witness the undoing of all his labors, and to lead in obscurity the remaining days of his life, till he tottered to his grave abandoned alike by his friends and his enemies. Ḥájibu'd-Dawlih, that bloodthirsty fiend, who had strenuously hounded down so many innocent and defenseless Bábís, fell in his turn a victim to the fury of the turbulent Lurs, who, after despoiling him of his property, cut off his beard, and forced him to eat it, saddled and bridled him, and rode him before the eyes of the people, after which they inflicted under his very eyes shameful atrocities upon his womenfolk and children. The Sa'ídu'l-'Ulamá, the fanatical, the ferocious and shameless mujtahid of Bárfurúsh, whose unquenchable hostility had heaped such insults upon, and caused such sufferings to, the heroes of Ṭabarsí, fell, soon after the abominations he had perpetrated, a prey to a strange disease, provoking an unquenchable thirst and producing such icy chills that neither the furs he wrapped himself in, nor the fire that continually burned in his room could alleviate his sufferings. The spectacle of his ruined and once luxurious home, fallen into such ill use after his death as to become the refuse-heap of the people of his town, impressed so profoundly the inhabitants of Mázindarán that in their mutual vituperations they would often invoke upon each other's home the same fate as that which had befallen that accursed habitation. The false-hearted and ambitious Maḥmúd Khán-i-Kalantar, into whose custody Ṭáhirih had been delivered before her martyrdom, incurred, nine years later, the wrath of his royal master, was dragged feet first by ropes through the bazaars to a place outside the city gates, and there hung on the gallows. Mírzá Ḥasan Khán, who carried out the execution of the Báb under orders from his brother, the Amír-Niẓám, was, within two years of that unpardonable act, subjected to a dreadful punishment which ended in his death. The Shaykhu'l-Islám of Tabríz, the insolent, the avaricious and tyrannical Mírzá 'Ali Aṣghar, who, after the refusal of the bodyguard of the governor of that city to inflict the bastinado on the Báb, proceeded to apply eleven times the rods to the feet of his Prisoner with his own hand, was, in that same year, struck with paralysis, and, after enduring the most excruciating ordeal, died a miserable death—a death that was soon followed by the abolition of the function of the Shaykhu'l-Islám in that city. The haughty and perfidious Mírzá Abú-Ṭálib Khán who, disregarding the counsels of moderation given him by Mírzá Áqá Khán, the Grand Vizir, ordered the plunder and burning of the village of Tákur, as well as the destruction of the house of Bahá'u'lláh, was, a year later, stricken with plague and perished wretchedly, shunned by even his nearest kindred. Mihr-'Alí Khán, the Shujá'u'l-Mulk, who, after the attempt on the Sháh's life, so savagely persecuted the remnants of the Bábí community in Nayríz, fell ill, according to the testimony of his own grandson, and was stricken with dumbness, which was never relieved till the day of his death. His accomplice, Mírzá Na'ím, fell into disgrace, was twice heavily fined, dismissed from office, and subjected to exquisite tortures. The regiment which, scorning the miracle that warned Sám Khán and his men to dissociate themselves from any further attempt to destroy the life of the Báb, volunteered to take their place and riddled His body with its bullets, lost, in that same year, no less than two hundred and fifty of its officers and men, in a terrible earthquake between Ardibíl and Tabríz; two years later the remaining five hundred were mercilessly shot in Tabríz for mutiny, and the people, gazing on their exposed and mutilated bodies, recalled their savage act, and indulged in such expressions of condemnation and wonder as to induce the leading mujtahids to chastise and silence them. The head of that regiment, Áqá Ján Big, lost his life, six years after the Báb's martyrdom, during the bombardment of Muḥammarih by the British naval forces.

The judgment of God, so rigorous and unsparing in its visitations on those who took a leading or an active part in the crimes committed against the Báb and His followers, was not less severe in its dealings with the mass of the people—a people more fanatical than the Jews in the days of Jesus—a people notorious for their gross ignorance, their ferocious bigotry, their willful perversity and savage cruelty, a people mercenary, avaricious, egotistical and cowardly. I can do no better than quote what the Báb Himself has written in the Dalá'il-i-Sab'ih (Seven Proofs) during the last days of His ministry: "*Call thou to remembrance the early days of the Revelation. How great the number of those who died of cholera! That was indeed one of the prodigies of the Revelation, and yet none recognized it! During four years the scourge raged among Shí'ah Muslims without any one grasping its significance!*" "As to the great mass of its people (Persia)," Nabíl has recorded in his immortal narrative, "who watched with sullen indifference the tragedy that was being enacted before their eyes, and who failed to raise a finger in protest against the hideousness of those cruelties, they fell, in their turn, victims to a misery which all the resources of the land and the energy of its statesmen were powerless to alleviate. . . . From the very day the hand of the assailant was stretched forth against the Báb . . . visitation upon visitation crushed the spirit out of that ungrateful people, and brought them to the very brink of national bankruptcy. Plagues, the very names of which were almost unknown to them except for a cursory reference in the dust-covered books which few cared to read, fell upon them with a fury that none could escape. That scourge scattered devastation wherever it spread. Prince and peasant alike felt its sting and bowed to its yoke. It held the populace in its grip, and refused to relax its hold upon them. As malignant as the fever which decimated the province of Gílán, these sudden afflictions continued to lay waste the land. Grievous as were these calamities, the avenging wrath of God did not stop at the misfortunes that befell a perverse and faithless people. It made itself felt in every living being that breathed on the surface of that stricken land. It afflicted the life of plants and animals alike, and made the people feel the magnitude of their distress. Famine added its horrors to the stupendous weight of afflictions under which the people were groaning. The gaunt spectre of starvation stalked abroad amidst them, and the prospect of a slow and painful death haunted their vision. . . . People and government alike sighed for the relief which they could nowhere obtain. They drank the cup of woe to its dregs, utterly unregardful of the Hand which had brought it to their lips, and of the Person for Whose sake they were made to suffer."

SECOND PERIOD

# THE MINISTRY OF BAHÁ'U'LLÁH
1853-1892

## CHAPTER VI

# The Birth of The Bahá'í Revelation

The train of dire events that followed in swift succession the calamitous attempt on the life of Náṣiri'd-Dín S͟háh mark, as already observed, the termination of the Bábí Dispensation and the closing of the initial, the darkest and bloodiest chapter of the history of the first Bahá'í century. A phase of measureless tribulation had been ushered in by these events, in the course of which the fortunes of the Faith proclaimed by the Báb sank to their lowest ebb. Indeed ever since its inception trials and vexations, setbacks and disappointments, denunciations, betrayals and massacres had, in a steadily rising crescendo, contributed to the decimation of the ranks of its followers, strained to the utmost the loyalty of its stoutest upholders, and all but succeeded in disrupting the foundations on which it rested.

From its birth, government, clergy and people had risen as one man against it and vowed eternal enmity to its cause. Muḥammad S͟háh, weak alike in mind and will, had, under pressure, rejected the overtures made to him by the Báb Himself, had declined to meet Him face to face, and even refused Him admittance to the capital. The youthful Náṣiri'd-Dín S͟háh, of a cruel and imperious nature, had, both as crown prince and as reigning sovereign, increasingly evinced the bitter hostility which, at a later stage in his reign, was to blaze forth in all its dark and ruthless savagery. The powerful and sagacious Mu'tamid, the one solitary figure who could have extended Him the support and protection He so sorely needed, was taken from Him by a sudden death. The Sherif of Mecca, who through the mediation of Quddús had been made acquainted with the new Revelation on the occasion of the Báb's pilgrimage to Mecca, had turned a deaf ear to the Divine Message, and received His messenger with curt indifference. The prearranged gathering that was to have taken place in the holy city of Karbilá, in the course of the Báb's return journey from Ḥijáz, had, to the disappointment of His followers who had been eagerly awaiting His arrival, to be definitely abandoned. The eighteen Letters of the Living, the principal bastions that buttressed the infant strength of the Faith, had for the most part fallen. The "Mirrors," the "Guides," the "Witnesses" comprising the Bábí hierarchy had either been put to the sword, or hounded from their native soil, or bludgeoned into silence. The program, whose essentials had been communicated to the foremost among them, had, owing to their excessive zeal, remained for the most part unfulfilled. The attempts which two of those disciples had made to establish the Faith in Turkey and India had signally failed at the very outset of their mission. The tempests that had swept Mázindarán, Nayríz and Zanján had, in addition to blasting to their roots the promising careers of the venerated Quddús, the lion-hearted Mullá Ḥusayn, the erudite Vaḥíd, and the indomitable Ḥujjat, cut short the lives of an alarmingly large number of the most resourceful and most valiant of their fellow-disciples. The hideous outrages associated with the death of the Seven Martyrs of Ṭihrán had been responsible for the extinction of yet another living symbol of the Faith, who, by reason of his close kinship to, and intimate association with, the Báb, no less than by virtue of his inherent qualities, would if spared have decisively contributed to the protection and furtherance of a struggling Cause.

The storm which subsequently burst, with unexampled violence, on a community already beaten to its knees, had, moreover, robbed it of its greatest heroine, the incomparable Ṭáhirih, still in the full tide of her victories, had sealed the doom of Siyyid Ḥusayn, the Báb's trusted amanuensis and chosen repository of His last wishes, had laid low Mullá 'Abdu'l-Karím-i-Qasvíní, admittedly one of the very few who could claim to possess a profound knowledge of the origins of the Faith, and had plunged into a dungeon Bahá'u'lláh, the sole survivor among the towering figures of the new Dispensation. The Báb—the Fountainhead from whence the vitalizing energies of a newborn Revelation had flowed—had Himself, ere the outburst of that hurricane, succumbed, in harrowing circumstances, to the volleys of a firing squad leaving behind, as titular head of a well-nigh disrupted community, a mere figurehead, timid in the extreme, good-natured yet susceptible to the slightest influence, devoid of any outstanding qualities, who now (loosed from the controlling hand of Bahá'u'lláh, the real Leader) was seeking, in the guise of a dervish, the protection afforded by the hills of his native Mázindarán against the threatened assaults of a deadly enemy. The voluminous writings of the Founder of the Faith—in manuscript, dispersed, unclassified, poorly transcribed and ill-preserved, were in part, owing to the fever and tumult of the times, either deliberately destroyed, confiscated, or hurriedly dispatched to places of safety beyond the confines of the land in which they were revealed. Powerful adversaries, among whom towered the figure of the inordinately ambitious and hypocritical Ḥájí Mírzá Karím Khán, who at the special request of the Sháh had in a treatise viciously attacked the new Faith and its doctrines, had now raised their heads, and, emboldened by the reverses it had sustained, were heaping abuse and calumnies upon it. Furthermore, under the stress of intolerable circumstances, a few of the Bábís were constrained to recant their faith, while others went so far as to apostatize and join the ranks of the enemy. And now to the sum of these dire misfortunes a monstrous calumny, arising from the outrage perpetrated by a handful of irresponsible enthusiasts, was added, branding a holy and innocent Faith with an infamy that seemed indelible, and which threatened to loosen it from its foundations.

And yet the Fire which the Hand of Omnipotence had lighted, though smothered by this torrent of tribulations let loose upon it, was not quenched. The flame which for nine years had burned with such brilliant intensity was indeed momentarily extinguished, but the embers which that great conflagration had left behind still glowed, destined, at no distant date, to blaze forth once again, through the reviving breezes of an incomparably greater Revelation, and to shed an illumination that would not only dissipate the surrounding darkness but project its radiance as far as the extremities of both the Eastern and Western Hemispheres. Just as the enforced captivity and isolation of the Báb had, on the one hand, afforded Him the opportunity of formulating His doctrine, of unfolding the full implications of His Revelation, of formally and publicly declaring His station and of establishing His Covenant, and, on the other hand, had been instrumental in the proclamation of the laws of His Dispensation through the voice of His disciples assembled in Badasht, so did the crisis of unprecedented magnitude, culminating in the execution of the Báb and the imprisonment of Bahá'u'lláh, prove to be the prelude of a revival which, through the quickening power of a far mightier Revelation, was to immortalize the fame, and fix on a still more enduring foundation, far beyond the confines of His native land, the original Message of the Prophet of Shíráz.

At a time when the Cause of the Báb seemed to be hovering on the brink of extinction, when the hopes and ambitions which animated it had, to all human seeming, been frustrated, when the colossal sacrifices of its unnumbered lovers appeared to have been made in vain, the Divine Promise enshrined within it was about to be suddenly redeemed, and its final perfection mysteriously manifested. The Bábí Dispensation was being brought to its close (not prematurely but in its own appointed time), and was yielding its destined fruit and revealing its ultimate purpose—the birth of the Mission of Bahá'u'lláh. In this most dark and dreadful hour a New Light was about to break in glory on Persia's somber horizon. As a result of what was in fact an evolving, ripening process, the most momentous if not the most spectacular stage in the Heroic Age of the Faith was now about to open.

During nine years, as foretold by the Báb Himself, swiftly, mysteriously and irresistibly the embryonic Faith conceived by Him had been developing until, at the fixed hour, the burden of the promised Cause of God was cast amidst the gloom and agony of the Síyáh-Chál of Ṭihrán. *"Behold,"* Bahá'u'lláh Himself, years later, testified, in refutation of the claims of those who had rejected the validity of His mission following so closely upon that of the Báb, *"how immediately upon the completion of the ninth year of this wondrous, this most holy and merciful Dispensation, the requisite number of pure, of wholly consecrated and sanctified souls has been most secretly consummated." "That so brief an interval,"* He, moreover has asserted, *"should have separated this most mighty and wondrous Revelation from Mine own previous Manifestation is a secret that no man can unravel, and a mystery such as no mind can fathom. Its duration had been foreordained."*

St. John the Divine had himself, with reference to these two successive Revelations, clearly prophesied: "The second woe is past; and, behold the third woe cometh quickly." *"This third woe,"* 'Abdu'l-Bahá, commenting upon this verse, has explained, *"is the day of the Manifestation of Bahá'u'lláh, the Day of God, and it is near to the day of the appearance of the Báb." "All the peoples of the world,"* He moreover has asserted, *"are awaiting two Manifestations, Who must be contemporaneous; all wait for the fulfillment of this promise."* And again: *"The essential fact is that all are promised two Manifestations, Who will come one following on the other."* Shaykh Aḥmad-i-Aḥsá'í, that luminous star of Divine guidance who had so clearly perceived, before the year sixty, the approaching glory of Bahá'u'lláh, and laid stress upon "the twin Revelations which are to follow each other in rapid succession," had, on his part, made this significant statement regarding the approaching hour of that supreme Revelation, in an epistle addressed in his own hand to Siyyid Kaẓím: "The mystery of this Cause must needs be made manifest, and the secret of this Message must needs be divulged. I can say no more.

I can appoint no time. His Cause will be made known after Ḥín (68)."

The circumstances in which the Vehicle of this newborn Revelation, following with such swiftness that of the Báb, received the first intimations of His sublime mission recall, and indeed surpass in poignancy the soul-shaking experience of Moses when confronted by the Burning Bush in the wilderness of Sinai; of Zoroaster when awakened to His mission by a succession of seven visions; of Jesus when coming out of the waters of the Jordan He saw the heavens opened and the Holy Ghost descend like a dove and light upon Him; of Muḥammad when in the Cave of Hira, outside of the holy city of Mecca, the voice of Gabriel bade Him *"cry in the name of Thy Lord"*; and of the Báb when in a dream He approached the bleeding head of the Imám Ḥusayn, and, quaffing the blood that dripped from his lacerated throat, awoke to find Himself the chosen recipient of the outpouring grace of the Almighty.

What, we may well inquire at this juncture, were the nature and implications of that Revelation which, manifesting itself so soon after the Declaration of the Báb, abolished, at one stroke, the Dispensation which that Faith had so newly proclaimed, and upheld, with such vehemence and force, the Divine authority of its Author? What, we may well pause to consider, were the claims of Him Who, Himself a disciple of the Báb, had, at such an early stage, regarded Himself as empowered to abrogate the Law identified with His beloved Master? What, we may further reflect, could be the relationship between the religious Systems established before Him and His own Revelation—a Revelation which, flowing out, in that extremely perilous hour, from His travailing soul, pierced the gloom that had settled upon that pestilential pit, and, bursting through its walls, and propagating itself as far as the ends of the earth, infused into the entire body of mankind its boundless potentialities, and is now under our very eyes, shaping the course of human society?

He Who in such dramatic circumstances was made to sustain the overpowering weight of so glorious a Mission was none other than the One Whom posterity will acclaim, and Whom innumerable followers already recognize, as the Judge, the Lawgiver and Redeemer of all mankind, as the Organizer of the entire planet, as the Unifier of the children of men, as the Inaugurator of the long-awaited millennium, as the Originator of a new "Universal Cycle," as the Establisher of the Most Great Peace, as the Fountain of the Most Great Justice, as the Proclaimer of the coming of age of the entire human race, as the Creator of a new World Order, and as the Inspirer and Founder of a world civilization.

To Israel He was neither more nor less than the incarnation of the "Everlasting Father," the "Lord of Hosts" come down "with ten thousands of saints"; to Christendom Christ returned "in the glory of the Father," to Shí'ah Islám the return of the Imám Ḥusayn; to Sunní Islám the descent of the "Spirit of God" (Jesus Christ); to the Zoroastrians the promised Sháh-Bahrám; to the Hindus the reincarnation of Krishna; to the Buddhists the fifth Buddha.

In the name He bore He combined those of the Imám Ḥusayn, the most illustrious of the successors of the Apostle of God—the brightest "star" shining in the "crown" mentioned in the Revelation of St. John—and of the Imám 'Alí, the Commander of the Faithful, the second of the two "witnesses" extolled in that same Book. He was formally designated Bahá'u'lláh, an appellation specifically recorded in the Persian Bayán, signifying at once the glory, the light and the splendor of God, and was styled the "Lord of Lords," the "Most Great Name," the "Ancient Beauty," the "Pen of the Most High," the "Hidden Name," the "Preserved Treasure," "He Whom God will make manifest," the "Most Great Light," the "All-Highest Horizon," the "Most Great Ocean," the "Supreme Heaven," the "Pre-Existent Root," the "Self-Subsistent," the "Day-Star of the Universe," the "Great Announcement," the "Speaker on Sinai," the "Sifter of Men," the "Wronged One of the World," the "Desire of the Nations," the "Lord of the Covenant," the "Tree beyond which there is no passing." He derived His descent, on the one hand, from Abraham (the Father of the Faithful) through his wife Katurah, and on the other from Zoroaster, as well as from Yazdigird, the last king of the Sásáníyán dynasty. He was moreover a descendant of Jesse, and belonged, through His father, Mírzá 'Abbás, better known as Mírzá Buzurg—a nobleman closely associated with the ministerial circles of the Court of Fatḥ-'Alí Sháh—to one of the most ancient and renowned families of Mázindarán.

To Him Isaiah, the greatest of the Jewish prophets, had alluded as the *"Glory of the Lord,"* the *"Everlasting Father,"* the *"Prince of Peace,"* the *"Wonderful,"* the *"Counsellor,"* the *"Rod come forth out of the stem of Jesse"* and the *"Branch grown out of His roots,"* Who *"shall be established upon the throne of David,"* Who *"will come with strong hand,"* Who *"shall judge among the nations,"* Who *"shall smite the earth with the rod of His mouth, and with the breath of His lips slay the wicked,"* and Who *"shall assemble the outcasts of Israel, and gather together the dispersed of Judah from the four corners of the earth."* Of Him David had sung in his Psalms, acclaiming Him as the *"Lord of Hosts"* and the *"King of Glory."* To Him Haggai had referred as the *"Desire of all nations,"* and Zechariah as the *"Branch"* Who *"shall grow up out of His place,"* and *"shall build the Temple of the Lord."* Zechariah had extolled Him as the *"Lord"* Who *"shall be king over all the earth,"* while to His day Joel and Zephaniah had both referred as the *"day of Jehovah,"* the latter describing it as *"a day of wrath, a day of trouble and distress, a day of wasteness and desolation, a day of darkness and gloominess, a day of clouds and thick darkness, a day of the trumpet and alarm against the fenced cities, and against the high towers."* His Day Ezekiel and Daniel had, moreover, both acclaimed as the *"day of the Lord,"* and Malachi described as *"the great and dreadful day of the Lord"* when *"the Sun of Righteousness"* will *"arise, with healing in His wings,"* whilst Daniel had pronounced His advent as signalizing the end of the *"abomination that maketh desolate."*

To His Dispensation the sacred books of the followers of Zoroaster had referred as that in which the sun must needs be brought to a standstill for no less than one whole month. To Him Zoroaster must have alluded when, according to tradition, He foretold that a period of three thousand years of conflict and contention must needs precede the advent of the World-Savior Sháh-Bahrám, Who would triumph over Ahriman and usher in an era of blessedness and peace.

He alone is meant by the prophecy attributed to Gautama Buddha Himself, that *"a Buddha named Maitreye, the Buddha of universal fellowship"* should, in the fullness of time, arise and reveal *"His boundless glory."* To Him the Bhagavad-Gita of the Hindus had referred as the *"Most Great Spirit,"* the *"Tenth Avatar,"* the *"Immaculate Manifestation of Krishna."*

To Him Jesus Christ had referred as the *"Prince of this world,"* as the *"Comforter"* Who will *"reprove the world of sin, and of righteousness, and of judgment,"* as the *"Spirit of Truth"* Who *"will guide you into all truth,"* Who *"shall not speak of Himself, but whatsoever He shall hear, that shall He speak,"* as the *"Lord of the Vineyard,"* and as the *"Son of Man"* Who *"shall come in the glory of His Father"* *"in the clouds of heaven with power and great glory,"* with *"all the holy angels"* about Him, and *"all nations"* gathered before His throne. To Him the Author of the Apocalypse had alluded as the *"Glory of God,"* as *"Alpha and Omega,"* *"the Beginning and the End,"* *"the First and the Last."* Identifying His Revelation with the *"third woe,"* he, moreover, had extolled His Law as *"a new heaven and a new earth,"* as the *"Tabernacle of God,"* as the *"Holy City,"* as the *"New Jerusalem, coming down from God out of heaven, prepared as a bride adorned for her husband."* To His Day Jesus Christ Himself had referred as *"the regeneration when the Son of Man shall sit in the throne of His glory."* To the hour of His advent St. Paul had alluded as the hour of the "last trump," the "trump of God," whilst St. Peter had spoken of it as the "Day of God, wherein the heavens being on fire shall be dissolved, and the elements shall melt with fervent heat." His Day he, furthermore, had described as "the times of refreshing," "the times of restitution of all things, which God hath spoken by the mouth of all His holy Prophets since the world began."

To Him Muḥammad, the Apostle of God, had alluded in His Book as the *"Great Announcement,"* and declared His Day to be the Day whereon *"God"* will *"come down"* *"overshadowed with clouds,"* the Day whereon *"thy Lord shall come and the angels rank on rank,"* and *"The Spirit shall arise and the angels shall be ranged in order."* His advent He, in that Book, in a súrih said to have been termed by Him *"the heart of the Qur'án,"* had foreshadowed as that of the *"third"* Messenger, sent down to *"strengthen"* the two who preceded Him. To His Day He, in the pages of that same Book, had paid a glowing tribute, glorifying it as the *"Great Day,"* the *"Last Day,"* the *"Day of God,"* the *"Day of Judgment,"* the *"Day of Reckoning,"* the *"Day of Mutual Deceit,"* the *"Day of Severing,"* the *"Day of Sighing,"* the *"Day of Meeting,"* the Day *"when the Decree shall be accomplished,"* the Day whereon the second *"Trumpet blast"* will be sounded, the *"Day when mankind shall stand before the Lord of the world,"* and *"all shall come to Him in humble guise,"* the Day when *"thou shalt see the mountains, which thou thinkest so firm, pass away with the passing of a cloud,"* the Day *"wherein account shall be taken,"* *"the approaching Day, when men's hearts shall rise up, choking them, into their throats,"* the Day when *"all that are in the heavens and all that are on the earth shall be terror-stricken, save him whom God pleaseth to deliver,"* the Day whereon *"every suckling woman shall forsake her sucking babe, and every woman that hath a burden in her womb shall cast her burden,"* the Day *"when the earth shall shine with the light of her Lord, and the Book shall be set, and the Prophets shall be brought up, and the witnesses; and judgment shall be given between them with equity; and none shall be wronged."*

The plenitude of His glory the Apostle of God had, moreover, as attested by Bahá'u'lláh Himself, compared to the *"full moon on its fourteenth night."* His station the Imám 'Alí, the Commander of the Faithful, had, according to the same testimony, identified with *"Him Who conversed with Moses from the Burning Bush on Sinai."* To the transcendent character of His mission the Imám Ḥusayn had, again according to Bahá'u'lláh, borne witness as a *"Revelation whose Revealer will be He Who revealed"* the Apostle of God Himself.

About Him Shaykh Aḥmad-i-Aḥsá'í, the herald of the Bábí Dispensation, who had foreshadowed the "strange happenings" that would transpire "between the years sixty and sixty-seven," and had categorically affirmed the inevitability of His Revelation had, as previously mentioned, written the following: "The Mystery of this Cause must needs be made manifest, and the Secret of this Message must needs be divulged. I can say no more, I can appoint no time. His Cause will be made known after Ḥín (68)" (i.e., after a while).

Siyyid Káẓim-i-Rashtí, Shaykh Aḥmad's disciple and successor, had likewise written: "The Qá'im must needs be put to death. After He has been slain the world will have attained the age of eighteen." In his Sharḥ-i-Qaṣídiy-i-Lámíyyih he had even alluded to the name "Bahá." Furthermore, to his disciples, as his days drew to a close, he had significantly declared: "Verily, I say, after the Qá'im the Qayyúm will be made manifest. For when the star of the former has set the sun of the beauty of Ḥusayn will rise and illuminate the whole world. Then will be unfolded in all its glory the 'Mystery' and the 'Secret' spoken of by Shaykh Aḥmad. . . . To have attained unto that Day of Days is to have attained unto the crowning glory of past generations, and one goodly deed performed in that age is equal to the pious worship of countless centuries."

The Báb had no less significantly extolled Him as the *"Essence of Being,"* as the *"Remnant of God,"* as the *"Omnipotent Master,"* as the *"Crimson, all-encompassing Light,"* as *"Lord of the visible and invisible,"* as the *"sole Object of all previous Revelations, including The Revelation of the Qá'im Himself."* He had formally designated Him as *"He Whom God shall make manifest,"* had alluded to Him as the *"Abhá Horizon"* wherein He Himself lived and dwelt, had specifically recorded His title, and eulogized His *"Order"* in His best-known work, the Persian Bayán, had disclosed His name through His allusion to the *"Son of 'Alí, a true and undoubted Leader of men,"* had, repeatedly, orally and in writing, fixed, beyond the shadow of a doubt, the time of His Revelation, and warned His followers lest *"the Bayán and all that hath been revealed therein"* should *"shut them out as by a veil"* from Him. He had, moreover, declared that He was the *"first servant to believe in Him,"* that He bore Him allegiance *"before all things were created,"* that *"no allusion"* of His *"could allude unto Him,"* that *"the year-old germ that holdeth within itself the potentialities of the Revelation that is to come is endowed with a potency superior to the combined forces of the whole of the Bayán."* He had, moreover, clearly asserted that He had *"covenanted with all created things"* concerning Him Whom God shall make manifest ere the covenant concerning His own mission had been established. He had readily acknowledged that He was but *"a letter"* of that *"Most Mighty Book," "a dew-drop"* from that *"Limitless Ocean,"* that His Revelation was *"only a leaf amongst the leaves of His Paradise,"* that *"all that hath been exalted in the Bayán"* was but *"a ring"* upon His own hand, and He Himself *"a ring upon the hand of Him Whom God shall make manifest,"* Who, *"turneth it as He pleaseth, for whatsoever He pleaseth, and through whatsoever He pleaseth."* He had unmistakably declared that He had *"sacrificed"* Himself *"wholly"* for Him, that He had *"consented to be cursed"* for His sake, and to have *"yearned for naught but martyrdom"* in the path of His love. Finally, He had unequivocally prophesied: *"Today the Bayán is in the stage of seed; at the beginning of the manifestation of Him Whom God shall make manifest its ultimate perfection will become apparent." "Ere nine will have elapsed from the inception of this Cause the realities of the created things will not be made manifest. All that thou hast as yet seen is but the stage from the moist-germ until We clothed it with flesh. Be patient until thou beholdest a new creation. Say: Blessed, therefore, be God, the Most Excellent of Makers!"*

*"He around Whom the Point of the Bayán* (Báb) *hath revolved is come"* is Bahá'u'lláh's confirmatory testimony to the inconceivable greatness and preeminent character of His own Revelation. *"If all who are in heaven and on earth,"* He moreover affirms, *"be invested in this day with the powers and attributes destined for the Letters of the Bayán, whose station is ten thousand times more glorious than that of the Letters of the Qur'ánic Dispensation, and if they one and all should, swift as the twinkling of an eye, hesitate to recognize My Revelation, they shall be accounted, in the sight of God, of those that have gone astray, and regarded as 'Letters of Negation.'" "Powerful is He, the King of Divine might,"* He, alluding to Himself in the Kitáb-i-Íqán, asserts, *"to extinguish with one letter of His wondrous*

*words, the breath of life in the whole of the Bayán and the people thereof, and with one letter bestow upon them a new and everlasting life, and cause them to arise and speed out of the sepulchers of their vain and selfish desires.*" "*This,*" He furthermore declares, "*is the king of days,*" the "*Day of God Himself,*" the "*Day which shall never be followed by night,*" the "*Springtime which autumn will never overtake,*" "*the eye to past ages and centuries,*" for which "*the soul of every Prophet of God, of every Divine Messenger, hath thirsted,*" for which "*all the divers kindreds of the earth have yearned,*" through which '*God hath proved the hearts of the entire company of His Messengers and Prophets, and beyond them those that stand guard over His sacred and inviolable Sanctuary, the inmates of the Celestial Pavilion and dwellers of the Tabernacle of Glory.*" "*In this most mighty Revelation,*" He moreover, states, "*all the Dispensations of the past have attained their highest, their final consummation.*" And again: "*None among the Manifestations of old, except to a prescribed degree, hath ever completely apprehended the nature of this Revelation.*" Referring to His own station He declares: "*But for Him no Divine Messenger would have been invested with the Robe of Prophethood, nor would any of the sacred Scriptures have been revealed.*"

And last but not least is 'Abdu'l-Bahá's own tribute to the transcendent character of the Revelation identified with His Father: "*Centuries, nay ages, must pass away, ere the Day-Star of Truth shineth again in its mid-summer splendor, or appeareth once more in the radiance of its vernal glory.*" "*The mere contemplation of the Dispensation inaugurated by the Blessed Beauty,*" He furthermore affirms, "*would have sufficed to overwhelm the saints of bygone ages—saints who longed to partake for one moment of its great glory.*" "*Concerning the Manifestations that will come down in the future 'in the shadows of the clouds,' know verily,*" is His significant statement, "*that in so far as their relation to the source of their inspiration is concerned they are under the shadow of the Ancient Beauty. In their relation, however, to the age in which they appear, each and every one of them 'doeth whatsoever He willeth.'* " And finally stands this, His illuminating explanation, setting forth conclusively the true relationship between the Revelation of Bahá'u'lláh and that of the Báb: "*The Revelation of the Báb may be likened to the sun, its station corresponding to the first sign of the Zodiac—the sign Aries—which the sun enters at the vernal equinox. The station of Bahá'u'lláh's Revelation, on the other hand, is represented by the sign Leo, the sun's mid-summer and highest station. By this is meant that this holy Dispensation is illumined with the light of the Sun of Truth shining from its most exalted station, and in the plenitude of its resplendency, its heat and glory."*

To attempt an exhaustive survey of the prophetic references to Bahá'u'lláh's Revelation would indeed be an impossible task. To this the pen of Bahá'u'lláh Himself bears witness: *"All the Divine Books and Scriptures have predicted and announced unto men the advent of the Most Great Revelation. None can adequately recount the verses recorded in the Books of former ages which forecast this supreme Bounty, this most mighty Bestowal."*

In conclusion of this theme, I feel, it should be stated that the Revelation identified with Bahá'u'lláh abrogates unconditionally all the Dispensations gone before it, upholds uncompromisingly the eternal verities they enshrine, recognizes firmly and absolutely the Divine origin of their Authors, preserves inviolate the sanctity of their authentic Scriptures, disclaims any intention of lowering the status of their Founders or of abating the spiritual ideals they inculcate, clarifies and correlates their functions, reaffirms their common, their unchangeable and fundamental purpose, reconciles their seemingly divergent claims and doctrines, readily and gratefully recognizes their respective contributions to the gradual unfoldment of one Divine Revelation, unhesitatingly acknowledges itself to be but one link in the chain of continually progressive Revelations, supplements their teachings with such laws and ordinances as conform to the imperative needs, and are dictated by the growing receptivity, of a fast evolving and constantly changing society, and proclaims its readiness and ability to fuse and incorporate the contending sects and factions into which they have fallen into a universal Fellowship, functioning within the framework, and in accordance with the precepts, of a divinely conceived, a world-unifying, a world-redeeming Order.

A Revelation, hailed as the promise and crowning glory of past ages and centuries, as the consummation of all the Dispensations within the Adamic Cycle, inaugurating an era of at least a thousand years' duration, and a cycle destined to last no less than five thousand centuries, signalizing the end of the Prophetic Era and the beginning of the Era of Fulfillment, unsurpassed alike in the duration of its Author's ministry and the fecundity and splendor of His mission—such a Revelation was, as already noted, born amidst the darkness of a subterranean dungeon in Ṭihrán—an abominable pit that had once served as a reservoir of water for one of the public baths of the city.

Wrapped in its stygian gloom, breathing its fetid air, numbed by its humid and icy atmosphere, His feet in stocks, His neck weighed down by a mighty chain, surrounded by criminals and miscreants of the worst order, oppressed by the consciousness of the terrible blot that had stained the fair name of His beloved Faith, painfully aware of the dire distress that had overtaken its champions, and of the grave dangers that faced the remnant of its followers—at so critical an hour and under such appalling circumstances the *"Most Great Spirit,"* as designated by Himself, and symbolized in the Zoroastrian, the Mosaic, the Christian, and Muḥammadan Dispensations by the Sacred Fire, the Burning Bush, the Dove and the Angel Gabriel respectively, descended upon, and revealed itself, personated by a *"Maiden,"* to the agonized soul of Bahá'u'lláh.

*"One night in a dream,"* He Himself, calling to mind, in the evening of His life, the first stirrings of God's Revelation within His soul, has written, *"these exalted words were heard on every side: 'Verily, We shall render Thee victorious by Thyself and by Thy pen. Grieve Thou not for that which hath befallen Thee, neither be Thou afraid, for Thou art in safety. Ere long will God raise up the treasures of the earth—men who will aid Thee through Thyself and through Thy Name, wherewith God hath revived the hearts of such as have recognized Him.'"* In another passage He describes, briefly and graphically, the impact of the onrushing force of the Divine Summons upon His entire being—an experience vividly recalling the vision of God that caused Moses to fall in a swoon, and the voice of Gabriel which plunged Muḥammad into such consternation that, hurrying to the shelter of His home, He bade His wife, Khadíjih, envelop Him in His mantle. *"During the days I lay in the prison of Ṭihrán,"* are His own memorable words, *"though the galling weight of the chains and the stench-filled air allowed Me but little sleep, still in those infrequent moments of slumber I felt as if something flowed from the crown of My head over My breast, even as a mighty torrent that precipitateth itself upon the earth from the summit of a lofty mountain. Every limb of My body would, as a result, be set afire. At such moments My tongue recited what no man could bear to hear."*

In His Súratu'l-Haykal (the Súrih of the Temple) He thus describes those breathless moments when the Maiden, symbolizing the *"Most Great Spirit"* proclaimed His mission to the entire creation: *"While engulfed in tribulations I heard a most wondrous, a most sweet voice, calling above My head. Turning My face, I beheld a Maiden—the embodiment of the remembrance of the name of My Lord—sus-*

*pended in the air before Me. So rejoiced was she in her very soul that her countenance shone with the ornament of the good-pleasure of God, and her cheeks glowed with the brightness of the All-Merciful. Betwixt earth and heaven she was raising a call which captivated the hearts and minds of men. She was imparting to both My inward and outer being tidings which rejoiced My soul, and the souls of God's honored servants. Pointing with her finger unto My head, she addressed all who are in heaven and all who are on earth, saying: 'By God! This is the Best-Beloved of the worlds, and yet ye comprehend not. This is the Beauty of God amongst you, and the power of His sovereignty within you, could ye but understand. This is the Mystery of God and His Treasure, the Cause of God and His glory unto all who are in the kingdoms of Revelation and of creation, if ye be of them that perceive.'*"

In His Epistle to Náṣiri'd-Dín S͟háh, His royal adversary, revealed at the height of the proclamation of His Message, occur these passages which shed further light on the Divine origin of His mission: "*O King! I was but a man like others, asleep upon My couch, when lo, the breezes of the All-Glorious were wafted over Me, and taught Me the knowledge of all that hath been. This thing is not from Me, but from One Who is Almighty and All-Knowing. And he bade Me lift up My voice between earth and heaven, and for this there befell Me what hath caused the tears of every man of understanding to flow. . . . This is but a leaf which the winds of the will of Thy Lord, the Almighty, the All-Praised, have stirred. . . . His all-compelling summons hath reached Me, and caused Me to speak His praise amidst all people. I was indeed as one dead when His behest was uttered. The hand of the will of Thy Lord, the Compassionate, the Merciful, transformed Me.*" "*By My Life!*" He asserts in another Tablet, "*Not of Mine own volition have I revealed Myself, but God, of His own choosing, hath manifested Me.*" And again: "*Whenever I chose to hold My peace and be still, lo, the Voice of the Holy Spirit, standing on My right hand, aroused Me, and the Most Great Spirit appeared before My face, and Gabriel overshadowed Me, and the Spirit of Glory stirred within My bosom, bidding Me arise and break My silence.*"

Such were the circumstances in which the Sun of Truth arose in the city of Ṭihrán—a city which, by reason of so rare a privilege conferred upon it, had been glorified by the Báb as the "*Holy Land,*" and surnamed by Bahá'u'lláh "*the Mother of the world,*" the "*Day-spring of Light,*" the "*Dawning-Place of the signs of the Lord,*" the "*Source of the joy of all mankind.*" The first dawnings of that Light of peerless splendor had, as already described, broken in the city of Shíráz. The rim of that Orb had now appeared above the horizon of the Síyáh-Chál of Ṭihrán. Its rays were to burst forth, a decade later, in Baghdád, piercing the clouds which immediately after its rise in those somber surroundings obscured its splendor. It was destined to mount to its zenith in the far-away city of Adrianople, and ultimately to set in the immediate vicinity of the fortress-town of 'Akká.

The process whereby the effulgence of so dazzling a Revelation was unfolded to the eyes of men was of necessity slow and gradual. The first intimation which its Bearer received did not synchronize with, nor was it followed immediately by, a disclosure of its character to either His own companions or His kindred. A period of no less than ten years had to elapse ere its far-reaching implications could be directly divulged to even those who had been intimately associated with Him—a period of great spiritual ferment, during which the Recipient of so weighty a Message restlessly anticipated the hour at which He could unburden His heavily laden soul, so replete with the potent energies released by God's nascent Revelation. All He did, in the course of this pre-ordained interval, was to hint, in veiled and allegorical language, in epistles, commentaries, prayers and treatises, which He was moved to reveal, that the Báb's promise had already been fulfilled, and that He Himself was the One Who had been chosen to redeem it. A few of His fellow-disciples, distinguished by their sagacity, and their personal attachment and devotion to Him, perceived the radiance of the as yet unrevealed glory that had flooded His soul, and would have, but for His restraining influence, divulged His secret and proclaimed it far and wide.

## CHAPTER VII

# Bahá'u'lláh's Banishment to 'Iráq

The attempt on the life of Náṣiri'd-Dín Sháh, as stated in a previous chapter, was made on the 28th of the month of Shavvál, 1268 A.H., corresponding to the 15th of August, 1852. Immediately after, Bahá'u'lláh was arrested in Níyávarán, was conducted with the greatest ignominy to Ṭihrán and cast into the Síyáh-Chál. His imprisonment lasted for a period of no less than four months, in the middle of which the "year nine" (1269), anticipated in such glowing terms by the Báb, and alluded to as the year "after Ḥín" by Shaykh Aḥmad-i-Aḥsá'í, was ushered in, endowing with undreamt-of potentialities the whole world. Two months after that year was born, Bahá'u'lláh, the purpose of His imprisonment now accomplished, was released from His confinement, and set out, a month later, for Baghdád, on the first stage of a memorable and life-long exile which was to carry Him, in the course of years, as far as Adrianople in European Turkey, and which was to end with His twenty-four years' incarceration in 'Akká.

Now that He had been invested, in consequence of that potent dream, with the power and sovereign authority associated with His Divine mission, His deliverance from a confinement that had achieved its purpose, and which if prolonged would have completely fettered Him in the exercise of His newly-bestowed functions, became not only inevitable, but imperative and urgent. Nor were the means and instruments lacking whereby his emancipation from the shackles that restrained Him could be effected. The persistent and decisive intervention of the Russian Minister, Prince Dolgorouki, who left no stone unturned to establish the innocence of Bahá'u'lláh; the public confession of Mullá Shaykh 'Alíy-i-Turshízí, surnamed 'Aẓím, who, in the Síyáh-Chál, in the presence of the Ḥájibu'd-Dawlih and the Russian Minister's interpreter and of the government's representative, emphatically exonerated Him, and acknowledged his own complicity; the indisputable testimony established by competent tribunals; the unrelaxing efforts exerted by His own brothers, sisters and kindred,—all these combined to effect His ultimate deliverance from the hands of His rapacious enemies. Another potent if less evident influence which must be acknowledged as having had a share in His liberation was the fate suffered by so large a number of His self-sacrificing fellow-disciples who languished with Him in that same prison. For, as Nabíl truly remarks, "the blood, shed in the course of that fateful year in Ṭihrán by that heroic band with whom Bahá'u'lláh had been imprisoned, was the ransom paid for His deliverance from the hand of a foe that sought to prevent Him from achieving the purpose for which God had destined Him."

With such overwhelming testimonies establishing beyond the shadow of a doubt the non-complicity of Bahá'u'lláh, the Grand Vizir, after having secured the reluctant consent of his sovereign to set free his Captive, was now in a position to dispatch his trusted representative, Ḥájí 'Alí, to the Síyáh-Chál, instructing him to deliver to Bahá'u'lláh the order for His release. The sight which that emissary beheld upon his arrival evoked in him such anger that he cursed his master for the shameful treatment of a man of such high position and stainless renown. Removing his mantle from his shoulders he presented it to Bahá'u'lláh, entreating Him to wear it when in the presence of the Minister and his counsellors, a request which He emphatically refused, preferring to appear, attired in the garb of a prisoner, before the members of the Imperial government.

No sooner had He presented Himself before them than the Grand Vizir addressed Him saying: "Had you chosen to take my advice, and had you dissociated yourself from the Faith of the Siyyid-i-Báb, you would never have suffered the pains and indignities that have been heaped upon you." *"Had you, in your turn,"* Bahá'u'lláh retorted, *"followed My counsels, the affairs of the government would not have reached so critical a stage."* Mírzá Áqá Khán was thereupon reminded of the conversation he had had with Him on the occasion of the Báb's martyrdom, when he had been warned that *"the flame that has been kindled will blaze forth more fiercely than ever."* "What is it that you advise me now to do?" he inquired from Bahá'u'lláh. *"Command the governors of the realm,"* was the instant reply, *"to cease shedding the blood of the innocent, to cease plundering their property, to cease dishonoring their women, and injuring their children."* That same day the Grand Vizir acted on the advice thus given him; but any effect it had, as the course of subsequent events amply demonstrated, proved to be momentary and negligible.

The relative peace and tranquillity accorded Bahá'u'lláh after His tragic and cruel imprisonment was destined, by the dictates of an unerring Wisdom, to be of an extremely short duration. He had hardly rejoined His family and kindred when a decree from Náṣiri'd-Dín S͟háh was communicated to Him, bidding Him leave the territory of Persia, fixing a time-limit of one month for His departure and allowing Him the right to choose the land of His exile.

The Russian Minister, as soon as he was informed of the Imperial decision, expressed the desire to take Bahá'u'lláh under the protection of his government, and offered to extend every facility for His removal to Russia. This invitation, so spontaneously extended, Bahá'u'lláh declined, preferring, in pursuance of an unerring instinct, to establish His abode in Turkish territory, in the city of Bag͟hdád. *"Whilst I lay chained and fettered in the prison,"* He Himself, years after, testified in His Epistle addressed to the Czar of Russia, Nicolaevitch Alexander II, *"one of thy ministers extended Me his aid. Whereupon God hath ordained for thee a station which the knowledge of none can comprehend except His knowledge. Beware lest thou barter away this sublime station." "In the days,"* is yet another illuminating testimony revealed by His pen, *"when this Wronged One was sore-afflicted in prison, the minister of the highly esteemed government* (of Russia)*—may God, glorified and exalted be He, assist him!—exerted his utmost endeavor to compass My deliverance. Several times permission for My release was granted. Some of the 'ulamás of the city, however, would prevent it. Finally, My freedom was gained through the solicitude and the endeavor of His Excellency the Minister. . . . His Imperial Majesty, the Most Great Emperor—may God, exalted and glorified be He, assist him!—extended to Me for the sake of God his protection—a protection which has excited the envy and enmity of the foolish ones of the earth."*

The S͟háh's edict, equivalent to an order for the immediate expulsion of Bahá'u'lláh from Persian territory, opens a new and glorious chapter in the history of the first Bahá'í century. Viewed in its proper perspective it will be even recognized to have ushered in one of the most eventful and momentous epochs in the world's religious history. It coincides with the inauguration of a ministry extending over a period of almost forty years—a ministry which, by virtue of its creative power, its cleansing force, its healing influences, and the irresistible operation of the world-directing, world-shaping forces it released, stands unparalleled in the religious annals of the entire human race. It marks the opening phase in a series of banishments, ranging over a period of four decades, and terminating only with the death of Him Who was the Object of that cruel edict. The process which it set in motion, gradually progressing and unfolding, began by establishing

His Cause for a time in the very midst of the jealously-guarded stronghold of Shí'ah Islám, and brought Him in personal contact with its highest and most illustrious exponents; then, at a later stage, it confronted Him, at the seat of the Caliphate, with the civil and ecclesiastical dignitaries of the realm and the representatives of the Sultán of Turkey, the most powerful potentate in the Islamic world; and finally carried Him as far as the shores of the Holy Land, thereby fulfilling the prophecies recorded in both the Old and the New Testaments, redeeming the pledge enshrined in various traditions attributed to the Apostle of God and the Imáms who succeeded Him, and ushering in the long-awaited restoration of Israel to the ancient cradle of its Faith. With it, may be said to have begun the last and most fruitful of the four stages of a life, the first twenty-seven years of which were characterized by the care-free enjoyment of all the advantages conferred by high birth and riches, and by an unfailing solicitude for the interests of the poor, the sick and the down-trodden; followed by nine years of active and exemplary discipleship in the service of the Báb; and finally by an imprisonment of four months' duration, overshadowed throughout by mortal peril, embittered by agonizing sorrows, and immortalized, as it drew to a close, by the sudden eruption of the forces released by an overpowering, soul-revolutionizing Revelation.

This enforced and hurried departure of Bahá'u'lláh from His native land, accompanied by some of His relatives, recalls in some of its aspects, the precipitate flight of the Holy Family into Egypt; the sudden migration of Muḥammad, soon after His assumption of the prophetic office, from Mecca to Medina; the exodus of Moses, His brother and His followers from the land of their birth, in response to the Divine summons, and above all the banishment of Abraham from Ur of the Chaldees to the Promised Land—a banishment which, in the multitudinous benefits it conferred upon so many divers peoples, faiths and nations, constitutes the nearest historical approach to the incalculable blessings destined to be vouchsafed, in this day, and in future ages, to the whole human race, in direct consequence of the exile suffered by Him Whose Cause is the flower and fruit of all previous Revelations.

'Abdu'l-Bahá, after enumerating in His "Some Answered Questions" the far-reaching consequences of Abraham's banishment, significantly affirms that *"since the exile of Abraham from Ur to Aleppo in Syria produced this result, we must consider what will be the effect of the exile of Bahá'u'lláh in His several removes from*

*Tihrán to Baghdád, from thence to Constantinople, to Rumelia and to the Holy Land.*"

On the first day of the month of Rabí'u'th-Thání, of the year 1269 A.H., (January 12, 1853), nine months after His return from Karbilá, Bahá'u'lláh, together with some of the members of His family, and escorted by an officer of the Imperial body-guard and an official representing the Russian Legation, set out on His three months' journey to Baghdád. Among those who shared His exile was His wife, the saintly Navváb, entitled by Him the "Most Exalted Leaf," who, during almost forty years, continued to evince a fortitude, a piety, a devotion and a nobility of soul which earned her from the pen of her Lord the posthumous and unrivalled tribute of having been made His "*perpetual consort in all the worlds of God.*" His nine-year-old son, later surnamed the "Most Great Branch," destined to become the Center of His Covenant and authorized Interpreter of His teachings, together with His seven-year-old sister, known in later years by the same title as that of her illustrious mother, and whose services until the ripe old age of four score years and six, no less than her exalted parentage, entitle her to the distinction of ranking as the outstanding heroine of the Bahá'í Dispensation, were also included among the exiles who were now bidding their last farewell to their native country. Of the two brothers who accompanied Him on that journey the first was Mírzá Músá, commonly called Áqáy-i-Kalím, His staunch and valued supporter, the ablest and most distinguished among His brothers and sisters, and one of the "*only two persons who,*" according to Bahá'u'lláh's testimony, "*were adequately informed of the origins*" of His Faith. The other was Mírzá Muḥammad-Qulí, a half-brother, who, in spite of the defection of some of his relatives, remained to the end loyal to the Cause he had espoused.

The journey, undertaken in the depth of an exceptionally severe winter, carrying the little band of exiles, so inadequately equipped, across the snow-bound mountains of Western Persia, though long and perilous, was uneventful except for the warm and enthusiastic reception accorded the travelers during their brief stay in Karand by its governor Hayát-Qulí Khán, of the 'Allíyu'lláhí sect. He was shown, in return, such kindness by Bahá'u'lláh that the people of the entire village were affected, and continued, long after, to extend such hospitality to His followers on their way to Baghdád that they gained the reputation of being known as Bábís.

In a prayer revealed by Him at that time, Bahá'u'lláh, expatiating upon the woes and trials He had endured in the Síyáh-Chál, thus bears witness to the hardships undergone in the course of that *"terrible journey": "My God, My Master, My Desire! . . . Thou hast created this atom of dust through the consummate power of Thy might, and nurtured Him with Thine hands which none can chain up. . . . Thou hast destined for Him trials and tribulations which no tongue can describe, nor any of Thy Tablets adequately recount. The throat Thou didst accustom to the touch of silk Thou hast, in the end, clasped with strong chains, and the body Thou didst ease with brocades and velvets Thou hast at last subjected to the abasement of a dungeon. Thy decree hath shackled Me with unnumbered fetters, and cast about My neck chains that none can sunder. A number of years have passed during which afflictions have, like showers of mercy, rained upon Me. . . . How many the nights during which the weight of chains and fetters allowed Me no rest, and how numerous the days during which peace and tranquillity were denied Me, by reason of that wherewith the hands and tongues of men have afflicted Me! Both bread and water which Thou hast, through Thy all-embracing mercy, allowed unto the beasts of the field, they have, for a time, forbidden unto this servant, and the things they refused to inflict upon such as have seceded from Thy Cause, the same have they suffered to be inflicted upon Me, until, finally, Thy decree was irrevocably fixed, and Thy behest summoned this servant to depart out of Persia, accompanied by a number of frail-bodied men and children of tender age, at this time when the cold is so intense that one cannot even speak, and ice and snow so abundant that it is impossible to move."*

Finally, on the 28th of Jamádíyu'th-Thání 1269 A.H. (April 8, 1853), Bahá'u'lláh arrived in Baghdád, the capital city of what was then the Turkish province of 'Iráq. From there He proceeded, a few days after, to Káẓimayn, about three miles north of the city, a town inhabited chiefly by Persians, and where the two Káẓims, the seventh and the ninth Imáms, are buried. Soon after His arrival the representative of the Sháh's government, stationed in Baghdád, called on Him, and suggested that it would be advisable for Him, in view of the many visitors crowding that center of pilgrimage, to establish His residence in Old Baghdád, a suggestion with which He readily concurred. A month later, towards the end of Rajab, He rented the house of Ḥájí 'Alí Madad, in an old quarter of the city, into which He moved with His family.

In that city, described in Islamic traditions as "Ẓahru'l-Kúfih," designated for centuries as the "Abode of Peace," and immortalized by Bahá'u'lláh as the *"City of God,"* He, except for His two year retirement to the mountains of Kurdistán and His occasional visits to Najaf, Karbilá and Káẓimayn, continued to reside until His banishment to Constantinople. To that city the Qur'án had alluded as the *"Abode of Peace"* to which God Himself *"calleth."* To it, in that same Book, further allusion had been made in the verse *"For them is a Dwelling of Peace with their Lord . . . on the Day whereon God shall gather them all together."* From it radiated, wave after wave, a power, a radiance and a glory which insensibly reanimated a languishing Faith, sorely-stricken, sinking into obscurity, threatened with oblivion. From it were diffused, day and night, and with ever-increasing energy, the first emanations of a Revelation which, in its scope, its copiousness, its driving force and the volume and variety of its literature, was destined to excel that of the Báb Himself. Above its horizon burst forth the rays of the Sun of Truth, Whose rising glory had for ten long years been overshadowed by the inky clouds of a consuming hatred, an ineradicable jealousy, an unrelenting malice. In it the Tabernacle of the promised *"Lord of Hosts"* was first erected, and the foundations of the long-awaited Kingdom of the *"Father"* unassailably established. Out of it went forth the earliest tidings of the Message of Salvation which, as prophesied by Daniel, was to mark, after the lapse of *"a thousand two hundred and ninety days"* (1280 A.H.), the end of *"the abomination that maketh desolate."* Within its walls the *"Most Great House of God,"* His *"Footstool"* and the *"Throne of His Glory," "the Cynosure of an adoring world,"* the *"Lamp of Salvation between earth and heaven,"* the *"Sign of His remembrance to all who are in heaven and on earth,"* enshrining the *"Jewel whose glory hath irradiated all creation,"* the *"Standard"* of His Kingdom, the *"Shrine round which will circle the concourse of the faithful"* was irrevocably founded and permanently consecrated. Upon it, by virtue of its sanctity as Bahá'u'lláh's *"Most Holy Habitation"* and *"Seat of His transcendent glory,"* was conferred the honor of being regarded as a center of pilgrimage second to none except the city of 'Akká, His *"Most Great Prison,"* in whose immediate vicinity His holy Sepulcher, the Qiblih of the Bahá'í world, is enshrined. Around the heavenly Table, spread in its very heart, clergy and laity, Sunnís and S͟hí'ahs, Kurds, Arabs, and Persians, princes and nobles, peasants and dervishes, gathered in increasing numbers from far and near, all partaking, according to their needs and capacities, of a measure of that Divine sustenance which was to enable them, in the course of time, to noise abroad the fame of that bountiful Giver, swell the ranks of His admirers, scatter far and wide His writings, enlarge the limits of His congregation, and lay a firm foundation for the future erection of the institutions of His Faith. And finally, before the gaze of the diversified communities that dwelt within its gates, the first phase in the gradual unfoldment of a newborn Revelation was ushered in, the first effusions from the inspired pen of its Author were recorded, the first principles of His slowly crystallizing doctrine were formulated, the first implications of His august station were apprehended, the first attacks aiming at the disruption of His Faith from within were launched, the first victories over its internal enemies were registered, and the first pilgrimages to the Door of His Presence were undertaken.

This life-long exile to which the Bearer of so precious a Message was now providentially condemned did not, and indeed could not, manifest, either suddenly or rapidly, the potentialities latent within it. The process whereby its unsuspected benefits were to be manifested to the eyes of men was slow, painfully slow, and was characterized, as indeed the history of His Faith from its inception to the present day demonstrates, by a number of crises which at times threatened to arrest its unfoldment and blast all the hopes which its progress had engendered.

One such crisis which, as it deepened, threatened to jeopardize His newborn Faith and to subvert its earliest foundations, overshadowed the first years of His sojourn in 'Iráq, the initial stage in His life-long exile, and imparted to them a special significance. Unlike those which preceded it, this crisis was purely internal in character, and was occasioned solely by the acts, the ambitions and follies of those who were numbered among His recognized fellow-disciples.

The external enemies of the Faith, whether civil or ecclesiastical, who had thus far been chiefly responsible for the reverses and humiliations it had suffered, were by now relatively quiescent. The public appetite for revenge, which had seemed insatiable, had now, to some extent, in consequence of the torrents of blood that had flowed, abated. A feeling, bordering on exhaustion and despair, had, moreover, settled on some of its most inveterate enemies, who were astute enough to perceive that though the Faith had bent beneath the grievous blows their hands had dealt it, its structure had remained essentially unimpaired and its spirit unbroken. The orders issued to the governors of the provinces by the Grand Vizir had had, furthermore, a sobering effect on the local authorities, who were now dissuaded from venting their fury upon, and from indulging in their sadistic cruelties against, a hated adversary.

A lull had, in consequence, momentarily ensued, which was destined to be broken, at a later stage, by a further wave of repressive measures in which the Sulṭán of Turkey and his ministers, as well as the Sunní sacerdotal order, were to join hands with the S͟háh and the S͟hí'ah clericals of Persia and 'Iráq in an endeavor to stamp out, once and for all, the Faith and all it stood for. While this lull persisted the initial manifestations of the internal crisis, already mentioned, were beginning to reveal themselves—a crisis which, though less spectacular in the public eye, proved itself, as it moved to its climax, to be one of unprecedented gravity, reducing the numerical strength of the infant community, imperiling its unity, causing immense damage to its prestige, and tarnishing for a considerable period of time its glory.

This crisis had already been brewing in the days immediately following the execution of the Báb, was intensified during the months when the controlling hand of Bahá'u'lláh was suddenly withdrawn as a result of His confinement in the Síyáh-C͟hál of Ṭihrán, was further aggravated by His precipitate banishment from Persia, and began to protrude its disturbing features during the first years of His sojourn in Bag͟hdád. Its devastating force gathered momentum during His two year retirement to the mountains of Kurdistán, and though it was checked, for a time, after His return from Sulaymáníyyih, under the overmastering influences exerted preparatory to the Declaration of His Mission, it broke out later, with still greater violence, and reached its climax in Adrianople, only to receive finally its death-blow under the impact of the irresistible forces released through the proclamation of that Mission to all mankind.

Its central figure was no less a person than the nominee of the Báb Himself, the credulous and cowardly Mírzá Yaḥyá, to certain traits of whose character reference has already been made in the foregoing pages. The black-hearted scoundrel who befooled and manipulated this vain and flaccid man with consummate skill and unyielding persistence was a certain Siyyid Muḥammad, a native of Iṣfahán, notorious for his inordinate ambition, his blind obstinacy and uncontrollable jealousy. To him Bahá'u'lláh had later referred in the Kitáb-i-Aqdas as the one who had *"led astray"* Mírzá Yaḥyá, and stigmatized him, in one of His Tablets, as the *"source of envy and the quintessence of mischief,"* while 'Abdu'l-Bahá had described the relationship existing between these two as that of *"the sucking child"* to the *"much-prized breast"* of its mother. Forced to abandon his studies in the madrisiyi-i-Ṣadr of Iṣfahán, this Siyyid had migrated, in shame and remorse, to Karbilá, had there joined the ranks of the Báb's followers, and shown, after His martyrdom, signs of vacillation which exposed the shallowness of his faith and the fundamental weakness of his convictions. Bahá'u'lláh's first visit to Karbilá and the marks of undisguised reverence, love and admiration shown Him by some of the most distinguished among the former disciples and companions of Siyyid Káẓim, had aroused in this calculating and unscrupulous schemer an envy, and bred in his soul an animosity, which the forbearance and patience shown him by Bahá'u'lláh had served only to inflame. His deluded helpers, willing tools of his diabolical designs, were the not inconsiderable number of Bábís who, baffled, disillusioned and leaderless, were already predisposed to be beguiled by him into pursuing a path diametrically opposed to the tenets and counsels of a departed Leader.

For, with the Báb no longer in the midst of His followers; with His nominee, either seeking a safe hiding place in the mountains of Mázindarán, or wearing the disguise of a dervish or of an Arab wandering from town to town; with Bahá'u'lláh imprisoned and subsequently banished beyond the limits of His native country; with the flower of the Faith mown down in a seemingly unending series of slaughters, the remnants of that persecuted community were sunk in a distress that appalled and paralyzed them, that stifled their spirit, confused their minds and strained to the utmost their loyalty. Reduced to this extremity they could no longer rely on any voice that commanded sufficient authority to still their forebodings, resolve their problems, or prescribe to them their duties and obligations.

Nabíl, traveling at that time through the province of Khurásán, the scene of the tumultuous early victories of a rising Faith, had himself summed up his impressions of the prevailing condition. "The fire of the Cause of God," he testifies in his narrative, "had been well-nigh quenched in every place. I could detect no trace of warmth anywhere." In Qasvín, according to the same testimony, the remnant of the community had split into four factions, bitterly opposed to one another, and a prey to the most absurd doctrines and fancies. Bahá'u'lláh upon His arrival in Baghdád, a city which had witnessed the glowing evidences of the indefatigable zeal of Ṭáhirih, found among His countrymen residing in that city no more than a single Bábí, while in Káẓimayn inhabited chiefly by Persians, a mere handful of His compatriots remained who still professed, in fear and obscurity, their faith in the Báb.

The morals of the members of this dwindling community, no less than their numbers, had sharply declined. Such was their *"waywardness and folly,"* to quote Bahá'u'lláh's own words, that upon His release from prison, His first decision was *"to arise . . . and undertake, with the utmost vigor, the task of regenerating this people."*

As the character of the professed adherents of the Báb declined and as proofs of the deepening confusion that afflicted them multiplied, the mischief-makers, who were lying in wait, and whose sole aim was to exploit the progressive deterioration in the situation for their own benefit, grew ever more and more audacious. The conduct of Mírzá Yaḥyá, who claimed to be the successor of the Báb, and who prided himself on his high sounding titles of Mir'átu'l-Azalíyyih (Everlasting Mirror), of Ṣubḥ-i-Azal (Morning of Eternity), and of Ismu'l-Azal (Name of Eternity), and particularly the machinations of Siyyid Muḥammad, exalted by him to the rank of the first among the "Witnesses" of the Bayán, were by now assuming such a character that the prestige of the Faith was becoming directly involved, and its future security seriously imperiled.

The former had, after the execution of the Báb, sustained such a violent shock that his faith almost forsook him. Wandering for a time, in the guise of a dervish, in the mountains of Mázindarán, he, by his behavior, had so severely tested the loyalty of his fellow-believers in Núr, most of whom had been converted through the indefatigable zeal of Bahá'u'lláh, that they too wavered in their convictions, some of them going so far as to throw in their lot with the enemy. He subsequently proceeded to Rasht, and remained concealed in the province of Gílán until his departure for Kirmánsháh, where in order the better to screen himself he entered the service of a certain 'Abdu'lláh-i-Qasvíní, a maker of shrouds, and became a vendor of his goods. He was still there when Bahá'u'lláh passed through that city on His way to Baghdád, and expressing a desire to live in close proximity to Bahá'u'lláh but in a house by himself where he could ply some trade incognito, he succeeded in obtaining from Him a sum of money with which he purchased several bales of cotton and then proceeded, in the garb of an Arab, by way of Mandalíj to Baghdád. He established himself there in the street of the Charcoal Dealers, situated in a dilapidated quarter of the city, and placing a turban upon his head, and assuming the name of Ḥájí 'Alíy-i-Lás-Furúsh, embarked on his newly-chosen occupation.

Siyyid Muḥammad had meanwhile settled in Karbilá, and was busily engaged, with Mírzá Yaḥyá as his lever, in kindling dissensions and in deranging the life of the exiles and of the community that had gathered about them.

Little wonder that from the pen of Bahá'u'lláh, Who was as yet unable to divulge the Secret that stirred within His bosom, these words of warning, of counsel and of assurance should, at a time when the shadows were beginning to deepen around Him, have proceeded: *"The days of tests are now come. Oceans of dissension and tribulation are surging, and the Banners of Doubt are, in every nook and corner, occupied in stirring up mischief and in leading men to perdition. . . . Suffer not the voice of some of the soldiers of negation to cast doubt into your midst, neither allow yourselves to become heedless of Him Who is the Truth, inasmuch as in every Dispensation such contentions have been raised. God, however, will establish His Faith, and manifest His light albeit the stirrers of sedition abhor it. . . . Watch ye every day for the Cause of God. . . . All are held captive in His grasp. No place is there for any one to flee to. Think not the Cause of God to be a thing lightly taken, in which any one can gratify his whims. In various quarters a number of souls have, at the present time, advanced this same claim. The time is approaching when . . . every one of them will have perished and been lost, nay will have come to naught and become a thing unremembered, even as the dust itself."*

To Mírzá Áqá Ján, "the first to believe" in Him, designated later as Khádimu'lláh (Servant of God)—a Bábí youth, aflame with devotion, who, under the influence of a dream he had of the Báb, and as a result of the perusal of certain writings of Bahá'u'lláh, had precipitately forsaken his home in Káshan and traveled to 'Iráq, in the hope of attaining His presence, and who from then on served Him assiduously for a period of forty years in his triple function of amanuensis, companion and attendant—to him Bahá'u'lláh, more than to any one else, was moved to disclose, at this critical juncture, a glimpse of the as yet unrevealed glory of His station. This same Mírzá Áqá Ján, recounting to Nabíl his experiences, on that first and never to be forgotten night spent in Karbilá, in the presence of his newly-found Beloved, Who was then a guest of Ḥájí Mírzá Ḥasan-i-Ḥakím-Báshí, had given the following testimony: "As it was summer-time Bahá'u'lláh was in the habit of passing His evenings and of sleeping on the roof of the House. . . . That night, when He had gone to sleep, I, according to His directions, lay down for a brief rest, at a distance of a few feet from Him. No sooner had I risen, and . . . started to offer my prayers, in a corner of the roof which adjoined a wall, than I beheld His blessed Person rise and walk towards me. When He reached me He said: '*You, too, are awake.*' Whereupon He began to chant and pace back and forth. How shall I ever describe that voice and the verses it intoned, and His gait, as He strode before me! Methinks, with every step He took and every word He uttered thousands of oceans of light surged before my face, and thousands of worlds of incomparable splendor were unveiled to my eyes, and thousands of suns blazed their light upon me! In the moonlight that streamed upon Him, He thus continued to walk and to chant. Every time He approached me He would pause, and, in a tone so wondrous that no tongue can describe it, would say: '*Hear Me, My son. By God, the True One! This Cause will assuredly be made manifest. Heed thou not the idle talk of the people of the Bayán, who pervert the meaning of every word.*' In this manner He continued to walk and chant, and to address me these words until the first streaks of dawn appeared. . . . Afterwards I removed His bedding to His room, and, having prepared His tea for Him, was dismissed from His presence."

The confidence instilled in Mírzá Áqá Ján by this unexpected and sudden contact with the spirit and directing genius of a new-born Revelation stirred his soul to its depths—a soul already afire with a consuming love born of his recognition of the ascendancy which his newly-found Master had already achieved over His fellow-disciples in both 'Iráq and Persia. This intense adoration that informed his whole being, and which could neither be suppressed nor concealed, was instantly detected by both Mírzá Yaḥyá and his fellow-conspirator Siyyid Muḥammad. The circumstances leading to the revelation of the Tablet of Kullu'ṭ-Ṭa'ám, written during that period, at the request of Ḥájí Mírzá Kamálu'd-Dín-i-Naráqí, a Bábí of honorable rank and high culture, could not but aggravate a situation that had already become serious and menacing. Impelled by a desire to receive illumination from Mírzá Yaḥyá concerning the meaning of the Qur'ánic verse "*All food was allowed to the children of Israel,*" Ḥájí Mírzá Kamálu'd-Dín had requested him to write a commentary upon it—a request which was granted, but with reluctance and in a manner which showed such incompetence and superficiality as to disillusion Ḥájí Mírzá Kamálu'd-Dín, and to destroy his confidence in its author. Turning to Bahá'u'lláh and repeating his request, he was honored by a Tablet, in which Israel and his children were identified with the Báb and His followers respectively—a Tablet which by reason of the allusions it contained, the beauty of its language and the cogency of its argument, so enraptured the soul of its recipient that he would have, but for the restraining hand of Bahá'u'lláh, proclaimed forthwith his discovery of God's hidden Secret in the person of the One Who had revealed it.

To these evidences of an ever deepening veneration for Bahá'u'lláh and of a passionate attachment to His person were now being added further grounds for the outbreak of the pent-up jealousies which His mounting prestige evoked in the breasts of His ill-wishers and enemies. The steady extension of the circle of His acquaintances and admirers; His friendly intercourse with officials including the governor of the city; the unfeigned homage offered Him, on so many occasions and so spontaneously, by men who had once been distinguished companions of Siyyid Káẓim; the disillusionment which the persistent concealment of Mírzá Yaḥyá, and the unflattering reports circulated regarding his character and abilities, had engendered; the signs of increasing independence, of innate sagacity and inherent superiority and capacity for leadership unmistakably exhibited by Bahá'u'lláh Himself—all combined to widen the breach which the infamous and crafty Siyyid Muḥammad had sedulously contrived to create.

A clandestine opposition, whose aim was to nullify every effort exerted, and frustrate every design conceived, by Bahá'u'lláh for the rehabilitation of a distracted community, could now be clearly discerned. Insinuations, whose purpose was to sow the seeds of doubt and suspicion and to represent Him as a usurper, as the subverter of the laws instituted by the Báb, and the wrecker of His Cause, were being incessantly circulated. His Epistles, interpretations, invocations and commentaries were being covertly and indirectly criticized, challenged and misrepresented. An attempt to injure His person was even set afoot but failed to materialize.

The cup of Bahá'u'lláh's sorrows was now running over. All His exhortations, all His efforts to remedy a rapidly deteriorating situation, had remained fruitless. The velocity of His manifold woes was hourly and visibly increasing. Upon the sadness that filled His soul and the gravity of the situation confronting Him, His writings, revealed during that somber period, throw abundant light. In some of His prayers He poignantly confesses that "*tribulation upon tribulation*" had gathered about Him, that "*adversaries with one consent*" had fallen upon Him, that "*wretchedness*" had grievously touched

Him, and that *"woes at their blackest"* had befallen Him. God Himself He calls upon as a Witness to His *"sighs and lamentations,"* His *"powerlessness, poverty and destitution,"* to the *"injuries"* He sustained, and the *"abasement"* He suffered. *"So grievous hath been My weeping,"* He, in one of these prayers, avows, *"that I have been prevented from making mention of Thee and singing Thy praises." "So loud hath been the voice of My lamentation,"* He, in another passage, avers, *"that every mother mourning for her child would be amazed, and would still her weeping and her grief." "The wrongs which I suffer,"* He, in His Lawḥ-i-Maryam, laments, *"have blotted out the wrongs suffered by My First Name* (the Báb) *from the Tablet of creation." "O Maryam!"* He continues, *"From the Land of Ṭá* (Ṭihrán), *after countless afflictions, We reached 'Iráq, at the bidding of the Tyrant of Persia, where, after the fetters of Our foes, We were afflicted with the perfidy of Our friends. God knoweth what befell Me thereafter!"* And again: *"I have borne what no man, be he of the past or of the future, hath borne or will bear." "Oceans of sadness,"* He testifies in the Tablet of Kullu'ṭ-Ṭa'ám, *"have surged over Me, a drop of which no soul could bear to drink. Such is My grief that My soul hath well nigh departed from My body." "Give ear, O Kamál!"* He, in that same Tablet, depicting His plight, exclaims, *"to the voice of this lowly, this forsaken ant, that hath hid itself in its hole, and whose desire is to depart from your midst, and vanish from your sight, by reason of that which the hands of men have wrought. God, verily, hath been witness between Me and His servants."* And again: *"Woe is Me, woe is Me! . . . All that I have seen from the day on which I first drank the pure milk from the breast of My mother until this moment hath been effaced from My memory, in consequence of that which the hands of the people have committed."* Furthermore, in His Qaṣídiy-i-Varqá'íyyih, an ode revealed during the days of His retirement to the mountains of Kurdistán, in praise of the Maiden personifying the Spirit of God recently descended upon Him, He thus gives vent to the agonies of His sorrow-laden heart: *"Noah's flood is but the measure of the tears I have shed, and Abraham's fire an ebullition of My soul. Jacob's grief is but a reflection of My sorrows, and Job's afflictions a fraction of my calamity." "Pour out patience upon Me, O My Lord!"*—such is His supplication in one of His prayers, *"and render Me victorious over the transgressors." "In these days,"* He, describing in the Kitáb-i-Íqán the virulence of the jealousy which, at that time, was beginning to bare its venomous fangs, has written, *"such odors of jealousy are diffused, that . . . from the beginning of the foundation of the world . . . until the present day, such malice, envy and hate have in no wise appeared, nor will they ever be witnessed in the future." "For two years or rather less,"* He, likewise, in another Tablet, declares, *"I shunned all else but God, and closed Mine eyes to all except Him, that haply the fire of hatred may die down and the heat of jealousy abate."*

Mírzá Áqá Ján himself has testified: "That Blessed Beauty evinced such sadness that the limbs of my body trembled." He has, likewise, related, as reported by Nabíl in his narrative, that, shortly before Bahá'u'lláh's retirement, he had on one occasion seen Him, between dawn and sunrise, suddenly come out from His house, His night-cap still on His head, showing such signs of perturbation that he was powerless to gaze into His face, and while walking, angrily remark: *"These creatures are the same creatures who for three thousand years have worshipped idols, and bowed down before the Golden Calf. Now, too, they are fit for nothing better. What relation can there be between this people and Him Who is the Countenance of Glory? What ties can bind them to the One Who is the supreme embodiment of all that is lovable?"* "I stood," declared Mírzá Áqá Ján, "rooted to the spot, lifeless, dried up as a dead tree, ready to fall under the impact of the stunning power of His words. Finally, He said: *'Bid them recite: "Is there any Remover of difficulties save God? Say: Praised be God! He is God! All are His servants, and all abide by His bidding!" Tell them to repeat it five hundred times, nay, a thousand times, by day and by night, sleeping and waking, that haply the Countenance of Glory may be unveiled to their eyes, and tiers of light descend upon them.'* He Himself, I was subsequently informed, recited this same verse, His face betraying the utmost sadness. . . . Several times during those days, He was heard to remark: *'We have, for a while, tarried amongst this people, and failed to discern the slightest response on their part.'* Oftentimes He alluded to His disappearance from our midst, yet none of us understood His meaning."

Finally, discerning, as He Himself testifies in the Kitáb-i-Íqán, *"the signs of impending events,"* He decided that before they happened He would retire. *"The one object of Our retirement,"* He, in that same Book affirms, *"was to avoid becoming a subject of discord among the faithful, a source of disturbance unto Our companions, the means of injury to any soul, or the cause of sorrow to any heart." "Our withdrawal,"* He, moreover, in that same passage emphatically asserts, *"contemplated no return, and Our separation hoped for no reunion."*

Suddenly, and without informing any one even among the members of His own family, on the 12th of Rajab 1270 A.H. (April 10, 1854), He departed, accompanied by an attendant, a Muḥammadan named Abu'l-Qásim-i-Hamadání, to whom He gave a sum of money, instructing him to act as a merchant and use it for his own purposes. Shortly after, that servant was attacked by thieves and killed, and Bahá'u'lláh was left entirely alone in His wanderings through the wastes of Kurdistán, a region whose sturdy and warlike people were known for their age-long hostility to the Persians, whom they regarded as seceders from the Faith of Islám, and from whom they differed in their outlook, race and language.

Attired in the garb of a traveler, coarsely clad, taking with Him nothing but his kas͟hkúl (alms-bowl) and a change of clothes, and assuming the name of Darvís͟h Muḥammad, Bahá'u'lláh retired to the wilderness, and lived for a time on a mountain named Sar-Galú, so far removed from human habitations that only twice a year, at seed sowing and harvest time, it was visited by the peasants of that region. Alone and undisturbed, He passed a considerable part of His retirement on the top of that mountain in a rude structure, made of stone, which served those peasants as a shelter against the extremities of the weather. At times His dwelling-place was a cave to which He refers in His Tablets addressed to the famous S͟hayk͟h 'Abdu'r-Raḥmán and to Maryam, a kinswoman of His. *"I roamed the wilderness of resignation"* He thus depicts, in the Lawḥ-i-Maryam, the rigors of His austere solitude, *"traveling in such wise that in My exile every eye wept sore over Me, and all created things shed tears of blood because of My anguish. The birds of the air were My companions and the beasts of the field My associates."* *"From My eyes,"* He, referring in the Kitáb-i-Íqán to those days, testifies, *"there rained tears of anguish, and in My bleeding heart surged an ocean of agonizing pain. Many a night I had no food for sustenance, and many a day My body found no rest. . . . Alone I communed with My spirit, oblivious of the world and all that is therein."*

In the odes He revealed, whilst wrapped in His devotions during those days of utter seclusion, and in the prayers and soliloquies which, in verse and prose, both in Arabic and Persian, poured from His sorrow-laden soul, many of which He was wont to chant aloud to Himself, at dawn and during the watches of the night, He lauded the names and attributes of His Creator, extolled the glories and mysteries of His own Revelation, sang the praises of that Maiden that personified the Spirit of God within Him, dwelt on His loneliness and His past and future tribulations, expatiated upon the blindness of His generation, the perfidy of His friends and the perversity of His enemies, affirmed His determination to arise and, if needs be, offer up His life for the vindication of His Cause, stressed those essential pre-requisites which every seeker after Truth must possess, and recalled, in anticipation of the lot that was to be His, the tragedy of the Imám Ḥusayn in Karbilá, the plight of Muḥammad in Mecca, the sufferings of Jesus at the hands of the Jews, the trials of Moses inflicted by Pharaoh and his people and the ordeal of Joseph as He languished in a pit by reason of the treachery of His brothers. These initial and impassioned outpourings of a Soul struggling to unburden itself, in the solitude of a self-imposed exile (many of them, alas lost to posterity) are, with the Tablet of Kullu'ṭ-Ṭa'ám and the poem entitled Rashḥ-i-'Amá, revealed in Ṭihrán, the first fruits of His Divine Pen. They are the forerunners of those immortal works—the Kitáb-i-Íqán, the Hidden Words and the Seven Valleys—which in the years preceding His Declaration in Baghdád, were to enrich so vastly the steadily swelling volume of His writings, and which paved the way for a further flowering of His prophetic genius in His epoch-making Proclamation to the world, couched in the form of mighty Epistles to the kings and rulers of mankind, and finally for the last fruition of His Mission in the Laws and Ordinances of His Dispensation formulated during His confinement in the Most Great Prison of 'Akká.

Bahá'u'lláh was still pursuing His solitary existence on that mountain when a certain Shaykh, a resident of Sulaymáníyyih, who owned a property in that neighborhood, sought Him out, as directed in a dream he had of the Prophet Muḥammad. Shortly after this contact was established, Shaykh Ismá'íl, the leader of the Khálidíyyih Order, who lived in Sulaymáníyyih, visited Him, and succeeded, after repeated requests, in obtaining His consent to transfer His residence to that town. Meantime His friends in Baghdád had discovered His whereabouts, and had dispatched Shaykh Sulṭán, the father-in-law of Áqáy-i-Kalím, to beg Him to return; and it was now while He was living in Sulaymáníyyih, in a room belonging to the Takyiy-i-Mawláná Khálid (theological seminary) that their messenger arrived. "I found," this same Shaykh Sulṭán, recounting his experiences to Nabíl, has stated, "all those who lived with Him in that place, from their Master down to the humblest neophyte, so enamoured of, and carried away by their love for Bahá'u'lláh, and so unprepared to contemplate the possibility of His departure that I felt certain that were I to inform them of the purpose of my visit, they would not have hesitated to put an end to my life."

Not long after Bahá'u'lláh's arrival in Kurdistán, Shaykh Sulṭán has related, He was able, through His personal contacts with Shaykh 'Uthmán, Shaykh 'Abdu'r-Raḥmán, and Shaykh Ismá'íl, the honored and undisputed leaders of the Naqshbandíyyih, the Qádiríyyih and the Khálidíyyih Orders respectively, to win their hearts completely and establish His ascendancy over them. The first of these, Shaykh 'Uthmán, included no less a person than the Sulṭán himself and his entourage among his adherents. The second, in reply to whose query the "Four Valleys" was later revealed, commanded the unwavering allegiance of at least a hundred thousand devout followers, while the third was held in such veneration by his supporters that they regarded him as co-equal with Khálid himself, the founder of the Order.

When Bahá'u'lláh arrived in Sulaymáníyyih none at first, owing to the strict silence and reserve He maintained, suspected Him of being possessed of any learning or wisdom. It was only accidentally, through seeing a specimen of His exquisite penmanship shown to them by one of the students who waited upon Him, that the curiosity of the learned instructors and students of that seminary was aroused, and they were impelled to approach Him and test the degree of His knowledge and the extent of His familiarity with the arts and sciences current amongst them. That seat of learning had been renowned for its vast endowments, its numerous takyihs, and its association with Ṣaláḥí'd-Dín-i-Ayyúbí and his descendants; from it some of the most illustrious exponents of Sunní Islám had gone forth to teach its precepts, and now a delegation, headed by Shaykh Ismá'íl himself, and consisting of its most eminent doctors and most distinguished students, called upon Bahá'u'lláh, and, finding Him willing to reply to any questions they might wish to address Him, they requested Him to elucidate for them, in the course of several interviews, the abstruse passages contained in the Futúḥát-i-Makkíyyih, the celebrated work of the famous Shaykh Muḥyi'd-Dín-i-'Arabí. *"God is My witness,"* was Bahá'u'lláh's instant reply to the learned delegation, *"that I have never seen the book you refer to. I regard, however, through the power of God, . . . whatever you wish me to do as easy of accomplishment."* Directing one of them to read aloud to Him, every day, a page of that book, He was able to resolve their perplexities in so amazing a fashion that they were lost in admiration. Not contenting Himself with a mere clarification of the obscure passages of the text, He would interpret for them the mind of its author, and expound his doctrine, and unfold his purpose. At times He would even go so far as to question the soundness of certain views propounded in that book, and would Himself vouchsafe a correct presentation of the issues that had been misunderstood, and would support it with proofs and evidences that were wholly convincing to His listeners.

Amazed by the profundity of His insight and the compass of His understanding, they were impelled to seek from Him what they considered to be a conclusive and final evidence of the unique power and knowledge which He now appeared in their eyes to possess. "No one among the mystics, the wise, and the learned," they claimed, while requesting this further favor from Him, "has hitherto proved himself capable of writing a poem in a rhyme and meter identical with that of the longer of the two odes, entitled Qaṣídiy-i-Tá'íyyih composed by Ibn-i-Fárid. We beg you to write for us a poem in that same meter and rhyme." This request was complied with, and no less than two thousand verses, in exactly the manner they had specified, were dictated by Him, out of which He selected one hundred and twenty-seven, which He permitted them to keep, deeming the subject matter of the rest premature and unsuitable to the needs of the times. It is these same one hundred and twenty-seven verses that constitute the Qaṣídiy-i-Varqá'íyyih, so familiar to, and widely circulated amongst, His Arabic speaking followers.

Such was their reaction to this marvelous demonstration of the sagacity and genius of Bahá'u'lláh that they unanimously acknowledged every single verse of that poem to be endowed with a force, beauty and power far surpassing anything contained in either the major or minor odes composed by that celebrated poet.

This episode, by far the most outstanding among the events that transpired during the two years of Bahá'u'lláh's absence from Baghdád, immensely stimulated the interest with which an increasing number of the 'ulamás, the scholars, the shaykhs, the doctors, the holy men and princes who had congregated in the seminaries of Sulaymáníyyih and Karkúk, were now following His daily activities. Through His numerous discourses and epistles He disclosed new vistas to their eyes, resolved the perplexities that agitated their minds, unfolded the inner meaning of many hitherto obscure passages in the writings of various commentators, poets and theologians, of which they had remained unaware, and reconciled the seemingly contradictory assertions which abounded in these dissertations, poems and treatises. Such was the esteem and respect entertained for Him that some held Him as One of the "Men of the Unseen," others accounted Him an adept in alchemy and the science of divination, still others designated Him "a pivot of the universe," whilst a not inconsiderable number among His admirers went so far as to believe that His station was no less than that of a prophet. Kurds, Arabs, and Persians, learned and illiterate, both high and low, young and old, who had come to know Him, regarded Him with equal reverence, and not a few among them with genuine and profound affection, and this despite certain assertions and allusions to His station He had made in public, which, had they fallen from the lips of any other member of His race, would have provoked such fury as to endanger His life. Small wonder that Bahá'u'lláh Himself should have, in the Lawḥ-i-Maryam, pronounced the period of His retirement as *"the mightiest testimony"* to, and *"the most perfect and conclusive evidence"* of, the truth of His Revelation. *"In a short time,"* is 'Abdu'l-Bahá's own testimony, *"Kurdistán was magnetized with His love. During this period Bahá'u'lláh lived in poverty. His garments were those of the poor and needy. His food was that of the indigent and lowly. An atmosphere of majesty haloed Him as the sun at midday. Everywhere He was greatly revered and loved."*

While the foundations of Bahá'u'lláh's future greatness were being laid in a strange land and amidst a strange people, the situation of the Bábí community was rapidly going from bad to worse. Pleased and emboldened by His unexpected and prolonged withdrawal from the scene of His labors, the stirrers of mischief with their deluded associates were busily engaged in extending the range of their nefarious activities. Mírzá Yaḥyá, closeted most of the time in his house, was secretly directing, through his correspondence with those Bábís whom he completely trusted, a campaign designed to utterly discredit Bahá'u'lláh. In his fear of any potential adversary he had dispatched Mírzá Muḥammad-i-Mázindarání, one of his supporters, to Ádhirbáyján for the express purpose of murdering Dayyán, the "repository of the knowledge of God," whom he surnamed "Father of Iniquities" and stigmatized as "Ṭághút," and whom the Báb had extolled as the *"Third Letter to believe in Him Whom God shall make manifest."* In his folly he had, furthermore, induced Mírzá Áqá Ján to proceed to Núr, and there await a propitious moment when he could make a successful attempt on the life of the sovereign.

His shamelessness and effrontery had waxed so great as to lead him to perpetrate himself, and permit Siyyid Muḥammad to repeat after him, an act so odious that Bahá'u'lláh characterized it as *"a most grievous betrayal,"* inflicting dishonor upon the Báb, and which *"overwhelmed all lands with sorrow."* He even, as a further evidence of the enormity of his crimes, ordered that the cousin of the Báb, Mírzá 'Alí-Akbar, a fervent admirer of Dayyán, be secretly put to death—a command which was carried out in all its iniquity. As to Siyyid Muḥammad, now given free rein by his master, Mírzá Yaḥyá, he had surrounded himself, as Nabíl who was at that time with him in Karbilá categorically asserts, with a band of ruffians, whom he allowed, and even encouraged, to snatch at night the turbans from the heads of wealthy pilgrims who had congregated in Karbilá, to steal their shoes, to rob the shrine of the Imám Ḥusayn of its divans and candles, and seize the drinking cups from the public fountains. The depths of degradation to which these so-called adherents of the Faith of the Báb had sunk could not but evoke in Nabíl the memory of the sublime renunciation shown by the conduct of the companions of Mullá Ḥusayn, who, at the suggestion of their leader, had scornfully cast by the wayside the gold, the silver and turquoise in their possession, or shown by the behavior of Vaḥíd who refused to allow even the least valuable amongst the treasures which his sumptuously furnished house in Yazd contained to be removed ere it was pillaged by the mob, or shown by the decision of Ḥujjat not to permit his companions, who were on the brink of starvation, to lay hands on the property of others, even though it were to save their own lives.

Such was the audacity and effrontery of these demoralized and misguided Bábís that no less than twenty-five persons, according to 'Abdu'l-Bahá's testimony, had the presumption to declare themselves to be the Promised One foretold by the Báb! Such was the decline in their fortunes that they hardly dared show themselves in public. Kurds and Persians vied with each other, when confronting them in the streets, in heaping abuse upon them, and in vilifying openly the Cause which they professed. Little wonder that on His return to Baghdád Bahá'u'lláh should have described the situation then existing in these words: *"We found no more than a handful of souls, faint and dispirited, nay utterly lost and dead. The Cause of God had ceased to be on any one's lips, nor was any heart receptive to its message."* Such was the sadness that overwhelmed Him on His arrival that He refused for some time to leave His house, except for His visits to Káẓimayn and for His occasional meeting with a few of His friends who resided in that town and in Baghdád.

The tragic situation that had developed in the course of His two years' absence now imperatively demanded His return. *"From the Mystic Source,"* He Himself explains in the Kitáb-i-Íqán, *"there came the summons bidding Us return whence We came. Surrendering Our will to His, We submitted to His injunction." "By God besides Whom there is none other God!"* is His emphatic assertion to Shaykh Sulṭán, as reported by Nabíl in his narrative, *"But for My recognition of the fact that the blessed Cause of the Primal Point was on the verge of being completely obliterated, and all the sacred blood poured out in the path of God would have been shed in vain, I would in no wise have consented to return to the people of the Bayán, and would have abandoned them to the worship of the idols their imaginations had fashioned."*

Mírzá Yaḥyá, realizing full well to what a pass his unrestrained leadership of the Faith had brought him, had, moreover, insistently and in writing, besought Him to return. No less urgent were the pleadings of His own kindred and friends, particularly His twelve-year old Son, 'Abdu'l-Bahá, Whose grief and loneliness had so consumed His soul that, in a conversation recorded by Nabíl in his narrative, He had avowed that subsequent to the departure of Bahá'u'lláh He had in His boyhood grown old.

Deciding to terminate the period of His retirement Bahá'u'lláh bade farewell to the shaykhs of Sulaymáníyyih, who now numbered among His most ardent and, as their future conduct demonstrated, staunchest admirers. Accompanied by Shaykh Sulṭán, He retraced His steps to Baghdád, on *"the banks of the River of Tribulations,"* as He Himself termed it, proceeding by slow stages, realizing, as He declared to His fellow-traveler, that these last days of His retirement would be *"the only days of peace and tranquillity"* left to Him, *"days which will never again fall to My lot."*

On the 12th of Rajab 1272 A.H. (March 19, 1856) He arrived in Baghdád, exactly two lunar years after His departure for Kurdistán.

## CHAPTER VIII

# Bahá'u'lláh's Banishment to 'Iráq

*(Continued)*

The return of Bahá'u'lláh from Sulaymáníyyih to Baghdád marks a turning point of the utmost significance in the history of the first Bahá'í century. The tide of the fortunes of the Faith, having reached its lowest ebb, was now beginning to surge back, and was destined to roll on, steadily and mightily, to a new high water-mark, associated this time with the Declaration of His Mission, on the eve of His banishment to Constantinople. With His return to Baghdád a firm anchorage was now being established, an anchorage such as the Faith had never known in its history. Never before, except during the first three years of its life, could that Faith claim to have possessed a fixed and accessible center to which its adherents could turn for guidance, and from which they could derive continuous and unobstructed inspiration. No less than half of the Báb's short-lived ministry was spent on the remotest border of His native country, where He was concealed and virtually cut off from the vast majority of His disciples. The period immediately after His martyrdom was marked by a confusion that was even more deplorable than the isolation caused by His enforced captivity. Nor when the Revelation which He had foretold made its appearance was it succeeded by an immediate declaration that could enable the members of a distracted community to rally round the person of their expected Deliverer. The prolonged self-concealment of Mírzá Yaḥyá, the center provisionally appointed pending the manifestation of the Promised One; the nine months' absence of Bahá'u'lláh from His native land, while on a visit to Karbilá, followed swiftly by His imprisonment in the Síyáh-Chál, by His banishment to 'Iráq, and afterwards by His retirement to Kurdistán—all combined to prolong the phase of instability and suspense through which the Bábí community had to pass.

Now at last, in spite of Bahá'u'lláh's reluctance to unravel the mystery surrounding His own position, the Bábís found themselves able to center both their hopes and their movements round One Whom they believed (whatever their views as to His station) capable of insuring the stability and integrity of their Faith. The orientation which the Faith had thus acquired and the fixity of the center towards which it now gravitated continued, in one form or another, to be its outstanding features, of which it was never again to be deprived.

The Faith of the Báb, as already observed, had, in consequence of the successive and formidable blows it had received, reached the verge of extinction. Nor was the momentous Revelation vouchsafed to Bahá'u'lláh in the Síyáh-Chál productive at once of any tangible results of a nature that would exercise a stabilizing influence on a well-nigh disrupted community. Bahá'u'lláh's unexpected banishment had been a further blow to its members, who had learned to place their reliance upon Him. Mírzá Yaḥyá's seclusion and inactivity further accelerated the process of disintegration that had set in. Bahá'u'lláh's prolonged retirement to Kurdistán seemed to have set the seal on its complete dissolution.

Now, however, the tide that had ebbed in so alarming a measure was turning, bearing with it, as it rose to flood point, those inestimable benefits that were to herald the announcement of the Revelation already secretly disclosed to Bahá'u'lláh.

During the seven years that elapsed between the resumption of His labors and the declaration of His prophetic mission—years to which we now direct our attention—it would be no exaggeration to say that the Bahá'í community, under the name and in the shape of a re-arisen Bábí community was born and was slowly taking shape, though its Creator still appeared in the guise of, and continued to labor as, one of the foremost disciples of the Báb. It was a period during which the prestige of the community's nominal head steadily faded from the scene, paling before the rising splendor of Him Who was its actual Leader and Deliverer. It was a period in the course of which the first fruits of an exile, endowed with incalculable potentialities, ripened and were garnered. It was a period that will go down in history as one during which the prestige of a recreated community was immensely enhanced, its morals entirely reformed, its recognition of Him who rehabilitated its fortunes enthusiastically affirmed, its literature enormously enriched, and its victories over its new adversaries universally acknowledged.

The prestige of the community, and particularly that of Bahá'u'lláh, now began from its first inception in Kurdistán to mount in a steadily rising crescendo. Bahá'u'lláh had scarcely gathered up again the reins of the authority he had relinquished when the devout admirers He had left behind in Sulaymáníyyih started to flock to Baghdád, with the name of "Darvísh Muḥammad" on their lips, and the "house of Mírzá Músá the Bábí" as their goal. Astonished at the sight of so many 'ulamás and Ṣúfís of Kurdish origin, of both the Qádiríyyih and Khálidíyyih Orders, thronging the house of Bahá'u'lláh, and impelled by racial and sectarian rivalry, the religious leaders of the city, such as the renowned Ibn-i-Álúsí, the Muftí of Baghdád, together with Shaykh 'Abdu's-Salám, Shaykh 'Abdu'l-Qádir and Siyyid Dáwúdí, began to seek His presence, and, having obtained completely satisfying answers to their several queries, enrolled themselves among the band of His earliest admirers. The unqualified recognition by these outstanding leaders of those traits that distinguished the character and conduct of Bahá'u'lláh stimulated the curiosity, and later evoked the unstinted praise, of a great many observers of less conspicuous position, among whom figured poets, mystics and notables, who either resided in, or visited, the city. Government officials, foremost among whom were 'Abdu'lláh Páshá and his lieutenant Maḥmúd Áqá, and Mullá 'Alí Mardán, a Kurd well-known in those circles, were gradually brought into contact with Him, and lent their share in noising abroad His fast-spreading fame. Nor could those distinguished Persians, who either lived in Baghdád and its environs or visited as pilgrims the holy places, remain impervious to the spell of His charm. Princes of the royal blood, amongst whom were such personages as the Ná'ibu'l-Íyálih, the Shujá'u'd-Dawlih, the Sayfu'd-Dawlih, and Zaynu'l-'Ábidín Khán, the Fakhru'd-Dawlih, were, likewise, irresistibly drawn into the ever-widening circle of His associates and acquaintances.

Those who, during Bahá'u'lláh's two years' absence from Baghdád, had so persistently reviled and loudly derided His companions and kindred were, by now, for the most part, silenced. Not an inconsiderable number among them feigned respect and esteem for Him, a few claimed to be His defenders and supporters, while others professed to share His beliefs, and actually joined the ranks of the community to which He belonged. Such was the extent of the reaction that had set in that one of them was even heard to boast that, as far back as the year 1250 A.H.—a decade before the Báb's Declaration—he had already perceived and embraced the truth of His Faith!

Within a few years after Bahá'u'lláh's return from Sulaymáníyyih the situation had been completely reversed. The house of Sulaymán-i-Ghannám, on which the official designation of the Bayt-i-A'ẓam (the Most Great House) was later conferred, known, at that time, as the house of Mírzá Músá, the Bábí, an extremely modest residence, situated in the Karkh quarter, in the neighborhood of the western bank of the river, to which Bahá'u'lláh's family had moved prior to His return from Kurdistán, had now become the focal center of a great number of seekers, visitors and pilgrims, including Kurds, Persians, Arabs and Turks, and derived from the Muslim, the Jewish and Christian Faiths. It had, moreover, become a veritable sanctuary to which the victims of the injustice of the official representative of the Persian government were wont to flee, in the hope of securing redress for the wrongs they had suffered.

At the same time an influx of Persian Bábís, whose sole object was to attain the presence of Bahá'u'lláh, swelled the stream of visitors that poured through His hospitable doors. Carrying back, on their return to their native country, innumerable testimonies, both oral and written, to His steadily rising power and glory, they could not fail to contribute, in a vast measure, to the expansion and progress of a newly-reborn Faith. Four of the Báb's cousins and His maternal uncle, Ḥájí Mírzá Siyyid Muḥammad; a grand-daughter of Fatḥ-'Alí Shah and fervent admirer of Ṭáhirih, surnamed Varaqatu'r-Riḍván; the erudite Mullá Muḥammad-i-Qá'iní, surnamed Nabíl-i-Akbar; the already famous Mullá Ṣadiq-i-Khurásání, surnamed Ismu'lláhu'l-Aṣdaq, who with Quddús had been ignominiously persecuted in Shíráz; Mullá Báqir, one of the Letters of the Living; Siyyid Asadu'lláh, surnamed Dayyán; the revered Siyyid Javád-i-Karbilá'í; Mírzá Muḥammad-Ḥasan and Mírzá Muḥammad-Ḥusayn, later immortalized by the titles of Sulṭánu'sh-Shuhadá and Maḥbúbu'sh-Shuhadá (King of Martyrs and Beloved of Martyrs) respectively; Mírzá Muḥammad-'Alíy-i-Nahrí, whose daughter, at a later date, was joined in wedlock to 'Abdu'l-Bahá; the immortal Siyyid Ismá'íl-i-Zavári'í; Ḥájí Shaykh Muḥammad, surnamed Nabíl by the Báb; the accomplished Mírzá Áqáy-i-Munír, surnamed Ismu'-lláhu'l-Muníb; the long-suffering Ḥájí Muḥammad-Taqí, surnamed Ayyúb; Mullá Zaynu'l-'Ábidín, surnamed Zaynu'l-Muqarrabín, who had ranked as a highly esteemed mujtahid—all these were numbered among the visitors and fellow-disciples who crossed His threshold, caught a glimpse of the splendor of His majesty, and communicated far and wide the creative influences instilled into them through their contact with His spirit. Mullá Muḥammad-i-Zarandí, surnamed Nabíl-i-A'ẓam, who may well rank as His Poet-Laureate, His chronicler and His indefatigable disciple, had already joined the exiles, and had launched out on His long and arduous series of journeys to Persia in furtherance of the Cause of his Beloved.

Even those who, in their folly and temerity had, in Baghdád, in Karbilá, in Qum, in Káshán, in Tabríz and in Ṭihrán, arrogated to themselves the rights, and assumed the title of "Him Whom God shall make manifest" were for the most part instinctively led to seek His presence, confess their error and supplicate His forgiveness. As time went on, fugitives, driven by the ever-present fear of persecution, sought, with their wives and children, the relative security afforded them by close proximity to One who had already become the rallying point for the members of a sorely-vexed community. Persians of high eminence, living in exile, rejecting, in the face of the mounting prestige of Bahá'u'lláh, the dictates of moderation and prudence, sat, forgetful of their pride, at His feet, and imbibed, each according to his capacity, a measure of His spirit and wisdom. Some of the more ambitious among them, such as 'Abbás Mírzá, a son of Muḥammad Sháh, the Vazír-Niẓám, and Mírzá Malkam Khán, as well as certain functionaries of foreign governments, attempted, in their short-sightedness, to secure His support and assistance for the furtherance of the designs they cherished, designs which He unhesitatingly and severely condemned. Nor was the then representative of the British government, Colonel Sir Arnold Burrows Kemball, consul-general in Baghdád, insensible of the position which Bahá'u'lláh now occupied. Entering into friendly correspondence with Him, he, as testified by Bahá'u'lláh Himself, offered Him the protection of British citizenship, called on Him in person, and undertook to transmit to Queen Victoria any communication He might wish to forward to her. He even expressed his readiness to arrange for the transfer of His residence to India, or to any place agreeable to Him. This suggestion Bahá'u'lláh declined, choosing to abide in the dominions of the Sulṭán of Turkey. And finally, during the last year of His sojourn in Baghdád the governor Námiq-Páshá, impressed by the many signs of esteem and veneration in which He was held, called upon Him to pay his personal tribute to One Who had already achieved so conspicuous a victory over the hearts and souls of those who had met Him. So profound was the respect the governor entertained for Him, Whom he regarded as one of the Lights of the Age, that it was not until the end of three months, during which he had received five successive commands from 'Álí Páshá, that he could bring himself to inform Bahá'u'lláh that it was the wish of the Turkish government that He should proceed to the capital. On one occasion, when 'Abdu'l-Bahá and Áqáy-i-Kalím had been delegated by Bahá'u'lláh to visit him, he entertained them with such elaborate ceremonial that the Deputy-Governor stated that so far as he knew no notable of the city had ever been accorded by any governor so warm and courteous a reception. So struck, indeed, had the Sulṭán 'Abdu'l-Majíd been by the favorable reports received about Bahá'u'lláh from successive governors of Baghdád (this is the personal testimony given by the Governor's deputy to Bahá'u'lláh himself) that he consistently refused to countenance the requests of the Persian government either to deliver Him to their representative or to order His expulsion from Turkish territory.

On no previous occasion, since the inception of the Faith, not even during the days when the Báb in Isfahán, in Tabríz and in Chihríq was acclaimed by the ovations of an enthusiastic populace, had any of its exponents risen to such high eminence in the public mind, or exercised over so diversified a circle of admirers an influence so far reaching and so potent. Yet unprecedented as was the sway which Bahá'u'lláh held while, in that primitive age of the Faith, He was dwelling in Baghdád, its range at that time was modest when compared with the magnitude of the fame which, at the close of that same age, and through the immediate inspiration of the Center of His Covenant, the Faith acquired in both the European and American continents.

The ascendancy achieved by Bahá'u'lláh was nowhere better demonstrated than in His ability to broaden the outlook and transform the character of the community to which He belonged. Though Himself nominally a Bábí, though the provisions of the Bayán were still regarded as binding and inviolable, He was able to inculcate a standard which, while not incompatible with its tenets, was ethically superior to the loftiest principles which the Bábí Dispensation had established. The salutary and fundamental truths advocated by the Báb, that had either been obscured, neglected or misrepresented, were moreover elucidated by Bahá'u'lláh, reaffirmed and instilled afresh into the corporate life of the community, and into the souls of the individuals who comprised it. The dissociation of the Bábí Faith from every form of political activity and from all secret associations and factions; the emphasis placed on the principle of non-violence; the necessity of strict obedience to established authority; the ban imposed on all forms of sedition, on back-biting, retaliation, and dispute; the stress laid on godliness, kindliness, humility and piety, on honesty and truthfulness, chastity and fidelity, on justice, toleration, sociability, amity and concord, on the acquisition of arts and sciences, on self-sacrifice and detachment, on patience, steadfastness and resignation to the will of God—all these constitute the salient features of a code of ethical conduct to which the books, treatises and epistles, revealed during those years, by the indefatigable pen of Bahá'u'lláh, unmistakably bear witness.

*"By the aid of God and His divine grace and mercy,"* He Himself has written with reference to the character and consequences of His own labors during that period, *"We revealed, as a copious rain, Our verses, and sent them to various parts of the world. We exhorted all men, and particularly this people, through Our wise counsels and loving admonitions, and forbade them to engage in sedition, quarrels, disputes or conflict. As a result of this, and by the grace of God, waywardness and folly were changed into piety and understanding, and weapons of war converted into instruments of peace."* *"Bahá'u'lláh,"* 'Abdu'l-Bahá affirmed, *"after His return* (from Sulaymáníyyih) *made such strenuous efforts in educating and training this community, in reforming its manners, in regulating its affairs and in rehabilitating its fortunes, that in a short while all these troubles and mischiefs were quenched, and the utmost peace and tranquillity reigned in men's hearts."* And again: *"When these fundamentals were established in the hearts of this people, they everywhere acted in such wise that, in the estimation of those in authority, they became famous for the integrity of their character, the steadfastness of their hearts, the purity of their motives, the praiseworthiness of their deeds, and the excellence of their conduct."*

The exalted character of the teachings of Bahá'u'lláh propounded during that period is perhaps best illustrated by the following statement made by Him in those days to an official who had reported to Him that, because of the devotion to His person which an evildoer had professed, he had hesitated to inflict upon that criminal the punishment he deserved: *"Tell him, no one in this world can claim any relationship to Me except those who, in all their deeds and in their conduct, follow My example, in such wise that all the peoples of the earth would be powerless to prevent them from doing and saying that which is meet and seemly."* *"This brother of Mine,"* He further declared to that official, *"this Mírzá Músá, who is from the same mother and father as Myself, and who from his earliest childhood has kept Me company, should he perpetrate an act contrary to the interests of either the state or religion, and his guilt be established in your sight, I would be pleased and appreciate your action were you to bind his hands and cast him into the river to drown, and refuse to consider the intercession of any one on his behalf."* In another connection He, wishing to stress His strong condemnation of all acts of violence, had written: *"It would be more acceptable in My sight for a person to harm one of My own sons or relatives rather than inflict injury upon any soul."*

"Most of those who surrounded Bahá'u'lláh," wrote Nabíl, describing the spirit that animated the reformed Bábí community in Baghdád, "exercised such care in sanctifying and purifying their souls, that they would suffer no word to cross their lips that might not conform to the will of God, nor would they take a single step that might be contrary to His good-pleasure." "Each one," he relates, "had entered into a pact with one of his fellow-disciples, in which they agreed to admonish one another, and, if necessary, chastise one another with a number of blows on the soles of the feet, proportioning the number of strokes to the gravity of the offense against the lofty standards they had sworn to observe." Describing the fervor of their zeal, he states that "not until the offender had suffered the punishment he had solicited, would he consent to either eat or drink."

The complete transformation which the written and spoken word of Bahá'u'lláh had effected in the outlook and character of His companions was equalled by the burning devotion which His love had kindled in their souls. A passionate zeal and fervor, that rivalled the enthusiasm that had glowed so fiercely in the breasts of the Báb's disciples in their moments of greatest exaltation, had now seized the hearts of the exiles of Baghdád and galvanized their entire beings. "So inebriated," Nabíl, describing the fecundity of this tremendously dynamic spiritual revival, has written, "so carried away was every one by the sweet savors of the Morn of Divine Revelation that, methinks, out of every thorn sprang forth heaps of blossoms, and every seed yielded innumerable harvests." "The room of the Most Great House," that same chronicler has recorded, "set apart for the reception of Bahá'u'lláh's visitors, though dilapidated, and having long since outgrown its usefulness, vied, through having been trodden by the blessed footsteps of the Well Beloved, with the Most Exalted Paradise. Low-roofed, it yet seemed to reach to the stars, and though it boasted but a single couch, fashioned from the branches of palms, whereon He Who is the King of Names was wont to sit, it drew to itself, even as a loadstone, the hearts of the princes."

It was this same reception room which, in spite of its rude simplicity, had so charmed the Shujá'u'd-Dawlih that he had expressed to his fellow-princes his intention of building a duplicate of it in his home in Káẓimayn. *"He may well succeed,"* Bahá'u'lláh is reported to have smilingly remarked when apprized of this intention, *"in reproducing outwardly the exact counterpart of this low-roofed room made of mud and straw with its diminutive garden. What of his ability to open onto it the spiritual doors leading to the hidden worlds of God?"* "I know not how to explain it," another prince, Zaynu'l-'Abidín K͟hán, the Fak͟hru'd-Dawlih, describing the atmosphere which pervaded that reception-room, had affirmed, "were all the sorrows of the world to be crowded into my heart they would, I feel, all vanish, when in the presence of Bahá'u'lláh. It is as if I had entered Paradise itself."

The joyous feasts which these companions, despite their extremely modest earnings, continually offered in honor of their Beloved; the gatherings, lasting far into the night, in which they loudly celebrated, with prayers, poetry and song, the praises of the Báb, of Quddús and of Bahá'u'lláh; the fasts they observed; the vigils they kept; the dreams and visions which fired their souls, and which they recounted to each other with feelings of unbounded enthusiasm; the eagerness with which those who served Bahá'u'lláh performed His errands, waited upon His needs, and carried heavy skins of water for His ablutions and other domestic purposes; the acts of imprudence which, in moments of rapture, they occasionally committed; the expressions of wonder and admiration which their words and acts evoked in a populace that had seldom witnessed such demonstrations of religious transport and personal devotion—these, and many others, will forever remain associated with the history of that immortal period, intervening between the birth hour of Bahá'u'lláh's Revelation and its announcement on the eve of His departure from 'Iráq.

Numerous and striking are the anecdotes which have been recounted by those whom duty, accident, or inclination had, in the course of these poignant years, brought into direct contact with Bahá'u'lláh. Many and moving are the testimonies of bystanders who were privileged to gaze on His countenance, observe His gait, or overhear His remarks, as He moved through the lanes and streets of the city, or paced the banks of the river; of the worshippers who watched Him pray in their mosques; of the mendicant, the sick, the aged, and the unfortunate whom He succored, healed, supported and comforted; of the visitors, from the haughtiest prince to the meanest beggar, who crossed His threshold and sat at His feet; of the merchant, the artisan, and the shopkeeper who waited upon Him and supplied His daily needs; of His devotees who had perceived the signs of His hidden glory; of His adversaries who were confounded or disarmed by the power of His utterance and the warmth of His love; of the priests and laymen, the noble and learned, who besought Him with the intention of either challenging His authority, or testing His knowledge, or investigating His claims, or confessing their shortcomings, or declaring their conversion to the Cause He had espoused.

From such a treasury of precious memories it will suffice my purpose to cite but a single instance, that of one of His ardent lovers, a native of Zavárih, Siyyid Ismá'íl by name, surnamed Dhabíḥ (the Sacrifice), formerly a noted divine, taciturn, meditative and wholly severed from every earthly tie, whose self-appointed task, on which he prided himself, was to sweep the approaches of the house in which Bahá'u'lláh was dwelling. Unwinding his green turban, the ensign of his holy lineage, from his head, he would, at the hour of dawn, gather up, with infinite patience, the rubble which the footsteps of his Beloved had trodden, would blow the dust from the crannies of the wall adjacent to the door of that house, would collect the sweepings in the folds of his own cloak, and, scorning to cast his burden for the feet of others to tread upon, would carry it as far as the banks of the river and throw it into its waters. Unable, at length, to contain the ocean of love that surged within his soul, he, after having denied himself for forty days both sleep and sustenance, and rendering for the last time the service so dear to his heart, betook himself, one day, to the banks of the river, on the road to Káẓimayn, performed his ablutions, lay down on his back, with his face turned towards Baghdád, severed his throat with a razor, laid the razor upon his breast, and expired. (1275 A.H.)

Nor was he the only one who had meditated such an act and was determined to carry it out. Others were ready to follow suit, had not Bahá'u'lláh promptly intervened, and ordered the refugees living in Baghdád to return immediately to their native land. Nor could the authorities, when it was definitely established that Dhabíḥ had died by his own hand, remain indifferent to a Cause whose Leader could inspire so rare a devotion in, and hold such absolute sway over, the hearts of His lovers. Apprized of the apprehensions that episode had evoked in certain quarters in Baghdád, Bahá'u'lláh is reported to have remarked: *"Siyyid Ismá'íl was possessed of such power and might that were he to be confronted by all the peoples of the earth, he would, without doubt, be able to establish his ascendancy over them."* *"No blood,"* He is reported to have said with reference to this same Dhabíḥ, whom He extolled as *"King and*

*Beloved of Martyrs," "has, till now, been poured upon the earth as pure as the blood he shed."*

"So intoxicated were those who had quaffed from the cup of Bahá'u'lláh's presence," is yet another testimony from the pen of Nabíl, who was himself an eye-witness of most of these stirring episodes, "that in their eyes the palaces of kings appeared more ephemeral than a spider's web. . . . The celebrations and festivities that were theirs were such as the kings of the earth had never dreamt of." "I, myself with two others," he relates, "lived in a room which was devoid of furniture. Bahá'u'lláh entered it one day, and, looking about Him, remarked: 'Its emptiness pleases Me. In My estimation it is preferable to many a spacious palace, inasmuch as the beloved of God are occupied in it with the remembrance of the Incomparable Friend, with hearts that are wholly emptied of the dross of this world.' " His own life was characterized by that same austerity, and evinced that same simplicity which marked the lives of His beloved companions. *"There was a time in 'Iráq,"* He Himself affirms, in one of His Tablets, *"when the Ancient Beauty . . . had no change of linen. The one shirt He possessed would be washed, dried and worn again."*

"Many a night," continues Nabíl, depicting the lives of those self-oblivious companions, "no less than ten persons subsisted on no more than a pennyworth of dates. No one knew to whom actually belonged the shoes, the cloaks, or the robes that were to be found in their houses. Whoever went to the bazaar could claim that the shoes upon his feet were his own, and each one who entered the presence of Bahá'u'lláh could affirm that the cloak and robe he then wore belonged to him. Their own names they had forgotten, their hearts were emptied of aught else except adoration for their Beloved. . . . O, for the joy of those days, and the gladness and wonder of those hours!"

The enormous expansion in the scope and volume of Bahá'u'lláh's writings, after His return from Sulaymáníyyih, is yet another distinguishing feature of the period under review. The verses that streamed during those years from His pen, described as *"a copious rain"* by Himself, whether in the form of epistles, exhortations, commentaries, apologies, dissertations, prophecies, prayers, odes or specific Tablets, contributed, to a marked degree, to the reformation and progressive unfoldment of the Bábí community, to the broadening of its outlook, to the expansion of its activities and to the enlightenment of the minds of its members. So prolific was this period, that during the first two years after His return from His retirement, according to the testimony of Nabíl, who was at that time living in Baghdád, the unrecorded verses that streamed from His lips averaged, in a single day and night, the equivalent of the Qur'án! As to those verses which He either dictated or wrote Himself, their number was no less remarkable than either the wealth of material they contained, or the diversity of subjects to which they referred. A vast, and indeed the greater, proportion of these writings were, alas, lost irretrievably to posterity. No less an authority than Mírzá Áqá Ján, Bahá'u'lláh's amanuensis, affirms, as reported by Nabíl, that by the express order of Bahá'u'lláh, hundreds of thousands of verses, mostly written by His own hand, were obliterated and cast into the river. "Finding me reluctant to execute His orders," Mírzá Áqá Ján has related to Nabíl, "Bahá'u'lláh would reassure me saying: 'None is to be found at this time worthy to hear these melodies.' . . . Not once, or twice, but innumerable times, was I commanded to repeat this act." A certain Muḥammad Karím, a native of Shíráz, who had been a witness to the rapidity and the manner in which the Báb had penned the verses with which He was inspired, has left the following testimony to posterity, after attaining, during those days, the presence of Bahá'u'lláh, and beholding with his own eyes what he himself had considered to be the only proof of the mission of the Promised One: "I bear witness that the verses revealed by Bahá'u'lláh were superior, in the rapidity with which they were penned, in the ease with which they flowed, in their lucidity, their profundity and sweetness to those which I, myself saw pour from the pen of the Báb when in His presence. Had Bahá'u'lláh no other claim to greatness, this were sufficient, in the eyes of the world and its people, that He produced such verses as have streamed this day from His pen."

Foremost among the priceless treasures cast forth from the billowing ocean of Bahá'u'lláh's Revelation ranks the Kitáb-i-Íqán (Book of Certitude), revealed within the space of two days and two nights, in the closing years of that period (1278 A.H.—1862 A.D.). It was written in fulfillment of the prophecy of the Báb, Who had specifically stated that the Promised One would complete the text of the unfinished Persian Bayán, and in reply to the questions addressed to Bahá'u'lláh by the as yet unconverted maternal uncle of the Báb, Ḥájí Mírzá Siyyid Muḥammad, while on a visit, with his brother, Ḥájí Mírzá Ḥasan-'Alí, to Karbilá. A model of Persian prose, of a style at once original, chaste and vigorous, and remarkably lucid, both cogent in argument and matchless in its irresistible eloquence, this Book, setting forth in outline the Grand Redemptive Scheme of God, occupies a position unequalled by any work in the entire range of Bahá'í literature, except the Kitáb-i-Aqdas, Bahá'u'lláh's Most Holy Book. Revealed on the eve of the declaration of His Mission, it proffered to mankind the *"Choice Sealed Wine,"* whose seal is of *"musk,"* and broke the *"seals"* of the *"Book"* referred to by Daniel, and disclosed the meaning of the *"words"* destined to remain *"closed up"* till the *"time of the end."*

Within a compass of two hundred pages it proclaims unequivocally the existence and oneness of a personal God, unknowable, inaccessible, the source of all Revelation, eternal, omniscient, omnipresent and almighty; asserts the relativity of religious truth and the continuity of Divine Revelation; affirms the unity of the Prophets, the universality of their Message, the identity of their fundamental teachings, the sanctity of their scriptures, and the twofold character of their stations; denounces the blindness and perversity of the divines and doctors of every age; cites and elucidates the allegorical passages of the New Testament, the abstruse verses of the Qur'án, and the cryptic Muḥammadan traditions which have bred those age-long misunderstandings, doubts and animosities that have sundered and kept apart the followers of the world's leading religious systems; enumerates the essential prerequisites for the attainment by every true seeker of the object of his quest; demonstrates the validity, the sublimity and significance of the Báb's Revelation; acclaims the heroism and detachment of His disciples; foreshadows, and prophesies the world-wide triumph of the Revelation promised to the people of the Bayán; upholds the purity and innocence of the Virgin Mary; glorifies the Imáms of the Faith of Muḥammad; celebrates the martyrdom, and lauds the spiritual sovereignty, of the Imám Ḥusayn; unfolds the meaning of such symbolic terms as *"Return," "Resurrection," "Seal of the Prophets"* and *"Day of Judgment"*; adumbrates and distinguishes between the three stages of Divine Revelation; and expatiates, in glowing terms, upon the glories and wonders of the *"City of God,"* renewed, at fixed intervals, by the dispensation of Providence, for the guidance, the benefit and salvation of all mankind. Well may it be claimed that of all the books revealed by the Author of the Bahá'í Revelation, this Book alone, by sweeping away the age-long barriers that have so insurmountably separated the great religions of the world, has laid down a broad and unassailable foundation for the complete and permanent reconciliation of their followers.

Next to this unique repository of inestimable treasures must rank that marvelous collection of gem-like utterances, the "Hidden Words" with which Bahá'u'lláh was inspired, as He paced, wrapped in His meditations, the banks of the Tigris. Revealed in the year 1274 A.H., partly in Persian, partly in Arabic, it was originally designated the "Hidden Book of Fáṭimih," and was identified by its Author with the Book of that same name, believed by Shí'ah Islám to be in the possession of the promised Qá'im, and to consist of words of consolation addressed by the angel Gabriel, at God's command, to Fáṭimih, and dictated to the Imám 'Alí, for the sole purpose of comforting her in her hour of bitter anguish after the death of her illustrious Father. The significance of this dynamic spiritual leaven cast into the life of the world for the reorientation of the minds of men, the edification of their souls and the rectification of their conduct can best be judged by the description of its character given in the opening passage by its Author: *"This is that which hath descended from the Realm of Glory, uttered by the tongue of power and might, and revealed unto the Prophets of old. We have taken the inner essence thereof and clothed it in the garment of brevity, as a token of grace unto the righteous, that they may stand faithful unto the Covenant of God, may fulfill in their lives His trust, and in the realm of spirit obtain the gem of Divine virtue."*

To these two outstanding contributions to the world's religious literature, occupying respectively, positions of unsurpassed preeminence among the doctrinal and ethical writings of the Author of the Bahá'í Dispensation, was added, during that same period, a treatise that may well be regarded as His greatest mystical composition, designated as the "Seven Valleys," which He wrote in answer to the questions of Shaykh Muḥyi'd-Dín, the Qáḍí of Kháníqayn, in which He describes the seven stages which the soul of the seeker must needs traverse ere it can attain the object of its existence.

The "Four Valleys," an epistle addressed to the learned Shaykh 'Abdu'r-Raḥmán-i-Karkútí; the "Tablet of the Holy Mariner," in which Bahá'u'lláh prophesies the severe afflictions that are to befall Him; the "Lawḥ-i-Ḥúríyyih" (Tablet of the Maiden), in which events of a far remoter future are foreshadowed; the "Súriy-i-Ṣabr" (Súrih of Patience), revealed on the first day of Riḍván which extols Vaḥíd and his fellow-sufferers in Nayríz; the commentary on the Letters prefixed to the Súrihs of the Qur'án; His interpretation of the letter Váv, mentioned in the writings of Shaykh Aḥmad-i-Aḥsá'í, and of other abstruse passages in the works of Siyyid Káẓim-i-Rashtí; the "Lawḥ-i-Madínatu't-Tawḥíd" (Tablet of the

City of Unity); the "Ṣaḥífiy-i-Shaṭṭíyyih"; the "Muṣíbát-i-Ḥurúfát-i-'Álíyát"; the "Tafsír-i-Hú"; the "Javáhiru'l-Asrár" and a host of other writings, in the form of epistles, odes, homilies, specific Tablets, commentaries and prayers, contributed, each in its own way, to swell the *"rivers of everlasting life"* which poured forth from the *"Abode of Peace"* and lent a mighty impetus to the expansion of the Báb's Faith in both Persia and 'Iráq, quickening the souls and transforming the character of its adherents.

The undeniable evidences of the range and magnificence of Bahá'u'lláh's rising power; His rapidly waxing prestige; the miraculous transformation which, by precept and example, He had effected in the outlook and character of His companions from Baghdád to the remotest towns and hamlets in Persia; the consuming love for Him that glowed in their bosoms; the prodigious volume of writings that streamed day and night from His pen, could not fail to fan into flame the animosity which smouldered in the breasts of His Shí'ah and Sunní enemies. Now that His residence was transferred to the vicinity of the strongholds of Shí'ah Islám, and He Himself brought into direct and almost daily contact with the fanatical pilgrims who thronged the holy places of Najaf, Karbilá and Káẓimayn, a trial of strength between the growing brilliance of His glory and the dark and embattled forces of religious fanaticism could no longer be delayed. A spark was all that was required to ignite this combustible material of all the accumulated hatreds, fears and jealousies which the revived activities of the Bábís had inspired. This was provided by a certain Shaykh 'Abdu'l-Ḥusayn, a crafty and obstinate priest, whose consuming jealousy of Bahá'u'lláh was surpassed only by his capacity to stir up mischief both among those of high degree and also amongst the lowest of the low, Arab or Persian, who thronged the streets and markets of Káẓimayn, Karbilá and Baghdád. He it was whom Bahá'u'lláh had stigmatized in His Tablets by such epithets as the *"scoundrel,"* the *"schemer,"* the *"wicked one,"* who *"drew the sword of his self against the face of God," "in whose soul Satan hath whispered,"* and *"from whose impiety Satan flies,"* the *"depraved one," "from whom originated and to whom will return all infidelity, cruelty and crime."* Largely through the efforts of the Grand Vizir, who wished to get rid of him, this troublesome mujtahid had been commissioned by the Sháh to proceed to Karbilá to repair the holy sites in that city. Watching for his opportunity, he allied himself with Mírzá Buzurg Khán, a newly-appointed Persian consul-general, who being of the same iniquitous turn of mind as himself, a man of mean intelligence, insincere, without foresight or honor, and a confirmed drunkard, soon fell a prey to the influence of that vicious plotter, and became the willing instrument of his designs.

Their first concerted endeavor was to obtain from the governor of Baghdád, Muṣṭafá Páshá, through a gross distortion of the truth, an order for the extradition of Bahá'u'lláh and His companions, an effort which miserably failed. Recognizing the futility of any attempt to achieve his purpose through the intervention of the local authorities, Shaykh 'Abdu'l-Ḥusayn began, through the sedulous circulation of dreams which he first invented and then interpreted, to excite the passions of a superstitious and highly inflammable population. The resentment engendered by the lack of response he met with was aggravated by his ignominious failure to meet the challenge of an interview pre-arranged between himself and Bahá'u'lláh. Mírzá Buzurg Khán, on his part, used his influence in order to arouse the animosity of the lower elements of the population against the common Adversary, by inciting them to affront Him in public, in the hope of provoking some rash retaliatory act that could be used as a ground for false charges through which the desired order for Bahá'u'lláh's extradition might be procured. This attempt too proved abortive, as the presence of Bahá'u'lláh, Who, despite the warnings and pleadings of His friends, continued to walk unescorted, both by day and by night, through the streets of the city, was enough to plunge His would-be molesters into consternation and shame. Well aware of their motives, He would approach them, rally them on their intentions, joke with them, and leave them covered with confusion and firmly resolved to abandon whatever schemes they had in mind. The consul-general had even gone so far as to hire a ruffian, a Turk, named Riḍá, for the sum of one hundred túmáns, provide him with a horse and with two pistols, and order him to seek out and kill Bahá'u'lláh, promising him that his own protection would be fully assured. Riḍá, learning one day that his would-be-victim was attending the public bath, eluded the vigilance of the Bábís in attendance, entered the bath with a pistol concealed in his cloak, and confronted Bahá'u'lláh in the inner chamber, only to discover that he lacked the courage to accomplish his task. He himself, years later, related that on another occasion he was lying in wait for Bahá'u'lláh, pistol in hand, when, on Bahá'u'lláh's approach, he was so overcome with fear that the pistol dropped from his hand; whereupon Bahá'u'lláh bade Áqáy-i-Kalím, who accompanied Him, to hand it back to him, and show him the way to his home.

Balked in his repeated attempts to achieve his malevolent purpose, Shaykh 'Abdu'l-Ḥusayn now diverted his energies into a new channel. He promised his accomplice he would raise him to the rank of a minister of the crown, if he succeeded in inducing the government to recall Bahá'u'lláh to Ṭihrán, and cast Him again into prison. He despatched lengthy and almost daily reports to the immediate entourage of the Sháh. He painted extravagant pictures of the ascendancy enjoyed by Bahá'u'lláh by representing Him as having won the allegiance of the nomadic tribes of 'Iráq. He claimed that He was in a position to muster, in a day, fully one hundred thousand men ready to take up arms at His bidding. He accused Him of meditating, in conjunction with various leaders in Persia, an insurrection against the sovereign. By such means as these he succeeded in bringing sufficient pressure on the authorities in Ṭihrán to induce the Sháh to grant him a mandate, bestowing on him full powers, and enjoining the Persian 'ulamás and functionaries to render him every assistance. This mandate the Shaykh instantly forwarded to the ecclesiastics of Najaf and Karbilá, asking them to convene a gathering in Káẓimayn, the place of his residence. A concourse of shaykhs, mullás and mujtahids, eager to curry favor with the sovereign, promptly responded. Upon being informed of the purpose for which they had been summoned, they determined to declare a holy war against the colony of exiles, and by launching a sudden and general assault on it to destroy the Faith at its heart. To their amazement and disappointment, however, they found that the leading mujtahid amongst them, the celebrated Shaykh Murtaḍáy-i-Anṣárí, a man renowned for his tolerance, his wisdom, his undeviating justice, his piety and nobility of character, refused, when apprized of their designs, to pronounce the necessary sentence against the Bábís. He it was whom Bahá'u'lláh later extolled in the "Lawḥ-i-Sulṭán," and numbered among *"those doctors who have indeed drunk of the cup of renunciation,"* and *"never interfered with Him,"* and to whom 'Abdu'l-Bahá referred as *"the illustrious and erudite doctor, the noble and celebrated scholar, the seal of seekers after truth."* Pleading insufficient knowledge of the tenets of this community, and claiming to have witnessed no act on the part of its members at variance with the Qur'án, he, disregarding the remonstrances of his colleagues, abruptly left the gathering, and returned to Najaf, after having expressed, through a messenger, his regret to Bahá'u'lláh for what had happened, and his devout wish for His protection.

Frustrated in their designs, but unrelenting in their hostility, the assembled divines delegated the learned and devout Ḥájí Mullá Ḥasan-i-'Ammú, recognized for his integrity and wisdom, to submit various questions to Bahá'u'lláh for elucidation. When these were submitted, and answers completely satisfactory to the messenger were given, Ḥájí Mullá Ḥasan, affirming the recognition by the 'ulamás of the vastness of the knowledge of Bahá'u'lláh, asked, as an evidence of the truth of His mission, for a miracle that would satisfy completely all concerned. *"Although you have no right to ask this,"* Bahá'u'lláh replied, *"for God should test His creatures, and they should not test God, still I allow and accept this request. . . . The 'ulamás must assemble, and, with one accord, choose one miracle, and write that, after the performance of this miracle they will no longer entertain doubts about Me, and that all will acknowledge and confess the truth of My Cause. Let them seal this paper, and bring it to Me. This must be the accepted criterion: if the miracle is performed, no doubt will remain for them; and if not, We shall be convicted of imposture."* This clear, challenging and courageous reply, unexampled in the annals of any religion, and addressed to the most illustrious Shí'ah divines, assembled in their time-honored stronghold, was so satisfactory to their envoy that he instantly arose, kissed the knee of Bahá'u'lláh, and departed to deliver His message. Three days later he sent word that that august assemblage had failed to arrive at a decision, and had chosen to drop the matter, a decision to which he himself later gave wide publicity, in the course of his visit to Persia, and even communicated it in person to the then Minister of Foreign Affairs, Mírzá Sa'íd Khán. *"We have,"* Bahá'u'lláh is reported to have commented, when informed of their reaction to this challenge, *"through this all-satisfying, all-embracing message which We sent, revealed and vindicated the miracles of all the Prophets, inasmuch as We left the choice to the 'ulamás themselves, undertaking to reveal whatever they would decide upon." "If we carefully examine the text of the Bible,"* 'Abdu'l-Bahá has written concerning a similar challenge made later by Bahá'u'lláh in the "Lawḥ-i-Sulṭán," *"we see that the Divine Manifestation never said to those who denied Him, 'whatever miracle you desire, I am ready to perform, and I will submit to whatever test you propose.' But in the Epistle to the Sháh Bahá'u'lláh said clearly, 'Gather the 'ulamás and summon Me, that the evidences and proofs may be established.'"*

Seven years of uninterrupted, of patient and eminently successful consolidation were now drawing to a close. A shepherdless community, subjected to a prolonged and tremendous strain, from both within and without, and threatened with obliteration, had been resuscitated, and risen to an ascendancy without example in the course of its twenty years' history. Its foundations reinforced, its spirit exalted, its outlook transformed, its leadership safeguarded, its fundamentals restated, its prestige enhanced, its enemies discomfited, the Hand of Destiny was gradually preparing to launch it on a new phase in its checkered career, in which weal and woe alike were to carry it through yet another stage in its evolution. The Deliverer, the sole hope, and the virtually recognized leader of this community, Who had consistently overawed the authors of so many plots to assassinate Him, Who had scornfully rejected all the timid advice that He should flee from the scene of danger, Who had firmly declined repeated and generous offers made by friends and supporters to insure His personal safety, Who had won so conspicuous a victory over His antagonists—He was, at this auspicious hour, being impelled by the resistless processes of His unfolding Mission, to transfer His residence to the center of still greater preeminence, the capital city of the Ottoman Empire, the seat of the Caliphate, the administrative center of Sunní Islám, the abode of the most powerful potentate in the Islamic world.

He had already flung a daring challenge to the sacerdotal order represented by the eminent ecclesiastics residing in Najaf, Karbilá and Káẓimayn. He was now, while in the vicinity of the court of His royal adversary, to offer a similar challenge to the recognized head of Sunní Islám, as well as to the sovereign of Persia, the trustee of the hidden Imám. The entire company of the kings of the earth, and in particular the Sulṭán and his ministers, were, moreover, to be addressed by Him, appealed to and warned, while the kings of Christendom and the Sunní hierarchy were to be severely admonished. Little wonder that the exiled Bearer of a newly-announced Revelation should have, in anticipation of the future splendor of the Lamp of His Faith, after its removal from 'Iráq, uttered these prophetic words: *"It will shine resplendently within another globe, as predestined by Him who is the Omnipotent, the Ancient of Days. . . . That the Spirit should depart out of the body of 'Iráq is indeed a wondrous sign unto all who are in heaven and all who are on earth. Erelong will ye behold this Divine Youth riding upon the steed of victory. Then will the hearts of the envious be seized with trembling."*

The predestined hour of Bahá'u'lláh's departure from 'Iráq having now struck, the process whereby it could be accomplished was set in motion. The nine months of unremitting endeavor exerted by His enemies, and particularly by Sh̲ayk̲h̲ 'Abdu'l-Ḥusayn and his confederate Mírzá Buzurg K̲h̲án, were about to yield their fruit. Náṣiri'd-Dín Sh̲áh and his ministers, on the one hand, and the Persian Ambassador in Constantinople, on the other, were incessantly urged to take immediate action to insure Bahá'u'lláh's removal from Bag̲h̲dád. Through gross misrepresentation of the true situation and the dissemination of alarming reports a malignant and energetic enemy finally succeeded in persuading the Sh̲áh to instruct his foreign minister, Mírzá Sa'íd K̲h̲án, to direct the Persian Ambassador at the Sublime Porte, Mírzá Ḥusayn K̲h̲án, a close friend of 'Álí Páshá, the Grand Vizir of the Sulṭán, and of Fu'ád Páshá, the Minister of foreign affairs, to induce Sulṭán 'Abdu'l-'Azíz to order the immediate transfer of Bahá'u'lláh to a place remote from Bag̲h̲dád, on the ground that His continued residence in that city, adjacent to Persian territory and close to so important a center of Sh̲í'ah pilgrimage, constituted a direct menace to the security of Persia and its government.

Mírzá Sa'íd K̲h̲án, in his communication to the Ambassador, stigmatized the Faith as a "misguided and detestable sect," deplored Bahá'u'lláh's release from the Síyáh-Ch̲ál, and denounced Him as one who did not cease from "secretly corrupting and misleading foolish persons and ignorant weaklings." "In accordance with the royal command," he wrote, "I, your faithful friend, have been ordered . . . to instruct you to seek, without delay, an appointment with their Excellencies, the Ṣadr-i-A'ẓam and the Minister of Foreign Affairs . . . to request . . . the removal of this source of mischief from a center like Bag̲h̲dád, which is the meeting-place of many different peoples, and is situated near the frontiers of the provinces of Persia." In that same letter, quoting a celebrated verse, he writes: " 'I see beneath the ashes the glow of fire, and it wants but little to burst into a blaze,' " thus betraying his fears and seeking to instill them into his correspondent.

Encouraged by the presence on the throne of a monarch who had delegated much of his powers to his ministers, and aided by certain foreign ambassadors and ministers in Constantinople, Mírzá Ḥusayn K̲h̲án, by dint of much persuasion and the friendly pressure he brought to bear on these ministers, succeeded in securing the sanction of the Sulṭán for the transfer of Bahá'u'lláh and His companions (who had in the meantime been forced by circumstances to change their citizenship) to Constantinople. It is even reported that the first request the Persian authorities made of a friendly Power, after the accession of the new Sulṭán to the throne, was for its active and prompt intervention in this matter.

It was on the fifth of Naw-Rúz (1863), while Bahá'u'lláh was celebrating that festival in the Mazra'iy-i-Vashsháṣh, in the outskirts of Baghdád, and had just revealed the "Tablet of the Holy Mariner," whose gloomy prognostications had aroused the grave apprehensions of His Companions, that an emissary of Námiq Páshá arrived and delivered into His hands a communication requesting an interview between Him and the governor.

Already, as Nabíl has pointed out in his narrative, Bahá'u'lláh had, in the course of His discourses, during the last years of His sojourn in Baghdád, alluded to the period of trial and turmoil that was inexorably approaching, exhibiting a sadness and heaviness of heart which greatly perturbed those around Him. A dream which He had at that time, the ominous character of which could not be mistaken, served to confirm the fears and misgivings that had assailed His companions. *"I saw,"* He wrote in a Tablet, *"the Prophets and the Messengers gather and seat themselves around Me, moaning, weeping and loudly lamenting. Amazed, I inquired of them the reason, whereupon their lamentation and weeping waxed greater, and they said unto Me: 'We weep for Thee, O Most Great Mystery, O Tabernacle of Immortality!' They wept with such a weeping that I too wept with them. Thereupon the Concourse on high addressed Me saying: '. . . Erelong shalt Thou behold with Thine own eyes what no Prophet hath beheld. . . . Be patient, be patient.' . . . They continued addressing Me the whole night until the approach of dawn."* "Oceans of sorrow," Nabíl affirms, "surged in the hearts of the listeners when the Tablet of the Holy Mariner was read aloud to them. . . . It was evident to every one that the chapter of Baghdád was about to be closed, and a new one opened, in its stead. No sooner had that Tablet been chanted than Bahá'u'lláh ordered that the tents which had been pitched should be folded up, and that all His companions should return to the city. While the tents were being removed He observed: *'These tents may be likened to the trappings of this world, which no sooner are they spread out than the time cometh for them to be rolled up.'* From these words of His they who heard them perceived that these tents would never again be pitched on that spot. They had not yet been taken away when the messenger arrived from Baghdád to deliver the afore-mentioned communication from the governor."

By the following day the Deputy-Governor had delivered to

Bahá'u'lláh in a mosque, in the neighborhood of the governor's house, 'Álí Pás͟há's letter, addressed to Námiq Pás͟há, couched in courteous language, inviting Bahá'u'lláh to proceed, as a guest of the Ottoman government, to Constantinople, placing a sum of money at His disposal, and ordering a mounted escort to accompany Him for His protection. To this request Bahá'u'lláh gave His ready assent, but declined to accept the sum offered Him. On the urgent representations of the Deputy that such a refusal would offend the authorities, He reluctantly consented to receive the generous allowance set aside for His use, and distributed it, that same day, among the poor.

The effect upon the colony of exiles of this sudden intelligence was instantaneous and overwhelming. "That day," wrote an eyewitness, describing the reaction of the community to the news of Bahá'u'lláh's approaching departure, "witnessed a commotion associated with the turmoil of the Day of Resurrection. Methinks, the very gates and walls of the city wept aloud at their imminent separation from the Abhá Beloved. The first night mention was made of His intended departure His loved ones, one and all, renounced both sleep and food. . . . Not a soul amongst them could be tranquillized. Many had resolved that in the event of their being deprived of the bounty of accompanying Him, they would, without hesitation, kill themselves. . . . Gradually, however, through the words which He addressed them, and through His exhortations and His loving-kindness, they were calmed and resigned themselves to His good-pleasure." For every one of them, whether Arab or Persian, man or woman, child or adult, who lived in Bag͟hdád, He revealed during those days, in His own hand, a separate Tablet. In most of these Tablets He predicted the appearance of the *"Calf"* and of the *"Birds of the Night,"* allusions to those who, as anticipated in the Tablet of the Holy Mariner, and foreshadowed in the dream quoted above, were to raise the standard of rebellion and precipitate the gravest crisis in the history of the Faith.

Twenty-seven days after that mournful Tablet had been so unexpectedly revealed by Bahá'u'lláh, and the fateful communication, presaging His departure to Constantinople had been delivered into His hands, on a Wednesday afternoon (April 22, 1863), thirty-one days after Naw-Rúz, on the third of D͟hi'l-Qa'dih, 1279 A.H., He set forth on the first stage of His four months' journey to the capital of the Ottoman Empire. That historic day, forever after designated as the first day of the Riḍván Festival, the culmination of innumerable farewell visits which friends and acquaintances of every class and denomination, had been paying him, was one the like of which the inhabitants of Baghdád had rarely beheld. A concourse of people of both sexes and of every age, comprising friends and strangers Arabs, Kurds and Persians, notables and clerics, officials and merchants, as well as many of the lower classes, the poor, the orphaned, the outcast, some surprised, others heartbroken, many tearful and apprehensive, a few impelled by curiosity or secret satisfaction, thronged the approaches of His house, eager to catch a final glimpse of One Who, for a decade, had, through precept and example, exercised so potent an influence on so large a number of the heterogeneous inhabitants of their city.

Leaving for the last time, amidst weeping and lamentation, His "*Most Holy Habitation,*" out of which had "*gone forth the breath of the All-Glorious,*" and from which had poured forth, in "*ceaseless strains,*" the "*melody of the All-Merciful,*" and dispensing on His way with a lavish hand a last alms to the poor He had so faithfully befriended, and uttering words of comfort to the disconsolate who besought Him on every side, He, at length, reached the banks of the river, and was ferried across, accompanied by His sons and amanuensis, to the Najíbíyyih Garden, situated on the opposite shore. "*O My companions,*" He thus addressed the faithful band that surrounded Him before He embarked, "*I entrust to your keeping this city of Baghdád, in the state ye now behold it, when from the eyes of friends and strangers alike, crowding its housetops, its streets and markets, tears like the rain of spring are flowing down, and I depart. With you it now rests to watch lest your deeds and conduct dim the flame of love that gloweth within the breasts of its inhabitants.*"

The muezzin had just raised the afternoon call to prayer when Bahá'u'lláh entered the Najíbíyyih Garden, where He tarried twelve days before His final departure from the city. There His friends and companions, arriving in successive waves, attained His presence and bade Him, with feelings of profound sorrow, their last farewell. Outstanding among them was the renowned Álúsí, the Muftí of Baghdád, who, with eyes dimmed with tears, execrated the name of Náṣiri'd-Dín Sháh, whom he deemed to be primarily responsible for so unmerited a banishment. "I have ceased to regard him," he openly asserted, "as Náṣiri'd-Dín (the helper of the Faith), but consider him rather to be its wrecker." Another distinguished visitor was the governor himself, Námiq Páshá, who, after expressing in the most respectful terms his regret at the developments which had precipitated Bahá'u'lláh's departure, and assuring Him of his readiness to aid Him in any way he could, handed to the officer appointed to accompany Him a written order, commanding the governors of the provinces through which the exiles would be passing to extend to them the utmost consideration. "Whatever you require," he, after profuse apologies, informed Bahá'u'lláh, "you have but to command. We are ready to carry it out." *"Extend thy consideration to Our loved ones,"* was the reply to his insistent and reiterated offers, *"and deal with them with kindness"*—a request to which he gave his warm and unhesitating assent.

Small wonder that, in the face of so many evidences of deep-seated devotion, sympathy and esteem, so strikingly manifested by high and low alike, from the time Bahá'u'lláh announced His contemplated journey to the day of His departure from the Najíbíyyih Garden—small wonder that those who had so tirelessly sought to secure the order for His banishment, and had rejoiced at the success of their efforts, should now have bitterly regretted their act. *"Such hath been the interposition of God,"* 'Abdu'l-Bahá, in a letter written by Him from that garden, with reference to these enemies, affirms, *"that the joy evinced by them hath been turned to chagrin and sorrow, so much so that the Persian consul-general in Baghdád regrets exceedingly the plans and plots the schemers had devised. Námiq Pás͟há himself, on the day he called on Him* (Bahá'u'lláh) *stated: 'Formerly they insisted upon your departure. Now, however, they are even more insistent that you should remain.'"*

## CHAPTER IX

# The Declaration of Bahá'u'lláh's Mission and His Journey to Constantinople

The arrival of Bahá'u'lláh in the Najíbíyyih Garden, subsequently designated by His followers the Garden of Riḍván, signalizes the commencement of what has come to be recognized as the holiest and most significant of all Bahá'í festivals, the festival commemorating the Declaration of His Mission to His companions. So momentous a Declaration may well be regarded both as the logical consummation of that revolutionizing process which was initiated by Himself upon His return from Sulaymáníyyih, and as a prelude to the final proclamation of that same Mission to the world and its rulers from Adrianople.

Through that solemn act the *"delay,"* of no less than a decade, divinely interposed between the birth of Bahá'u'lláh's Revelation in the Síyáh-Chál and its announcement to the Báb's disciples, was at long last terminated. The *"set time of concealment,"* during which as He Himself has borne witness, the *"signs and tokens of a divinely-appointed Revelation"* were being showered upon Him, was fulfilled. The *"myriad veils of light,"* within which His glory had been wrapped, were, at that historic hour, partially lifted, vouchsafing to mankind *"an infinitesimal glimmer"* of the effulgence of His *"peerless, His most sacred and exalted Countenance."* The *"thousand two hundred and ninety days,"* fixed by Daniel in the last chapter of His Book, as the duration of the *"abomination that maketh desolate"* had now elapsed. The *"hundred lunar years,"* destined to immediately precede that blissful consummation (1335 days), announced by Daniel in that same chapter, had commenced. The nineteen years, constituting the first "Váḥid," preordained in the Persian Bayán by the pen of the Báb, had been completed. The Lord of the Kingdom, Jesus Christ returned in the glory of the Father, was about to ascend His throne, and assume the sceptre of a world-embracing, indestructible sovereignty. The community of the Most Great Name, the *"companions of the Crimson Colored Ark,"* lauded in glowing terms in the Qayyúmu'l-Asmá', had visibly emerged. The Báb's own prophecy regarding the *"Riḍván,"* the scene of the unveiling of Bahá'u'lláh's transcendent glory, had been literally fulfilled.

Undaunted by the prospect of the appalling adversities which, as predicted by Himself, were soon to overtake Him; on the eve of a second banishment which would be fraught with many hazards and perils, and would bring Him still farther from His native land, the cradle of His Faith, to a country alien in race, in language and in culture; acutely conscious of the extension of the circle of His adversaries, among whom were soon to be numbered a monarch more despotic than Náṣiri'd-Dín Sháh, and ministers no less unyielding in their hostility than either Ḥájí Mírzá Áqásí or the Amír-Niẓám; undeterred by the perpetual interruptions occasioned by the influx of a host of visitors who thronged His tent, Bahá'u'lláh chose in that critical and seemingly unpropitious hour to advance so challenging a claim, to lay bare the mystery surrounding His person, and to assume, in their plenitude, the power and the authority which were the exclusive privileges of the One Whose advent the Báb had prophesied.

Already the shadow of that great oncoming event had fallen upon the colony of exiles, who awaited expectantly its consummation. As the year *"eighty"* steadily and inexorably approached, He Who had become the real leader of that community increasingly experienced, and progressively communicated to His future followers, the onrushing influences of its informing force. The festive, the soul-entrancing odes which He revealed almost every day; the Tablets, replete with hints, which streamed from His pen; the allusions which, in private converse and public discourse, He made to the approaching hour; the exaltation which in moments of joy and sadness alike flooded His soul; the ecstasy which filled His lovers, already enraptured by the multiplying evidences of His rising greatness and glory; the perceptible change noted in His demeanor; and finally, His adoption of the táj (tall felt head-dress), on the day of His departure from His Most Holy House—all proclaimed unmistakably His imminent assumption of the prophetic office and of His open leadership of the community of the Báb's followers.

"Many a night," writes Nabíl, depicting the tumult that had seized the hearts of Bahá'u'lláh's companions, in the days prior to the declaration of His mission, "would Mírzá Áqá Ján gather them together in his room, close the door, light numerous camphorated candles, and chant aloud to them the newly revealed odes and Tablets in his possession. Wholly oblivious of this contingent world, completely immersed in the realms of the spirit, forgetful of the necessity for food, sleep or drink, they would suddenly discover that night had become day, and that the sun was approaching its zenith."

Of the exact circumstances attending that epoch-making Declaration we, alas, are but scantily informed. The words Bahá'u'lláh actually uttered on that occasion, the manner of His Declaration, the reaction it produced, its impact on Mírzá Yaḥyá, the identity of those who were privileged to hear Him, are shrouded in an obscurity which future historians will find it difficult to penetrate. The fragmentary description left to posterity by His chronicler Nabíl is one of the very few authentic records we possess of the memorable days He spent in that garden. "Every day," Nabíl has related, "ere the hour of dawn, the gardeners would pick the roses which lined the four avenues of the garden, and would pile them in the center of the floor of His blessed tent. So great would be the heap that when His companions gathered to drink their morning tea in His presence, they would be unable to see each other across it. All these roses Bahá'u'lláh would, with His own hands, entrust to those whom He dismissed from His presence every morning to be delivered, on His behalf, to His Arab and Persian friends in the city." "One night," he continues, "the ninth night of the waxing moon, I happened to be one of those who watched beside His blessed tent. As the hour of midnight approached, I saw Him issue from His tent, pass by the places where some of His companions were sleeping, and begin to pace up and down the moonlit, flower-bordered avenues of the garden. So loud was the singing of the nightingales on every side that only those who were near Him could hear distinctly His voice. He continued to walk until, pausing in the midst of one of these avenues, He observed: 'Consider these nightingales. So great is their love for these roses, that sleepless from dusk till dawn, they warble their melodies and commune with burning passion with the object of their adoration. How then can those who claim to be afire with the rose-like beauty of the Beloved choose to sleep?' For three successive nights I watched and circled round His blessed tent. Every time I passed by the couch whereon He lay, I would find Him wakeful, and every day, from morn till eventide, I would see Him ceaselessly engaged in conversing with the stream of visitors who kept flowing in from Baghdád. Not once could I discover in the words He spoke any trace of dissimulation."

As to the significance of that Declaration let Bahá'u'lláh Himself reveal to us its import. Acclaiming that historic occasion as the *"Most Great Festival,"* the *"King of Festivals,"* the *"Festival of God,"*

He has, in His Kitáb-i-Aqdas, characterized it as the Day whereon "*all created things were immersed in the sea of purification,*" whilst in one of His specific Tablets, He has referred to it as the Day whereon "*the breezes of forgiveness were wafted over the entire creation.*" "*Rejoice, with exceeding gladness, O people of Bahá!*", He, in another Tablet, has written, "*as ye call to remembrance the Day of supreme felicity, the Day whereon the Tongue of the Ancient of Days hath spoken, as He departed from His House proceeding to the Spot from which He shed upon the whole of creation the splendors of His Name, the All-Merciful . . . Were We to reveal the hidden secrets of that Day, all that dwell on earth and in the heavens would swoon away and die, except such as will be preserved by God, the Almighty, the All-Knowing, the All-Wise. Such is the inebriating effect of the words of God upon the Revealer of His undoubted proofs that His pen can move no longer.*" And again: "*The Divine Springtime is come, O Most Exalted Pen, for the Festival of the All-Merciful is fast approaching. . . . The Day-Star of Blissfulness shineth above the horizon of Our Name, the Blissful, inasmuch as the Kingdom of the Name of God hath been adorned with the ornament of the Name of Thy Lord, the Creator of the heavens. . . . Take heed lest anything deter Thee from extolling the greatness of this Day—the Day whereon the Finger of Majesty and Power hath opened the seal of the Wine of Reunion, and called all who are in the heavens and all who are on earth. . . . This is the Day whereon the unseen world crieth out: 'Great is thy blessedness, O earth, for thou hast been made the footstool of thy God, and been chosen as the seat of His mighty throne' . . . Say . . . He it is Who hath laid bare before you the hidden and treasured Gem, were ye to seek it. He it is who is the One Beloved of all things, whether of the past or of the future.*" And yet again: "*Arise, and proclaim unto the entire creation the tidings that He who is the All-Merciful hath directed His steps towards the Riḍván and entered it. Guide, then, the people unto the Garden of Delight which God hath made the Throne of His Paradise . . . Within this Paradise, and from the heights of its loftiest chambers, the Maids of Heaven have cried out and shouted: 'Rejoice, ye dwellers of the realms above, for the fingers of Him Who is the Ancient of Days are ringing, in the name of the All-Glorious, the Most Great Bell, in the midmost heart of the heavens. The hands of bounty have borne round the cups of everlasting life. Approach, and quaff your fill.'*" And finally: "*Forget the world of creation, O Pen, and turn Thou towards the face of Thy Lord, the Lord of all names. Adorn, then, the world with the ornament of the favors of Thy Lord, the King of everlasting days. For We perceive the fragrance of the Day whereon He Who is the Desire of all nations hath shed upon the kingdoms of the unseen and of the seen the splendors of the light of His most excellent names, and enveloped them with the radiance of the luminaries of His most gracious favors, favors which none can reckon except Him Who is the Omnipotent Protector of the entire creation."*

The departure of Bahá'u'lláh from the Garden of Riḍván, at noon, on the 14th of Dhi'l-Qa'dih 1279 A.H. (May 3, 1863), witnessed scenes of tumultuous enthusiasm no less spectacular, and even more touching, than those which greeted Him when leaving His Most Great House in Baghdád. "The great tumult," wrote an eyewitness, "associated in our minds with the Day of Gathering, the Day of Judgment, we beheld on that occasion. Believers and unbelievers alike sobbed and lamented. The chiefs and notables who had congregated were struck with wonder. Emotions were stirred to such depths as no tongue can describe, nor could any observer escape their contagion."

Mounted on His steed, a red roan stallion of the finest breed, the best His lovers could purchase for Him, and leaving behind Him a bowing multitude of fervent admirers, He rode forth on the first stage of a journey that was to carry Him to the city of Constantinople. "Numerous were the heads," Nabíl himself a witness of that memorable scene, recounts, "which, on every side, bowed to the dust at the feet of His horse, and kissed its hoofs, and countless were those who pressed forward to embrace His stirrups." "How great the number of those embodiments of fidelity," testifies a fellow-traveler, "who, casting themselves before that charger, preferred death to separation from their Beloved! Methinks, that blessed steed trod upon the bodies of those pure-hearted souls." *"He* (God) *it was,"* Bahá'u'lláh Himself declares, *"Who enabled Me to depart out of the city* (Baghdád), *clothed with such majesty as none, except the denier and the malicious, can fail to acknowledge."* These marks of homage and devotion continued to surround Him until He was installed in Constantinople. Mírzá Yaḥyá, while hurrying on foot, by his own choice, behind Bahá'u'lláh's carriage, on the day of His arrival in that city, was overheard by Nabíl to remark to Siyyid Muḥammad: "Had I not chosen to hide myself, had I revealed my identity, the honor accorded Him (Bahá'u'lláh) on this day would have been mine too."

The same tokens of devotion shown Bahá'u'lláh at the time of

His departure from His House, and later from the Garden of Riḍván, were repeated when, on the 20th of Dh͟hi'l-Qa'dih (May 9, 1863), accompanied by members of His family and twenty-six of His disciples, He left Firayját, His first stopping-place in the course of that journey. A caravan, consisting of fifty mules, a mounted guard of ten soldiers with their officer, and seven pairs of howdahs, each pair surmounted by four parasols, was formed, and wended its way, by easy stages, and in the space of no less than a hundred and ten days, across the uplands, and through the defiles, the woods, valleys and pastures, comprising the picturesque scenery of eastern Anatolia, to the port of Sámsún, on the Black Sea. At times on horseback, at times resting in the howdah reserved for His use, and which was oftentimes surrounded by His companions, most of whom were on foot, He, by virtue of the written order of Námiq Pás͟há, was accorded, as He traveled northward, in the path of spring, an enthusiastic reception by the válís, the mutiṣarrifs, the qá'im-maqáms, the mudírs, the s͟hayk͟hs, the muftís and qaḍís, the government officials and notables belonging to the districts through which He passed. In Karkúk, in Irbíl, in Mosul, where He tarried three days, in Níṣíbín, in Márdín, in Díyár-Bakr, where a halt of a couple of days was made, in K͟hárpút, in Sívas, as well as in other villages and hamlets, He would be met by a delegation immediately before His arrival, and would be accompanied, for some distance, by a similar delegation upon His departure. The festivities which, at some stations, were held in His honor, the food the villagers prepared and brought for His acceptance, the eagerness which time and again they exhibited in providing the means for His comfort, recalled the reverence which the people of Baghdád had shown Him on so many occasions.

"As we passed that morning through the town of Márdín," that same fellow-traveler relates, "we were preceded by a mounted escort of government soldiers, carrying their banners, and beating their drums in welcome. The mutiṣarrif, together with officials and notables, accompanied us, while men, women and children, crowding the housetops and filling the streets, awaited our arrival. With dignity and pomp we traversed that town, and resumed our journey, the mutiṣarrif and those with him escorting us for a considerable distance." "According to the unanimous testimony of those we met in the course of that journey," Nabíl has recorded in his narrative, "never before had they witnessed along this route, over which governors and mus͟hírs continually passed back and forth between Constantinople and Bag͟hdád, any one travel in such state, dispense such hospitality to all, and accord to each so great a share of his bounty." Sighting from His howdah the Black Sea, as He approached the port of Sámsún, Bahá'u'lláh, at the request of Mírzá Áqá Ján, revealed a Tablet, designated Lawḥ-i-Hawdaj (Tablet of the Howdah), which by such allusions as the *"Divine Touchstone," "the grievous and tormenting Mischief,"* reaffirmed and supplemented the dire predictions recorded in the recently revealed Tablet of the Holy Mariner.

In Sámsún the Chief Inspector of the entire province, extending from Baghdád to Constantinople, accompanied by several páshás, called on Him, showed Him the utmost respect, and was entertained by Him at luncheon. But seven days after His arrival, He, as foreshadowed in the Tablet of the Holy Mariner, was put on board a Turkish steamer and three days later was disembarked, at noon, together with His fellow-exiles, at the port of Constantinople, on the first of Rabí'u'l-Avval 1280 A.H. (August 16, 1863). In two special carriages, which awaited Him at the landing-stage He and His family drove to the house of Shamsí Big, the official who had been appointed by the government to entertain its guests, and who lived in the vicinity of the Khirqiy-i-Sharíf mosque. Later they were transferred to the more commodious house of Vísí Páshá, in the neighborhood of the mosque of Sulṭán Muḥammad.

With the arrival of Bahá'u'lláh at Constantinople, the capital of the Ottoman Empire and seat of the Caliphate (acclaimed by the Muḥammadans as "the Dome of Islam," but stigmatized by Him as the spot whereon the *"throne of tyranny"* had been established) the grimmest and most calamitous and yet the most glorious chapter in the history of the first Bahá'í century may be said to have opened. A period in which untold privations and unprecedented trials were mingled with the noblest spiritual triumphs was now commencing. The day-star of Bahá'u'lláh's ministry was about to reach its zenith. The most momentous years of the Heroic Age of His Dispensation were at hand. The catastrophic process, foreshadowed as far back as the year sixty by His Forerunner in the Qayyúmu'l-Asmá', was beginning to be set in motion.

Exactly two decades earlier the Bábí Revelation had been born in darkest Persia, in the city of Shíráz. Despite the cruel captivity to which its Author had been subjected, the stupendous claims He had voiced had been proclaimed by Him before a distinguished assemblage in Tabríz, the capital of Ádhirbáyján. In the hamlet of Badasht the Dispensation which His Faith had ushered in had been fearlessly inaugurated by the champions of His Cause. In the midst of the hopelessness and agony of the Síyáh-Chál of Ṭihrán, nine years later, that Revelation had, swiftly and mysteriously been brought to sudden fruition. The process of rapid deterioration in the fortunes of that Faith, which had gradually set in, and was alarmingly accelerated during the years of Bahá'u'lláh's withdrawal to Kurdistán, had, in a masterly fashion after His return from Sulaymáníyyih, been arrested and reversed. The ethical, the moral and doctrinal foundations of a nascent community had been subsequently, in the course of His sojourn in Baghdád, unassailably established. And finally, in the Garden of Riḍván, on the eve of His banishment to Constantinople, the ten-year delay, ordained by an inscrutable Providence, had been terminated through the Declaration of His Mission and the visible emergence of what was to become the nucleus of a world-embracing Fellowship. What now remained to be achieved was the proclamation, in the city of Adrianople, of that same Mission to the world's secular and ecclesiastical leaders, to be followed, in successive decades, by a further unfoldment, in the prison-fortress of 'Akká, of the principles and precepts constituting the bedrock of that Faith, by the formulation of the laws and ordinances designed to safeguard its integrity, by the establishment, immediately after His ascension, of the Covenant designed to preserve its unity and perpetuate its influence, by the prodigious and world-wide extension of its activities, under the guidance of 'Abdu'l-Bahá, the Center of that Covenant, and lastly, by the rise, in the Formative Age of that Faith, of its Administrative Order, the harbinger of its Golden Age and future glory.

This historic Proclamation was made at a time when the Faith was in the throes of a crisis of extreme violence, and it was in the main addressed to the kings of the earth, and to the Christian and Muslim ecclesiastical leaders who, by virtue of their immense prestige, ascendancy and authority, assumed an appalling and inescapable responsibility for the immediate destinies of their subjects and followers.

The initial phase of that Proclamation may be said to have opened in Constantinople with the communication (the text of which we, alas, do not possess) addressed by Bahá'u'lláh to Sulṭán 'Abdu'l-'Azíz himself, the self-styled vicar of the Prophet of Islám and the absolute ruler of a mighty empire. So potent, so august a personage was the first among the sovereigns of the world to receive the Divine Summons, and the first among Oriental monarchs to sustain the impact of God's retributive justice. The occasion for this communication was provided by the infamous edict the Sulṭán had promulgated, less than four months after the arrival of the exiles in his capital, banishing them, suddenly and without any justification whatsoever, in the depth of winter, and in the most humiliating circumstances, to Adrianople, situated on the extremities of his empire.

That fateful and ignominious decision, arrived at by the Sulṭán and his chief ministers, 'Álí Pá<u>sh</u>á and Fu'ád Pá<u>sh</u>á, was in no small degree attributable to the persistent intrigues of the Mu<u>sh</u>íru'd-Dawlih, Mírzá Ḥusayn <u>Kh</u>án, the Persian Ambassador to the Sublime Porte, denounced by Bahá'u'lláh as His *"calumniator,"* who awaited the first opportunity to strike at Him and the Cause of which He was now the avowed and recognized leader. This Ambassador was pressed continually by his government to persist in the policy of arousing against Bahá'u'lláh the hostility of the Turkish authorities. He was encouraged by the refusal of Bahá'u'lláh to follow the invariable practice of government guests, however highly placed, of calling in person, upon their arrival at the capital, on the <u>Sh</u>ay<u>kh</u>u'l-Islám, on the Ṣadr-i-A'ẓam, and on the Foreign Minister—Bahá'u'lláh did not even return the calls paid Him by several ministers, by Kamál Pá<u>sh</u>á and by a former Turkish envoy to the court of Persia. He was not deterred by Bahá'u'lláh's upright and independent attitude which contrasted so sharply with the mercenariness of the Persian princes who were wont, on their arrival, to "solicit at every door such allowances and gifts as they might obtain." He resented Bahá'u'lláh's unwillingness to present Himself at the Persian Embassy, and to repay the visit of its representative; and, being seconded, in his efforts, by his accomplice, Ḥájí Mírzá Ḥasan-i-Ṣafá, whom he instructed to circulate unfounded reports about Him, he succeeded through his official influence, as well as through his private intercourse with ecclesiastics, notables and government officials, in representing Bahá'u'lláh as a proud and arrogant person, Who regarded Himself as subject to no law, Who entertained designs inimical to all established authority, and Whose forwardness had precipitated the grave differences that had arisen between Himself and the Persian Government. Nor was he the only one who indulged in these nefarious schemes. Others, according to 'Abdu'l-Bahá, *"condemned and vilified"* the exiles, as *"a mischief to all the world,"* as *"destructive of treaties and covenants,"* as *"baleful to all lands"* and as *"deserving of every chastisement and punishment."*

No less a personage than the highly-respected brother-in-law of the Ṣadr-i-A'ẓam was commissioned to apprize the Captive of the edict pronounced against Him—an edict which evinced a virtual coalition of the Turkish and Persian imperial governments against a common adversary, and which in the end brought such tragic consequences upon the Sultanate, the Caliphate and the Qájár dynasty. Refused an audience by Bahá'u'lláh that envoy had to content himself with a presentation of his puerile observations and trivial arguments to 'Abdu'l-Bahá and Áqáy-i-Kalím, who were delegated to see him, and whom he informed that, after three days, he would return to receive the answer to the order he had been bidden to transmit.

That same day a Tablet, severely condemnatory in tone, was revealed by Bahá'u'lláh, was entrusted by Him, in a sealed envelope, on the following morning, to S͟hamsí Big, who was instructed to deliver it into the hands of 'Álí Pás͟há, and to say that it was sent down from God. "I know not what that letter contained," S͟hamsí Big subsequently informed Áqáy-i-Kalím, "for no sooner had the Grand Vizir perused it than he turned the color of a corpse, and remarked: 'It is as if the King of Kings were issuing his behest to his humblest vassal king and regulating his conduct.' So grievous was his condition that I backed out of his presence." *"Whatever action,"* Bahá'u'lláh, commenting on the effect that Tablet had produced, is reported to have stated, *"the ministers of the Sulṭán took against Us, after having become acquainted with its contents, cannot be regarded as unjustifiable. The acts they committed before its perusal, however, can have no justification."*

That Tablet, according to Nabíl, was of considerable length, opened with words directed to the sovereign himself, severely censured his ministers, exposed their immaturity and incompetence, and included passages in which the ministers themselves were addressed, in which they were boldly challenged, and sternly admonished not to pride themselves on their worldly possessions, nor foolishly seek the riches of which time would inexorably rob them.

Bahá'u'lláh was on the eve of His departure, which followed almost immediately upon the promulgation of the edict of His banishment, when, in a last and memorable interview with the aforementioned Háji Mírzá Ḥasan-i-Ṣafá, He sent the following message to the Persian Ambassador: *"What did it profit thee, and such as are like thee, to slay, year after year, so many of the oppressed, and to inflict upon them manifold afflictions, when they have increased a hundredfold, and ye find yourselves in complete bewilderment, knowing not how to relieve your minds of this oppressive thought. . . . His Cause transcends any and every plan ye devise. Know this much: Were all the governments on earth to unite and take My life and the lives of all who bear this Name, this Divine Fire would never be quenched. His Cause will rather encompass all the kings of the earth, nay all that hath been created from water and clay. . . . Whatever may yet befall Us, great shall be our gain, and manifest the loss wherewith they shall be afflicted."*

Pursuant to the peremptory orders issued for the immediate departure of the already twice banished exiles, Bahá'u'lláh, His family, and His companions, some riding in wagons, others mounted on pack animals, with their belongings piled in carts drawn by oxen, set out, accompanied by Turkish officers, on a cold December morning, amidst the weeping of the friends they were leaving behind, on their twelve-day journey, across a bleak and windswept country, to a city characterized by Bahá'u'lláh as *"the place which none entereth except such as have rebelled against the authority of the sovereign." "They expelled Us,"* is His own testimony in the Súriy-i-Múlúk, *"from thy city* (Constantinople) *with an abasement with which no abasement on earth can compare." "Neither My family, nor those who accompanied Me,"* He further states, *"had the necessary raiment to protect them from the cold in that freezing weather."* And again: *"The eyes of Our enemies wept over Us, and beyond them those of every discerning person."* "A banishment," laments Nabíl, "endured with such meekness that the pen sheddeth tears when recounting it, and the page is ashamed to bear its description." "A cold of such intensity," that same chronicler records, "prevailed that year, that nonagenarians could not recall its like. In some regions, in both Turkey and Persia, animals succumbed to its severity and perished in the snows. The upper reaches of the Euphrates, in Ma'dan-Nuqrih, were covered with ice for several days—an unprecedented phenomenon—while in Díyár-Bakr the river froze over for no less than forty days." "To obtain water from the springs," one of the exiles of Adrianople recounts, "a great fire had to be lighted in their immediate neighborhood, and kept burning for a couple of hours before they thawed out."

Traveling through rain and storm, at times even making night marches, the weary travelers, after brief halts at Kúchik-Chakmachih, Búyúk-Chakmachih, Salvarí, Birkás, and Bábá-Ískí, arrived at their destination, on the first of Rajab 1280 A.H. (December 12, 1863), and were lodged in the Khán-i-'Arab, a two-story caravanserai, near the house of 'Izzat-Áqá. Three days later, Bahá'u'lláh and His family were consigned to a house suitable only for summer habitation, in the Murádíyyih quarter, near the Takyiy-i-Mawlaví, and were moved again, after a week, to another house, in the vicinity of a mosque in that same neighborhood. About six months later they transferred to more commodious quarters, known as the house of Amru'lláh (House of God's command) situated on the northern side of the mosque of Sulṭán Salím.

Thus closes the opening scene of one of the most dramatic episodes in the ministry of Bahá'u'lláh. The curtain now rises on what is admittedly the most turbulent and critical period of the first Bahá'í century—a period that was destined to precede the most glorious phase of that ministry, the proclamation of His Message to the world and its rulers.

## CHAPTER X

# The Rebellion of Mírzá Yaḥyá and the Proclamation of Bahá'u'lláh's Mission in Adrianople

A twenty-year-old Faith had just begun to recover from a series of successive blows when a crisis of the first magnitude overtook it and shook it to its roots. Neither the tragic martyrdom of the Báb nor the ignominious attempt on the life of the sovereign, nor its bloody aftermath, nor Bahá'u'lláh's humiliating banishment from His native land, nor even His two-year withdrawal to Kurdistán, devastating though they were in their consequences, could compare in gravity with this first major internal convulsion which seized a newly rearisen community, and which threatened to cause an irreparable breach in the ranks of its members. More odious than the unrelenting hostility which Abú-Jahl, the relative of Muḥammad, had exhibited, more shameful than the betrayal of Jesus Christ by His disciple, Judas Iscariot, more perfidious than the conduct of the sons of Jacob towards Joseph their brother, more abhorrent than the deed committed by one of the sons of Noah, more infamous than even the criminal act perpetrated by Cain against Abel, the monstrous behavior of Mírzá Yaḥyá, one of the half-brothers of Bahá'u'lláh, the nominee of the Báb, and recognized chief of the Bábí community, brought in its wake a period of travail which left its mark on the fortunes of the Faith for no less than half a century. This supreme crisis Bahá'u'lláh Himself designated as the Ayyám-i-Shidád (Days of Stress), during which *"the most grievous veil"* was torn asunder, and the *"most great separation"* was irrevocably effected. It immensely gratified and emboldened its external enemies, both civil and ecclesiastical, played into their hands, and evoked their unconcealed derision. It perplexed and confused the friends and supporters of Bahá'u'lláh, and seriously damaged the prestige of the Faith in the eyes of its western admirers. It had been brewing ever since the early days of Bahá'u'lláh's sojourn in Baghdád, was temporarily suppressed by the creative forces which, under His as yet unproclaimed leadership, reanimated a disintegrating community, and finally broke out, in all its violence, in the years immediately preceding the proclamation of His Message. It brought incalculable sorrow to Bahá'u'lláh, visibly aged Him, and inflicted, through its repercussions, the heaviest blow ever sustained by Him in His lifetime. It was engineered throughout by the tortuous intrigues and incessant machinations of that same diabolical Siyyid Muḥammad, that vile whisperer who, disregarding Bahá'u'lláh's advice, had insisted on accompanying Him to Constantinople and Adrianople, and was now redoubling his efforts, with unrelaxing vigilance, to bring it to a head.

Mírzá Yaḥyá had, ever since the return of Bahá'u'lláh from Sulaymáníyyih, either chosen to maintain himself in an inglorious seclusion in his own house, or had withdrawn, whenever danger threatened, to such places of safety as Ḥillih and Basra. To the latter town he had fled, disguised as a Baghdád Jew, and become a shoe merchant. So great was his terror that he is reported to have said on one occasion: "Whoever claims to have seen me, or to have heard my voice, I pronounce an infidel." On being informed of Bahá'u'lláh's impending departure for Constantinople, he at first hid himself in the garden of Huvaydar, in the vicinity of Baghdád, meditating meanwhile on the advisability of fleeing either to Ábyssinia, India or some other country. Refusing to heed Bahá'u'lláh's advice to proceed to Persia, and there disseminate the writings of the Báb, he sent a certain Ḥájí Muḥammad Káẓim, who resembled him, to the government-house to procure for him a passport in the name of Mírzá 'Alíy-i-Kirmánsháhí, and left Baghdád, abandoning the writings there, and proceeded in disguise, accompanied by an Arab Bábí, named Ẓáhir, to Mosul, where he joined the exiles who were on their way to Constantinople.

A constant witness of the ever deepening attachment of the exiles to Bahá'u'lláh and of their amazing veneration for Him; fully aware of the heights to which his Brother's popularity had risen in Baghdád, in the course of His journey to Constantinople, and later through His association with the notables and governors of Adrianople; incensed by the manifold evidences of the courage, the dignity, and independence which that Brother had demonstrated in His dealings with the authorities in the capital; provoked by the numerous Tablets which the Author of a newly-established Dispensation had been ceaselessly revealing; allowing himself to be duped by the enticing prospects of unfettered leadership held out to him by Siyyid Muḥammad, the Antichrist of the Bahá'í Revelation, even as Muḥammad Sháh had been misled by the Antichrist of the Bábí Revelation, Ḥájí Mírzá Áqásí; refusing to be admonished by prominent members of the community who advised him, in writing, to exercise wisdom and restraint; forgetful of the kindness and counsels of Bahá'u'lláh, who, thirteen years his senior, had watched over his early youth and manhood; emboldened by the sin-covering eye of his Brother, Who, on so many occasions, had drawn a veil over his many crimes and follies, this arch-breaker of the Covenant of the Báb, spurred on by his mounting jealousy and impelled by his passionate love of leadership, was driven to perpetrate such acts as defied either concealment or toleration.

Irremediably corrupted through his constant association with Siyyid Muḥammad, that living embodiment of wickedness, cupidity and deceit, he had already in the absence of Bahá'u'lláh from Ba<u>gh</u>dád, and even after His return from Sulaymáníyyih, stained the annals of the Faith with acts of indelible infamy. His corruption, in scores of instances, of the text of the Báb's writings; the blasphemous addition he made to the formula of the a<u>dh</u>án by the introduction of a passage in which he identified himself with the Godhead; his insertion of references in those writings to a succession in which he nominated himself and his descendants as heirs of the Báb; the vacillation and apathy he had betrayed when informed of the tragic death which his Master had suffered; his condemnation to death of all the Mirrors of the Bábí Dispensation, though he himself was one of those Mirrors; his dastardly act in causing the murder of Dayyán, whom he feared and envied; his foul deed in bringing about, during the absence of Bahá'u'lláh from Ba<u>gh</u>dád, the assassination of Mírzá 'Alí-Akbar, the Báb's cousin; and, most heinous of all, his unspeakably repugnant violation, during that same period, of the honor of the Báb Himself—all these, as attested by Áqáy-i-Kalím, and reported by Nabíl in his Narrative, were to be thrown into a yet more lurid light by further acts the perpetration of which were to seal irretrievably his doom.

Desperate designs to poison Bahá'u'lláh and His companions, and thereby reanimate his own defunct leadership, began, approximately a year after their arrival in Adrianople, to agitate his mind. Well aware of the erudition of his half-brother, Áqáy-i-Kalím, in matters pertaining to medicine, he, under various pretexts, sought enlightenment from him regarding the effects of certain herbs and poisons, and then began, contrary to his wont, to invite Bahá'u'lláh to his home, where, one day, having smeared His tea-cup with a substance he had concocted, he succeeded in poisoning Him sufficiently to produce a serious illness which lasted no less than a month, and which was accompanied by severe pains and high fever, the aftermath of which left Bahá'u'lláh with a shaking hand till the end of His life.

So grave was His condition that a foreign doctor, named Shíshmán, was called in to attend Him. The doctor was so appalled by His livid hue that he deemed His case hopeless, and, after having fallen at His feet, retired from His presence without prescribing a remedy. A few days later that doctor fell ill and died. Prior to his death Bahá'u'lláh had intimated that doctor Shíshmán had sacrificed his life for Him. To Mírzá Áqá Ján, sent by Bahá'u'lláh to visit him, the doctor had stated that God had answered his prayers, and that after his death a certain Dr. Chúpán, whom he knew to be reliable, should, whenever necessary, be called in his stead.

On another occasion this same Mírzá Yaḥyá had, according to the testimony of one of his wives, who had temporarily deserted him and revealed the details of the above-mentioned act, poisoned the well which provided water for the family and companions of Bahá'u'lláh, in consequence of which the exiles manifested strange symptoms of illness. He even had, gradually and with great circumspection, disclosed to one of the companions, Ustád Muḥammad-'Alíy-i-Salmání, the barber, on whom he had lavished great marks of favor, his wish that he, on some propitious occasion, when attending Bahá'u'lláh in His bath, should assassinate Him. "So enraged was Ustád Muḥammad-'Alí," Áqáy-i-Kalím, recounting this episode to Nabíl in Adrianople, has stated, "when apprized of this proposition, that he felt a strong desire to kill Mírzá Yaḥyá on the spot, and would have done so but for his fear of Bahá'u'lláh's displeasure. I happened to be the first person he encountered as he came out of the bath weeping. . . . I eventually succeeded, after much persuasion, in inducing him to return to the bath and complete his unfinished task." Though ordered subsequently by Bahá'u'lláh not to divulge this occurrence to any one, the barber was unable to hold his peace and betrayed the secret, plunging thereby the community into great consternation. *"When the secret nursed in his* (Mírzá Yaḥyá) *bosom was revealed by God,"* Bahá'u'lláh Himself affirms, *"he disclaimed such an intention, and imputed it to that same servant* (Ustád Muḥammad-'Alí)."

The moment had now arrived for Him Who had so recently, both verbally and in numerous Tablets, revealed the implications of the claims He had advanced, to acquaint formally the one who was the nominee of the Báb with the character of His Mission. Mírzá Áqá Ján was accordingly commissioned to bear to Mírzá Yaḥyá the newly revealed Súriy-i-Amr, which unmistakably affirmed those claims, to read aloud to him its contents, and demand an unequivocal and conclusive reply. Mírzá Yaḥyá's request for a one day respite, during which he could meditate his answer, was granted. The only reply, however, that was forthcoming was a counter-declaration, specifying the hour and the minute in which he had been made the recipient of an independent Revelation, necessitating the unqualified submission to him of the peoples of the earth in both the East and the West.

So presumptuous an assertion, made by so perfidious an adversary to the envoy of the Bearer of so momentous a Revelation was the signal for the open and final rupture between Bahá'u'lláh and Mírzá Yaḥyá—a rupture that marks one of the darkest dates in Bahá'í history. Wishing to allay the fierce animosity that blazed in the bosom of His enemies, and to assure to each one of the exiles a complete freedom to choose between Him and them, Bahá'u'lláh withdrew with His family to the house of Riḍá Big (S͟havvál 22, 1282 A.H.), which was rented by His order, and refused, for two months, to associate with either friend or stranger, including His own companions. He instructed Áqáy-i-Kalím to divide all the furniture, bedding, clothing and utensils that were to be found in His home, and send half to the house of Mírzá Yaḥyá; to deliver to him certain relics he had long coveted, such as the seals, rings, and manuscripts in the handwriting of the Báb; and to insure that he received his full share of the allowance fixed by the government for the maintenance of the exiles and their families. He, moreover, directed Áqáy-i-Kalím to order to attend to Mírza Yaḥyá's shopping, for several hours a day, any one of the companions whom he himself might select, and to assure him that whatever would henceforth be received in his name from Persia would be delivered into his own hands.

"That day," Áqáy-i-Kalím is reported to have informed Nabíl, "witnessed a most great commotion. All the companions lamented in their separation from the Blessed Beauty." "Those days," is the written testimony of one of those companions, "were marked by tumult and confusion. We were sore-perplexed, and greatly feared lest we be permanently deprived of the bounty of His presence."

This grief and perplexity were, however, destined to be of short duration. The calumnies with which both Mírzá Yaḥyá and Siyyid Muḥammad now loaded their letters, which they disseminated in Persia and 'Iráq, as well as the petitions, couched in obsequious language, which the former had addressed to K͟hurs͟híd Pás͟há, the governor of Adrianople, and to his assistant 'Azíz Pás͟há, impelled Bahá'u'lláh to emerge from His retirement. He was soon after informed that this same brother had despatched one of his wives to the government house to complain that her husband had been cheated of his rights, and that her children were on the verge of starvation—an accusation that spread far and wide and, reaching Constantinople, became, to Bahá'u'lláh's profound distress, the subject of excited discussion and injurious comment in circles that had previously been greatly impressed by the high standard which His noble and dignified behavior had set in that city. Siyyid Muḥammad journeyed to the capital, begged the Persian Ambassador, the Mus͟hír'd-Dawlih, to allot Mírzá Yaḥyá and himself a stipend, accused Bahá'u'lláh of sending an agent to assassinate Náṣiri'd-Dín-S͟háh, and spared no effort to heap abuse and calumny on One Who had, for so long and so patiently, forborne with him, and endured in silence the enormities of which he had been guilty.

After a stay of about one year in the house of Riḍá Big Bahá'u'lláh returned to the house He had occupied before His withdrawal from His companions, and thence, after three months, He transferred His residence to the house of 'Izzat Áqá, in which He continued to live until His departure from Adrianople. It was in this house, in the month of Jamádíyu'l-Avval 1284 A.H. (Sept. 1867) that an event of the utmost significance occurred, which completely discomfited Mírzá Yaḥyá and his supporters, and proclaimed to friend and foe alike Bahá'u'lláh's triumph over them. A certain Mír Muḥammad, a Bábí of S͟híráz, greatly resenting alike the claims and the cowardly seclusion of Mírzá Yaḥyá, succeeded in forcing Siyyid Muḥammad to induce him to meet Bahá'u'lláh face to face, so that a discrimination might be publicly effected between the true and the false. Foolishly assuming that his illustrious Brother would never countenance such a proposition, Mírzá Yaḥyá appointed the mosque of Sulṭán Salím as the place for their encounter. No sooner had Bahá'u'lláh been informed of this arrangement than He set forth, on foot, in the heat of midday, and accompanied by this same Mír Muḥammad, for the afore-mentioned mosque, which was situated in a distant part of the city, reciting, as He walked, through the streets and markets, verses, in a voice and in a manner that greatly astonished those who saw and heard Him.

"O *Muḥammad!*", are some of the words He uttered on that memorable occasion, as testified by Himself in a Tablet, "*He Who is the Spirit hath, verily, issued from His habitation, and with Him have come forth the souls of God's chosen ones and the realities of His Messengers. Behold, then, the dwellers of the realms on high above Mine head, and all the testimonies of the Prophets in My grasp.*

*Say: Were all the divines, all the wise men, all the kings and rulers on earth to gather together, I, in very truth, would confront them, and would proclaim the verses of God, the Sovereign, the Almighty, the All-Wise. I am He Who feareth no one, though all who are in heaven and all who are on earth rise up against Me. . . . This is Mine hand which God hath turned white for all the worlds to behold. This is My staff; were We to cast it down, it would, of a truth, swallow up all created things."* Mír Muḥammad, who had been sent ahead to announce Bahá'u'lláh's arrival, soon returned, and informed Him that he who had challenged His authority wished, owing to unforeseen circumstances, to postpone for a day or two the interview. Upon His return to His house Bahá'u'lláh revealed a Tablet, wherein He recounted what had happened, fixed the time for the postponed interview, sealed the Tablet with His seal, entrusted it to Nabíl, and instructed him to deliver it to one of the new believers, Mullá Muḥammad-i-Tabrízí, for the information of Siyyid Muḥammad, who was in the habit of frequenting that believer's shop. It was arranged to demand from Siyyid Muḥammad, ere the delivery of that Tablet, a sealed note pledging Mírzá Yaḥyá, in the event of failing to appear at the trysting-place, to affirm in writing that his claims were false. Siyyid Muḥammad promised that he would produce the next day the document required, and though Nabíl, for three successive days, waited in that shop for the reply, neither did the Siyyid appear, nor was such a note sent by him. That undelivered Tablet, Nabíl, recording twenty-three years later this historic episode in his chronicle, affirms was still in his possession, "as fresh as the day on which the Most Great Branch had penned it, and the seal of the Ancient Beauty had sealed and adorned it," a tangible and irrefutable testimony to Bahá'u'lláh's established ascendancy over a routed opponent.

Bahá'u'lláh's reaction to this most distressful episode in His ministry was, as already observed, characterized by acute anguish. *"He who for months and years,"* He laments, *"I reared with the hand of loving-kindness hath risen to take My life." "The cruelties inflicted by My oppressors,"* He wrote, in allusion to these perfidious enemies, *"have bowed Me down, and turned My hair white. Shouldst thou present thyself before My throne, thou wouldst fail to recognize the Ancient Beauty, for the freshness of His countenance is altered, and its brightness hath faded, by reason of the oppression of the infidels." "By God!"* He cries out, *"No spot is left on My body that hath not been touched by the spears of thy machinations."* And again: *"Thou hast perpetrated against thy Brother what no man hath perpetrated against another.*" "*What hath proceeded from thy pen,*" He, furthermore, has affirmed, "*hath caused the Countenances of Glory to be prostrated upon the dust, hath rent in twain the Veil of Grandeur in the Sublime Paradise, and lacerated the hearts of the favored ones established upon the loftiest seats.*" And yet, in the Kitáb-i-Aqdas, a forgiving Lord assures this same brother, this "*source of perversion,*" "*from whose own soul the winds of passion had risen and blown upon him,*" to "*fear not because of thy deeds,*" bids him "*return unto God, humble, submissive and lowly,*" and affirms that "*He will put away from thee thy sins,*" and that "*thy Lord is the Forgiving, the Mighty, the All-Merciful.*"

The "*Most Great Idol*" had at the bidding and through the power of Him Who is the Fountain-head of the Most Great Justice been cast out of the community of the Most Great Name, confounded, abhorred and broken. Cleansed from this pollution, delivered from this horrible possession, God's infant Faith could now forge ahead, and, despite the turmoil that had convulsed it, demonstrate its capacity to fight further battles, capture loftier heights, and win mightier victories.

A temporary breach had admittedly been made in the ranks of its supporters. Its glory had been eclipsed, and its annals stained forever. Its name, however, could not be obliterated, its spirit was far from broken, nor could this so-called schism tear its fabric asunder. The Covenant of the Báb, to which reference has already been made, with its immutable truths, incontrovertible prophecies, and repeated warnings, stood guard over that Faith, insuring its integrity, demonstrating its incorruptibility, and perpetuating its influence.

Though He Himself was bent with sorrow, and still suffered from the effects of the attempt on His life, and though He was well aware a further banishment was probably impending, yet, undaunted by the blow which His Cause had sustained, and the perils with which it was encompassed, Bahá'u'lláh arose with matchless power, even before the ordeal was overpast, to proclaim the Mission with which He had been entrusted to those who, in East and West, had the reins of supreme temporal authority in their grasp. The day-star of His Revelation was, through this very Proclamation, destined to shine in its meridian glory, and His Faith manifest the plenitude of its divine power.

A period of prodigious activity ensued which, in its repercussions, outshone the vernal years of Bahá'u'lláh's ministry. "Day and night," an eye-witness has written, "the Divine verses were raining down in such number that it was impossible to record them. Mírzá Áqá Ján wrote them as they were dictated, while the Most Great Branch was continually occupied in transcribing them. There was not a moment to spare." "A number of secretaries," Nabíl has testified, "were busy day and night and yet they were unable to cope with the task. Among them was Mírzá Báqir-i-S͟hírází. . . . He alone transcribed no less than two thousand verses every day. He labored during six or seven months. Every month the equivalent of several volumes would be transcribed by him and sent to Persia. About twenty volumes, in his fine penmanship, he left behind as a remembrance for Mírzá Áqá Ján." Bahá'u'lláh, Himself, referring to the verses revealed by Him, has written: *"Such are the outpourings . . . from the clouds of Divine Bounty that within the space of an hour the equivalent of a thousand verses hath been revealed." "So great is the grace vouchsafed in this day that in a single day and night, were an amanuensis capable of accomplishing it to be found, the equivalent of the Persian Bayán would be sent down from the heaven of Divine holiness." "I swear by God!"* He, in another connection has affirmed, *"In those days the equivalent of all that hath been sent down aforetime unto the Prophets hath been revealed." "That which hath already been revealed in this land* (Adrianople)," He, furthermore, referring to the copiousness of His writings, has declared, *"secretaries are incapable of transcribing. It has, therefore, remained for the most part untranscribed."*

Already in the very midst of that grievous crisis, and even before it came to a head, Tablets unnumbered were streaming from the pen of Bahá'u'lláh, in which the implications of His newly-asserted claims were fully expounded. The Súriy-i-Amr, the Lawḥ-i-Nuqṭih, the Lawḥ-i-Aḥmad, the Súriy-i-Aṣḥáb, the Lawḥ-i-Sayyáḥ, the Súriy-i-Damm, the Súriy-i-Ḥajj, the Lawḥu'r-Rúḥ, the Lawḥu'r-Riḍván, the Lawḥu't-Tuqá were among the Tablets which His pen had already set down when He transferred His residence to the house of 'Izzat Áqá. Almost immediately after the "Most Great Separation" had been effected, the weightiest Tablets associated with His sojourn in Adrianople were revealed. The Súriy-i-Múlúk, the most momentous Tablet revealed by Bahá'u'lláh (Súrih of Kings) in which He, for the first time, directs His words collectively to the entire company of the monarchs of East and West, and in which the Sulṭán of Turkey, and his ministers, the kings of Christendom, the French and Persian Ambassadors accredited to the Sublime Porte, the Muslim ecclesiastical leaders in Constantinople, its wise men and inhabitants, the people of Persia and the philosophers of the world are separately addressed; the Kitáb-i-Badí‘, His apologia, written to refute the accusations levelled against Him by Mírzá Mihdíy-i-Ra<u>sh</u>tí, corresponding to the Kitáb-i-Íqán, revealed in defense of the Bábí Revelation; the Munájátháy-i-Ṣíyám (Prayers for Fasting), written in anticipation of the Book of His Laws; the first Tablet to Napoleon III, in which the Emperor of the French is addressed and the sincerity of his professions put to the test; the Lawḥ-i-Sulṭán, His detailed epistle to Náṣiri'd-Dín <u>Sh</u>áh, in which the aims, purposes and principles of His Faith are expounded and the validity of His Mission demonstrated; the Súriy-i-Ra'ís, begun in the village of Ká<u>sh</u>ánih on His way to Gallipoli, and completed shortly after at Gyáwur-Kyuy—these may be regarded not only as the most outstanding among the innumerable Tablets revealed in Adrianople, but as occupying a foremost position among all the writings of the Author of the Bahá'í Revelation.

In His message to the kings of the earth, Bahá'u'lláh, in the Súriy-i-Múlúk, discloses the character of His Mission; exhorts them to embrace His Message; affirms the validity of the Báb's Revelation; reproves them for their indifference to His Cause; enjoins them to be just and vigilant, to compose their differences and reduce their armaments; expatiates on His afflictions; commends the poor to their care; warns them that *"Divine chastisement"* will *"assail"* them *"from every direction,"* if they refuse to heed His counsels, and prophesies His *"triumph upon earth"* though no king be found who would turn his face towards Him.

The kings of Christendom, more specifically, Bahá'u'lláh, in that same Tablet, censures for having failed to *"welcome"* and *"draw nigh"* unto Him Who is the *"Spirit of Truth,"* and for having persisted in *"disporting"* themselves with their *"pastimes and fancies,"* and declares to them that they *"shall be called to account"* for their doings, *"in the presence of Him Who shall gather together the entire creation."*

He bids Sulṭán 'Abdu'l-'Azíz *"hearken to the speech . . . of Him Who unerringly treadeth the Straight Path"*; exhorts him to direct in person the affairs of his people, and not to repose confidence in unworthy ministers; admonishes him not to rely on his treasures, nor to *"overstep the bounds of moderation"* but to deal with his subjects with *"undeviating justice"*; and acquaints him with the overwhelming burden of His own tribulations. In that same Tablet He asserts

His innocence and His loyalty to the Sulṭán and his ministers; describes the circumstances of His banishment from the capital; and assures him of His prayers to God on his behalf.

To this same Sulṭán He, moreover, as attested by the Súriy-i-Ra'ís, transmitted, while in Gallipoli, a verbal message through a Turkish officer named 'Umar, requesting the sovereign to grant Him a ten minute interview, *"so that he may demand whatsoever he would deem to be a sufficient testimony and would regard as proof of the veracity of Him Who is the Truth,"* adding that *"should God enable Him to produce it, let him, then, release these wronged ones and leave them to themselves."*

To Napoleon III Bahá'u'lláh addressed a specific Tablet, which was forwarded through one of the French ministers to the Emperor, in which He dwelt on the sufferings endured by Himself and His followers; avowed their innocence; reminded him of his two pronouncements on behalf of the oppressed and the helpless; and, desiring to test the sincerity of his motives, called upon him to *"inquire into the condition of such as have been wronged,"* and *"extend his care to the weak,"* and look upon Him and His fellow-exiles *"with the eye of loving-kindness."*

To Náṣiri'd-Dín Sháh He revealed a Tablet, the lengthiest epistle to any single sovereign, in which He testified to the unparalleled severity of the troubles that had touched Him; recalled the sovereign's recognition of His innocence on the eve of His departure for 'Iráq; adjured him to rule with justice; described God's summons to Himself to arise and proclaim His Message; affirmed the disinterestedness of His counsels; proclaimed His belief in the unity of God and in His Prophets; uttered several prayers on the Sháh's behalf; justified His own conduct in 'Iráq; stressed the beneficent influence of His teachings; and laid special emphasis on His condemnation of all forms of violence and mischief. He, moreover, in that same Tablet, demonstrated the validity of His Mission; expressed the wish to be *"brought face to face with the divines of the age, and produce proofs and testimonies in the presence of His Majesty,"* which would establish the truth of His Cause; exposed the perversity of the ecclesiastical leaders in His own days, as well as in the days of Jesus Christ and of Muḥammad; prophesied that His sufferings will be followed by the *"outpourings of a supreme mercy"* and by an *"overflowing prosperity"*; drew a parallel between the afflictions that had befallen His kindred and those endured by the relatives of the Prophet Muḥammad; expatiated on the instability of human affairs; depicted the city to which He was about to be banished; foreshadowed the future abasement of the 'ulamás; and concluded with yet another expression of hope that the sovereign might be assisted by God to *"aid His Faith and turn towards His justice."*

To 'Álí Pá<u>sh</u>á, the Grand Vizir, Bahá'u'lláh addressed the Súriy-i-Ra'ís. In this He bids him *"hearken to the voice of God"*; declares that neither his *"grunting,"* nor the *"barking"* of those around him, nor *"the hosts of the world"* can withhold the Almighty from achieving His purpose; accuses him of having perpetrated that which has caused *"the Apostle of God to lament in the most sublime Paradise,"* and of having conspired with the Persian Ambassador to harm Him; forecasts *"the manifest loss"* in which he would soon find himself; glorifies the Day of His own Revelation; prophesies that this Revelation will *"erelong encompass the earth and all that dwell therein,"* and that the *"Land of Mystery* (Adrianople) *and what is beside it . . . shall pass out of the hands of the King, and commotions shall appear, and the voice of lamentation shall be raised, and the evidences of mischief shall be revealed on all sides"*; identifies that same Revelation with the Revelations of Moses and of Jesus; recalls the *"arrogance"* of the Persian Emperor in the days of Muḥammad, the *"transgression"* of Pharaoh in the days of Moses, and of the *"impiety"* of Nimrod in the days of Abraham; and proclaims His purpose to *"quicken the world and unite all its peoples."*

The ministers of the Sulṭán, He, in the Súriy-i-Múlúk, reprimands for their conduct, in passages in which He challenges the soundness of their principles, predicts that they will be punished for their acts, denounces their pride and injustice, asserts His integrity and detachment from the vanities of the world, and proclaims His innocence.

The French Ambassador accredited to the Sublime Porte, He, in that same Súrih, rebukes for having combined with the Persian Ambassador against Him; reminds him of the counsels of Jesus Christ, as recorded in the Gospel of St. John; warns him that he will be held answerable for the things his hands have wrought; and counsels him, together with those like him, not to deal with any one as he has dealt with Him.

To the Persian Ambassador in Constantinople, He, in that same Tablet, addresses lengthy passages in which He exposes his delusions and calumnies, denounces his injustice and the injustice of his countrymen, assures him that He harbors no ill-will against him, declares that, should he realize the enormity of his deed, he would mourn all the days of his life, affirms that he will persist till his death in his heedlessness, justifies His own conduct in Ṭihrán and in 'Iráq, and bears witness to the corruption of the Persian minister in Baghdád and to his collusion with this minister.

To the entire company of the ecclesiastical leaders of Sunní Islám in Constantinople He addresses a specific message in the same Súriy-i-Múlúk in which He denounces them as heedless and spiritually dead; reproaches them for their pride and for failing to seek His presence; unveils to them the full glory and significance of His Mission; affirms that their leaders, had they been alive, would have *"circled around Him"*; condemns them as *"worshippers of names"* and lovers of leadership; and avows that God will find naught acceptable from them unless they *"be made new"* in His estimation.

To the wise men of the City of Constantinople and the philosophers of the world He devotes the concluding passages of the Súriy-i-Múlúk, in which He cautions them not to wax proud before God; reveals to them the essence of true wisdom; stresses the importance of faith and upright conduct; rebukes them for having failed to seek enlightenment from Him; and counsels them not to *"overstep the bounds of God,"* nor turn their gaze towards the *"ways of men and their habits."*

To the inhabitants of Constantinople He, in that same Tablet, declares that He *"feareth no one except God,"* that He speaks *"naught except at His* (God) *bidding,"* that He follows naught save God's truth, that He found the governors and elders of the city as *"children gathered about and disporting themselves with clay,"* and that He perceived no one sufficiently mature to acquire the truths which God had taught Him. He bids them take firm hold on the precepts of God; warns them not to wax proud before God and His loved ones; recalls the tribulations, and extols the virtues, of the Imám Ḥusayn; prays that He Himself may suffer similar afflictions; prophesies that erelong God will raise up a people who will recount His troubles and demand the restitution of His rights from His oppressors; and calls upon them to give ear to His words, and return unto God and repent.

And finally, addressing the people of Persia, He, in that same Tablet, affirms that were they to put Him to death God will assuredly raise up One in His stead, and asserts that the Almighty will *"perfect His light"* though they, in their secret hearts, abhor it.

So weighty a proclamation, at so critical a period, by the Bearer of so sublime a Message, to the kings of the earth, Muslim and Christian alike, to ministers and ambassadors, to the ecclesiastical heads of Sunní Islám, to the wise men and inhabitants of Constantinople—the seat of both the Sultanate and the Caliphate—to the philosophers of the world and the people of Persia, is not to be regarded as the only outstanding event associated with Bahá'u'lláh's sojourn in Adrianople. Other developments and happenings of great, though lesser, significance must be noted in these pages, if we would justly esteem the importance of this agitated and most momentous phase of Bahá'u'lláh's ministry.

It was at this period, and as a direct consequence of the rebellion and appalling downfall of Mírzá Yaḥyá, that certain disciples of Bahá'u'lláh (who may well rank among the *"treasures"* promised Him by God when bowed down with chains in the Síyáh-C͟hál of Ṭihrán), including among them one of the Letters of the Living, some survivors of the struggle of Ṭabarsí, and the erudite Mírzá Aḥmad-i-Azg͟handí, arose to defend the newborn Faith, to refute, in numerous and detailed apologies, as their Master had done in the Kitáb-i-Badí', the arguments of His opponents, and to expose their odious deeds. It was at this period that the limits of the Faith were enlarged, when its banner was permanently planted in the Caucasus by the hand of Mullá Abú-Ṭálib and others whom Nabíl had converted, when its first Egyptian center was established at the time when Siyyid Ḥusayn-i-Kás͟hání and Ḥájí Báqir-i-Kás͟hání took up their residence in that country, and when to the lands already warmed and illuminated by the early rays of God's Revelation—'Iráq, Turkey and Persia—Syria was added. It was in this period that the greeting of *"Alláh-u-Abhá"* superseded the old salutation of *"Alláh-u-Akbar,"* and was simultaneously adopted in Persia and Adrianople, the first to use it in the former country, at the suggestion of Nabíl, being Mullá Muḥammad-i-Fúrúg͟hí, one of the defenders of the Fort of S͟hayk͟h Ṭabarsí. It was in this period that the phrase *"the people of the Bayán,"* now denoting the followers of Mírzá Yaḥyá, was discarded, and was supplanted by the term *"the people of Bahá."* It was during those days that Nabíl, recently honored with the title of Nabíl-i-A'ẓam, in a Tablet specifically addressed to him, in which he was bidden to *"deliver the Message"* of his Lord *"to East and West,"* arose, despite intermittent persecutions, to tear asunder the *"most grievous veil,"* to implant the love of an adored Master in the hearts of His countrymen, and to champion the Cause which his Beloved had, under such tragic conditions, proclaimed. It was during those same days that Bahá'u'lláh instructed this same Nabíl to recite on His behalf the two newly revealed Tablets of the Pilgrimage, and to perform, in His stead, the rites prescribed in them, when visiting the Báb's House in Shíráz and the Most Great House in Baghdád—an act that marks the inception of one of the holiest observances, which, in a later period, the Kitáb-i-Aqdas was to formally establish. It was during this period that the "Prayers of Fasting" were revealed by Bahá'u'lláh, in anticipation of the Law which that same Book was soon to promulgate. It was, too, during the days of Bahá'u'lláh's banishment to Adrianople that a Tablet was addressed by Him to Mullá 'Alí-Akbar-i-Shahmírzádí and Jamál-i-Burújirdí, two of His well-known followers in Ṭihrán, instructing them to transfer, with the utmost secrecy, the remains of the Báb from the Imám-Zádih Ma'ṣúm, where they were concealed, to some other place of safety—an act which was subsequently proved to have been providential, and which may be regarded as marking another stage in the long and laborious transfer of those remains to the heart of Mt. Carmel, and to the spot which He, in His instructions to 'Abdu'l-Bahá, was later to designate. It was during that period that the Súriy-i-Ghuṣn (Súrih of the Branch) was revealed, in which 'Abdu'l-Bahá's future station is foreshadowed, and in which He is eulogized as the *"Branch of Holiness,"* the *"Limb of the Law of God,"* the *"Trust of God," "sent down in the form of a human temple"*—a Tablet which may well be regarded as the harbinger of the rank which was to be bestowed upon Him, in the Kitáb-i-Aqdas, and which was to be later elucidated and confirmed in the Book of His Covenant. And finally, it was during that period that the first pilgrimages were made to the residence of One Who was now the visible Center of a newly-established Faith—pilgrimages which by reason of their number and nature, an alarmed government in Persia was first impelled to restrict, and later to prohibit, but which were the precursors of the converging streams of Pilgrims who, from East and West, at first under perilous and arduous circumstances, were to direct their steps towards the prison-fortress of 'Akká—pilgrimages which were to culminate in the historic arrival of a royal convert at the foot of Mt. Carmel, who, at the very threshold of a longed-for and much advertised pilgrimage, was so cruelly thwarted from achieving her purpose.

These notable developments, some synchronizing with, and others flowing from, the proclamation of the Faith of Bahá'u'lláh, and from the internal convulsion which the Cause had undergone, could not escape the attention of the external enemies of the Movement, who were bent on exploiting to the utmost every crisis which the folly of its friends or the perfidy of renegades might at any time precipitate. The thick clouds had hardly been dissipated by the sudden outburst of the rays of a Sun, now shining from its meridian, when the darkness of another catastrophe—the last the Author of that Faith was destined to suffer—fell upon it, blackening its firmament and subjecting it to one of the severest trials it had as yet experienced.

Emboldened by the recent ordeals with which Bahá'u'lláh had been so cruelly afflicted, these enemies, who had been momentarily quiescent, began to demonstrate afresh, and in a number of ways, the latent animosity they nursed in their hearts. A persecution, varying in the degree of its severity, began once more to break out in various countries. In Ádhirbáyján and Zanján, in Níshápúr and Ṭihrán, the adherents of the Faith were either imprisoned, vilified, penalized, tortured or put to death. Among the sufferers may be singled out the intrepid Najaf-'Alíy-i-Zanjání, a survivor of the struggle of Zanján, and immortalized in the "Epistle to the Son of the Wolf," who, bequeathing the gold in his possession to his executioner, was heard to shout aloud "Yá Rabbíya'l-Abhá" before he was beheaded. In Egypt, a greedy and vicious consul-general extorted no less than a hundred thousand túmáns from a wealthy Persian convert, named Ḥájí Abu'l-Qásim-i-Shírází; arrested Ḥájí Mírzá Ḥaydar-'Alí and six of his fellow-believers, and instigated their condemnation to a nine year exile in Khartúm, confiscating all the writings in their possession, and then threw into prison Nabíl, whom Bahá'u'lláh had sent to appeal to the Khedive on their behalf. In Baghdád and Káẓimayn indefatigable enemies, watching their opportunity, subjected Bahá'u'lláh's faithful supporters to harsh and ignominious treatment; savagely disemboweled 'Abdu'r-Rasúl-i-Qumí, as he was carrying water in a skin, at the hour of dawn, from the river to the Most Great House, and banished, amidst scenes of public derision, about seventy companions to Mosul, including women and children.

No less active were Mírzá Ḥusayn-Khán, the Mushíru'd-Dawlih, and his associates, who, determined to take full advantage of the troubles that had recently visited Bahá'u'lláh, arose to encompass His destruction. The authorities in the capital were incensed by the esteem shown Him by the governor Muḥammad Páshá-y-i-Qibrisí, a former Grand Vizir, and his successors Sulaymán Páshá, of the Qádiríyyih Order, and particularly Khurshíd Páshá, who, openly and on many occasions, frequented the house of Bahá'u'lláh, entertained

Him in the days of Ramaḍán, and evinced a fervent admiration for 'Abdu'l-Bahá. They were well aware of the challenging tone Bahá'u'lláh had assumed in some of His newly revealed Tablets, and conscious of the instability prevailing in their own country. They were disturbed by the constant comings and goings of pilgrims in Adrianople, and by the exaggerated reports of Fu'ád Pás͟há, who had recently passed through on a tour of inspection. The petitions of Mírzá Yaḥyá which reached them through Siyyid Muḥammad, his agent, had provoked them. Anonymous letters (written by this same Siyyid and by an accomplice, Áqá Ján, serving in the Turkish artillery) which perverted the writings of Bahá'u'lláh, and which accused Him of having conspired with Bulgarian leaders and certain ministers of European powers to achieve, with the help of some thousands of His followers, the conquest of Constantinople, had filled their breasts with alarm. And now, encouraged by the internal dissensions which had shaken the Faith, and irritated by the evident esteem in which Bahá'u'lláh was held by the consuls of foreign powers stationed in Adrianople, they determined to take drastic and immediate action which would extirpate that Faith, isolate its Author and reduce Him to powerlessness. The indiscretions committed by some of its over-zealous followers, who had arrived in Constantinople, no doubt, aggravated an already acute situation.

The fateful decision was eventually arrived at to banish Bahá'u'lláh to the penal colony of 'Akká, and Mírzá Yahyá to Famagusta in Cyprus. This decision was embodied in a strongly worded Farmán, issued by Sulṭán 'Abdu'l-'Azíz. The companions of Bahá'u'lláh, who had arrived in the capital, together with a few who later joined them, as well as Áqá Ján, the notorious mischief-maker, were arrested, interrogated, deprived of their papers and flung into prison. The members of the community in Adrianople were, several times, summoned to the governorate to ascertain their number, while rumors were set afloat that they were to be dispersed and banished to different places or secretly put to death.

Suddenly, one morning, the house of Bahá'u'lláh was surrounded by soldiers, sentinels were posted at its gates, His followers were again summoned by the authorities, interrogated, and ordered to make ready for their departure. *"The loved ones of God and His kindred,"* is Bahá'u'lláh's testimony in the Súriy-i-Ra'ís, *"were left on the first night without food . . . The people surrounded the house, and Muslims and Christians wept over Us . . . We perceived that the weeping of the people of the Son* (Christians) *exceeded the weeping of others—*

*a sign for such as ponder.*" "A great tumult seized the people," writes Áqá Riḍá, one of the stoutest supporters of Bahá'u'lláh, exiled with him all the way from Baghdád to 'Akká, "All were perplexed and full of regret . . . Some expressed their sympathy, others consoled us, and wept over us . . . Most of our possessions were auctioned at half their value." Some of the consuls of foreign powers called on Bahá'u'lláh, and expressed their readiness to intervene with their respective governments on His behalf—suggestions for which He expressed appreciation, but which He firmly declined. "*The consuls of that city* (Adrianople) *gathered in the presence of this Youth at the hour of His departure,*" He Himself has written, "*and expressed their desire to aid Him. They, verily, evinced towards Us manifest affection.*"

The Persian Ambassador promptly informed the Persian consuls in 'Iráq and Egypt that the Turkish government had withdrawn its protection from the Bábís, and that they were free to treat them as they pleased. Several pilgrims, among whom was Ḥájí Muḥammad Ismá'íl-i-Káshání, surnamed Anís in the Lawḥ-i-Ra'ís, had, in the meantime, arrived in Adrianople, and had to depart to Gallipoli, without even beholding the face of their Master. Two of the companions were forced to divorce their wives, as their relatives refused to allow them to go into exile. Khurshíd Páshá, who had already several times categorically denied the written accusations sent him by the authorities in Constantinople, and had interceded vigorously on behalf of Bahá'u'lláh, was so embarrassed by the action of his government that he decided to absent himself when informed of His immediate departure from the city, and instructed the Registrar to convey to Him the purport of the Sulṭán's edict. Ḥájí Ja'far-i-Tabrízí, one of the believers, finding that his name had been omitted from the list of the exiles who might accompany Bahá'u'lláh, cut his throat with a razor, but was prevented in time from ending his life—an act which Bahá'u'lláh, in the Súriy-i-Ra'ís, characterizes as "*unheard of in bygone centuries,*" and which "*God hath set apart for this Revelation, as an evidence of the power of His might.*"

On the twenty-second of the month of Rabí'u'th-Thání 1285 A.H. (August 12, 1868) Bahá'u'lláh and His family, escorted by a Turkish captain, Ḥasan Effendi by name, and other soldiers appointed by the local government, set out on their four-day journey to Gallipoli, riding in carriages and stopping on their way at Uzún-Kúprú and Káshánih, at which latter place the Súriy-i-Ra'ís was revealed. "The inhabitants of the quarter in which Bahá'u'lláh had been living, and the neighbors who had gathered to bid Him farewell, came one after the other," writes an eye-witness, "with the utmost sadness and regret to kiss His hands and the hem of His robe, expressing meanwhile their sorrow at His departure. That day, too, was a strange day. Methinks the city, its walls and its gates bemoaned their imminent separation from Him." "On that day," writes another eye-witness, "there was a wonderful concourse of Muslims and Christians at the door of our Master's house. The hour of departure was a memorable one. Most of those present were weeping and wailing, especially the Christians." *"Say,"* Bahá'u'lláh Himself declares in the Súriy-i-Ra'ís, *"this Youth hath departed out of this country and deposited beneath every tree and every stone a trust, which God will erelong bring forth through the power of truth."*

Several of the companions who had been brought from Constantinople were awaiting them in Gallipoli. On his arrival Bahá'u'lláh made the following pronouncement to Ḥasan Effendi, who, his duty discharged, was taking his leave: *"Tell the king that this territory will pass out of his hands, and his affairs will be thrown into confusion."* "To this," Áqá Riḍá, the recorder of that scene has written, "Bahá'u'lláh furthermore added: 'Not I speak these words, but God speaketh them.' In those moments He was uttering verses which we, who were downstairs, could overhear. They were spoken with such vehemence and power that, methinks, the foundations of the house itself trembled."

Even in Gallipoli, where three nights were spent, no one knew what Bahá'u'lláh's destination would be. Some believed that He and His brothers would be banished to one place, and the remainder dispersed, and sent into exile. Others thought that His companions would be sent back to Persia, while still others expected their immediate extermination. The government's original order was to banish Bahá'u'lláh, Áqáy-i-Kalím and Mírzá Muḥammad-Qulí, with a servant to 'Akká, while the rest were to proceed to Constantinople. This order, which provoked scenes of indescribable distress, was, however, at the insistence of Bahá'u'lláh, and by the instrumentality of 'Umar Effendi, a major appointed to accompany the exiles, revoked. It was eventually decided that all the exiles, numbering about seventy, should be banished to 'Akká. Instructions were, moreover, issued that a certain number of the adherents of Mírzá Yaḥyá, among whom were Siyyid Muḥammad and Áqá Ján, should accompany these exiles, whilst four of the companions of Bahá'u'lláh were ordered to depart with the Azalís for Cyprus.

So grievous were the dangers and trials confronting Bahá'u'lláh at the hour of His departure from Gallipoli that He warned His companions that *"this journey will be unlike any of the previous journeys,"* and that whoever did not feel himself *"man enough to face the future"* had best *"depart to whatever place he pleaseth, and be preserved from tests, for hereafter he will find himself unable to leave"*—a warning which His companions unanimously chose to disregard.

On the morning of the 2nd of Jamádíyu'l-Avval 1285 A.H. (August 21, 1868) they all embarked in an Austrian-Lloyd steamer for Alexandria, touching at Madellí, and stopping for two days at Smyrna, where Jináb-i-Munír, surnamed Ismu'lláhu'l-Muníb, became gravely ill, and had, to his great distress, to be left behind in a hospital where he soon after died. In Alexandria they transhipped into a steamer of the same company, bound for Haifa, where, after brief stops at Port Said and Jaffa, they landed, setting out, a few hours later, in a sailing vessel, for 'Akká, where they disembarked, in the course of the afternoon of the 12th of Jamádíyu'l-Avval 1285 A.H. (August 31, 1868). It was at the moment when Bahá'u'lláh had stepped into the boat which was to carry Him to the landing-stage in Haifa that 'Abdu'l-Ghaffár, one of the four companions condemned to share the exile of Mírzá Yaḥyá, and whose *"detachment, love and trust in God"* Bahá'u'lláh had greatly praised, cast himself, in his despair, into the sea, shouting "Yá Bahá'u'l-Abhá," and was subsequently rescued and resuscitated with the greatest difficulty, only to be forced by adamant officials to continue his voyage, with Mírzá Yaḥyá's party, to the destination originally appointed for him.

## CHAPTER XI

# Bahá'u'lláh's Incarceration in 'Akká

The arrival of Bahá'u'lláh in 'Akká marks the opening of the last phase of His forty-year long ministry, the final stage, and indeed the climax, of the banishment in which the whole of that ministry was spent. A banishment that had, at first, brought Him to the immediate vicinity of the strongholds of Shí'ah orthodoxy and into contact with its outstanding exponents, and which, at a later period, had carried Him to the capital of the Ottoman empire, and led Him to address His epoch-making pronouncements to the Sulṭán, to his ministers and to the ecclesiastical leaders of Sunní Islám, had now been instrumental in landing Him upon the shores of the Holy Land—the Land promised by God to Abraham, sanctified by the Revelation of Moses, honored by the lives and labors of the Hebrew patriarchs, judges, kings and prophets, revered as the cradle of Christianity, and as the place where Zoroaster, according to 'Abdu'l-Bahá's testimony, had *"held converse with some of the Prophets of Israel,"* and associated by Islám with the Apostle's night-journey, through the seven heavens, to the throne of the Almighty. Within the confines of this holy and enviable country, *"the nest of all the Prophets of God," "the Vale of God's unsearchable Decree, the snow-white Spot, the Land of unfading splendor"* was the Exile of Baghdád, of Constantinople and Adrianople condemned to spend no less than a third of the allotted span of His life, and over half of the total period of His Mission. *"It is difficult,"* declares 'Abdu'l-Bahá, *"to understand how Bahá'u'lláh could have been obliged to leave Persia, and to pitch His tent in this Holy Land, but for the persecution of His enemies, His banishment and exile."*

Indeed such a consummation, He assures us, had been actually prophesied *"through the tongue of the Prophets two or three thousand years before."* God, *"faithful to His promise,"* had, *"to some of the Prophets" "revealed and given the good news that the 'Lord of Hosts should be manifested in the Holy Land.'"* Isaiah had, in this connection, announced in his Book: *"Get thee up into the high mountain, O Zion that bringest good tidings; lift up thy voice with strength, O Jerusalem, that bringest good tidings. Lift it up, be not afraid;*

*say unto the cities of Judah: 'Behold your God! Behold the Lord God will come with strong hand, and His arm shall rule for Him.'"* David, in his Psalms, had predicted: *"Lift up your heads, O ye gates; even lift them up, ye everlasting doors; and the King of Glory shall come in. Who is this King of Glory? The Lord of Hosts, He is the King of Glory." "Out of Zion, the perfection of beauty, God hath shined. Our God shall come, and shall not keep silence."* Amos had, likewise, foretold His coming: *"The Lord will roar from Zion, and utter His voice from Jerusalem; and the habitations of the shepherds shall mourn, and the top of Carmel shall wither."*

'Akká, itself, flanked by the *"glory of Lebanon,"* and lying in full view of the *"splendor of Carmel,"* at the foot of the hills which enclose the home of Jesus Christ Himself, had been described by David as *"the Strong City,"* designated by Hosea as *"a door of hope,"* and alluded to by Ezekiel as *"the gate that looketh towards the East,"* whereunto *"the glory of the God of Israel came from the way of the East,"* His voice *"like a noise of many waters."* To it the Arabian Prophet had referred as *"a city in Syria to which God hath shown His special mercy,"* situated *"betwixt two mountains . . . in the middle of a meadow," "by the shore of the sea . . . suspended beneath the Throne," "white, whose whiteness is pleasing unto God." "Blessed the man,"* He, moreover, as confirmed by Bahá'u'lláh, had declared, *"that hath visited 'Akká, and blessed he that hath visited the visitor of 'Akká."* Furthermore, *"He that raiseth therein the call to prayer, his voice will be lifted up unto Paradise."* And again: *"The poor of 'Akká are the kings of Paradise and the princes thereof. A month in 'Akká is better than a thousand years elsewhere."* Moreover, in a remarkable tradition, which is contained in Shaykh Ibnu'l-'Arabí's work, entitled "Futúḥát-i-Makkíyyih," and which is recognized as an authentic utterance of Muḥammad, and is quoted by Mírzá Abu'l-Faḍl in his "Fará'id," this significant prediction has been made: *"All of them* (the companions of the Qá'im) *shall be slain except One Who shall reach the plain of 'Akká, the Banquet-Hall of God."*

Bahá'u'lláh Himself, as attested by Nabíl in his narrative, had, as far back as the first years of His banishment to Adrianople, alluded to that same city in His Lawḥ-i-Sayyáḥ, designating it as the "Vale of Nabíl," the word Nabíl being equal in numerical value to that of 'Akká. *"Upon Our arrival,"* that Tablet had predicted, *"We were welcomed with banners of light, whereupon the Voice of the Spirit cried out saying: 'Soon will all that dwell on earth be enlisted under these banners.'"*

The banishment, lasting no less than twenty-four years, to which two Oriental despots had, in their implacable enmity and shortsightedness, combined to condemn Bahá'u'lláh, will go down in history as a period which witnessed a miraculous and truly revolutionizing change in the circumstances attending the life and activities of the Exile Himself, will be chiefly remembered for the widespread recrudescence of persecution, intermittent but singularly cruel, throughout His native country and the simultaneous increase in the number of His followers, and, lastly, for an enormous extension in the range and volume of His writings.

His arrival at the penal colony of 'Akká, far from proving the end of His afflictions, was but the beginning of a major crisis, characterized by bitter suffering, severe restrictions, and intense turmoil, which, in its gravity, surpassed even the agonies of the Síyáh-Chál of Ṭihrán, and to which no other event, in the history of the entire century can compare, except the internal convulsion that rocked the Faith in Adrianople. *"Know thou,"* Bahá'u'lláh, wishing to emphasize the criticalness of the first nine years of His banishment to that prison-city, has written, *"that upon Our arrival at this Spot, We chose to designate it as the 'Most Great Prison.' Though previously subjected in another land* (Ṭihrán) *to chains and fetters, We yet refused to call it by that name. Say: Ponder thereon, O ye endued with understanding!"*

The ordeal He endured, as a direct consequence of the attempt on the life of Náṣiri'd-Dín Sháh, was one which had been inflicted upon Him solely by the external enemies of the Faith. The travail in Adrianople, the effects of which all but sundered the community of the Báb's followers, was, on the other hand, purely internal in character. This fresh crisis which, during almost a decade, agitated Him and His companions, was, however, marked throughout not only by the assaults of His adversaries from without, but by the machinations of enemies from within, as well as by the grievous misdeeds of those who, though bearing His name, perpetrated what made His heart and His pen alike to lament.

'Akká, the ancient Ptolemais, the St. Jean d'Acre of the Crusaders, that had successfully defied the siege of Napoleon, had sunk, under the Turks, to the level of a penal colony to which murderers, highway robbers and political agitators were consigned from all parts of the Turkish empire. It was girt about by a double system of ramparts; was inhabited by a people whom Bahá'u'lláh stigmatized as *"the generation of vipers"*; was devoid of any source of water within its gates;

was flea-infested, damp and honey-combed with gloomy, filthy and tortuous lanes. *"According to what they say,"* the Supreme Pen has recorded in the Lawḥ-i-Sulṭán, *"it is the most desolate of the cities of the world, the most unsightly of them in appearance, the most detestable in climate, and the foulest in water. It is as though it were the metropolis of the owl."* So putrid was its air that, according to a proverb, a bird when flying over it would drop dead.

Explicit orders had been issued by the Sulṭán and his ministers to subject the exiles, who were accused of having grievously erred and led others far astray, to the strictest confinement. Hopes were confidently expressed that the sentence of life-long imprisonment pronounced against them would lead to their eventual extermination. The farmán of Sulṭán 'Abdu'l-'Azíz, dated the fifth of Rabí'u'th-Thání 1285 A.H. (July 26, 1868), not only condemned them to perpetual banishment, but stipulated their strict incarceration, and forbade them to associate either with each other or with the local inhabitants. The text of the farmán itself was read publicly, soon after the arrival of the exiles, in the principal mosque of the city as a warning to the population. The Persian Ambassador, accredited to the Sublime Porte, had thus assured his government, in a letter, written a little over a year after their banishment to 'Akká: "I have issued telegraphic and written instructions, forbidding that He (Bahá'u'lláh) associate with any one except His wives and children, or leave under any circumstances, the house wherein He is imprisoned. 'Abbás-Qulí Khán, the Consul-General in Damascus . . . I have, three days ago, sent back, instructing him to proceed direct to 'Akká . . . confer with its governor regarding all necessary measures for the strict maintenance of their imprisonment . . . and appoint, before his return to Damascus, a representative on the spot to insure that the orders issued by the Sublime Porte will, in no wise, be disobeyed. I have, likewise, instructed him that once every three months he should proceed from Damascus to 'Akká, and personally watch over them, and submit his report to the Legation." Such was the isolation imposed upon them that the Bahá'ís of Persia, perturbed by the rumors set afloat by the Azalís of Iṣfahán that Bahá'u'lláh had been drowned, induced the British Telegraph office in Julfá to ascertain on their behalf the truth of the matter.

Having, after a miserable voyage, disembarked at 'Akká, all the exiles, men, women and children, were, under the eyes of a curious and callous population that had assembled at the port to behold the "God of the Persians," conducted to the army barracks, where they were locked in, and sentinels detailed to guard them. "*The first night,*" Bahá'u'lláh testifies in the Lawḥ-i-Ra'ís, "*all were deprived of either food or drink . . . They even begged for water, and were refused.*" So filthy and brackish was the water in the pool of the courtyard that no one could drink it. Three loaves of black and salty bread were assigned to each, which they were later permitted to exchange, when escorted by guards to the market, for two of better quality. Subsequently they were allowed a mere pittance as substitute for the allotted dole of bread. All fell sick, except two, shortly after their arrival. Malaria, dysentery, combined with the sultry heat, added to their miseries. Three succumbed, among them two brothers, who died the same night, "*locked,*" as testified by Bahá'u'lláh, "*in each other's arms.*" The carpet used by Him He gave to be sold in order to provide for their winding-sheets and burial. The paltry sum obtained after it had been auctioned was delivered to the guards, who had refused to bury them without first being paid the necessary expenses. Later, it was learned that, unwashed and unshrouded, they had buried them, without coffins, in the clothes they wore, though, as affirmed by Bahá'u'lláh, they were given twice the amount required for their burial. "*None,*" He Himself has written, "*knoweth what befell Us, except God, the Almighty, the All-Knowing . . . From the foundation of the world until the present day a cruelty such as this hath neither been seen nor heard of.*" "*He hath, during the greater part of His life,*" He, referring to Himself, has, moreover, recorded, "*been sore-tried in the clutches of His enemies. His sufferings have now reached their culmination in this afflictive Prison, into which His oppressors have so unjustly thrown Him.*"

The few pilgrims who, despite the ban that had been so rigidly imposed, managed to reach the gates of the Prison—some of whom had journeyed the entire distance from Persia on foot—had to content themselves with a fleeting glimpse of the face of the Prisoner, as they stood, beyond the second moat, facing the window of His Prison. The very few who succeeded in penetrating into the city had, to their great distress, to retrace their steps without even beholding His countenance. The first among them, the self-denying Ḥájí Abu'l-Ḥasan-i-Ardikání, surnamed Amín-i-Iláhí (Trusted of God), to enter His presence was only able to do so in a public bath, where it had been arranged that he should see Bahá'u'lláh without approaching Him or giving any sign of recognition. Another pilgrim, Ustád Ismá'íl-i-Ká<u>sh</u>í, arriving from Mosul, posted himself on the far side of the moat, and, gazing for hours, in rapt adoration, at the window of his Beloved, failed in the end, owing to the feebleness of his sight, to discern His face, and had to turn back to the cave which served as his dwelling-place on Mt. Carmel—an episode that moved to tears the Holy Family who had been anxiously watching from afar the frustration of his hopes. Nabíl himself had to precipitately flee the city, where he had been recognized, had to satisfy himself with a brief glimpse of Bahá'u'lláh from across that same moat, and continued to roam the countryside around Nazareth, Haifa, Jerusalem and Hebron, until the gradual relaxation of restrictions enabled him to join the exiles.

To the galling weight of these tribulations was now added the bitter grief of a sudden tragedy—the premature loss of the noble, the pious Mírzá Mihdí, the Purest Branch, 'Abdu'l-Bahá's twenty-two year old brother, an amanuensis of Bahá'u'lláh and a companion of His exile from the days when, as a child, he was brought from Ṭihrán to Baghdád to join his Father after His return from Sulaymáníyyih. He was pacing the roof of the barracks in the twilight, one evening, wrapped in his customary devotions, when he fell through the unguarded skylight onto a wooden crate, standing on the floor beneath, which pierced his ribs, and caused, twenty-two hours later, his death, on the 23rd of Rabí'u'l-Avval 1287 A.H. (June 23, 1870). His dying supplication to a grieving Father was that his life might be accepted as a ransom for those who were prevented from attaining the presence of their Beloved.

In a highly significant prayer, revealed by Bahá'u'lláh in memory of His son—a prayer that exalts his death to the rank of those great acts of atonement associated with Abraham's intended sacrifice of His son, with the crucifixion of Jesus Christ and the martyrdom of the Imám Ḥusayn—we read the following: *"I have, O my Lord, offered up that which Thou hast given Me, that Thy servants may be quickened, and all that dwell on earth be united."* And, likewise, these prophetic words, addressed to His martyred son: *"Thou art the Trust of God and His Treasure in this Land. Erelong will God reveal through thee that which He hath desired."*

After he had been washed in the presence of Bahá'u'lláh, he *"that was created of the light of Bahá,"* to whose *"meekness"* the Supreme Pen had testified, and of the *"mysteries"* of whose ascension that same Pen had made mention, was borne forth, escorted by the fortress guards, and laid to rest, beyond the city walls, in a spot adjacent to the shrine of Nabí Ṣáliḥ, from whence, seventy years later, his remains, simultaneously with those of his illustrious mother, were to be translated to the slopes of Mt. Carmel, in the precincts of the grave of his sister, and under the shadow of the Báb's holy sepulcher.

Nor was this the full measure of the afflictions endured by the Prisoner of 'Akká and His fellow-exiles. Four months after this tragic event a mobilization of Turkish troops necessitated the removal of Bahá'u'lláh and all who bore Him company from the barracks. He and His family were accordingly assigned the house of Malik, in the western quarter of the city, whence, after a brief stay of three months, they were moved by the authorities to the house of Khavvám which faced it, and from which, after a few months, they were again obliged to take up new quarters in the house of Rábi'ih, being finally transferred, four months later, to the house of 'Údí Khammár, which was so insufficient to their needs that in one of its rooms no less than thirteen persons of both sexes had to accommodate themselves. Some of the companions had to take up their residence in other houses, while the remainder were consigned to a caravanserai named the Khán-i-'Avámíd.

Their strict confinement had hardly been mitigated, and the guards who had kept watch over them been dismissed, when an internal crisis, which had been brewing in the midst of the community, was brought to a sudden and catastrophic climax. Such had been the conduct of two of the exiles, who had been included in the party that accompanied Bahá'u'lláh to 'Akká, that He was eventually forced to expel them, an act of which Siyyid Muḥammad did not hesitate to take the fullest advantage. Reinforced by these recruits, he, together with his old associates, acting as spies, embarked on a campaign of abuse, calumny and intrigue, even more pernicious than that which had been launched by him in Constantinople, calculated to arouse an already prejudiced and suspicious populace to a new pitch of animosity and excitement. A fresh danger now clearly threatened the life of Bahá'u'lláh. Though He Himself had stringently forbidden His followers, on several occasions, both verbally and in writing, any retaliatory acts against their tormentors, and had even sent back to Beirut an irresponsible Arab convert, who had meditated avenging the wrongs suffered by his beloved Leader, seven of the companions clandestinely sought out and slew three of their persecutors, among whom were Siyyid Muḥammad and Áqá Ján.

The consternation that seized an already oppressed community was indescribable. Bahá'u'lláh's indignation knew no bounds. *"Were We,"* He thus voices His emotions, in a Tablet revealed shortly after this act had been committed, *"to make mention of what befell Us, the heavens would be rent asunder and the mountains would crumble.*" "*My captivity,*" He wrote on another occasion, "*cannot harm Me. That which can harm Me is the conduct of those who love Me, who claim to be related to Me, and yet perpetrate what causeth My heart and My pen to groan.*" And again: "*My captivity can bring on Me no shame. Nay, by My life, it conferreth on Me glory. That which can make Me ashamed is the conduct of such of My followers as profess to love Me, yet in fact follow the Evil One.*"

He was dictating His Tablets to His amanuensis when the governor, at the head of his troops, with drawn swords, surrounded His house. The entire populace, as well as the military authorities, were in a state of great agitation. The shouts and clamor of the people could be heard on all sides. Bahá'u'lláh was peremptorily summoned to the Governorate, interrogated, kept in custody the first night, with one of His sons, in a chamber in the Khán-i-Shávirdí, transferred for the following two nights to better quarters in that neighborhood, and allowed only after the lapse of seventy hours to regain His home. 'Abdu'l-Bahá was thrown into prison and chained during the first night, after which He was permitted to join His Father. Twenty-five of the companions were cast into another prison and shackled, all of whom, except those responsible for that odious deed, whose imprisonment lasted several years, were, after six days, moved to the Khán-i-Shávirdí, and there placed, for six months, under confinement.

"Is it proper," the Commandant of the city, turning to Bahá'u'lláh, after He had arrived at the Governorate, boldly inquired, "that some of your followers should act in such a manner?" "*If one of your soldiers,*" was the swift rejoinder, "*were to commit a reprehensible act, would you be held responsible, and be punished in his place?*" When interrogated, He was asked to state His name and that of the country from which He came. "*It is more manifest than the sun,*" He answered. The same question was put to Him again, to which He gave the following reply: "*I deem it not proper to mention it. Refer to the farmán of the government which is in your possession.*" Once again they, with marked deference, reiterated their request, whereupon Bahá'u'lláh spoke with majesty and power these words: "*My name is Bahá'u'lláh* (Light of God), *and My country is Núr* (Light). *Be ye apprized of it.*" Turning then, to the Muftí, He addressed him words of veiled rebuke, after which He spoke to the entire gathering, in such vehement and exalted language that none made bold to answer Him. Having quoted verses from the Súriy-i-

Múlúk, He, afterwards, arose and left the gathering. The Governor, soon after, sent word that He was at liberty to return to His home, and apologized for what had occurred.

A population, already ill-disposed towards the exiles, was, after such an incident, fired with uncontrollable animosity for all those who bore the name of the Faith which those exiles professed. The charges of impiety, atheism, terrorism and heresy were openly and without restraint flung into their faces. 'Abbúd, who lived next door to Bahá'u'lláh, reinforced the partition that separated his house from the dwelling of his now much-feared and suspected Neighbor. Even the children of the imprisoned exiles, whenever they ventured to show themselves in the streets during those days, would be pursued, vilified and pelted with stones.

The cup of Bahá'u'lláh's tribulations was now filled to overflowing. A situation, greatly humiliating, full of anxieties and even perilous, continued to face the exiles, until the time, set by an inscrutable Will, at which the tide of misery and abasement began to ebb, signalizing a transformation in the fortunes of the Faith even more conspicuous than the revolutionary change effected during the latter years of Bahá'u'lláh's sojourn in Baghdád.

The gradual recognition by all elements of the population of Bahá'u'lláh's complete innocence; the slow penetration of the true spirit of His teachings through the hard crust of their indifference and bigotry; the substitution of the sagacious and humane governor, Aḥmad Big Tawfíq, for one whose mind had been hopelessly poisoned against the Faith and its followers; the unremitting labors of 'Abdu'l-Bahá, now in the full flower of His manhood, Who, through His contacts with the rank and file of the population, was increasingly demonstrating His capacity to act as the shield of His Father; the providential dismissal of the officials who had been instrumental in prolonging the confinement of the innocent companions—all paved the way for the reaction that was now setting in, a reaction with which the period of Bahá'u'lláh's banishment to 'Akká will ever remain indissolubly associated.

Such was the devotion gradually kindled in the heart of that governor, through his association with 'Abdu'l-Bahá, and later through his perusal of the literature of the Faith, which mischief-makers, in the hope of angering him, had submitted for his consideration, that he invariably refused to enter His presence without first removing his shoes, as a token of his respect for Him. It was even bruited about that his favored counselors were those very exiles who were the followers of the Prisoner in his custody. His own son he was wont to send to 'Abdu'l-Bahá for instruction and enlightenment. It was on the occasion of a long-sought audience with Bahá'u'lláh that, in response to a request for permission to render Him some service, the suggestion was made to him to restore the aqueduct which for thirty years had been allowed to fall into disuse—a suggestion which he immediately arose to carry out. To the inflow of pilgrims, among whom were numbered the devout and venerable Mullá Ṣádiq-i-Khurásání and the father of Badí, both survivors of the struggle of Ṭabarsí, he offered scarcely any opposition, though the text of the imperial farmán forbade their admission into the city. Muṣṭafá Ḍíyá Pásḥá, who became governor a few years later, had even gone so far as to intimate that his Prisoner was free to pass through its gates whenever He pleased, a suggestion which Bahá'u'lláh declined. Even the Muftí of 'Akká, Shaykh Maḥmúd, a man notorious for his bigotry, had been converted to the Faith, and, fired by his newborn enthusiasm, made a compilation of the Muḥammadan traditions related to 'Akká. Nor were the occasionally unsympathetic governors, despatched to that city, able, despite the arbitrary power they wielded, to check the forces which were carrying the Author of the Faith towards His virtual emancipation and the ultimate accomplishment of His purpose. Men of letters, and even 'ulamás residing in Syria, were moved, as the years rolled by, to voice their recognition of Bahá'u'lláh's rising greatness and power. 'Azíz Páshá, who, in Adrianople, had evinced a profound attachment to 'Abdu'l-Bahá, and had in the meantime been promoted to the rank of Válí, twice visited 'Akká for the express purpose of paying his respects to Bahá'u'lláh, and to renew his friendship with One Whom he had learned to admire and revere.

Though Bahá'u'lláh Himself practically never granted personal interviews, as He had been used to do in Baghdád, yet such was the influence He now wielded that the inhabitants openly asserted that the noticeable improvement in the climate and water of their city was directly attributable to His continued presence in their midst. The very designations by which they chose to refer to him, such as the "august leader," and "his highness" bespoke the reverence with which He inspired them. On one occasion, a European general who, together with the governor, was granted an audience by Him, was so impressed that he "remained kneeling on the ground near the door." Shaykh 'Alíy-i-Mírí, the Muftí of 'Akká, had even, at the suggestion of 'Abdu'l-Bahá, to plead insistently that He might permit the termination of His nine-year confinement within the walls of the prison-city, before He would consent to leave its gates. The garden of Na'mayn, a small island, situated in the middle of a river to the east of the city, honored with the appellation of Riḍván, and designated by Him the *"New Jerusalem"* and *"Our Verdant Isle,"* had, together with the residence of 'Abdu'lláh Pá<u>sh</u>á,—rented and prepared for Him by 'Abdu'l-Bahá, and situated a few miles north of 'Akká—become by now the favorite retreats of One Who, for almost a decade, had not set foot beyond the city walls, and Whose sole exercise had been to pace, in monotonous repetition, the floor of His bed-chamber.

Two years later the palace of 'Údí <u>Kh</u>ammár, on the construction of which so much wealth had been lavished, while Bahá'u'lláh lay imprisoned in the barracks, and which its owner had precipitately abandoned with his family owing to the outbreak of an epidemic disease, was rented and later purchased for Him—a dwelling-place which He characterized as the *"lofty mansion,"* the spot which *"God hath ordained as the most sublime vision of mankind."* 'Abdu'l-Bahá's visit to Beirut, at the invitation of Midḥat Pá<u>sh</u>á, a former Grand Vizir of Turkey, occurring about this time; His association with the civil and ecclesiastical leaders of that city; His several interviews with the well-known <u>Sh</u>ay<u>kh</u> Muḥammad 'Abdu served to enhance immensely the growing prestige of the community and spread abroad the fame of its most distinguished member. The splendid welcome accorded him by the learned and highly esteemed <u>Sh</u>ay<u>kh</u> Yúsuf, the Muftí of Nazareth, who acted as host to the válís of Beirut, and who had despatched all the notables of the community several miles on the road to meet Him as He approached the town, accompanied by His brother and the Muftí of 'Akká, as well as the magnificent reception given by 'Abdu'l-Bahá to that same <u>Sh</u>ay<u>kh</u> Yúsuf when the latter visited Him in 'Akká, were such as to arouse the envy of those who, only a few years before, had treated Him and His fellow-exiles with feelings compounded of condescension and scorn.

The drastic farmán of Sulṭán 'Abdu'l-'Azíz, though officially unrepealed, had by now become a dead letter. Though "Bahá'u'lláh was still nominally a prisoner, *"the doors of majesty and true sovereignty were,"* in the words of 'Abdu'l-Bahá, *"flung wide open."* *"The rulers of Palestine,"* He moreover has written, *"envied His influence and power. Governors and mutiṣarrifs, generals and local officials, would humbly request the honor of attaining His presence—a request to which He seldom acceded."*

It was in that same mansion that the distinguished Orientalist, Prof. E. G. Browne of Cambridge, was granted his four successive interviews with Bahá'u'lláh, during the five days he was His guest at Bahjí (April 15-20, 1890), interviews immortalized by the Exile's historic declaration that *"these fruitless strifes, these ruinous wars shall pass away and the 'Most Great Peace' shall come."* "The face of Him on Whom I gazed," is the interviewer's memorable testimony for posterity, "I can never forget, though I cannot describe it. Those piercing eyes seemed to read one's very soul; power and authority sat on that ample brow. . . . No need to ask in whose presence I stood, as I bowed myself before one who is the object of a devotion and love which kings might envy and emperors sigh for in vain." "Here," the visitor himself has testified, "did I spend five most memorable days, during which I enjoyed unparalleled and unhoped-for opportunities of holding intercourse with those who are the fountain-heads of that mighty and wondrous spirit, which works with invisible but ever-increasing force for the transformation and quickening of a people who slumber in a sleep like unto death. It was, in truth, a strange and moving experience, but one whereof I despair of conveying any save the feeblest impression."

In that same year Bahá'u'lláh's tent, the *"Tabernacle of Glory,"* was raised on Mt. Carmel, *"the Hill of God and His Vineyard,"* the home of Elijah, extolled by Isaiah as the *"mountain of the Lord,"* to which *"all nations shall flow."* Four times He visited Haifa, His last visit being no less than three months long. In the course of one of these visits, when His tent was pitched in the vicinity of the Carmelite Monastery, He, the *"Lord of the Vineyard,"* revealed the Tablet of Carmel, remarkable for its allusions and prophecies. On another occasion He pointed out Himself to 'Abdu'l-Bahá, as He stood on the slopes of that mountain, the site which was to serve as the permanent resting-place of the Báb, and on which a befitting mausoleum was later to be erected.

Properties, bordering on the Lake associated with the ministry of Jesus Christ, were, moreover, purchased at Bahá'u'lláh's bidding, designed to be consecrated to the glory of His Faith, and to be the forerunners of those *"noble and imposing structures"* which He, in His Tablets, had anticipated would be raised *"throughout the length and breadth"* of the Holy Land, as well as of the *"rich and sacred territories adjoining the Jordan and its vicinity,"* which, in those Tablets, He had permitted to be dedicated *"to the worship and service of the one true God."*

The enormous expansion in the volume of Bahá'u'lláh's correspondence; the establishment of a Bahá'í agency in Alexandria for its despatch and distribution; the facilities provided by His staunch follower, Muḥammad Muṣṭafá, now established in Beirut to safeguard the interests of the pilgrims who passed through that city; the comparative ease with which a titular Prisoner communicated with the multiplying centers in Persia, 'Iráq, Caucasus, Turkistán, and Egypt; the mission entrusted by Him to Sulaymán Khán-i-Tanakábuní, known as Jamál Effendi, to initiate a systematic campaign of teaching in India and Burma; the appointment of a few of His followers as *"Hands of the Cause of God"*; the restoration of the Holy House in Shíráz, whose custodianship was now formally entrusted by Him to the Báb's wife and her sister; the conversion of a considerable number of the adherents of the Jewish, Zoroastrian and Buddhist Faiths, the first fruits of the zeal and the perseverance which itinerant teachers in Persia, India and Burma were so strikingly displaying—conversions that automatically resulted in a firm recognition by them of the Divine origin of both Christianity and Islám—all these attested the vitality of a leadership that neither kings nor ecclesiastics, however powerful or antagonistic, could either destroy or undermine.

Nor should reference be omitted to the emergence of a prosperous community in the newly laid out city of 'Ishqábád, in Russian Turkistán, assured of the good will of a sympathetic government, enabling it to establish a Bahá'í cemetery and to purchase property and erect thereon structures that were to prove the precursors of the first Mashriqu'l-Adhkár of the Bahá'í world; or to the establishment of new outposts of the Faith in far-off Samarqand and Bukhárá, in the heart of the Asiatic continent, in consequence of the discourses and writings of the erudite Fáḍil-i-Qá'iní and the learned apologist Mírzá Abu'l-Faḍl; or to the publication in India of five volumes of the writings of the Author of the Faith, including His "Most Holy Book"—publications which were to herald the vast multiplication of its literature, in various scripts and languages, and its dissemination, in later decades, throughout both the East and the West.

*"Sulṭán 'Abdu'l-'Azíz,"* Bahá'u'lláh is reported by one of His fellow-exiles to have stated, *"banished Us to this country in the greatest abasement, and since his object was to destroy Us and humble Us, whenever the means of glory and ease presented themselves, We did not reject them." "Now, praise be to God,"* He, moreover, as reported by Nabíl in his narrative, once remarked, *"it has reached*

*the point when all the people of these regions are manifesting their submissiveness unto Us."* And again, as recorded in that same narrative: *"The Ottoman Sulṭán, without any justification, or reason, arose to oppress Us, and sent Us to the fortress of 'Akká. His imperial farmán decreed that none should associate with Us, and that We should become the object of the hatred of every one. The Hand of Divine power, therefore, swiftly avenged Us. It first loosed the winds of destruction upon his two irreplaceable ministers and confidants, 'Alí and Fu'ád, after which that Hand was stretched out to roll up the panoply of 'Azíz himself, and to seize him, as He only can seize, Who is the Mighty, the Strong."*

*"His enemies,"* 'Abdu'l-Bahá, referring to this same theme, has written, *"intended that His imprisonment should completely destroy and annihilate the blessed Cause, but this prison was, in reality, of the greatest assistance, and became the means of its development." ". . . This illustrious Being,"* He, moreover has affirmed, *"uplifted His Cause in the Most Great Prison. From this Prison His light was shed abroad; His fame conquered the world, and the proclamation of His glory reached the East and the West." "His light at first had been a star; now it became a mighty sun." "Until our time,"* He, moreover has affirmed, *"no such thing has ever occurred."*

Little wonder that, in view of so remarkable a reversal in the circumstances attending the twenty-four years of His banishment to 'Akká, Bahá'u'lláh Himself should have penned these weighty words: *"The Almighty . . . hath transformed this Prison-House into the Most Exalted Paradise, the Heaven of Heavens."*

## CHAPTER XII

# Bahá'u'lláh's Incarceration in 'Akká

### (Continued)

While Bahá'u'lláh and the little band that bore Him company were being subjected to the severe hardships of a banishment intended to blot them from the face of the earth, the steadily expanding community of His followers in the land of His birth were undergoing a persecution more violent and of longer duration than the trials with which He and His companions were being afflicted. Though on a far smaller scale than the blood baths which had baptized the birth of the Faith, when in the course of a single year, as attested by 'Abdu'l-Bahá, *"more than four thousand souls were slain, and a great multitude of women and children left without protector and helper,"* the murderous and horrible acts subsequently perpetrated by an insatiable and unyielding enemy covered as wide a range and were marked by an even greater degree of ferocity.

Náṣiri'd-Dín S͟háh, stigmatized by Bahá'u'lláh as the *"Prince of Oppressors,"* as one who had *"perpetrated what hath caused the denizens of the cities of justice and equity to lament,"* was, during the period under review, in the full tide of his manhood and had reached the plenitude of his despotic power. The sole arbiter of the fortunes of a country "firmly stereotyped in the immemorial traditions of the East"; surrounded by "venal, artful and false" ministers whom he could elevate or abase at his pleasure; the head of an administration in which "every actor was, in different aspects, both the briber and the bribed"; allied, in his opposition to the Faith, with a sacerdotal order which constituted a veritable "church-state"; supported by a people preeminent in atrocity, notorious for its fanaticism, its servility, cupidity and corrupt practices, this capricious monarch, no longer able to lay hands upon the person of Bahá'u'lláh, had to content himself with the task of attempting to stamp out in his own dominions the remnants of a much-feared and newly resuscitated community. Next to him in rank and power were his three eldest sons, to whom, for purposes of internal administration, he had practically delegated his authority, and in whom he had invested the governorship of all the provinces of his kingdom. The province of

Á<u>dh</u>irbáyján he had entrusted to the weak and timid Muẓaffari'd-Dín Mírzá, the heir to his throne, who had fallen under the influence of the <u>Sh</u>ay<u>kh</u>í sect, and was showing a marked respect to the mullás. To the stern and savage rule of the astute Mas'úd Mírzá, commonly known as Ẓillu's-Sulṭán, his eldest surviving son, whose mother had been of plebeian origin, he had committed over two-fifths of his kingdom, including the provinces of Yazd and Iṣfahán, whilst upon Kámrán Mírzá, his favorite son, commonly called by his title the Náyibu's-Salṭanih, he had bestowed the rulership of Gílán and Mázindarán, and made him governor of Ṭihrán, his minister of war and the commander-in-chief of his army. Such was the rivalry between the last two princes, who vied with each other in courting the favor of their father, that each endeavored, with the support of the leading mujtahids within his jurisdiction, to outshine the other in the meritorious task of hunting, plundering and exterminating the members of a defenseless community, who, at the bidding of Bahá'u'lláh, had ceased to offer armed resistance even in self-defense, and were carrying out His injunction that *"it is better to be killed than kill."* Nor were the clerical firebrands, Ḥájí Mullá 'Alíy-i-Kaní and Siyyid Ṣádiq-i-Ṭabáṭabá'í, the two leading mujtahids of Ṭihrán, together with <u>Sh</u>ay<u>kh</u> Muḥammad-Báqir, their colleague in Iṣfahán, and Mír Muḥammad-Ḥusayn, the Imám-Jum'ih of that city, willing to allow the slightest opportunity to pass without striking, with all the force and authority they wielded, at an adversary whose liberalizing influences they had even more reason to fear than the sovereign himself.

Little wonder that, confronted by a situation so full of peril, the Faith should have been driven underground, and that arrests, interrogations, imprisonment, vituperation, spoliation, tortures and executions should constitute the outstanding features of this convulsive period in its development. The pilgrimages that had been initiated in Adrianople, and which later assumed in 'Akká impressive proportions, together with the dissemination of the Tablets of Bahá'u'lláh and the circulation of enthusiastic reports through the medium of those who had attained His presence served, moreover, to inflame the animosity of clergy and laity alike, who had foolishly imagined that the breach which had occurred in the ranks of the followers of the Faith in Adrianople and the sentence of life banishment pronounced subsequently against its Leader, would seal irretrievably its fate.

In Ábádih a certain Ustád 'Alí-Akbar was, at the instigation of a local Siyyid, apprehended and so ruthlessly thrashed that he was covered from head to foot with his own blood. In the village of Tákur, at the bidding of the Sháh, the property of the inhabitants was pillaged, Ḥájí Mírzá Riḍá-Qulí, a half-brother of Bahá'u'lláh, was arrested, conducted to the capital and thrown into the Síyáh-Chál, where he remained for a month, whilst the brother-in-law of Mírzá Ḥasan, another half-brother of Bahá'u'lláh, was seized and branded with red-hot irons, after which the neighboring village of Dár-Kalá was delivered to the flames.

Áqá Buzurg of Khurásán, the illustrious "Badí'" (Wonderful); converted to the Faith by Nabíl; surnamed the "Pride of Martyrs"; the seventeen-year old bearer of the Tablet addressed to Náṣiri'd-Dín Sháh; in whom, as affirmed by Bahá'u'lláh, *"the spirit of might and power was breathed,"* was arrested, branded for three successive days, his head beaten to a pulp with the butt of a rifle, after which his body was thrown into a pit and earth and stones heaped upon it. After visiting Bahá'u'lláh in the barracks, during the second year of His confinement, he had arisen with amazing alacrity to carry that Tablet, alone and on foot, to Tihrán and deliver it into the hands of the sovereign. A four months' journey had taken him to that city, and, after passing three days in fasting and vigilance, he had met the Sháh proceeding on a hunting expedition to Shimírán. He had calmly and respectfully approached His Majesty, calling out, "O King! I have come to thee from Sheba with a weighty message"; whereupon at the Sovereign's order, the Tablet was taken from him and delivered to the mujtahids of Tihrán who were commanded to reply to that Epistle—a command which they evaded, recommending instead that the messenger should be put to death. That Tablet was subsequently forwarded by the Sháh to the Persian Ambassador in Constantinople, in the hope that its perusal by the Sulṭán's ministers might serve to further inflame their animosity. For a space of three years Bahá'u'lláh continued to extol in His writings the heroism of that youth, characterizing the references made by Him to that sublime sacrifice as the *"salt of My Tablets."*

Abá-Baṣír and Siyyid Ashraf, whose fathers had been slain in the struggle of Zanján, were decapitated on the same day in that city, the former going so far as to instruct, while kneeling in prayer, his executioner as to how best to deal his blow, while the latter, after having been so brutally beaten that blood flowed from under his nails, was beheaded, as he held in his arms the body of his martyred companion. It was the mother of this same Ashraf who, when sent to the prison in the hope that she would persuade her only son to recant, had warned him that she would disown him were he to denounce his faith, had bidden him follow the example of Abá-Baṣír, and had even watched him expire with eyes undimmed with tears. The wealthy and prominent Muḥammad-Ḥasan K͟hán-i-Kás͟hí was so mercilessly bastinadoed in Burújird that he succumbed to his ordeal. In S͟híráz Mírzá Áqáy-i-Rikáb-Sáz, together with Mírzá Rafí'-i-K͟hayyáṭ and Mas͟hhadí Nabí, were by order of the local mujtahid simultaneously strangled in the dead of night, their graves being later desecrated by a mob who heaped refuse upon them. S͟hayk͟h Abu'l-Qásim-i-Mázkání in Kás͟hán, who had declined a drink of water that was offered him before his death, affirming that he thirsted for the cup of martyrdom, was dealt a fatal blow on the nape of his neck, whilst he was prostrating himself in prayer.

Mírzá Báqir-i-S͟hírází, who had transcribed the Tablets of Bahá'-u'lláh in Adrianople with such unsparing devotion, was slain in Kirmán, while in Ardikán the aged and infirm Gul-Muḥammad was set upon by a furious mob, thrown to the ground, and so trampled upon by the hob-nailed boots of two siyyids that his ribs were crushed in and his teeth broken, after which his body was taken to the outskirts of the town and buried in a pit, only to be dug up the next day, dragged through the streets, and finally abandoned in the wilderness. In the city of Mas͟hhad, notorious for its unbridled fanaticism, Ḥájí 'Abdu'l-Majíd, who was the eighty-five year old father of the afore-mentioned Badí' and a survivor of the struggle of Tabarsí, and who, after the martyrdom of his son, had visited Bahá-'u'lláh and returned afire with zeal to K͟hurásán, was ripped open from waist to throat, and his head exposed on a marble slab to the gaze of a multitude of insulting onlookers, who, after dragging his body ignominiously through the bazaars, left it at the morgue to be claimed by his relatives.

In Iṣfahán Mullá Káẓim was beheaded by order of S͟hayk͟h Muḥammad-Báqir, and a horse made to gallop over his corpse, which was then delivered to the flames, while Siyyid Áqá Ján had his ears cut off, and was led by a halter through the streets and bazaars. A month later occurred in that same city the tragedy of the two famous brothers Mírzá Muḥammad-Ḥasan and Mírzá Muḥammad-Ḥusayn, the "twin shining lights," respectively surnamed "Sulṭánu's͟h-S͟huhadá" (King of Martyrs) and "Maḥbúbu's͟h-S͟huhadá" (Beloved of Martyrs), who were celebrated for their generosity, trustworthiness, kindliness and piety. Their martyrdom was instigated by the wicked and dishonest Mír Muḥammad-Ḥusayn, the Imám-Jum'ih, stigmatized by

Bahá'u'lláh as the "she-serpent," who, in view of a large debt he had incurred in his transactions with them, schemed to nullify his obligations by denouncing them as Bábís, and thereby encompassing their death. Their richly-furnished houses were plundered, even to the trees and flowers in their gardens, all their remaining possessions were confiscated; Shaykh Muḥammad-Báqir, denounced by Bahá'u'lláh as the "wolf," pronounced their death-sentence; the Ẓillu's-Sulṭán ratified the decision, after which they were put in chains, decapitated, dragged to the Maydán-i-Sháh, and there exposed to the indignities heaped upon them by a degraded and rapacious populace. *"In such wise,"* 'Abdu'l-Bahá has written, *"was the blood of these two brothers shed that the Christian priest of Julfá cried out, lamented and wept on that day."* For several years Bahá'u'lláh in His Tablets continued to make mention of them, to voice His grief over their passing and to extol their virtues.

Mullá 'Alí Ján was conducted on foot from Mázindarán to Ṭihrán, the hardships of that journey being so severe that his neck was wounded and his body swollen from the waist to the feet. On the day of his martyrdom he asked for water, performed his ablutions, recited his prayers, bestowed a considerable gift of money on his executioner, and was still in the act of prayer when his throat was slit by a dagger, after which his corpse was spat upon, covered with mud, left exposed for three days, and finally hewn to pieces. In Námiq Mullá 'Alí, converted to the Faith in the days of the Báb, was so severely attacked and his ribs so badly broken with a pick-axe that he died immediately. Mírzá Ashraf was slain in Iṣfahán, his corpse trampled under foot by Shaykh Muḥammad Taqíy-i-Najafí, the "son of the wolf," and his pupils, savagely mutilated, and delivered to the mob to be burnt, after which his charred bones were buried beneath the ruins of a wall that was pulled down to cover them.

In Yazd, at the instigation of the mujtahid of that city, and by order of the callous Maḥmúd Mírzá, the Jalúlu'l-Dawlih, the governor, a son of Ẓillu's-Sulṭán, seven were done to death in a single day in horrible circumstances. The first of these, a twenty-seven year old youth, 'Alí-Aṣghar, was strangled, his body delivered into the hands of some Jews who, forcing the dead man's six companions to come with them, dragged the corpse through the streets, surrounded by a mob of people and soldiers beating drums and blowing trumpets, after which, arriving near the Telegraph Office, they beheaded the eighty-five year old Mullá Mihdí and dragged him in the same manner to another quarter of the city, where, in view of a great throng of onlookers, frenzied by the throbbing strains of the music, they executed Áqá 'Alí in like manner. Proceeding thence to the house of the local mujtahid, and carrying with them the four remaining companions, they cut the throat of Mullá 'Alíy-i-Sabzivárí, who had been addressing the crowd and glorying in his imminent martyrdom, hacked his body to pieces with a spade, while he was still alive, and pounded his skull to a pulp with stones. In another quarter, near the Mihríz gate, they slew Muḥammad-Báqir, and afterwards, in the Maydán-i-Khán, as the music grew wilder and drowned the yells of the people, they beheaded the survivors who remained, two brothers in their early twenties, 'Alí-Aṣghar and Muḥammad-Ḥasan. The stomach of the latter was ripped open and his heart and liver plucked out, after which his head was impaled on a spear, carried aloft, to the accompaniment of music, through the streets of the city, and suspended on a mulberry tree, and stoned by a great concourse of people. His body was cast before the door of his mother's house, into which women deliberately entered to dance and make merry. Even pieces of their flesh were carried away to be used as a medicament. Finally, the head of Muḥammad-Ḥasan was attached to the lower part of his body and, together with those of the other martyrs, was borne to the outskirts of the city and so viciously pelted with stones that the skulls were broken, whereupon they compelled the Jews to carry the remains and throw them into a pit in the plain of Salsabíl. A holiday was declared by the governor for the people, all the shops were closed by his order, the city was illuminated at night, and festivities proclaimed the consummation of one of the most barbarous acts perpetrated in modern times.

Nor were the Jews and the Parsis who had been newly converted to the Faith, and were living, the former in Hamadán, and the latter in Yazd, immune to the assaults of enemies whose fury was exasperated by the evidences of the penetration of the light of the Faith in quarters they had fondly imagined to be beyond its reach. Even in the city of 'Ishqábád the newly established Shí'ah community, envious of the rising prestige of the followers of Bahá'u'lláh who were living in their midst, instigated two ruffians to assault the seventy-year old Ḥájí Muḥammad-Riḍáy-i-Iṣfáhání, whom, in broad day and in the midst of the bazaar, they stabbed in no less than thirty-two places, exposing his liver, lacerating his stomach and tearing open his breast. A military court dispatched by the Czar to 'Ishqábád established, after prolonged investigation, the guilt of the

S͟hí'ahs, sentencing two to death and banishing six others—a sentence which neither Náṣiri'd-Dín S͟háh, nor the 'ulamás of Ṭihrán, of Mas͟hhad and of Tabríz, who were appealed to, could mitigate, but which the representatives of the aggrieved community, through their magnanimous intercession which greatly surprised the Russian authorities, succeeded in having commuted to a lighter punishment.

Such are some typical examples of the treatment meted out by the adversaries of the Faith to the newly resurgent community of its followers during the period of Bahá'u'lláh's banishment to 'Akká—a treatment which it may be truly said testified alternately to "the callousness of the brute and the ingenuity of the fiend."

The "inquisition and appalling tortures," following the attempt on the life of Náṣiri'd-Dín S͟háh, had already, in the words of no less eminent an observer than Lord Curzon of Kedleston, imparted to the Faith "a vitality which no other impulse could have secured." This recrudescence of persecution, this fresh outpouring of the blood of martyrs, served to further enliven the roots which that holy Sapling had already struck in its native soil. Careless of the policy of fire and blood which aimed at their annihilation, undismayed by the tragic blows rained upon a Leader so far removed from their midst, uncorrupted by the foul and seditious acts perpetrated by the Arch-Breaker of the Báb's Covenant, the followers of Bahá'u'lláh were multiplying in number and silently gathering the necessary strength that was to enable them, at a later stage, to lift their heads in freedom, and rear the fabric of their institutions.

Soon after his visit to Persia in the autumn of 1889 Lord Curzon of Kedleston wrote, in the course of references designed to dispel the "great confusion" and "error" prevailing "among European and specially English writers" regarding the Faith, that "the Bahá'ís are now believed to comprise nineteen-twentieths of the Bábí persuasion." Count Gobineau, writing as far back as the year 1865, testified as follows: "L'opinion générale est que les Bábís sont répandus dans toutes les classes de la population et parmi tous les religionnaires de la Perse, sauf les Nuṣayrís et les Chrétiens; mais ce sont surtout les classes éclairées, les hommes pratiquant les sciences du pays, qui sont donnés comme très suspects. On pense, et avec raison, ce semble, que beaucoup de mullás, et parmi eux des mujtahids considérables, des magistrats d'un rang élevé, des hommes qui occupent à la cour des fonctions importantes et qui approchent de près la personne du Roi, sont des Bábís. D'après un calcul fait récemment, il y aurait a Ṭihrán cinq milles de ces religionnaires sur une population de quatre-vingt milles âmes a peu près." Furthermore: ". . . Le Bábisme a pris une action considérable sur l'intelligence de la nation persane, et, se rependant même au delà des limites du territoire, il a débordé dans le pachalik de Baghdád, et passé aussi dans l'Inde." And again: ". . . Un mouvement religieux tout particulier dont l'Asie Centrale, c'est-à-dire la Perse, quelques points de l'Inde et une partie de la Turquie d'Asie, aux environs de Baghdád, est aujourd'hui vivement préoccupée, mouvement remarquable et digne d'être étudié à tous les titres. Il permet d'assister à des développements de faits, à des manifestations, à des catastrophes telles que l'on n'est pas habitué à les imaginer ailleurs que dans les temps reculés où se sont produites les grandes religions."

"These changes, however," Lord Curzon, alluding to the Declaration of the Mission of Bahá'u'lláh and the rebellion of Mírzá Yaḥyá, has, moreover written, "have in no wise impaired, but appear on the contrary, to have stimulated its propaganda, which has advanced with a rapidity inexplicable to those who can only see therein a crude form of political or even of metaphysical fermentation. The lowest estimate places the present number of Bábís in Persia at half a million. I am disposed to think, from conversations with persons well qualified to judge, that the total is nearer one million." "They are to be found," he adds, "in every walk of life, from the ministers and nobles of the Court to the scavenger or the groom, not the least arena of their activity being the Musulmán priesthood itself." "From the facts," is another testimony of his, "that Bábism in its earliest years found itself in conflict with the civil powers, and that an attempt was made by Bábís upon the life of the Sháh, it has been wrongly inferred that the movement was political in origin and Nihilist in character . . . At the present time the Bábís are equally loyal with any other subjects of the Crown. Nor does there appear to be any greater justice in the charges of socialism, communism and immorality that have so freely been levelled at the youthful persuasion . . . The only communism known to and recommended by Him (the Báb) was that of the New Testament and the early Christian Church, viz., the sharing of goods in common by members of the Faith, and the exercise of alms-giving, and an ample charity. The charge of immorality seems to have arisen partly from the malignant inventions of opponents, partly from the much greater freedom claimed for women by the Báb, which in the oriental mind is scarcely dissociable from profligacy of conduct." And, finally, the following prognostication from his pen: "If Bábism continues to grow at its present rate of progression, a time may conceivably come when it will oust Muḥammadanism from the field in Persia. This, I think, it would be unlikely to do, did it appear upon the ground under the flag of a hostile faith. But since its recruits are won from the best soldiers of the garrison whom it is attacking, there is greater reason to believe that it may ultimately prevail."

Bahá'u'lláh's incarceration in the prison-fortress of 'Akká, the manifold tribulations He endured, the prolonged ordeal to which the community of His followers in Persia was being subjected, did not arrest, nor could they even impede, to the slightest degree, the mighty stream of Divine Revelation, which, without interruption, had been flowing from His pen, and on which the future orientation, the integrity, the expansion and the consolidation of His Faith directly depended. Indeed, in their scope and volume, His writings, during the years of His confinement in the Most Great Prison, surpassed the outpourings of His pen in either Adrianople or Ba<u>gh</u>dád. More remarkable than the radical transformation in the circumstances of His own life in 'Akká, more far-reaching in its spiritual consequences than the campaign of repression pursued so relentlessly by the enemies of His Faith in the land of His birth, this unprecedented extension in the range of His writings, during His exile in that Prison, must rank as one of the most vitalizing and fruitful stages in the evolution of His Faith.

The tempestuous winds that swept the Faith at the inception of His ministry and the wintry desolation that marked the beginnings of His prophetic career, soon after His banishment from Ṭihrán, were followed during the latter part of His sojourn in Ba<u>gh</u>dád, by what may be described as the vernal years of His Mission—years which witnessed the bursting into visible activity of the forces inherent in that Divine Seed that had lain dormant since the tragic removal of His Forerunner. With His arrival in Adrianople and the proclamation of His Mission the Orb of His Revelation climbed as it were to its zenith, and shone, as witnessed by the style and tone of His writings, in the plenitude of its summer glory. The period of His incarceration in 'Akká brought with it the ripening of a slowly maturing process, and was a period during which the choicest fruits of that mission were ultimately garnered.

The writings of Bahá'u'lláh during this period, as we survey the vast field which they embrace, seem to fall into three distinct categories. The first comprises those writings which constitute the sequel to the proclamation of His Mission in Adrianople. The second includes the laws and ordinances of His Dispensation, which, for the most part, have been recorded in the Kitáb-i-Aqdas, His Most Holy Book. To the third must be assigned those Tablets which partly enunciate and partly reaffirm the fundamental tenets and principles underlying that Dispensation.

The Proclamation of His Mission had been, as already observed, directed particularly to the kings of the earth, who, by virtue of the power and authority they wielded, were invested with a peculiar and inescapable responsibility for the destinies of their subjects. It was to these kings, as well as to the world's religious leaders, who exercised a no less pervasive influence on the mass of their followers, that the Prisoner of 'Akká directed His appeals, warnings, and exhortations during the first years of His incarceration in that city. *"Upon Our arrival at this Prison,"* He Himself affirms, *"We purposed to transmit to the kings the messages of their Lord, the Mighty, the All-Praised. Though We have transmitted to them, in several Tablets, that which We were commanded, yet We do it once again, as a token of God's grace."*

To the kings of the earth, both in the East and in the West, both Christian and Muslim, who had already been collectively admonished and warned in the Súriy-i-Múlúk revealed in Adrianople, and had been so vehemently summoned by the Báb, in the opening chapter of the Qayyúmu'l-Asmá', on the very night of the Declaration of His Mission, Bahá'u'lláh, during the darkest days of His confinement in 'Akká, addressed some of the noblest passages of His Most Holy Book. In these passages He called upon them to take fast hold of the *"Most Great Law"*; proclaimed Himself to be *"the King of Kings"* and *"the Desire of all Nations"*; declared them to be His *"vassals"* and *"emblems of His sovereignty"*; disclaimed any intention of laying hands on their kingdoms; bade them forsake their palaces, and hasten to gain admittance into His Kingdom; extolled the king who would arise to aid His Cause as *"the very eye of mankind"*; and finally arraigned them for the things which had befallen Him at their hands.

In His Tablet to Queen Victoria He, moreover, invites these kings to hold fast to *"the Lesser Peace,"* since they had refused *"the Most Great Peace"*; exhorts them to be reconciled among themselves, to unite and to reduce their armaments; bids them refrain from laying excessive burdens on their subjects, who, He informs them, are their *"wards"* and *"treasures"*; enunciates the principle that should any one among them take up arms against another, all should rise against him;

and warns them not to deal with Him as the *"King of Islám"* and his ministers had dealt.

To the Emperor of the French, Napoleon III, the most prominent and influential monarch of his day in the West, designated by Him as the *"Chief of Sovereigns,"* and who, to quote His words, had *"cast behind his back"* the Tablet revealed for him in Adrianople, He, while a prisoner in the army barracks, addressed a second Tablet and transmitted it through the French agent in 'Akká. In this He announces the coming of *"Him Who is the Unconstrained,"* whose purpose is to *"quicken the world"* and unite its peoples; unequivocally asserts that Jesus Christ was the Herald of His Mission; proclaims the fall of *"the stars of the firmament of knowledge,"* who have turned aside from Him; exposes that monarch's insincerity; and clearly prophesies that his kingdom shall be *"thrown into confusion,"* that his *"empire shall pass"* from his hands, and that *"commotions shall seize all the people in that land,"* unless he arises to help the Cause of God and follow Him Who is His Spirit.

In memorable passages addressed to *"the Rulers of America and the Presidents of the Republics therein"* He, in His Kitáb-i-Aqdas, calls upon them to *"adorn the temple of dominion with the ornament of justice and of the fear of God, and its head with the crown of remembrance"* of their Lord; declares that *"the Promised One"* has been made manifest; counsels them to avail themselves of the *"Day of God"*; and bids them *"bind with the hands of justice the broken"* and *"crush"* the *"oppressor"* with *"the rod of the commandments of their Lord, the Ordainer, the All-Wise."*

To Nicolaevitch Alexander II, the all-powerful Czar of Russia, He addressed, as He lay a prisoner in the barracks, an Epistle wherein He announces the advent of the promised Father, Whom *"the tongue of Isaiah hath extolled,"* and *"with Whose name both the Torah and the Evangel were adorned"*; commands him to *"arise . . . and summon the nations unto God"*; warns him to beware lest his sovereignty withhold him from *"Him Who is the Supreme Sovereign"*; acknowledges the aid extended by his Ambassador in Ṭihrán; and cautions him not to forfeit the station ordained for him by God.

To Queen Victoria He, during that same period, addressed an Epistle in which He calls upon her to incline her ear to the voice of her Lord, the Lord of all mankind; bids her *"cast away all that is on earth,"* and set her heart towards her Lord, the Ancient of Days; asserts that *"all that hath been mentioned in the Gospel hath been fulfilled"*; assures her that God would reward her for having *"for-*

*bidden the trading in slaves,"* were she to follow what has been sent unto her by Him; commends her for having *"entrusted the reins of counsel into the hands of the representatives of the people"*; and exhorts them to *"regard themselves as the representatives of all that dwell on earth,"* and to judge between men with *"pure justice."*

In a celebrated passage addressed to William I, King of Prussia and newly-acclaimed emperor of a unified Germany, He, in His Kitáb-i-Aqdas, bids the sovereign hearken to His Voice, the Voice of God Himself; warns him to take heed lest his pride debar him from recognizing *"the Day-Spring of Divine Revelation,"* and admonishes him to *"remember the one* (Napoleon III) *whose power transcended"* his power, and who *"went down to dust in great loss."* Furthermore, in that same Book, apostrophizing the *"banks of the Rhine,"* He predicts that *"the swords of retribution"* would be drawn against them, and that *"the lamentations of Berlin"* would be raised, though at that time she was *"in conspicuous glory."*

In another notable passage of that same Book, addressed to Francis-Joseph, the Austrian Emperor and heir of the Holy Roman Empire, Bahá'u'lláh reproves the sovereign for having neglected to inquire about Him in the course of a pilgrimage to Jerusalem; takes God to witness that He had found him *"clinging unto the Branch and heedless of the Root"*; grieves to observe his waywardness; and bids him open his eyes and gaze on *"the Light that shineth above this luminous Horizon."*

To 'Álí Pás͟há, the Grand Vizir of the Sulṭán of Turkey He addressed, shortly after His arrival in 'Akká, a second Tablet, in which He reprimands him for his cruelty *"that hath made hell to blaze and the Spirit to lament"*; recounts his acts of oppression; condemns him as one of those who, from time immemorial, have denounced the Prophets as stirrers of mischief; prophesies his downfall; expatiates on His own sufferings and those of His fellow-exiles; extolls their fortitude and detachment; predicts that God's *"wrathful anger"* will seize him and his government, that *"sedition will be stirred up"* in their midst, and that their *"dominions will be disrupted"*; and affirms that were he to awake, he would abandon all his possessions, and would *"choose to abide in one of the dilapidated rooms of this Most Great Prison."* In the Lawḥ-i-Fu'ád, in the course of His reference to the premature death of the Sulṭán's Foreign Minister, Fu'ád Pás͟há, He thus confirms His above-mentioned prediction: *"Soon will We dismiss the one* ('Álí Pás͟há) *who was like unto him and will lay hold on their Chief* (Sulṭán 'Abdu'l-'Azíz) *who ruleth the land, and I, verily, am the Almighty, the All-Compelling.*"

No less outspoken and emphatic are the messages, some embodied in specific Tablets, others interspersed through His writings, which Bahá'u'lláh addressed to the world's ecclesiastical leaders of all denominations—messages in which He discloses, clearly and unreservedly, the claims of His Revelation, summons them to heed His call, and denounces, in certain specific cases, their perversity, their extreme arrogance and tyranny.

In immortal passages of His Kitáb-i-Aqdas and other Tablets He bids the entire company of these ecclesiastical leaders to "*fear God,*" to "*rein in*" their pens, "*fling away idle fancies and imaginings, and turn then towards the Horizon of Certitude*"; warns them to "*weigh not the Book of God* (Kitáb-i-Aqdas) *with such standards and sciences as are current*" amongst them; designates that same Book as the "*Unerring Balance established amongst men*"; laments over their blindness and waywardness; asserts His superiority in vision, insight, utterance and wisdom; proclaims His innate and God-given knowledge; cautions them not to "*shut out the people by yet another veil,*" after He Himself had "*rent the veils asunder*"; accuses them of having been "*the cause of the repudiation of the Faith in its early days*"; and adjures them to "*peruse with fairness and justice that which hath been sent down*" by Him, and to "*nullify not the Truth*" with the things they possess.

To Pope Pius IX, the undisputed head of the most powerful Church in Christendom, possessor of both temporal and spiritual authority, He, a Prisoner in the army barracks of the penal-colony of 'Akká, addressed a most weighty Epistle, in which He announces that "*He Who is the Lord of Lords is come overshadowed with clouds,*" and that "*the Word which the Son concealed is made manifest.*" He, moreover, warns him not to dispute with Him even as the Pharisees of old disputed with Jesus Christ; bids him leave his palaces unto such as desire them, "*sell all the embellished ornaments*" in his possession, "*expend them in the path of God,*" abandon his kingdom unto the kings, "*arise . . . amidst the peoples of the earth,*" and summon them to His Faith. Regarding him as one of the suns of the heaven of God's names, He cautions him to guard himself lest "*darkness spread its veils*" over him; calls upon him to "*exhort the kings*" to "*deal equitably with men*"; and counsels him to walk in the footsteps of his Lord, and follow His example.

To the patriarchs of the Christian Church He issued a specific summons in which He proclaims the coming of the Promised One; exhorts them to *"fear God"* and not to follow *"the vain imaginings of the superstitious"*; and directs them to lay aside the things they possess and *"take fast hold of the Tablet of God by His sovereign power."* To the archbishops of that Church He similarly declares that *"He Who is the Lord of all men hath appeared,"* that they are *"numbered with the dead,"* and that great is the blessedness of him who is *"stirred by the breeze of God, and hath arisen from amongst the dead in this perspicuous Name."* In passages addressed to its bishops He proclaims that *"the Everlasting Father calleth aloud between earth and heaven,"* pronounces them to be the fallen stars of the heaven of His knowledge, and affirms that His body *"yearneth for the cross"* and His head is *"eager for the spear in the path of the All-Merciful."* The concourse of Christian priests He bids *"leave the bells,"* and come forth from their churches; exhorts them to *"proclaim aloud the Most Great Name among the nations"*; assures them that whoever will summon men in His Name will *"show forth that which is beyond the power of all that are on earth"*; warns them that the *"Day of Reckoning hath appeared"*; and counsels them to turn with their hearts to their *"Lord, the Forgiving, the Generous."* In numerous passages addressed to the *"concourse of monks"* He bids them not to seclude themselves in churches and cloisters, but to occupy themselves with that which will profit their souls and the souls of men; enjoins them to enter into wedlock; and affirms that if they choose to follow Him He will make them heirs of His Kingdom, and that if they transgress against Him, He will, in His long-suffering, endure it patiently.

And finally, in several passages addressed to the entire body of the followers of Jesus Christ He identifies Himself with the *"Father"* spoken of by Isaiah, with the *"Comforter"* Whose Covenant He Who is the Spirit (Jesus) had Himself established, and with the *"Spirit of Truth"* Who will guide them *"into all truth"*; proclaims His Day to be the Day of God; announces the conjunction of the river Jordan with the *"Most Great Ocean"*; asserts their heedlessness as well as His own claim to have opened unto them *"the gates of the kingdom"*; affirms that the promised *"Temple"* has been built *"with the hands of the will"* of their Lord, the Mighty, the Bounteous; bids them *"rend the veils assunder,"* and enter in His name His Kingdom; recalls the saying of Jesus to Peter; and assures them that, if they choose to follow Him, He will make them to become *"quickeners of mankind."*

To the entire body of Muslim ecclesiastics Bahá'u'lláh specifically devoted innumerable passages in His Books and Tablets, wherein He, in vehement language, denounces their cruelty; condemns their pride and arrogance; calls upon them to lay aside the things they possess, to hold their peace, and give ear to the words He has spoken; and asserts that, by reason of their deeds, *"the exalted station of the people hath been abased, the standard of Islám hath been reversed, and its mighty throne hath fallen."* To the *"concourse of Persian divines"* He more particularly addressed His condemnatory words in which He stigmatizes their deeds, and prophesies that their *"glory will be turned into the most wretched abasement,"* and that they shall behold the punishment which will be inflicted upon them, *"as decreed by God, the Ordainer, the All-Wise."*

To the Jewish people, He, moreover, announced that the Most Great Law has come, that *"the Ancient Beauty ruleth upon the throne of David,"* Who cries aloud and invokes His Name, that *"from Zion hath appeared that which was hidden,"* and that *"from Jerusalem is heard the Voice of God, the One, the Incomparable, the Omniscient."*

To the *"high priests"* of the Zoroastrian Faith He, furthermore, proclaimed that *"the Incomparable Friend"* is manifest, that He *"speaketh that wherein lieth salvation,"* that *"the Hand of Omnipotence is stretched forth from behind the clouds,"* that the tokens of His majesty and greatness are unveiled; and declared that *"no man's acts shall be acceptable in this day unless he forsaketh mankind and all that men possess, and setteth his face towards the Omnipotent One."*

Some of the weightiest passages of His Epistle to Queen Victoria are addressed to the members of the British Legislature, the Mother of Parliaments, as well as to the elected representatives of the peoples in other lands. In these He asserts that His purpose is to quicken the world and unite its peoples; refers to the treatment meted out to Him by His enemies; exhorts the legislators to *"take counsel together,"* and to concern themselves only *"with that which profiteth mankind"*; and affirms that the *"sovereign remedy"* for the *"healing of all the world"* is the *"union of all its peoples in one universal Cause, one common Faith,"* which can *"in no wise be achieved except through the power of a skilled and all-powerful and inspired Physician."* He, moreover, in His Most Holy Book, has enjoined the selection of a single language and the adoption of a common script for all on earth to use, an injunction which, when carried out, would, as He Himself affirms in that Book, be one of the signs of the *"coming of age of the human race."*

No less significant are the words addressed separately by Him to the *"people of the Bayán,"* to the wise men of the world, to its poets, to its men of letters, to its mystics and even to its tradesmen, in which

He exhorts them to be attentive to His voice, to recognize His Day, and to follow His bidding.

Such in sum are the salient features of the concluding utterances of that historic Proclamation, the opening notes of which were sounded during the latter part of Bahá'u'lláh's banishment to Adrianople, and which closed during the early years of His incarceration in the prison-fortress of 'Akká. Kings and emperors, severally and collectively; the chief magistrates of the Republics of the American continent; ministers and ambassadors; the Sovereign Pontiff himself; the Vicar of the Prophet of Islám; the royal Trustee of the Kingdom of the Hidden Imám; the monarchs of Christendom, its patriarchs, archbishops, bishops, priests and monks; the recognized leaders of both the Sunní and Shí'ah sacerdotal orders; the high priests of the Zoroastrian religion; the philosophers, the ecclesiastical leaders, the wise men and the inhabitants of Constantinople—that proud seat of both the Sultanate and the Caliphate; the entire company of the professed adherents of the Zoroastrian, the Jewish, the Christian and Muslim Faiths; the people of the Bayán; the wise men of the world, its men of letters, its poets, its mystics, its tradesmen, the elected representatives of its peoples; His own countrymen—all have, at one time or another, in books, Epistles, and Tablets, been brought directly within the purview of the exhortations, the warnings, the appeals, the declarations and the prophecies which constitute the theme of His momentous summons to the leaders of mankind—a summons which stands unparalleled in the annals of any previous religion, and to which the messages directed by the Prophet of Islám to some of the rulers among His contemporaries alone offer a faint resemblance.

*"Never since the beginning of the world,"* Bahá'u'lláh Himself affirms, *"hath the Message been so openly proclaimed."* *"Each one of them,"* He, specifically referring to the Tablets addressed by Him to the sovereigns of the earth—Tablets acclaimed by 'Abdu'l-Bahá as a *"miracle"*—has written, *"hath been designated by a special name. The first hath been named 'The Rumbling,' the second 'The Blow,' the third 'The Inevitable,' the fourth 'The Plain,' the fifth 'The Catastrophe,' and the others 'The Stunning Trumpet-Blast,' 'The Near Event,' 'The Great Terror,' 'The Trumpet,' 'The Bugle,' and the like, so that all the peoples of the earth may know, of a certainty, and may witness, with outward and inner eyes, that He Who is the Lord of Names hath prevailed, and will continue to prevail, under all conditions, over all men."* The most important of these Tablets, together with the celebrated Súriy-i-Haykal (the Súrih of the Temple), He,

moreover, ordered to be written in the shape of a pentacle, symbolizing the temple of man, and which He identified, when addressing the followers of the Gospel in one of His Tablets, with the "Temple" mentioned by the Prophet Zechariah, and designated as *"the resplendent dawning-place of the All-Merciful,"* and which *"the hands of the power of Him Who is the Causer of Causes"* had built.

Unique and stupendous as was this Proclamation, it proved to be but a prelude to a still mightier revelation of the creative power of its Author, and to what may well rank as the most signal act of His ministry—the promulgation of the Kitáb-i-Aqdas. Alluded to in the Kitáb-i-Íqán; the principal repository of that Law which the Prophet Isaiah had anticipated, and which the writer of the Apocalypse had described as the *"new heaven"* and the *"new earth,"* as *"the Tabernacle of God,"* as the *"Holy City,"* as the *"Bride,"* the *"New Jerusalem coming down from God,"* this *"Most Holy Book,"* whose provisions must remain inviolate for no less than a thousand years, and whose system will embrace the entire planet, may well be regarded as the brightest emanation of the mind of Bahá'u'lláh, as the Mother Book of His Dispensation, and the Charter of His New World Order.

Revealed soon after Bahá'u'lláh had been transferred to the house of 'Údí Khammár (circa 1873), at a time when He was still encompassed by the tribulations that had afflicted Him, through the acts committed by His enemies and the professed adherents of His Faith, this Book, this treasury enshrining the priceless gems of His Revelation, stands out, by virtue of the principles it inculcates, the administrative institutions it ordains and the function with which it invests the appointed Successor of its Author, unique and incomparable among the world's sacred Scriptures. For, unlike the Old Testament and the Holy Books which preceded it, in which the actual precepts uttered by the Prophet Himself are non-existent; unlike the Gospels, in which the few sayings attributed to Jesus Christ afford no clear guidance regarding the future administration of the affairs of His Faith; unlike even the Qur'án which, though explicit in the laws and ordinances formulated by the Apostle of God, is silent on the all-important subject of the succession, the Kitáb-i-Aqdas, revealed from first to last by the Author of the Dispensation Himself, not only preserves for posterity the basic laws and ordinances on which the fabric of His future World Order must rest, but ordains, in addition to the function of interpretation which it confers upon His Successor, the necessary institutions through which the integrity and unity of His Faith can alone be safeguarded.

In this Charter of the future world civilization its Author—at once the Judge, the Lawgiver, the Unifier and Redeemer of mankind—announces to the kings of the earth the promulgation of the *"Most Great Law"*; pronounces them to be His vassals; proclaims Himself the *"King of Kings"*; disclaims any intention of laying hands on their kingdoms; reserves for Himself the right to *"seize and possess the hearts of men"*; warns the world's ecclesiastical leaders not to weigh the *"Book of God"* with such standards as are current amongst them; and affirms that the Book itself is the *"Unerring Balance"* established amongst men. In it He formally ordains the institution of the *"House of Justice,"* defines its functions, fixes its revenues, and designates its members as the *"Men of Justice,"* the *"Deputies of God,"* the *"Trustees of the All-Merciful,"* alludes to the future Center of His Covenant, and invests Him with the right of interpreting His holy Writ; anticipates by implication the institution of Guardianship; bears witness to the revolutionizing effect of His World Order; enunciates the doctrine of the *"Most Great Infallibility"* of the Manifestation of God; asserts this infallibility to be the inherent and exclusive right of the Prophet; and rules out the possibility of the appearance of another Manifestation ere the lapse of at least one thousand years.

In this Book He, moreover, prescribes the obligatory prayers; designates the time and period of fasting; prohibits congregational prayer except for the dead; fixes the Qiblih; institutes the Ḥuqúqu'lláh (Right of God); formulates the law of inheritance; ordains the institution of the Mas̲h̲riqu'l-Ad̲h̲kár; establishes the Nineteen Day Feasts, the Bahá'í festivals and the Intercalary Days; abolishes the institution of priesthood; prohibits slavery, asceticism, mendicancy, monasticism, penance, the use of pulpits and the kissing of hands; prescribes monogamy; condemns cruelty to animals, idleness and sloth, backbiting and calumny; censures divorce; interdicts gambling, the use of opium, wine and other intoxicating drinks; specifies the punishments for murder, arson, adultery and theft; stresses the importance of marriage and lays down its essential conditions; imposes the obligation of engaging in some trade or profession, exalting such occupation to the rank of worship; emphasizes the necessity of providing the means for the education of children; and lays upon every person the duty of writing a testament and of strict obedience to one's government.

Apart from these provisions Bahá'u'lláh exhorts His followers to consort, with amity and concord and without discrimination, with the adherents of all religions; warns them to guard against fanaticism, sedition, pride, dispute and contention; inculcates upon them immaculate cleanliness, strict truthfulness, spotless chastity, trustworthiness; hospitality, fidelity, courtesy, forbearance, justice and fairness; counsels them to be *"even as the fingers of one hand and the limbs of one body"*; calls upon them to arise and serve His Cause; and assures them of His undoubted aid. He, furthermore, dwells upon the instability of human affairs; declares that true liberty consists in man's submission to His commandments; cautions them not to be indulgent in carrying out His statutes; prescribes the twin inseparable duties of recognizing the *"Dayspring of God's Revelation"* and of observing all the ordinances revealed by Him, neither of which, He affirms, is acceptable without the other.

The significant summons issued to the Presidents of the Republics of the American continent to seize their opportunity in the Day of God and to champion the cause of justice; the injunction to the members of parliaments throughout the world, urging the adoption of a universal script and language; His warnings to William I, the conqueror of Napoleon III; the reproof He administers to Francis Joseph, the Emperor of Austria; His reference to *"the lamentations of Berlin"* in His apostrophe to *"the banks of the Rhine"*; His condemnation of *"the throne of tyranny"* established in Constantinople, and His prediction of the extinction of its *"outward splendor"* and of the tribulations destined to overtake its inhabitants; the words of cheer and comfort He addresses to His native city, assuring her that God had chosen her to be *"the source of the joy of all mankind"*; His prophecy that *"the voice of the heroes of Khurásán"* will be raised in glorification of their Lord; His assertion that men *"endued with mighty valor"* will be raised up in Kirmán who will make mention of Him; and finally, His magnanimous assurance to a perfidious brother who had afflicted Him with such anguish, that an *"ever-forgiving, all-bounteous"* God would forgive him his iniquities were he only to repent—all these further enrich the contents of a Book designated by its Author as *"the source of true felicity,"* as the *"Unerring Balance,"* as the *"Straight Path"* and as the *"quickener of mankind."*

The laws and ordinances that constitute the major theme of this Book, Bahá'u'lláh, moreover, has specifically characterized as *"the breath of life unto all created things,"* as *"the mightiest stronghold,"* as the *"fruits"* of His *"Tree,"* as *"the highest means for the maintenance of order in the world and the security of its peoples,"* as *"the lamps of His wisdom and loving-providence,"* as *"the sweet smelling savor of*

*His garment,"* as the *"keys"* of His *"mercy"* to His creatures. *"This Book,"* He Himself testifies, *"is a heaven which We have adorned with the stars of Our commandments and prohibitions." "Blessed the man,"* He, moreover, has stated, *"who will read it, and ponder the verses sent down in it by God, the Lord of Power, the Almighty. Say, O men! Take hold of it with the hand of resignation . . . By My life! It hath been sent down in a manner that amazeth the minds of men. Verily, it is My weightiest testimony unto all people, and the proof of the All-Merciful unto all who are in heaven and all who are on earth."* And again: *"Blessed the palate that savoreth its sweetness, and the perceiving eye that recognizeth that which is treasured therein, and the understanding heart that comprehendeth its allusions and mysteries. By God! Such is the majesty of what hath been revealed therein, and so tremendous the revelation of its veiled allusions that the loins of utterance shake when attempting their description."* And finally: *"In such a manner hath the Kitáb-i-Aqdas been revealed that it attracteth and embraceth all the divinely appointed Dispensations. Blessed those who peruse it! Blessed those who apprehend it! Blessed those who meditate upon it! Blessed those who ponder its meaning! So vast is its range that it hath encompassed all men ere their recognition of it. Erelong will its sovereign power, its pervasive influence and the greatness of its might be manifested on earth."*

The formulation by Bahá'u'lláh, in His Kitáb-i-Aqdas, of the fundamental laws of His Dispensation was followed, as His Mission drew to a close, by the enunciation of certain precepts and principles which lie at the very core of His Faith, by the reaffirmation of truths He had previously proclaimed, by the elaboration and elucidation of some of the laws He had already laid down, by the revelation of further prophecies and warnings, and by the establishment of subsidiary ordinances designed to supplement the provisions of His Most Holy Book. These were recorded in unnumbered Tablets, which He continued to reveal until the last days of His earthly life, among which the "Ishráqát" (Splendors), the "Bishárát" (Glad Tidings), the "Ṭarázát" (Ornaments), the "Tajallíyát" (Effulgences), the "Kalimát-i-Firdawsíyyih" (Words of Paradise), the "Lawḥ-i-Aqdas" (Most Holy Tablet), the "Lawḥ-i-Dunyá" (Tablet of the World), the "Lawḥ-i-Maqsúd" (Tablet of Maqsúd), are the most noteworthy. These Tablets—mighty and final effusions of His indefatigable pen—must rank among the choicest fruits which His mind has yielded, and mark the consummation of His forty-year-long ministry.

Of the principles enshrined in these Tablets the most vital of them all is the principle of the oneness and wholeness of the human race, which may well be regarded as the hall-mark of Bahá'u'lláh's Revelation and the pivot of His teachings. Of such cardinal importance is this principle of unity that it is expressly referred to in the Book of His Covenant, and He unreservedly proclaims it as the central purpose of His Faith. "*We, verily,*" He declares, "*have come to unite and weld together all that dwell on earth.*" "*So potent is the light of unity,*" He further states, "*that it can illuminate the whole earth.*" "*At one time,*" He has written with reference to this central theme of His Revelation, "*We spoke in the language of the lawgiver; at another in that of the truth seeker and the mystic, and yet Our supreme purpose and highest wish hath always been to disclose the glory and sublimity of this station.*" Unity, He states, is the goal that "*excelleth every goal*" and an aspiration which is "*the monarch of all aspirations.*" "*The world,*" He proclaims, "*is but one country, and mankind its citizens.*" He further affirms that the unification of mankind, the last stage in the evolution of humanity towards maturity is inevitable, that "*soon will the present day order be rolled up, and a new one spread out in its stead,*" that "*the whole earth is now in a state of pregnancy,*" that "*the day is approaching when it will have yielded its noblest fruits, when from it will have sprung forth the loftiest trees, the most enchanting blossoms, the most heavenly blessings.*" He deplores the defectiveness of the prevailing order, exposes the inadequacy of patriotism as a directing and controlling force in human society, and regards the "*love of mankind*" and service to its interests as the worthiest and most laudable objects of human endeavor. He, moreover, laments that "*the vitality of men's belief in God is dying out in every land,*" that the "*face of the world*" is turned towards "*waywardness and unbelief*"; proclaims religion to be "*a radiant light and an impregnable stronghold for the protection and welfare of the peoples of the world*" and "*the chief instrument for the establishment of order in the world*"; affirms its fundamental purpose to be the promotion of union and concord amongst men; warns lest it be made "*a source of dissension, of discord and hatred*"; commands that its principles be taught to children in the schools of the world, in a manner that would not be productive of either prejudice or fanaticism; attributes "*the waywardness of the ungodly*" to the "*decline of religion*"; and predicts "*convulsions*" of such severity as to "*cause the limbs of mankind to quake.*"

The principle of collective security He unreservedly urges; recommends the reduction in national armaments; and proclaims as necessary and inevitable the convening of a world gathering at which the kings and rulers of the world will deliberate for the establishment of peace among the nations.

Justice He extols as *"the light of men"* and their *"guardian,"* as *"the revealer of the secrets of the world of being, and the standard-bearer of love and bounty"*; declares its radiance to be incomparable; affirms that upon it must depend *"the organization of the world and the tranquillity of mankind."* He characterizes its *"two pillars"*—*"reward and punishment"*—as *"the sources of life"* to the human race; warns the peoples of the world to bestir themselves in anticipation of its advent; and prophesies that, after an interval of great turmoil and grievous injustice, its day-star will shine in its full splendor and glory.

He, furthermore, inculcates the principle of *"moderation in all things"*; declares that whatsoever, be it *"Liberty, civilization and the like,"* *"passeth beyond the limits of moderation"* must *"exercise a pernicious influence upon men"*; observes that western civilization has gravely perturbed and alarmed the peoples of the world; and predicts that the day is approaching when the *"flame"* of a civilization *"carried to excess"* *"will devour the cities."*

Consultation He establishes as one of the fundamental principles of His Faith; describes it as *"the lamp of guidance,"* as *"the bestower of understanding,"* and as one of the two *"luminaries"* of the *"heaven of Divine wisdom."* Knowledge, He states, is *"as wings to man's life and a ladder for his ascent"*; its acquisition He regards as *"incumbent upon every one"*; considers *"arts, crafts and sciences"* to be conducive to the exaltation of the world of being; commends the wealth acquired through crafts and professions; acknowledges the indebtedness of the peoples of the world to scientists and craftsmen; and discourages the study of such sciences as are unprofitable to men, and *"begin with words and end with words."*

The injunction to *"consort with all men in a spirit of friendliness and fellowship"* He further emphasizes, and recognizes such association to be conducive to *"union and concord,"* which, He affirms, are the establishers of order in the world and the quickeners of nations. The necessity of adopting a universal tongue and script He repeatedly stresses; deplores the waste of time involved in the study of divers languages; affirms that with the adoption of such a language and script the whole earth will be considered as *"one city and one land"*; and claims to be possessed of the knowledge of both, and ready to impart it to any one who might seek it from Him.

To the trustees of the House of Justice He assigns the duty of legislating on matters not expressly provided in His writings, and promises that God will *"inspire them with whatsoever He willeth."* The establishment of a constitutional form of government, in which the ideals of republicanism and the majesty of kingship, characterized by Him as *"one of the signs of God,"* are combined, He recommends as a meritorious achievement; urges that special regard be paid to the interests of agriculture; and makes specific reference to *"the swiftly appearing newspapers,"* describes them as *"the mirror of the world"* and as *"an amazing and potent phenomenon,"* and prescribes to all who are responsible for their production the duty to be sanctified from malice, passion and prejudice, to be just and fair-minded, to be painstaking in their inquiries, and ascertain all the facts in every situation.

The doctrine of the Most Great Infallibility He further elaborates; the obligation laid on His followers to "behave towards the government of the country in which they reside with loyalty, honesty and truthfulness," He reaffirms; the ban imposed upon the waging of holy war and the destruction of books He reemphasizes; and He singles out for special praise men of learning and wisdom, whom He extols as *"eyes"* to the body of mankind, and as the *"greatest gifts"* conferred upon the world.

Nor should a review of the outstanding features of Bahá'u'lláh's writings during the latter part of His banishment to 'Akká fail to include a reference to the Lawḥ-i-Ḥikmat (Tablet of Wisdom), in which He sets forth the fundamentals of true philosophy, or to the Tablet of Visitation revealed in honor of the Imám Ḥusayn, whose praises He celebrates in glowing language; or to the "Questions and Answers" which elucidates the laws and ordinances of the Kitáb-i-Aqdas; or to the "Lawḥ-i-Burhán" (Tablet of the Proof) in which the acts perpetrated by Shaykh Muḥammad-Báqir, surnamed *"Dhi'b"* (Wolf), and Mír Muḥammad-Ḥusayn, the Imám-Jum'ih of Iṣfahán, surnamed *"Raqshá"* (She-Serpent), are severely condemned; or to the Lawḥ-i-Karmil (Tablet of Carmel) in which the Author significantly makes mention of *"the City of God that hath descended from heaven,"* and prophesies that *"erelong will God sail His Ark"* upon that mountain, and *"will manifest the people of Bahá."* Finally, mention must be made of His Epistle to Shaykh Muḥammad-Taqí, surnamed "Ibn-i-Dhi'b" (Son of the Wolf), the last outstanding Tablet revealed by the pen of Bahá'u'lláh, in which He calls upon that rapacious priest to repent of his acts, quotes some of the most characteristic and celebrated passages of His own writings, and adduces proofs establishing the validity of His Cause.

With this book, revealed about one year prior to His ascension, the prodigious achievement as author of a hundred volumes, repositories of the priceless pearls of His Revelation, may be said to have practically terminated—volumes replete with unnumbered exhortations, revolutionizing principles, world-shaping laws and ordinances, dire warnings and portentous prophecies, with soul-uplifting prayers and meditations, illuminating commentaries and interpretations, impassioned discourses and homilies, all interspersed with either addresses or references to kings, to emperors and to ministers, of both the East and the West, to ecclesiastics of divers denominations, and to leaders in the intellectual, political, literary, mystical, commercial and humanitarian spheres of human activity.

*"We, verily,"* wrote Bahá'u'lláh, surveying, in the evening of His life, from His Most Great Prison, the entire range of this vast and weighty Revelation, *"have not fallen short of Our duty to exhort men, and to deliver that whereunto I was bidden by God, the Almighty, the All-Praised." "Is there any excuse,"* He further has stated, *"left for any one in this Revelation? No, by God, the Lord of the Mighty Throne! My signs have encompassed the earth, and my power enveloped all mankind."*

## CHAPTER XIII

# Ascension of Bahá'u'lláh

Well nigh half a century had passed since the inception of the Faith. Cradled in adversity, deprived in its infancy of its Herald and Leader, it had been raised from the dust, in which a hostile despot had thrown it, by its second and greatest Luminary Who, despite successive banishments, had, in less than half a century, succeeded in rehabilitating its fortunes, in proclaiming its Message, in enacting its laws and ordinances, in formulating its principles and in ordaining its institutions, and it had just begun to enjoy the sunshine of a prosperity never previously experienced, when suddenly it was robbed of its Author by the Hand of Destiny, its followers were plunged into sorrow and consternation, its repudiators found their declining hopes revive, and its adversaries, political as well as ecclesiastical, began to take heart again.

Already nine months before His ascension Bahá'u'lláh, as attested by 'Abdu'l-Bahá, had voiced His desire to depart from this world. From that time onward it became increasingly evident, from the tone of His remarks to those who attained His presence, that the close of His earthly life was approaching, though He refrained from mentioning it openly to any one. On the night preceding the eleventh of Shavvál 1309 A.H. (May 8, 1892) He contracted a slight fever which, though it mounted the following day, soon after subsided. He continued to grant interviews to certain of the friends and pilgrims, but it soon became evident that He was not well. His fever returned in a more acute form than before, His general condition grew steadily worse, complications ensued which at last culminated in His ascension, at the hour of dawn, on the 2nd of Dhi'l-Qa'dih 1309 A.H. (May 29, 1892), eight hours after sunset, in the 75th year of His age. His spirit, at long last released from the toils of a life crowded with tribulations, had winged its flight to His *"other dominions,"* dominions *"whereon the eyes of the people of names have never fallen,"* and to which the *"Luminous Maid," "clad in white,"* had bidden Him hasten, as described by Himself in the Lawḥ-i-Ru'yá (Tablet of the Vision), revealed nineteen years previously, on the anniversary of the birth of His Forerunner.

Six days before He passed away He summoned to His presence, as He lay in bed leaning against one of His sons, the entire company of believers, including several pilgrims, who had assembled in the Mansion, for what proved to be their last audience with Him. *"I am well pleased with you all,"* He gently and affectionately addressed the weeping crowd that gathered about Him. *"Ye have rendered many services, and been very assiduous in your labors. Ye have come here every morning and every evening. May God assist you to remain united. May He aid you to exalt the Cause of the Lord of being."* To the women, including members of His own family, gathered at His bedside, He addressed similar words of encouragement, definitely assuring them that in a document entrusted by Him to the Most Great Branch He had commended them all to His care.

The news of His ascension was instantly communicated to Sulṭán 'Abdu'l-Ḥamíd in a telegram which began with the words "the Sun of Bahá has set" and in which the monarch was advised of the intention of interring the sacred remains within the precincts of the Mansion, an arrangement to which he readily assented. Bahá'u'lláh was accordingly laid to rest in the northernmost room of the house which served as a dwelling-place for His son-in-law, the most northerly of the three houses lying to the west of, and adjacent to, the Mansion. His interment took place shortly after sunset, on the very day of His ascension.

The inconsolable Nabíl, who had had the privilege of a private audience with Bahá'u'lláh during the days of His illness; whom 'Abdu'l-Bahá had chosen to select those passages which constitute the text of the Tablet of Visitation now recited in the Most Holy Tomb; and who, in his uncontrollable grief, drowned himself in the sea shortly after the passing of his Beloved, thus describes the agony of those days: "Methinks, the spiritual commotion set up in the world of dust had caused all the worlds of God to tremble. . . . My inner and outer tongue are powerless to portray the condition we were in. . . . In the midst of the prevailing confusion a multitude of the inhabitants of 'Akká and of the neighboring villages, that had thronged the fields surrounding the Mansion, could be seen weeping, beating upon their heads, and crying aloud their grief."

For a full week a vast number of mourners, rich and poor alike, tarried to grieve with the bereaved family, partaking day and night of the food that was lavishly dispensed by its members. Notables, among whom were numbered Shí'ahs, Sunnís, Christians, Jews and Druzes, as well as poets, 'ulamás and government officials, all joined in lamenting the loss, and in magnifying the virtues and greatness of Bahá'u'lláh, many of them paying to Him their written tributes, in verse and in prose, in both Arabic and Turkish. From cities as far afield as Damascus, Aleppo, Beirut and Cairo similar tributes were received. These glowing testimonials were, without exception, submitted to 'Abdu'l-Bahá, Who now represented the Cause of the departed Leader, and Whose praises were often mingled in these eulogies with the homage paid to His Father.

And yet these effusive manifestations of sorrow and expressions of praise and of admiration, which the ascension of Bahá'u'lláh had spontaneously evoked among the unbelievers in the Holy Land and the adjoining countries, were but a drop when compared with the ocean of grief and the innumerable evidences of unbounded devotion which, at the hour of the setting of the Sun of Truth, poured forth from the hearts of the countless thousands who had espoused His Cause, and were determined to carry aloft its banner in Persia, India, Russia, 'Iráq, Turkey, Palestine, Egypt and Syria.

With the ascension of Bahá'u'lláh draws to a close a period which, in many ways, is unparalleled in the world's religious history. The first century of the Bahá'í Era had by now run half its course. An epoch, unsurpassed in its sublimity, its fecundity and duration by any previous Dispensation, and characterized, except for a short interval of three years, by half a century of continuous and progressive Revelation, had terminated. The Message proclaimed by the Báb had yielded its golden fruit. The most momentous, though not the most spectacular phase of the Heroic Age had ended. The Sun of Truth, the world's greatest Luminary, had risen in the Síyáh-Chál of Ṭihrán, had broken through the clouds which enveloped it in Baghdád, had suffered a momentary eclipse whilst mounting to its zenith in Adrianople and had set finally in 'Akká, never to reappear ere the lapse of a full millennium. God's newborn Faith, the cynosure of all past Dispensations, had been fully and unreservedly proclaimed. The prophecies announcing its advent had been remarkably fulfilled. Its fundamental laws and cardinal principles, the warp and woof of the fabric of its future World Order, had been clearly enunciated. Its organic relation to, and its attitude towards, the religious systems which preceded it had been unmistakably defined. The primary institutions, within which an embryonic World Order was destined to mature, had been unassailably established. The Covenant designed to safeguard the unity and integrity of its world-embracing system had been irrevocably bequeathed to posterity. The promise of the unification of the whole human race, of the inauguration of the Most Great Peace, of the unfoldment of a world civilization, had been incontestably given. The dire warnings, foreshadowing catastrophes destined to befall kings, ecclesiastics, governments and peoples, as a prelude to so glorious a consummation, had been repeatedly uttered. The significant summons to the Chief Magistrates of the New World, forerunner of the Mission with which the North American continent was to be later invested, had been issued. The initial contact with a nation, a descendant of whose royal house was to espouse its Cause ere the expiry of the first Bahá'í century, had been established. The original impulse which, in the course of successive decades, has conferred, and will continue to confer, in the years to come, inestimable benefits of both spiritual and institutional significance upon God's holy mountain, overlooking the Most Great Prison, had been imparted. And finally, the first banners of a spiritual conquest which, ere the termination of that century, was to embrace no less than sixty countries in both the Eastern and Western hemispheres had been triumphantly planted.

In the vastness and diversity of its Holy Writ; in the number of its martyrs; in the valor of its champions; in the example set by its followers; in the condign punishment suffered by its adversaries; in the pervasiveness of its influence; in the incomparable heroism of its Herald; in the dazzling greatness of its Author; in the mysterious operation of its irresistible spirit; the Faith of Bahá'u'lláh, now standing at the threshold of the sixth decade of its existence, had amply demonstrated its capacity to forge ahead, indivisible and incorruptible, along the course traced for it by its Founder, and to display, before the gaze of successive generations, the signs and tokens of that celestial potency with which He Himself had so richly endowed it.

To the fate that has overtaken those kings, ministers and ecclesiastics, in the East as well as in the West, who have, at various stages of Bahá'u'lláh's ministry, either deliberately persecuted His Cause, or have neglected to heed the warnings He had uttered, or have failed in their manifest duty to respond to His summons or to accord Him and His message the treatment they deserved, particular attention, I feel, should at this juncture be directed. Bahá'u'lláh Himself, referring to those who had actively arisen to destroy or harm His Faith, had declared that *"God hath not blinked, nor will He ever blink His eyes at the tyranny of the oppressor. More particularly in this Revelation hath He visited each and every tyrant with His vengeance."* Vast and awful is, indeed, the spectacle which meets our eyes, as we survey the field over which the retributory winds of God have, since the inception of the ministry of Bahá'u'lláh, furiously swept, dethroning monarchs, extinguishing dynasties, uprooting ecclesiastical hierarchies, precipitating wars and revolutions, driving from office princes and ministers, dispossessing the usurper, casting down the tyrant, and chastising the wicked and the rebellious.

Sulṭán 'Abdu'l-'Azíz, who with Náṣiri'd-Dín S̲h̲áh was the author of the calamities heaped upon Bahá'u'lláh, and was himself responsible for three decrees of banishment against the Prophet; who had been stigmatized, in the Kitáb-i-Aqdas, as occupying the *"throne of tyranny,"* and whose fall had been prophesied in the Lawḥ-i-Fu'ád, was deposed in consequence of a palace revolution, was condemned by a fatvá (sentence) of the Muftí in his own capital, was four days later assassinated (1876), and was succeeded by a nephew who was declared to be imbecile. The war of 1877-78 emancipated eleven million people from the Turkish yoke; Adrianople was occupied by the Russian forces; the empire itself was dissolved as a result of the war of 1914-18; the sultanate was abolished; a republic was proclaimed; and a rulership that had endured above six centuries was ended.

The vain and despotic Náṣiri'd-Dín S̲h̲áh, denounced by Bahá'u'lláh as the *"Prince of Oppressors"*; of whom He had written that he would soon be made *"an object-lesson for the world"*; whose reign was stained by the execution of the Báb and the imprisonment of Bahá'u'lláh; who had persistently instigated his subsequent banishments to Constantinople, Adrianople and 'Akká; who, in collusion with a vicious sacerdotal order, had vowed to strangle the Faith in its cradle, was dramatically assassinated, in the shrine of S̲h̲áh 'Abdu'l-'Aẓím, on the very eve of his jubilee, which, as ushering in a new era, was to have been celebrated with the most elaborate magnificence, and was to go down in history as the greatest day in the annals of the Persian nation. The fortunes of his house thereafter steadily declined, and finally through the scandalous misconduct of the dissipated and irresponsible Aḥmad S̲h̲áh, led to the eclipse and disappearance of the Qájár dynasty.

Napoleon III, the foremost monarch of his day in the West, excessively ambitious, inordinately proud, tricky and superficial, who is reported to have contemptuously flung down the Tablet sent to him by Bahá'u'lláh, who was tested by Him and found wanting, and whose downfall was explicitly predicted in a subsequent Tablet, was ignominiously defeated in the Battle of Sedan (1870), marking the greatest military capitulation recorded in modern history; lost his kingdom and spent the remaining years of his life in exile. His hopes were utterly blasted, his only son, the Prince Imperial, was killed in the Zulu War, his much vaunted empire collapsed, a civil war ensued more ferocious than the Franco-German war itself, and William I, the Prussian king, was hailed emperor of a unified Germany in the Palace of Versailles.

William I, the pride-intoxicated newly-acclaimed conqueror of Napoleon III, admonished in the Kitáb-i-Aqdas and bidden to ponder the fate that had overtaken *"one whose power transcended"* his own, warned in that same Book, that the *"lamentations of Berlin"* would be raised and that the banks of the Rhine would be *"covered with gore,"* sustained two attempts on his life, and was succeeded by a son who died of a mortal disease, three months after his accession to the throne, bequeathing the throne to the arrogant, the headstrong and short-sighted William II. The pride of the new monarch precipitated his downfall. Revolution, swiftly and suddenly, broke out in his capital, communism reared its head in a number of cities; the princes of the German states abdicated, and he himself, fleeing ignominiously to Holland, was compelled to relinquish his right to the throne. The constitution of Weimar sealed the fate of the empire, whose birth had been so loudly proclaimed by his grandfather, and the terms of an oppressively severe treaty provoked *"the lamentations"* which, half a century before, had been ominously prophesied.

The arbitrary and unyielding Francis Joseph, emperor of Austria and king of Hungary, who had been reproved in the Kitáb-i-Aqdas, for having neglected his manifest duty to inquire about Bahá'u'lláh during his pilgrimage to the Holy Land, was so engulfed by misfortunes and tragedies that his reign came to be regarded as one unsurpassed by any other reign in the calamities it inflicted upon the nation. His brother, Maximilian, was put to death in Mexico; the Crown Prince Rudolph perished in ignominious circumstances; the Empress was assassinated; Archduke Francis Ferdinand and his wife were murdered in Serajevo; the "ramshackle empire" itself disintegrated, was carved up, and a shrunken republic was set up on the ruins of a vanished Holy Roman Empire—a republic which, after a brief and precarious existence, was blotted out from the political map of Europe.

Nicolaevitch Alexander II, the all-powerful Czar of Russia, who, in a Tablet addressed to him by name had been thrice warned by Bahá'u'lláh, had been bidden to *"summon the nations unto God,"* and had been cautioned not to allow his sovereignty to prevent him from recognizing *"the Supreme Sovereign,"* suffered several attempts on his life, and at last died at the hand of an assassin. A harsh policy of repression, initiated by himself and followed by his successor, Alexander III, paved the way for a revolution which, in the reign of Nicholas II, swept away on a bloody tide the empire of the Czars, brought in its wake war, disease and famine, and established a militant proletariat which massacred the nobility, persecuted the clergy, drove away the intellectuals, disendowed the state religion, executed the Czar with his consort and his family, and extinguished the dynasty of the Romanoffs.

Pope Pius IX, the undisputed head of the most powerful Church in Christendom, who had been commanded, in an Epistle addressed to him by Bahá'u'lláh, to leave his *"palaces unto such as desire them,"* to *"sell all the embellished ornaments"* in his possession, to *"expend them in the path of God,"* and hasten towards *"the Kingdom,"* was compelled to surrender, in distressing circumstances, to the besieging forces of King Victor Emmanuel, and to submit himself to be depossessed of the Papal States and of Rome itself. The loss of "the Eternal City," over which the Papal flag had flown for one thousand years, and the humiliation of the religious orders under his jurisdiction, added mental anguish to his physical infirmities and embittered the last years of his life. The formal recognition of the Kingdom of Italy subsequently exacted from one of his successors in the Vatican, confirmed the virtual extinction of the Pope's temporal sovereignty.

But the rapid dissolution of the Ottoman, the Napoleonic, the German, the Austrian and the Russian empires, the demise of the Qájár dynasty and the virtual extinction of the temporal sovereignty of the Roman Pontiff do not exhaust the story of the catastrophes that befell the monarchies of the world through the neglect of Bahá'u'lláh's warnings conveyed in the opening passages of His Súriy-i-Múlúk. The conversion of the Portuguese and Spanish monarchies, as well as the Chinese empire, into republics; the strange fate that has, more recently, been pursuing the sovereigns of Holland, of Norway, of Greece, of Yugoslavia and of Albania now living in exile; the virtual abdication of the authority exercised by the kings of Denmark, of Belgium, of Bulgaria, of Rumania and of Italy; the apprehension with which their fellow sovereigns must be viewing the convulsions that have seized so many thrones; the shame and acts of violence which, in some instances, have darkened the annals of the reigns of certain monarchs in both the East and the West, and still more recently the sudden downfall of the Founder of the newly established dynasty in Persia—these are yet further instances of the infliction of the *"Divine Chastisement"* foreshadowed by Bahá'u'lláh in that immortal Súrih, and show forth the divine reality of the arraignment pronounced by Him against the rulers of the earth in His Most Holy Book.

No less arresting has been the extinction of the all-pervasive influence exerted by the Muslim ecclesiastical leaders, both Sunní and Shí'ah, in the two countries in which the mightiest institutions of Islám had been reared, and which have been directly associated with the tribulations heaped upon the Báb and Bahá'u'lláh.

The Caliph, the self-styled vicar of the Prophet of Islám, known also as the "Commander of the Faithful," the protector of the holy cities of Mecca and Medina, whose spiritual jurisdiction extended over more than two hundred million Muḥammadans, was by the abolition of the Sultanate in Turkey, divested of his temporal authority, hitherto regarded as inseparable from his high office. The Caliph himself, after having occupied for a brief period, an anomalous and precarious position, fled to Europe; the Caliphate, the most august and powerful institution of Islám, was, without consultation with any community in the Sunní world, summarily abolished; the unity of the most powerful branch of the Islamic Faith was thereby shattered; a formal, a complete and permanent separation of the Turkish state from the Sunní faith was proclaimed; the Sharí'ah canonical Law was annulled; ecclesiastical institutions were disendowed; a civil code was promulgated; religious orders were suppressed; the Sunní hierarchy was dissolved; the Arabic tongue, the language of the Prophet of Islám, fell into disuse, and its script was superseded by the Latin alphabet; the Qur'án itself was translated into Turkish; Constantinople, the "Dome of Islám," sank to the level of a provincial city, and its peerless jewel, the Mosque of St. Sophia, was converted into a museum—a series of degradations recalling the fate which, in the first century of the Christian Era, befell the Jewish people, the city of Jerusalem, the Temple of Solomon, the Holy of Holies, and an ecclesiastical hierarchy, whose members were the avowed persecutors of the religion of Jesus Christ.

A similar convulsion shook the foundations of the entire sacerdotal order in Persia, though its formal divorce from the Persian state is as yet unproclaimed. A "church-state," that had been firmly rooted in the life of the nation and had extended its ramifications to every sphere of life in that country, was virtually disrupted. A sacerdotal order, the rock wall of Shí'ah Islám in that land, was paralyzed and discredited; its mujtahids, the favorite ministers of the hidden Imám, were reduced to an insignificant number; all its be-turbaned officers, except for a handful, were ruthlessly forced to exchange their traditional head-dress and robes for the European clothes they themselves anathematized; the pomp and pageantry that marked their ceremonials vanished; their fatvás (sentences) were nullified; their endowments were handed over to a civil administration; their mosques and seminaries were deserted; the right of sanctuary accorded to their shrines ceased to be recognized; their religious plays were banned; their takyihs were closed and even their pilgrimages to Najaf and Karbilá were discouraged and curtailed. The disuse of the veil; the recognition of the equality of sexes; the establishment of civil tribunals; the abolition of concubinage; the disparagement of the use of the Arabic tongue, the language of Islám and of the Qur'án, and the efforts exerted to divorce it from Persian —all these further proclaim the degradation, and foreshadow the final extinction, of that infamous crew, whose leaders had dared style themselves "servants of the Lord of Saintship" (Imám 'Alí), who had so often received the homage of the pious kings of the Ṣafaví dynasty, and whose anathemas, ever since the birth of the Faith of the Báb, had been chiefly responsible for the torrents of blood which had been shed, and whose acts have blackened the annals of both their religion and nation.

A crisis, not indeed as severe as that which shook the Islamic sacerdotal orders—the inveterate adversaries of the Faith—has, moreover, afflicted the ecclesiastical institutions of Christendom, whose influence, ever since Bahá'u'lláh's summons was issued and His warning was sounded, has visibly deteriorated, whose prestige has been gravely damaged, whose authority has steadily declined, and whose power, rights and prerogatives have been increasingly circumscribed. The virtual extinction of the temporal sovereignty of the Roman Pontiff, to which reference has already been made; the wave of anticlericalism that brought in its wake the separation of the Catholic Church from the French Republic; the organized assault launched by a triumphant Communist state upon the Greek Orthodox Church in Russia, and the consequent disestablishment, disendowment and persecution of the state religion; the dismemberment of the Austro-Hungarian monarchy which owed its allegiance to the Church of Rome and powerfully supported its institutions; the ordeal to which that same Church has been subjected in Spain and in Mexico; the wave of secularization which, at present, is engulfing the Catholic, the

Anglican and the Presbyterian Missions in non-Christian lands; the forces of an aggressive paganism which are assailing the ancient citadels of the Catholic, the Greek Orthodox and the Lutheran Churches in Western, in Central and Eastern Europe, in the Balkans and in the Baltic and Scandinavian states—these stand out as the most conspicuous manifestations of the decline in the fortunes of the ecclesiastical leaders of Christendom, leaders who, heedless of the voice of Bahá'u'lláh, have interposed themselves between the Christ returned in the glory of the Father and their respective congregations.

Nor can we fail to note the progressive deterioration in the authority, wielded by the ecclesiastical leaders of the Jewish and Zoroastrian Faiths, ever since the voice of Bahá'u'lláh was raised, announcing, in no uncertain terms, that the *"Most Great Law is come,"* that the Ancient Beauty *"ruleth upon the throne of David,"* and that *"whatsoever hath been announced in the Books* (Zoroastrian Holy Writ) *hath been revealed and made clear."* The evidences of increasing revolt against clerical authority; the disrespect and indifference shown to time-honored observances, rituals and ceremonials; the repeated inroads made by the forces of an aggressive and often hostile nationalism into the spheres of clerical jurisdiction; and the general apathy with which, particularly in the case of the professed adherents of the Zoroastrian Faith, these encroachments are regarded —all provide, beyond the shadow of a doubt, further justification of the warnings and predictions uttered by Bahá'u'lláh in His historic addresses to the world's ecclesiastical leaders.

Such in sum are the awful evidences of God's retributive justice that have afflicted kings as well as ecclesiastics, in both the East and the West, as a direct consequence of either their active opposition to the Faith of Bahá'u'lláh, or of their lamentable failure to respond to His call, to inquire into His Message, to avert the sufferings He endured, or to heed the marvelous signs and prodigies which, during a hundred years, have accompanied the birth and rise of His Revelation.

*"From two ranks amongst men,"* is His terse and prophetic utterance, *"power hath been seized: kings and ecclesiastics." "If ye pay no heed,"* He thus warned the kings of the earth, *"unto the counsels which . . . We have revealed in this Tablet, Divine chastisement will assail you from every direction . . . On that day ye shall . . . recognize your own impotence."* And again: *"Though aware of most of Our afflictions, ye, nevertheless, have failed to stay the hand of the aggressor."* And, furthermore, this arraignment: *". . . We . . . will*

*be patient, as We have been patient in that which hath befallen Us at your hands, O concourse of kings!"*

Condemning specifically the world's ecclesiastical leaders, He has written: *"The source and origin of tyranny have been the divines . . . God, verily, is clear of them, and We, too, are clear of them." "When We observed carefully,"* He openly affirms, *"We discovered that Our enemies are, for the most part, the divines." "O concourse of divines!"* He thus addresses them, *"Ye shall not henceforth behold yourselves possessed of any power, inasmuch as We have seized it from you . . ." "Had ye believed in God when He revealed Himself,"* He explains, *"the people would not have turned aside from Him, nor would the things ye witness today have befallen Us." "They,"* referring more specifically to Muslim ecclesiastics, He asserts, *"rose up against Us with such cruelty as hath sapped the strength of Islám . . ." "The divines of Persia,"* He affirms, *"committed that which no people amongst the peoples of the world hath committed."* And again: *". . . The divines of Persia . . . have perpetrated what the Jews have not perpetrated during the Revelation of Him Who is the Spirit* (Jesus)." And finally, these portentous prophecies: *"Because of you the people were abased, and the banner of Islám was hauled down, and its mighty throne subverted." "Erelong will all that ye possess perish, and your glory be turned into the most wretched abasement, and ye shall behold the punishment for what ye have wrought . . ." "Erelong,"* the Báb Himself, even more openly prophesies, *"We will, in very truth, torment such as waged war against Ḥusayn* (Imám Ḥusayn) *. . . with the most afflictive torment . . ." "Erelong will God wreak His vengeance upon them, at the time of Our return, and He hath, in very truth, prepared for them, in the world to come, a severe torment."*

Nor should, in a review of this nature, reference be omitted to those princes, ministers and ecclesiastics who have individually been responsible for the afflictive trials which Bahá'u'lláh and His followers have suffered. Fu'ád Pá<u>sh</u>á, the Turkish Minister for Foreign Affairs, denounced by Him as the *"instigator"* of His banishment to the Most Great Prison, who had so assiduously striven with his colleague 'Álí Pá<u>sh</u>á, to excite the fears and suspicions of a despot already predisposed against the Faith and its Leader, was, about a year after he had succeeded in executing his design, struck down, while on a trip to Paris, by the avenging rod of God, and died at Nice (1869). 'Álí Pá<u>sh</u>á, the Ṣadr-i-A'ẓam (Prime Minister), denounced in such forceful language in the Lawḥ-i-Ra'ís, whose downfall the Lawḥ-i-

Fu'ád had unmistakably predicted, was, a few years after Bahá'u'lláh's banishment to 'Akká, dismissed from office, was shorn of all power, and sank into complete oblivion. The tyrannical Prince Mas'úd Mírzá, the Ẓillu's-Sulṭán, Náṣiri'd-Dín S͟háh's eldest son and ruler over more than two-fifths of his kingdom, stigmatized by Bahá'u'lláh as *"the Infernal Tree,"* fell into disgrace, was deprived of all his governorships, except that of Iṣfahán, and lost all chances of future eminence or promotion. The rapacious Prince Jalálu'd-Dawlih, branded by the Supreme Pen as *"the tyrant of Yazd,"* was, about a year after the iniquities he had perpetrated, deprived of his post, recalled to Ṭihrán, and forced to return a part of the property he had stolen from his victims.

The scheming, the ambitious and profligate Mírzá Buzurg K͟hán, the Persian Consul General in Bag͟hdád, was eventually dismissed from office, "overwhelmed with disaster, filled with remorse and plunged into confusion." The notorious Mujtahid Siyyid Ṣádiq-i-Ṭabáṭabá'í, denounced by Bahá'u'lláh as *"the Liar of Ṭihrán,"* the author of the monstrous decree condemning every male member of the Bahá'í community in Persia, young or old, high or low, to be put to death, and all its women to be deported, was suddenly taken ill, fell a prey to a disease that ravaged his heart, his brain and his limbs, and precipitated eventually his death. The high-handed Ṣubḥí Pás͟há, who had peremptorily summoned Bahá'u'lláh to the government house in 'Akká, lost the position he occupied, and was recalled under circumstances highly detrimental to his reputation. Nor were the other governors of the city, who had dealt unjustly with the exalted Prisoner in their charge and His fellow-exiles, spared a like fate. "Every pás͟há," testifies Nabíl in his narrative, "whose conduct in 'Akká was commendable enjoyed a long term of office, and was bountifully favored by God, whereas every hostile Mutiṣarrif (governor) was speedily deposed by the Hand of Divine power, even as 'Abdu'r-Raḥmán Pás͟há and Muḥammad-Yúsuf Pás͟há who, on the morrow of the very night they had resolved to lay hands on the loved ones of Bahá'u'lláh, were telegraphically advised of their dismissal. Such was their fate that they were never again given a position."

S͟hayk͟h Muḥammad-Báqir, surnamed the "Wolf," who, in the strongly condemnatory Lawḥ-i-Burhán addressed to him by Bahá'u'lláh, had been compared to *"the last trace of sunlight upon the mountain-top,"* witnessed the steady decline of his prestige, and died in a miserable state of acute remorse. His accomplice, Mír Muḥammad-Ḥusayn, surnamed the "She-Serpent," whom Bahá'u'lláh described as one *"infinitely more wicked than the oppressor of Karbilá,"* was, about that same time, expelled from Iṣfahán, wandered from village to village, contracted a disease that engendered so foul an odor that even his wife and daughter could not bear to approach him, and died in such ill-favor with the local authorities that no one dared to attend his funeral, his corpse being ignominiously interred by a few porters.

Mention should, moreover, be made of the devastating famine which, about a year after the illustrious Badí' had been tortured to death, ravaged Persia and reduced the population to such extremities that even the rich went hungry, and hundreds of mothers ghoulishly devoured their own children.

Nor can this subject be dismissed without special reference being made to the Arch-Breaker of the Covenant of the Báb, Mírzá Yaḥyá, who lived long enough to witness, while eking out a miserable existence in Cyprus, termed by the Turks "the Island of Satan," every hope he had so maliciously conceived reduced to naught. A pensioner first of the Turkish and later of the British Government, he was subjected to the further humiliation of having his application for British citizenship refused. Eleven of the eighteen "Witnesses" he had appointed forsook him and turned in repentance to Bahá'u'lláh. He himself became involved in a scandal which besmirched his reputation and that of his eldest son, deprived that son and his descendants of the successorship with which he had previously invested him, and appointed, in his stead, the perfidious Mírzá Hádíy-i-Dawlat-Ábádí, a notorious Azalí, who, on the occasion of the martyrdom of the aforementioned Mírzá As̱hraf, was seized with such fear that during four consecutive days he proclaimed from the pulpit-top, and in a most vituperative language, his complete repudiation of the Bábí Faith, as well as of Mírzá Yaḥyá, his benefactor, who had reposed in him such implicit confidence. It was this same eldest son who, through the workings of a strange destiny, sought years after, together with his nephew and niece, the presence of 'Abdu'l-Bahá, the appointed Successor of Bahá'u'lláh and Center of His Covenant, expressed repentance, prayed for forgiveness, was graciously accepted by Him, and remained, till the hour of his death, a loyal follower of the Faith which his father had so foolishly, so shamelessly and so pitifully striven to extinguish.

## THIRD PERIOD

# THE MINISTRY OF ‘ABDU’L-BAHÁ

## 1892-1921

## CHAPTER XIV

# The Covenant of Bahá'u'lláh

I have in the preceding chapters endeavored to trace the rise and progress of the Faith associated with the Báb and Bahá'u'lláh during the first fifty years of its existence. If I have dwelt too long on the events connected with the life and mission of these twin Luminaries of the Bahá'í Revelation, if I have at times indulged in too circumstantial a narrative of certain episodes related to their ministries, it is solely because these happenings proclaim the birth, and signalize the establishment, of an epoch which future historians will acclaim as the most heroic, the most tragic and the most momentous period in the Apostolic Age of the Bahá'í Dispensation. Indeed the tale which the subsequent decades of the century under review unfold to our eyes is but the record of the manifold evidences of the resistless operation of those creative forces which the revolution of fifty years of almost uninterrupted Revelation had released.

A dynamic process, divinely propelled, possessed of undreamt-of potentialities, world-embracing in scope, world-transforming in its ultimate consequences, had been set in motion on that memorable night when the Báb communicated the purpose of His mission to Mullá Ḥusayn in an obscure corner of S͟híráz. It acquired a tremendous momentum with the first intimations of Bahá'u'lláh's dawning Revelation amidst the darkness of the Síyáh-C͟hál of Ṭihrán. It was further accelerated by the Declaration of His mission on the eve of His banishment from Bag͟hdád. It moved to a climax with the proclamation of that same mission during the tempestuous years of His exile in Adrianople. Its full significance was disclosed when the Author of that Mission issued His historic summonses, appeals and warnings to the kings of the earth and the world's ecclesiastical leaders. It was finally consummated by the laws and ordinances which He formulated, by the principles which He enunciated and by the institutions which He ordained during the concluding years of His ministry in the prison-city of 'Akká.

To direct and canalize these forces let loose by this Heaven-sent process, and to insure their harmonious and continuous operation after His ascension, an instrument divinely ordained, invested with indisputable authority, organically linked with the Author of the Revelation Himself, was clearly indispensable. That instrument Bahá'u'lláh had expressly provided through the institution of the Covenant, an institution which He had firmly established prior to His ascension. This same Covenant He had anticipated in His Kitáb-i-Aqdas, had alluded to it as He bade His last farewell to the members of His family, who had been summoned to His bed-side, in the days immediately preceding His ascension, and had incorporated it in a special document which He designated as "the Book of My Covenant," and which He entrusted, during His last illness, to His eldest son 'Abdu'l-Bahá.

Written entirely in His own hand; unsealed, on the ninth day after His ascension in the presence of nine witnesses chosen from amongst His companions and members of His Family; read subsequently, on the afternoon of that same day, before a large company assembled in His Most Holy Tomb, including His sons, some of the Báb's kinsmen, pilgrims and resident believers, this unique and epoch-making Document, designated by Bahá'u'lláh as His "Most Great Tablet," and alluded to by Him as the "Crimson Book" in His "Epistle to the Son of the Wolf," can find no parallel in the Scriptures of any previous Dispensation, not excluding that of the Báb Himself. For nowhere in the books pertaining to any of the world's religious systems, not even among the writings of the Author of the Bábí Revelation, do we find any single document establishing a Covenant endowed with an authority comparable to the Covenant which Bahá'u'lláh had Himself instituted.

*"So firm and mighty is this Covenant,"* He Who is its appointed Center has affirmed, *"that from the beginning of time until the present day no religious Dispensation hath produced its like." "It is indubitably clear,"* He, furthermore, has stated, *"that the pivot of the oneness of mankind is nothing else but the power of the Covenant." "Know thou,"* He has written, *"that the 'Sure Handle' mentioned from the foundation of the world in the Books, the Tablets and the Scriptures of old is naught else but the Covenant and the Testament."* And again: *"The lamp of the Covenant is the light of the world, and the words traced by the Pen of the Most High a limitless ocean." "The Lord, the All-Glorified,"* He has moreover declared, *"hath, beneath the shade of the Tree of Anísá* (Tree of Life), *made a new Covenant and established a great Testament . . . Hath such a Covenant been established in any previous Dispensation, age, period or century? Hath such a Testament, set down by the Pen of the Most*

*High, ever been witnessed? No, by God!"* And finally: *"The power of the Covenant is as the heat of the sun which quickeneth and promoteth the development of all created things on earth. The light of the Covenant, in like manner, is the educator of the minds, the spirits, the hearts and souls of men."* To this same Covenant He has in His writings referred as the *"Conclusive Testimony,"* the *"Universal Balance,"* the *"Magnet of God's grace,"* the *"Upraised Standard,"* the *"Irrefutable Testament," "the all-mighty Covenant, the like of which the sacred Dispensations of the past have never witnessed"* and *"one of the distinctive features of this most mighty cycle."*

Extolled by the writer of the Apocalypse as "the Ark of His (God) Testament"; associated with the gathering beneath the *"Tree of Anísá"* (Tree of Life) mentioned by Bahá'u'lláh in the Hidden Words; glorified by Him, in other passages of His writings, as the *"Ark of Salvation"* and as *"the Cord stretched betwixt the earth and the Abhá Kingdom,"* this Covenant has been bequeathed to posterity in a Will and Testament which, together with the Kitáb-i-Aqdas and several Tablets, in which the rank and station of 'Abdu'l-Bahá are unequivocally disclosed, constitute the chief buttresses designed by the Lord of the Covenant Himself to shield and support, after His ascension, the appointed Center of His Faith and the Delineator of its future institutions.

In this weighty and incomparable Document its Author discloses the character of that *"excellent and priceless heritage"* bequeathed by Him to His *"heirs"*; proclaims afresh the fundamental purpose of His Revelation; enjoins the *"peoples of the world"* to hold fast to that which will *"elevate"* their *"station"*; announces to them that *"God hath forgiven what is past"*; stresses the sublimity of man's station; discloses the primary aim of the Faith of God; directs the faithful to pray for the welfare of the kings of the earth, *"the manifestations of the power, and the daysprings of the might and riches, of God"*; invests them with the rulership of the earth; singles out as His special domain the hearts of men; forbids categorically strife and contention; commands His followers to aid those rulers who are *"adorned with the ornament of equity and justice"*; and directs, in particular, the Aghṣán (His sons) to ponder the *"mighty force and the consummate power that lieth concealed in the world of being."* He bids them, moreover, together with the Afnán (the Báb's kindred) and His own relatives, to *"turn, one and all, unto the Most Great Branch* ('Abdu'l-Bahá)"; identifies Him with *"the One Whom God hath purposed," "Who hath branched from this pre-existent Root,"* referred to in the

Kitáb-i-Aqdas; ordains the station of the *"Greater Branch"* (Mírzá Muḥammad-'Alí) to be beneath that of the *"Most Great Branch"* ('Abdu'l-Bahá); exhorts the believers to treat the Aghsán with consideration and affection; counsels them to respect His family and relatives, as well as the kindred of the Báb; denies His sons *"any right to the property of others"*; enjoins on them, on His kindred and on that of the Báb to *"fear God, to do that which is meet and seemly"* and to follow the things that will *"exalt"* their station; warns all men not to allow *"the means of order to be made the cause of confusion, and the instrument of union an occasion for discord"*; and concludes with an exhortation calling upon the faithful to *"serve all nations,"* and to strive for the *"betterment of the world."*

That such a unique and sublime station should have been conferred upon 'Abdu'l-Bahá did not, and indeed could not, surprise those exiled companions who had for so long been privileged to observe His life and conduct, nor the pilgrims who had been brought, however fleetingly, into personal contact with Him, nor indeed the vast concourse of the faithful who, in distant lands, had grown to revere His name and to appreciate His labors, nor even the wide circle of His friends and acquaintances who, in the Holy Land and the adjoining countries, were already well familiar with the position He had occupied during the lifetime of His Father.

He it was Whose auspicious birth occurred on that never-to-be-forgotten night when the Báb laid bare the transcendental character of His Mission to His first disciple Mullá Ḥusayn. He it was Who, as a mere child, seated on the lap of Ṭáhirih, had registered the thrilling significance of the stirring challenge which that indomitable heroine had addressed to her fellow-disciple, the erudite and far-famed Vaḥíd. He it was Whose tender soul had been seared with the ineffaceable vision of a Father, haggard, dishevelled, freighted with chains, on the occasion of a visit, as a boy of nine, to the Síyáh-Chál of Ṭihrán. Against Him, in His early childhood, whilst His Father lay a prisoner in that dungeon, had been directed the malice of a mob of street urchins who pelted Him with stones, vilified Him and overwhelmed Him with ridicule. His had been the lot to share with His Father, soon after His release from imprisonment, the rigors and miseries of a cruel banishment from His native land, and the trials which culminated in His enforced withdrawal to the mountains of Kurdistán. He it was Who, in His inconsolable grief at His separation from an adored Father, had confided to Nabíl, as attested by him in his narrative, that He felt Himself to have grown old though still but a child of tender years. His had been the unique distinction of recognizing, while still in His childhood, the full glory of His Father's as yet unrevealed station, a recognition which had impelled Him to throw Himself at His feet and to spontaneously implore the privilege of laying down His life for His sake. From His pen, while still in His adolescence in Baghdád, had issued that superb commentary on a well-known Muḥammadan tradition, written at the suggestion of Bahá'u'lláh, in answer to a request made by 'Alí-Shawkat Páshá, which was so illuminating as to excite the unbounded admiration of its recipient. It was His discussions and discourses with the learned doctors with whom He came in contact in Baghdád that first aroused that general admiration for Him and for His knowledge which was steadily to increase as the circle of His acquaintances was widened, at a later date, first in Adrianople and then in 'Akká. It was to Him that the highly accomplished Khurshíd Páshá, the governor of Adrianople, had been moved to pay a public and glowing tribute when, in the presence of a number of distinguished divines of that city, his youthful Guest had, briefly and amazingly, resolved the intricacies of a problem that had baffled the minds of the assembled company—an achievement that affected so deeply the Páshá that from that time onwards he could hardly reconcile himself to that Youth's absence from such gatherings.

On Him Bahá'u'lláh, as the scope and influence of His Mission extended, had been led to place an ever greater degree of reliance, by appointing Him, on numerous occasions, as His deputy, by enabling Him to plead His Cause before the public, by assigning Him the task of transcribing His Tablets, by allowing Him to assume the responsibility of shielding Him from His enemies, and by investing Him with the function of watching over and promoting the interests of His fellow-exiles and companions. He it was Who had been commissioned to undertake, as soon as circumstances might permit, the delicate and all-important task of purchasing the site that was to serve as the permanent resting-place of the Báb, of insuring the safe transfer of His remains to the Holy Land, and of erecting for Him a befitting sepulcher on Mt. Carmel. He it was Who had been chiefly instrumental in providing the necessary means for Bahá'u'lláh's release from His nine-year confinement within the city walls of 'Akká, and in enabling Him to enjoy, in the evening of His life, a measure of that peace and security from which He had so long been debarred. It was through His unremitting efforts that the illustrious Badí' had been granted his memorable interviews with Bahá'u'lláh, that the hostility evinced by several governors of 'Akká towards the exiled community had been transmuted into esteem and admiration, that the purchase of properties adjoining the Sea of Galilee and the River Jordan had been effected, and that the ablest and most valuable presentation of the early history of the Faith and of its tenets had been transmitted to posterity. It was through the extraordinarily warm reception accorded Him during His visit to Beirut, through His contact with Midhat Páshá, a former Grand Vizir of Turkey, through His friendship with 'Azíz Páshá, whom He had previously known in Adrianople, and who had subsequently been promoted to the rank of Valí, and through His constant association with officials, notables and leading ecclesiastics who, in increasing number had besought His presence, during the final years of His Father's ministry, that He had succeeded in raising the prestige of the Cause He had championed to a level it had never previously attained.

He alone had been accorded the privilege of being called *"the Master,"* an honor from which His Father had strictly excluded all His other sons. Upon Him that loving and unerring Father had chosen to confer the unique title of *"Sirru'lláh"* (the Mystery of God), a designation so appropriate to One Who, though essentially human and holding a station radically and fundamentally different from that occupied by Bahá'u'lláh and His Forerunner, could still claim to be the perfect Exemplar of His Faith, to be endowed with superhuman knowledge, and to be regarded as the stainless mirror reflecting His light. To Him, whilst in Adrianople, that same Father had, in the Súriy-i-Ghusn (Tablet of the Branch), referred as *"this sacred and glorious Being, this Branch of Holiness,"* as *"the Limb of the Law of God,"* as His *"most great favor"* unto men, as His *"most perfect bounty"* conferred upon them, as One through Whom *"every mouldering bone is quickened,"* declaring that *"whoso turneth towards Him hath turned towards God,"* and that *"they who deprive themselves of the shadow of the Branch are lost in the wilderness of error."* To Him He, whilst still in that city, had alluded (in a Tablet addressed to Ḥájí Muḥammad Ibráhím-i-Khalíl) as the one amongst His sons *"from Whose tongue God will cause the signs of His power to stream forth,"* and as the one Whom *"God hath specially chosen for His Cause."* On Him, at a later period, the Author of the Kitáb-i-Aqdas, in a celebrated passage, subsequently elucidated in the "Book of My Covenant," had bestowed the function of interpreting His Holy Writ, proclaiming Him, at the same time, to be the One *"Whom God hath purposed, Who hath branched from this Ancient Root."*

To Him in a Tablet, revealed during that same period and addressed to Mírzá Muḥammad Qulíy-i-Sabzivárí, He had referred as *"the Gulf that hath branched out of this Ocean that hath encompassed all created things,"* and bidden His followers to turn their faces towards it. To Him, on the occasion of His visit to Beirut, His Father had, furthermore, in a communication which He dictated to His amanuensis, paid a glowing tribute, glorifying Him as the One *"round Whom all names revolve,"* as *"the Most Mighty Branch of God,"* and as *"His ancient and immutable Mystery."* He it was Who, in several Tablets which Bahá'u'lláh Himself had penned, had been personally addressed as *"the Apple of Mine eye,"* and been referred to as *"a shield unto all who are in heaven and on earth,"* as *"a shelter for all mankind"* and *"a stronghold for whosoever hath believed in God."* It was on His behalf that His Father, in a prayer revealed in His honor, had supplicated God to *"render Him victorious,"* and to *"ordain . . . for Him, as well as for them that love Him,"* the things destined by the Almighty for His *"Messengers"* and the *"Trustees"* of His Revelation. And finally in yet another Tablet these weighty words had been recorded: *"The glory of God rest upon Thee, and upon whosoever serveth Thee and circleth around Thee. Woe, great woe, betide him that opposeth and injureth Thee. Well is it with him that sweareth fealty to Thee; the fire of hell torment him who is Thy enemy."*

And now to crown the inestimable honors, privileges and benefits showered upon Him, in ever increasing abundance, throughout the forty years of His Father's ministry in Baghdád, in Adrianople and in 'Akká, He had been elevated to the high office of Center of Bahá'u'lláh's Covenant, and been made the successor of the Manifestation of God Himself—a position that was to empower Him to impart an extraordinary impetus to the international expansion of His Father's Faith, to amplify its doctrine, to beat down every barrier that would obstruct its march, and to call into being, and delineate the features of, its Administrative Order, the Child of the Covenant, and the Harbinger of that World Order whose establishment must needs signalize the advent of the Golden Age of the Bahá'í Dispensation.

## CHAPTER XV

# The Rebellion of Mírzá Muḥammad-'Alí

The immediate effect of the ascension of Bahá'u'lláh had been, as already observed, to spread grief and bewilderment among His followers and companions, and to inspire its vigilant and redoubtable adversaries with fresh hope and renewed determination. At a time when a grievously traduced Faith had triumphantly emerged from the two severest crises it had ever known, one the work of enemies without, the other the work of enemies within, when its prestige had risen to a height unequalled in any period during its fifty-year existence, the unerring Hand which had shaped its destiny ever since its inception was suddenly removed, leaving a gap which friend and foe alike believed could never again be filled.

Yet, as the appointed Center of Bahá'u'lláh's Covenant and the authorized Interpreter of His teaching had Himself later explained, the dissolution of the tabernacle wherein the soul of the Manifestation of God had chosen temporarily to abide signalized its release from the restrictions which an earthly life had, of necessity, imposed upon it. Its influence no longer circumscribed by any physical limitations, its radiance no longer beclouded by its human temple, that soul could henceforth energize the whole world to a degree unapproached at any stage in the course of its existence on this planet.

Bahá'u'lláh's stupendous task on this earthly plane had, moreover, at the time of His passing, been brought to its final consummation. His mission, far from being in any way inconclusive, had, in every respect, been carried through to a full end. The Message with which He had been entrusted had been disclosed to the gaze of all mankind. The summons He had been commissioned to issue to its leaders and rulers had been fearlessly voiced. The fundamentals of the doctrine destined to recreate its life, heal its sicknesses and redeem it from bondage and degradation had been impregnably established. The tide of calamity that was to purge and fortify the sinews of His Faith had swept on with unstemmed fury. The blood which was to fertilize the soil out of which the institutions of His World Order were destined to spring had been profusely shed. Above all the Covenant that was to perpetuate the influence of that Faith, insure its integrity, safeguard it from schism, and stimulate its world-wide expansion, had been fixed on an inviolable basis.

His Cause, precious beyond the dreams and hopes of men; enshrining within its shell that pearl of great price to which the world, since its foundation, had been looking forward; confronted with colossal tasks of unimaginable complexity and urgency, was beyond a peradventure in safe keeping. His own beloved Son, the apple of His eye, His vicegerent on earth, the Executive of His authority, the Pivot of His Covenant, the Shepherd of His flock, the Exemplar of His faith, the Image of His perfections, the Mystery of His Revelation, the Interpreter of His mind, the Architect of His World Order, the Ensign of His Most Great Peace, the Focal Point of His unerring guidance—in a word, the occupant of an office without peer or equal in the entire field of religious history—stood guard over it, alert, fearless and determined to enlarge its limits, blazon abroad its fame, champion its interests and consummate its purpose.

The stirring proclamation ʻAbdu'l-Bahá had penned, addressed to the rank and file of the followers of His Father, on the morrow of His ascension, as well as the prophecies He Himself had uttered in His Tablets, breathed a resolve and a confidence which the fruits garnered and the triumphs achieved in the course of a thirty-year ministry have abundantly justified.

The cloud of despondency that had momentarily settled on the disconsolate lovers of the Cause of Bahá'u'lláh was lifted. The continuity of that unerring guidance vouchsafed to it since its birth was now assured. The significance of the solemn affirmation that this is *"the Day which shall not be followed by night"* was now clearly apprehended. An orphan community had recognized in ʻAbdu'l-Bahá, in its hour of desperate need, its Solace, its Guide, its Mainstay and Champion. The Light that had glowed with such dazzling brightness in the heart of Asia, and had, in the lifetime of Bahá'u'lláh, spread to the Near East, and illuminated the fringes of both the European and African continents, was to travel, through the impelling influence of the newly proclaimed Covenant, and almost immediately after the death of its Author, as far West as the North American continent, and from thence diffuse itself to the countries of Europe, and subsequently shed its radiance over both the Far East and Australasia.

Before the Faith, however, could plant its banner in the midmost heart of the North American continent, and from thence establish its outposts over so vast a portion of the Western world, the newly born Covenant of Bahá'u'lláh had, as had been the case with the

Faith that had given it birth, to be baptized with a fire which was to demonstrate its solidity and proclaim its indestructibility to an unbelieving world. A crisis, almost as severe as that which had assailed the Faith in its earliest infancy in Baghdád, was to shake that Covenant to its foundations at the very moment of its inception, and subject afresh the Cause of which it was the noblest fruit to one of the most grievous ordeals experienced in the course of an entire century.

This crisis, misconceived as a schism, which political as well as ecclesiastical adversaries, no less than the fast dwindling remnant of the followers of Mírza Yaḥyá hailed as a signal for the immediate disruption and final dissolution of the system established by Bahá'u'lláh, was precipitated at the very heart and center of His Faith, and was provoked by no one less than a member of His own family, a half-brother of 'Abdu'l-Bahá, specifically named in the book of the Covenant, and holding a rank second to none except Him Who had been appointed as the Center of that Covenant. For no less than four years that emergency fiercely agitated the minds and hearts of a vast proportion of the faithful throughout the East, eclipsed, for a time, the Orb of the Covenant, created an irreparable breach within the ranks of Bahá'u'lláh's own kindred, sealed ultimately the fate of the great majority of the members of His family, and gravely damaged the prestige, though it never succeeded in causing a permanent cleavage in the structure, of the Faith itself. The true ground of this crisis was the burning, the uncontrollable, the soul-festering jealousy which the admitted preeminence of 'Abdu'l-Bahá in rank, power, ability, knowledge and virtue, above all the other members of His Father's family, had aroused not only in Mírzá Muḥammad-'Alí, the archbreaker of the Covenant, but in some of his closest relatives as well. An envy as blind as that which had possessed the soul of Mírzá Yaḥyá, as deadly as that which the superior excellence of Joseph had kindled in the hearts of his brothers, as deep-seated as that which had blazed in the bosom of Cain and prompted him to slay his brother Abel, had, for several years, prior to Bahá'u'lláh's ascension, been smouldering in the recesses of Mírzá Muḥammad-'Alí's heart and had been secretly inflamed by those unnumbered marks of distinction, of admiration and favor accorded to 'Abdu'l-Bahá not only by Bahá'u'lláh Himself, His companions and His followers, but by the vast number of unbelievers who had come to recognize that innate greatness which 'Abdu'l-Bahá had manifested from childhood.

Far from being allayed by the provisions of a Will which had elevated him to the second-highest position within the ranks of the faithful, the fire of unquenchable animosity that glowed in the breast of Mírzá Muḥammad-'Alí burned even more fiercely as soon as he came to realize the full implications of that Document. All that 'Abdu'l-Bahá could do, during a period of four distressful years, His incessant exhortations, His earnest pleadings, the favors and kindnesses He showered upon him, the admonitions and warnings He uttered, even His voluntary withdrawal in the hope of averting the threatening storm, proved to be of no avail. Gradually and with unyielding persistence, through lies, half-truths, calumnies and gross exaggerations, this "Prime Mover of sedition" succeeded in ranging on his side almost the entire family of Bahá'u'lláh, as well as a considerable number of those who had formed his immediate entourage. Bahá'u'lláh's two surviving wives, His two sons, the vacillating Mírzá Ḍíyá'u'lláh and the treacherous Mírzá Badí'u'lláh, with their sister and half-sister and their husbands, one of them the infamous Siyyid 'Alí, a kinsman of the Báb, the other the crafty Mírzá Majdi'd-Dín, together with his sister and half-brothers—the children of the noble, the faithful and now deceased Áqáy-i-Kalím—all united in a determined effort to subvert the foundations of the Covenant which the newly proclaimed Will had laid. Even Mírzá Áqá Ján, who for forty years had labored as Bahá'u'lláh's amanuensis, as well as Muḥammad-Javád-i-Qasvíní, who ever since the days of Adrianople, had been engaged in transcribing the innumerable Tablets revealed by the Supreme Pen, together with his entire family, threw in their lot with the Covenant-breakers, and allowed themselves to be ensnared by their machinations.

Forsaken, betrayed, assaulted by almost the entire body of His relatives, now congregated in the Mansion and the neighboring houses clustering around the most Holy Tomb, 'Abdu'l-Bahá, already bereft of both His mother and His sons, and without any support at all save that of an unmarried sister, His four unmarried daughters, His wife and His uncle (a half-brother of Bahá'u'lláh), was left alone to bear, in the face of a multitude of enemies arrayed against Him from within and from without, the full brunt of the terrific responsibilities which His exalted office had laid upon Him.

Closely-knit by one common wish and purpose; indefatigable in their efforts; assured of the backing of the powerful and perfidious Jamál-i-Burújirdí and his henchmen, Ḥájí Ḥusayn-i-Káshí, Khalíl-i-Khu'í and Jalíl-i-Tabrízí who had espoused their cause; linked by a vast system of correspondence with every center and individual they could reach; seconded in their labors by emissaries whom they dispatched to Persia, 'Iráq, India and Egypt; emboldened in their designs by the attitude of officials whom they bribed or seduced, these repudiators of a divinely-established Covenant arose, as one man, to launch a campaign of abuse and vilification which compared in virulence with the infamous accusations which Mírza Yaḥyá and Siyyid Muḥammad had jointly levelled at Bahá'u'lláh. To friend and stranger, believer and unbeliever alike, to officials both high and low, openly and by insinuation, verbally as well as in writing, they represented 'Abdu'l-Bahá as an ambitious, a self-willed, an unprincipled and pitiless usurper, Who had deliberately disregarded the testamentary instructions of His Father; Who had, in language intentionally veiled and ambiguous, assumed a rank co-equal with the Manifestation Himself; Who in His communications with the West was beginning to claim to be the return of Jesus Christ, the Son of God, who had come *"in the glory of the Father"*; Who, in His letters to the Indian believers, was proclaiming Himself as the promised S͟háh Bahrám, and arrogating to Himself the right to interpret the writing of His Father, to inaugurate a new Dispensation, and to share with Him the Most Great Infallibility, the exclusive prerogative of the holders of the prophetic office. They, furthermore, affirmed that He had, for His private ends, fomented discord, fostered enmity and brandished the weapon of excommunication; that He had perverted the purpose of a Testament which they alleged to be primarily concerned with the private interests of Bahá'u'lláh's family by acclaiming it as a Covenant of world importance, prë-existent, peerless and unique in the history of all religions; that He had deprived His brothers and sisters of their lawful allowance, and expended it on officials for His personal advancement; that He had declined all the repeated invitations made to Him to discuss the issues that had arisen and to compose the differences which prevailed; that He had actually corrupted the Holy Text, interpolated passages written by Himself, and perverted the purpose and meaning of some of the weightiest Tablets revealed by the pen of His Father; and finally, that the standard of rebellion had, as a result of such conduct, been raised by the Oriental believers, that the community of the faithful had been rent asunder, was rapidly declining and was doomed to extinction.

And yet it was this same Mírzá Muḥammad-'Alí who, regarding himself as the exponent of fidelity, the standard-bearer of the "Unitarians," the "Finger who points to his Master," the champion of the Holy Family, the spokesman of the Ag͟hṣán, the upholder of the

Holy Writ, had, in the lifetime of Bahá'u'lláh, so openly and shamelessly advanced in a written statement, signed and sealed by him, the very claim now falsely imputed by him to 'Abdu'l-Bahá, that his Father had, with His own hand, chastised him. He it was who, when sent on a mission to India, had tampered with the text of the holy writings entrusted to his care for publication. He it was who had the impudence and temerity to tell 'Abdu'l-Bahá to His face that just as 'Umar had succeeded in usurping the successorship of the Prophet Muḥammad, he, too, felt himself able to do the same. He it was who, obsessed by the fear that he might not survive 'Abdu'l-Bahá, had, the moment he had been assured by Him that all the honor he coveted would, in the course of time, be his, swiftly rejoined that he had no guarantee that he would outlive Him. He it was who, as testified by Mírzá Badí''ulláh in his confession, written and published on the occasion of his repentance and his short-lived reconciliation with 'Abdu'l-Bahá, had, while Bahá'u'lláh's body was still awaiting interment, carried off, by a ruse, the two satchels containing his Father's most precious documents, entrusted by Him, prior to His ascension, to 'Abdu'l-Bahá. He it was who, by an exceedingly adroit and simple forgery of a word recurring in some of the denunciatory passages addressed by the Supreme Pen to Mírzá Yaḥyá, and by other devices such as mutilation and interpolation, had succeeded in making them directly applicable to a Brother Whom he hated with such consuming passion. And lastly, it was this same Mírzá Muḥammad-'Alí who, as attested by 'Abdu'l-Bahá in His Will, had, with circumspection and guile, conspired to take His life, an intention indicated by the allusions made in a letter written by S͟hú'á'u'lláh (Son of Mírzá Muḥammad-'Alí), the original of which was enclosed in that same Document by 'Abdu'l-Bahá.

The Covenant of Bahá'u'llah had, by acts such as these, and others too numerous to recount, been manifestly violated. Another blow, stunning in its first effects, had been administered to the Faith and had caused its structure momentarily to tremble. The storm foreshadowed by the writer of the Apocalypse had broken. The *"lightnings,"* the *"thunders,"* the *"earthquake"* which must needs accompany the revelation of the *"Ark of His Testament,"* had all come to pass.

'Abdu'l-Bahá's grief over so tragic a development, following so swiftly upon His Father's ascension, was such that, despite the triumphs witnessed in the course of His ministry, it left its traces upon Him till the end of His days. The intensity of the emotions which this somber episode aroused within Him were reminiscent of the effect produced upon Bahá'u'lláh by the dire happenings precipitated by the rebellion of Mírzá Yaḥyá. *"I swear by the Ancient Beauty!,"* He wrote in one of His Tablets, *"So great is My sorrow and regret that My pen is paralyzed between My fingers." "Thou seest Me,"* He, in a prayer recorded in His Will, thus laments, *"submerged in an ocean of calamities that overwhelm the soul, of afflictions that oppress the heart . . . Sore trials have compassed Me round, and perils have from all sides beset Me. Thou seest Me immersed in a sea of unsurpassed tribulation, sunk into a fathomless abyss, afflicted by Mine enemies and consumed with the flame of hatred kindled by My kinsmen with whom Thou didst make Thy strong Covenant and Thy firm Testament . . ."* And again in that same Will: *"Lord! Thou seest all things weeping over Me, and My kindred rejoicing in My woes. By Thy glory, O my God! Even amongst Mine enemies some have lamented My troubles and My distress, and of the envious ones a number have shed tears because of My cares, My exile and My afflictions." "O Thou the Glory of Glories!,"* He, in one of His last Tablets, had cried out, *"I have renounced the world and its people, and am heart-broken and sorely afflicted because of the unfaithful. In the cage of this world I flutter even as a frightened bird, and yearn every day to take My flight unto Thy Kingdom."*

Bahá'u'lláh Himself had significantly revealed in one of His Tablets—a Tablet that sheds an illuminating light on the entire episode: *"By God, O people! Mine eye weepeth, and the eye of 'Alí* (the Báb) *weepeth amongst the Concourse on high, and Mine heart crieth out, and the heart of Muḥammad crieth out within the Most Glorious Tabernacle, and My soul shouteth and the souls of the Prophets shout before them that are endued with understanding . . . My sorrow is not for Myself, but for Him Who shall come after Me, in the shadow of My Cause, with manifest and undoubted sovereignty, inasmuch as they will not welcome His appearance, will repudiate His signs, will dispute His sovereignty, will contend with Him, and will betray His Cause . . ." "Can it be possible,"* He, in a no less significant Tablet, had observed, *"that after the dawning of the day-star of Thy Testament above the horizon of Thy Most Great Tablet, the feet of any one shall slip in Thy Straight Path? Unto this We answered: 'O My most exalted Pen! It behoveth Thee to occupy Thyself with that whereunto Thou hast been bidden by God, the Exalted, the Great. Ask not of that which will consume Thine heart and the hearts of the denizens of Paradise, who have circled round My wondrous Cause. It behoveth Thee not to be acquainted with that which We have veiled from Thee. Thy Lord is, verily, the Concealer, the All-Knowing!'"* More specifically Bahá'u'lláh had, referring to Mírzá Muḥammad-'Alí in clear and unequivocal language, affirmed: *"He, verily, is but one of My servants . . . Should he for a moment pass out from under the shadow of the Cause, he surely shall be brought to naught."* Furthermore, in a no less emphatic language, He, again in connection with Mírzá Muḥammad-'Alí had stated: *"By God, the True One! Were We, for a single instant, to withhold from him the outpourings of Our Cause, he would wither, and would fall upon the dust."* 'Abdu'l-Bahá Himself had, moreover, testified: *"There is no doubt that in a thousand passages in the sacred writings of Bahá'u'lláh the breakers of the Covenant have been execrated."* Some of these passages He Himself compiled, ere His departure from this world, and incorporated them in one of His last Tablets, as a warning and safeguard against those who, throughout His ministry, had manifested so implacable a hatred against Him, and had come so near to subverting the foundations of a Covenant on which not only His own authority but the integrity of the Faith itself depended.

## CHAPTER XVI

# The Rise and Establishment of the Faith in the West

Though the rebellion of Mírzá Muhammad-'Alí precipitated many sombre and distressing events, and though its dire consequences continued for several years to obscure the light of the Covenant, to endanger the life of its appointed Center, and to distract the thoughts and retard the progress of the activities of its supporters in both the East and the West, yet the entire episode, viewed in its proper perspective, proved to be neither more nor less than one of those periodic crises which, since the inception of the Faith of Bahá'u'lláh, and throughout a whole century, have been instrumental in weeding out its harmful elements, in fortifying its foundations, in demonstrating its resilience, and in releasing a further measure of its latent powers.

Now that the provisions of a divinely appointed Covenant had been indubitably proclaimed; now that the purpose of the Covenant was clearly apprehended and its fundamentals had become immovably established in the hearts of the overwhelming majority of the adherents of the Faith; and now that the first assaults launched by its would-be subverters had been successfully repulsed, the Cause for which that Covenant had been designed could forge ahead along the course traced for it by the finger of its Author. Shining exploits and unforgettable victories had already signalized the birth of that Cause and accompanied its rise in several countries of the Asiatic continent, and particularly in the homeland of its Founder. The mission of its newly-appointed Leader, the steward of its glory and the diffuser of its light, was, as conceived by Himself, to enrich and extend the bounds of the incorruptible patrimony entrusted to His hands by shedding the illumination of His Father's Faith upon the West, by expounding the fundamental precepts of that Faith and its cardinal principles, by consolidating the activities which had already been initiated for the promotion of its interests, and, finally, by ushering in, through the provisions of His own Will, the Formative Age in its evolution.

A year after the ascension of Bahá'u'lláh, 'Abdul-Bahá had, in a verse which He had revealed, and which had evoked the derision of the Covenant-breakers, already foreshadowed an auspicious event which posterity would recognize as one of the greatest triumphs of His ministry, which in the end would confer an inestimable blessing upon the western world, and which erelong was to dispel the grief and the apprehensions that had surrounded the community of His fellow-exiles in 'Akká. The Great Republic of the West, above all the other countries of the Occident, was singled out to be the first recipient of God's inestimable blessing, and to become the chief agent in its transmission to so many of her sister nations throughout the five continents of the earth.

The importance of so momentous a development in the evolution of the Faith of Bahá'u'lláh—the establishment of His Cause in the North American continent—at a time when 'Abdu'l-Bahá had just inaugurated His Mission, and was still in the throes of the most grievous crisis with which He was ever confronted, can in no wise be overestimated. As far back as the year which witnessed the birth of the Faith in Shíráz the Báb had, in the Qayyúmu'l-Asmá', after having warned in a memorable passage the peoples of both the Orient and the Occident, directly addressed the *"peoples of the West,"* and significantly bidden them *"issue forth"* from their *"cities"* to aid God, and *"become as brethren"* in His *"one and indivisible religion."* *"In the East,"* Bahá'u'lláh Himself had, in anticipation of this development, written, *"the light of His Revelation hath broken; in the West the signs of His dominion have appeared."* *"Should they attempt,"* He, moreover, had predicted, *"to conceal its light on the continent, it will assuredly rear its head in the midmost heart of the ocean, and, raising its voice, proclaim: 'I am the lifegiver of the world!'"* *"Had this Cause been revealed in the West,"* He, shortly before His ascension, is reported by Nabíl in his narrative to have stated, *"had Our verses been sent from the West to Persia and other countries of the East, it would have become evident how the people of the Occident would have embraced Our Cause. The people of Persia, however, have failed to appreciate it."* *"From the beginning of time until the present day,"* is 'Abdu'l-Bahá's own testimony, *"the light of Divine Revelation hath risen in the East and shed its radiance upon the West. The illumination thus shed hath, however, acquired in the West an extraordinary brilliancy. Consider the Faith proclaimed by Jesus. Though it first appeared in the East, yet not until its light had been shed upon the West did the full measure of its potentialities become manifest."* *"The day is approaching,"* He has affirmed, *"when ye shall witness how, through the splendor of the Faith of Bahá'u'lláh, the West will have replaced the East, radiating the light of Divine guidance."* And again: *"The West hath acquired illumination from the East, but, in some respects, the reflection of the light hath been greater in the Occident."* Furthermore, *"The East hath, verily, been illumined with the light of the Kingdom. Erelong will this same light shed a still greater illumination upon the West."*

More specifically has the Author of the Bahá'í Revelation Himself chosen to confer upon the rulers of the American continent the unique honor of addressing them collectively in the Kitáb-i-Aqdas, His most Holy Book, significantly exhorting them to *"adorn the temple of dominion with the ornament of justice and of the fear of God, and its head with the crown of the remembrance"* of their Lord, and bidding them *"bind with the hands of justice the broken,"* and *"crush the oppressor"* with the *"rod of the commandments"* of their *"Lord, the Ordainer, the All-Wise." "The continent of America,"* wrote 'Abdu'l-Bahá, *"is, in the eyes of the one true God, the land wherein the splendors of His light shall be revealed, where the mysteries of His Faith shall be unveiled, where the righteous will abide and the free assemble." "The American continent,"* He has furthermore predicted, *"giveth signs and evidences of very great advancement. Its future is even more promising, for its influence and illumination are far reaching. It will lead all nations spiritually."*

*"The American people,"* 'Abdu'l-Bahá, even more distinctly, singling out for His special favor the Great Republic of the West, the leading nation of the American continent, has revealed, *"are indeed worthy of being the first to build the Tabernacle of the Most Great Peace, and proclaim the oneness of mankind."* And again: *"This American nation is equipped and empowered to accomplish that which will adorn the pages of history, to become the envy of the world, and be blest in both the East and the West for the triumph of its people."* Furthermore: *"May this American democracy be the first nation to establish the foundation of international agreement. May it be the first nation to proclaim the unity of mankind. May it be the first to unfurl the standard of the Most Great Peace." "May the inhabitants of this country,"* He, moreover has written, *". . . rise from their present material attainment to such heights that heavenly illumination may stream from this center to all the peoples of the world."*

*"O ye apostles of Bahá'u'lláh!,"* 'Abdu'l-Bahá has thus addressed the believers of the North American continent, *". . . consider how exalted and lofty is the station you are destined to attain . . . The full measure of your success is as yet unrevealed, its significance still unapprehended."* And again: *"Your mission is unspeakably glorious.*

*Should success crown your enterprise, America will assuredly evolve into a center from which waves of spiritual power will emanate, and the throne of the Kingdom of God, will in the plenitude of its majesty and glory, be firmly established."* And finally, this stirring affirmation: *"The moment this Divine Message is carried forward by the American believers from the shores of America, and is propagated through the continents of Europe, of Asia, of Africa and of Australasia, and as far as the islands of the Pacific, this community will find itself securely established upon the throne of an everlasting dominion . . . Then will the whole earth resound with the praises of its majesty and greatness."*

Little wonder that a community belonging to a nation so abundantly blessed, a nation occupying so eminent a position in a continent so richly endowed, should have been able to add, during the fifty years of its existence, many a page rich with victories to the annals of the Faith of Bahá'u'lláh. This is the community, it should be remembered, which, ever since it was called into being through the creative energies released by the proclamation of the Covenant of Bahá'u'lláh, was nursed in the lap of 'Abdu'l-Bahá's unfailing solicitude, and was trained by Him to discharge its unique mission through the revelation of innumerable Tablets, through the instructions issued to returning pilgrims, through the despatch of special messengers, through His own travels at a later date, across the North American continent, through the emphasis laid by Him on the institution of the Covenant in the course of those travels, and finally through His mandate embodied in the Tablets of the Divine Plan. This is the community which, from its earliest infancy until the present day, has unremittingly labored and succeeded, through its own unaided efforts, in implanting the banner of Bahá'u'lláh in the vast majority of the sixty countries which, in both the East and the West, can now claim the honor of being included within the pale of His Faith. To this community belongs the distinction of having evolved the pattern, and of having been the first to erect the framework, of the administrative institutions that herald the advent of the World Order of Bahá'u'llah. Through the efforts of its members the Mother Temple of the West, the Harbinger of that Order, one of the noblest institutions ordained in the Kitáb-i-Aqdas, and the most stately edifice reared in the entire Bahá'í world, has been erected in the very heart of the North American continent. Through the assiduous labors of its pioneers, its teachers and its administrators, the literature of the Faith has been enormously expanded, its aims and purposes fearlessly defended, and its nascent institutions solidly established. In direct consequence of the unsupported and indefatigable endeavors of the most distinguished of its itinerant teachers the spontaneous allegiance of Royalty to the Faith of Bahá'u'lláh has been secured and unmistakably proclaimed in several testimonies transmitted to posterity by the pen of the royal convert herself. And finally, to the members of this community, the spiritual descendants of the dawn-breakers of the Heroic Age of the Bahá'í Dispensation, must be ascribed the eternal honor of having arisen, on numerous occasions, with marvelous alacrity, zeal and determination, to champion the cause of the oppressed, to relieve the needy, and to defend the interests of the edifices and institutions reared by their brethren in countries such as Persia, Russia, Egypt, 'Iráq and Germany, countries where the adherents of the Faith have had to sustain, in varying measure, the rigors of racial and religious persecution.

Strange, indeed, that in a country, invested with such a unique function among its sister-nations throughout the West, the first public reference to the Author of so glorious a Faith should have been made through the mouth of one of the members of that ecclesiastical order with which that Faith has had so long to contend, and from which it has frequently suffered. Stranger still that he who first established it in the city of Chicago, fifty years after the Báb had declared His Mission in Shíráz, should himself have forsaken, a few years later, the standard which he, single-handed, had implanted in that city.

It was on September 23, 1893, a little over a year after Bahá'u'llah's ascension, that, in a paper written by Rev. Henry H. Jessup, D.D., Director of Presbyterian Missionary Operations in North Syria, and read by Rev. George A. Ford of Syria, at the World Parliament of Religions, held in Chicago, in connection with the Columbian Exposition, commemorating the four-hundredth anniversary of the discovery of America, it was announced that "a famous Persian Sage," "the Bábí Saint," had died recently in 'Akká, and that two years previous to His ascension "a Cambridge scholar" had visited Him, to whom He had cxpressed "sentiments so noble, so Christ-like" that the author of the paper, in his "closing words," wished to share them with his audience. Less than a year later, in February 1894, a Syrian doctor, named Ibráhím Khayru'lláh, who, while residing in Cairo, had been converted by Ḥájí 'Abdu'l-Karím-i-Ṭihrání to the Faith, had received a Tablet from Bahá'u'lláh, had communicated with 'Abdu'l-Bahá, and reached New York in December 1892, established his residence in Chicago, and began to teach actively and systematically the Cause he had espoused. Within the space of two years he had communicated his impressions to 'Abdu'l-Bahá, and reported on the remarkable success that had attended his efforts. In 1895 an opening was vouchsafed to him in Kenosha, which he continued to visit once a week, in the course of his teaching activities. By the following year the believers in these two cities, it was reported, were counted by hundreds. In 1897 he published his book, entitled the Bábu'd-Dín, and visited Kansas City, New York City, Ithaca and Philadelphia, where he was able to win for the Faith a considerable number of supporters. The stout-hearted Thornton Chase, surnamed Th͟ábit (Steadfast) by 'Abdu'l-Bahá and designated by Him *"the first American believer,"* who became a convert to the Faith in 1894, the immortal Louisa A. Moore, the mother teacher of the West, surnamed Livá (Banner) by 'Abdu'l-Bahá, Dr. Edward Getsinger, to whom she was later married, Howard MacNutt, Arthur P. Dodge, Isabella D. Brittingham, Lillian F. Kappes, Paul K. Dealy, Chester I. Thacher and Helen S. Goodall, whose names will ever remain associated with the first stirrings of the Faith of Bahá'u'lláh in the North American continent, stand out as the most prominent among those who, in those early years, awakened to the call of the New Day, and consecrated their lives to the service of the newly proclaimed Covenant.

By 1898 Mrs. Phoebe Hearst, the well-known philanthropist (wife of Senator George F. Hearst), whom Mrs. Getsinger had, while on a visit to California, attracted to the Faith, had expressed her intention of visiting 'Abdu'l-Bahá in the Holy Land, had invited several believers, among them Dr. and Mrs. Getsinger, Dr. K͟hayru'lláh and his wife, to join her, and had completed the necessary arrangements for their historic pilgrimage to 'Akká. In Paris several resident Americans, among whom were May Ellis Bolles, whom Mrs. Getsinger had won over to the Faith, Miss Pearson, and Ann Apperson, both nieces of Mrs. Hearst, with Mrs. Thornburgh and her daughter, were added to the party, the number of which was later swelled in Egypt by the addition of Dr. K͟hayru'lláh's daughters and their grand-mother whom he had recently converted.

The arrival of fifteen pilgrims, in three successive parties, the first of which, including Dr. and Mrs. Getsinger, reached the prison-city of 'Akká on December 10, 1898; the intimate personal contact established between the Center of Bahá'u'lláh's Covenant and the newly arisen heralds of His Revelation in the West; the moving circumstances attending their visit to His Tomb and the great honor bestowed upon them of being conducted by 'Abdu'l-Bahá Himself into its innermost chamber; the spirit which, through precept and example, despite the briefness of their stay, a loving and bountiful Host so powerfully infused into them; and the passionate zeal and unyielding resolve which His inspiring exhortations, His illuminating instructions and the multiple evidences of His divine love kindled in their hearts—all these marked the opening of a new epoch in the development of the Faith in the West, an epoch whose significance the acts subsequently performed by some of these same pilgrims and their fellow-disciples have amply demonstrated.

"Of that first meeting," one of these pilgrims, recording her impressions, has written, "I can remember neither joy nor pain, nor anything that I can name. I had been carried suddenly to too great a height, my soul had come in contact with the Divine Spirit, and this force, so pure, so holy, so mighty, had overwhelmed me . . . We could not remove our eyes from His glorious face; we heard all that He said; we drank tea with Him at His bidding; but existence seemed suspended; and when He arose and suddenly left us, we came back with a start to life; but never again, oh! never again, thank God, the same life on this earth." "In the might and majesty of His presence," that same pilgrim, recalling the last interview accorded the party of which she was a member, has testified, "our fear was turned to perfect faith, our weakness into strength, our sorrow into hope, and ourselves forgotten in our love for Him. As we all sat before Him, waiting to hear His words, some of the believers wept bitterly. He bade them dry their tears, but they could not for a moment. So again He asked them for His sake not to weep, nor would He talk to us and teach us until all tears were banished . . ."

. . . "Those three days," Mrs. Hearst herself has, in one of her letters, testified, "were the most memorable days of my life . . . The Master I will not attempt to describe: I will only state that I believe with all my heart that He is the Master, and my greatest blessing in this world is that I have been privileged to be in His presence, and look upon His sanctified face . . . Without a doubt 'Abbás Effendi is the Messiah of this day and generation, and we need not look for another." "I must say," she, moreover, has in another letter written, "He is the most wonderful Being I have ever met or ever expect to meet in this world . . . The spiritual atmosphere which surrounds Him and most powerfully affects all those who are blest by being near Him, is indescribable . . . I believe in Him with all my heart and soul, and I hope all who call themselves believers will concede to Him all the greatness, all the glory, and all the praise, for surely He is the Son of God—and 'the spirit of the Father abideth in Him.' "

Even Mrs. Hearst's butler, a negro named Robert Turner, the first member of his race to embrace the Cause of Bahá'u'lláh in the West, had been transported by the influence exerted by 'Abdu'l-Bahá in the course of that epoch-making pilgrimage. Such was the tenacity of his faith that even the subsequent estrangement of his beloved mistress from the Cause she had spontaneously embraced failed to becloud its radiance, or to lessen the intensity of the emotions which the loving-kindness showered by 'Abdu'l-Bahá upon him had excited in his breast.

The return of these God-intoxicated pilgrims, some to France, others to the United States, was the signal for an outburst of systematic and sustained activity, which, as it gathered momentum, and spread its ramifications over Western Europe and the states and provinces of the North American continent, grew to so great a scale that 'Abdu'l-Bahá Himself resolved that, as soon as He should be released from His prolonged confinement in 'Akká, He would undertake a personal mission to the West. Undeflected in its course by the devastating crisis which the ambition of Dr. Khayru'lláh had, upon his return from the Holy Land (December, 1899) precipitated; undismayed by the agitation which he, working in collaboration with the arch-breaker of the Covenant and his messengers, had provoked; disdainful of the attacks launched by him and his fellow-seceders, as well as by Christian ecclesiastics increasingly jealous of the rising power and extending influence of the Faith; nourished by a continual flow of pilgrims who transmitted the verbal messages and special instructions of a vigilant Master; invigorated by the effusions of His pen recorded in innumerable Tablets; instructed by the successive messengers and teachers dispatched at His behest for its guidance, edification and consolidation, the community of the American believers arose to initiate a series of enterprises which, blessed and stimulated a decade later by 'Abdu'l-Bahá Himself, were to be but a prelude to the unparalleled services destined to be rendered by its members during the Formative Age of His Father's Dispensation.

No sooner had one of these pilgrims, the afore-mentioned May Bolles, returned to Paris than she succeeded, in compliance with 'Abdu'l-Bahá's emphatic instructions, in establishing in that city the first Bahá'í center to be formed on the European continent. This center was, shortly after her arrival, reinforced by the conversion of the illumined Thomas Breakwell, the first English believer, immortalized by 'Abdu'l-Bahá's fervent eulogy revealed in his memory; of Hippolyte Dreyfus, the first Frenchman to embrace the Faith, who, through his writings, translations, travels and other pioneer services, was able to consolidate, as the years went by, the work which had been initiated in his country; and of Laura Barney, whose imperishable service was to collect and transmit to posterity in the form of a book, entitled "Some Answered Questions," 'Abdu'l-Bahá's priceless explanations, covering a wide variety of subjects, given to her in the course of an extended pilgrimage to the Holy Land. Three years later, in 1902, May Bolles, now married to a Canadian, transferred her residence to Montreal, and succeeded in laying the foundations of the Cause in that Dominion.

In London Mrs. Thornburgh-Cropper, as a consequence of the creative influences released by that never-to-be-forgotten pilgrimage, was able to initiate activities which, stimulated and expanded through the efforts of the first English believers, and particularly of Ethel J. Rosenberg, converted in 1899, enabled them to erect, in later years, the structure of their administrative institutions in the British Isles. In the North American continent, the defection and the denunciatory publications of Dr. Khayru'lláh (encouraged as he was by Mírzá Muḥammad-'Alí and his son Shu'á'u'lláh, whom he had despatched to America) tested to the utmost the loyalty of the newly fledged community; but successive messengers despatched by 'Abdu'l-Bahá (such as Ḥájí 'Abdu'l-Karím-i-Ṭihrání, Ḥájí Mírzá Ḥasan-i-Khurásání, Mírzá Asadu'lláh and Mírzá Abu'l-Faḍl) succeeded in rapidly dispelling the doubts, and in deepening the understanding, of the believers, in holding the community together, and in forming the nucleus of those administrative institutions which, two decades later, were to be formally inaugurated through the explicit provisions of 'Abdu'l-Bahá's Will and Testament. As far back as the year 1899 a council board of seven officers, the forerunner of a series of Assemblies which, ere the close of the first Bahá'í Century, were to cover the North American Continent from coast to coast, was established in the city of Kenosha. In 1902 a Bahá'í Publishing Society, designed to propagate the literature of a gradually expanding community, was formed in Chicago. A Bahá'í Bulletin, for the purpose of disseminating the teachings of the Faith was inaugurated in New York. The "Bahá'í News," another periodical, subsequently appeared in Chicago, and soon developed into a magazine entitled "Star of the West." The translation of some of the most important writings of Bahá'u'lláh, such as the "Hidden Words," the "Kitáb-i-Íqán," the "Tablets to the Kings," and the "Seven Valleys," together with the Tablets of 'Abdu'l-Bahá, as well as several treatises and pamphlets written by Mírzá Abu'l-Faḍl and others, was energetically undertaken. A considerable correspondence with various centers throughout the Orient was initiated, and grew steadily in scope and importance. Brief histories of the Faith, books and pamphlets written in its defence, articles for the press, accounts of travels and pilgrimages, eulogies and poems, were likewise published and widely disseminated.

Simultaneously, travellers and teachers, emerging triumphantly from the storms of tests and trials which had threatened to engulf their beloved Cause, arose, of their own accord, to reinforce and multiply the strongholds of the Faith already established. Centers were opened in the cities of Washington, Boston, San Francisco, Los Angeles, Cleveland, Baltimore, Minneapolis, Buffalo, Rochester, Pittsburgh, Seattle, St. Paul and in other places. Audacious pioneers, whether as visitors or settlers, eager to spread the new born Evangel beyond the confines of their native country, undertook journeys, and embarked on enterprises which carried its light to the heart of Europe, to the Far East, and as far as the islands of the Pacific. Mason Remey voyaged to Russia and Persia, and later, with Howard Struven, circled, for the first time in Bahá'í history, the globe, visiting on his way the Hawaiian Islands, Japan, China, India and Burma. Hooper Harris and Harlan Ober traveled, during no less than seven months, in India and Burma, visiting Bombay, Poona, Lahore, Calcutta, Rangoon and Mandalay. Alma Knobloch, following on the heels of Dr. K. E. Fisher, hoisted the standard of the Faith in Germany, and carried its light to Austria. Dr. Susan I. Moody, Sydney Sprague, Lillian F. Kappes, Dr. Sarah Clock, and Elizabeth Stewart transferred their residence to Ṭihrán for the purpose of furthering the manifold interests of the Faith, in collaboration with the Bahá'ís of that city. Sarah Farmer, who had already initiated in 1894, at Green Acre, in the State of Maine, summer conferences and established a center for the promotion of unity and fellowship between races and religions, placed, after her pilgrimage to 'Akká in 1900, the facilities these conferences provided at the disposal of the followers of the Faith which she had herself recently embraced.

And last but not least, inspired by the example set by their fellow-disciples in 'Is͟hqábád, who had already commenced the construction of the first Mas͟hriqu'l-Ad͟hkár of the Bahá'í world, and afire with the desire to demonstrate, in a tangible and befitting manner, the quality of their faith and devotion, the Bahá'ís of Chicago, having petitioned 'Abdu'l-Bahá for permission to erect a House of Worship, and secured, in a Tablet revealed in June 1903, His ready and enthusiastic approval, arose, despite the smallness of their numbers and their limited resources, to initiate an enterprise which must rank as the greatest single contribution which the Bahá'ís of America, and indeed of the West, have as yet made to the Cause of Bahá'u'lláh. The subsequent encouragement given them by 'Abdu'l-Bahá, and the contributions raised by various Assemblies decided the members of this Assembly to invite representatives of their fellow-believers in various parts of the country to meet in Chicago for the initiation of the stupendous undertaking they had conceived. On November 26, 1907, the assembled representatives, convened for that purpose, appointed a committee of nine to locate a suitable site for the proposed Temple. By April 9, 1908, the sum of two thousand dollars had been paid for the purchase of two building lots, situated near the shore of Lake Michigan. In March 1909, a convention representative of various Bahá'í centers was called, in pursuance of instructions received from 'Abdu'l-Bahá. The thirty-nine delegates, representing thirty-six cities, who had assembled in Chicago, on the very day the remains of the Báb were laid to rest by 'Abdu'l-Bahá in the specially erected mausoleum on Mt. Carmel, established a permanent national organization, known as the Bahá'í Temple Unity, which was incorporated as a religious corporation, functioning under the laws of the State of Illinois, and invested with full authority to hold title to the property of the Temple and to provide ways and means for its construction. At this same convention a constitution was framed, the Executive Board of the Bahá'í Temple Unity was elected, and was authorized by the delegates to complete the purchase of the land recommended by the previous Convention. Contributions for this historic enterprise, from India, Persia, Turkey, Syria, Palestine, Russia, Egypt, Germany, France, England, Canada, Mexico, the Hawaiian Islands, and even Mauritius, and from no less than sixty American cities, amounted by 1910, two years previous to 'Abdu'l-Bahá's arrival in America, to no less than twenty thousand dollars, a remarkable testimony alike to the solidarity of the followers of Bahá'u'lláh in both the East and the West, and to the self-sacrificing efforts exerted by the American believers who, as the work progressed, assumed a preponderating share in providing the sum of over a million dollars required for the erection of the structure of the Temple and its external ornamentation.

## CHAPTER XVII

# Renewal of 'Abdu'l-Bahá's Incarceration

The outstanding accomplishments of a valiant and sorely-tested community, the first fruits of Bahá'u'lláh's newly established Covenant in the Western world, had laid a foundation sufficiently imposing to invite the presence of the appointed Center of that Covenant, Who had called that Community into being and watched, with such infinite care and foresight, over its budding destinies. Not until, however, 'Abdu'l-Bahá had emerged from the severe crisis which had already for several years been holding Him in its toils could He undertake His memorable voyage to the shores of a continent where the rise and establishment of His Father's Faith had been signalized by such magnificent and enduring achievements.

This second major crisis of His ministry, external in nature and hardly less severe than the one precipitated by the rebellion of Mírzá Muḥammad-'Alí, gravely imperiled His life, deprived Him, for a number of years, of the relative freedom He had enjoyed, plunged into anguish His family and the followers of the Faith in East and West, and exposed as never before, the degradation and infamy of His relentless adversaries. It originated two years after the departure of the first American pilgrims from the Holy Land. It persisted, with varying degrees of intensity, during more than seven years, and was directly attributable to the incessant intrigues and monstrous misrepresentations of the Arch-Breaker of Bahá'u'lláh's Covenant and his supporters.

Embittered by his abject failure to create a schism on which he had fondly pinned his hopes; stung by the conspicuous success which the standard-bearers of the Covenant had, despite his machinations, achieved in the North American continent; encouraged by the existence of a régime that throve in an atmosphere of intrigue and suspicion, and which was presided over by a cunning and cruel potentate; determined to exploit to the full the opportunities for mischief afforded him by the arrival of Western pilgrims at the prison-fortress of 'Akká, as well as by the commencement of the construction of the Báb's sepulcher on Mt. Carmel, Mírzá Muḥammad-'Alí, seconded by his brother, Mírzá Badí'u'lláh, and aided by his brother-in-law,

Mírzá Majdi'd-Dín, succeeded through strenuous and persistent endeavors in exciting the suspicion of the Turkish government and its officials, and in inducing them to reimpose on 'Abdu'l-Bahá the confinement from which, in the days of Bahá'u'lláh, He had so grievously suffered.

This very brother, Mírzá Muhammad-'Alí's chief accomplice, in a written confession signed, sealed and published by him, on the occasion of his reconciliation with 'Abdu'l-Bahá, has borne testimony to the wicked plots that had been devised. "What I have heard from others," wrote Mírzá Badí'u'lláh, "I will ignore. I will only recount what I have seen with my own eyes, and heard from his (Mírzá Muḥammad-'Alí) lips." "It was arranged by him (Mírzá Muḥammad-'Alí)," he, then, proceeds to relate, "to dispatch Mírzá Majdi'd-Dín with a gift and a letter written in Persian to Naẓim Páshá, the Válí (governor) of Damascus, and to seek his assistance. . . . As he (Mírzá Majdi'd-Dín) himself informed me in Haifa he did all he could to acquaint him (governor) fully with the construction work on Mt. Carmel, with the comings and goings of the American believers, and with the gatherings held in 'Akká. The Páshá, in his desire to know all the facts, was extremely kind to him, and assured him of his aid. A few days after Mírzá Majdi'd-Dín's return a cipher telegram was received from the Sublime Porte, transmitting the Sulṭán's orders to incarcerate 'Abdu'l-Bahá, myself and the others." "In those days," he, furthermore, in that same document, testifies, "a man who came to 'Akká from Damascus stated to outsiders that Náẓim Páshá had been the cause of the incarceration of 'Abbás Effendi. The strangest thing of all is this that Mírzá Muḥammad-'Alí, after he had been incarcerated, wrote a letter to Naẓim Páshá for the purpose of achieving his own deliverance. . . . The Páshá, however, did not write even a word in answer to either the first or the second letter."

It was in 1901, on the fifth day of the month of Jamádíyu'l-Avval 1319 A.H. (August 20) that 'Abdu'l-Bahá, upon His return from Bahjí where He had participated in the celebration of the anniversary of the Báb's Declaration, was informed, in the course of an interview with the governor of 'Akká, of Sulṭán 'Abdu'l-Hamíd's instructions ordering that the restrictions which had been gradually relaxed should be reimposed, and that He and His brothers should be strictly confined within the walls of that city. The Sulṭán's edict was at first rigidly enforced, the freedom of the exiled community was severely curtailed, while 'Abdu'l-Bahá had to submit, alone and unaided, to the prolonged interrogation of judges and officials, who required His presence for several consecutive days at government headquarters for the purpose of their investigations. One of His first acts was to intercede on behalf of His brothers, who had been peremptorily summoned and informed by the governor of the orders of the sovereign, an act which failed to soften their hostility or lessen their malevolent activities. Subsequently, through His intervention with the civil and military authorities, He succeeded in obtaining the freedom of His followers who resided in 'Akká, and in enabling them to continue to earn, without interference, the means of livelihood.

The Covenant-breakers were unappeased by the measures taken by the authorities against One Who had so magnanimously intervened on their behalf. Aided by the notorious Yaḥyá Bey, the chief of police, and other officials, civil as well as military, who, in consequence of their representations, had replaced those who had been friendly to 'Abdu'l-Bahá, and by secret agents who traveled back and forth between 'Akká and Constantinople, and who even kept a vigilant watch over everything that went on in His household, they arose to encompass His ruin. They lavished on officials gifts which included possessions sacred to the memory of Bahá'u'lláh, and shamelessly proffered to high and low alike bribes drawn, in some instances, from the sale of properties associated with Him or bestowed upon some of them by 'Abdu'l-Bahá. Relaxing nothing of their efforts they pursued relentlessly the course of their nefarious activities, determined to leave no stone unturned until they had either brought about His execution or ensured His deportation to a place remote enough to enable them to wrest the Cause from His grasp. The Válí of Damascus, the Muftí of Beirut, members of the Protestant missions established in Syria and 'Akká, even the influential S͟hayk͟h Abu'l-Hudá, in Constantinople, whom the Sulṭán held in as profound an esteem as that in which Muḥammad S͟háh had held his Grand Vizir, Ḥájí Mírzá Áqásí, were, on various occasions, approached, appealed to, and urged to lend their assistance for the prosecution of their odious designs.

Through verbal messages, formal communications and by personal interviews the Covenant-breakers impressed upon these notables the necessity of immediate action, shrewdly adapting their arguments to the particular interests and prejudices of those whose aid they solicited. To some they represented 'Abdu'l-Bahá as a callous usurper Who had trampled upon their rights, robbed them of their heritage, reduced them to poverty, made their friends in Persia their enemies, accumulated for Himself a vast fortune, and acquired no less than two-thirds of the land in Haifa. To others they declared that 'Abdu'l-Bahá contemplated making of 'Akká and Haifa a new Mecca and Medina. To still others they affirmed that Bahá'u'lláh was no more than a retired dervish, who professed and promoted the Faith of Islám, Whom 'Abbás Effendi, His son, had, for the purpose of self-glorification, exalted to the rank of God-head, whilst claiming Himself to be the Son of God and the return of Jesus Christ. They further accused Him of harboring designs inimical to the interests of the state, of meditating a rebellion against the Sulṭán, of having already hoisted the banner of Yá Bahá'u'l-Abhá, the ensign of revolt, in distant villages in Palestine and Syria, of having raised surreptitiously an army of thirty thousand men, of being engaged in the construction of a fortress and a vast ammunition depot on Mt. Carmel, of having secured the moral and material support of a host of English and American friends, amongst whom were officers of foreign powers, who were arriving, in large numbers and in disguise, to pay Him their homage, and of having already, in conjunction with them, drawn up His plans for the subjugation of the neighboring provinces, for the expulsion of the ruling authorities, and for the ultimate seizure of the power wielded by the Sulṭán himself. Through misrepresentation and bribery they succeeded in inducing certain people to affix their signatures as witnesses to the documents which they had drawn up, and which they despatched, through their agents, to the Sublime Porte.

Such grave accusations, embodied in numerous reports, could not fail to perturb profoundly the mind of a despot already obsessed by the fear of impending rebellion among his subjects. A commission was accordingly appointed to inquire into the matter, and report the result of its investigations. Each of the charges brought against 'Abdu'l-Bahá, when summoned to the court, on several occasions, He carefully and fearlessly refuted. He exposed the absurdity of these accusations, acquainted the members of the Commission, in support of His argument, with the provisions of Bahá'u'lláh's Testament, expressed His readiness to submit to any sentence the court might decide to pass upon Him, and eloquently affirmed that if they should chain Him, drag Him through the streets, execrate and ridicule Him, stone and spit upon Him, suspend Him in the public square, and riddle Him with bullets, He would regard it as a signal honor, inasmuch as He would thereby be following in the footsteps, and sharing the sufferings, of His beloved Leader, the Báb.

The gravity of the situation confronting 'Abdu'l-Bahá; the rumors that were being set afloat by a population that anticipated the gravest developments; the hints and allusions to the dangers threatening Him contained in newspapers published in Egypt and Syria; the aggressive attitude which His enemies increasingly assumed; the provocative behavior of some of the inhabitants of 'Akká and Haifa who had been emboldened by the predictions and fabrications of these enemies regarding the fate awaiting a suspected community and its Leader, led Him to reduce the number of pilgrims, and even to suspend, for a time, their visits, and to issue special instructions that His mail be handled through an agent in Egypt rather than in Haifa; for a time He ordered that it should be held there pending further advice from Him. He, moreover, directed the believers, as well as His own secretaries, to collect and remove to a place of safety all the Bahá'í writings in their possession, and, urging them to transfer their residence to Egypt, went so far as to forbid their gathering, as was their wont, in His house. Even His numerous friends and admirers refrained, during the most turbulent days of this period, from calling upon Him, for fear of being implicated and of incurring the suspicion of the authorities. On certain days and nights, when the outlook was at its darkest, the house in which He was living, and which had for many years been a focus of activity, was completely deserted. Spies, secretly and openly, kept watch around it, observing His every movement and restricting the freedom of His family.

The construction of the Báb's sepulcher, whose foundation-stone had been laid by Him on the site blessed and selected by Bahá'u'lláh, He, however, refused to suspend, or even interrupt, for however brief a period. Nor would He allow any obstacle, however formidable, to interfere with the daily flow of Tablets which poured forth, with prodigious rapidity and ever increasing volume, from His indefatigable pen, in answer to the vast number of letters, reports, inquiries, prayers, confessions of faith, apologies and eulogies received from countless followers and admirers in both the East and the West. Eye-witnesses have testified that, during that agitated and perilous period of His life, they had known Him to pen, with His own Hand, no less than ninety Tablets in a single day, and to pass many a night, from dusk to dawn, alone in His bed-chamber engaged in a correspondence which the pressure of His manifold responsibilities had prevented Him from attending to in the day-time.

It was during these troublous times, the most dramatic period of His ministry, when, in the hey-day of His life and in the full tide of

His power, He, with inexhaustible energy, marvelous serenity and unshakable confidence, initiated and resistlessly prosecuted the varied enterprises associated with that ministry. It was during these times that the plan of the first Mashriqu'l-Adhkár of the Bahá'í world was conceived by Him, and its construction undertaken by His followers in the city of 'Ishqábád in Turkistán. It was during these times, despite the disturbances that agitated His native country, that instructions were issued by Him for the restoration of the holy and historic House of the Báb in Shíráz. It was during these times that the initial measures, chiefly through His constant encouragement, were taken which paved the way for the laying of the dedication stone, which He, in later years, placed with His own hands when visiting the site of the Mother Temple of the West on the shore of Lake Michigan. It was at this juncture that that celebrated compilation of His table talks, published under the title "Some Answered Questions," was made, talks given during the brief time He was able to spare, in the course of which certain fundamental aspects of His Father's Faith were elucidated, traditional and rational proofs of its validity adduced, and a great variety of subjects regarding the Christian Dispensation, the Prophets of God, Biblical prophecies, the origin and condition of man and other kindred themes authoritatively explained.

It was during the darkest hours of this period that, in a communication addressed to the Báb's cousin, the venerable Ḥájí Mírzá Muḥammad-Taqí, the chief builder of the Temple of 'Ishqábád, 'Abdu'l-Bahá, in stirring terms, proclaimed the immeasurable greatness of the Revelation of Bahá'u'lláh, sounded the warnings foreshadowing the turmoil which its enemies, both far and near, would let loose upon the world, and prophesied, in moving language, the ascendancy which the torchbearers of the Covenant would ultimately achieve over them. It was at an hour of grave suspense, during that same period, that He penned His Will and Testament, that immortal Document wherein He delineated the features of the Administrative Order which would arise after His passing, and would herald the establishment of that World Order, the advent of which the Báb had announced, and the laws and principles of which Bahá'u'lláh had already formulated. It was in the course of these tumultuous years that, through the instrumentality of the heralds and champions of a firmly instituted Covenant, He reared the embryonic institutions, administrative, spiritual, and educational, of a steadily expanding Faith in Persia, the cradle of that Faith, in the Great Republic of the West, the cradle of its Administrative Order, in the Dominion of Canada, in France, in England, in Germany, in Egypt, in 'Iráq, in Russia, in India, in Burma, in Japan, and even in the remote Pacific Islands. It was during these stirring times that a tremendous impetus was lent by Him to the translation, the publication and dissemination of Bahá'í literature, whose scope now included a variety of books and treatises, written in the Persian, the Arabic, the English, the Turkish, the French, the German, the Russian and Burmese languages. At His table, in those days, whenever there was a lull in the storm raging about Him, there would gather pilgrims, friends and inquirers from most of the afore-mentioned countries, representative of the Christian, the Muslim, the Jewish, the Zoroastrian, the Hindu and Buddhist Faiths. To the needy thronging His doors and filling the courtyard of His house every Friday morning, in spite of the perils that environed Him, He would distribute alms with His own hands, with a regularity and generosity that won Him the title of "Father of the Poor." Nothing in those tempestuous days could shake His confidence, nothing would be allowed to interfere with His ministrations to the destitute, the orphan, the sick, and the down-trodden, nothing could prevent Him from calling in person upon those who were either incapacitated, or ashamed to solicit His aid. Adamant in His determination to follow the example of both the Báb and Bahá'u'lláh, nothing would induce Him to flee from His enemies, or escape from imprisonment, neither the advice tendered Him by the leading members of the exiled community in 'Akká, nor the insistent pleas of the Spanish Consul—a kinsman of the agent of an Italian steamship company—who, in his love for 'Abdu'l-Bahá and his anxiety to avert the threatening danger, had gone so far as to place at His disposal an Italian freighter, ready to provide Him a safe passage to any foreign port He might name.

So imperturbable was 'Abdu'l-Bahá's equanimity that, while rumors were being bruited about that He might be cast into the sea, or exiled to Fízán in Tripolitania, or hanged on the gallows, He, to the amazement of His friends and the amusement of His enemies, was to be seen planting trees and vines in the garden of His house, whose fruits when the storm had blown over, He would bid His faithful gardener, Ismá'íl Áqá, pluck and present to those same friends and enemies on the occasion of their visits to Him.

In the early part of the winter of 1907 another Commission of four officers, headed by 'Árif Bey, and invested with plenary powers, was suddenly dispatched to 'Akká by order of the Sulṭán. A few days before its arrival 'Abdul'-Bahá had a dream, which He recounted to the believers, in which He saw a ship cast anchor off 'Akká, from which flew a few birds, resembling sticks of dynamite, and which, circling about His head, as He stood in the midst of a multitude of the frightened inhabitants of the city, returned without exploding to the ship.

No sooner had the members of the Commission landed than they placed under their direct and exclusive control both the Telegraph and Postal services in 'Akká; arbitrarily dismissed officials suspected of being friendly to 'Abdu'l-Bahá, including the governor of the city; established direct and secret contact with the government in Constantinople; took up their residence in the home of the neighbors and intimate associates of the Covenant-breakers; set guards over the house of 'Abdu'l-Bahá to prevent any one from seeing Him; and started the strange procedure of calling up as witnesses the very people, among whom were Christians and Moslems, orientals and westerners, who had previously signed the documents forwarded to Constantinople, and which they had brought with them for the purpose of their investigations.

The activities of the Covenant-breakers, and particularly of Mírzá Muḥammad-'Alí, now jubilant and full of hope, rose in this hour of extreme crisis, to the highest pitch. Visits, interviews and entertainments multiplied, in an atmosphere of fervid expectation, now that the victory was seen to be at hand. Not a few among the lower elements of the population were led to believe that their acquisition of the property which would be left behind by the deported exiles was imminent. Insults and calumnies markedly increased. Even some of the poor, so long and so bountifully succored by 'Abdu'l-Bahá, forsook Him for fear of reprisals.

'Abdu'l-Bahá, while the members of the Commission were carrying on their so-called investigations, and throughout their stay of about one month in 'Akká, consistently refused to meet or have any dealings with any of them, in spite of the veiled threats and warnings conveyed by them to Him through a messenger, an attitude which greatly surprised them and served to inflame their animosity and reinforce their determination to execute their evil designs. Though the perils and tribulations which had encompassed Him were now at their thickest, though the ship on which He was supposed to embark with the members of the Commission was waiting in readiness, at times in 'Akká, at times in Haifa, and the wildest rumors were being spread about Him, the serenity He had invariably maintained, ever since His incarceration had been reimposed, remained unclouded, and His confidence unshaken. *"The meaning of the dream I dreamt,"* He, at that time, told the believers who still remained in 'Akká, *"is now clear and evident. Please God this dynamite will not explode."*

Meanwhile the members of the Commission had, on a certain Friday, gone to Haifa and inspected the Báb's sepulcher, the construction of which had been proceeding without any interruption on Mt. Carmel. Impressed by its solidity and dimensions, they had inquired of one of the attendants as to the number of vaults that had been built beneath that massive structure.

Shortly after the inspection had been made it was suddenly observed, one day at about sunset, that the ship, which had been lying off Haifa, had weighed anchor, and was heading towards 'Akká. The news spread rapidly among an excited population that the members of the Commission had embarked upon it. It was anticipated that it would stop long enough at 'Akká to take 'Abdu'l-Bahá on board, and then proceed to its destination. Consternation and anguish seized the members of His family when informed of the approach of the ship. The few believers who were left wept with grief at their impending separation from their Master. 'Abdu'l-Bahá could be seen, at that tragic hour, pacing, alone and silent, the courtyard of His house.

As dusk fell, however, it was suddenly noticed that the lights of the ship had swung round, and the vessel had changed her course. It now became evident that she was sailing direct for Constantinople. The intelligence was instantly communicated to 'Abdu'l-Bahá, Who, in the gathering darkness, was still pacing His courtyard. Some of the believers who had posted themselves at different points to watch the progress of the ship hurried to confirm the joyful tidings. One of the direst perils that had ever threatened 'Abdu'l-Bahá's precious life was, on that historic day, suddenly, providentially and definitely averted.

Soon after the precipitate and wholly unexpected sailing of that ship news was received that a bomb had exploded in the path of the Sulṭán while he was returning to his palace from the mosque where he had been offering his Friday prayers.

A few days after this attempt on his life the Commission submitted its report to him; but he and his government were too preoccupied to consider the matter. The case was laid aside, and when, some months later, it was again brought forward it was abruptly closed forever by an event which, once and for all, placed the Prisoner of 'Akká beyond the power of His royal enemy. The "Young Turk" Revolution, breaking out swiftly and decisively in 1908, forced a reluctant despot to promulgate the constitution which he had suspended, and to release all religious and political prisoners held under the old régime. Even then a telegram had to be sent to Constantinople to inquire specifically whether 'Abdu'l-Bahá was included in the category of these prisoners, to which an affirmative reply was promptly received.

Within a few months, in 1909, the Young Turks obtained from the Shaykhu'l-Islám the condemnation of the Sulṭán himself who, as a result of further attempts to overthrow the constitution, was finally and ignominiously deposed, deported and made a prisoner of state. On one single day of that same year there were executed no less than thirty-one leading ministers, pá<u>sh</u>ás and officials, among whom were numbered notorious enemies of the Faith. Tripolitania itself, the scene of 'Abdu'l-Bahá's intended exile was subsequently wrested from the Turks by Italy. Thus ended the reign of the "Great Assassin," "the most mean, cunning, untrustworthy and cruel intriguer of the long dynasty of 'Uthmán," a reign "more disastrous in its immediate losses of territory and in the certainty of others to follow, and more conspicuous for the deterioration of the condition of his subjects, than that of any other of his twenty-three degenerate predecessors since the death of Sulaymán the Magnificent."

## CHAPTER XVIII

# Entombment of the Báb's Remains on Mt. Carmel

'Abdu'l-Bahá's unexpected and dramatic release from His forty-year confinement dealt a blow to the ambitions cherished by the Covenant-breakers as devastating as that which, a decade before, had shattered their hopes of undermining His authority and of ousting Him from His God-given position. Now, on the very morrow of His triumphant liberation a third blow befell them as stunning as those which preceded it and hardly less spectacular than they. Within a few months of the historic decree which set Him free, in the very year that witnessed the downfall of Sulṭán 'Abdu'l-Ḥamíd, that same power from on high which had enabled 'Abdu'l-Bahá to preserve inviolate the rights divinely conferred on Him, to establish His Father's Faith in the North American continent, and to triumph over His royal oppressor, enabled Him to achieve one of the most signal acts of His ministry: the removal of the Báb's remains from their place of concealment in Ṭihrán to Mt. Carmel. He Himself testified, on more than one occasion, that the safe transfer of these remains, the construction of a befitting mausoleum to receive them, and their final interment with His own hands in their permanent resting-place constituted one of the three principal objectives which, ever since the inception of His mission, He had conceived it His paramount duty to achieve. This act indeed deserves to rank as one of the outstanding events in the first Bahá'í century.

As observed in a previous chapter the mangled bodies of the Báb and His fellow-martyr, Mírzá Muḥammad-'Alí, were removed, in the middle of the second night following their execution, through the pious intervention of Ḥájí Sulaymán Khán, from the edge of the moat where they had been cast to a silk factory owned by one of the believers of Mílán, and were laid the next day in a wooden casket, and thence carried to a place of safety. Subsequently, according to Bahá'u'lláh's instructions, they were transported to Ṭihrán and placed in the shrine of Imám-Zádih Ḥasan. They were later removed to the residence of Hájí Sulaymán Khán himself in the Sar-Chashmih quarter of the city, and from his house were taken to the shrine of Imám-Zádih Ma'ṣúm, where they remained concealed until the year

1284 A.H. (1867-1868), when a Tablet, revealed by Bahá'u'lláh in Adrianople, directed Mullá 'Alí-Akbar-i-Shahmírzádí and Jamál-i-Burújirdí to transfer them without delay to some other spot, an instruction which, in view of the subsequent reconstruction of that shrine, proved to have been providential.

Unable to find a suitable place in the suburb of Sháh 'Abdu'l-'Aẓím, Mullá 'Alí-Akbar and his companion continued their search until, on the road leading to Chashmih-'Alí, they came upon the abandoned and dilapidated Masjid-i-Mashá'u'lláh, where they deposited, within one of its walls, after dark, their precious burden, having first re-wrapt the remains in a silken shroud brought by them for that purpose. Finding the next day to their consternation that the hiding-place had been discovered, they clandestinely carried the casket through the gate of the capital direct to the house of Mírzá Ḥasan-i-Vazír, a believer and son-in-law of Ḥájí Mírzá Siyyid 'Alíy-i-Tafríshí, the Majdu'l-Ashráf, where it remained for no less than fourteen months. The long-guarded secret of its whereabouts becoming known to the believers, they began to visit the house in such numbers that a communication had to be addressed by Mullá 'Alí-Akbar to Bahá'u'lláh, begging for guidance in the matter. Ḥájí Sháh Muḥammad-i-Manshádí, surnamed Amínu'l-Bayán, was accordingly commissioned to receive the Trust from him, and bidden to exercise the utmost secrecy as to its disposal.

Assisted by another believer, Ḥájí Sháh Muḥammad buried the casket beneath the floor of the inner sanctuary of the shrine of Imám-Zádih Zayd, where it lay undetected until Mírzá Asadu'lláh-i-Iṣfahání was informed of its exact location through a chart forwarded to him by Bahá'u'lláh. Instructed by Bahá'u'lláh to conceal it elsewhere, he first removed the remains to his own house in Ṭihrán, after which they were deposited in several other localities such as the house of Ḥusayn-'Alíy-i-Iṣfahání and that of Muḥammad-Karím-i-'Aṭṭár, where they remained hidden until the year 1316 (1899) A.H., when, in pursuance of directions issued by 'Abdu'l-Bahá, this same Mírzá Asadu'lláh, together with a number of other believers, transported them by way of Iṣfahán, Kirmánsháh, Baghdád and Damascus, to Beirut and thence by sea to 'Akká, arriving at their destination on the 19th of the month of Ramaḍán 1316 A.H. (January 31, 1899), fifty lunar years after the Báb's execution in Tabríz.

In the same year that this precious Trust reached the shores of the Holy Land and was delivered into the hands of 'Abdu'l-Bahá, He, accompanied by Dr. Ibráhím Khayru'lláh, whom He had already honored with the titles of *"Bahá's Peter," "The Second Columbus"* and *"Conqueror of America,"* drove to the recently purchased site which had been blessed and selected by Bahá'u'lláh on Mt. Carmel, and there laid, with His own hands, the foundation-stone of the edifice, the construction of which He, a few months later, was to commence. About that same time, the marble sarcophagus, designed to receive the body of the Báb, an offering of love from the Bahá'ís of Rangoon, had, at 'Abdu'l-Bahá's suggestion, been completed and shipped to Haifa.

No need to dwell on the manifold problems and preoccupations which, for almost a decade, continued to beset 'Abdu'l-Bahá until the victorious hour when He was able to bring to a final consummation the historic task entrusted to Him by His Father. The risks and perils with which Bahá'u'lláh and later His Son had been confronted in their efforts to insure, during half a century, the protection of those remains were but a prelude to the grave dangers which, at a later period, the Center of the Covenant Himself had to face in the course of the construction of the edifice designed to receive them, and indeed until the hour of His final release from His incarceration.

The long-drawn out negotiations with the shrewd and calculating owner of the building-site of the holy Edifice, who, under the influence of the Covenant-breakers, refused for a long time to sell; the exorbitant price at first demanded for the opening of a road leading to that site and indispensable to the work of construction; the interminable objections raised by officials, high and low, whose easily aroused suspicions had to be allayed by repeated explanations and assurances given by 'Abdu'l-Bahá Himself; the dangerous situation created by the monstrous accusations brought by Mírzá Muḥammad-'Alí and his associates regarding the character and purpose of that building; the delays and complications caused by 'Abdu'l-Bahá's prolonged and enforced absence from Haifa, and His consequent inability to supervise in person the vast undertaking He had initiated—all these were among the principal obstacles which He, at so critical a period in His ministry, had to face and surmount ere He could execute in its entirety the Plan, the outline of which Bahá'u'lláh had communicated to Him on the occasion of one of His visits to Mt. Carmel.

*"Every stone of that building, every stone of the road leading to it,"* He, many a time was heard to remark, *"I have with infinite tears and at tremendous cost, raised and placed in position." "One night,"* He, according to an eye-witness, once observed, *"I was so hemmed in by My anxieties that I had no other recourse than to recite and*

*repeat over and over again a prayer of the Báb which I had in My possession, the recital of which greatly calmed Me. The next morning the owner of the plot himself came to Me, apologized and begged Me to purchase his property."*

Finally, in the very year His royal adversary lost his throne, and at the time of the opening of the first American Bahá'í Convention, convened in Chicago for the purpose of creating a permanent national organization for the construction of the Mas͟hriqu'l-Ad͟hkár, 'Abdu'l-Bahá brought His undertaking to a successful conclusion, in spite of the incessant machinations of enemies both within and without. On the 28th of the month of Ṣafar 1327 A.H., the day of the first Naw-Rúz (1909), which He celebrated after His release from His confinement, 'Abdu'l-Bahá had the marble sarcophagus transported with great labor to the vault prepared for it, and in the evening, by the light of a single lamp, He laid within it, with His own hands—in the presence of believers from the East and from the West and in circumstances at once solemn and moving—the wooden casket containing the sacred remains of the Báb and His companion.

When all was finished, and the earthly remains of the Martyr-Prophet of S͟hiráz were, at long last, safely deposited for their everlasting rest in the bosom of God's holy mountain, 'Abdu'l-Bahá, Who had cast aside His turban, removed His shoes and thrown off His cloak, bent low over the still open sarcophagus, His silver hair waving about His head and His face transfigured and luminous, rested His forehead on the border of the wooden casket, and, sobbing aloud, wept with such a weeping that all those who were present wept with Him. That night He could not sleep, so overwhelmed was He with emotion.

*"The most joyful tidings is this,"* He wrote later in a Tablet announcing to His followers the news of this glorious victory, *"that the holy, the luminous body of the Báb . . . after having for sixty years been transferred from place to place, by reason of the ascendancy of the enemy, and from fear of the malevolent, and having known neither rest nor tranquillity has, through the mercy of the Abhá Beauty, been ceremoniously deposited, on the day of Naw-Rúz, within the sacred casket, in the exalted Shrine on Mt. Carmel . . . By a strange coincidence, on that same day of Naw-Rúz, a cablegram was received from Chicago, announcing that the believers in each of the American centers had elected a delegate and sent to that city . . . and definitely decided on the site and construction of the Mas͟hriqu'l-Ad͟hkár."*

With the transference of the remains of the Báb—Whose advent marks the return of the Prophet Elijah—to Mt. Carmel, and their interment in that holy mountain, not far from the cave of that Prophet Himself, the Plan so gloriously envisaged by Bahá'u'lláh, in the evening of His life, had been at last executed, and the arduous labors associated with the early and tumultuous years of the ministry of the appointed Center of His Covenant crowned with immortal success. A focal center of Divine illumination and power, the very dust of which 'Abdu'l-Bahá averred had inspired Him, yielding in sacredness to no other shrine throughout the Bahá'í world except the Sepulcher of the Author of the Bahá'í Revelation Himself, had been permanently established on that mountain, regarded from time immemorial as sacred. A structure, at once massive, simple and imposing; nestling in the heart of Carmel, the "Vineyard of God"; flanked by the Cave of Elijah on the west, and by the hills of Galilee on the east; backed by the plain of Sharon, and facing the silver-city of 'Akká, and beyond it the Most Holy Tomb, the Heart and Qiblih of the Bahá'í world; overshadowing the colony of German Templars who, in anticipation of the "coming of the Lord," had forsaken their homes and foregathered at the foot of that mountain, in the very year of Bahá'u'lláh's Declaration in Baghdád (1863), the mausoleum of the Báb had now, with heroic effort and in impregnable strength been established as *"the Spot round which the Concourse on high circle in adoration."* Events have already demonstrated through the extension of the Edifice itself, through the embellishment of its surroundings, through the acquisition of extensive endowments in its neighborhood, and through its proximity to the resting-places of the wife, the son and daughter of Bahá'u'lláh Himself, that it was destined to acquire with the passing of the years a measure of fame and glory commensurate with the high purpose that had prompted its founding. Nor will it, as the years go by, and the institutions revolving around the World Administrative Center of the future Bahá'í Commonwealth are gradually established, cease to manifest the latent potentialities with which that same immutable purpose has endowed it. Resistlessly will this Divine institution flourish and expand, however fierce the animosity which its future enemies may evince, until the full measure of its splendor will have been disclosed before the eyes of all mankind.

*"Haste thee, O Carmel!"* Bahá'u'lláh, significantly addressing that holy mountain, has written, *"for lo, the light of the Countenance of God . . . hath been lifted upon thee . . . Rejoice, for God hath, in this Day, established upon thee His throne, hath made thee the dawning-place of His signs and the dayspring of the evidences of His*

*Revelation. Well is it with him that circleth around thee, that proclaimeth the revelation of thy glory, and recounteth that which the bounty of the Lord thy God hath showered upon thee." "Call out to Zion, O Carmel!"* He, furthermore, has revealed in that same Tablet, *"and announce the joyful tidings: He that was hidden from mortal eyes is come! His all-conquering sovereignty is manifest; His all-encompassing splendor is revealed. Beware lest thou hesitate or halt. Hasten forth and circumambulate the City of God that hath descended from heaven, the celestial Kaaba round which have circled in adoration the favored of God, the pure in heart, and the company of the most exalted angels."*

## CHAPTER XIX

# 'Abdu'l-Bahá's Travels in Europe and America

The establishment of the Faith of Bahá'u'lláh in the Western Hemisphere—the most outstanding achievement that will forever be associated with 'Abdu'l-Bahá's ministry—had, as observed in the preceding pages, set in motion such tremendous forces, and been productive of such far-reaching results, as to warrant the active and personal participation of the Center of the Covenant Himself in those epoch-making activities which His Western disciples had, through the propelling power of that Covenant, boldly initiated and were vigorously prosecuting.

The crisis which the blindness and perversity of the Covenant-breakers had precipitated, and which, for several years, had so tragically interfered with the execution of 'Abdu'l-Bahá's purpose, was now providentially resolved. An unsurmountable barrier had been suddenly lifted from His path, His fetters were unlocked, and God's avenging wrath had taken the chains from His neck and placed them upon that of 'Abdu'l-Ḥamíd, His royal adversary and the dupe of His most implacable enemy. The sacred remains of the Báb, entrusted to His hands by His departed Father, had, moreover, with immense difficulty been transferred from their hiding-place in far-off Ṭihrán to the Holy Land, and deposited ceremoniously and reverently by Him in the bosom of Mt. Carmel.

'Abdu'l-Bahá was at this time broken in health. He suffered from several maladies brought on by the strains and stresses of a tragic life spent almost wholly in exile and imprisonment. He was on the threshold of three-score years and ten. Yet as soon as He was released from His forty-year long captivity, as soon as He had laid the Báb's body in a safe and permanent resting-place, and His mind was free of grievous anxieties connected with the execution of that priceless Trust, He arose with sublime courage, confidence and resolution to consecrate what little strength remained to Him, in the evening of His life, to a service of such heroic proportions that no parallel to it is to be found in the annals of the first Bahá'í century.

Indeed His three years of travel, first to Egypt, then to Europe and later to America, mark, if we would correctly appraise their historic importance, a turning point of the utmost significance in the history of the century. For the first time since the inception of the Faith, sixty-six years previously, its Head and supreme Representative burst asunder the shackles which had throughout the ministries of both the Báb and Bahá'u'lláh so grievously fettered its freedom. Though repressive measures still continued to circumscribe the activities of the vast majority of its adherents in the land of its birth, its recognized Leader was now vouchsafed a freedom of action which, with the exception of a brief interval in the course of the War of 1914-18, He was to continue to enjoy to the end of His life, and which has never since been withdrawn from its institutions at its world center.

So momentous a change in the fortunes of the Faith was the signal for such an outburst of activity on His part as to dumbfound His followers in East and West with admiration and wonder, and exercise an imperishable influence on the course of its future history. He Who, in His own words, had entered prison as a youth and left it an old man, Who never in His life had faced a public audience, had attended no school, had never moved in Western circles, and was unfamiliar with Western customs and language, had arisen not only to proclaim from pulpit and platform, in some of the chief capitals of Europe and in the leading cities of the North American continent, the distinctive verities enshrined in His Father's Faith, but to demonstrate as well the Divine origin of the Prophets gone before Him, and to disclose the nature of the tie binding them to that Faith.

Inflexibly resolved to undertake this arduous voyage, at whatever cost to His strength, at whatever risk to His life, He, quietly and without any previous warning, on a September afternoon, of the year 1910, the year following that which witnessed the downfall of Sulṭán 'Abdu'l-Ḥamíd and the formal entombment of the Báb's remains on Mt. Carmel, sailed for Egypt, sojourned for about a month in Port Said, and from thence embarked with the intention of proceeding to Europe, only to discover that the condition of His health necessitated His landing again at Alexandria and postponing His voyage. Fixing His residence in Ramleh, a suburb of Alexandria, and later visiting Zaytún and Cairo, He, on August 11 of the ensuing year, sailed with a party of four, on the S. S. Corsica, for Marseilles, and proceeded, after a brief stop at Thonon-les-Bains, to London, where He arrived on September 4, 1911. After a visit of about a month, He went to Paris, where He stayed for a period of nine weeks, returning to Egypt in December, 1911. Again taking up His residence in Ramleh, where He passed the winter, He embarked, on

His second journey to the West, on the steamship Cedric, on March 25, 1912, sailing via Naples direct to New York where He arrived on April 11. After a prolonged tour of eight months' duration, which carried Him from coast to coast, and in the course of which He visited Washington, Chicago, Cleveland, Pittsburgh, Montclair, Boston, Worcester, Brooklyn, Fanwood, Milford, Philadelphia, West Englewood, Jersey City, Cambridge, Medford, Morristown, Dublin, Green Acre, Montreal, Malden, Buffalo, Kenosha, Minneapolis, St. Paul, Omaha, Lincoln, Denver, Glenwood Springs, Salt Lake City, San Francisco, Oakland, Palo Alto, Berkeley, Pasadena, Los Angeles, Sacramento, Cincinnati, and Baltimore, He sailed, on the S. S. Celtic, on December 5, from New York for Liverpool; and landing there He proceeded by train to London. Later He visited Oxford, Edinburgh and Bristol, and thence returning to London, left for Paris on January 21, 1913. On March 30 He traveled to Stuttgart, and from there proceeded, on April 9, to Budapest, visited Vienna nine days later, returned to Stuttgart on April 25, and to Paris on May first, where He remained until June 12, sailing the following day, on the S. S. Himalaya from Marseilles bound for Egypt, arriving in Port Said four days later, where after short visits to Ismá'ílíyyih and Abúqír, and a prolonged stay in Ramleh, He returned to Haifa, concluding His historic journeys on December 5, 1913.

It was in the course of these epoch-making journeys and before large and representative audiences, at times exceeding a thousand people, that 'Abdu'l-Bahá expounded, with brilliant simplicity, with persuasiveness and force, and for the first time in His ministry, those basic and distinguishing principles of His Father's Faith, which together with the laws and ordinances revealed in the Kitáb-i-Aqdas constitute the bed-rock of God's latest Revelation to mankind. The independent search after truth, unfettered by superstition or tradition; the oneness of the entire human race, the pivotal principle and fundamental doctrine of the Faith; the basic unity of all religions; the condemnation of all forms of prejudice, whether religious, racial, class or national; the harmony which must exist between religion and science; the equality of men and women, the two wings on which the bird of human kind is able to soar; the introduction of compulsory education; the adoption of a universal auxiliary language; the abolition of the extremes of wealth and poverty; the institution of a world tribunal for the adjudication of disputes between nations; the exaltation of work, performed in the spirit of service, to the rank of worship; the glorification of justice as the ruling principle in human society, and of religion as a bulwark for the protection of all peoples and nations; and the establishment of a permanent and universal peace as the supreme goal of all mankind—these stand out as the essential elements of that Divine polity which He proclaimed to leaders of public thought as well as to the masses at large in the course of these missionary journeys. The exposition of these vitalizing truths of the Faith of Bahá'u'lláh, which He characterized as the *"spirit of the age,"* He supplemented with grave and reiterated warnings of an impending conflagration which, if the statesmen of the world should fail to avert, would set ablaze the entire continent of Europe. He, moreover, predicted, in the course of these travels, the radical changes which would take place in that continent, foreshadowed the movement of the decentralization of political power which would inevitably be set in motion, alluded to the troubles that would overtake Turkey, anticipated the persecution of the Jews on the European continent, and categorically asserted that the *"banner of the unity of mankind would be hoisted, that the tabernacle of universal peace would be raised and the world become another world."*

During these travels 'Abdu'l-Bahá displayed a vitality, a courage, a single-mindedness, a consecration to the task He had set Himself to achieve that excited the wonder and admiration of those who had the privilege of observing at close hand His daily acts. Indifferent to the sights and curiosities which habitually invite the attention of travelers and which the members of His entourage often wished Him to visit; careless alike of His comfort and His health; expending every ounce of His energy day after day from dawn till late at night; consistently refusing any gifts or contributions towards the expenses of His travels; unfailing in His solicitude for the sick, the sorrowful and the down-trodden; uncompromising in His championship of the underprivileged races and classes; bountiful as the rain in His generosity to the poor; contemptuous of the attacks launched against Him by vigilant and fanatical exponents of orthodoxy and sectarianism; marvelous in His frankness while demonstrating, from platform and pulpit, the prophetic Mission of Jesus Christ to the Jews, of the Divine origin of Islám in churches and synagogues, or the truth of Divine Revelation and the necessity of religion to materialists, atheists or agnostics; unequivocal in His glorification of Bahá'u'lláh at all times and within the sanctuaries of divers sects and denominations; adamant in His refusal, on several occasions, to curry the favor of people of title and wealth both in England and in the

United States; and last but not least incomparable in the spontaneity, the genuineness and warmth of His sympathy and loving-kindness shown to friend and stranger alike, believer and unbeliever, rich and poor, high and low, whom He met, either intimately or casually, whether on board ship, or whilst pacing the streets, in parks or public squares, at receptions or banquets, in slums or mansions, in the gatherings of His followers or the assemblage of the learned, He, the incarnation of every Bahá'í virtue and the embodiment of every Bahá'í ideal, continued for three crowded years to trumpet to a world sunk in materialism and already in the shadow of war, the healing, the God-given truths enshrined in His Father's Revelation.

In the course of His several visits to Egypt He had more than one interview with the Khedive, 'Abbás Ḥilmí Pá<u>sh</u>á II, was introduced to Lord Kitchener, met the Muftí, <u>Sh</u>ay<u>kh</u> Muḥammad Ba<u>kh</u>ít, as well as the Khedive's Imám, <u>Sh</u>ay<u>kh</u> Muḥammad Rá<u>sh</u>id, and associated with several 'ulamás, pá<u>sh</u>ás, Persian notables, members of the Turkish Parliament, editors of leading newspapers in Cairo and Alexandria, and other leaders and representatives of well-known institutions, both religious and secular.

Whilst He sojourned in England the house placed at His disposal in Cadogan Gardens became a veritable mecca to all sorts and conditions of men, thronging to visit the Prisoner of 'Akká Who had chosen their great city as the first scene of His labors in the West. "O, these pilgrims, these guests, these visitors!" thus bears witness His devoted hostess during the time He spent in London, "Remembering those days, our ears are filled with the sound of their footsteps—as they came from every country in the world. Every day, all day long, a constant stream, an interminable procession! Ministers and missionaries, oriental scholars and occult students, practical men of affairs and mystics, Anglicans, Catholics, and Non-conformists, Theosophists and Hindus, Christian Scientists and doctors of medicine, Muslims, Buddhists and Zoroastrians. There also called: politicians, Salvation Army soldiers, and other workers for human good, women suffragists, journalists, writers, poets and healers, dressmakers and great ladies, artists and artisans, poor workless people and prosperous merchants, members of the dramatic and musical world, these all came; and none were too lowly, nor too great, to receive the sympathetic consideration of this holy Messenger, Who was ever giving His life for others' good."

'Abdu'l-Bahá's first public appearance before a western audience significantly enough took place in a Christian house of worship, when, on September 10, 1911, He addressed an overflowing congregation from the pulpit of the City Temple. Introduced by the Pastor, the Reverend R. J. Campbell, He, in simple and moving language, and with vibrant voice, proclaimed the unity of God, affirmed the fundamental oneness of religion, and announced that the hour of the unity of the sons of men, of all races, religions and classes had struck. On another occasion, on September 17, at the request of the Venerable Archdeacon Wilberforce, He addressed the congregation of St. John the Divine, at Westminster, after evening service, choosing as His theme the transcendental greatness of the Godhead, as affirmed and elucidated by Bahá'u'lláh in the Kitáb-i-Íqán. "The Archdeacon," wrote a contemporary of that event, "had the Bishop's chair placed for his Guest on the chancel steps, and, standing beside Him, read the translation of 'Abdu'l-Bahá's address himself. The congregation was profoundly moved, and, following the Archdeacon's example, knelt to receive the blessing of the Servant of God—Who stood with extended arms—His wonderful voice rising and falling in the silence with the power of His invocation."

At the invitation of the Lord Mayor of London He breakfasted with him at the Mansion House; addressed the Theosophical Society at their headquarters, at the express request of their President, and also a Meeting of the Higher Thought center in London; was invited by a deputation from the Bramo-Somaj Society to deliver a lecture under their auspices; visited and delivered an address on world unity at the Mosque at Woking, at the invitation of the Muslim Community of Great Britain, and was entertained by Persian princes, noblemen, ex-ministers and members of the Persian Legation in London. He stayed as a guest in Dr. T. K. Cheyne's home in Oxford, and He delivered an address to "a large and deeply interested audience," highly academic in character, gathered at Manchester College in that city, and presided over by Dr. Estlin Carpenter. He also spoke from the pulpit of a Congregational Church in the East End of London, in response to the request of its Pastor; addressed gatherings in Caxton Hall and Westminster Hall, the latter under the chairmanship of Sir Thomas Berkeley, and witnessed a performance of "Eager Heart," a Christmas mystery play at the Church House, Westminster, the first dramatic performance He had ever beheld, and which in its graphic depiction of the life and sufferings of Jesus Christ moved Him to tears. In the Hall of the Passmore Edwards' Settlement, in Tavistock Place, he spoke to an audience of about four hundred and sixty representative people, presided over by Prof. Michael Sadler, called on a number of working women of that Settlement, who were on holiday at Vanners', in Byfleet, some twenty miles out of London, and paid a second visit there, meeting on that occasion people of every condition who had specially gathered to see Him, among whom were "the clergy of several denominations, a headmaster of a boys' public school, a member of Parliament, a doctor, a famous political writer, the vice-chancellor of a university, several journalists, a well-known poet, and a magistrate from London." "He will long be remembered," wrote a chronicler of His visit to England, describing that occasion, "as He sat in the bow window in the afternoon sunshine, His arm round a very ragged but very happy little boy who had come to ask 'Abdu'l-Bahá for sixpence for his money box and for his invalid mother, whilst round Him in the room were gathered men and women discussing Education, Socialism, the first Reform Bill, and the relation of submarines and wireless telegraphy to the new era on which man is entering."

Among those who called on Him during the memorable days He spent in England and Scotland were the Reverend Archdeacon Wilberforce, the Reverend R. J. Campbell, the Reverend Rhonddha Williams, the Reverend Roland Corbet, Lord Lamington, Sir Richard and Lady Stapley, Sir Michael Sadler, the Jalálu'd-Dawlih, son of the Ẓillu's-Sulṭán, Sir Ameer Ali, the late Maharaja of Jalawar, who paid Him many visits and gave an elaborate dinner and reception in His honor, the Maharaja of Rajputana, the Ranee of Sarawak, Princess Karadja, Baroness Barnekov, Lady Wemyss and her sister, Lady Glencomer, Lady Agnew, Miss Constance Maud, Prof. E. G. Browne, Prof. Patrick Geddes, Mr. Albert Dawson, editor of the Christian Commonwealth, Mr. David Graham Pole, Mrs. Annie Besant, Mrs. Pankhurst, and Mr. Stead, who had long and earnest conversations with Him. "Very numerous," His hostess, describing the impression produced on those who were accorded by Him the privilege of a private audience, has written, "were these applicants for so unique an experience, how unique only those knew when in the presence of the Master, and we could partly divine, as we saw the look on their faces as they emerged—a look as though blended of awe, of marveling, and of a certain calm joy. Sometimes we were conscious of reluctance in them to come forth into the outer world, as though they would hold fast to their beatitude, lest the return of things of earth should wrest it from them." "A profound impression," the aforementioned chronicler has recorded, summing up the results produced by that memorable visit, "remained in the minds and memories of all sorts and conditions of men and women. . . . Very greatly was 'Abdu'l-Bahá's sojourn in London appreciated; very greatly His departure regretted. He left behind Him many, many friends. His love had kindled love. His heart had opened to the West, and the Western heart had closed around this patriarchal presence from the East. His words had in them something that appealed not only to their immediate hearers, but to men and women generally."

His visits to Paris, where for a time He occupied an apartment in the Avenue de Camoens, were marked by a warmth of welcome no less remarkable than the reception accorded Him by His friends and followers in London. "During the Paris visit," that same devoted English hostess, Lady Blomfield, who had followed Him to that city, has testified, "as it had been in London, daily happenings took on the atmosphere of spiritual events. . . . Every morning, according to His custom, the Master expounded the principles of the teaching of Bahá'u'lláh to those who gathered round Him, the learned and the unlearned, eager and respectful. They were of all nationalities and creeds, from the East and from the West, including Theosophists, agnostics, materialists, spiritualists, Christian Scientists, social reformers, Hindus, Sufis, Muslims, Buddhists, Zoroastrians and many others." And again: "Interview followed interview. Church dignitaries of various branches of the Christian Tree came, some earnestly desirous of finding new aspects of the Truth. . . . Others there were who stopped their ears, lest they should hear and understand."

Persian princes, noblemen and ex-ministers, among them the Ẓillu's-Sulṭán, the Persian Minister, the Turkish Ambassador in Paris, Ras̲h̲íd Pás̲h̲á, an ex-válí of Beirut, Turkish pás̲h̲ás and ex-ministers, and Viscount Arawaka, Japanese Ambassador to the Court of Spain, were among those who had the privilege of attaining His presence. Gatherings of Esperantists and Theosophists, students of the Faculty of Theology and large audiences at l'Alliance Spiritualiste were addressed by Him; at a Mission Hall, in a very poor quarter of the city, He addressed a congregation at the invitation of the Pastor, whilst in numerous meetings of His followers those already familiar with His teachings were privileged to hear from His lips detailed and frequent expositions of certain aspects of His Father's Faith.

In Stuttgart, where He made a brief but never-to-be-forgotten stay, and to which He traveled in spite of ill-health in order to establish personal contact with the members of the community of His enthusiastic and dearly beloved German friends, He, apart from attending the gatherings of His devoted followers, bestowed His abundant blessings on the members of the Youth group, gathered at Esslingen, and addressed, at the invitation of Professor Christale, President of the Esperantists of Europe, a large meeting of Esperantists at their club. He, moreover, visited Bad Mergentheim, in Württemberg, where a few years later (1915) a monument was erected in memory of His visit by one of His grateful disciples. "The humility, love and devotion of the German believers," wrote an eyewitness, "rejoiced the heart of 'Abdu'l-Bahá, and they received His blessings and His words of encouraging counsel in complete submissiveness. . . . Friends came from far and near to see the Master. There was a constant flow of visitors at the Hotel Marquart. There 'Abdu'l-Bahá received them with such love and graciousness that they became radiant with joy and happiness."

In Vienna, where He stayed a few days, 'Abdu'l-Bahá addressed a gathering of Theosophists in that city, whilst in Budapest He granted an interview to the President of the University, met on a number of occasions the famous Orientalist Prof. Arminius Vambery, addressed the Theosophical Society, and was visited by the President of the Turanian, and representatives of the Turkish Societies, army officers, several members of Parliament, and a deputation of Young Turks, led by Prof. Julius Germanus, who accorded Him a hearty welcome to the city. "During this time," is the written testimony of Dr. Rusztem Vambery, "His ('Abdu'l-Bahá) room in the Dunapalota Hotel became a veritable mecca for all those whom the mysticism of the East and the wisdom of its Master attracted into its magic circle. Among His visitors were Count Albert Apponyi, Prelate Alexander Giesswein, Professor Ignatius Goldziher, the Orientalist of world-wide renown, Professor Robert A. Nadler, the famous Budapest painter, and leader of the Hungarian Theosophical Society."

It was reserved, however, for the North American continent to witness the most astonishing manifestation of the boundless vitality 'Abdu'l-Bahá exhibited in the course of these journeys. The remarkable progress achieved by the organized community of His followers in the United States and Canada, the marked receptivity of the American public to His Message, as well as His consciousness of the high destiny awaiting the people of that continent, fully warranted the expenditure of time and energy which he devoted to this most important phase of His travels. A visit which entailed a journey of over five thousand miles, which lasted from April to December, which carried Him from the Atlantic to the Pacific coast and back, which elicited discourses of such number as to fill no less than three volumes, was to mark the climax of those journeys, and was fully justified by the far-reaching results which He well knew such labors on His part would produce. *"This long voyage,"* He told His assembled followers on the occasion of His first meeting with them in New York, *"will prove how great is My love for you. There were many troubles and vicissitudes, but in the thought of meeting you, all these things vanished and were forgotten."*

The character of the acts He performed fully demonstrated the importance He attached to that visit. The laying, with His own hands, of the dedication stone of the Mas̲h̲riqu'l-Ad̲h̲kár, by the shore of Lake Michigan, in the vicinity of Chicago, on the recently purchased property, and in the presence of a representative gathering of Bahá'ís from East and West; the dynamic affirmation by Him of the implications of the Covenant instituted by Bahá'u'lláh, following the reading of the newly translated Tablet of the Branch, in a general assembly of His followers in New York, designated henceforth as the "City of the Covenant"; the moving ceremony in Inglewood, California, marking His special pilgrimage to the grave of Thornton Chase, the "first American believer," and indeed the first to embrace the Cause of Bahá'u'lláh in the Western world; the symbolic Feast He Himself offered to a large gathering of His disciples assembled in the open air, and in the green setting of a June day at West Englewood, in New Jersey; the blessing He bestowed on the Open Forum at Green Acre, in Maine, on the banks of the Piscataqua River, where many of His followers had gathered, and which was to evolve into one of the first Bahá'í summer schools of the Western Hemisphere and be recognized as one of the earliest endowments established in the American continent; His address to an audience of several hundred attending the last session of the newly-founded Bahá'í Temple Unity held in Chicago; and, last but not least, the exemplary act He performed by uniting in wedlock two of His followers of different nationalities, one of the white, the other of the Negro race—these must rank among the outstanding functions associated with His visit to the community of the American believers, functions designed to pave the way for the erection of their central House of Worship, to fortify them against the tests they were soon to endure, to cement their unity, and to bless the beginnings of that Administrative Order which they were soon to initiate and champion.

No less remarkable were 'Abdu'l-Bahá's public activities in the course of His association with the multitude of people with whom He came in contact during His tour across a continent. A full account of these diversified activities which crowded His days during no less than eight months, would be beyond the scope of this survey. Suffice it to say that in the city of New York alone He delivered public addresses in, and made formal visits to, no less than fifty-five different places. Peace societies, Christian and Jewish congregations, colleges and universities, welfare and charitable organizations, members of ethical cults, New Thought centers, metaphysical groups, Women's clubs, scientific associations, gatherings of Esperantists, Theosophists, Mormons, and agnostics, institutions for the advancement of the colored people, representatives of the Syrian, the Armenian, the Greek, the Chinese, and Japanese communities—all were brought into contact with His dynamic presence, and were privileged to hear from His lips His Father's Message. Nor was the press either in its editorial comment or in the publication of reports of His lectures, slow to appreciate the breadth of His vision or the character of His summons.

His discourse at the Peace Conferences at Lake Mohonk; His addresses to large gatherings at Columbia, Howard and New York Universities; His participation in the fourth annual conference of the National Association for the Advancement of the Colored People; His fearless assertion of the truth of the prophetic Missions of both Jesus Christ and Muḥammad in Temple Emmanu-El, a Jewish synagogue in San Francisco, where no less than two thousand people were gathered; His illuminating discourse before an audience of eighteen hundred students and one hundred and eighty teachers and professors at Leland Stanford University; His memorable visit to the Bowery Mission in the slums of New York; the brilliant reception given in His honor in Washington, at which many outstanding figures in the social life of the capital were presented to Him—these stand out as the highlights of the unforgettable Mission He undertook in the service of His Father's Cause. Secretaries of State, Ambassadors, Congressmen, distinguished rabbis and churchmen, and other people of eminence attained His presence, among whom were such figures as Dr. D. S. Jordan, President of Leland Stanford University, Prof. Jackson of Columbia University, Prof. Jack of Oxford University, Rabbi Stephen Wise of New York, Dr. Martin A. Meyer, Rabbi Joseph L. Levy, Rabbi Abram Simon, Alexander Graham Bell, Rabindranath Tagore, Hon. Franklin K. Lane, Mrs. William Jennings Bryan, Andrew Carnegie, Hon. Franklin MacVeagh, Secretary of the United States Treasury, Lee McClung, Mr. Roosevelt, Admiral Wain Wright, Admiral Peary, the British, Dutch and Swiss Ministers in Washington, Yúsuf Ḍíyá Pás͟há, the Turkish Ambassador in that city, Thomas Seaton, Hon. William Sulzer and Prince Muḥammad-'Alí of Egypt, the Khedive's brother.

"When 'Abdu'l-Bahá visited this country for the first time in 1912," a commentator on His American travels has written, "He found a large and sympathetic audience waiting to greet Him personally and to receive from His own lips His loving and spiritual message. . . . Beyond the words spoken there was something indescribable in His personality that impressed profoundly all who came into His presence. The dome-like head, the patriarchal beard, the eyes that seemed to have looked beyond the reach of time and sense, the soft yet clearly penetrating voice, the translucent humility, the never failing love,—but above all, the sense of power mingled with gentleness that invested His whole being with a rare majesty of spiritual exaltation that both set Him apart, and yet that brought Him near to the lowliest soul,—it was all this, and much more that can never be defined, that have left with His many . . . friends, memories that are ineffaceable and unspeakably precious."

A survey, however inadequate of the varied and immense activities of 'Abdu'l-Bahá in His tour of Europe and America cannot leave without mention some of the strange incidents that would often accompany personal contact with Him. The bold determination of a certain indomitable youth who, fearing 'Abdu'l-Bahá would not be able to visit the Western states, and unable himself to pay for a train journey to New England, had traveled all the way from Minneapolis to Maine lying on the rods between the wheels of a train; the transformation effected in the life of the son of a country rector in England, who, in his misery and poverty, had resolved, whilst walking along the banks of the Thames, to put an end to his existence, and who, at the sight of 'Abdu'l-Bahá's photograph displayed in a shop window, had inquired about Him, hurried to His residence, and been so revived by His words of cheer and comfort as to abandon all thought of self-destruction; the extraordinary experience of a woman whose little girl, as the result of a dream she had had, insisted that Jesus Christ was in the world, and who, at the sight of 'Abdu'l-Bahá's picture exposed in the window of a magazine store, had instantly identified it as that of the Jesus Christ of her dream—an act which impelled her mother, after reading that 'Abdu'l-Bahá was in Paris, to take the next boat for Europe and hasten to attain His presence; the decision of the editor of a journal printed in Japan to break his journey to Tokyo at Constantinople, and travel to London for "the joy of spending one evening in His presence"; the touching scene when 'Abdu'l-Bahá, receiving from the hands of a Persian friend, recently arrived in London from 'Ishqábád, a cotton handkerchief containing a piece of dry black bread and a shrivelled apple—the offering of a poor Bahá'í workman in that city—opened it before His assembled guests, and, leaving His luncheon untouched, broke pieces off that bread, and partaking Himself of it shared it with those who were present—these are but a few of a host of incidents that shed a revealing light on some personal aspects of His memorable journeys.

Nor can certain scenes revolving around that majestic and patriarchal Figure, as He moved through the cities of Europe and America, be ever effaced from memory. The remarkable interview at which 'Abdu'l-Bahá, while placing lovingly His hand on the head of Archdeacon Wilberforce, answered his many questions, whilst that distinguished churchman sat on a low chair by His side; the still more remarkable scene when that same Archdeacon, after having knelt with his entire congregation to receive His benediction at St. John's the Divine, passed down the aisle to the vestry hand in hand with his Guest, whilst a hymn was being sung by the entire assembly standing; the sight of Jalálu'd-Dawlih, fallen prostrate at His feet, profuse in his apologies and imploring His forgiveness for his past iniquities; the enthusiastic reception accorded Him at Leland Stanford University when, before the gaze of well nigh two thousand professors and students, He discoursed on some of the noblest truths underlying His message to the West; the touching spectacle at Bowery Mission when four hundred of the poor of New York filed past Him, each receiving a piece of silver from His blessed hands; the acclamation of a Syrian woman in Boston who, pushing aside the crowd that had gathered around Him, flung herself at His feet, exclaiming, "I confess that in Thee I have recognized the Spirit of God and Jesus Christ Himself"; the no less fervent tribute paid Him by two admiring Arabs who, as He was leaving that city for Dublin, N. H., cast themselves before Him, and, sobbing aloud, avowed that He was God's own Messenger to mankind; the vast congregation of two thousand Jews assembled in a synagogue in San Francisco, intently listening to His discourse as He demonstrated the validity of the claims advanced by both Jesus Christ and Muḥammad; the gathering He addressed one night in Montreal, at which, in the course of His speech, His turban fell from His head, so carried away was He by the theme He was expounding; the boisterous crowd in a very poor quarter of Paris, who, awed by His presence, reverently and silently made way for Him as He passed through their midst, while returning from a Mission Hall whose congregation He had been addressing; the characteristic gesture of a Zoroastrian physician who, arriving in breathless haste on the morning of Abdu'l-Bahá's departure from London to bid Him farewell, anointed with fragrant oil first His head and His breast, and then, touching the hands of all present, placed round His neck and shoulders a garland of rosebuds and lilies; the crowd of visitors arriving soon after dawn, patiently waiting on the doorsteps of His house in Cadogan Gardens until the door would be opened for their admittance; His majestic figure as He paced with a vigorous step the platform, or stood with hands upraised to pronounce the benediction, in church and synagogue alike, and before vast audiences of reverent listeners; the unsolicited mark of respect shown Him by distinguished society women in London, who would spontaneously curtsy when ushered into His presence; the poignant sight when He stooped low to the grave of His beloved disciple, Thornton Chase, in Inglewood Cemetery, and kissed his tombstone, an example which all those present hastened to follow; the distinguished gathering of Christians, Jews and Muslims, men and women and representative of both the East and the West, assembled to hear His discourse on world unity in the mosque at Woking—such scenes as these, even in the cold record of the printed page, must still have much of their original impressiveness and power.

Who knows what thoughts flooded the heart of 'Abdu'l-Bahá as He found Himself the central figure of such memorable scenes as these? Who knows what thoughts were uppermost in His mind as He sat at breakfast beside the Lord Mayor of London, or was received with extraordinary deference by the Khedive himself in his palace, or as He listened to the cries of "Alláh-u-Abhá" and to the hymns of thanksgiving and praise that would herald His approach to the numerous and brilliant assemblages of His enthusiastic followers and friends organized in so many cities of the American continent? Who knows what memories stirred within Him as He stood before the thundering waters of Niagara, breathing the free air of a far distant land, or gazed, in the course of a brief and much-needed rest, upon the green woods and countryside in Glenwood Springs, or moved with a retinue of Oriental believers along the paths of the Trocadero gardens in Paris, or walked alone in the evening beside the majestic Hudson on Riverside Drive in New York, or as He paced the terrace of the Hotel du Parc at Thonon-les-Bains, overlooking the Lake of Geneva, or as He watched from Serpentine Bridge in London the pearly chain of lights beneath the trees stretching as far as the eye could see? Memories of the sorrows, the poverty, the overhanging doom of His earlier years; memories of His mother who sold her gold buttons to provide Him, His brother and His sister with sustenance, and who was forced, in her darkest hours, to place a handful of dry flour in the palm of His hand to appease His hunger; of His own childhood when pursued and derided by a mob of ruffians in the streets of Ṭihrán; of the damp and gloomy room, formerly a morgue, which He occupied in the barracks of 'Akká and of His imprisonment in the dungeon of that city—memories such as these must surely have thronged His mind. Thoughts, too, must have visited Him of the Báb's captivity in the mountain fastnesses of Ádhirbáyján, when at night time He was refused even a lamp, and of His cruel and tragic execution when hundreds of bullets riddled His youthful breast. Above all His thoughts must have centered on Bahá'u'lláh, Whom He loved so passionately and Whose trials He had witnessed and had shared from His boyhood. The vermin-infested Síyáh-Chál of Ṭihrán; the bastinado inflicted upon Him in Ámul; the humble fare which filled His kashkúl while He lived for two years the life of a dervish in the mountains of Kurdistán; the days in Baghdád when He did not even possess a change of linen, and when His followers subsisted on a handful of dates; His confinement behind the prison-walls of 'Akká, when for nine years even the sight of verdure was denied Him; and the public humiliation to which He was subjected at government headquarters in that city—pictures from the tragic past such as these must have many a time overpowered Him with feelings of mingled gratitude and sorrow, as He witnessed the many marks of respect, of esteem, and honor now shown Him and the Faith which He represented. *"O Bahá'u'lláh! What hast Thou done?"* He, as reported by the chronicler of His travels, was heard to exclaim one evening as He was being swiftly driven to fulfil His third engagement of the day in Washington, *"O Bahá'u'lláh! May my life be sacrificed for Thee! O Bahá'u'lláh! May my soul be offered up for Thy sake! How full were Thy days with trials and tribulations! How severe the ordeals Thou didst endure! How solid the foundation Thou hast finally laid, and how glorious the banner Thou didst hoist!"* "One day, as He was strolling," that same chronicler has testified, "He called to remembrance the days of the Blessed Beauty, referring with sadness to His sojourn in Sulaymáníyyih, to His loneliness and to the wrongs inflicted upon Him. Though He had often recounted that episode, that day He was so overcome with emotion that He sobbed aloud in His grief. . . . All His attendants wept with Him, and were plunged into sorrow as they heard the tale of the woeful trials endured by the Ancient Beauty, and witnessed the tenderness of heart manifested by His Son."

A most significant scene in a century-old drama had been enacted. A glorious chapter in the history of the first Bahá'í century had been written. Seeds of undreamt-of potentialities had, with the hand of the Center of the Covenant Himself, been sown in some of the fertile fields of the Western world. Never in the entire range of religious history had any Figure of comparable stature arisen to perform a labor of such magnitude and imperishable worth. Forces were unleashed through those fateful journeys which even now, at a distance of well nigh thirty-five years, we are unable to measure or comprehend. Already a Queen, inspired by the powerful arguments adduced by 'Abdu'l-Bahá in the course of His addresses in support of the Divinity of Muḥammad, has proclaimed her faith, and borne public testimony to the Divine origin of the Prophet of Islám. Already a President of the United States, imbibing some of the principles so clearly enunciated by Him in His discourses, has incorporated them in a Peace Program which stands out as the boldest and noblest proposal yet made for the well-being and security of mankind. And already, alas! a world which proved deaf to His warnings and refused to heed His summons has plunged itself into two global wars of unprecedented severity, the repercussions of which none as yet can even dimly visualize.

# CHAPTER XX

## Growth and Expansion of the Faith in East and West

'Abdu'l-Bahá's historic journeys to the West, and in particular His eight-month tour of the United States of America, may be said to have marked the culmination of His ministry, a ministry whose untold blessings and stupendous achievements only future generations can adequately estimate. As the day-star of Bahá'u'lláh's Revelation had shone forth in its meridian splendor at the hour of the proclamation of His Message to the rulers of the earth in the city of Adrianople, so did the Orb of His Covenant mount its zenith and shed its brightest rays when He Who was its appointed Center arose to blazon the glory and greatness of His Father's Faith among the peoples of the West.

That divinely instituted Covenant had, shortly after its inception, demonstrated beyond the shadow of a doubt its invincible strength through its decisive triumph over the dark forces which its Arch-Breaker had with such determination arrayed against it. Its energizing power had soon after been proclaimed through the signal victories which its torch-bearers had so rapidly and courageously won in the far-off cities of Western Europe and the United States of America. Its high claims had, moreover, been fully vindicated through its ability to safeguard the unity and integrity of the Faith in both the East and the West. It had subsequently given further proof of its indomitable strength by the memorable victory it registered through the downfall of Sulṭán 'Abdu'l-Ḥamíd, and the consequent release of its appointed Center from a forty-year captivity. It had provided for those still inclined to doubt its Divine origin yet another indisputable testimony to its solidity by enabling 'Abdu'l-Bahá, in the face of formidable obstacles, to effect the transfer and the final entombment of the Báb's remains in a mausoleum on Mt. Carmel. It had manifested also before all mankind, with a force and in a measure hitherto unapproached, its vast potentialities when it empowered Him in Whom its spirit and its purpose were enshrined to embark on a three-year-long mission to the Western world—a mission so momentous that it deserves to rank as the greatest exploit ever to be associated with His ministry.

Nor were these, preeminent though they were, the sole fruits garnered through the indefatigable efforts exerted so heroically by the Center of that Covenant. The progress and extension of His Father's Faith in the East; the initiation of activities and enterprises which may be said to signalize the beginnings of a future Administrative Order; the erection of the first Mas͟hriqu'l-Ad͟hkár of the Bahá'í world in the city of 'Is͟hqábád in Russian Turkistán; the expansion of Bahá'í literature; the revelation of the Tablets of the Divine Plan; and the introduction of the Faith in the Australian continent—these may be regarded as the outstanding achievements that have embellished the brilliant record of 'Abdu'l-Bahá's unique ministry.

In Persia, the cradle of the Faith, despite the persecutions which, throughout the years of that ministry, persisted with unabated violence, a noticeable change, marking the gradual emergence of a proscribed community from its hitherto underground existence, could be clearly discerned. Náṣiri'd-Dín S͟háh, four years after Bahá'u'lláh's ascension, had, on the eve of his jubilee, designed to mark a turning-point in the history of his country, met his death at the hands of an assassin, named Mírzá Riḍá, a follower of the notorious Siyyid Jamálu'd-Dín-i-Afg͟hání, an enemy of the Faith and one of the originators of the constitutional movement which, as it gathered momentum, during the reign of the S͟háh's son and successor, Muẓaffari'd-Dín, was destined to involve in further difficulties an already hounded and persecuted community. Even the S͟háh's assassination had at first been laid at the door of that community, as evidenced by the cruel death suffered, immediately after the murder of the sovereign, by the renowned teacher and poet, Mírzá 'Alí-Muḥammad, surnamed "Varqá" (Dove) by Bahá'u'lláh, who, together with his twelve-year-old son, Rúḥu'lláh, was inhumanly put to death in the prison of Ṭihrán, by the brutal Ḥájibu'd-Dawlih, who, after thrusting his dagger into the belly of the father and cutting him into pieces, before the eyes of his son, adjured the boy to recant, and, meeting with a blunt refusal, strangled him with a rope.

Three years previously a youth, named Muḥammad-Riḍáy-i-Yazdí, was shot in Yazd, on the night of his wedding while proceeding from the public bath to his home, the first to suffer martyrdom during 'Abdu'l-Bahá's ministry. In Turbat-i-Ḥaydaríyyih, in consequence of the S͟háh's assassination, five persons, known as the S͟huhadáy-i-K͟hamsih (Five Martyrs), were put to death. In Mas͟hhad a well-known merchant, Ḥájí Muḥammad-i-Tabrízí, was murdered and his corpse set on fire. An interview was granted by the new sovereign and his Grand Vizir, the unprincipled and reactionary Mírzá 'Alí-Asghar Khán, the Atábik-i-A'ẓam, to two representative followers of the Faith in Paris (1902), but it produced no real results whatever. On the contrary, a fresh storm of persecutions broke out a few years later, persecutions which, as the constitutional movement developed in that country, grew ever fiercer as reactionaries brought groundless accusations against the Bahá'ís, and publicly denounced them as supporters and inspirers of the nationalist cause.

A certain Muḥammad-Javád was stripped naked in Iṣfahán, and was severely beaten with a whip of braided wires, while in Káshán the adherents of the Faith of Jewish extraction were fined, beaten and chained at the instigation of both the Muḥammadan clergy and the Jewish doctors. It was, however, in Yazd and its environs that the most bloody outrages committed during 'Abdu'l-Bahá's ministry occurred. In that city Ḥájí Mírzáy-i-Ḥalabí-Sáz was so mercilessly flogged that his wife flung herself upon his body, and was in her turn severely beaten, after which his skull was lacerated by the cleaver of a butcher. His eleven-year-old son was pitilessly thrashed, stabbed with penknives and tortured to death. Within the space of half a day nine people met their death. A crowd of about six thousand people, of both sexes, vented their fury upon the helpless victims, a few going so far as to drink their blood. In some instances, as was the case with a man named Mírzá Asadu'lláh-i-Ṣabbágh, they plundered their property and fought over its possession. They evinced such cruelty that some of the government officials were moved to tears at the sight of the harrowing scenes in which the women of that city played a conspicuously shameful part.

In Taft several people were put to death, some of whom were shot and their bodies dragged through the streets. A newly converted eighteen-year-old youth, named Ḥusayn, was denounced by his own father, and torn to pieces before the eyes of his mother, whilst Muḥammad-Kamál was hacked into bits with knife, spade and pickaxe. In Manshád, where the persecutions lasted nineteen days, similar atrocities were perpetrated. An eighty-year-old man, named Siyyid Mírzá, was instantly killed in his sleep by two huge stones which were thrown on him; a Mírzá Ṣádiq, who asked for water, had a knife plunged into his breast, his executioner afterwards licking the blood from the blade, while Sháṭir-Ḥasan, one of the victims, was seen before his death distributing some candy in his possession among the executioners and dividing among them his clothing. A sixty-five year old woman, Khadíjih-Sulṭán, was hurled from the roof of a house; a believer named Mírzá Muḥammad was tied to a tree, made a target for hundreds of bullets and his body set on fire, whilst another, named Ustád Riḍáy-i-Ṣaffár, was seen to kiss the hand of his murderer, after which he was shot and his corpse heaped with insults.

In Banáduk, in Dih-Bálá, in Farásẖáh, in ʻAbbás-Ábád, in Hanzá, in Ardikán, in Dawlat-Ábád and in Hamadán crimes of similar nature were committed, an outstanding case being that of a highly respected and courageous woman, named Fáṭimih-Bagum, who was ignominiously dragged from her house, her veil was torn from her head, her throat cut across, her belly ripped open; and having been beaten by the savage crowd with every weapon they could lay hands on, she was finally suspended from a tree and delivered to the flames.

In Sárí, in the days when the agitation for the constitution was moving towards a climax, five believers of recognized standing, known later as the Sẖuhadáy-i-Kẖamsih (Five Martyrs), were done to death, whilst in Nayríz a ferocious assault, recalling that of Yazd, was launched by the enemy, in which nineteen lost their lives, among them the sixty-five year old Mullá ʻAbduʼl-Ḥamíd, a blind man who was shot and his body foully abused, and in the course of which a considerable amount of property was plundered, and numerous women and children had to flee for their lives, or seek refuge in mosques, or live in the ruins of their houses, or remain shelterless by the wayside.

In Sírján, in Dúgẖ-Ábád, in Tabríz, in Ávih, in Qum, in Najaf-Ábád, in Sangsar, in Sẖahmírzád, in Iṣfahán, and in Jahrum redoubtable and remorseless enemies, both religious and political, continued, under various pretexts, and even after the signing of the Constitution by the Sẖáh in 1906, and during the reign of his successors, Muḥammad-ʻAlí Sẖáh and Aḥmad Sẖáh, to slay, torture, plunder and abuse the members of a community who resolutely refused to either recant or deviate a hair's breadth from the path laid down for them by their Leaders. Even during ʻAbduʼl-Baháʼs journeys to the West, and after His return to the Holy Land, and indeed till the end of His life, He continued to receive distressing news of the martyrdom of His followers, and of the outrages perpetrated against them by an insatiable enemy. In Dawlat-Ábád, a prince of the royal blood, Ḥabíbuʼlláh Mírzá by name, a convert to the Faith who had consecrated his life to its service, was slain with a hatchet and his corpse set on fire. In Masẖhad the learned and pious Sẖaykẖ

'Alí-Akbar-i-Qú<u>ch</u>ání was shot to death. In Sulṭán-Ábád, Mírzá 'Alí-Akbar and seven members of his family including a forty day old infant were barbarously massacred. Persecutions of varying degrees of severity broke out in Ná'ín, in <u>Sh</u>ahmírzád, in Bandar-i-Jaz and in Qamsar. In Kirmán<u>sh</u>áh, the martyr Mírzá Ya'qúb-i-Muttaḥidih, the ardent twenty-five year old Jewish convert to the Faith, was the last to lay down his life during 'Abdu'l-Bahá's ministry; and his mother, according to his own instructions, celebrated his martyrdom in Hamadán with exemplary fortitude. In every instance the conduct of the believers testified to the indomitable spirit and unyielding tenacity that continued to distinguish the lives and services of the Persian followers of the Faith of Bahá'u'lláh.

Despite these intermittent severe persecutions the Faith that had evoked in its heroes so rare a spirit of self-sacrifice was steadily and silently growing. Engulfed for a time and almost extinguished in the sombre days following the martyrdom of the Báb, driven underground throughout the period of Bahá'u'lláh's ministry, it began, after His ascension, under the unerring guidance, and as a result of the unfailing solicitude, of a wise, a vigilant and loving Master, to gather its forces, and gradually to erect the embryonic institutions which were to pave the way for the establishment, at a later period, of its Administrative Order. It was during this period that the number of its adherents rapidly multiplied, that its range, now embracing every province of that kingdom, steadily widened, and the rudimentary forms of its future Assemblies were inaugurated. It was during this period, at a time when state schools and colleges were practically non-existent in that country, and when the education given in existing religious institutions was lamentably defective, that its earliest schools were established, beginning with the Tarbíyat, schools in Ṭihrán for both boys and girls, and followed by the Ta'yíd and Mawhibat schools in Hamadán, the Vaḥdat-i-Ba<u>sh</u>ar school in Ká<u>sh</u>án and other similar educational institutions in Bárfurú<u>sh</u> and Qazvín. It was during these years that concrete and effectual assistance, both spiritual and material, in the form of visiting teachers from both Europe and America, of nurses, instructors, and physicians, was first extended to the Bahá'í community in that land, these workers constituting the vanguard of that host of helpers which 'Abdu'l-Bahá promised would arise in time to further the interests of the Faith as well as those of the country in which it was born. It was in the course of these years that the term Bábí, as an appellation, designating the followers of Bahá'u'lláh in that country, was universally discarded by the masses in favor of the word Bahá'í, the former henceforth being exclusively applied to the fast dwindling number of the followers of Mírzá Yaḥyá. During this period, moreover, the first systematic attempts were made to organize and stimulate the teaching work undertaken by the Persian believers, attempts which, apart from reinforcing the foundations of the community, were instrumental in attracting to its cause several outstanding figures in the public life of that country, not excluding certain prominent members of the Shí'ah sacerdotal order, and even descendants of some of the worst persecutors of the Faith. It was during the years of that ministry that the House of the Báb in Shíráz, ordained by Bahá'u'lláh as a center of pilgrimage for His followers, and now so recognized, was by order of 'Abdu'l-Bahá and through His assistance, restored, and that it became increasingly a focus of Bahá'í life and activity for those who were deprived by circumstances of visiting either the Most Great House in Baghdád or the Most Holy Tomb in 'Akká.

More conspicuous than any of these undertakings, however, was the erection of the first Mashriqu'l-Adhkár of the Bahá'í world in the city of 'Ishqábád, a center founded in the days of Bahá'u'lláh, where the initial steps preparatory to its construction, had been already undertaken during His lifetime. Initiated at about the close of the first decade of 'Abdu'l-Bahá's ministry (1902); fostered by Him at every stage in its development; personally supervised by the venerable Ḥájí Mírzá Muḥammad-Taqí, the Vakílu'd-Dawlih, a cousin of the Báb, who dedicated his entire resources to its establishment, and whose dust now reposes at the foot of Mt. Carmel under the shadow of the Tomb of his beloved Kinsman; carried out according to the directions laid down by the Center of the Covenant Himself; a lasting witness to the fervor and the self-sacrifice of the Oriental believers who were resolved to execute the bidding of Bahá'u'lláh as revealed in the Kitáb-i-Aqdas, this enterprise must rank not only as the first major undertaking launched through the concerted efforts of His followers in the Heroic Age of His Faith, but as one of the most brilliant and enduring achievements in the history of the first Bahá'í century.

The edifice itself, the foundation stone of which was laid in the presence of General Krupatkin, the governor-general of Turkistán, who had been delegated by the Czar to represent him at the ceremony, has thus been minutely described by a Bahá'í visitor from the West: "The Mashriqu'l-Adhkár stands in the heart of the city; its high dome standing out above the trees and house tops being visible for miles to the travelers as they approach the town. It is in the center of a garden bounded by four streets. In the four corners of this enclosure are four buildings: one is the Bahá'í school; one is the traveler's house, where pilgrims and wayfarers are lodged; one is for the keepers, while the fourth one is to be used as a hospital. Nine radial avenues approach the Temple from the several parts of the grounds, one of which, the principal approach to the building, leads from the main gateway of the grounds to the principal portal of the Temple." "In plan," he further adds, "the building is composed of three sections; namely, the central rotunda, the aisle or ambulatory which surrounds it, and the loggia which surrounds the entire building. It is built on the plan of a regular polygon of nine sides. One side is occupied by the monumental main entrance, flanked by minarets—a high arched portico extending two stories in height recalling in arrangement the architecture of the world famous Taj Mahal at Agra in India, the delight of the world to travelers, many of whom pronounce it to be the most beautiful temple in the world. Thus the principal doorway opens toward the direction of the Holy land. The entire building is surrounded by two series of loggias—one upper and one lower—which opens out upon the garden giving a very beautiful architectural effect in harmony with the luxuriant semi-tropical vegetation which fills the garden . . . The interior walls of the rotunda are treated in five distinct stories. First, a series of nine arches and piers which separate the rotunda from the ambulatory. Second, a similar treatment with balustrades which separate the triforium gallery (which is above the ambulatory and is reached by two staircases in the loggias placed one on either side of the main entrance) from the well of the rotunda. Third, a series of nine blank arches filled with fretwork, between which are escutcheons bearing the Greatest Name. Fourth, a series of nine large arched windows. Fifth, a series of eighteen bull's eye windows. Above and resting on a cornice surmounting this last story rises the inner hemispherical shell of the dome. The interior is elaborately decorated in plaster relief work . . . The whole structure impresses one by its mass and strength."

Nor should mention be omitted of the two schools for boys and girls which were established in that city, of the pilgrim house instituted in the close vicinity of the Temple, of the Spiritual Assembly and its auxiliary bodies formed to administer the affairs of a growing community, and of the new centers of activity inaugurated in various towns and cities in the province of Turkistán—all testifying to the vitality which the Faith had displayed ever since its inception in that land.

A parallel if less spectacular development could be observed in the Caucasus. After the establishment of the first center and the formation of an Assembly in Bákú, a city which Bahá'í pilgrims, traveling in increasing numbers from Persia to the Holy Land via Turkey, invariably visited, new groups began to be organized, and, evolving later into well-established communities, cooperated in increasing measure with their brethren both in Turkistán and Persia.

In Egypt a steady increase in the number of the adherents of the Faith was accompanied by a general expansion in its activities. The establishments of new centers; the consolidation of the chief center established in Cairo; the conversion, largely through the indefatigable efforts of the learned Mírzá Abu'l-Faḍl, of several prominent students and teachers of the Azhar University—premonitory symptoms foreshadowing the advent of the promised day on which, according to 'Abdu'l-Bahá, the standard and emblem of the Faith would be implanted in the heart of that time-honored Islamic seat of learning; the translation into Arabic and the dissemination of some of the most important writings of Bahá'u'lláh revealed in Persian, together with other Bahá'í literature; the printing of books, treatises and pamphlets by Bahá'í authors and scholars; the publication of articles in the Press written in defense of the Faith and for the purpose of broadcasting its message; the formation of rudimentary administrative institutions in the capital as well as in nearby centers; the enrichment of the life of the community through the addition of converts of Kurdish, Coptic, and Armenian origin—these may be regarded as the first fruits garnered in a country which, blessed by the footsteps of 'Abdu'l-Bahá, was, in later years, to play a historic part in the emancipation of the Faith, and which, by virtue of its unique position as the intellectual center of both the Arab and Islamic worlds, must inevitably assume a notable and decisive share of responsibility in the final establishment of that Faith throughout the East.

Even more remarkable was the expansion of Bahá'í activity in India and Burma, where a steadily growing community, now including among its members representatives of the Zoroastrian, the Islamic, the Hindu and the Buddhist Faiths, as well as members of the Sikh community, succeeded in establishing its outposts, as far as Mandalay and the village of Daidanaw Kalazoo, in the Hanthawaddy district of Burma, at which latter place no less than eight hundred Bahá'ís resided, possessing a school, a court, and a hospital of their own, as well as land for community cultivation, the proceeds of which they devoted to the furtherance of the interests of their Faith.

In 'Iráq, where the House occupied by Bahá'u'lláh was entirely restored and renovated, and where a small yet intrepid community struggled in the face of constant opposition to regulate and administer its affairs; in Constantinople, where a Bahá'í center was established; in Tunis where the foundations of a local community were firmly laid; in Japan, in China, and in Honolulu to which Bahá'í teachers traveled, and where they settled and taught—in all of these places the manifold evidences of the guiding hand of 'Abdu'l-Bahá and the tangible effects of His sleepless vigilance and unfailing care could be clearly perceived.

Nor did the nascent communities established in France, England, Germany and the United States cease to receive, after His memorable visits to those countries, further tokens of His special interest in, and solicitude for, their welfare and spiritual advancement. It was in consequence of His directions and the unceasing flow of His Tablets, addressed to the members of these communities, as well as His constant encouragement of the efforts they were exerting, that Bahá'í centers steadily multiplied, that public meetings were organized, that new periodicals were published, that translations of some of the best known works of Bahá'u'lláh and of the Tablets of 'Abdu'l-Bahá were printed and circulated in the English, the French, and German languages, and that the initial attempts to organize the affairs, and consolidate the foundations, of these newly established communities were undertaken.

In the North American continent, more particularly, the members of a flourishing community, inspired by the blessings bestowed by 'Abdu'l-Bahá, as well as by His example and the acts He performed in the course of His prolonged visit to their country, gave an earnest of the magnificent enterprise they were to carry through in later years. They purchased the twelve remaining lots forming part of the site of their projected Temple, selected, during the sessions of their 1920 Convention, the design of the French Canadian Bahá'í architect, Louis Bourgeois, placed the contract for the excavation and the laying of its foundations, and succeeded soon after in completing the necessary arrangements for the construction of its basement: measures which heralded the stupendous efforts which, after 'Abdu'l-Bahá's ascension, culminated in the erection of its superstructure and the completion of its exterior ornamentation.

The war of 1914-18, repeatedly foreshadowed by 'Abdu'l-Bahá in the dark warnings He uttered in the course of His western travels, and which broke out eight months after His return to the Holy Land, once more cast a shadow of danger over His life, the last that was to darken the years of His agitated yet glorious ministry.

The late entry of the United States of America in that world-convulsing conflict, the neutrality of Persia, the remoteness of India and of the Far East from the theater of operations, insured the protection of the overwhelming majority of His followers, who, though for the most part entirely cut off for a number of years from the spiritual center of their Faith, were still able to conduct their affairs and safeguard the fruits of their recent achievements in comparative safety and freedom.

In the Holy Land, however, though the outcome of that tremendous struggle was to liberate once and for all the Heart and Center of the Faith from the Turkish yoke, a yoke which had imposed for so long upon its Founder and His Successor such oppressive and humiliating restrictions, yet severe privations and grave dangers continued to surround its inhabitants during the major part of that conflict, and renewed, for a time, the perils which had confronted 'Abdu'l-Bahá during the years of His incarceration in 'Akká. The privations inflicted on the inhabitants by the gross incompetence, the shameful neglect, the cruelty and callous indifference of both the civil and military authorities, though greatly alleviated through the bountiful generosity, the foresight and the tender care of 'Abdu'l-Bahá, were aggravated by the rigors of a strict blockade. A bombardment of Haifa by the Allies was a constant threat, at one time so real that it necessitated the temporary removal of 'Abdu'l-Bahá, His family and members of the local community to the village of Abú-Sinán at the foot of the hills east of 'Akká. The Turkish Commander-in-Chief, the brutal, the all-powerful and unscrupulous Jamál Pá<u>sh</u>á, an inveterate enemy of the Faith, through his own ill-founded suspicions and the instigation of its enemies, had already grievously afflicted 'Abdu'l-Bahá, and even expressed his intention of crucifying Him and of razing to the ground the Tomb of Bahá'u'lláh. 'Abdu'l-Bahá Himself still suffered from the ill-health and exhaustion brought on by the fatigues of His three-year journeys. He felt acutely the virtual stoppage of all communication with most of the Bahá'í centers throughout the world. Agony filled His soul at the spectacle of human slaughter precipitated through humanity's failure to respond to the summons He had issued, or to heed the warnings He had given. Surely sorrow upon sorrow was added to the burden of trials and vicissitudes which He, since His boyhood, had borne so heroically for the sake, and in the service, of His Father's Cause.

And yet during these somber days, the darkness of which was reminiscent of the tribulations endured during the most dangerous period of His incarceration in the prison-fortress of 'Akká, 'Abdu'l-Bahá, whilst in the precincts of His Father's Shrine, or when dwelling in the House He occupied in 'Akká, or under the shadow of the Báb's sepulcher on Mt. Carmel, was moved to confer once again, and for the last time in His life, on the community of His American followers a signal mark of His special favor by investing them, on the eve of the termination of His earthly ministry, through the revelation of the Tablets of the Divine Plan, with a world mission, whose full implications even now, after the lapse of a quarter of a century, still remain undisclosed, and whose unfoldment thus far, though as yet in its initial stages, has so greatly enriched the spiritual as well as the administrative annals of the first Bahá'í century.

The conclusion of this terrible conflict, the first stage in a titanic convulsion long predicted by Bahá'u'lláh, not only marked the extinction of Turkish rule in the Holy Land and sealed the doom of that military despot who had vowed to destroy 'Abdu'l-Bahá, but also shattered once and for all the last hopes still entertained by the remnant of Covenant-breakers who, untaught by the severe retribution that had already overtaken them, still aspired to witness the extinction of the light of Bahá'u'lláh's Covenant. Furthermore, it produced those revolutionary changes which, on the one hand, fulfilled the ominous predictions made by Bahá'u'lláh in the Kitáb-i-Aqdas, and enabled, according to Scriptural prophecy, so large an element of the *"outcasts of Israel,"* the *"remnant"* of the *"flock,"* to *"assemble"* in the Holy Land, and to be brought back to *"their folds"* and *"their own border,"* beneath the shadow of the *"Incomparable Branch,"* referred to by 'Abdu'l-Bahá in His "Some Answered Questions," and which, on the other hand, gave birth to the institution of the League of Nations, the precursor of that World Tribunal which, as prophesied by that same "Incomparable Branch," the peoples and nations of the earth must needs unitedly establish.

No need to dwell on the energetic steps which the English believers as soon as they had been apprized of the dire peril threatening the life of 'Abdu'l-Bahá undertook to insure His security; on the measures independently taken whereby Lord Curzon and others in the British Cabinet were advised as to the critical situation at Haifa;

on the prompt intervention of Lord Lamington, who immediately wrote to the Foreign Office to "explain the importance of 'Abdu'l-Bahá's position;" on the despatch which the Foreign Secretary, Lord Balfour, on the day of the receipt of this letter, sent to General Allenby, instructing him to "extend every protection and consideration to 'Abdu'l-Bahá, His family and His friends;" on the cablegram subsequently sent by the General, after the capture of Haifa, to London, requesting the authorities to "notify the world that 'Abdu'l-Bahá is safe;" on the orders which that same General issued to the General Commanding Officer in command of the Haifa operations to insure 'Abdu'l-Bahá's safety, thus frustrating the express intention of the Turkish Commander-in-Chief (according to information which had reached the British Intelligence Service) to "crucify 'Abdu'l-Bahá and His family on Mt. Carmel" in the event of the Turkish army being compelled to evacuate Haifa and retreat northwards.

The three years which elapsed between the liberation of Palestine by the British forces and the passing of 'Abdu'l-Bahá were marked by a further enhancement of the prestige which the Faith, despite the persecutions to which it had been subjected, had acquired at its world center, and by a still greater extension in the range of its teaching activities in various parts of the world. The danger which, for no less than three score years and five, had threatened the lives of the Founders of the Faith and of the Center of His Covenant, was now at long last through the instrumentality of that war completely and definitely lifted. The Head of the Faith, and its twin holy Shrines, in the plain of 'Akká and on the slopes of Mt. Carmel, were henceforth to enjoy for the first time, through the substitution of a new and liberal régime for the corrupt administration of the past, a freedom from restrictions which was later expanded into a clearer recognition of the institutions of the Cause. Nor were the British authorities slow to express their appreciation of the rôle which 'Abdu'l-Bahá had played in allaying the burden of suffering that had oppressed the inhabitants of the Holy Land during the dark days of that distressing conflict. The conferment of a knighthood upon Him at a ceremony specially held for His sake in Haifa, at the residence of the British Governor, at which notables of various communities had assembled; the visit paid Him by General and Lady Allenby, who were His guests at luncheon in Bahjí, and whom He conducted to the Tomb of Bahá'u'lláh; the interview at His Haifa residence between Him and King Feisal who shortly after became the ruler of 'Iráq; the several calls paid Him by Sir Herbert Samuel (later

Viscount Samuel of Carmel) both before and after his appointment as High Commissioner for Palestine; His meeting with Lord Lamington who, likewise, called upon Him in Haifa, as well as with the then Governor of Jerusalem, Sir Ronald Storrs; the multiplying evidences of the recognition of His high and unique position by all religious communities, whether Muslim, Christian or Jewish; the influx of pilgrims who, from East and West, flocked to the Holy Land in comparative ease and safety to visit the Holy Tombs in 'Akká and Haifa, to pay their share of homage to Him, to celebrate the signal protection vouchsafed by Providence to the Faith and its followers, and to give thanks for the final emancipation of its Head and world Center from Turkish yoke—these contributed, each in its own way, to heighten the prestige which the Faith of Bahá'u'lláh had been steadily and gradually acquiring through the inspired leadership of 'Abdu'l-Bahá.

As the ministry of 'Abdu'l-Bahá drew to a close signs multiplied of the resistless and manifold unfoldment of the Faith both in the East and in the West, both in the shaping and consolidation of its institutions and in the widening range of its activities and its influence. In the city of 'Ishqábád the construction of the Mashriqu'l-Adhkár, which He Himself had initiated, was successfully consummated. In Wilmette the excavations for the Mother Temple of the West were carried out and the contract placed for the construction of the basement of the building. In Baghdád the initial steps were taken, according to His special instructions, to reinforce the foundations and restore the Most Great House associated with the memory of His Father. In the Holy Land an extensive property east of the Báb's Sepulcher was purchased through the initiative of the Holy Mother with the support of contributions from Bahá'ís in both the East and the West to serve as a site for the future erection of the first Bahá'í school at the world Administrative Center of the Faith. The site for a Western Pilgrim House was acquired in the neighborhood of 'Abdu'l-Bahá's residence, and the building was erected soon after His passing by American believers. The Oriental Pilgrim House, erected on Mt. Carmel by a believer from 'Ishqábád, soon after the entombment of the Báb's remains, for the convenience of visiting pilgrims, was granted tax exemption by the civil authorities (the first time such a privilege had been conceded since the establishment of the Faith in the Holy Land). The famous scientist and entomologist, Dr. Auguste Forel, was converted to the Faith through the influence of a Tablet sent him by 'Abdu'l-Bahá—one of the most weighty the Master ever wrote. Another Tablet of far-reaching importance was His reply to a communication addressed to Him by the Executive Committee of the "Central Organization for a Durable Peace," which He dispatched to them at The Hague by the hands of a special delegation. A new continent was opened to the Cause when, in response to the Tablets of the Divine Plan unveiled at the first Convention after the war, the great-hearted and heroic Hyde Dunn, at the advanced age of sixty-two, promptly forsook his home in California, and, seconded and accompanied by his wife, settled as a pioneer in Australia, where he was able to carry the Message to no less than seven hundred towns throughout that Commonwealth. A new episode began when, in quick response to those same Tablets and their summons, that star-servant of Bahá'u'lláh, the indomitable and immortal Martha Root, designated by her Master *"herald of the Kingdom"* and *"harbinger of the Covenant,"* embarked on the first of her historic journeys which were to extend over a period of twenty years, and to carry her several times around the globe, and which ended only with her death far from home and in the active service of the Cause she loved so greatly. These events mark the closing stage of a ministry which sealed the triumph of the Heroic Age of the Bahá'í Dispensation, and which will go down in history as one of the most glorious and fruitful periods of the first Bahá'í century.

## CHAPTER XXI

# The Passing of 'Abdu'l-Bahá

'Abdu'l-Bahá's great work was now ended. The historic Mission with which His Father had, twenty-nine years previously, invested Him had been gloriously consummated. A memorable chapter in the history of the first Bahá'í century had been written. The Heroic Age of the Bahá'í Dispensation, in which He had participated since its inception, and played so unique a rôle, had drawn to a close. He had suffered as no disciple of the Faith, who had drained the cup of martyrdom, had suffered, He had labored as none of its greatest heroes had labored. He had witnessed triumphs such as neither the Herald of the Faith nor its Author had ever witnessed.

At the close of His strenuous Western tours, which had called forth the last ounce of His ebbing strength, He had written: *"Friends, the time is coming when I shall be no longer with you. I have done all that could be done. I have served the Cause of Bahá'u'lláh to the utmost of My ability. I have labored night and day all the years of My life. O how I long to see the believers shouldering the responsibilities of the Cause! . . . My days are numbered, and save this there remains none other joy for me."* Several years before He had thus alluded to His passing: "O *ye My faithful loved ones! Should at any time afflicting events come to pass in the Holy Land, never feel disturbed or agitated. Fear not, neither grieve. For whatsoever thing happeneth will cause the Word of God to be exalted, and His Divine fragrances to be diffused."* And again: *"Remember, whether or not I be on earth, My presence will be with you always." "Regard not the person of 'Abdu'l-Bahá,"* He thus counselled His friends in one of His last Tablets, *"for He will eventually take His leave of you all; nay, fix your gaze upon the Word of God . . . The loved ones of God must arise with such steadfastness that should, in one moment, hundreds of souls even as 'Abdu'l-Bahá Himself be made a target for the darts of woe, nothing whatsoever shall affect or lessen their . . . service to the Cause of God."*

In a Tablet addressed to the American believers, a few days before He passed away, He thus vented His pent-up longing to depart from this world: *"I have renounced the world and the people thereof . . . In the cage of this world I flutter even as a frightened bird, and yearn every day to take My flight unto Thy Kingdom. Yá Bahá'u'l-Abhá! Make Me drink of the cup of sacrifice, and set Me free."* He revealed a prayer less than six months before His ascension in honor of a kinsman of the Báb, and in it wrote: " '*O Lord! My bones are weakened, and the hoar hairs glisten on My head . . . and I have now reached old age, failing in My powers.' . . . No strength is there left in Me wherewith to arise and serve Thy loved ones . . . O Lord, My Lord! Hasten My ascension unto Thy sublime Threshold . . . and My arrival at the Door of Thy grace beneath the shadow of Thy most great mercy . . .*"

Through the dreams He dreamed, through the conversations He held, through the Tablets He revealed, it became increasingly evident that His end was fast approaching. Two months before His passing He told His family of a dream He had had. *"I seemed,"* He said, *"to be standing within a great mosque, in the inmost shrine, facing the Qiblih, in the place of the Imám himself. I became aware that a large number of people were flocking into the mosque. More and yet more crowded in, taking their places in rows behind Me, until there was a vast multitude. As I stood I raised loudly the call to prayer. Suddenly the thought came to Me to go forth from the mosque. When I found Myself outside I said within Myself: 'For what reason came I forth, not having led the prayer? But it matters not; now that I have uttered the Call to prayer, the vast multitude will of themselves chant the prayer.'"* A few weeks later, whilst occupying a solitary room in the garden of His house, He recounted another dream to those around Him. *"I dreamed a dream,"* He said, *"and behold, the Blessed Beauty* (Bahá'u'lláh) *came and said to Me: 'Destroy this room.'"* None of those present comprehended the significance of this dream until He Himself had soon after passed away, when it became clear to them all that by the "room" was meant the temple of His body.

A month before His death (which occurred in the 78th year of His age, in the early hours of the 28th of November, 1921) He had referred expressly to it in some words of cheer and comfort that He addressed to a believer who was mourning the loss of his brother. And about two weeks before His passing He had spoken to His faithful gardener in a manner that clearly indicated He knew His end to be nigh. *"I am so fatigued,"* He observed to him, *"the hour is come when I must leave everything and take My flight. I am too weary to walk."* He added: *"It was during the closing days of the Blessed Beauty, when I was engaged in gathering together His papers which were strewn over the sofa in His writing chamber in Bahjí, that He turned to Me and said: 'It is of no use to gather them, I must leave them and flee away.' I also have finished My work. I can do nothing more. Therefore must I leave it, and take My departure."*

Till the very last day of His earthly life 'Abdu'l-Bahá continued to shower that same love upon high and low alike, to extend that same assistance to the poor and the down-trodden, and to carry out those same duties in the service of His Father's Faith, as had been His wont from the days of His boyhood. On the Friday before His passing, despite great fatigue, He attended the noonday prayer at the mosque, and distributed afterwards alms, as was His custom, among the poor; dictated some Tablets—the last ones He revealed—; blessed the marriage of a trusted servant, which He had insisted should take place that day; attended the usual meeting of the friends in His home; felt feverish the next day, and being unable to leave the house on the following Sunday, sent all the believers to the Tomb of the Báb to attend a feast which a Parsí pilgrim was offering on the occasion of the anniversary of the Declaration of the Covenant; received with His unfailing courtesy and kindness that same afternoon, and despite growing weariness, the Muftí of Haifa, the Mayor and the Head of the Police; and inquired that night—the last of His life—before He retired after the health of every member of His household, of the pilgrims and of the friends in Haifa.

At 1:15 A.M. He arose, and, walking to a table in His room, drank some water, and returned to bed. Later on, He asked one of His two daughters who had remained awake to care for Him, to lift up the net curtains, complaining that He had difficulty in breathing. Some rose-water was brought to Him, of which He drank, after which He again lay down, and when offered food, distinctly remarked: *"You wish Me to take some food, and I am going?"* A minute later His spirit had winged its flight to its eternal abode, to be gathered, at long last, to the glory of His beloved Father, and taste the joy of everlasting reunion with Him.

The news of His passing, so sudden, so unexpected, spread like wildfire throughout the town, and was flashed instantly over the wires to distant parts of the globe, stunning with grief the community of the followers of Bahá'u'lláh in East and West. Messages from far and near, from high and low alike, through cablegrams and letters, poured in conveying to the members of a sorrow-stricken and disconsolate family expressions of praise, of devotion, of anguish and of sympathy.

The British Secretary of State for the Colonies, Mr. Winston Churchill, telegraphed immediately to the High Commissioner for Palestine, Sir Herbert Samuel, instructing him to "convey to the Bahá'í Community, on behalf of His Majesty's Government, their sympathy and condolence." Viscount Allenby, the High Commissioner for Egypt, wired the High Commissioner for Palestine asking him to "convey to the relatives of the late Sir 'Abdu'l-Bahá 'Abbás Effendi and to the Bahá'í Community" his "sincere sympathy in the loss of their revered leader." The Council of Ministers in Baghdád instructed the Prime Minister Siyyid 'Abdu'r-Raḥmán to extend their "sympathy to the family of His Holiness 'Abdu'l-Bahá in their bereavement." The Commander-in-Chief of the Egyptian Expeditionary Force, General Congreve, addressed to the High Commissioner for Palestine a message requesting him to "convey his deepest sympathy to the family of the late Sir 'Abbás Bahá'í." General Sir Arthur Money, former Chief Administrator of Palestine, wrote expressing his sadness, his profound respect and his admiration for Him as well as his sympathy in the loss which His family had sustained. One of the distinguished figures in the academic life of the University of Oxford, a famous professor and scholar, wrote on behalf of himself and his wife: "The passing beyond the veil into fuller life must be specially wonderful and blessed for One Who has always fixed His thoughts on high, and striven to lead an exalted life here below."

Many and divers newspapers, such as the London "Times," the "Morning Post," the "Daily Mail," the "New York World," "Le Temps," the "Times of India" and others, in different languages and countries, paid their tribute to One Who had rendered the Cause of human brotherhood and peace such signal and imperishable services.

The High Commissioner, Sir Herbert Samuel, sent immediately a message conveying his desire to attend the funeral in person, in order as he himself later wrote, to "express my respect for His creed and my regard for His person." As to the funeral itself, which took place on Tuesday morning—a funeral the like of which Palestine had never seen—no less than ten thousand people participated representing every class, religion and race in that country. "A great throng," bore witness at a later date, the High Commissioner himself, "had gathered together, sorrowing for His death, but rejoicing also for His life." Sir Ronald Storrs, Governor of Jerusalem at the time, also wrote in describing the funeral: "I have never known a more united expression of regret and respect than was called forth by the utter simplicity of the ceremony."

The coffin containing the remains of 'Abdu'l-Bahá was borne to its last resting-place on the shoulders of His loved ones. The cortège which preceded it was led by the City Constabulary Force, acting as a Guard of Honor, behind which followed in order the Boy Scouts of the Muslim and Christian communities holding aloft their banners, a company of Muslim choristers chanting their verses from the Qur'án, the chiefs of the Muslim community headed by the Muftí, and a number of Christian priests, Latin, Greek and Anglican. Behind the coffin walked the members of His family, the British High Commissioner, Sir Herbert Samuel, the Governor of Jerusalem, Sir Ronald Storrs, the Governor of Phoenicia, Sir Stewart Symes, officials of the government, consuls of various countries resident in Haifa, notables of Palestine, Muslim, Jewish, Christian and Druze, Egyptians, Greeks, Turks, Arabs, Kurds, Europeans and Americans, men, women and children. The long train of mourners, amid the sobs and moans of many a grief-stricken heart, wended its slow way up the slopes of Mt. Carmel to the Mausoleum of the Báb.

Close to the eastern entrance of the Shrine, the sacred casket was placed upon a plain table, and, in the presence of that vast concourse, nine speakers, who represented the Muslim, the Jewish and Christian Faiths, and who included the Muftí of Haifa, delivered their several funeral orations. These concluded, the High Commissioner drew close to the casket, and, with bowed head fronting the Shrine, paid his last homage of farewell to 'Abdu'l-Bahá: the other officials of the Government followed his example. The coffin was then removed to one of the chambers of the Shrine, and there lowered, sadly and reverently, to its last resting-place in a vault adjoining that in which were laid the remains of the Báb.

During the week following His passing, from fifty to a hundred of the poor of Haifa were daily fed at His house, whilst on the seventh day corn was distributed in His memory to about a thousand of them irrespective of creed or race. On the fortieth day an impressive memorial feast was held in His memory, to which over six hundred of the people of Haifa, 'Akká and the surrounding parts of Palestine and Syria, including officials and notables of various religions and races, were invited. More than one hundred of the poor were also fed on that day.

One of the assembled guests, the Governor of Phoenicia, paid a last tribute to the memory of 'Abdu'l-Bahá in the following words: "Most of us here have, I think, a clear picture of Sir 'Abdu'l-Bahá 'Abbás, of His dignified figure walking thoughtfully in our streets, of His courteous and gracious manner, of His kindness, of His love for little children and flowers, of His generosity and care for the poor and suffering. So gentle was He, and so simple, that in His presence one almost forgot that He was also a great teacher, and that His writings and His conversations have been a solace and an inspiration to hundreds and thousands of people in the East and in the West."

Thus was brought to a close the ministry of One Who was the incarnation, by virtue of the rank bestowed upon Him by His Father, of an institution that has no parallel in the entire field of religious history, a ministry that marks the final stage in the Apostolic, the Heroic and most glorious Age of the Dispensation of Bahá'u'lláh.

Through Him the Covenant, that *"excellent and priceless Heritage"* bequeathed by the Author of the Bahá'í Revelation, had been proclaimed, championed and vindicated. Through the power which that Divine Instrument had conferred upon Him the light of God's infant Faith had penetrated the West, had diffused itself as far as the Islands of the Pacific, and illumined the fringes of the Australian continent. Through His personal intervention the Message, Whose Bearer had tasted the bitterness of a life-long captivity, had been noised abroad, and its character and purpose disclosed, for the first time in its history, before enthusiastic and representative audiences in the chief cities of Europe and of the North American continent. Through His unrelaxing vigilance the holy remains of the Báb, brought forth at long last from their fifty-year concealment, had been safely transported to the Holy Land and permanently and befittingly enshrined in the very spot which Bahá'u'lláh Himself had designated for them and had blessed with His presence. Through His bold initiative the first Mas͟hriqu'l-Ad͟hkár of the Bahá'í world had been reared in Central Asia, in Russian Turkistán, whilst through His unfailing encouragement a similar enterprise, of still vaster proportions, had been undertaken, and its land dedicated by Himself in the heart of the North American continent. Through the sustaining grace overshadowing Him since the inception of His ministry His royal adversary had been humbled to the dust, the arch-breaker of His Father's Covenant had been utterly routed, and the danger which, ever since Bahá'u'lláh had been banished to Turkish soil, had been threatening the heart of the Faith, definitely removed. In pursuance of His instructions, and in conformity with the principles enunciated and the laws ordained by His Father, the rudimentary institutions, heralding the formal inauguration of the Administrative Order to be founded after His passing, had taken shape and been established. Through His unremitting labors, as reflected in the treatises He composed, the thousands of Tablets He revealed, the discourses He delivered, the prayers, poems and commentaries He left to posterity, mostly in Persian, some in Arabic and a few in Turkish, the laws and principles, constituting the warp and woof of His Father's Revelation, had been elucidated, its fundamentals restated and interpreted, its tenets given detailed application and the validity and indispensability of its verities fully and publicly demonstrated. Through the warnings He sounded, an unheeding humanity, steeped in materialism and forgetful of its God, had been apprized of the perils threatening to disrupt its ordered life, and made, in consequence of its persistent perversity, to sustain the initial shocks of that world upheaval which continues, until the present day, to rock the foundations of human society. And lastly, through the mandate He had issued to a valiant community, the concerted achievements of whose members had shed so great a lustre on the annals of His own ministry, He had set in motion a Plan which, soon after its formal inauguration, achieved the opening of the Australian continent, which, in a later period, was to be instrumental in winning over the heart of a royal convert to His Father's Cause, and which, today, through the irresistible unfoldment of its potentialities, is so marvellously quickening the spiritual life of all the Republics of Latin America as to constitute a befitting conclusion to the records of an entire century.

Nor should a survey of the outstanding features of so blessed and fruitful a ministry omit mention of the prophecies which the unerring pen of the appointed Center of Bahá'u'lláh's Covenant has recorded. These foreshadow the fierceness of the onslaught that the resistless march of the Faith must provoke in the West, in India and in the Far East when it meets the time-honored sacerdotal orders of the Christian, the Buddhist and Hindu religions. They foreshadow the turmoil which its emancipation from the fetters of religious orthodoxy will cast in the American, the European, the Asiatic and African continents. They foreshadow the gathering of the children of Israel in their ancient homeland; the erection of the banner of Bahá'u'lláh in the Egyptian citadel of Sunní Islám; the extinction of the powerful influence wielded by the Shí'ah ecclesiastics in Persia; the load of misery which must needs oppress the pitiful remnants of the breakers of Bahá'u'lláh's Covenant at the world center of His Faith; the splendor of the institutions which that triumphant Faith must erect on the slopes of a mountain, destined to be so linked with the city of 'Akká that a single grand metropolis will be formed to enshrine the spiritual as well as the administrative seats of the future Bahá'í Commonwealth; the conspicuous honor which the inhabitants of Bahá'u'lláh's native land in general, and its government in particular, must enjoy in a distant future; the unique and enviable position which the community of the Most Great Name in the North American continent must occupy, as a direct consequence of the execution of the world mission which He entrusted to them: finally they foreshadow, as the sum and summit of all, the "*hoisting of the standard of God among all nations*" and the unification of the entire human race, when "*all men will adhere to one religion . . . will be blended into one race, and become a single people.*"

Nor can the revolutionary changes in the great world which that ministry has witnessed be allowed to pass unnoticed—most of them flowing directly from the warnings which were uttered by the Báb, in the first chapter of His Qayyumu'l-Asmá', on the very night of the Declaration of His Mission in Shíráz, and which were later reinforced by the pregnant passages addressed by Bahá'u'lláh to the kings of the earth and the world's religious leaders, in both the Súriy-i-Mulúk and the Kitáb-i-Aqdas. The conversion of the Portuguese monarchy and the Chinese empire into republics; the collapse of the Russian, the German and Austrian empires, and the ignominious fate which befell their rulers; the assassination of Náṣiri'd-Dín Sháh, the fall of Sulṭán 'Abdu'l-Ḥamíd—these may be said to have marked further stages in the operation of that catastrophic process the inception of which was signalized in the lifetime of Bahá'u'lláh by the murder of Sulṭán 'Abdu'l-'Azíz, by the dramatic downfall of Napoleon III, and the extinction of the Third Empire, and by the self-imposed imprisonment and virtual termination of the temporal sovereignty of the Pope himself. Later, after 'Abdu'l-Bahá's passing, the same process was to be accelerated by the demise of the Qájár dynasty in Persia, by the overthrow of the Spanish monarchy, by the collapse of both the Sultanate and the Caliphate in Turkey, by a swift decline in the fortunes of Shí'ah Islám and of the Christian Missions in the East, and by the cruel fate that is now overtaking so many of the crowned heads of Europe.

Nor can this subject be dismissed without special reference to the names of those men of eminence and learning who were moved, at various stages of 'Abdu'l-Bahá's ministry, to pay tribute not only to 'Abdu'l-Bahá Himself but also to the Faith of Bahá'u'lláh. Such names as Count Leo Tolstoy, Prof. Arminius Vambery, Prof. Auguste Forel, Dr. David Starr Jordan, the Venerable Archdeacon Wilberforce, Prof.

Jowett of Balliol, Dr. T. K. Cheyne, Dr. Estlin Carpenter of Oxford University, Viscount Samuel of Carmel, Lord Lamington, Sir Valentine Chirol, Rabbi Stephen Wise, Prince Muḥammad-'Alí of Egypt, S͟hayk͟h Muḥammad 'Abdu, Midḥat Pás͟há, and K͟hurs͟híd Pás͟há attest, by virtue of the tributes associated with them, the great progress made by the Faith of Bahá'u'lláh under the brilliant leadership of His exalted Son—tributes whose impressiveness was, in later years, to be heightened by the historic, the repeated and written testimonies which a famous Queen, a grand-daughter of Queen Victoria, was impelled to bequeath to posterity as a witness of her recognition of the prophetic mission of Bahá'u'lláh.

As for those enemies who have sedulously sought to extinguish the light of Bahá'u'lláh's Covenant, the condign punishment they have been made to suffer is no less conspicuous than the doom which overtook those who, in an earlier period, had so basely endeavored to crush the hopes of a rising Faith and destroy its foundations.

To the assassination of the tyrannical Náṣiri'd-Dín S͟háh and the subsequent extinction of the Qájár dynasty reference has already been made. Sulṭán 'Abdu'l-Ḥamíd, after his deposition, was made a prisoner of state and condemned to a life of complete obscurity and humiliation, scorned by his fellow-rulers and vilified by his subjects. The bloodthirsty Jamál Pás͟há, who had resolved to crucify 'Abdu'l-Bahá and raze to the ground Bahá'u'lláh's holy Tomb, had to flee for his life and was slain, while a refugee in the Caucasus, by the hand of an Armenian whose fellow-compatriots he had so pitilessly persecuted. The scheming Jamálu'd-Dín Afg͟hání, whose relentless hostility and powerful influence had been so gravely detrimental to the progress of the Faith in Near Eastern countries, was, after a checkered career filled with vicissitudes, stricken with cancer, and having had a major part of his tongue cut away in an unsuccessful operation perished in misery. The four members of the ill-fated Commission of Inquiry, despatched from Constantinople to seal the fate of 'Abdu'l-Bahá, suffered, each in his turn, a humiliation hardly less drastic than that which they had planned for Him. 'Árif Bey, the head of the Commission, seeking stealthily at midnight to flee from the wrath of the Young Turks, was shot dead by a sentry. Adham Bey succeeded in escaping to Egypt, but was robbed of his possessions by his servant on the way, and was in the end compelled to seek financial assistance from the Bahá'ís of Cairo, a request which was not refused. Later he sought help from 'Abdu'l-Bahá, Who immediately directed the believers to present him with a sum on His behalf, an instruction which they were unable to carry out owing to his sudden disappearance. Of the other two members, one was exiled to a remote place, and the other died soon after in abject poverty. The notorious Yaḥyá Bey, the Chief of the Police in 'Akká, a willing and powerful tool in the hand of Mírzá Muḥammad-'Alí, the arch-breaker of Bahá'u'lláh's Covenant, witnessed the frustration of all the hopes he had cherished, lost his position, and had eventually to beg for pecuniary assistance from 'Abdu'l-Bahá. In Constantinople, in the year which witnessed the downfall of 'Abdu'l-Ḥamíd, no less than thirty-one dignitaries of the state, including ministers and other high officers of the government, among whom numbered redoubtable enemies of the Faith, were, in a single day, arrested and condemned to the gallows, a spectacular retribution for the part they had played in upholding a tyrannical régime and in endeavoring to extirpate the Faith and its institutions.

In Persia, apart from the sovereign who had, in the full tide of his hopes and the plenitude of his power, been removed from the scene in so startling a manner, a number of princes, ministers and mujtahids, who had actively participated in the suppression of a persecuted community, including Kámrán Mírzá, the Ná'ibu's-Salṭanih, the Jalálu'd-Dawlih and Mírzá 'Alí-Aṣghar Khán, the Atábik-i-A'ẓam, and Shaykh Muḥammad-Taqíy-i-Najafí, the "Son of the Wolf," lost, one by one, their prestige and authority, sank into obscurity, abandoned all hope of achieving their malevolent purpose, and lived, some of them, long enough to behold the initial evidences of the ascendancy of a Cause they had so greatly feared and so vehemently hated.

When we note that in the Holy Land, in Persia, and in the United States of America certain exponents of Christian ecclesiasticism such as Vatralsky, Wilson, Richardson or Easton, observing, and in some cases fearing, the vigorous advances made by the Faith of Bahá'u'lláh in Christian lands, arose to stem its progress; and when we watch the recent and steady deterioration of their influence, the decline of their power, the confusion in their ranks and the dissolution of some of their old standing missions and institutions, in Europe, in the Middle East and in Eastern Asia—may we not attribute this weakening to the opposition which members of various Christian sacerdotal orders began, in the course of 'Abdu'l-Bahá's ministry, to evince towards the followers and institutions of a Faith which claims to be no less than the fulfilment of the Promise given by Jesus Christ, and the establisher of the Kingdom He Himself had prayed for and foretold?

And finally, he who, from the moment the Divine Covenant was born until the end of his life, showed a hatred more unrelenting than that which animated the afore-mentioned adversaries of 'Abdu'l-Bahá, who plotted more energetically than any one of them against Him, and afflicted his Father's Faith with a shame more grievous than any which its external enemies had inflicted upon it—such a man, together with the infamous crew of covenant-breakers whom he had misled and instigated, was condemned to witness, in a growing measure, as had been the case with Mírzá Yaḥyá and his henchmen, the frustration of his evil designs, the evaporation of all his hopes, the exposition of his true motives and the complete extinction of his erstwhile honor and glory. His brother, Mírzá Ḍíyá'u'lláh, died prematurely; Mírzá Áqá Ján, his dupe, followed that same brother, three years later, to the grave; and Mírzá Badí'u'lláh, his chief accomplice, betrayed his cause, published a signed denunciation of his evil acts, but rejoined him again, only to be alienated from him in consequence of the scandalous behavior of his own daughter. Mírzá Muḥammad-'Alí's half-sister, Furúghíyyih, died of cancer, whilst her husband, Siyyid 'Alí, passed away from a heart attack before his sons could reach him, the eldest being subsequently stricken in the prime of life, by the same malady. Muḥammad-Javád-i-Qazvíní, a notorious Covenant-breaker, perished miserably. Shu'á'u'lláh who, as witnessed by 'Abdu'l-Bahá in His Will, had counted on the murder of the Center of the Covenant, and who had been despatched to the United States by his father to join forces with Ibráhím Khayru'lláh, returned crestfallen and empty-handed from his inglorious mission. Jamál-i-Burújirdí, Mírzá Muḥammad-'Alí's ablest lieutenant in Persia, fell a prey to a fatal and loathsome disease; Siyyid Mihdíy-i-Dahají, who, betraying 'Abdu'l-Bahá, joined the Covenant-breakers, died in obscurity and poverty, followed by his wife and his two sons; Mírzá Ḥusayn-'Alíy-i-Jahrumí, Mírzá Ḥusayn-i-Shírázíy-i-Khurṭúmí and Ḥájí Muḥammad-Ḥusayn-i-Káshání, who represented the arch-breaker of the Covenant in Persia, India and Egypt, failed utterly in their missions; whilst the greedy and conceited Ibráhím-i-Khayru'lláh, who had chosen to uphold the banner of his rebellion in America for no less than twenty years, and who had the temerity to denounce, in writing, 'Abdu'l-Bahá, His "false teachings, His misrepresentations of Bahaism, His dissimulation," and to stigmatize His visit to America as "a death-blow" to the "Cause of God," met his death soon after he had uttered these denunciations, utterly abandoned and despised by the entire body of the members of a community, whose founders he himself had converted to the Faith, and in the very land that bore witness to the multiplying evidences of the established ascendancy of 'Abdu'l-Bahá, Whose authority he had, in his later years, vowed to uproot.

As to those who had openly espoused the cause of this arch-breaker of Bahá'u'lláh's Covenant, or who had secretly sympathized with him, whilst outwardly supporting 'Abdu'l-Bahá, some eventually repented and were forgiven; others became disillusioned and lost their faith entirely; a few apostatized, whilst the rest dwindled away, leaving him in the end, except for a handful of his relatives, alone and unsupported. Surviving 'Abdu'l-Bahá by almost twenty years, he who had so audaciously affirmed to His face that he had no assurance he might outlive Him, lived long enough to witness the utter bankruptcy of his cause, leading meanwhile a wretched existence within the walls of a Mansion that had once housed a crowd of his supporters; was denied by the civil authorities, as a result of the crisis he had after 'Abdu'l-Bahá's passing foolishly precipitated, the official custody of his Father's Tomb; was compelled, a few years later, to vacate that same Mansion, which, through his flagrant neglect, had fallen into a dilapidated condition; was stricken with paralysis which crippled half his body; lay bedridden in pain for months before he died; and was buried according to Muslim rites, in the immediate vicinity of a local Muslim shrine, his grave remaining until the present day devoid of even a tombstone—a pitiful reminder of the hollowness of the claims he had advanced, of the depths of infamy to which he had sunk, and of the severity of the retribution his acts had so richly merited.

FOURTH PERIOD

# THE INCEPTION OF THE FORMATIVE AGE OF THE BAHÁ'Í FAITH

1921 - 1944

## CHAPTER XXII

# The Rise and Establishment of the Administrative Order

With the passing of 'Abdu'l-Bahá the first century of the Bahá'í era, whose inception had synchronized with His birth, had run more than three quarters of its course. Seventy-seven years previously the light of the Faith proclaimed by the Báb had risen above the horizon of Shíráz and flashed across the firmament of Persia, dispelling the age-long gloom which had enveloped its people. A blood bath of unusual ferocity, in which government, clergy and people, heedless of the significance of that light and blind to its splendor, had jointly participated, had all but extinguished the radiance of its glory in the land of its birth. Bahá'u'lláh had at the darkest hour in the fortunes of that Faith been summoned, while Himself a prisoner in Ṭihrán, to reinvigorate its life, and been commissioned to fulfil its ultimate purpose. In Baghdád, upon the termination of the ten-year delay interposed between the first intimation of that Mission and its Declaration, He had revealed the Mystery enshrined in the Báb's embryonic Faith, and disclosed the fruit which it had yielded. In Adrianople Bahá'u'lláh's Message, the promise of the Bábí as well as of all previous Dispensations, had been proclaimed to mankind, and its challenge voiced to the rulers of the earth in both the East and the West. Behind the walls of the prison-fortress of 'Akká the Bearer of God's newborn Revelation had ordained the laws and formulated the principles that were to constitute the warp and woof of His World Order. He had, moreover, prior to His ascension, instituted the Covenant that was to guide and assist in the laying of its foundations and to safeguard the unity of its builders. Armed with that peerless and potent Instrument, 'Abdu'l-Bahá, His eldest Son and Center of His Covenant, had erected the standard of His Father's Faith in the North American continent, and established an impregnable basis for its institutions in Western Europe, in the Far East and in Australia. He had, in His works, Tablets and addresses, elucidated its principles, interpreted its laws, amplified its doctrine, and erected the rudimentary institutions of its future Administrative Order. In Russia He had raised its first House of Worship, whilst on the slopes of Mt. Carmel He had reared a befitting mausoleum for its Herald, and deposited His remains therein with His Own hands. Through His visits to several cities in Europe and the North American continent He had broadcast Bahá'u'lláh's Message to the peoples of the West, and heightened the prestige of the Cause of God to a degree it had never previously experienced. And lastly, in the evening of His life, He had through the revelation of the Tablets of the Divine Plan issued His mandate to the community which He Himself had raised up, trained and nurtured, a Plan that must in the years to come enable its members to diffuse the light, and erect the administrative fabric, of the Faith throughout the five continents of the globe.

The moment had now arrived for that undying, that world-vitalizing Spirit that was born in Shíráz, that had been rekindled in Ṭihrán, that had been fanned into flame in Baghdád and Adrianople, that had been carried to the West, and was now illuminating the fringes of five continents, to incarnate itself in institutions designed to canalize its outspreading energies and stimulate its growth. The Age that had witnessed the birth and rise of the Faith had now closed. The Heroic, the Apostolic Age of the Dispensation of Bahá'u'lláh, that primitive period in which its Founders had lived, in which its life had been generated, in which its greatest heroes had struggled and quaffed the cup of martyrdom, and its pristine foundations been established—a period whose splendors no victories in this or any future age, however brilliant, can rival—had now terminated with the passing of One Whose mission may be regarded as the link binding the Age in which the seed of the newborn Message had been incubating and those which are destined to witness its efflorescence and ultimate fruition.

The Formative Period, the Iron Age, of that Dispensation was now beginning, the Age in which the institutions, local, national and international, of the Faith of Bahá'u'lláh were to take shape, develop and become fully consolidated, in anticipation of the third, the last, the Golden Age destined to witness the emergence of a world-embracing Order enshrining the ultimate fruit of God's latest Revelation to mankind, a fruit whose maturity must signalize the establishment of a world civilization and the formal inauguration of the Kingdom of the Father upon earth as promised by Jesus Christ Himself.

To this World Order the Báb Himself had, whilst a prisoner in the mountain fastnesses of Adhirbáyján, explicitly referred in His Persian Bayán, the Mother-Book of the Bábí Dispensation, had announced its advent, and associated it with the name of Bahá'u'lláh, Whose Mission He Himself had heralded. *"Well is it with Him,"* is His remarkable statement in the sixteenth chapter of the third Váḥid, *"who fixeth his gaze upon the Order of Bahá'u'lláh, and rendereth thanks unto his Lord! For He will assuredly be made manifest . . .* " To this same Order Bahá'u'lláh Who, in a later period, revealed the laws and principles that must govern the operation of that Order, had thus referred in the Kitáb-i-Aqdas, the Mother-Book of His Dispensation: *"The world's equilibrium hath been upset through the vibrating influence of this Most Great Order. Mankind's ordered life hath been revolutionized through the agency of this unique, this wondrous System, the like of which mortal eyes have never witnessed."* Its features 'Abdu'l-Bahá, its great Architect, delineated in His Will and Testament, whilst the foundations of its rudimentary institutions are now being laid after Him by His followers in the East and in the West in this, the Formative Age of the Bahá'í Dispensation.

The last twenty-three years of the first Bahá'í century may thus be regarded as the initial stage of the Formative Period of the Faith, an Age of Transition to be identified with the rise and establishment of the Administrative Order, upon which the institutions of the future Bahá'í World Commonwealth must needs be ultimately erected in the Golden Age that must witness the consummation of the Bahá'í Dispensation. The Charter which called into being, outlined the features and set in motion the processes of, this Administrative Order is none other than the Will and Testament of 'Abdu'l-Bahá, His greatest legacy to posterity, the brightest emanation of His mind and the mightiest instrument forged to insure the continuity of the three ages which constitute the component parts of His Father's Dispensation.

The Covenant of Bahá'u'lláh had been instituted solely through the direct operation of His Will and purpose. The Will and Testament of 'Abdu'l-Bahá, on the other hand, may be regarded as the offspring resulting from that mystic intercourse between Him Who had generated the forces of a God-given Faith and the One Who had been made its sole Interpreter and was recognized as its perfect Exemplar. The creative energies unleashed by the Originator of the Law of God in this age gave birth, through their impact upon the mind of Him Who had been chosen as its unerring Expounder, to that Instrument, the vast implications of which the present generation, even after the lapse of twenty-three years, is still incapable of fully apprehending. This Instrument can, if we would correctly appraise it, no more be divorced from the One Who provided the motivating impulse for its creation than from Him Who directly conceived it. The purpose of the Author of the Bahá'í Revelation had, as already observed, been so thoroughly infused into the mind of 'Abdu'l-Bahá, and His Spirit had so profoundly impregnated His being, and their aims and motives been so completely blended, that to dissociate the doctrine laid down by the former from the supreme act associated with the mission of the latter would be tantamount to a repudiation of one of the most fundamental verities of the Faith.

The Administrative Order which this historic Document has established, it should be noted, is, by virtue of its origin and character, unique in the annals of the world's religious systems. No Prophet before Bahá'u'lláh, it can be confidently asserted, not even Muḥammad Whose Book clearly lays down the laws and ordinances of the Islamic Dispensation, has established, authoritatively and in writing, anything comparable to the Administrative Order which the authorized Interpreter of Bahá'u'lláh's teachings has instituted, an Order which, by virtue of the administrative principles which its Author has formulated, the institutions He has established, and the right of interpretation with which He has invested its Guardian, must and will, in a manner unparalleled in any previous religion, safeguard from schism the Faith from which it has sprung. Nor is the principle governing its operation similar to that which underlies any system, whether theocratic or otherwise, which the minds of men have devised for the government of human institutions. Neither in theory nor in practice can the Administrative Order of the Faith of Bahá'u'lláh be said to conform to any type of democratic government, to any system of autocracy, to any purely aristocratic order, or to any of the various theocracies, whether Jewish, Christian or Islamic which mankind has witnessed in the past. It incorporates within its structure certain elements which are to be found in each of the three recognized forms of secular government, is devoid of the defects which each of them inherently possesses, and blends the salutary truths which each undoubtedly contains without vitiating in any way the integrity of the Divine verities on which it is essentially founded. The hereditary authority which the Guardian of the Administrative Order is called upon to exercise, and the right of the interpretation of the Holy Writ solely conferred upon him; the powers and prerogatives of the Universal House of Justice, possessing the exclusive right to legislate on matters not explicitly revealed in the Most Holy Book; the ordinance exempting its members from any responsibility to those whom they represent, and from the obligation to conform to their views, convictions or sentiments; the specific provisions requiring the free and democratic election by the mass of the faithful of the Body that constitutes the sole legislative organ in the world-wide Bahá'í community—these are among the features which combine to set apart the Order identified with the Revelation of Bahá'u'lláh from any of the existing systems of human government.

Nor have the enemies who, at the hour of the inception of this Administrative Order, and in the course of its twenty-three year existence, both in the East and in the West, from within and from without, misrepresented its character, or derided and vilified it, or striven to arrest its march, or contrived to create a breach in the ranks of its supporters, succeeded in achieving their malevolent purpose. The strenuous exertions of an ambitious Armenian, who, in the course of the first years of its establishment in Egypt, endeavored to supplant it by the "Scientific Society" which in his short-sightedness he had conceived and was sponsoring, failed utterly in its purpose. The agitation provoked by a deluded woman who strove diligently both in the United States and in England to demonstrate the unauthenticity of the Charter responsible for its creation, and even to induce the civil authorities of Palestine to take legal action in the matter—a request which to her great chagrin was curtly refused—as well as the defection of one of the earliest pioneers and founders of the Faith in Germany, whom that same woman had so tragically misled, produced no effect whatsoever. The volumes which a shameless apostate composed and disseminated, during that same period in Persia, in his brazen efforts not only to disrupt that Order but to undermine the very Faith which had conceived it, proved similarly abortive. The schemes devised by the remnants of the Covenant-breakers, who immediately the aims and purposes of 'Abdu'l-Bahá's Will became known arose, headed by Mírzá Badí'u'lláh, to wrest the custodianship of the holiest shrine in the Bahá'í world from its appointed Guardian, likewise came to naught and brought further discredit upon them. The subsequent attacks launched by certain exponents of Christian orthodoxy, in both Christian and non-Christian lands, with the object of subverting the foundations, and distorting the features, of this same Order were powerless to sap the loyalty of its upholders or to deflect them from their high purpose. Not even the infamous and insidious machinations of a former secretary of 'Abdu'l-Bahá, who, untaught by the retribution that befell Bahá'u'lláh's amanuensis, as well as by the fate that overtook several other secretaries and interpreters of His Master, in both the East and the West, has arisen, and is still exerting himself, to pervert the purpose and nullify the essential provisions of the immortal Document from which that Order derives its authority, have been able to stay even momentarily the march of its institutions along the course set for it by its Author, or to create anything that might, however remotely, resemble a breach in the ranks of its assured, its wide-awake and stalwart supporters.

The Document establishing that Order, the Charter of a future world civilization, which may be regarded in some of its features as supplementary to no less weighty a Book than the Kitáb-i-Aqdas; signed and sealed by 'Abdu'l-Bahá; entirely written with His own hand; its first section composed during one of the darkest periods of His incarceration in the prison-fortress of 'Akká, proclaims, categorically and unequivocally, the fundamental beliefs of the followers of the Faith of Bahá'u'lláh; reveals, in unmistakable language, the two-fold character of the Mission of the Báb; discloses the full station of the Author of the Bahá'í Revelation; asserts that "all others are servants unto Him and do His bidding"; stresses the importance of the Kitáb-i-Aqdas; establishes the institution of the Guardianship as a hereditary office and outlines its essential functions; provides the measures for the election of the International House of Justice, defines its scope and sets forth its relationship to that Institution; prescribes the obligations, and emphasizes the responsibilities, of the Hands of the Cause of God; and extolls the virtues of the indestructible Covenant established by Bahá'u'lláh. That Document, furthermore, lauds the courage and constancy of the supporters of Bahá'u'lláh's Covenant; expatiates on the sufferings endured by its appointed Center; recalls the infamous conduct of Mírzá Yaḥyá and his failure to heed the warnings of the Báb; exposes, in a series of indictments, the perfidy and rebellion of Mírzá Muḥammad-'Alí, and the complicity of his son Shu'á'u'lláh and of his brother Mírzá Badí'u'lláh; reaffirms their excommunication, and predicts the frustration of all their hopes; summons the Afnán (the Báb's kindred), the Hands of the Cause and the entire company of the followers of Bahá'u'lláh to arise unitedly to propagate His Faith, to disperse far and wide, to labor tirelessly and to follow the heroic example of the Apostles of Jesus Christ; warns them against the dangers of association with the Covenant-breakers, and bids them shield the Cause from the assaults of the insincere and the hypocrite; and counsels them to demonstrate by their conduct the universality of the Faith they have espoused, and vindicate its high principles. In that same Document its Author reveals the significance and purpose of the Ḥuqúqu'lláh (Right of God), already instituted in the Kitáb-i-Aqdas; enjoins submission and fidelity towards all monarchs who are just; expresses His longing for martyrdom, and voices His prayers for the repentance as well as the forgiveness of His enemies.

Obedient to the summons issued by the Author of so momentous a Document; conscious of their high calling; galvanized into action by the shock sustained through the unexpected and sudden removal of 'Abdu'l-Bahá; guided by the Plan which He, the Architect of the Administrative Order, had entrusted to their hands; undeterred by the attacks directed against it by betrayers and enemies, jealous of its gathering strength and blind to its unique significance, the members of the widely-scattered Bahá'í communities, in both the East and the West, arose with clear vision and inflexible determination to inaugurate the Formative Period of their Faith by laying the foundations of that world-embracing Administrative system designed to evolve into a World Order which posterity must acclaim as the promise and crowning glory of all the Dispensations of the past. Not content with the erection and consolidation of the administrative machinery provided for the preservation of the unity and the efficient conduct of the affairs of a steadily expanding community, the followers of the Faith of Bahá'u'lláh resolved, in the course of the two decades following 'Abdu'l-Bahá's passing, to assert and demonstrate by their acts the independent character of that Faith, to enlarge still further its limits and swell the number of its avowed supporters.

In this triple world-wide effort, it should be noted, the rôle played by the American Bahá'í community, since the passing of 'Abdu'l-Bahá until the termination of the first Bahá'í century, has been such as to lend a tremendous impetus to the development of the Faith throughout the world, to vindicate the confidence placed in its members by 'Abdu'l-Bahá Himself, and to justify the high praise He bestowed upon them and the fond hopes He entertained for their future. Indeed so preponderating has been the influence of its members in both the initiation and the consolidation of Bahá'í administrative institutions that their country may well deserve to be recognized as the cradle of the Administrative Order which Bahá'u'lláh Himself had envisaged and which the Will of the Center of His Covenant had called into being.

It should be borne in mind in this connection that the preliminary steps aiming at the disclosure of the scope and working of this Administrative Order, which was now to be formally established after 'Abdu'l-Bahá's passing, had already been taken by Him, and even by Bahá'u'lláh in the years preceding His ascension. The appointment by Him of certain outstanding believers in Persia as "Hands of the Cause"; the initiation of local Assemblies and boards of consultation by 'Abdu'l-Bahá in leading Bahá'í centers in both the East and the West;

the formation of the Bahá'í Temple Unity in the United States of America; the establishment of local funds for the promotion of Bahá'í activities; the purchase of property dedicated to the Faith and its future institutions; the founding of publishing societies for the dissemination of Bahá'í literature; the erection of the first Mashriqu'l-Adhkár of the Bahá'í world; the construction of the Báb's mausoleum on Mt. Carmel; the institution of hostels for the accommodation of itinerant teachers and pilgrims—these may be regarded as the precursors of the institutions which, immediately after the closing of the Heroic Age of the Faith, were to be permanently and systematically established throughout the Bahá'í world.

No sooner had the provisions of that Divine Charter, delineating the features of the Administrative Order of the Faith of Bahá'u'lláh been disclosed to His followers than they set about erecting, upon the foundations which the lives of the heroes, the saints and martyrs of that Faith had laid, the first stage of the framework of its administrative institutions. Conscious of the necessity of constructing, as a first step, a broad and solid base upon which the pillars of that mighty structure could subsequently be raised; fully aware that upon these pillars, when firmly established, the dome, the final unit crowning the entire edifice, must eventually rest; undeflected in their course by the crisis which the Covenant-breakers had precipitated in the Holy Land, or the agitation which the stirrers of mischief had provoked in Egypt, or the disturbances resulting from the seizure by the Shí'ah community of the House of Bahá'u'lláh in Baghdád, or the growing dangers confronting the Faith in Russia, or the scorn and ridicule which had greeted the initial activities of the American Bahá'í community from certain quarters that had completely misapprehended their purpose, the pioneer builders of a divinely-conceived Order undertook, in complete unison, and despite the great diversity in their outlook, customs and languages, the double task of establishing and of consolidating their local councils, elected by the rank and file of the believers, and designed to direct, coordinate and extend the activities of the followers of a far-flung Faith. In Persia, in the United States of America, in the Dominion of Canada, in the British Isles, in France, in Germany, in Austria, in India, in Burma, in Egypt, in 'Iráq, in Russian Turkistán, in the Caucasus, in Australia, in New Zealand, in South Africa, in Turkey, in Syria, in Palestine, in Bulgaria, in Mexico, in the Philippine Islands, in Jamaica, in Costa Rica, in Guatemala, in Honduras, in San Salvador, in Argentina, in Uruguay, in Chile, in Brazil, in Ecuador, in Colombia, in Paraguay, in Peru, in Alaska, in Cuba, in Haiti, in

Japan, in the Hawaiian Islands, in Tunisia, in Puerto Rico, in Balúchistán, in Russia, in Transjordan, in Lebanon, and in Abyssinia such councils, constituting the basis of the rising Order of a long-persecuted Faith, were gradually established. Designated as "Spiritual Assemblies"—an appellation that must in the course of time be replaced by their permanent and more descriptive title of "Houses of Justice," bestowed upon them by the Author of the Bahá'í Revelation; instituted, without any exception, in every city, town and village where nine or more adult believers are resident; annually and directly elected, on the first day of the greatest Bahá'í Festival by all adult believers, men and women alike; invested with an authority rendering them unanswerable for their acts and decisions to those who elect them; solemnly pledged to follow, under all conditions, the dictates of the "Most Great Justice" that can alone usher in the reign of the "Most Great Peace" which Bahá'u'lláh has proclaimed and must ultimately establish; charged with the responsibility of promoting at all times the best interests of the communities within their jurisdiction, of familiarizing them with their plans and activities and of inviting them to offer any recommendations they might wish to make; cognizant of their no less vital task of demonstrating, through association with all liberal and humanitarian movements, the universality and comprehensiveness of their Faith; dissociated entirely from all sectarian organizations, whether religious or secular; assisted by committees annually appointed by, and directly responsible to, them, to each of which a particular branch of Bahá'í activity is assigned for study and action; supported by local funds to which all believers voluntarily contribute; these Assemblies, the representatives and custodians of the Faith of Bahá'u'lláh, numbering, at the present time, several hundred, and whose membership is drawn from the diversified races, creeds and classes constituting the world-wide Bahá'í community, have, in the course of the last two decades, abundantly demonstrated, by virtue of their achievements, their right to be regarded as the chief sinews of Bahá'í society, as well as the ultimate foundation of its administrative structure.

*"The Lord hath ordained,"* is Bahá'u'lláh's injunction in His Kitáb-i-Aqdas, *"that in every city a House of Justice be established, wherein shall gather counsellors to the number of Bahá* (9), *and should it exceed this number, it doth not matter. It behoveth them to be the trusted ones of the Merciful among men, and to regard themselves as the guardians appointed of God for all that dwell on earth. It is incumbent upon them to take counsel together, and to have regard*

*for the interests of the servants of God, for His sake, even as they regard their own interests, and to choose that which is meet and seemly.*" "*These Spiritual Assemblies,*" is 'Abdu'l-Bahá's testimony, in a Tablet addressed to an American believer, "*are aided by the Spirit of God. Their defender is 'Abdu'l-Bahá. Over them He spreadeth His Wings. What bounty is there greater than this?*" "*These Spiritual Assemblies,*" He, in that same Tablet has declared, "*are shining lamps and heavenly gardens, from which the fragrances of holiness are diffused over all regions, and the lights of knowledge are shed abroad over all created things. From them the spirit of life streameth in every direction. They, indeed, are the potent sources of the progress of man, at all times and under all conditions.*" Establishing beyond any doubt their God-given authority, He has written: "*It is incumbent upon every one not to take any step without consulting the Spiritual Assembly, and all must assuredly obey with heart and soul its bidding, and be submissive unto it, that things may be properly ordered and well arranged.*" "*If after discussion,*" He, furthermore has written, "*a decision be carried unanimously, well and good; but if, the Lord forbid, differences of opinion should arise, a majority of voices must prevail.*"

Having established the structure of their local Assemblies—the base of the edifice which the Architect of the Administrative Order of the Faith of Bahá'u'lláh had directed them to erect—His disciples, in both the East and the West, unhesitatingly embarked on the next and more difficult stage, of their high enterprise. In countries where the local Bahá'í communities had sufficiently advanced in number and in influence measures were taken for the initiation of National Assemblies, the pivots round which all national undertakings must revolve. Designated by 'Abdu'l-Bahá in His Will as the "*Secondary Houses of Justice,*" they constitute the electoral bodies in the formation of the International House of Justice, and are empowered to direct, unify, coordinate and stimulate the activities of individuals as well as local Assemblies within their jurisdiction. Resting on the broad base of organized local communities, themselves pillars sustaining the institution which must be regarded as the apex of the Bahá'í Administrative Order, these Assemblies are elected, according to the principle of proportional representation, by delegates representative of Bahá'í local communities assembled at Convention during the period of the Ridván Festival; are possessed of the necessary authority to enable them to insure the harmonious and efficient development of Bahá'í activity within their respective spheres; are freed from all direct responsibility for their policies and decisions to their electorates; are charged with the sacred duty of consulting the views, of inviting the recommendations and of securing the confidence and cooperation of the delegates and of acquainting them with their plans, problems and actions; and are supported by the resources of national funds to which all ranks of the faithful are urged to contribute. Instituted in the United States of America (1925) (the National Assembly superseding in that country the institution of Bahá'í Temple Unity formed during 'Abdu'l-Bahá's ministry), in the British Isles (1923), in Germany (1923), in Egypt (1924), in 'Iráq (1931), in India (1923), in Persia (1934) and in Australia (1934); their election renewed annually by delegates whose number has been fixed, according to national requirements, at 9, 19, 95, or 171 (9 times 19), these national bodies have through their emergence signalized the birth of a new epoch in the Formative Age of the Faith, and marked a further stage in the evolution, the unification and consolidation of a continually expanding community. Aided by national committees responsible to and chosen by them, without discrimination, from among the entire body of the believers within their jurisdiction, and to each of which a particular sphere of Bahá'í service is allocated, these Bahá'í National Assemblies have, as the scope of their activities steadily enlarged, proved themselves, through the spirit of discipline which they have inculcated and through their uncompromising adherence to principles which have enabled them to rise above all prejudices of race, nation, class and color, capable of administering, in a remarkable fashion, the multiplying activities of a newly-consolidated Faith.

Nor have the national committees themselves been less energetic and devoted in the discharge of their respective functions. In the defense of the Faith's vital interests, in the exposition of its doctrine; in the dissemination of its literature; in the consolidation of its finances; in the organization of its teaching force; in the furtherance of the solidarity of its component parts; in the purchase of its historic sites; in the preservation of its sacred records, treasures and relics; in its contacts with the various institutions of the society of which it forms a part; in the education of its youth; in the training of its children; in the improvement of the status of its women adherents in the East; the members of these diversified agencies, operating under the aegis of the elected national representatives of the Bahá'í community, have amply demonstrated their capacity to promote effectively its vital and manifold interests. The mere enumeration of the national committees which, originating mostly in the West and functioning with exemplary efficiency in the United States and Canada, now carry on their activities with a vigor and a unity of purpose which sharply contrast with the effete institutions of a moribund civilization, would suffice to reveal the scope of these auxiliary institutions which an evolving Administrative Order, still in the secondary stage of its development, has set in motion: The Teaching Committee, the Regional Teaching Committees; the Inter-America Committee; the Publishing Committee; the Race Unity Committee; the Youth Committee; the Reviewing Committee; The Temple Maintenance Committee; the Temple Program Committee; the Temple Guides Committee; the Temple Librarian and Sales Committee; the Boys' and Girls' Service Committees; the Child Education Committee; the Women's Progress, Teaching, and Program Committees; the Legal Committee; the Archives and History Committee; the Census Committee; the Bahá'í Exhibits Committee; the Bahá'í News Committee; the Bahá'í News Service Committee; the Braille Transcriptions Committee; the Contacts Committee; the Service Committee; the Editorial Committee; the Index Committee; the Library Committee; the Radio Committee; the Accountant Committee; the Annual Souvenir Committee; the Bahá'í World Editorial Committee; the Study Outline Committee; the International Auxiliary Language Committee; the Institute of Bahá'í Education Committee; the World Order Magazine Committee; the Bahá'í Public Relations Committee; the Bahá'í Schools Committee; the Summer Schools Committees; the International School Committee; the Pamphlet Literature Committee; the Bahá'í Cemetery Committee; the Ḥazíratu'l-Quds Committee; the Mas͟hriqu'l-Ad͟hkár Committee; the Assembly Development Committee; the National History Committee; the Miscellaneous Materials Committee; the Free Literature Committee; the Translation Committee; the Cataloguing Tablets Committee; the Editing Tablets Committee; the Properties Committee; the Adjustments Committee; the Publicity Committee; the East and West Committee; the Welfare Committee; the Transcription of Tablets Committee; the Traveling Teachers Committee; the Bahá'í Education Committee; the Holy Sites Committee; the Children's Savings Bank Committee.

The establishment of local and national Assemblies and the subsequent formation of local and national committees, acting as necessary adjuncts to the elected representatives of Bahá'í communities in both the East and the West, however remarkable in themselves, were but a prelude to a series of undertakings on the part of the newly formed National Assemblies, which have contributed in no small measure to the unification of the Bahá'í world community and the consolidation of its Administrative Order. The initial step taken in that direction was the drafting and adoption of a Bahá'í National constitution, first framed and promulgated by the elected representatives of the American Bahá'í Community in 1927, the text of which has since, with slight variations suited to national requirements, been translated into Arabic, German and Persian, and constitutes, at the present time, the charter of the National Spiritual Assemblies of the Bahá'ís of the United States and Canada, of the British Isles, of Germany, of Persia, of 'Iráq, of India and Burma, of Egypt and the Sudan and of Australia and New Zealand. Heralding the formulation of the constitution of the future Bahá'í World Community; submitted for the consideration of all local Assemblies and ratified by the entire body of the recognized believers in countries possessing national Assemblies, this national constitution has been supplemented by a similar document, containing the by-laws of Bahá'í local assemblies, first drafted by the New York Bahá'í community in November, 1931, and accepted as a pattern for all local Bahá'í constitutions. The text of this national constitution comprises a Declaration of Trust, whose articles set forth the character and objects of the national Bahá'í community, establish the functions, designate the central office, and describe the official seal, of the body of its elected representatives, as well as a set of by-laws which define the status, the mode of election, the powers and duties of both local and national Assemblies, describe the relation of the National Assembly to the International House of Justice as well as to local Assemblies and individual believers, outline the rights and obligations of the National Convention and its relation to the National Assembly, disclose the character of Bahá'í elections, and lay down the requirements of voting membership in all Bahá'í communities.

The framing of these constitutions, both local and national, identical to all intents and purposes in their provisions, provided the necessary foundation for the legal incorporation of these administrative institutions in accordance with civil statutes controlling religious or commercial bodies. Giving these Assemblies a legal standing, this incorporation greatly consolidated their power and enlarged their capacity, and in this regard the achievement of the National Spiritual Assembly of the Bahá'ís of the United States and Canada and the Spiritual Assembly of the Bahá'ís of New York again set an example worthy of emulation by their sister Assemblies in both the East and the West. The incorporation of the American National Spiritual Assembly as a voluntary Trust, a species of corporation recognized under the common law, enabling it to enter into contract, hold property and receive bequests by virtue of a certificate issued in May, 1929, under the seal of the Department of State in Washington and bearing the signature of the Secretary of State, Henry L. Stimson, was followed by the adoption of similar legal measures resulting in the successive incorporation of the National Spiritual Assembly of the Bahá'ís of India and Burma, in January, 1933, in Lahore, in the state of Punjab, according to the provisions of the Societies Registration Act of 1860; of the National Spiritual Assembly of the Bahá'ís of Egypt and the Sudan, in December, 1934, as certified by the Mixed Court in Cairo; of the National Spiritual Assembly of the Bahá'ís of Australia and New Zealand, in January, 1938, as witnessed by the Deputy Registrar at the General Registry Office for the state of South Australia; and more recently of the National Spiritual Assembly of the Bahá'ís of the British Isles, in August, 1939, as an unlimited non-profit company, under the Companies Act, 1929, and certified by the Assistant Registrar of Companies in the City of London.

Parallel with the legal incorporation of these National Assemblies a far larger number of Bahá'í local Assemblies were similarly incorporated, following the example set by the Chicago Bahá'í Assembly in February, 1932, in countries as far apart as the United States of America, India, Mexico, Germany, Canada, Australia, New Zealand, Burma, Costa Rica, Balúchistán and the Hawaiian Islands. The Spiritual Assemblies of the Bahá'ís of Esslingen in Germany, of Mexico City in Mexico, of San José in Costa Rica, of Sydney and Adelaide in Australia, of Auckland in New Zealand, of Delhi, Bombay, Karachi, Poona, Calcutta, Secunderabad, Bangalore, Vellore, Ahmedabad, Serampore, Andheri and Baroda in India, of Tuetta in Balúchistán, of Rangoon, Mandalay and Daidanow-Kalazoo in Burma, of Montreal and Vancouver in Canada, of Honolulu in the Hawaiian Islands, and of Chicago, New York, Washington, D. C., Boston, San Francisco, Philadelphia, Kenosha, Teaneck, Racine, Detroit, Cleveland, Los Angeles, Milwaukee, Minneapolis, Cincinnati, Winnetka, Phoenix, Columbus, Lima, Portland, Jersey City, Wilmette, Peoria, Seattle, Binghamton, Helena, Richmond Highlands, Miami, Pasadena, Oakland, Indianapolis, St. Paul, Berkeley, Urbana, Springfield and Flint in the United States of America—all these succeeded, gradually and after submitting the text of almost identical Bahá'í local constitutions to the civil authorities in their respective states or provinces, in constituting themselves into societies and corporations recognized by law, and protected by the civil statutes operating in their respective countries.

Just as the formulation of Bahá'í constitutions had provided the foundation for the incorporation of Bahá'í Spiritual Assemblies, so did the recognition accorded by local and national authorities to the elected representatives of Bahá'í communities pave the way for the establishment of national and local Bahá'í endowments—a historic undertaking which, as had been the case with previous achievements of far-reaching importance, the American Bahá'í Community was the first to initiate. In most cases these endowments, owing to their religious character, have been exempted from both government and municipal taxes, as a result of representations made by the incorporated Bahá'í bodies to the civil authorities, though the value of the properties thus exempted has, in more than one country, amounted to a considerable sum.

In the United States of America the national endowments of the Faith, already representing one and three-quarter million dollars of assets, and established through a series of Indentures of Trust, created in 1928, 1929, 1935, 1938, 1939, 1941 and 1942 by the National Spiritual Assembly in that country, acting as Trustees of the American Bahá'í Community, now include the land and structure of the Mas̲h̲riqu'l-Ad̲h̲kár, and the caretaker's cottage in Wilmette, Ill.; the adjoining Ḥazíratu'l-Quds (Bahá'í National Headquarters) and its supplementary administrative office; the Inn, the Fellowship House, the Bahá'í Hall, the Arts and Crafts Studio, a farm, a number of cottages, several parcels of land, including the holding on Monsalvat, blessed by the footsteps of 'Abdu'l-Bahá, in Green Acre, in the state of Maine; Bosch House, the Bahá'í Hall, a fruit orchard, the Redwood Grove, a dormitory and Ranch Buildings in Geyserville, Calif.; Wilhelm House, Evergreen Cabin, a pine grove and seven lots with buildings at West Englewood, N. J., the scene of the memorable Unity Feast given by 'Abdu'l-Bahá, in June, 1912, to the Bahá'ís of the New York Metropolitan district; Wilson House, blessed by His presence, and land in Malden, Mass.; Mathews House and Ranch Buildings in Pine Valley, Colo.; land in Muskegon, Mich., and a cemetery lot in Portsmouth, N. H.

Of even greater importance, and in their aggregate far surpassing in value the national endowments of the American Bahá'í community, though their title-deeds are, owing to the inability of the Persian Bahá'í community to incorporate its national and local assemblies, held in trust by individuals, are the assets which the Faith now possesses in the land of its origin. To the House of the Báb in S̲h̲íráz and the ancestral Home of Bahá'u'lláh in Tákur, Mázindarán, already in the possession of the community in the days of 'Abdu'l-Bahá's ministry, have, since His ascension, been added extensive properties, in the outskirts of the capital, situated on the slopes of Mt. Alburz, overlooking the native city of Bahá'u'lláh, including a farm, a garden and vineyard, comprising an area of over three million and a half square meters, preserved as the future site of the first Mas͟hriqu'l-Ad͟hkár in Persia. Other acquisitions that have greatly extended the range of Bahá'í endowments in that country include the House in which Bahá'u'lláh was born in Ṭihrán; several buildings adjoining the House of the Báb in S͟híráz, including the house owned by His maternal uncle; the Ḥaẓíratu'l-Quds in Ṭihrán; the shop occupied by the Báb during the years He was a merchant in Bús͟hihr; a quarter of the village of C͟hihríq, where He was confined; the house of Ḥájí Mírzá Jání, where He tarried on His way to Tabríz; the public bath used by Him in S͟híráz and some adjacent houses; half of the house owned by Vaḥíd in Nayríz and part of the house owned by Ḥujjat in Zanján; the three gardens rented by Bahá'u'lláh in the hamlet of Badas͟ht; the burial-place of Quddús in Bárfurús͟h; the house of Kalantar in Ṭihrán, the scene of Ṭáhirih's confinement; the public bath visited by the Báb when in Urúmíyyih, Ád͟hirbáyján; the house owned by Mírzá Husayn-'Alíy-i-Núr, where the Báb's remains had been concealed; the Bábíyyih and the house owned by Mullá Ḥusayn in Mas͟hhad; the residence of the Sulṭánu's͟h-S͟huhadá (King of Martyrs) and of the Maḥbúbu's͟h-S͟huhadá (Beloved of Martyrs) in Iṣfahán, as well as a considerable number of sites and houses, including burial-places, associated with the heroes and martyrs of the Faith. These holdings which, with very few exceptions, have been recently acquired in Persia, are now being preserved and yearly augmented, and, whenever necessary, carefully restored, through the assiduous efforts of a specially appointed national committee, acting under the constant and general supervision of the elected representatives of the Persian believers.

Nor should mention be omitted of the varied and multiplying national assets which, ever since the inception of the Administrative Order of the Faith of Bahá'u'lláh, have been steadily acquired in other countries such as India, Burma, the British Isles, Germany, 'Iráq, Egypt, Australia, Transjordan and Syria. Among these may be specially mentioned the Ḥaẓíratu'l-Quds of the Bahá'ís of 'Iráq, the Ḥaẓíratu'l-Quds of the Bahá'ís of Egypt, the Ḥaẓíratu'l-Quds of the Bahá'ís of India, the Ḥaẓíratu'l-Quds of the Bahá'ís of Australia, the Bahá'í Home in Esslingen, the Publishing Trust of the Bahá'ís of the

British Isles, the Bahá'í Pilgrim House in Baghdád, and the Bahá'í Cemeteries established in the capitals of Persia, Egypt and Turkistán. Whether in the form of land, schools, administrative headquarters, secretariats, libraries, cemeteries, hostels or publishing companies, these widely scattered assets, partly registered in the name of incorporated National Assemblies, and partly held in trust by individual recognized believers, have contributed their share to the uninterrupted expansion of national Bahá'í endowments in recent years as well as to the consolidation of their foundations. Of vital importance, though less notable in significance, have been, moreover, the local endowments which have supplemented the national assets of the Faith and which, in consequence of the incorporation of Bahá'í local Assemblies, have been legally established and safeguarded in various countries in both the East and the West. Particularly in Persia these holdings, whether in the form of land, administrative buildings, schools or other institutions, have greatly enriched and widened the scope of the local endowments of the world-wide Bahá'í community.

Simultaneous with the establishment and incorporation of local and national Bahá'í Assemblies, with the formation of their respective committees, the formulation of national and local Bahá'í constitutions and the founding of Bahá'í endowments, undertakings of great institutional significance were initiated by these newly founded Assemblies, among which the institution of the Ḥazíratu'l-Quds—the seat of the Bahá'í National Assembly and pivot of all Bahá'í administrative activity in future—must rank as one of the most important. Originating first in Persia, now universally known by its official and distinctive title signifying "the Sacred Fold," marking a notable advance in the evolution of a process whose beginnings may be traced to the clandestine gatherings held at times underground and in the dead of night, by the persecuted followers of the Faith in that country, this institution, still in the early stages of its development, has already lent its share to the consolidation of the internal functions of the organic Bahá'í community, and provided a further visible evidence of its steady growth and rising power. Complementary in its functions to those of the Mashriqu'l-Adhkár—an edifice exclusively reserved for Bahá'í worship—this institution, whether local or national, will, as its component parts, such as the Secretariat, the Treasury, the Archives, the Library, the Publishing Office, the Assembly Hall, the Council Chamber, the Pilgrims' Hostel, are brought together and made jointly to operate in one spot, be increasingly regarded as the focus of all Bahá'í administrative activity, and symbolize, in a befitting manner, the ideal of service animating the Bahá'í community in its relation alike to the Faith and to mankind in general.

From the Mas͟hriqu'l-Ad͟hkár, ordained as a house of worship by Bahá'u'lláh in the Kitáb-i-Aqdas, the representatives of Bahá'í communities, both local and national, together with the members of their respective committees, will, as they gather daily within its walls at the hour of dawn, derive the necessary inspiration that will enable them to discharge, in the course of their day-to-day exertions in the Ḥaẓíratu'l-Quds—the scene of their administrative activities—their duties and responsibilities as befits the chosen stewards of His Faith.

Already on the shores of Lake Michigan, in the outskirts of the first Bahá'í center established in the American continent and under the shadow of the first Mas͟hriqu'l-Ad͟hkár of the West; in the capital city of Persia, the cradle of the Faith; in the vicinity of the Most Great House in Bag͟hdád; in the city of 'Is͟hqábad, adjoining the first Mas͟hriqu'l-Ad͟hkár of the Bahá'í world; in the capital of Egypt, the foremost center of both the Arab and Islamic worlds; in Delhi, the capital city of India and even in Sydney in far-off Australia, initial steps have been taken which must eventually culminate in the establishment, in all their splendor and power, of the national administrative seats of the Bahá'í communities established in these countries.

Locally, moreover, in the above-mentioned countries, as well as in several others, the preliminary measures for the establishment of this institution, in the form of a house, either owned or rented by the local Bahá'í community, have been taken, foremost among them being the numerous administrative buildings which, in various provinces of Persia, the believers have, despite the disabilities from which they suffer, succeeded in either purchasing or constructing.

Equally important as a factor in the evolution of the Administrative Order has been the remarkable progress achieved, particularly in the United States of America, by the institution of the summer schools designed to foster the spirit of fellowship in a distinctly Bahá'í atmosphere, to afford the necessary training for Bahá'í teachers, and to provide facilities for the study of the history and teachings of the Faith, and for a better understanding of its relation to other religions and to human society in general.

Established in three regional centers, for the three major divisions of the North American continent, in Geyserville, in the Californian hills (1927), at Green Acre, situated on the banks of the Piscataqua in the state of Maine (1929), and at Louhelen Ranch near Davison, Michigan (1931), and recently supplemented by the International

School founded at Pine Valley, Colorado Springs, dedicated to the training of Bahá'í teachers wishing to serve in other lands and especially in Latin America, these three embryonic Bahá'í educational institutions have, through a steady expansion of their programs, set an example worthy of emulation by other Bahá'í communities in both the East and the West. Through the intensive study of Bahá'í Scriptures and of the early history of the Faith; through the organization of courses on the teachings and history of Islám; through conferences for the promotion of inter-racial amity; through laboratory courses designed to familiarize the participants with the processes of the Bahá'í Administrative Order; through special sessions devoted to Youth and child training; through classes in public speaking; through lectures on Comparative Religion; through group discussion on the manifold aspects of the Faith; through the establishment of libraries; through teaching classes; through courses on Bahá'í ethics and on Latin America; through the introduction of winter school sessions; through forums and devotional gatherings; through plays and pageants; through picnics and other recreational activities, these schools, open to Bahá'ís and non-Bahá'ís alike, have set so noble an example as to inspire other Bahá'í communities in Persia, in the British Isles, in Germany, in Australia, in New Zealand, in India, in 'Iráq and in Egypt to undertake the initial measures designed to enable them to build along the same lines institutions that bid fair to evolve into the Bahá'í universities of the future.

Among other factors contributing to the expansion and establishment of the Administrative Order may be mentioned the organized activities of the Bahá'í Youth, already much advanced in Persia and in the United States of America, and launched more recently in India, in the British Isles, in Germany, in 'Iráq, in Egypt, in Australia, in Bulgaria, in the Hawaiian Islands, in Hungary and in Havana. These activities comprise annual world-wide Bahá'í Youth Symposiums, Youth sessions at Bahá'í summer schools, youth bulletins and magazines, an international correspondence Bureau, facilities for the registration of young people desiring to join the Faith, the publication of outlines and references for the study of the teachings and the organization of a Bahá'í study group as an official university activity in a leading American university. They include, moreover, "study days" held in Bahá'í homes and centers, classes for the study of Esperanto and other languages, the organization of Bahá'í libraries, the opening of reading rooms, the production of Bahá'í plays and pageants, the holding of oratorical contests, the education of orphans, the organization of classes in public speaking, the holding of gatherings to perpetuate the memory of historical Bahá'í personalities, inter-group regional conferences and youth sessions held in connection with Bahá'í annual conventions.

Still other factors promoting the development of that Order and contributing to its consolidation have been the systematic institution of the Nineteen Day Feast, functioning in most Bahá'í communities in East and West, with its threefold emphasis on the devotional, the administrative and the social aspects of Bahá'í community life; the initiation of activities designed to prepare a census of Bahá'í children, and provide for them laboratory courses, prayer books and elementary literature, and the formulation and publication of a body of authoritative statements on the non-political character of the Faith, on membership in non-Bahá'í religious organizations, on methods of teaching, on the Bahá'í attitude towards war, on the institutions of the Annual Convention, of the Bahá'í Spiritual Assembly, of the Nineteen Day Feast and of the National Fund. Reference should, moreover, be made to the establishment of National Archives for the authentication, the collection, the translation, the cataloguing and the preservation of the Tablets of Bahá'u'lláh and of 'Abdu'l-Bahá and for the preservation of sacred relics and historical documents; to the verification and transcription of the original Tablets of the Báb, of Bahá'u'lláh and of 'Abdu'l-Bahá in the possession of Oriental believers; to the compilation of a detailed history of the Faith since its inception until the present day; to the opening of a Bahá'í International Bureau in Geneva; to the holding of Bahá'í district conventions; to the purchase of historic sites; to the establishment of Bahá'í memorial libraries, and to the initiation of a flourishing children's Savings Bank in Persia.

Nor should mention be omitted of the participation, whether official or non-official, of representatives of these newly founded national Bahá'í communities in the activities and proceedings of a great variety of congresses, associations, conventions and conferences, held in various countries of Europe, Asia and America for the promotion of religious unity, peace, education, international cooperation, inter-racial amity and other humanitarian purposes. With organizations such as the Conference of some Living Religions within the British Empire, held in London in 1924 and the World Fellowship of Faiths held in that same city in 1936; with the Universal Esperanto Congresses held annually in various capitals of Europe; with the Institute of Intellectual Cooperation; with the Century of Progress Exhibition held in Chicago in 1933; with the World's Fair held in New

York in 1938 and 1939; with the Golden Gate International Exposition held in San Francisco in 1939; with the First Convention of the Religious Congress held in Calcutta; with the Second All-India Cultural Conference convened in that same city; with the All-Faiths' League Convention in Indore; with the Arya Samaj and the Brahmo Samaj Conferences as well as those of the Theosophical Society and the All-Asian Women's Conference, held in various cities of India; with the World Council of Youth; with the Eastern Women's Congress in Ṭihrán; with the Pan-Pacific Women's Conference in Honolulu; with the Women's International League for Peace and with the Peoples Conference at Buenos Aires in Argentina—with these and others, relationships have, in one form or another, been cultivated which have served the twofold purpose of demonstrating the universality and comprehensiveness of the Faith of Bahá'u'lláh and of forging vital and enduring links between them and the far-flung agencies of its Administrative Order.

Nor should we ignore or underestimate the contacts established between these same agencies and some of the highest governmental authorities, in both the East and the West, as well as with the heads of Islám in Persia, and with the League of Nations, and with even royalty itself for the purpose of defending the rights, or of presenting the literature, or of setting forth the aims and purposes of the followers of the Faith in their unremitting efforts to champion the cause of an infant Administrative Order. The communications addressed by the members of the National Spiritual Assembly of the Bahá'ís of the United States and Canada—the champion builders of that Order—to the Palestine High Commissioner for the restitution of the keys of the Tomb of Bahá'u'lláh to its custodian; to the Sh͟áh of Persia, on four occasions, pleading for justice on behalf of their persecuted brethren within his domains; to the Persian Prime Minister on that same subject; to Queen Marie of Rumania, expressing gratitude for her historic tributes to the Bahá'í Faith; to the Heads of Islám in Persia, appealing for harmony and peace among religions; to King Feisal of 'Iráq for the purpose of insuring the security of the Most Great House in Bag͟hdád; to the Soviet Authorities on behalf of the Bahá'í communities in Russia; to the German authorities regarding the disabilities suffered by their German brethren; to the Egyptian Government concerning the emancipation of their co-religionists from the yoke of Islamic orthodoxy; to the Persian Cabinet in connection with the closing of Persian Bahá'í educational institutions; to the State Department of the United States Government and the Turkish Ambassador in Washington and the Turkish Cabinet in Ankara, in defense of the interests of the Faith in Turkey; to that same State Department in order to facilitate the transfer of the remains of Lua Getsinger from the Protestant Cemetery in Cairo to the first Bahá'í burial-ground established in Egypt; to the Persian Minister in Washington regarding the mission of Keith Ransom-Kehler; to the King of Egypt with accompanying Bahá'í literature; to the Government of the United States and the Canadian Government, setting forth the Bahá'í teachings on Universal Peace; to the Rumanian Minister in Washington on behalf of the American Bahá'ís, on the occasion of the death of Queen Marie of Rumania; and to President Franklin D. Roosevelt, acquainting him with Bahá'u'lláh's summons issued in His Kitáb-i-Aqdas to the Presidents of the American Republics and with certain prayers revealed by 'Abdu'l-Bahá—such communications constitute in themselves a notable and illuminating chapter in the history of the unfoldment of the Bahá'í Administrative Order.

To these must be added the communications addressed from the world center of the Faith as well as by Bahá'í national and local assemblies, whether telegraphically or in writing, to the Palestine High Commissioner, pleading for the delivery of the keys of the Tomb of Bahá'u'lláh to its original keeper; the appeals made by Bahá'í centers in East and West to the 'Iráqí authorities for the restoration of the House of Bahá'u'lláh in Baghdád; the subsequent appeal made to the British Secretary of State for the Colonies, following the verdict of the Baghdád Court of Appeals in that connection; the messages despatched to the League of Nations on behalf of Bahá'í communities in the East and in the West, in appreciation of the official pronouncement of the Council of the League in favor of the claims presented by the Bahá'í petitioners, as well as several letters exchanged between the International Center of the Faith, on the one hand, and that archetype of Bahá'í teachers, Martha Root, on the other, with Queen Marie of Rumania, following the publication of her historic appreciations of the Faith, and the messages of sympathy addressed to Queen Marie of Yugoslavia, on behalf of the world-wide Bahá'í Community, on the occasion of the passing of her mother, and to the Duchess of Kent following the tragic death of her husband.

Nor should we fail to make special mention of the petition forwarded by the National Spiritual Assembly of the Bahá'ís of 'Iráq to the Mandates Commission of the League of Nations, as a result of the seizure of Bahá'u'lláh's house in Baghdád, or of the written messages sent to King Ghází I of 'Iráq by that same Assembly, after the death of his father and on the occasion of his marriage, or of its condolences conveyed in writing to the present Regent of 'Iráq at the time of the sudden death of that King, or of the communications of the National Spiritual Assembly of the Bahá'ís of Egypt submitted to the Egyptian Prime Minister, the Minister of the Interior, and the Minister of Justice, following the verdict of the Muslim ecclesiastical court in Egypt, or of the letters addressed by the National Spiritual Assembly of the Bahá'ís of Persia to the Sháh and to the Persian Cabinet in connection with the closing of Bahá'í schools and the ban imposed on Bahá'í literature in that country. Mention should, moreover, be made of the written messages despatched by the National Spiritual Assembly of the Bahá'ís of Persia to the King of Rumania and the Royal Family on the occasion of the death of his mother, Queen Marie, as well as to the Turkish Ambassador in Ṭihrán enclosing the contribution of the Persian believers for the sufferers of the earthquake in Turkey; of Martha Root's letters to the late President Von Hindenburg and to Dr. Streseman, the German Foreign Minister, accompanying the presentation to them of Bahá'í literature; of Keith Ransom-Kehler's seven successive petitions addressed to the Sháh of Persia, and of her numerous communications to various ministers and high dignitaries of the realm, during her memorable visit to that land.

Collateral with these first stirrings of the Bahá'í Administrative Order, and synchronizing with the emergence of National Bahá'í communities and with the institution of their administrative, educational, and teaching agencies, the mighty process set in motion in the Holy Land, the heart and nerve-center of that Administrative Order, on the memorable occasions when Bahá'u'lláh revealed the Tablet of Carmel and visited the future site of the Báb's sepulcher, was irresistibly unfolding. That process had received a tremendous impetus through the purchase of that site, shortly after Bahá'u'lláh's ascension, through the subsequent transfer of the Báb's remains from Ṭihrán to 'Akká, through the construction of that sepulcher during the most distressful years of 'Abdu'l-Bahá's incarceration, and lastly through the permanent interment of those remains in the heart of Mt. Carmel, through the establishment of a pilgrim house in the immediate vicinity of that sepulcher, and the selection of the future site of the first Bahá'í educational institution on that mountain.

Profiting from the freedom accorded the world center of the Faith of Bahá'u'lláh, ever since the ignominious defeat of the decrepit Ottoman empire during the war of 1914-18, the forces released through the inception of the stupendous Plan conceived by Him could now flow unchecked, under the beneficent influence of a sympathetic régime, into channels designed to disclose to the world at large the potencies with which that Plan had been endowed. The interment of 'Abdu'l-Bahá Himself within a vault of the Báb's mausoleum, enhancing still further the sacredness of that mountain; the installment of an electric plant, the first of its kind established in the city of Haifa, flooding with illumination the Grave of One Who, in His own words, had been denied even "a lighted lamp" in His fortress-prison in Á<u>dh</u>irbáyján; the construction of three additional chambers adjoining His sepulcher, thereby completing 'Abdu'l-Bahá's plan for the first unit of that Edifice; the vast extension, despite the machinations of the Covenant-breakers, of the properties surrounding that resting-place, sweeping from the ridge of Carmel down to the Templar colony nestling at its foot, and representing assets estimated at no less than four hundred thousand pounds, together with the acquisition of four tracts of land, dedicated to the Bahá'í Shrines, and situated in the plain of 'Akká to the north, in the district of Beersheba to the south, and in the valley of the Jordan to the east, amounting to approximately six hundred acres; the opening of a series of terraces which, as designed by 'Abdu'l-Bahá, are to provide a direct approach to the Báb's Tomb from the city lying under its shadow; the beautification of its precincts through the laying out of parks and gardens, open daily to the public, and attracting tourists and residents alike to its gates—these may be regarded as the initial evidences of the marvelous expansion of the international institutions and endowments of the Faith at its world center. Of particular significance, moreover, has been the exemption granted by the Palestine High Commissioner to the entire area of land surrounding and dedicated to the Shrine of the Báb, to the school property and the archives in its vicinity, to the Western pilgrim-house situated in its neighborhood, and to such historic sites as the Mansion in Bahjí, the House of Bahá'u'lláh in 'Akká, and the garden of Riḍván to the east of that city; the establishment, as a result of two formal applications submitted to the civil authorities, of the Palestine Branches of the American and Indian National Spiritual Assemblies, as recognized religious societies in Palestine (to be followed, for purposes of internal consolidation, by a similar incorporation of the branches of other National Spiritual Assemblies throughout the Bahá'í world); and the transfer to the Branch of the American National Spiritual Assembly, through a series of no less than thirty transactions, of properties dedicated to the Tomb of the Báb, and approximating in their aggregate fifty thousand square meters, the majority of the title-deeds of which bear the signature of the son of the Arch-breaker of Bahá'u'lláh's Covenant in his capacity as Registrar of lands in Haifa.

Equally significant has been the founding on Mt. Carmel of two international Archives, the one adjoining the shrine of the Báb, the other in the immediate vicinity of the resting-place of the Greatest Holy Leaf, where, for the first time in Bahá'í history, priceless treasures, hitherto scattered and often hidden for safekeeping, have been collected and are now displayed to visiting pilgrims. These treasures include portraits of both the Báb and Bahá'u'lláh; personal relics such as the hair, the dust and garments of the Báb; the locks and blood of Bahá'u'lláh and such articles as His pen-case, His garments, His brocaded tájes (head dresses), the kas͟hkúl of His Sulaymáníyyih days, His watch and His Qur'án; manuscripts and Tablets of inestimable value, some of them illuminated, such as part of the Hidden Words written in Bahá'u'lláh's own hand, the Persian Bayán, in the handwriting of Siyyid Ḥusayn, the Báb's amanuensis, the original Tablets to the Letters of the Living penned by the Báb, and the manuscript of "Some Answered Questions." This precious collection, moreover, includes objects and effects associated with 'Abdu'l-Bahá; the blood-stained garment of the Purest Branch, the ring of Quddús, the sword of Mullá Ḥusayn, the seals of the Vazír, the father of Bahá'u'lláh, the brooch presented by the Queen of Rumania to Martha Root, the originals of the Queen's letters to her and to others, and of her tributes to the Faith, as well as no less than twenty volumes of prayers and Tablets revealed by the Founders of the Faith, authenticated and transcribed by Bahá'í Assemblies throughout the Orient, and supplementing the vast collection of their published writings.

Moreover, as a further testimony to the majestic unfoldment and progressive consolidation of the stupendous undertaking launched by Bahá'u'lláh on that holy mountain, may be mentioned the selection of a portion of the school property situated in the precincts of the Shrine of the Báb as a permanent resting-place for the Greatest Holy Leaf, the *"well-beloved"* sister of 'Abdu'l-Bahá, the *"Leaf that hath sprung"* from the *"Pre-existent Root,"* the *"fragrance"* of Bahá'u'lláh's *"shining robe,"* elevated by Him to a *"station such as none other woman hath surpassed,"* and comparable in rank to those immortal heroines such as Sarah, Ásíyih, the Virgin Mary, Fáṭimih and Ṭáhirih, each of whom has outshone every member of her sex in previous Dispensations. And lastly, there should be mentioned, as a further evidence of the blessings flowing from the Divine Plan, the transfer, a few years later, to that same hallowed spot, after a separation in death of above half a century, and notwithstanding the protests voiced by the brother and lieutenant of the arch-breaker of Bahá'u'lláh's Covenant, of the remains of the Purest Branch, the martyred son of Bahá'u'lláh, *"created of the light of Bahá,"* the *"Trust of God"* and His *"Treasure"* in the Holy Land, and offered up by his Father as a *"ransom"* for the regeneration of the world and the unification of its peoples. To this same burial-ground, and on the same day the remains of the Purest Branch were interred, was transferred the body of his mother, the saintly Navváb, she to whose dire afflictions, as attested by 'Abdu'l-Bahá in a Tablet, the 54th chapter of the Book of Isaiah has, in its entirety, borne witness, whose *"Husband,"* in the words of that Prophet, is *"the Lord of Hosts,"* whose *"seed shall inherit the Gentiles,"* and whom Bahá'u'lláh in His Tablet, has destined to be *"His consort in every one of His worlds."*

The conjunction of these three resting-places, under the shadow of the Báb's own Tomb, embosomed in the heart of Carmel, facing the snow-white city across the bay of 'Akká, the Qiblih of the Bahá'í world, set in a garden of exquisite beauty, reinforces, if we would correctly estimate its significance, the spiritual potencies of a spot, designated by Bahá'u'lláh Himself the seat of God's throne. It marks, too, a further milestone in the road leading eventually to the establishment of that permanent world Administrative Center of the future Bahá'í Commonwealth, destined never to be separated from, and to function in the proximity of, the Spiritual Center of that Faith, in a land already revered and held sacred alike by the adherents of three of the world's outstanding religious systems.

Scarcely less significant has been the erection of the superstructure and the completion of the exterior ornamentation of the first Mas͟hriqu'l-Ad͟hkár of the West, the noblest of the exploits which have immortalized the services of the American Bahá'í community to the Cause of Bahá'u'lláh. Consummated through the agency of an efficiently functioning and newly established Administrative Order, this enterprise has itself immensely enhanced the prestige, consolidated the strength and expanded the subsidiary institutions of the community that made its building possible.

Conceived forty-one years ago; originating with the petition spontaneously addressed, in March 1903 to 'Abdu'l-Bahá by the "House of Spirituality" of the Bahá'ís of Chicago—the first Bahá'í center established in the Western world—the members of which, inspired by the example set by the builders of the Mas͟hriqu'l-Ad͟hkár of 'Is͟hqábád, had appealed for permission to construct a similar Temple in

America; blessed by His approval and high commendation in a Tablet revealed by Him in June of that same year; launched by the delegates of various American Assemblies, assembled in Chicago in November, 1907, for the purpose of choosing the site of the Temple; established on a national basis through a religious corporation known as the "Bahá'í Temple Unity," which was incorporated shortly after the first American Bahá'í Convention held in that same city in March, 1909; honored through the dedication ceremony presided over by 'Abdu'l-Bahá Himself when visiting that site in May, 1912, this enterprise—the crowning achievement of the Administrative Order of the Faith of Bahá'u'lláh in the first Bahá'í century—had, ever since that memorable occasion, been progressing intermittently until the time when the foundations of that Order having been firmly laid in the North American continent the American Bahá'í community was in a position to utilize the instruments which it had forged for the efficient prosecution of its task.

At the 1914 American Bahá'í Convention the purchase of the Temple property was completed. The 1920 Convention, held in New York, having been previously directed by 'Abdu'l-Bahá to select the design of that Temple, chose from among a number of designs competitively submitted to it that of Louis J. Bourgeois, a French-Canadian architect, a selection that was later confirmed by 'Abdu'l-Bahá Himself. The contracts for the sinking of the nine great caissons supporting the central portion of the building, extending to rock at a depth of 120 feet below the ground level, and for the construction of the basement structure, were successively awarded in December, 1920 and August, 1921. In August, 1930, in spite of the prevailing economic crisis, and during a period of unemployment unparalleled in American history, another contract, with twenty-four additional sub-contracts, for the erection of the superstructure was placed, and the work completed by May 1, 1931, on which day the first devotional service in the new structure was celebrated, coinciding with the 19th anniversary of the dedication of the grounds by 'Abdu'l-Bahá. The ornamentation of the dome was started in June, 1932 and finished in January, 1934. The ornamentation of the clerestory was completed in July, 1935, and that of the gallery unit below it in November, 1938. The mainstory ornamentation was, despite the outbreak of the present war, undertaken in April, 1940, and completed in July, 1942; whilst the eighteen circular steps were placed in position by December, 1942, seventeen months in advance of the centenary celebration of the Faith, by which time the exterior of the Temple was scheduled to be finished, and forty years after the petition of the Chicago believers had been submitted to and granted by 'Abdu'l-Bahá.

This unique edifice, the first fruit of a slowly maturing Administrative Order, the noblest structure reared in the first Bahá'í century, and the symbol and precursor of a future world civilization, is situated in the heart of the North American continent, on the western shore of Lake Michigan, and is surrounded by its own grounds comprising a little less than seven acres. It has been financed, at cost of over a million dollars, by the American Bahá'í community, assisted at times by voluntary contributions of recognized believers in East and West, of Christian, of Muslim, of Jewish, of Zoroastrian, of Hindu and Buddhist extraction. It has been associated, in its initial phase, with 'Abdu'l-Bahá, and in the concluding stages of its construction with the memory of the Greatest Holy Leaf, the Purest Branch and their mother. The structure itself is a pure white nonagonal building, of original and unique design, rising from a flight of white stairs encircling its base; and surmounted by a majestic and beautifully proportioned dome, bearing nine tapering symmetrically placed ribs of decorative as well as structural significance, which soar to its apex and finally merge into a common unit pointing skyward. Its framework is constructed of structural steel enclosed in concrete, the material of its ornamentation consisting of a combination of crystalline quartz, opaque quartz and white Portland cement, producing a composition clear in texture, hard and enduring as stone, impervious to the elements, and cast into a design as delicate as lace. It soars 191 feet from the floor of its basement to the culmination of the ribs, clasping the hemispherical dome which is forty-nine feet high, with an external diameter of ninety feet, and one-third of the surface of which is perforated to admit light during the day and emit light at night. It is buttressed by pylons forty-five feet in height, and bears above its nine entrances, one of which faces 'Akká, nine selected quotations from the writings of Bahá'u'lláh, as well as the Greatest Name in the center of each of the arches over its doors. It is consecrated exclusively to worship, devoid of all ceremony and ritual, is provided with an auditorium which can seat 1600 people, and is to be supplemented by accessory institutions of social service to be established in its vicinity, such as an orphanage, a hospital, a dispensary for the poor, a home for the incapacitated, a hostel for travelers and a college for the study of arts and sciences. It had already, long before its construction, evoked, and is now increasingly evoking, though its interior ornamentation is as yet unbegun, such interest and comment, in the public press, in technical journals and in magazines, of both the United States and other countries, as to justify the hopes and expectations entertained for it by 'Abdu'l-Bahá. Its model exhibited at Art centers, galleries, state fairs and national expositions—among which may be mentioned the Century of Progress Exhibition, held in Chicago in 1933, where no less than ten thousand people, passing through the Hall of Religions, must have viewed it every day—its replica forming a part of the permanent exhibit of the Museum of Science and Industry in Chicago; its doors now thronged by visitors from far and near, whose number, during the period from June, 1932 to October, 1941 has exceeded 130,000 people, representing almost every country in the world, this great "Silent Teacher" of the Faith of Bahá'u'lláh, it may be confidently asserted, has contributed to the diffusion of the knowledge of His Faith and teachings in a measure which no other single agency, operating within the framework of its Administrative Order, has ever remotely approached.

*"When the foundation of the Mas͟hriqu'l-Ad͟hkár is laid in America,"* 'Abdu'l-Bahá Himself has predicted, *"and that Divine Edifice is completed, a most wonderful and thrilling motion will appear in the world of existence . . . From that point of light the spirit of teaching, spreading the Cause of God and promoting the teachings of God, will permeate to all parts of the world." "Out of this Mas͟hriqu'l-Ad͟hkár,"* He has affirmed in the Tablets of the Divine Plan, *"without doubt, thousands of Mas͟hriqu'l-Ad͟hkárs will be born." "It marks,"* He, furthermore, has written, *"the inception of the Kingdom of God on earth."* And again: *"It is the manifest Standard waving in the center of that great continent." "Thousands of Mas͟hriqu'l-Ad͟hkárs,"* He, when dedicating the grounds of the Temple, declared, *" . . . will be built in the East and in the West, but this, being the first erected in the Occident, has great importance." "This organization of the Mas͟hriqu'l-Ad͟hkár,"* He, referring to that edifice, has moreover stated, *"will be a model for the coming centuries, and will hold the station of the mother."*

"Its inception," the architect of the Temple has himself testified, "was not from man, for, as musicians, artists, poets receive their inspiration from another realm, so the Temple's architect, through all his years of labor, was ever conscious that Bahá'u'lláh was the creator of this building to be erected to His glory." "Into this new design," he, furthermore, has written, " . . . is woven, in symbolic form, the great Bahá'í teaching of unity—the unity of all religions and of all mankind. There are combinations of mathematical lines, symbolizing those of the universe, and in their intricate merging of circle into circle, and circle within circle, we visualize the merging of all the religions into one." And again: "A circle of steps, eighteen in all, will surround the structure on the outside, and lead to the auditorium floor. These eighteen steps represent the eighteen first disciples of the Báb, and the door to which they lead stands for the Báb Himself." "As the essence of the pure original teachings of the historic religions was the same . . . in the Bahá'í Temple is used a composite architecture, expressing the essence in the line of each of the great architectural styles, harmonizing them into one whole."

"It is the first new idea in architecture since the 13th century," declared a distinguished architect, H. Van Buren Magonigle, President of the Architectural League, after gazing upon a plaster model of the Temple on exhibition in the Engineering Societies Building in New York, in June 1920. "The Architect," he, moreover, has stated, "has conceived a Temple of Light in which structure, as usually understood, is to be concealed, visible support eliminated as far as possible, and the whole fabric to take on the airy substance of a dream. It is a lacy envelope enshrining an idea, the idea of light, a shelter of cobweb interposed between earth and sky, struck through and through with light—light which shall partly consume the forms and make of it a thing of faery."

"In the geometric forms of the ornamentation," a writer in the well-known publication "Architectural Record" has written, "covering the columns and surrounding windows and doors of the Temple, one deciphers all the religious symbols of the world. Here are the swastika, the circle, the cross, the triangle, the double triangle or six pointed star (Solomon's seal)—but more than this—the noble symbol of the spiritual orb . . . the five pointed star; the Greek Cross, the Roman cross, and supreme above all, the wonderful nine pointed star, figured in the structure of the Temple itself, and appearing again and again in its ornamentation as significant of the spiritual glory in the world today."

"The greatest creation since the Gothic period," is the testimony of George Grey Barnard, one of the most widely-known sculptors in the United States of America, "and the most beautiful I have ever seen."

"This is a new creation," Prof. Luigi Quaglino, ex-professor of Architecture from Turin declared, after viewing the model, "which will revolutionize architecture in the world, and it is the most beautiful I have ever seen. Without doubt it will have a lasting page in history. It is a revelation from another world."

"Americans," wrote Sherwin Cody, in the magazine section of the

New York Times, of the model of the Temple, when exhibited in the Kevorkian Gallery in New York, "will have to pause long enough to find that an artist has wrought into this building the conception of a Religious League of Nations." And lastly, this tribute paid to the features of, and the ideals embodied in, this Temple—the most sacred House of Worship in the Bahá'í world, whether of the present or of the future—by Dr. Rexford Newcomb, Dean of the College of Fine and Applied Arts at the University of Illinois: "This 'Temple of Light' opens upon the terrain of human experience nine great doorways which beckon men and women of every race and clime, of every faith and conviction, of every condition of freedom or servitude to enter here into a recognition of that kinship and brotherhood without which the modern world will be able to make little further progress . . . The dome, pointed in form, aiming as assuredly as did the aspiring lines of the medieval cathedrals toward higher and better things, achieves not only through its symbolism but also through its structural propriety and sheer loveliness of form, a beauty not matched by any domical structure since the construction of Michelangelo's dome on the Basilica of St. Peter in Rome."

## CHAPTER XXIII

# Attacks on Bahá'í Institutions

The institutions signalizing the rise and establishment of the Administrative Order of the Faith of Bahá'u'lláh did not (as the history of their unfoldment abundantly demonstrates) remain immune against the assaults and persecutions to which the Faith itself, the progenitor of that Order, had, for over seventy years, been subjected, and from which it is still suffering. The emergence of a firmly knit community, advancing the claims of a world religion, with ramifications spread over five continents representing a great variety of races, languages, classes and religious traditions; provided with a literature scattered over the surface of the earth, and expounding in several languages its doctrine; clear-visioned, unafraid, alert and determined to achieve at whatever sacrifice its goal; organically united through the machinery of a divinely appointed Administrative Order; non-sectarian, non-political, faithful to its civil obligations yet supra-national in character; tenacious in its adherence to the laws and ordinances regulating its community life—the emergence of such a community, in a world steeped in prejudice, worshipping false gods, torn by intestine divisions, and blindly clinging to obsolescent doctrines and defective standards, could not but precipitate, sooner or later, crises no less grave, though less spectacular, than the persecutions which, in an earlier age, had raged around the Founders of that community and their early disciples. Assailed by enemies within, who have either rebelled against its God-given authority or wholly renounced their faith, or by adversaries from without, whether political or ecclesiastical, the infant Order identified with this community has, since its inception, and throughout every stage in its evolution, felt severely the impact of the forces which have sought in vain to strangle its budding life or to obscure its purpose.

To these attacks, destined to grow in scope and severity, and to arouse a tumult that will reverberate throughout the world, 'Abdu'l-Bahá Himself had already, at the time the outlines of that Divine order were being delineated by Him in His Will, significantly alluded: *"Erelong shall the clamor of the multitude throughout Africa, throughout America, the cry of the European and of the Turk, the groaning of India and China, be heard from far and near. One and all, they shall arise with all their power to resist His Cause. Then shall the knights of the Lord . . . reinforced by the legions of the Covenant, arise and manifest the truth of the verse: 'Behold the confusion that hath befallen the tribes of the defeated!'"*

Already in more than one country the trustees and elected representatives of this indestructible world-embracing Order have been summoned by civil authorities or ecclesiastical courts, ignorant of its claims, or hostile to its principles or fearful of its rising strength, to defend its cause, or to renounce their allegiance to it, or to curtail the range of its operation. Already an aggressive hand, unmindful of God's avenging wrath, has been stretched out against its sanctuaries and edifices. Already its defenders and champions have, in some countries, been declared heretics, or stigmatized as subverters of law and order, or branded as visionaries, unpatriotic and careless of their civic duties and responsibilities, or peremptorily ordered to suspend their activities and dissolve their institutions.

In the Holy Land, the world seat of this System, where its heart pulsates, where the dust of its Founders reposes, where the processes disclosing its purposes, energizing its life and shaping its destiny all originate, there fell, at the very hour of its inception, the first blow which served to proclaim to high and low alike the solidity of the foundations on which it has been established. The Covenant-breakers, now dwindled to a mere handful, instigated by Mírzá Muḥammad-'Alí, the Arch-rebel, whose dormant hopes had been awakened by 'Abdu'l-Bahá's sudden ascension, and headed by the arrogant Mírzá Badí'u'lláh, seized forcibly the keys of the Tomb of Bahá'u'lláh, expelled its keeper, the brave-souled Abu'l-Qásim-i-Khurásání, and demanded that their chief be recognized by the authorities as the legal custodian of that Shrine. Unadmonished by their abject failure, as witnessed by the firm action of the Palestine authorities, who, after prolonged investigations, instructed the British officer in 'Akká to deliver the keys into the hands of that same keeper, they resorted to other methods in the hope of creating a cleavage in the ranks of the bereaved yet resolute disciples of 'Abdu'l-Bahá and of ultimately undermining the foundations of the institutions His followers were laboring to erect. Through their mischievous misrepresentations of the ideals animating the builders of the Bahá'í Administrative Order; through the maintenance, though not on its original scale, of a subversive correspondence with individuals whose loyalty they hoped they could sap; through deliberate distortions of the truth in their contact with officials and notables whom they could approach; through attempts, made through bribery and intimidation, to purchase a part of the Mansion of Bahá'u'lláh; through efforts directed at preventing the acquisition by the Bahá'í community of certain properties situated in the vicinity of the Tomb of the Báb, and at frustrating the design to consolidate the foundation of some of these properties by transferring their title-deeds to incorporated Bahá'í assemblies, they continued to labor intermittently for several years until the extinction of the life of the Arch-breaker of the Covenant himself virtually sealed their doom.

The evacuation of the Mansion of Bahá'u'lláh by these Covenant-breakers, after their unchallenged occupancy of it since His ascension, a Mansion which, through their gross neglect, had fallen into a sad state of disrepair; its subsequent complete restoration, fulfilling a long cherished desire of 'Abdu'l-Bahá; its illumination through an electric plant installed by an American believer for that purpose; the refurnishing of all its rooms after it had been completely denuded by its former occupants of all the precious relics it contained, with the exception of a single candlestick in the room where Bahá'u'lláh had ascended; the collection within its walls of Bahá'í historic documents, of relics and of over five thousand volumes of Bahá'í literature, in no less than forty languages; the extension to it of the exemption from government taxes, already granted to other Bahá'í institutions and properties in 'Akká and on Mt. Carmel; and finally, its conversion from a private residence to a center of pilgrimage visited by Bahá'ís and non-Bahá'ís alike—these served to further dash the hopes of those who were still desperately striving to extinguish the light of the Covenant of Bahá'u'lláh. Furthermore, the success later achieved in purchasing and safeguarding the area forming the precincts of the resting-place of the Báb on Mt. Carmel, and the transfer of the title-deeds of some of these properties to the legally constituted Palestine Branch of the American Bahá'í National Spiritual Assembly, no less than the circumstances attending the death of the one who had been the prime mover of mischief throughout 'Abdu'l-Bahá's ministry, demonstrated to these enemies the futility of their efforts and the hopelessness of their cause.

Of a more serious nature, and productive of still greater repercussions, was the unlawful seizure by the Shí'ahs of 'Iráq, at about the same time that the keys of the Tomb of Bahá'u'lláh were wrested by the Covenant-breakers from its keeper, of yet another Bahá'í Shrine, the House occupied by Bahá'u'lláh for well nigh the whole period of

His exile in 'Iráq, which had been acquired by Him, and later had been ordained as a center of pilgrimage, and had continued in the unbroken and undisputed possession of His followers ever since His departure from Baghdád. This crisis, originating about a year prior to 'Abdu'l-Bahá's ascension, and precipitated by the measures which, after the change of régime in 'Iráq, had, according to His instructions, been taken for the reconstruction of that House, acquired as it developed a steadily widening measure of publicity. It became the object of the consideration of successive tribunals, first of the local Shí'ah Ja'faríy-yih court in Baghdád, second of the Peace court, then the court of First Instance, then of the court of Appeal in 'Iráq, and finally of the League of Nations, the greatest international body yet come into existence, and empowered to exercise supervision and control over all Mandated Territories. Though as yet unresolved through a combination of causes, religious as well as political, it has already remarkably fulfilled Bahá'u'lláh's own prediction, and will, in its own appointed time, as the means for its solution are providentially created, fulfill the high destiny ordained for it by Him in His Tablets. Long before its seizure by fanatical enemies, who had no conceivable claim to it whatever, He had prophesied that *"it shall be so abased in the days to come as to cause tears to flow from every discerning eye."*

The Spiritual Assembly of the Bahá'ís of Baghdád, deprived of the use of that sacred property through an adverse decision by a majority of the court of Appeal, which had reversed the verdict of the lower court and awarded the property to the Shí'ahs, and aroused by subsequent action of the Shí'ahs, soon after the execution of the judgment of that court, in converting the building into waqf property (pious foundation), designating it "Ḥusayníyyih," with the purpose of consolidating their gain, realized the futility of the three years of negotiations they had been conducting with the civil authorities in Baghdád for the righting of the wrong inflicted upon them. In their capacity as the national representatives of the Bahá'ís of 'Iráq, they, therefore, on September 11, 1928, through the High Commissioner for 'Iráq and in conformity with the provisions of Art. 22 of the Covenant of the League of Nations, approached the League's Permanent Mandates Commission, charged with the supervision of the administration of all Mandated Territories, and presented a petition that was accepted and approved by that body in November, 1928. A memorandum submitted, in connection with that petition, to that same Commission, by the Mandatory Power unequivocally stated that the Shí'ahs had "no conceivable claim whatever" to the House, that the decision of the judge of the Ja'faríyyih court was "obviously wrong," "unjust" and "undoubtedly actuated by religious prejudice," that the subsequent ejectment of the Bahá'ís was "illegal," that the action of the authorities had been "highly irregular," and that the verdict of the Court of Appeal was suspected of not being "uninfluenced by political consideration."

"The Commission," states the Report submitted by it to the Council of the League, and published in the Minutes of the 14th session of the Permanent Mandates Commission, held in Geneva in the fall of 1928, and subsequently translated into Arabic and published in 'Iráq, "draws the Council's attention to the considerations and conclusions suggested to it by an examination of the petition . . . It recommends that the Council should ask the British Government to make representations to the 'Iráq Government with a view to the immediate redress of the denial of justice from which the petitioners have suffered."

The British accredited representative present at the sessions of the Commission, furthermore, stated that "the Mandatory Power had recognized that the Bahá'ís had suffered an injustice," whilst allusion was made, in the course of that session, to the fact that the action of the Shí'ahs constituted a breach of the constitution and the Organic Law of 'Iráq. The Finnish representative, moreover, in his report to the Council, declared that this "injustice must be attributed solely to religious passion," and asked that "the petitioner's wrongs should be redressed."

The Council of the League, on its part, having considered this report as well as the joint observations and conclusions of the Commission, unanimously adopted, on March 4, 1929, a resolution, subsequently translated and published in the newspapers of Baghdád, directing the Mandatory Power "to make representations to the Government of 'Iráq with a view to the immediate redress of the injustice suffered by the Petitioners." It instructed, accordingly, the Secretary General to bring to the notice of the Mandatory Power, as well as to the petitioners concerned, the conclusions arrived at by the Commission, an instruction which was duly transmitted by the British Government through its High Commissioner to the 'Iráq Government.

A letter dated January 12, 1931, written on behalf of the British Foreign Minister, Mr. Arthur Henderson, addressed to the League Secretariat, stated that the conclusions reached by the Council had "received the most careful consideration by the Government of 'Iráq," who had "finally decided to set up a special committee . . . to consider the views expressed by the Bahá'í community in respect of certain houses in Baghdád, and to formulate recommendations for an equitable settlement of this question." That letter, moreover, pointed out that the committee had submitted its report in August, 1930, that it had been accepted by the government, that the Bahá'í community had "accepted in principle" its recommendations, and that the authorities in Baghdád had directed that "detailed plans and estimates shall be prepared with a view to carrying these recommendations into effect during the coming financial year."

No need to dwell on the subsequent history of this momentous case, on the long-drawn out negotiations, the delays and complications that ensued; on the consultations, "over a hundred" in number, in which the king, his ministers and advisers took part; on the expressions of "regret," of "surprise" and of "anxiety" placed on record at successive sessions of the Mandates Commission held in Geneva in 1929, 1930, 1931, 1932 and 1933; on the condemnation by its members of the "spirit of intolerance" animating the Shí'ah community, of the "partiality" of the 'Iráqí courts, of the "weakness" of the civil authorities and of the "religious passion at the bottom of this injustice"; on their testimony to the "extremely conciliatory disposition" of the petitioners, on their "doubt" regarding the adequacy of the proposals, and on their recognition of the "serious" character of the situation that had been created, of the "flagrant denial of justice" which the Bahá'ís had suffered, and of the "moral debt" which the 'Iráq Government had contracted, a debt which, whatever the changes in her status as a nation, it was her bounden duty to discharge.

Nor does it seem necessary to expatiate on the unfortunate consequences of the untimely death of both the British High Commissioner and the 'Iráqí Prime Minister; on the admission of 'Iráq as a member of the League, and the consequent termination of the mandate held by Great Britain; on the tragic and unexpected death of the King himself; on the difficulties raised owing to the existence of a town planning scheme; on the written assurance conveyed to the High Commissioner by the acting Premier in his letter of January, 1932; on the pledge given by the King, prior to his death, in the presence of the foreign minister, in February, 1933, that the House would be expropriated, and the necessary sum would be appropriated in the spring of the ensuing year; on the categorical statement made by that same foreign minister that the Prime Minister had given the necessary assurances that the promise already made by the acting

Premier would be redeemed; or on the positive statements made by that same Foreign Minister and his colleague, the Minister of Finance, when representing their country during the sessions of the League Assembly held in Geneva, that the promise given by their late King would be fully honored.

Suffice it to say that, despite these interminable delays, protests and evasions, and the manifest failure of the Authorities concerned to implement the recommendations made by both the Council of the League and the Permanent Mandates Commission, the publicity achieved for the Faith by this memorable litigation, and the defense of its cause—the cause of truth and justice—by the world's highest tribunal, have been such as to excite the wonder of its friends and to fill with consternation its enemies. Few episodes, if any, since the birth of the Formative Age of the Faith of Bahá'u'lláh, have given rise to repercussions in high places comparable to the effect produced on governments and chancelleries by this violent and unprovoked assault directed by its inveterate enemies against one of its holiest sanctuaries.

*"Grieve not, O House of God,"* Bahá'u'lláh Himself has significantly written, *"if the veil of thy sanctity be rent asunder by the infidels. God hath, in the world of creation, adorned thee with the jewel of His remembrance. Such an ornament no man can, at any time, profane. Towards thee the eyes of thy Lord shall, under all conditions, remain directed." "In the fullness of time,"* He, in another passage, referring to that same House, has prophesied, *"the Lord shall, by the power of truth, exalt it in the eyes of all men. He shall cause it to become the Standard of His Kingdom, the Shrine round which will circle the concourse of the faithful."*

To the bold onslaught made by the breakers of the Covenant of Bahá'u'lláh in their concerted efforts to secure the custodianship of His holy Tomb, to the arbitrary seizure of His holy House in Bag̲hdád by the S̲hí'ah community of 'Iráq, was to be added, a few years later, yet another grievous assault launched by a still more powerful adversary, directed against the very fabric of the Administrative Order as established by two long-flourishing Bahá'í communities of the East, culminating in the virtual disruption of these communities and the seizure of the first Mas̲hriqu'l-Ad̲hkár of the Bahá'í world and of the few accessory institutions already reared about it.

The courage, the fervor and the spiritual vitality evinced by these communities; the highly organized state of their administrative institutions; the facilities provided for the religious education and training of their youth; the conversion of a number of broad-minded Russian citizens, imbued with ideas closely related to the tenets of the Faith; the growing realization of the implications of its principles, with their emphasis on religion, on the sanctity of family life, on the institution of private property, and their repudiation of all discrimination between classes and of the doctrine of the absolute equality of men—these combined to excite the suspicion, and later to arouse the fierce antagonism, of the ruling authorities, and to precipitate one of the gravest crises in the history of the first Bahá'í century.

As the crisis developed and spread to even the outlying centers of both Turkistán and the Caucasus it resulted gradually in the imposition of restrictions limiting the freedom of these communities, in the interrogation and arrest of their elected representatives, in the dissolution of their local Assemblies and their respective committees in Moscow, in 'Ishqábád, in Bákú and in other localities in the above-mentioned provinces and in the suspension of all Bahá'í youth activities. It even led to the closing of Bahá'í schools, kindergartens, libraries and public reading-rooms, to the interception of all communication with foreign Bahá'í centers, to the confiscation of Bahá'í printing presses, books and documents, to the prohibition of all teaching activities, to the abrogation of the Bahá'í constitution, to the abolition of all national and local funds and to the ban placed on the attendance of non-believers at Bahá'í meetings.

In the middle of 1928 the law expropriating religious edifices was applied to the Mashriqu'l-Adhkár of 'Ishqábád. The use of this edifice as a house of worship, however, was continued, under a five-year lease, which was renewed by the local authorities in 1933, for a similar period. In 1938 the situation in both Turkistán and the Caucasus rapidly deteriorated, leading to the imprisonment of over five hundred believers—many of whom died—as well as a number of women, and the confiscation of their property, followed by the exile of several prominent members of these communities to Siberia, the polar forests and other places in the vicinity of the Arctic Ocean, the subsequent deportation of most of the remnants of these communities to Persia, on account of their Persian nationality, and lastly, the complete expropriation of the Temple itself and its conversion into an art gallery.

In Germany, likewise, the rise and establishment of the Administrative Order of the Faith, to whose expansion and consolidation the German believers were distinctively and increasingly contributing, was soon followed by repressive measures, which, though less grievous than the afflictions suffered by the Bahá'ís of Turkistán and the Caucasus, amounted to the virtual cessation, in the years immediately preceding the present conflict, of all organized Bahá'í activity throughout the length and breadth of that land. The public teaching of the Faith, with its unconcealed emphasis on peace and universality, and its repudiation of racialism, was officially forbidden; Bahá'í Assemblies and their committees were dissolved; the holding of Bahá'í conventions was interdicted; the Archives of the National Spiritual Assembly were seized; the summer school was abolished and the publication of all Bahá'í literature was suspended.

In Persia, moreover, apart from sporadic outbreaks of persecution in such places as S͟híráz, Ábádih, Ardibíl, Iṣfahán, and in certain districts of Ád͟hirbáyján and K͟hurásán—outbreaks greatly reduced in number and violence, owing to the marked decline in the fortunes of the erstwhile powerful S͟hí'ah ecclesiastics—the institutions of a newly-established and as yet unconsolidated Administrative Order were subjected by the civil authorities, in both the capital and the provinces, to restrictions designed to circumscribe their scope, to fetter their freedom and undermine their foundations.

The gradual and wholly unexpected emergence from obscurity of a firmly-welded national community, schooled in adversity and unbroken in spirit, with centers established in every province of that country, in spite of the successive waves of inhuman persecution which had, for three quarters of a century, swept over and had all but engulfed it; the determination of its members to diffuse the spirit and principles of their Faith, broadcast its literature, enforce its laws and ordinances, penalize those who would transgress them, maintain a steady intercourse with their fellow-believers in foreign lands, and erect the edifices and institutions of its Administrative Order, could not but arouse the apprehensions and the hostility of those placed in authority, who either misunderstood the aims of that community, or were bent upon stifling its life. The insistence of its members, while obedient in all matters of a purely administrative character to the civil statutes of their country, on adhering to the fundamental spiritual principles, precepts and laws revealed by Bahá'u'lláh, requiring them, among other things, to hold fast to truthfulness, not to dissimulate their faith, observe the ordinances prescribed for marriage and divorce, and suspend all manner of work on the Holy Days ordained by Him, brought them, sooner or later, into conflict with a régime which, owing to its formal recognition of Islám as the state religion of Persia, refused to extend any recognition to those whom the official exponents of that religion had already condemned as heretics.

The closing of all schools belonging to the Bahá'í community in that country, as a direct consequence of the refusal of the representatives of that community to permit official Bahá'í institutions, owned and entirely controlled by them, to transgress the clearly revealed law requiring the suspension of work on Bahá'í Holy Days; the rejection of all Bahá'í marriage certificates and the refusal to register them at government License Bureaus; the ban placed on the printing and circulation of all Bahá'í literature, as well as on its entry into the country; the seizure in various centers of Bahá'í documents, books and relics; the closing, in some of the provinces of the Ḥazíratu'l-Quds, and the confiscation in some localities of their furniture; the prohibition of all Bahá'í demonstrations, conferences and conventions; the strict censorship imposed on, and often the non-delivery of, communications between Bahá'í centers in Persia and between these centers and Bahá'í communities in foreign lands; the withholding of good-record certificates from loyal and law-abiding citizens on the ground of their avowed adherence to the Bahá'í Faith; the dismissal of Government employees, the demotion or discharge of army officers, the arrest, the interrogation, the imprisonment of, and the imposition of fines and other punishments upon, a number of believers who refused either to cast aside the moral obligation of adhering to the spiritual principles of their Faith, or to act in any manner that would conflict with its universal and non-political character—all these may be regarded as the initial attempts made in the country whose soil had already been imbued with the blood of countless Bahá'í martyrs, to resist the rise, and frustrate the struggle for the emancipation, of a nascent Administrative Order, whose very roots have sucked their strength from such heroic sacrifice.

## CHAPTER XXIV

# Emancipation and Recognition of the Faith and Its Institutions

While the initial steps aiming at the erection of the framework of the Administrative Order of the Faith of Bahá'u'lláh were being simultaneously undertaken by His followers in the East and in the West, a fierce attack was launched in an obscure village in Egypt on a handful of believers, who were trying to establish there one of the primary institutions of that Order—an attack which, viewed in the perspective of history, will be acclaimed by future generations as a landmark not only in the Formative Period of the Faith but in the history of the first Bahá'í century. Indeed, the sequel to this assault may be said to have opened a new chapter in the evolution of the Faith itself, an evolution which, carrying it through the successive stages of repression, of emancipation, of recognition as an independent Revelation, and as a state religion, must lead to the establishment of the Bahá'í state and culminate in the emergence of the Bahá'í World Commonwealth.

Originating in a country which can rightly boast of being the acknowledged center of both the Arab and Muslim worlds; precipitated by the action, taken on their own initiative, by the ecclesiastical representatives of the largest communion in Islám; the direct outcome of a series of disturbances instigated by some of the members of that communion designed to suppress the activities of certain followers of the Faith who had held a clerical rank among them, this momentous development in the fortunes of a struggling community has directly contributed, to a considerable degree, to the consolidation and the enhancement of the prestige of the Administrative Order which that community had begun to erect. It will, moreover, as its repercussions are more widely spread to other Islamic countries, and its vast significance is more clearly apprehended by the adherents of both Christianity and Islám, hasten the termination of the period of transition through which the Faith, now in the formative stage of its growth, is passing.

It was in the village of Kawmu'ṣ-Ṣa'áyidih, in the district of Beba, of the province of Beni Suef in Upper Egypt, that, as a result of the religious fanaticism which the formation of a Bahá'í assembly had kindled in the breast of the headman of that village, and of the grave accusations made by him to both the District Police Officer and the Governor of the province—accusations which aroused the Muḥammadans to such a pitch of excitement as to cause them to perpetrate shameful acts against their victims—that action was initiated by the notary of the village, in his capacity as a religious plaintiff authorized by the Ministry of Justice, against three Bahá'í residents of that village, demanding that their Muslim wives be divorced from them on the grounds that their husbands had abandoned Islám after their legal marriage as Muslims.

The Opinion and Judgment of the Appellate religious court of Beba, delivered on May 10, 1925, subsequently sanctioned by the highest ecclesiastical authorities in Cairo and upheld by them as final, printed and circulated by the Muslim authorities themselves, annulled the marriages contracted by the three Bahá'í defendants and condemned the mass heretics for having violated the laws and ordinances of Islám. It even went so far as to make the positive, the startling and indeed the historic assertion that the Faith embraced by these heretics is to be regarded as a distinct religion, wholly independent of the religious systems that have preceded it—an assertion which hitherto the enemies of the Faith, whether in the East or in the West, had either disputed or deliberately ignored.

Having expounded the fundamental tenets and ordinances of Islám, and given a detailed exposition of the Bahá'í teachings, supported by various quotations from the Kitáb-i-Aqdas, from the writings of 'Abdu'l-Bahá and of Mírzá Abu'l-Faḍl, with special reference to certain Bahá'í laws, and demonstrated that the defendants had, in the light of these statements, actually abjured the Faith of Muhammad, his formal verdict declares in the most unequivocal terms: "The Bahá'í Faith is a new religion, entirely independent, with beliefs, principles and laws of its own, which differ from, and are utterly in conflict with, the beliefs, principles and laws of Islám. No Bahá'í, therefore, can be regarded a Muslim or vice-versa, even as no Buddhist, Brahmin, or Christian can be regarded a Muslim or vice-versa." Ordering the dissolution of the contracts of marriage of the parties on trial, and the "separation" of the husbands from their wives, this official and memorable pronouncement concludes with the following words: "If any one of them (husbands) repents, believes in, and acknowledges whatsoever . . . Muḥammad, the Apostle of God . . . has brought from God . . . and returns to the august Faith of Islám . . . and testifies that . . . Muḥammad . . . is the Seal of the Prophets and Messengers, that no religion will succeed His religion, that no law will abrogate His law, that the Qur'án is the last of the Books of God and His last Revelation to His Prophets and His Messengers . . . he shall be accepted and shall be entitled to renew his marriage contract . . . "

This declaration of portentous significance, which was supported by incontrovertible proofs adduced by the avowed enemies of the Faith of Bahá'u'lláh themselves, which was made in a country that aspires to the headship of Islám through the restoration of the Caliphate, and which has received the sanction of the highest ecclesiastical authorities in that country, this official testimony which the leaders of S̲h̲í'ah Islám, in both Persia and 'Iráq, have, through a century, sedulously avoided voicing, and which, once and for all, silences those detractors, including Christian ecclesiastics in the West, who have in the past stigmatized that Faith as a cult, as a Bábí sect and as an offshoot of Islám or represented it as a synthesis of religions—such a declaration was acclaimed by all Bahá'í communities in the East and in the West as the first Charter of the emancipation of the Cause of Bahá'u'lláh from the fetters of Islamic orthodoxy, the first historic step taken, not by its adherents as might have been expected, but by its adversaries on the road leading to its ultimate and world-wide recognition.

Such a verdict, fraught with incalculable possibilities, was immediately recognized as a powerful challenge which the builders of the Administrative Order of the Faith of Bahá'u'lláh were not slow to face and accept. It imposed upon them a sacred obligation which they felt ready to discharge. Designed by its authors to deprive their adversaries of access to Muslim courts, and thereby place them in a perplexing and embarrassing situation, it became a lever which the Egyptian Bahá'í community, followed later by its sister-communities, readily utilized for the purpose of asserting the independence of its Faith and of seeking for it the recognition of its government. Translated into several languages, circulated among Bahá'í communities in East and West, it gradually paved the way for the initiation of negotiations between the elected representatives of these communities and the civil authorities in Egypt, in the Holy Land, in Persia and even in the United States of America, for the purpose of securing the official recognition by these authorities of the Faith as an independent religion.

In Egypt it was the signal for the adoption of a series of measures which have in their cumulative effect greatly facilitated the extension of such a recognition by a government which is still formally associated with the religion of Islám, and which suffers its laws and regulations to be shaped in a great measure by the views and pronouncements of its ecclesiastical leaders. The inflexible determination of the Egyptian believers not to deviate a hair's breadth from the tenets of their Faith, by avoiding all dealings with any Muslim ecclesiastical court in that country and by refusing any ecclesiastical post which might be offered them; the codification and publication of the fundamental laws of the Kitáb-i-Aqdas regarding matters of personal status, such as marriage, divorce, inheritance and burial, and the presentation of these laws to the Egyptian Cabinet; the issuance of marriage and divorce certificates by the Egyptian National Spiritual Assembly; the assumption by that Assembly of all the duties and responsibilities connected with the conduct of Bahá'í marriages and divorces, as well as with the burial of the dead; the observance by all members of that community of the nine Holy Days on which work, as prescribed in the Bahá'í teachings, must be completely suspended; the presentation of a petition addressed by the national elected representatives of that community to the Egyptian Prime Minister, the Minister of the Interior and the Minister of Justice (supported by a similar communication addressed by the American National Spiritual Assembly to the Egyptian Government), enclosing a copy of the judgment of the Court, and of their national Bahá'í constitution and by-laws, requesting them to recognize their Assembly as a body qualified to exercise the functions of an independent court and empowered to apply, in all matters affecting their personal status, the laws and ordinances revealed by the Author of their Faith—these stand out as the initial consequences of a historic pronouncement that must eventually lead to the establishment of that Faith on a basis of absolute equality with its sister religions in that land.

A corollary to this epoch-making declaration, and a direct consequence of the intermittent disturbances instigated in Port Said and Ismá'ílíyyih by a fanatical populace in connection with the burial of some of the members of the Bahá'í community, was the official and no less remarkable fatvá (judgment) issued, at the request of the Ministry of Justice, by the Grand Muftí of Egypt. This, soon after its pronouncement, was published in the Egyptian press and contributed to fortify further the independent status of the Faith. It followed upon the riots which broke out with exceptional fury in Ismá'íllíyyih, when angry crowds surrounded the funeral cortège of Muḥammad Sulaymán, a prominent Bahá'í resident of that town, creating such an uproar that the police had to intervene, and having rescued the body and brought it back to the home of the deceased, they were forced to carry it without escort, at night, to the edge of the desert and inter it in the wilderness.

This judgment was passed as a result of the inquiry addressed in writing, on January 24, 1939, by the Egyptian Ministry of the Interior to the Ministry of Justice, enclosing a copy of the compilation of Bahá'í laws related to matters of personal status published by the Egyptian Bahá'í National Spiritual Assembly, and asking for a pronouncement by the Muftí regarding the petition addressed by that Assembly to the Egyptian Government for the allocation of four plots to serve as cemeteries for the Bahá'í communities of Cairo, Alexandria, Port Said and Ismá'ílíyyih. "We are," wrote the Muftí in his reply of March 11, 1939, to the communication addressed to him by the Ministry of Justice, "in receipt of your letter . . . dated February 21, 1939, with its enclosures . . . inquiring whether or not it would be lawful to bury the Bahá'í dead in Muslim cemeteries. We hereby declare that this Community is not to be regarded as Muslim, as shown by the beliefs which it professes. The perusal of what they term 'The Bahá'í Laws affecting Matters of Personal Status,' accompanying the papers, is deemed sufficient evidence. Whoever among its members had formerly been a Muslim has, by virtue of his belief in the pretensions of this community, renounced Islám, and is regarded as beyond its pale, and is subject to the laws governing apostasy as established in the right Faith of Islám. This community not being Muslim, it would be unlawful to bury its dead in Muslim cemeteries, be they originally Muslims or otherwise . . ."

It was in consequence of this final, this clearly-worded and authoritative sentence by the highest exponent of Islamic Law in Egypt, and after prolonged negotiations, resulting at first in the allocation to the Cairo Bahá'í community of a cemetery plot forming a part of that set aside for free thinkers, residing in that city, that the Egyptian government consented to grant to that community, as well as to the Bahá'ís of Ismá'ílíyyih, two tracts of land to serve as burial grounds for their dead—an act of historic significance which was greatly welcomed by the members of sore-pressed and long-suffering communities, and which has served to demonstrate still further the independent character of their Faith and enlarge the sphere of the jurisdiction of its representative institutions.

It was to the first of these two officially designated Bahá'í cemeteries, following the decision of the Egyptian Bahá'í National Assembly aided by its sister-Assembly in Persia, that the remains of the illustrious Mírzá Abu'l-Faḍl were transferred and accorded a sepulture worthy of his high position, thereby inaugurating, in a befitting manner, the first official Bahá'í institution of its kind established in the East. This achievement was, soon after, enhanced by the exhumation from a Christian cemetery in Cairo of the body of that far-famed mother teacher of the West, Mrs. E. Getsinger, and its interment, through the assistance extended by the American Bahá'í National Assembly and the Department of State in Washington, in a spot in the heart of that cemetery and adjoining the resting-place of that distinguished author and champion of the Faith.

In the Holy Land, where a Bahá'í cemetery had, before these pronouncements, been established during 'Abdu'l-Bahá's ministry, the historic decision to bury the Bahá'í dead facing the Qiblih in 'Akká was taken—a measure whose significance was heightened by the resolution to cease having recourse, as had been previously the case, to any Muḥammadan court in all matters affecting marriage and divorce, and to carry out, in their entirety and without any concealment whatever, the rites prescribed by Bahá'u'lláh for the preparation and burial of the dead. This was soon after followed by the presentation of a formal petition addressed by the representatives of the local Bahá'í community of Haifa, dated May 4, 1929, to the Palestine Authorities, requesting them that, pending the adoption of a uniform civil law of personal status applicable to all residents of the country irrespective of their religious beliefs, the community be officially recognized by them and be granted "full powers to administer its own affairs now enjoyed by other religious communities in Palestine."

The acceptance of this petition—an act of tremendous significance and wholly unprecedented in the history of the Faith in any country—according official recognition by the civil authorities to marriage certificates issued by the representatives of the local community, the validity of which the official representative of the Persian Government in Palestine has tacitly recognized, was followed by a series of decisions exempting from government tax all properties and institutions regarded by the Bahá'í community as holy sites, or dedicated to the Tombs of its Founders at its world center. Moreover, through these decisions, all articles serving as ornaments or furniture for the Bahá'í shrines were exempted from customs duties, and the branches of both the American and Indian Bahá'í National Spiritual Assemblies were enabled to function as "religious societies," in accordance with the laws of the country, and to hold and administer property as agents of these Assemblies.

In Persia, where a far larger community, already numerically superior to the Christian, the Jewish and the Zoroastrian minorities living in that country, had, notwithstanding the traditionally hostile attitude of the civil and ecclesiastical authorities, succeeded in rearing the structure of its administrative institutions, the reaction to so momentous a declaration was such as to inspire its members and induce them to exploit, in the fullest measure possible, the enormous advantages which this wholly unexpected testimonial had conferred upon them. Having survived the fiery ordeals to which the cruel, the arrogant and implacable leaders of an all-powerful priesthood, now grievously humiliated, had subjected it, a triumphant community, just emerging from obscurity, was determined, more than ever before, to press, within the limits prescribed for it by its Founders, its claim to be regarded as an independent religious entity, and to safeguard, by all available means, its integrity, the solidarity of its members and the solidity of its elective institutions. It could no longer, now that its declared adversaries had, in such a country, in such a language, and on so important an issue, made so emphatic and sweeping a pronouncement, and torn asunder the veil that had for so long been drawn over some of the distinguishing verities lying at the core of its doctrine, keep silent or tolerate without any protest the imposition of restrictions calculated to circumscribe its powers, stifle its community life and deny it its right to be placed on a footing of unqualified equality with other religious communities in that land.

Inflexibly resolved to be classified no longer as Muslim, Jew, Christian or Zoroastrian, the members of this community determined, as a first step, to adopt such measures as would vindicate beyond challenge the distinctive position claimed for their religion by its avowed enemies. Mindful of their clear, their sacred and inescapable duty to obey unreservedly, in all matters of a purely administrative character, the laws of their country, but firmly determined to assert and demonstrate, through every legitimate means at their disposal, the independent character of their Faith, they formulated a policy and embarked in undertakings designed to carry them a stage further towards the goal they had set themselves to attain.

The steadfast resolution not to dissemble their faith, whatever the sacrifices it might entail; the uncompromising position that they would not refer any matters affecting their personal status to any Muslim, Christian, Rabbinical or Zoroastrian court; the refusal to affiliate with any organization, or accept any ecclesiastical post associated with any of the recognized religions in their country; the universal observance of the laws prescribed in the Kitáb-i-Aqdas relating to obligatory prayers, fasting, marriage, divorce, inheritance, burial of the dead, and the use of opium and alcoholic beverages; the issue and circulation of certificates of birth, death, marriage and divorce, at the direction and under the seal of recognized Bahá'í Assemblies; the translation into Persian of "The Bahá'í Laws affecting Matters of Personal Status," first published by the Egyptian Bahá'í National Assembly; the cessation of work on all Bahá'í Holy Days; the establishment of Bahá'í cemeteries in the capital as well as in the provinces, designed to provide a common burial ground for all ranks of the faithful, whatever their religious extraction; the insistence that they no longer be registered as Muslim, Christian, Jew or Zoroastrian on identity cards, marriage certificates, passports and other official documents; the emphasis placed on the institution of the Nineteen Day Feast, as established by Bahá'-u'lláh in His Most Holy Book; the imposition of sanctions by Bahá'í elective Assemblies, now assuming the duties and functions of religious courts, on recalcitrant members of the community by denying them the right to vote and of membership in these Assemblies and their committees—all these are to be associated with the first stirrings of a community that had erected the fabric of its Administrative Order, and was now, under the propelling influence of the historic judicial sentence passed in Egypt, intent upon obtaining, not by force but through persuasion, the recognition by the civil authorities of the status to which its ecclesiastical adversaries had so emphatically borne witness.

That its initial attempt should have met with partial success, that it should have aroused at times the suspicion of the ruling authorities, that it should have been grossly misrepresented by its vigilant enemies, is not a matter for surprise. It was successful in certain respects in its negotiations with the civil authorities, as in obtaining the government decree removing all references to religious affiliation in passports issued to Persian subjects, and in the tacit permission granted in certain localities that its members should not fill in the religious columns in certain state documents, but should register with their own Assemblies their marriage, their divorce, their birth and their death certificates, and should conduct their funerals according to their religious rites. In other respects, however, it has been subjected to grave disabilities: its schools, founded, owned and controlled exclusively by itself, were forcibly closed because they refused to remain open on Bahá'í holy days; its members, both men and women, were prosecuted; those who held army or civil service appointments were in some cases dismissed; a ban was placed on the import, on the printing and circulation of its literature; and all Bahá'í public gatherings were proscribed.

To all administrative regulations which the civil authorities have issued from time to time, or will issue in the future in that land, as in all other countries, the Bahá'í community, faithful to its sacred obligations towards its government, and conscious of its civic duties, has yielded, and will continue to yield implicit obedience. Its immediate closing of its schools in Persia is a proof of this. To such orders, however, as are tantamount to a recantation of their faith by its members, or constitute an act of disloyalty to its spiritual, its basic and God-given principles and precepts, it will stubbornly refuse to bow, preferring imprisonment, deportation and all manner of persecution, including death—as already suffered by the twenty thousand martyrs that have laid down their lives in the path of its Founders—rather than follow the dictates of a temporal authority requiring it to renounce its allegiance to its cause.

"If you cut us in pieces, men, women and children alike, in the entire district of Ábádih," was the memorable message sent by the fearless descendants of some of those martyrs in that turbulent center to the Governor of Fárs, who had intended to coerce them into declaring themselves as Muslims, "we will never submit to your wishes"—a message which, as soon as it was delivered to that defiant governor, induced him to desist from pressing the matter any further.

In the United States of America, the Bahá'í community, having already set an inspiring example, by erecting and perfecting the machinery of its Administrative Order, was alive to the far-reaching implications of the sentence passed by the Muslim court in Egypt, and to the significance of the reaction it had produced in the Holy Land, and was stimulated by the courageous persistence demonstrated by its sister-community in Persia. It determined to supplement its notable achievements with further acts designed to throw into sharper relief the status achieved by the Faith of Bahá'u'lláh in the North American continent. It was numerically smaller than the community of the Persian believers. Owing to the multiplicity of laws governing the states within the Union, it was faced, in matters affecting the personal status of its members, with a situation radically different from that confronting the believers in the East, and much more complex. But conscious of its responsibility to lend, once again, a powerful impetus to the unfoldment of a divinely appointed Order, it boldly undertook to initiate such measures as would accentuate the independent character of a Revelation it had already so nobly championed.

The recognition of its National Spiritual Assembly by the Federal authorities as a religious body entitled to hold as trustees properties dedicated to the interests of the Faith; the establishment of Bahá'í endowments and the exemption obtained for them from the civil authorities as properties owned by, and administered solely for the benefit of, a purely religious community, were now to be supplemented by decisions and measures designed to give further prominence to the nature of the ties uniting its members. The special stress laid on some of the fundamental laws contained in the Kitáb-i-Aqdas regarding daily obligatory prayers; the observance of the fast, the consent of the parents as a prerequisite of marriage; the one-year separation between husband and wife as an indispensable condition of divorce; abstinence from all alcoholic drinks; the emphasis placed on the institution of the Nineteen Day Feast as ordained by Bahá'u'lláh in that same Book; the discontinuation of membership in, and affiliation with, all ecclesiastical organizations, and the refusal to accept any ecclesiastical post—these have served to forcibly underline the distinctive character of the Bahá'í Fellowship, and to dissociate it, in the eyes of the public, from the rituals, the ceremonials and man-made institutions identified with the religious systems of the past.

Of particular and historic importance has been the application made by the Spiritual Assembly of the Bahá'ís of Chicago—the first center established in the North American continent, the first to be incorporated among its sister-Assemblies and the first to take the initiative in paving the way for the erection of a Bahá'í Temple in the West—to the civil authorities in the state of Illinois for civil recognition of the right to conduct legal marriages in accordance with the ordinances of the Kitáb-i-Aqdas, and to file marriage certificates that have previously received the official sanction of that Assembly. The acceptance of this petition by the authorities, necessitating an amendment of the by-laws of all local Assemblies to enable them to conduct Bahá'í legal marriages, and empowering the Chairman or secretary of the Chicago Assembly to represent that body in the conduct of all Bahá'í marriages; the issuance, on September 22, 1939, of the first Bahá'í Marriage License by the State of Illinois, authorizing the aforementioned Assembly to solemnize Bahá'í marriages and issue Bahá'í marriage certificates; the successful measures taken subsequently by Assemblies in other states of the Union, such as New York, New Jersey, Wisconsin and Ohio, to procure for themselves similar privileges, have, moreover, contributed their share in giving added prominence to the independent religious status of the Faith. To these must be added a similar and no less significant recognition extended, since the outbreak of the present conflict, by the United States War Department—as evidenced by the communication addressed to the American Bahá'í National Spiritual Assembly by the Quartermaster General of that Department, on August 14, 1942—approving the use of the symbol of the Greatest Name on stones marking the graves of Bahá'ís killed in the war and buried in military or private cemeteries, distinguishing thereby these graves from those bearing the Latin Cross or the Star of David assigned to those belonging to the Christian and Jewish Faiths respectively.

Nor should mention be omitted of the equally successful application made by the American Bahá'í National Spiritual Assembly to the Office of Price Administration in Washington, D. C., asking that the chairmen and secretaries of Bahá'í local Assemblies should, in their capacity as officers conducting religious meetings, and authorized, in certain states, to perform marriage services, be eligible for preferred mileage under the provisions of the Preferred Mileage Section of the Gasoline Regulations, for the purpose of meeting the religious needs of the localities they serve.

Nor have the Bahá'í communities in other countries such as India, 'Iráq, Great Britain and Australia, been slow to either appreciate the advantages derived from the publication of this historic verdict, or to exploit, each according to its capacity and within the limits imposed upon it by prevailing circumstances, the opportunities afforded by such public testimonial for a further demonstration on their part of the independent character of the Faith whose administrative structure they had already erected. Through the enforcement, to whatever extent deemed practicable, of the laws ordained in their Most Holy Book; through the severance of all ties of affiliation with, and membership in, ecclesiastical institutions of whatever denomination; through the formulation of a policy initiated for the sole purpose of giving further publicity to this mighty issue, marking a great turning-point in the evolution of the Faith, and of facilitating its ultimate settlement, these communities, and indeed all organized Bahá'í bodies, whether in the East or in the West, however isolated their position or immature their state of development, have, conscious of their solidarity and well aware of the glorious prospects opening before them, arisen to proclaim with one voice the independent character of the religion of Bahá'u'lláh and to pave the way for its emancipation from whatever fetters, be they ecclesiastical or otherwise, might hinder or delay its ultimate and world-wide recognition.

To the status already achieved by their Faith, largely through their own unaided efforts and accomplishments, tributes have been paid by observers in various walks of life, whose testimony they welcome and regard as added incentive to action in their steep and laborious ascent towards the heights which they must eventually capture.

"Palestine," is the testimony of Prof. Norman Bentwitch, a former Attorney-General of the Palestine Government, "may indeed be now regarded as the land not of three but of four Faiths, because the Bahá'í creed, which has its center of faith and pilgrimage in 'Akká and Haifa, is attaining to the character of a world religion. So far as its influence goes in the land, it is a factor making for international and inter-religious understanding." "In 1920," is the declaration made in his testament by the distinguished Swiss scientist and psychiatrist, Dr. Auguste Forel, "I learned at Karlsruhe of the supra-confessional world religion of the Bahá'ís, founded in the Orient seventy years ago by a Persian, Bahá'u'lláh. This is the real religion of 'Social Welfare' without dogmas or priests, binding together all men of this small terrestrial globe of ours. I have become a Bahá'í. May this religion live and prosper for the good of humanity! This is my most ardent desire." "There is bound to be a world state, a universal language, and a universal religion," he, moreover has stated, "The Bahá'í Movement for the oneness of mankind is, in my estimation, the greatest movement today working for universal peace and brotherhood." "A religion," is yet another testimony, from the pen of the late Queen Marie of Rumania, "which links all creeds . . . a religion based upon the inner spirit of God . . . It teaches that all hatreds, intrigues, suspicions, evil words, all aggressive patriotism even, are outside the one essential law of God, and that special beliefs are but surface things whereas the heart that beats with Divine love knows no tribe nor race."

## CHAPTER XXV

# International Expansion of Teaching Activities

While the fabric of the Administrative Order of the Faith of Bahá'u'lláh gradually arose, and while through the influence of unforeseen forces the independence of the Faith was more and more definitely acknowledged by its enemies and demonstrated by its friends, another development, no less pregnant with consequences, was at the same time being set in motion. The purpose of this was to extend the borders of the Faith, increasing the number of its declared supporters and of its administrative centers, and to give a new and ever growing impetus to the enriching, the expanding, the diversifying of its literature, and to the task of disseminating it farther and farther afield. Experience indeed proved that the very pattern of the Administrative Order, apart from other distinctive features, definitely encouraged efficiency and expedition in this work of teaching, and its builders found their zeal continually quickened and their missionary ardor heightened as the Faith moved forward to an ever fuller emancipation.

Nor were they unmindful of the exhortations, the appeals and the promises of the Founders of their Faith, Who, for three quarters of a century, had, each in His own way and within the limits circumscribing His activities, labored so heroically to noise abroad the fame of the Cause Whose destiny an almighty Providence had commissioned them to shape.

The Herald of their Faith had commanded the sovereigns of the earth themselves to arise and teach His Cause, writing in the Qayyúmu'l-Asmá': *"O concourse of kings! Deliver with truth and in all haste the verses sent down by Us to the peoples of Turkey and of India, and beyond them . . . to lands in both the East and the West." "Issue forth from your cities, O peoples of the West,"* He, in that same Book, had moreover written, *"to aid God." "We behold you from Our Most Glorious Horizon,"* Bahá'u'lláh had thus addressed His followers in His Kitáb-i-Aqdas, *"and will assist whosoever will arise to aid My Cause with the hosts of the Concourse on high, and a cohort of the angels, who are nigh unto Me." " . . . Teach ye the Cause of God, O people of Bahá!"* He, furthermore, had written, *"for God hath prescribed unto every one the duty of proclaiming His message, and regardeth it as the most meritorious of all deeds."* *"Should a man all alone,"* He had clearly affirmed, *"arise in the name of Bahá and put on the armor of His love, him will the Almighty cause to be victorious, though the forces of earth and heaven be arrayed against him."* *"Should any one arise for the triumph of Our Cause,"* He moreover had declared, *"him will God render victorious though tens of thousands of enemies be leagued against him."* And again: *"Center your energies in the propagation of the Faith of God. Whoso is worthy of so high a calling, let him arise and promote it. Whoso is unable, it is his duty to appoint him who will, in his stead, proclaim this Revelation . . . "* *"They that have forsaken their country,"* is His own promise, *"for the purpose of teaching Our Cause—these shall the Faithful Spirit strengthen through its power . . . Such a service is indeed the prince of all goodly deeds, and the ornament of every goodly act."* *"In these days,"* 'Abdu'l-Bahá had written in His Will, *"the most important of all things is the guidance of the nations and peoples of the world. Teaching the Cause is of the utmost importance, for it is the head corner-stone of the foundation itself."* *"The disciples of Christ,"* He had declared in that same Document, *"forgot themselves and all earthly things, forsook all their cares and belongings, purged themselves of self and passion, and, with absolute detachment, scattered far and wide, and engaged in guiding aright the peoples of the world, till at last they made the world another world, illumined the earth, and to their last hour proved self-sacrificing in the path of that Beloved One of God. Finally, in various lands they suffered martyrdom. Let men of action follow in their footsteps."* *"When the hour cometh,"* He had solemnly stated in that same Will, *"that this wronged and broken-winged bird will have taken its flight unto the celestial concourse . . . it is incumbent upon . . . the friends and loved ones, one and all, to bestir themselves and arise, with heart and soul, and in one accord . . . to teach His Cause and promote His Faith. It behoveth them not to rest for a moment . . . They must disperse themselves in every land . . . and travel throughout all regions. Bestirred, without rest, and steadfast to the end, they must raise in every land the cry of Yá Bahá'u'l-Abhá* (O Thou the Glory of Glories) . . . *that throughout the East and the West a vast concourse may gather under the shadow of the Word of God, that the sweet savors of holiness may be wafted, that men's faces may be illumined, that their hearts may be filled with the Divine Spirit and their souls become heavenly."*

Obedient to these repeated injunctions, mindful of these glowing promises, conscious of the sublimity of their calling, spurred on by the example which 'Abdu'l-Bahá Himself had set, undismayed by His sudden removal from their midst, undaunted by the attacks launched by their adversaries from within and from without, His followers in both the East and in the West arose, in the full strength of their solidarity, to promote, more vigorously than ever before, the international expansion of their Faith, an expansion which was now to assume such proportions as to deserve to be recognized as one of the most significant developments in the history of the first Bahá'í century.

Launched in every continent of the globe, at first intermittent, haphazard, and unorganized, and later, as a result of the emergence of a slowly developing Administrative Order, systematically conducted, centrally directed and efficiently prosecuted, the teaching enterprises which were undertaken by the followers of Bahá'u'lláh in many lands, but conspicuously in America, and which were pursued by members of all ages and of both sexes, by neophytes and by veterans, by itinerant teachers and by settlers, constitute, by virtue of their range and the blessings which have flowed from them, a shining episode that yields place to none except those associated with the exploits which have immortalized the early years of the primitive age of the Bahá'í Dispensation.

The light of the Faith which during the nine years of the Bábí Dispensation had irradiated Persia, and been reflected on the adjoining territory of 'Iráq; which in the course of Bahá'u'lláh's thirty-nine-year ministry had shed its splendor upon India, Egypt, Turkey, the Caucasus, Turkistán, the Súdán, Palestine, Syria, Lebanon and Burma, and which had subsequently, through the impulse of a divinely-instituted Covenant, traveled to the United States of America, Canada, France, Great Britain, Germany, Austria, Russia, Italy, Holland, Hungary, Switzerland, Arabia, Tunisia, China, Japan, the Hawaiian Islands, South Africa, Brazil and Australia, was now to be carried to, and illuminate, ere the termination of the first Bahá'í century, no less than thirty-four independent nations, as well as several dependencies situated in the American, the Asiatic and African continents, in the Persian Gulf, and in the Atlantic and the Pacific oceans. In Norway, in Sweden, in Denmark, in Belgium, in Finland, in Ireland, in Poland, in Czechoslovakia, in Rumania, in Yugoslavia, in Bulgaria, in Albania, in Afghanistan, in Abyssinia, in New Zealand and in nineteen Latin American Republics ensigns of the Revelation of Bahá'u'lláh have been raised since 'Abdu'l-Bahá's passing, and the structural basis of the Administrative Order of His Faith, in many of them, already established. In several dependencies, moreover, in both the East and the

West, including Alaska, Iceland, Jamaica, Porto Rico, the island of Solano in the Philippines, Java, Tasmania, the islands of Baḥrayn and of Tahiti, Baluchistan, South Rhodesia and the Belgian Congo, the bearers of the new born Gospel have established their residence, and are bending every effort to lay an impregnable basis for its institutions.

Through lectures and conferences, through the press and radio, through the organization of study classes and fire-side gatherings, through participation in the activities of societies, institutes and clubs animated by ideals akin to the principles of the Faith, through the dissemination of Bahá'í literature, through various exhibits, through the establishment of teacher training classes, through contact with statesmen, scholars, publicists, philanthropists and other leaders of public thought—most of which have been carried out through the resourcefulness of the members of the American Bahá'í community, who have assumed direct responsibility for the spiritual conquest of the vast majority of these countries and dependencies—above all through the inflexible resolution and unswerving fidelity of pioneers who, whether as visiting teachers or as residents, have participated in these crusades, have these signal victories been achieved during the closing decades of the first Bahá'í century.

Nor should reference be omitted to the international teaching activities of the western followers of the Faith of Bahá'u'lláh, and particularly the members of the stalwart American Bahá'í community, who, seizing every opportunity that presented itself to them, have either through example, precept or the circulation of literature carried the Faith to virgin fields, scattering the seeds which must eventually germinate and yield a harvest as notable as those already garnered in the aforementioned countries. Through such efforts as these the breezes of God's vitalizing Revelation have been blown upon the uttermost corners of the earth, bearing the germ of a new spiritual life to such distant climes and inhospitable regions as Lapland; the Island of Spitzbergen, the northernmost settlement in the world; Hammerfest, in Norway, and Magellanes, in the extremity of Chile—the most northerly and southerly cities of the globe respectively; Pago Pago and Fiji, in the Pacific Ocean; Chichen Itza, in the province of Yucatan; the Bahama Islands, Trinidad and Barbados in the West Indies; the Island of Bali and British North Borneo in the East Indies; Patagonia; British Guiana; Seychelles Islands; New Guinea and Ceylon.

Nor can we fail to notice the special endeavors that have been exerted by individuals as well as Assemblies for the purpose of establishing contact with minority groups and races in various parts of the world, such as the Jews and Negroes in the United States of America, the Eskimos in Alaska, the Patagonian Indians in Argentina, the Mexican Indians in Mexico, the Inca Indians in Peru, the Cherokee Indians in North Carolina, the Oneida Indians in Wisconsin, the Mayans in Yucatan, the Lapps in Northern Scandinavia, and the Maoris in Rotorua, New Zealand.

Of special and valuable assistance has been the institution of an international Bahá'í Bureau in Geneva, a center designed primarily to facilitate the expansion of the teaching activities of the Faith in the European continent, which, as an auxiliary to the world administrative center in the Holy Land, has maintained contact with Bahá'í communities in the East and in the West. Serving as a bureau of information on the Faith, as well as a distributing center for its literature, it has, through its free reading room and lending library, through the hospitality extended to itinerant teachers and visiting believers, and through its contact with various societies, contributed, in no small measure, to the consolidation of the teaching enterprises undertaken by individuals as well as Bahá'í National Assemblies.

Through these teaching activities, some initiated by individual believers, others conducted through plans launched by organized Assemblies, the Faith of Bahá'u'lláh which, in His lifetime, had included within its ranks Persians, Arabs, Turks, Russians, Kurds, Indians, Burmese and Negroes, and was later, in the days of 'Abdu'l-Bahá, reinforced by the inclusion of American, British, German, French, Italian, Japanese, Chinese, and Armenian converts, could now boast of having enrolled amongst its avowed supporters representatives of such widely dispersed ethnic groups and nationalities as Hungarians, Netherlanders, Irishmen, Scandinavians, Sudanese, Czechs, Bulgarians, Finns, Ethiopians, Albanians, Poles, Eskimos, American Indians, Yugoslavians, Latin Americans and Maoris.

So notable an enlargement of the limits of the Faith, so striking an increase in the diversity of the elements included within its pale, was accompanied by an enormous extension in the volume and the circulation of its literature, an extension that sharply contrasted with those initial measures undertaken for the publication of the few editions of Bahá'u'lláh's writing issued during the concluding years of His ministry. The range of Bahá'í literature, confined during half a century, in the days of the Báb and of Bahá'u'lláh, to the two languages in which their teachings were originally revealed, and subsequently extended, in the lifetime of 'Abdu'l-Bahá, to include editions published in the English, the French, the German, the Turkish, the Russian and Burmese languages, was steadily enlarged after His passing, through a vast multiplication in the number of books, treatises, pamphlets and leaflets, printed and circulated in no less than twenty-nine additional languages. In Spanish and in Portuguese; in the three Scandinavian languages, in Finnish and in Icelandic; in Dutch, Italian, Czech, Polish, Hungarian, Rumanian, Serbian, Bulgarian, Greek and Albanian; in Hebrew and in Esperanto, in Armenian, in Kurdish and in Amharic; in Chinese and in Japanese; as well as in five Indian languages, namely Urdu, Gujrati, Bengali, Hindi, and Sindhi, books, mostly through the initiative of individual Bahá'ís, and partly through the intermediary of Bahá'í assemblies, were published, widely distributed, and placed in private as well as public libraries in both the East and the West. The literature of the Faith, moreover, is being translated at present into Latvian, Lithuanian, Ukrainian, Tamil, Mahratti, Pushtoo, Telegu, Kinarese, Singhalese, Malyalan, Oriya, Punjabi and Rajasthani.

No less remarkable has been the range of the literature produced and placed at the disposal of the general public in every continent of the globe, and carried by resolute and indefatigable pioneers to the furthermost ends of the earth, an enterprise in which the members of the American Bahá'í community have again distinguished themselves. The publication of an English edition comprising selected passages from the more important and hitherto untranslated writings of Bahá'u'lláh, as well as of an English version of His "Epistle to the Son of the Wolf," and of a compilation, in the same language, of Prayers and Meditations revealed by His pen; the translation and publication of His "Hidden Words" in eight, of His "Kitáb-i-Íqán" in seven, and of 'Abdu'l-Bahá's "Some Answered Questions" in six, languages; the compilation of the third volume of 'Abdu'l-Bahá's Tablets translated into English; the publication of books and treatises related to the principles of Bahá'í belief and to the origin and development of the Administrative Order of the Faith; of an English translation of the Narrative of the early days of the Bahá'í Revelation, written by the chronicler and poet, Nabíl-i-Zarandí, subsequently published in Arabic and translated into German and Esperanto; of commentaries and of expositions of the Bahá'í teachings, of administrative institutions and of kindred subjects, such as world federation, race unity and comparative religion by western authors and by former ministers of the Church—all these attest the diversified character of Bahá'í publications, so closely paralleled by their extensive dissemination over the surface of the globe. Moreover, the printing of documents related to the laws of the Kitáb-i-Aqdas, of books and pamphlets dealing with Biblical prophecies, of revised editions of some of the writings of Bahá'u'lláh, of 'Abdu'l-Bahá and of several Bahá'í authors, of guides and study outlines for a wide variety of Bahá'í books and subjects, of lessons in Bahá'í Administration, of indexes to Bahá'í books and periodicals, of anniversary cards and of calendars, of poems, songs, plays and pageants, of study outlines and a prayer-book for the training of Bahá'í children, and of news letters, bulletins and periodicals issued in English, Persian, German, Esperanto, Arabic, French, Urdu, Burmese and Portuguese has contributed to swell the output and increase the diversity of Bahá'í publications.

Of particular value and significance has been the production, over a period of many years, of successive volumes of biennial international record of Bahá'í activity, profusely illustrated, fully documented, and comprising among other things a statement on the aims and purposes of the Faith and its Administrative Order, selections from its scriptures, a survey of its activities, a list of its centers in five continents, a bibliography of its literature, tributes paid to its ideals and achievements by prominent men and women in East and West, and articles dealing with its relation to present-day problems.

Nor would any survey of the Bahá'í literature produced during the concluding decades of the first Bahá'í century be complete without special reference being made to the publication of, and the far-reaching influence exerted by, that splendid, authoritative and comprehensive introduction to Bahá'í history and teachings, penned by that pure-hearted and immortal promoter of the Faith, J. E. Esslemont, which has already been printed in no less than thirty-seven languages, and is being translated into thirteen additional languages, whose English version has already run into tens of thousands, which has been reprinted no less than nine times in the United States of America, whose Esperanto, Japanese and English versions have been transcribed into Braille, and to which royalty has paid its tribute, characterizing it as "a glorious book of love and goodness, strength and beauty," commending it to all, and affirming that "no man could fail to be better because of this Book."

Deserving special mention, moreover, is the establishment by the British National Spiritual Assembly of a Publishing Trust, registered as "The Bahá'í Publishing Co." and acting as a publisher and wholesale distributor of Bahá'í literature throughout the British Isles; the compilation by various Bahá'í Assemblies throughout the East of no less than forty volumes in manuscript of the authenticated and unpublished writings of the Báb, of Bahá'u'lláh and of 'Abdu'l-Bahá; the translation into English of the Appendix to the Kitáb-i-Aqdas, entitled "Questions and Answers," as well as the publication in Arabic and Persian by the Egyptian and Indian Bahá'í National Spiritual Assemblies respectively of the Outline of Bahá'í Laws on Matters of Personal Status, and of a brief outline by the latter Assembly of the laws relating to the burial of the dead; and the translation of a pamphlet into Maori undertaken by a Maori Bahá'í in New Zealand. Reference should also be made to the collection and publication by the Spiritual Assembly of the Bahá'ís of Tihrán of a considerable number of the addresses delivered by 'Abdu'l-Bahá in the course of His Western tours; to the preparation of a detailed history of the Faith in Persian; to the printing of Bahá'í certificates of marriage and divorce, in both Persian and Arabic, by a number of National Spiritual Assemblies in the East; to the issuance of birth and death certificates by the Persian Bahá'í National Spiritual Assembly; to the preparation of forms of bequest available to believers wishing to make a legacy to the Faith; to the compilation of a considerable number of the unpublished Tablets of 'Abdu'l-Bahá by the American Bahá'í National Spiritual Assembly; to the translation into Esperanto, undertaken by the daughter of the famous Zamenhof, herself a convert to the Faith, of several Bahá'í books, including some of the more important writings of Bahá'u'lláh and of 'Abdu'l-Bahá; to the translation of a Bahá'í booklet into Serbian by Prof. Bogdan Popovitch, one of the most eminent scholars attached to the University of Belgrade, and to the offer spontaneously made by Princess Ileana of Rumania (now Arch-Duchess Anton of Austria) to render into her own native language a Bahá'í pamphlet written in English, and subsequently distributed in her native country.

The progress made in connection with the transcription of the Bahá'í writings into Braille, should also be noted—a transcription which already includes such works as the English versions of the "Kitáb-i-Íqán," of the "Hidden Words," of the "Seven Valleys," of the "Ishráqát," of the "Súriy-i-Haykal," of the "Words of Wisdom," of the "Prayers and Meditations of Bahá'u'lláh," of 'Abdu'l-Bahá's "Some Answered Questions," of the "Promulgation of Universal Peace," of the "Wisdom of 'Abdu'l-Bahá," of "The Goal of a New World Order," as well as of the English (two editions), the Esperanto and the Japanese versions of "Bahá'u'lláh and the New Era" and of pamphlets written in English, in French and in Esperanto.

Nor have those who have been primarily responsible for the enrichment of the literature of the Faith and its translation into so many languages, been slow to disseminate it, by every means in their power, in their daily intercourse with individuals as well as in their official contacts with organizations whom they have been seeking to acquaint with the aims and principles of their Faith. The energy, the vigilance, the steadfastness displayed by these heralds of the Faith of Bahá'u'lláh and their elected representatives, under whose auspices the circulation of Bahá'í literature has, of late years, assumed tremendous dimensions, merit the highest praise. From the reports prepared and circulated by the chief agencies entrusted with the task of the publication and distribution of this literature in the United States and Canada the remarkable facts emerge that, within the space of the eleven months ending February 28, 1943, over 19,000 books, 100,000 pamphlets, 3,000 study outlines, 4,000 sets of selected writings, and 1800 anniversary and Temple cards and folders had been either sold or distributed; that, in the course of two years, 376,000 pamphlets, outlining the character and purpose of the House of Worship, erected in the United States of America, had been printed; that over 300,000 pieces of literature had been distributed at the two World Fairs held in San Francisco and New York; that, in a period of twelve months, 1089 books had been donated to various libraries, and that, through the National Contacts Committee, during one year, more than 2,300 letters, with over 4,500 pamphlets, had reached authors, radio speakers, and representatives of the Jewish and Negro minorities, as well as various organizations interested in international affairs.

In the presentation of this vast literature to men of eminence and rank the elected representatives, as well as the traveling teachers, of the American Bahá'í community, aided by Assemblies in other lands, have, likewise, exhibited an energy and determination as laudable as the efforts exerted for its production. To the King of England, to Queen Marie of Rumania, to President Franklin D. Roosevelt, to the Emperor of Japan, to the late President von Hindenburg, to the King of Denmark, to the Queen of Sweden, to King Ferdinand of Bulgaria, to the Emperor of Abyssinia, to the King of Egypt, to the late King Feisal of 'Iráq, to King Zog of Albania, to the late President Masaryk of Czechoslovakia, to the Presidents of Mexico, of Honduras, of Panama, of El-Salvador, of Guatemala, and of Porto Rico, to General Chiang Kai-shek, to the Ex-Khedive of Egypt, to the Crown Prince of Sweden, to the Duke of Windsor, to the Duchess of Kent, to the Arch-Duchess Anton of Austria, to Princess Olga of Yugoslavia, to Princess Kadria of Egypt, to Princess Estelle Bernadotte of Wisborg, to Mahatma Gandhi, to several ruling princes of India and to the Prime Ministers of all the states of the Australian Commonwealth—to these, as well as to other personages of lesser rank, Bahá'í literature, touching various aspects of the Faith, has been presented, to some personally, to others through suitable intermediaries, either by individual believers or by the elected representatives of Bahá'í communities.

Nor have these individual teachers and Assemblies been neglectful of their duty to place this literature at the disposal of the public in state, university and public libraries, thereby extending the opportunity to the great mass of the reading public of familiarizing itself with the history and precepts of the Revelation of Bahá'u'lláh. A mere enumeration of a number of the more important of these libraries would suffice to reveal the scope of these activities extending over five continents: the British Museum in London, the Bodleian Library at Oxford, the Library of Congress in Washington, the Peace Palace Library at the Hague, the Nobel Peace Foundation and Nansen Foundation Libraries at Oslo, the Royal Library in Copenhagen, the League of Nations Library in Geneva, the Hoover Peace Library, the Amsterdam University Library, the Library of Parliament in Ottawa, the Allahabad University Library, the Aligarch University Library, the University of Madras Library, the Shantineketan International University Library in Bolepur, the 'Uthmáníyyih University Library in Hyderabad, the Imperial Library in Calcutta, the Jamia Milli Library in Delhi, the Mysore University Library, the Bernard Library in Rangoon, the Jerabia Wadia Library in Poona, the Lahore Public Library, the Lucknow and Delhi University Libraries, the Johannesburg Public Library, the Rio de Janeiro Circulating libraries, the Manila National Library, the Hong Kong University Library, the Reykjavik public libraries, the Carnegie Library in the Seychelles Islands, the Cuban National Library, the San Juan Public Library, the Ciudad Trujillo University Library, the University and Carnegie Public libraries in Porto Rico, the Library of Parliament in Canberra, the Wellington Parliamentary Library. In all these, as well as in all the chief libraries of Australia and New Zealand, nine libraries in Mexico, several libraries in Mukden, Manchukuo, and more than a thousand public libraries, a hundred service libraries and two hundred university and college libraries, including Indian colleges, in the United States and Canada, authoritative books on the Faith of Bahá'u'lláh have been placed.

State prisons and, since the outbreak of the war, army libraries have been included in the comprehensive scheme which the American Bahá'í community has, through a special committee, devised for the diffusion of the literature of the Faith. The interests of the blind, too, have not been neglected by that alert and enterprising community, as is shown by the placing of Bahá'í books, transcribed by its members in Braille, in thirty libraries and institutes, in eighteen states of the United States of America, in Honolulu (Hawaii), in Regina (Saskatchewan), and in the Tokyo and Geneva Libraries for the Blind, as well as in a large number of circulating libraries connected with public libraries in various large cities of the North American continent.

Nor can I dismiss this subject without singling out for special reference her who, not only through her preponderating share in initiating measures for the translation and dissemination of Bahá'í literature, but above all through her prodigious and indeed unique exertions in the international teaching field, has covered herself with a glory that has not only eclipsed the achievements of the teachers of the Faith among her contemporaries the globe around, but has outshone the feats accomplished by any of its propagators in the course of an entire century. To Martha Root, that archetype of Bahá'í itinerant teachers and the foremost Hand raised by Bahá'u'lláh since 'Abdu'l-Bahá's passing, must be awarded, if her manifold services and the supreme act of her life are to be correctly appraised, the title of Leading Ambassadress of His Faith and Pride of Bahá'í teachers, whether men or women, in both the East and the West.

The first to arise, in the very year the Tablets of the Divine Plan were unveiled in the United States of America, in response to the epoch-making summons voiced in them by 'Abdu'l-Bahá; embarking, with unswerving resolve and a spirit of sublime detachment, on her world journeys, covering an almost uninterrupted period of twenty years and carrying her four times round the globe, in the course of which she traveled four times to China and Japan and three times to India, visited every important city in South America, transmitted the message of the New Day to kings, queens, princes and princesses, presidents of republics, ministers and statesmen, publicists, professors, clergymen and poets, as well as a vast number of people in various walks of life, and contacted, both officially and informally, religious congresses, peace societies, Esperanto associations, socialist congresses, Theosophical societies, women's clubs and other kindred organizations, this indomitable soul has, by virtue of the character of her exertions and the quality of the victories she has won, established a record that constitutes the nearest approach to the example set by 'Abdu'l-Bahá

Himself to His disciples in the course of His journeys throughout the West.

Her eight successive audiences with Queen Marie of Rumania, the first of which took place in January, 1926 in Controceni Palace in Bucharest, the second in 1927 in Pelisor Palace in Sinaia, followed by a visit in January of the ensuing year to her Majesty and her daughter Princess Ileana, at the royal palace in Belgrade, where they were staying as guests of the King and Queen of Yugoslavia, and later, in October, 1929, at the Queen's summer palace "Tehna Yuva," at Balcic, on the Black Sea, and again, in August, 1932 and February, 1933, at the home of Princess Ileana (now Arch-Duchess Anton of Austria) at Mödling, near Vienna, followed a year later, in February, by another audience at Controceni Palace, and lastly, in February, 1936, in that same palace—these audiences stand out, by reason of the profound influence exerted by the visitor on her royal hostess, as witnessed by the successive encomiums from the Queen's own pen, as the most outstanding feature of those memorable journeys. The three invitations which that indefatigable champion of the Faith received to call on Prince Paul and Princess Olga of Yugoslavia at the Royal Palace in Belgrade; the lectures which she delivered in over four hundred universities and colleges in both the East and the West; her twice repeated visits to all German universities with the exception of two, as well as to nearly a hundred universities, colleges and schools in China; the innumerable articles which she published in newspapers and magazines in practically every country she visited; the numerous broadcasts which she delivered and the unnumbered books she placed in private and state libraries; her personal meetings with the statesmen of more than fifty countries, during her three-months stay in Geneva, in 1932, at the time of the Disarmament Conference; the painstaking efforts she exerted, while on her arduous journeys, in supervising the translation and production of a large number of versions of Dr. Esslemont's "Bahá'u'lláh and the New Era"; the correspondence exchanged with, and the presentation of Bahá'í books to, men of eminence and learning; her pilgrimage to Persia, and the touching homage paid by her to the memory of the heroes of the Faith when visiting the Bahá'í historic sites in that country; her visit to Adrianople, where, in her overflowing love for Bahá'u'lláh, she searched out the houses where He had dwelt and the people whom He had met during His exile to that city, and where she was entertained by its governor and mayor; the ready and unfailing assistance extended by her to the administrators of the Faith in all countries where its institutions had been erected or were being established—these may be regarded as the highlights of a service which, in many of its aspects, is without parallel in the entire history of the first Bahá'í century.

No less impressive is the list of the names of those whom she interviewed in the course of the execution of her mission, including, in addition to those already mentioned, such royal personages and distinguished figures as King Haakon of Norway; King Feisal of 'Iráq; King Zog of Albania and members of his family; Princess Marina of Greece (now the Duchess of Kent); Princess Elizabeth of Greece; President Thomas G. Masaryk and President Eduard Benes of Czechoslovakia; the President of Austria; Dr. Sun Yat Sen; Dr. Nicholas Murray Butler, President of Columbia University; Prof. Bogdan Popovitch of Belgrade University; the Foreign Minister of Turkey, Tawfíq Rushdí Bey; the Chinese Foreign Minister and Minister of Education; the Lithuanian Foreign Minister; Prince Muḥammad-'Alí of Egypt; Stephen Raditch; the Maharajas of Patiala, of Benares, and of Travancore; the Governor and the Grand Muftí of Jerusalem; Dr. Erling Eidem, Archbishop of Sweden; Sarojini Naidu; Sir Rabindranath Tagore; Madame Huda Sha'ráví, the Egyptian feminist leader; Dr. K. Ichiki, minister of the Japanese Imperial Household; Prof. Tetrujiro Inouye, Prof. Emeritus of the Imperial University of Tokyo; Baron Yoshiro Sakatani, member of the House of Peers of Japan and Mehmed Fuad, Doyen of the Faculty of Letters and President of the Institute of Turkish history.

Neither age nor ill-health, neither the paucity of literature which hampered her early efforts, nor the meager resources which imposed an added burden on her labors, neither the extremities of the climates to which she was exposed, nor the political disturbances which she encountered in the course of her journeys, could damp the zeal or deflect the purpose of this spiritually dynamic and saintly woman. Single-handed and, on more than one occasion, in extremely perilous circumstances, she continued to call, in clarion tones, men of diverse creeds, color and classes to the Message of Bahá'u'lláh, until, while in spite of a deadly and painful disease, the onslaught of which she endured with heroic fortitude, she hastened homeward to help in the recently launched Seven Year Plan, she was stricken down on her way, in far off Honolulu. There in that symbolic spot between the Eastern and Western Hemispheres, in both of which she had labored so mightily, she died, on September 28, 1939, and brought to its close a life which may well be regarded as the fairest fruit as yet yielded by the Formative Age of the Dispensation of Bahá'u'lláh.

To the injunction of 'Abdu'l-Bahá bequeathed in His Will to follow in the footsteps of the disciples of Jesus Christ, *"not to rest for a moment,"* to *"travel throughout all regions"* and to raise, *"without rest and steadfast to the end," "in every land, the cry of 'Yá Bahá'u'l-Abhá,'"* this immortal heroine yielded an obedience of which the present as well as future generations may well be proud, and which they may emulate.

*"Unrestrained as the wind,"* putting her *"whole trust"* in God, as *"the best provision"* for her journey, she fulfilled almost to the letter the wish so poignantly expressed by 'Abdu'l-Bahá in the Tablets, whose summons she had instantly arisen to carry out: *"O that I could travel, even though on foot and in the utmost poverty, to these regions, and, raising the call of 'Yá Bahá'u'l-Abhá' in cities, villages, mountains, deserts and oceans, promote the Divine teachings! This, alas, I cannot do. How intensely I deplore it! Please God, ye may achieve it."*

"I am deeply distressed to hear of the death of good Miss Martha Root," is the royal tribute paid to her memory by Princess Olga of Yugoslavia, on being informed of her death, "as I had no idea of it. We always enjoyed her visits in the past. She was so kind and gentle, and a real worker for peace. I am sure she will be sadly missed in her work."

*"Thou art, in truth, a herald of the Kingdom and a harbinger of the Covenant,"* is the testimony from the unerring pen of the Center of Bahá'u'lláh's Covenant Himself, *"Thou art truly self-sacrificing. Thou showest kindness unto all nations. Thou art sowing a seed that shall, in due time, give rise to thousands of harvests. Thou art planting a tree that shall eternally put forth leaves and blossoms and yield fruits, and whose shadow shall day by day grow in magnitude."*

Of all the services rendered the Cause of Bahá'u'lláh by this star servant of His Faith, the most superb and by far the most momentous has been the almost instantaneous response evoked in Queen Marie of Rumania to the Message which that ardent and audacious pioneer had carried to her during one of the darkest moments of her life, an hour of bitter need, perplexity and sorrow. "It came," she herself in a letter had testified, "as all great messages come, at an hour of dire grief and inner conflict and distress, so the seed sank deeply."

Eldest daughter of the Duke of Edinburgh, who was the second son of that Queen to whom Bahá'u'lláh had, in a significant Tablet, addressed words of commendation; granddaughter of Czar Alexander II to whom an Epistle had been revealed by that same Pen; related by both birth and marriage to Europe's most prominent families; born in the Anglican Faith; closely associated through her marriage with the

Greek Orthodox Church, the state religion of her adopted country; herself an accomplished authoress; possessed of a charming and radiant personality; highly talented, clear-visioned, daring and ardent by nature; keenly devoted to all enterprises of a humanitarian character, she, alone among her sister-queens, alone among all those of royal birth or station, was moved to spontaneously acclaim the greatness of the Message of Bahá'u'lláh, to proclaim His Fatherhood, as well as the Prophethood of Muḥammad, to commend the Bahá'í teachings to all men and women, and to extol their potency, sublimity and beauty.

Through the fearless acknowledgment of her belief to her own kith and kin, and particularly to her youngest daughter; through three successive encomiums that constitute her greatest and abiding legacy to posterity; through three additional appreciations penned by her as her contribution to Bahá'í publications; through several letters written to friends and associates, as well as those addressed to her guide and spiritual mother; through various tokens expressive of faith and gratitude for the glad-tidings that had been brought to her through the orders for Bahá'í books placed by her and her youngest daughter; and lastly through her frustrated pilgrimage to the Holy Land for the express purpose of paying homage at the graves of the Founders of the Faith—through such acts as these this illustrious queen may well deserve to rank as the first of those royal supporters of the Cause of God who are to arise in the future, and each of whom, in the words of Bahá'u'lláh Himself, is to be acclaimed as *"the very eye of mankind, the luminous ornament on the brow of creation, the fountainhead of blessings unto the whole world."*

"Some of those of my caste," she, in a personal letter, has significantly testified, "wonder at and disapprove my courage to step forward pronouncing words not habitual for crowned heads to pronounce, but I advance by an inner urge I cannot resist. With bowed head I recognize that I too am but an instrument in greater Hands, and I rejoice in the knowledge."

A note which Martha Root, upon her arrival in Bucharest, sent to her Majesty and a copy of "Bahá'u'lláh and the New Era," which accompanied the note, and which so absorbed the Queen's attention that she continued reading it into the small hours of the morning, led, two days later, to the Queen's granting Martha Root an audience, on January 30, 1926, in Controceni Palace in Bucharest, in the course of which her Majesty avowed her belief that "these teachings are the solution for the world's problems"; and from these followed her publication, that same year on her own initiative, of those three epoch-making testimonies which appeared in nearly two hundred newspapers of the United States and Canada, and which were subsequently translated and published in Europe, China, Japan, Australia, the Near East and the Islands of the seas.

In the first of these testimonies she affirmed that the writings of Bahá'u'lláh and 'Abdu'l-Bahá are "a great cry toward peace, reaching beyond all limits of frontiers, above all dissensions about rites and dogmas . . . It is a wondrous message that Bahá'u'lláh and His Son 'Abdu'l-Bahá have given us! They have not set it up aggressively, knowing that the germ of eternal truth which lies at its core cannot but take root and spread . . . It is Christ's message taken up anew, in the same words almost, but adapted to the thousand years and more difference that lies between the year one and today." She added a remarkable admonition, reminiscent of the telling words of Dr. Benjamin Jowett, who had hailed the Faith, in his conversation with his pupil, Prof. Lewis Campbell, as "the greatest light that has come into the world since the time of Jesus Christ," and cautioned him to "watch it" and never let it out of his sight. "If ever," wrote the Queen, "the name of Bahá'u'lláh or 'Abdu'l-Bahá comes to your attention, do not put their writings from you. Search out their books, and let their glorious, peace-bringing, love-creating words and lessons sink into your hearts as they have into mine . . . Seek them and be the happier."

In another of these testimonies, wherein she makes a significant comment on the station of the Arabian Prophet, she declared: "God is all. Everything. He is the power behind all beings . . . His is the voice within us that shows us good and evil. But mostly we ignore or misunderstand this voice. Therefore, did He choose His Elect to come down amongst us upon earth to make clear His Word, His real meaning. Therefore the Prophets; therefore Christ, Muḥammad, Bahá'u'lláh, for man needs from time to time a voice upon earth to bring God to him, to sharpen the realization of the existence of the true God. Those voices sent to us had to become flesh, so that with our earthly ears we should be able to hear and understand."

In appreciation of these testimonies a communication was addressed to her, in the name of the followers of Bahá'u'lláh in East and West, and in the course of the deeply touching letter which she sent in reply she wrote: "Indeed a great light came to me with the Message of Bahá'u'lláh and 'Abdu'l-Bahá . . . My youngest daughter finds also great strength and comfort in the teachings of the beloved Masters. We pass on the Message from mouth to mouth, and all those we give it to see a light suddenly lighting before them, and much that was obscure and perplexing becomes simple, luminous and full of hope as never before. That my open letter was a balm to those suffering for the Cause, is indeed a great happiness to me, and I take it as a sign that God accepted my humble tribute. The occasion given me to be able to express myself publicly was also His work, for indeed it was a chain of circumstances of which each link led me unwittingly one step further, till suddenly all was clear before my eyes and I understood why it had been. Thus does He lead us finally to our ultimate destiny . . . Little by little the veil is lifting, grief tore it in two. And grief was also a step leading me ever nearer truth; therefore do I not cry out against grief!"

In a significant and moving letter to an intimate American friend of hers, residing in Paris, she wrote: "Lately a great hope has come to me from one 'Abdu'l-Bahá. I have found in His and His Father, Bahá'u'lláh's Message of faith, all my yearning for real religion satisfied . . . What I mean: these Books have strengthened me beyond belief, and I am now ready to die any day full of hope. But I pray God not to take me away yet, for I still have a lot of work to do."

And again in one of her later appreciations of the Faith: "The Bahá'í teaching brings peace and understanding. It is like a wide embrace gathering all those who have long searched for words of hope . . . Saddened by the continual strife amongst believers of many confessions and wearied of their intolerance towards each other, I discovered in the Bahá'í teaching the real spirit of Christ so often denied and misunderstood." And again, this wonderful confession: "The Bahá'í teaching brings peace to the soul and hope to the heart. To those in search of assurance the words of the Father are as a fountain in the desert after long wandering."

"The beautiful truth of Bahá'u'lláh," she wrote to Martha Root, "is with me always, a help and an inspiration. What I wrote was because my heart overflowed with gratitude for the reflection you brought me. I am happy if you think I helped. I thought it might bring truth nearer because my words are read by so many."

In the course of a visit to the Near East she expressed her intention of visiting the Bahá'í Shrines, and, accompanied by her youngest daughter, actually passed through Haifa, and was within sight of her goal, when she was denied the right to make the pilgrimage she had planned—to the keen disappointment of the aged Greatest Holy Leaf who had eagerly expected her arrival. A few months later, in June, 1931, she wrote in the course of a letter to Martha Root: "Both Ileana and I were cruelly disappointed at having been prevented going to the holy Shrines . . . but at that time we were going through a cruel crisis, and every movement I made was being turned against me and being politically exploited in an unkind way. It caused me a good deal of suffering and curtailed my liberty most unkindly . . . But the beauty of truth remains, and I cling to it through all the vicissitudes of a life become rather sad . . . I am glad to hear that your traveling has been so fruitful, and I wish you continual success knowing what a beautiful Message you are carrying from land to land."

After this sad disappointment she wrote to a friend of her childhood who dwelt near 'Akká, in a house formerly occupied by Bahá'u'lláh: "It was indeed nice to hear from you, and to think that you are of all things living near Haifa and are, as I am, a follower of the Bahá'í teachings. It interests me that you are living in that special house . . . I was so intensely interested and studied each photo intently. It must be a lovely place . . . and the house you live in, so incredibly attractive and made precious by its associations with the Man we all venerate . . ."

Her last public tribute to the Faith she had dearly loved was made two years before her death. "More than ever today," she wrote, "when the world is facing such a crisis of bewilderment and unrest, must we stand firm in Faith seeking that which binds together instead of tearing asunder. To those searching for light, the Bahá'í teachings offer a star which will lead them to deeper understanding, to assurance, peace and goodwill with all men."

Martha Root's own illuminating record is given in one of her articles as follows: "For ten years Her Majesty and her daughter, H.R.H. Princess Ileana (now Arch-Duchess Anton) have read with interest each new book about the Bahá'í Movement, as soon as it came from the press . . . Received in audience by Her Majesty in Pelisor Palace, Sinaia, in 1927, after the passing of His Majesty King Ferdinand, her husband, she graciously gave me an interview, speaking of the Bahá'í teachings about immortality. She had on her table and on the divan a number of Bahá'í books, for she had just been reading in each of them the Teachings about life after death. She asked the writer to give her greeting to . . . the friends in Írán and to the many American Bahá'ís, who she said had been so remarkably kind to her during her trip through the United States the year before . . . Meeting the Queen again on January 19, 1928, in the Royal Palace in Belgrade, where she and H.R.H. Princess Ileana were guests of the Queen of Yugoslavia—and they had brought some of their Bahá'í books with them—the words that I shall remember longest of all that her dear Majesty said were these: 'The ultimate dream which we shall realize is that the Bahá'í channel of thought has such strength, it will serve little by little to become a light to all those searching for the real expression of Truth' . . . Then in the audience in Controceni Palace, on February 16, 1934, when her Majesty was told that the Rumanian translation of 'Bahá'u'lláh and the New Era' had just been published in Bucharest, she said she was so happy that her people were to have the blessing of reading this precious teaching . . . And now today, February 4, 1936, I have just had another audience with Her Majesty in Controceni Palace, in Bucharest . . . Again Queen Marie of Rumania received me cordially in her softly lighted library, for the hour was six o'clock . . . What a memorable visit it was! . . . She also told me that when she was in London she had met a Bahá'í, Lady Blomfield, who had shown her the original Message that Bahá'u'lláh had sent to her grand-mother, Queen Victoria, in London. She asked the writer about the progress of the Bahá'í Movement, especially in the Balkan countries . . . She spoke too of several Bahá'í books, the depths of "Íqán," and especially of "Gleanings from the Writings of Bahá'u'lláh," which she said was a wonderful book! To quote her own words: 'Even doubters would find a powerful strength in it, if they would read it alone, and would give their souls time to expand.' . . . I asked her if I could perhaps speak of the brooch which historically is precious to Bahá'ís, and she replied, 'Yes, you may.' Once, and it was in 1928, Her dear Majesty had given the writer a gift, a lovely and rare brooch which had been a gift to the Queen from her royal relatives in Russia some years ago. It was two little wings of wrought gold and silver, set with tiny diamond chips, and joined together with one large pearl. 'Always you are giving gifts to others, and I am going to give you a gift from me,' said the Queen smiling, and she herself clasped it onto my dress. The wings and the pearl made it seem 'Light-bearing' Bahá'í! It was sent the same week to Chicago as a gift to the Bahá'í Temple . . . and at the National Bahá'í Convention which was in session that spring, a demur was made—should a gift from the Queen be sold? Should it not be kept as a souvenir of the first Queen who arose to promote the Faith of Bahá'u'lláh? However, it was sold immediately and the money given to the Temple, for all Bahá'ís were giving to the utmost to forward this mighty structure, the first of its kind in the United States of America. Mr. Willard Hatch, a Bahá'í of Los Angeles, Calif., who bought the exquisite brooch, took it to Haifa, Palestine, in 1931, and placed it in the

Archives on Mt. Carmel, where down the ages it will rest with the Bahá'í treasures . . . "

In July, 1938, Queen Marie of Rumania passed away. A message of condolence was communicated, in the name of all Bahá'í communities in East and West, to her daughter, the Queen of Yugoslavia, to which she replied expressing "sincere thanks to all of Bahá'u'lláh's followers." The National Spiritual Assembly of the Bahá'ís of Persia addressed, on behalf of the followers of the Faith in Bahá'u'lláh's native land, a letter expressive of grief and sympathy to her son, the King of Rumania and the Rumanian Royal Family, the text of which was in both Persian and English. An expression of profound and loving sympathy was sent by Martha Root to Princess Ileana, and was gratefully acknowledged by her. Memorial gatherings were held in the Queen's memory, at which a meed of honor was paid to her bold and epochal confession of faith in the Fatherhood of Bahá'u'lláh, to her recognition of the station of the Prophet of Islám and to the several encomiums from her pen. On the first anniversary of her death the National Spiritual Assembly of the Bahá'ís of the United States and Canada demonstrated its grateful admiration and affection for the deceased Queen by associating itself, through an imposing floral offering, with the impressive memorial service, held in her honor, and arranged by the Rumanian Minister, in Bethlehem Chapel, at the Cathedral of Washington, D. C., at which the American delegation, headed by the Secretary of State and including government officials and representatives of the Army and Navy, the British, French and Italian Ambassadors, and representatives of other European embassies and legations joined in a common tribute to one who, apart from the imperishable renown achieved by her in the Kingdom of Bahá'u'lláh, had earned, in this earthly life, the esteem and love of many a soul living beyond the confines of her own country.

Queen Marie's acknowledgment of the Divine Message stands as the first fruits of the vision which Bahá'u'lláh had seen long before in His captivity, and had announced in His Kitáb-i-Aqdas. *"How great,"* He wrote, *"the blessedness that awaits the King who will arise to aid My Cause in My Kingdom, who will detach himself from all else but Me! . . . All must glorify his name, must reverence his station, and aid him to unlock the cities with the keys of My Name, the Omnipotent Protector of all that inhabit the visible and invisible kingdoms. Such a king is the very eye of mankind, the luminous ornament on the brow of creation, the fountain-head of blessings unto the whole world.*

*Offer up, O people of Bahá, your substance, nay your very lives for his assistance."*

The American Bahá'í community, crowned with imperishable glory by these signal international services of Martha Root, was destined, as the first Bahá'í century drew to a close, to distinguish itself, through the concerted efforts of its members, both at home and abroad, by further achievements of such scope and quality that no survey of the teaching activities of the Faith in the course of that century can afford to ignore them. It would be no exaggeration to say that these colossal achievements, with the amazing results which flowed from them, could only have been effected through the harnessing of all the agencies of a newly established Administrative Order, operating in conformity with a carefully conceived Plan, and that they constitute a befitting conclusion to the record of a hundred years of sublime endeavor in the service of the Cause of Bahá'u'lláh.

That the community of His followers in the United States and Canada should have carried off the palm of victory in the concluding years of such a glorious century is not a matter for surprise. Its accomplishments during the last two decades of the Heroic, and throughout the first fifteen years of the Formative Age of the Bahá'í Dispensation, had already augured well for its future, and had paved the way for its final victory ere the expiration of the first century of the Bahá'í Era.

The Báb had in His Qayyúmu'l-Asmá', almost a hundred years previously, sounded His specific summons to the "*peoples of the West*" to "*issue forth*" from their "*cities*" and aid His Cause. Bahá'u'lláh, in His Kitáb-i-Aqdas, had collectively addressed the Presidents of the Republics of the entire Americas, bidding them arise and "*bind with the hands of justice the broken,*" and "*crush the oppressor*" with the "*rod of the commandments*" of their Lord, and had, moreover, anticipated in His writings the appearance "*in the West*" of the "*signs of His Dominion.*" 'Abdu'l-Bahá had, on His part, declared that the "*illumination*" shed by His Father's Revelation upon the West would acquire an "*extraordinary brilliancy,*" and that the "*light of the Kingdom*" would "*shed a still greater illumination upon the West*" than upon the East. He had extolled the American continent in particular as "*the land wherein the splendors of His Light shall be revealed, where the mysteries of His Faith shall be unveiled,*" and affirmed that "*it will lead all nations spiritually.*" More specifically still, He had singled out the Great Republic of the West, the leading nation of that continent, declaring that its people were "*indeed worthy of being the first to build the Tabernacle of the Most Great Peace* and *proclaim the oneness of mankind,"* that it was *"equipped and empowered to accomplish that which will adorn the pages of history, to become the envy of the world, and be blest in both the East and the West."*

The first act of His ministry had been to unfurl the standard of Bahá'u'lláh in the very heart of that Republic. This was followed by His own prolonged visit to its shores, by His dedication of the first House of Worship to be built by the community of His disciples in that land, and finally by the revelation, in the evening of His life, of the Tablets of the Divine Plan, investing His disciples with a mandate to plant the banner of His Father's Faith, as He had planted it in their own land, in all the continents, the countries and islands of the globe. He had, furthermore, acclaimed one of their most celebrated presidents as one who, through the ideals he had expounded and the institutions he had inaugurated, had caused the *"dawn"* of the Peace anticipated by Bahá'u'lláh to break; had voiced the hope that from their country *"heavenly illumination"* may *"stream to all the peoples of the world"*; had designated them in those Tablets as *"Apostles of Bahá'u'lláh"*; had assured them that, *"should success crown"* their *"enterprise," "the throne of the Kingdom of God will, in the plenitude of its majesty and glory, be firmly established"*; and had made the stirring announcement that *"the moment this Divine Message is propagated"* by them *"through the continents of Europe, of Asia, of Africa and of Australasia, and as far as the islands of the Pacific, this community will find itself securely established upon the throne of an everlasting dominion,"* and that *"the whole earth"* would *"resound with the praises of its majesty and greatness."*

That Community had already, in the lifetime of Him Who had created it, tenderly nursed and repeatedly blessed it, and had at last conferred upon it so distinctive a mission, arisen to launch the enterprise of the Mashriqu'l-Adhkár through the purchase of its land and the laying of its foundations. It had despatched its teachers to the East and to the West to propagate the Cause it had espoused, had established the basis of its community life, and had, since His passing, erected the superstructure and commenced the external ornamentation of its Temple. It had, moreover, assumed a preponderating share in the task of erecting the framework of the Administrative Order of the Faith, of championing its cause, of demonstrating its independent character, of enriching and disseminating its literature, of lending moral and material assistance to its persecuted followers, of repelling the assaults of its adversaries and of winning the allegiance of royalty to its Founder. Such a splendid record was to culminate, as the century approached its end, in the initiation of a Plan—the first stage in the execution of the Mission entrusted to it by 'Abdu'l-Bahá—which, within the space of seven brief years, was to bring to a successful completion the exterior ornamentation of the Mas̲hriqu'l-Ad̲hkár, to almost double the number of Spiritual Assemblies functioning in the North American continent, to bring the total number of localities in which Bahá'ís reside to no less than thirteen hundred and twenty-two in that same continent, to establish the structural basis of the Administrative Order in every state of the United States and every province of Canada, and by laying a firm anchorage in each of the twenty Republics of Central and South America, to swell to sixty the number of the sovereign states included within its orbit.

Many and diverse forces combined now to urge the American Bahá'í community to strong action: the glowing exhortations and promises of Bahá'u'lláh and His behest to erect in His name Houses of Worship; the directions issued by 'Abdu'l-Bahá in fourteen Tablets addressed to the believers residing in the Western, the Central, the North Eastern and Southern States of the North American Republic and in the Dominion of Canada; His prophetic utterances regarding the future of the Mas̲hriqu'l-Ad̲hkár in America; the influence of the new Administrative Order in fostering and rendering effective an eager spirit of cooperation; the example of Martha Root who, though equipped with no more than a handful of inadequately translated leaflets, had traveled to South America and visited every important city in that continent; the tenacity and self-sacrifice of the fearless and brilliant Keith Ransom-Kehler, the first American martyr, who, journeying to Persia had pleaded in numerous interviews with ministers, ecclesiastics and government officials the cause of her down-trodden brethren in that land, had addressed no less than seven petitions to the S̲háh, and, heedless of the warnings of age and ill-health, had at last succumbed in Iṣfahán. Other factors which spurred the members of that community to fresh sacrifices and adventure were their eagerness to reinforce the work intermittently undertaken through the settlement and travels of a number of pioneers, who had established the first center of the Faith in Brazil, circumnavigated the South American continent and visited the West Indies and distributed literature in various countries of Central and South America: the consciousness of their pressing responsibilities in the face of a rapidly deteriorating international situation; the realization that the first Bahá'í century was fast speeding to a close and their anxiety to bring to a befitting conclusion an enterprise that had been launched thirty years previously. Undeterred by the immensity of the field, the power wielded by firmly entrenched ecclesiastical organizations, the political instability of some of the countries in which they were to settle, the climatic conditions they were to encounter, and the difference in language and custom of the people amongst whom they were to reside, and keenly aware of the crying needs of the Faith in the North American continent, the members of the American Bahá'í community arose, as one man, to inaugurate a threefold campaign, carefully planned and systematically conducted, designed to establish a Spiritual Assembly in every virgin state and province in North America, to form a nucleus of resident believers in each of the Republics of Central and South America, and to consummate the exterior ornamentation of the Mas͟hriqu'l-Ad͟hkár.

A hundred activities, administrative and educational, were devised and pursued for the prosecution of this noble Plan. Through the liberal contribution of funds; through the establishment of an Inter-America Committee and the formation of auxiliary Regional Teaching Committees; through the founding of an International School to provide training for Bahá'í teachers; through the settlement of pioneers in virgin areas and the visits of itinerant teachers; through the dissemination of literature in Spanish and Portuguese; through the initiation of teacher training courses and extension work by groups and local Assemblies; through newspaper and radio publicity; through the exhibition of Temple slides and models; through inter-community conferences and lectures delivered in universities and colleges; through the intensification of teaching courses and Latin American studies at summer schools—through these and other activities the prosecutors of this Seven-Year Plan have succeeded in sealing the triumph of what must be regarded as the greatest collective enterprise ever launched by the followers of Bahá'u'lláh in the entire history of the first Bahá'í century.

Indeed, ere the expiry of that century not only had the work on the Temple been completed sixteen months before the appointed time, but instead of one tiny nucleus in every Latin Republic, Spiritual Assemblies had already been established in Mexico City and Puebla (Mexico), in Buenos Aires (Argentina), in Guatemala City (Guatemala), in Santiago (Chile), in Montevideo (Uruguay), in Quito (Ecuador), in Bogotá (Colombia), in Lima (Peru), in Asuncion (Paraguay), in Tegucigalpa (Honduras), in San Salvador (El-Salvador), in San José and Puntarenas (Costa Rica), in Havana (Cuba) and in Port-au-Prince (Haiti). Extension work, in which newly fledged Latin American believers were participating, had, moreover, been initiated, and was being vigorously carried out, in the Republics of Mexico, Brazil, Argentina, Chile, Panama and Costa Rica; believers had established their residence not only in the capital cities of all the Latin American Republics, but also in such centers as Veracruz, Cananea and Tacubaya (Mexico), in Balboa and Christobal (Panama), in Recife (Brazil), in Guayaquil and Ambato (Ecuador), and in Temuco and Magellanes (Chile); the Spiritual Assemblies of the Bahá'ís of Mexico City and of San José had been incorporated; in the former city a Bahá'í center, comprising a library, a reading room and a lecture room, had been founded; Bahá'í Youth Symposiums had been observed in Havana, Buenos Aires and Santiago, whilst a distributing center of Bahá'í literature for Latin America had been established in Buenos Aires.

Nor was this gigantic enterprise destined to be deprived, in its initial stage, of a blessing that was to cement the spiritual union of the Americas—a blessing flowing from the sacrifice of one who, at the very dawn of the Day of the Covenant, had been responsible for the establishment of the first Bahá'í centers in both Europe and the Dominion of Canada, and who, though seventy years of age and suffering from ill-health, undertook a six thousand mile voyage to the capital of Argentina, where, while still on the threshold of her pioneer service, she suddenly passed away, imparting through such a death to the work initiated in that Republic an impetus which has already enabled it, through the establishment of a distributing center of Bahá'í literature for Latin America and through other activities, to assume the foremost position among its sister Republics.

To May Maxwell, laid to rest in the soil of Argentina; to Hyde Dunn, whose dust reposes in the Antipodes, in the city of Sydney; to Keith Ransom-Kehler, entombed in distant Iṣfahán; to Susan Moody and Lillian Kappes and their valiant associates who lie buried in Ṭihrán; to Lua Getsinger, reposing forever in the capital of Egypt, and last but not least to Martha Root, interred in an island in the bosom of the Pacific, belong the matchless honor of having conferred, through their services and sacrifice, a lustre upon the American Bahá'í community for which its representatives, while celebrating at their historic, their first All-American Convention, their hard-won victories, may well feel eternally grateful.

Gathered within the walls of its national Shrine—the most sacred Temple ever to be reared to the glory of Bahá'u'lláh; commemorating at once the centenary of the birth of the Bábí Dispensation, of the inauguration of the Bahá'í era, of the inception of the Bahá'í Cycle and of the birth of 'Abdu'l-Bahá, as well as the fiftieth anniversary of the establishment of the Faith in the Western Hemisphere; associated in its celebration with the representatives of American Republics, foregathered in the close vicinity of a city that may well pride itself on being the first Bahá'í center established in the Western world, this community may indeed feel, on this solemn occasion, that it has, in its turn, through the triumphal conclusion of the first stage of the Plan traced for it by 'Abdu'l-Bahá, shed a lasting glory upon its sister communities in East and West, and written, in golden letters, the concluding pages in the annals of the first Bahá'í century.

# Retrospect and Prospect

Thus drew to a close the first century of the Bahá'í era—an epoch which, in its sublimity and fecundity, is without parallel in the entire field of religious history, and indeed in the annals of mankind. A process, God-impelled, endowed with measureless potentialities, mysterious in its workings, awful in the retribution meted out to every one seeking to resist its operation, infinitely rich in its promise for the regeneration and redemption of human kind, had been set in motion in Shíráz, had gained momentum successively in Ṭihrán, Baghdád, Adrianople and 'Akká, had projected itself across the seas, poured its generative influences into the West, and manifested the initial evidences of its marvelous, world-energizing force in the midst of the North American continent.

It had sprung from the heart of Asia, and pressing westward had gathered speed in its resistless course, until it had encircled the earth with a girdle of glory. It had been generated by the son of a mercer in the province of Fárs, had been reshaped by a nobleman of Núr, had been reinforced through the exertions of One Who had spent the fairest years of His youth and manhood in exile and imprisonment, and had achieved its most conspicuous triumphs in a country and amidst a people living half the circumference of the globe distant from the land of its origin. It had repulsed every onslaught directed against it, torn down every barrier opposing its advance, abased every proud antagonist who had sought to sap its strength, and had exalted to heights of incredible courage the weakest and humblest among those who had arisen and become willing instruments of its revolutionizing power. Heroic struggles and matchless victories, interwoven with appalling tragedies and condign punishments, have formed the pattern of its hundred year old history.

A handful of students, belonging to the Shaykhí school, sprung from the Ithná-'Asharíyyih sect of Shí'ah Islám, had, in consequence of the operation of this process, been expanded and transformed into a world community, closely knit, clear of vision, alive, consecrated by the sacrifice of no less than twenty thousand martyrs; supranational; non-sectarian; non-political; claiming the status, and assuming the functions, of a world religion; spread over five continents and the islands of the seas; with ramifications extending over sixty sovereign states and seventeen dependencies; equipped with a literature translated and broadcast in forty languages; exercising control over endowments representing several million dollars; recognized by a number of governments in both the East and the West; integral in aim and outlook; possessing no professional clergy; professing a single belief; following a single law; animated by a single purpose; organically united through an Administrative Order, divinely ordained and unique in its features; including within its orbit representatives of all the leading religions of the world, of various classes and races; faithful to its civil obligations; conscious of its civic responsibilities, as well as of the perils confronting the society of which it forms a part; sharing the sufferings of that society and confident of its own high destiny.

The nucleus of this community had been formed by the Báb, soon after the night of the Declaration of His Mission to Mullá Ḥusayn in Shíráz. A clamor in which the Sháh, his government, his people and the entire ecclesiastical hierarchy of his country unanimously joined had greeted its birth. Captivity, swift and cruel, in the mountains of Ádhirbáyján, had been the lot of its youthful Founder, almost immediately after His return from His pilgrimage to Mecca. Amidst the solitude of Máh-Kú and Chihríq, He had instituted His Covenant, formulated His laws, and transmitted to posterity the overwhelming majority of His writings. A conference of His disciples, headed by Bahá'u'lláh, had, in the hamlet of Badasht, abrogated in dramatic circumstances the laws of the Islamic, and ushered in the new, Dispensation. In Tabríz He had, in the presence of the Heir to the Throne and the leading ecclesiastical dignitaries of Ádhirbáyján, publicly and unreservedly voiced His claim to be none other than the promised, the long-awaited Qá'im. Tempests of devastating violence in Mázindarán, Nayríz, Zanján and Ṭihrán had decimated the ranks of His followers and robbed Him of the noblest and most valuable of His supporters. He Himself had to witness the virtual annihilation of His Faith and the loss of most of the Letters of the Living, and, after experiencing, in His own person, a series of bitter humiliations, He had been executed by a firing squad in the barrack-square of Tabríz. A blood bath of unusual ferocity had engulfed the greatest heroine of His Faith, had further denuded it of its adherents, had extinguished the life of His trusted amanuensis and repository of His last wishes, and swept Bahá'u'lláh into the depths of the foulest dungeon of Ṭihrán.

In the pestilential atmosphere of the Síyáh-Chál, nine years after that historic Declaration, the Message proclaimed by the Báb had yielded its fruit, His promise had been redeemed, and the most glorious, the most momentous period of the Heroic Age of the Bahá'í era had dawned. A momentary eclipse of the newly risen Sun of Truth, the world's greatest Luminary, had ensued, as a result of Bahá'u'lláh's precipitate banishment to 'Iráq by order of Náṣiri'd-Dín Sh̲áh, of His sudden withdrawal to the mountains of Kurdistán, and of the degradation and confusion that afflicted the remnant of the persecuted community of His fellow-disciples in Bag̲hdád. A reversal in the fortunes of a fast declining community, following His return from His two-year retirement, had set in, bringing in its wake the recreation of that community, the reformation of its morals, the enhancement of its prestige, the enrichment of its doctrine, and culminating in the Declaration of His Mission in the garden of Najíbíyyih to His immediate companions on the eve of His banishment to Constantinople. Another crisis—the severest a struggling Faith was destined to experience in the course of its history—precipitated by the rebellion of the Báb's nominee and the iniquities perpetrated by him and by the evil genius that had seduced him, had, in Adrianople, well nigh disrupted the newly consolidated forces of the Faith and all but destroyed in a baptism of fire the community of the Most Great Name which Bahá'u'lláh had called into being. Cleansed of the pollution of this "Most Great Idol," undeterred by the convulsion that had seized it, an indestructible Faith had, in the strength of the Covenant instituted by the Báb, now surmounted the most formidable obstacles it was ever to meet; and in this very hour it reached its meridian glory through the proclamation of the Mission of Bahá'u'lláh to the kings, the rulers and ecclesiastical leaders of the world in both the East and the West. Close on the heels of this unprecedented victory had followed the climax of His sufferings, a banishment to the penal colony of 'Akká, decreed by Sulṭán 'Abdu'l-'Azíz. This had been hailed by vigilant enemies as the signal for the final extermination of a much feared and hated adversary, and it had heaped upon that Faith in this fortress-town, designated by Bahá'u'lláh as His *"Most Great Prison,"* calamities from both within and without, such as it had never before experienced. The formulation of the laws and ordinances of a newborn Dispensation and the enunciation and reaffirmation of its fundamental principles—the warp and woof of a future Administrative Order—had, however, enabled a slowly maturing Revelation, in spite of this tide of tribulations, to advance a stage further and yield its fairest fruit.

The ascension of Bahá'u'lláh had plunged into grief and bewilderment His loyal supporters, quickened the hopes of the betrayers of His Cause, who had rebelled against His God-given authority, and rejoiced and encouraged His political as well as ecclesiastical adversaries. The Instrument He had forged, the Covenant He had Himself instituted, had canalized, after His passing, the forces released by Him in the course of a forty-year ministry, had preserved the unity of His Faith and provided the impulse required to propel it forward to achieve its destiny. The proclamation of this new Covenant had been followed by yet another crisis, precipitated by one of His own sons on whom, according to the provisions of that Instrument, had been conferred a rank second to none except the Center of that Covenant Himself. Impelled by the forces engendered by the revelation of that immortal and unique Document, an unbreachable Faith (having registered its initial victory over the Covenant-breakers), had, under the leadership of 'Abdu'l-Bahá, irradiated the West, illuminated the Western fringes of Europe, hoisted its banner in the heart of the North American continent, and set in motion the processes that were to culminate in the transfer of the mortal remains of its Herald to the Holy Land and their entombment in a mausoleum on Mt. Carmel, as well as in the erection of its first House of Worship in Russian Turkistán. A major crisis, following swiftly upon the signal victories achieved in East and West, attributable to the monstrous intrigues of the Arch-breaker of Bahá'u'lláh's Covenant and to the orders issued by the tyrannical 'Abdu'l-Hamíd, had exposed, during more than seven years, the Heart and Center of the Faith to imminent peril, filled with anxiety and anguish its followers and postponed the execution of the enterprises conceived for its spread and consolidation. 'Abdu'l-Bahá's historic journeys in Europe and America, soon after the fall of that tyrant and the collapse of his régime, had dealt a staggering blow to the Covenant-breakers, had consolidated the colossal enterprise He had undertaken in the opening years of His ministry, had raised the prestige of His Father's Faith to heights it had never before attained, had been instrumental in proclaiming its verities far and wide, and had paved the way for the diffusion of its light over the Far East and as far as the Antipodes. Another major crisis—the last the Faith was to undergo at its world center—provoked by the cruel Jamál Pá<u>sh</u>á, and accentuated by the anxieties of a devastating world war, by the privations it entailed and the rupture of communications it brought about, had threatened with still graver peril the Head of the Faith Himself, as well as the holiest sanctuaries enshrining the remains of its twin Founders. The revelation of the Tablets of the

Divine Plan, during the somber days of that tragic conflict, had, in the concluding years of 'Abdu'l-Bahá's ministry, invested the members of the leading Bahá'í community in the West—the champions of a future Administrative Order—with a world mission which, in the concluding years of the first Bahá'í century, was to shed deathless glory upon the Faith and its administrative institutions. The conclusion of that long and distressing conflict had frustrated the hopes of that military despot and inflicted an ignominious defeat on him, had removed, once and for all, the danger that had overshadowed for sixty-five years the Founder of the Faith and the Center of His Covenant, fulfilled the prophecies recorded by Him in His writings, enhanced still further the prestige of His Faith and its Leader, and been signalized by the spread of His Message to the continent of Australia.

The sudden passing of 'Abdu'l-Bahá, marking the close of the Primitive Age of the Faith, had, as had been the case with the ascension of His Father, submerged in sorrow and consternation His faithful disciples, imparted fresh hopes to the dwindling followers of both Mírzá Yaḥyá and Mírzá Muḥammad-'Alí, and stirred to feverish activity political as well as ecclesiastical adversaries, all of whom anticipated the impending dismemberment of the communities which the Center of the Covenant had so greatly inspired and ably led. The promulgation of His Will and Testament, inaugurating the Formative Age of the Bahá'í era, the Charter delineating the features of an Order which the Báb had announced, which Bahá'u'lláh had envisioned, and whose laws and principles He had enunciated, had galvanized these communities in Europe, Asia, Africa and America into concerted action, enabling them to erect and consolidate the framework of this Order, by establishing its local and national Assemblies, by framing the constitutions of these Assemblies, by securing the recognition on the part of the civil authorities in various countries of these institutions, by founding administrative headquarters, by raising the superstructure of the first House of Worship in the West, by establishing and extending the scope of the endowments of the Faith and by obtaining the full recognition by the civil authorities of the religious character of these endowments at its world center as well as in the North American continent.

A severe, a historic censure pronounced by a Muslim ecclesiastical court in Egypt had, whilst this mighty process—the laying of the structural basis of the Bahá'í world Administrative Order—was being initiated, officially expelled all adherents of the Faith of Muslim extraction from Islám, had condemned them as heretics and brought the members of a proscribed community face to face with tests and perils of a character they had never known before. The unjust decision of a civil court in Baghdád, instigated by Shí'ah enemies, in 'Iráq, and the decree issued by a still more redoubtable adversary in Russia had, moreover, robbed the Faith, on the one hand, of one of its holiest centers of pilgrimage, and denied it, on the other, the use of its first House of Worship, initiated by 'Abdu'l-Bahá and erected in the course of His ministry. And finally, inspired by this unexpected declaration made by an age-long enemy—marking the first step in the march of their Faith towards total emancipation—and undaunted by this double blow struck at its institutions, the followers of Bahá'u'lláh, already united and fully equipped through the agencies of a firmly established Administrative Order, had arisen to crown the immortal records of the first Bahá'í century by vindicating the independent character of their Faith, by enforcing the fundamental laws ordained in their Most Holy Book, by demanding and in some cases obtaining, the recognition by the ruling authorities of their right to be classified as followers of an independent religion, by securing from the world's highest Tribunal its condemnation of the injustice they had suffered at the hands of their persecutors, by establishing their residence in no less than thirty-four additional countries, as well as in thirteen dependencies, by disseminating their literature in twenty-nine additional languages, by enrolling a Queen in the ranks of the supporters of their Cause, and lastly by launching an enterprise which, as that century approached its end, enabled them to complete the exterior ornamentation of their second House of Worship, and to bring to a successful conclusion the first stage of the Plan which 'Abdu'l-Bahá had conceived for the world-wide and systematic propagation of their Faith.

Kings, emperors, princes, whether of the East or of the West, had, as we look back upon the tumultuous record of an entire century, either ignored the summons of its Founders, or derided their Message, or decreed their exile and banishment, or barbarously persecuted their followers, or sedulously striven to discredit their teachings. They were visited by the wrath of the Almighty, many losing their thrones, some witnessing the extinction of their dynasties, a few being assassinated or covered with shame, others finding themselves powerless to avert the cataclysmic dissolution of their kingdoms, still others being degraded to positions of subservience in their own realms. The Caliphate, its arch-enemy, had unsheathed the sword against its Author and thrice pronounced His banishment. It was humbled to dust, and, in its ignominious collapse, suffered the same fate as the Jewish hierarchy, the chief persecutor of Jesus Christ, had suffered at the hands of its Roman masters, in the first century of the Christian Era, almost two thousand years before. Members of various sacerdotal orders, S͟hí'ah, Sunní, Zoroastrian and Christian, had fiercely assailed the Faith, branded as heretic its supporters, and labored unremittingly to disrupt its fabric and subvert its foundations. The most redoubtable and hostile amongst these orders were either overthrown or virtually dismembered, others rapidly declined in prestige and influence, all were made to sustain the impact of a secular power, aggressive and determined to curtail their privileges and assert its own authority. Apostates, rebels, betrayers, heretics, had exerted their utmost endeavors, privily or openly, to sap the loyalty of the followers of that Faith, to split their ranks or assault their institutions. These enemies were, one by one, some gradually, others with dramatic swiftness, confounded, dispersed, swept away and forgotten. Not a few among its leading figures, its earliest disciples, its foremost champions, the companions and fellow-exiles of its Founders, trusted amanuenses and secretaries of its Author and of the Center of His Covenant, even some of those who were numbered among the kindred of the Manifestation Himself, not excluding the nominee of the Báb and the son of Bahá'u'lláh, named by Him in the Book of His Covenant, had allowed themselves to pass out from under its shadow, to bring shame upon it, through acts of indelible infamy, and to provoke crises of such dimensions as have never been experienced by any previous religion. All were precipitated, without exception, from the enviable positions they occupied, many of them lived to behold the frustration of their designs, others were plunged into degradation and misery, utterly impotent to impair the unity, or stay the march, of the Faith they had so shamelessly forsaken. Ministers, ambassadors and other state dignitaries had plotted assiduously to pervert its purpose, had instigated the successive banishments of its Founders, and maliciously striven to undermine its foundations. They had, through such plottings, unwittingly brought about their own downfall, forfeited the confidence of their sovereigns, drunk the cup of disgrace to its dregs, and irrevocably sealed their own doom. Humanity itself, perverse and utterly heedless, had refused to lend a hearing ear to the insistent appeals and warnings sounded by the twin Founders of the Faith, and later voiced by the Center of the Covenant in His public discourses in the West. It had plunged into two desolating wars of unprecedented magnitude, which have deranged its equilibrium, mown down its youth, and shaken it to its roots. The weak, the obscure, the down-trodden had, on the other hand, through their allegiance to so mighty a Cause and their response to its summons, been enabled to accomplish such feats of valor and heroism as to equal, and in some cases to dwarf, the exploits of those men and women of undying fame whose names and deeds adorn the spiritual annals of mankind.

Despite the blows leveled at its nascent strength, whether by the wielders of temporal and spiritual authority from without, or by black-hearted foes from within, the Faith of Bahá'u'lláh had, far from breaking or bending, gone from strength to strength, from victory to victory. Indeed its history, if read aright, may be said to resolve itself into a series of pulsations, of alternating crises and triumphs, leading it ever nearer to its divinely appointed destiny. The outburst of savage fanaticism that greeted the birth of the Revelation proclaimed by the Báb, His subsequent arrest and captivity, had been followed by the formulation of the laws of His Dispensation, by the institution of His Covenant, by the inauguration of that Dispensation in Badasht, and by the public assertion of His station in Tabríz. Widespread and still more violent uprisings in the provinces, His own execution, the blood bath which followed it and Bahá'u'lláh's imprisonment in the Síyáh-Chál had been succeeded by the breaking of the dawn of the Bahá'í Revelation in that dungeon. Bahá'u'lláh's banishment to 'Iráq, His withdrawal to Kurdistán and the confusion and distress that afflicted His fellow-disciples in Baghdád had, in turn, been followed by the resurgence of the Bábí community, culminating in the Declaration of His Mission in the Najíbíyyih Garden. Sulṭán 'Abdu'l-'Azíz's decree summoning Him to Constantinople and the crisis precipitated by Mírzá Yaḥyá had been succeeded by the proclamation of that Mission to the crowned heads of the world and its ecclesiastical leaders. Bahá'u'lláh's banishment to the penal colony of 'Akká, with all its attendant troubles and miseries, had, in its turn, led to the promulgation of the laws and ordinances of His Revelation and to the institution of His Covenant, the last act of His life. The fiery tests engendered by the rebellion of Mírzá Muḥammad-'Alí and his associates had been succeeded by the introduction of the Faith of Bahá'u'lláh in the West and the transfer of the Báb's remains to the Holy Land. The renewal of 'Abdu'l-Bahá's incarceration and the perils and anxieties consequent upon it had resulted in the downfall of 'Abdu'l-Ḥamíd, in 'Abdu'l-Bahá's release from His confinement, in the entombment of the Báb's remains on Mt. Carmel, and in the triumphal journeys undertaken by the Center of the Covenant Himself in Europe and America. The outbreak of a devastating world war and the deepening of the dangers to which Jamál Pá<u>sh</u>á and the Covenant-breakers had exposed Him had led to the revelation of the Tablets of the Divine Plan, to the flight of that overbearing Commander, to the liberation of the Holy Land, to the enhancement of the prestige of the Faith at its world center, and to a marked expansion of its activities in East and West. 'Abdu'l-Bahá's passing and the agitation which His removal had provoked had been followed by the promulgation of His Will and Testament, by the inauguration of the Formative Age of the Bahá'í era and by the laying of the foundations of a world-embracing Administrative Order. And finally, the seizure of the keys of the Tomb of Bahá'u'lláh by the Covenant-breakers, the forcible occupation of His House in Ba<u>gh</u>dád by the <u>Sh</u>í'ah community, the outbreak of persecution in Russia and the expulsion of the Bahá'í community from Islám in Egypt had been succeeded by the public assertion of the independent religious status of the Faith by its followers in East and West, by the recognition of that status at its world center, by the pronouncement of the Council of the League of Nations testifying to the justice of its claims, by a remarkable expansion of its international teaching activities and its literature, by the testimonials of royalty to its Divine origin, and by the completion of the exterior ornamentation of its first House of Worship in the western world.

The tribulations attending the progressive unfoldment of the Faith of Bahá'u'lláh have indeed been such as to exceed in gravity those from which the religions of the past have suffered. Unlike those religions, however, these tribulations have failed utterly to impair its unity, or to create, even temporarily, a breach in the ranks of its adherents. It has not only survived these ordeals, but has emerged, purified and inviolate, endowed with greater capacity to face and surmount any crisis which its resistless march may engender in the future.

Mighty indeed have been the tasks accomplished and the victories achieved by this sorely-tried yet undefeatable Faith within the space of a century! Its unfinished tasks, its future victories, as it stands on the threshold of the second Bahá'í century, are greater still. In the brief space of the first hundred years of its existence it has succeeded in diffusing its light over five continents, in erecting its outposts in the furthermost corners of the earth, in establishing, on an impregnable basis its Covenant with all mankind, in rearing the fabric of its world-encompassing Administrative Order, in casting off many of the shackles hindering its total emancipation and world-wide recognition, in registering its initial victories over royal, political and ecclesiastical adversaries, and in launching the first of its systematic crusades for the spiritual conquest of the whole planet.

The institution, however, which is to constitute the last stage in the erection of the framework of its world Administrative Order, functioning in close proximity to its world spiritual center, is as yet unestablished. The full emancipation of the Faith itself from the fetters of religious orthodoxy, the essential prerequisite of its universal recognition and of the emergence of its World Order, is still unachieved. The successive campaigns, designed to extend the beneficent influence of its System, according to 'Abdu'l-Bahá's Plan, to every country and island where the structural basis of its Administrative Order has not been erected, still remain to be launched. The banner of Yá Bahá'u'l-Abhá which, as foretold by Him, must float from the pinnacles of the foremost seat of learning in the Islamic world is still unhoisted. The Most Great House, ordained as a center of pilgrimage by Bahá'u'lláh in His Kitáb-i-Aqdas, is as yet unliberated. The third Mashriqu'l-Adhkár to be raised to His glory, the site of which has recently been acquired, as well as the Dependencies of the two Houses of Worship already erected in East and West, are as yet unbuilt. The dome, the final unit which, as anticipated by 'Abdu'l-Bahá, is to crown the Sepulcher of the Báb is as yet unreared. The codification of the Kitáb-i-Aqdas, the Mother-Book of the Bahá'í Revelation, and the systematic promulgation of its laws and ordinances, are as yet unbegun. The preliminary measures for the institution of Bahá'í courts, invested with the legal right to apply and execute those laws and ordinances, still remain to be undertaken. The restitution of the first Mashriqu'l-Adhkár of the Bahá'í world and the recreation of the community that so devotedly reared it, have yet to be accomplished. The sovereign who, as foreshadowed in Bahá'u'lláh's Most Holy Book, must adorn the throne of His native land, and cast the shadow of royal protection over His long-persecuted followers, is as yet undiscovered. The contest that must ensue as a result of the concerted onslaughts which, as prophesied by 'Abdu'l-Bahá, are to be delivered by the leaders of religions as yet indifferent to the advance of the Faith, is as yet unfought. The Golden Age of the Faith itself that must witness the unification of all the peoples and nations of the world, the establishment of the Most Great Peace, the inauguration of the Kingdom of the Father upon earth, the coming of age of the entire human race and the birth of a world civilization, inspired and directed by the creative energies released by Bahá'u'lláh's World Order, shining in its meridian splendor, is still unborn and its glories unsuspected.

Whatever may befall this infant Faith of God in future decades or in succeeding centuries, whatever the sorrows, dangers and tribulations which the next stage in its world-wide development may engender, from whatever quarter the assaults to be launched by its present or future adversaries may be unleashed against it, however great the reverses and setbacks it may suffer, we, who have been privileged to apprehend, to the degree our finite minds can fathom, the significance of these marvelous phenomena associated with its rise and establishment, can harbor no doubt that what it has already achieved in the first hundred years of its life provides sufficient guarantee that it will continue to forge ahead, capturing loftier heights, tearing down every obstacle, opening up new horizons and winning still mightier victories until its glorious mission, stretching into the dim ranges of time that lie ahead, is totally fulfilled.

[End]

# INDEX

## INDEX